Jake

JAKE

Jake

World GEOGRAPHY

Authors

Dr. Linda L. Greenow
Associate Professor and Acting Chair,
Department of Geography
SUNY—The College at New Paltz
New Paltz, NY

Dr. W. Frank Ainsley
Professor of Geography
University of North Carolina
Wilmington, NC

Dr. Gary S. Elbow
Professor of Geography
Texas Tech University
Lubbock, TX

Series Consultants

Dr. James F. Baumann
Professor of Reading Education
Associate Director, National Reading
Research Center
The University of Georgia
Athens, GA

Dr. Theodore Kaltsounis
Professor of Social Studies Education
College of Education
University of Washington
Seattle, WA

Literature Consultants

Dr. Ben A. Smith
Assistant Professor of Social Studies Education
Kansas State University
Manhattan, KS

Dr. John C. Davis
Professor of Elementary Education
University of Southern Mississippi
Hattiesburg, MS

Dr. Jesse Palmer
Assistant Professor, Department of Curriculum and Instruction
University of Southern Mississippi
Hattiesburg, MS

Silver Burdett Ginn
Parsippany, NJ
Atlanta, GA   Deerfield, IL   Irving, TX   Needham, MA   Upland, CA

SERIES AUTHORS

Dr. W. Frank Ainsley, Professor of Geography, University of North Carolina, Wilmington, NC

Dr. Herbert J. Bass, Professor of History, Temple University, Philadelphia, PA

Dr. Kenneth S. Cooper, Professor of History, Emeritus, George Peabody College for Teachers, Venderbilt University, Nashville, TN

Dr. Claudia Crump, Professor of Elementary Social Studies Education, Indiana University Southeast, New Albany, IN

Dr. Gary S. Elbow, Professor of Geography Texas Tech University, Lubbock, TX

Roy Erickson, Program Specialist, K12 Social Studies and Multicultural Education, San Juan Unified School District, Carmichael, CA

Dr. Daniel B. Fleming, Professor of Social Studies Education, Virginia Polytechnic Institute and State University, Blacksburg, VA

Dr. Gerald Michael Greenfield, Professor and Director, Center for International Studies, University of Wisconsin — Parkside, Kenosha, WI

Dr. Linda Greenow, Associate Professor and Acting Chair, Department of Geography, SUNY — The College at New Paltz, New Paltz, NY

Dr. William W. Joyce, Professor of Education, Michigan State University, East Lansing, MI

Dr. Gail S. Ludwig, Former Geographer-in-Residence, National Geographic Society, Geography Education Program, Washington, D.C.

Dr. Michael B. Petrovich, Professor Emeritus of History, University of Wisconsin, Madison, WI

Dr. Norman J.G. Pounds, Former University Professor of History and Geography, Indiana University, Bloomington, IN

Dr. Arthur Roberts, Professor of Education, University of Connecticut, Storrs, CT

Dr. Christine L. Roberts, Professor of Education, University of Connecticut, Storrs, CT

Parke Rouse, Jr., Virginia Historian and Retired Executive Director of the Jamestown-Yorktown Foundation, Williamsburg, VA

Dr. Paul C. Slayton, Jr., Distinguished Professor of Education, Mary Washington College, Fredericksburg, VA

Dr. Edgar A. Toppin, Professor of History and Dean of the Graduate School, Virginia State University Petersburg, VA

GRADE LEVEL WRITERS/CONSULTANTS

Claudette Butler Hatfield, Social Studies Department Chairperson, Williams Middle School, Florence, South Carolina

Pat Kelly-Coupar, Teacher, Thomas Jefferson Middle School, Edison, New Jersey

Cay Hoh, Teacher, Hayes Junior High School, St. Albans, West Virginia

Alvin Lindsey, Teacher, Donnan Junior High School, Indianapolis, Indiana

ACKNOWLEDGMENTS

Page 29: *The Sea Around Us* by Rachel Carson. Copyright © 1950, 1951, 1961 by Rachel L. Carson; Renewed 1979 by Roger Christie. Oxford University Press.

Page 41: By M. Scott Carpenter et al. Used by permission of Simon & Schuster Inc.

Page 47: © Copyright 1971 Cherry Lane Music Publishing Company, Inc. All rights reserved. Used by permission.

Page 64: Copyright © 1992 by The New York Times Company. Reprinted by permission.

Page 102: Reprinted by permission of Macmillan Publishing Company from RICHARD HALLIBURTON'S COMPLETE BOOK OF MARVELS. © 1960, renewed 1988 by Macmillan Publishing Company.

Pages 134, 136: From THE BERNAL DIAZ CHRONICLES as translated by Albert Idell. Used by permission of Doubleday & Company.

Page 140: From *Anthology of Mexican Poets* translated by Edna W. Underwood.

Page 145: Reprinted with permission from book #60660 The Log of Christopher Columbus, by Robert Fuson. Copyright © 1987 by Robert Fuson. Published by International Marine Publishing Company, a division of TAB BOOKS, Blue Ridge Summit, PA 17294 (1-800-233-1128 or 717-794-2191).

Page 170: Copyright © 1987 by The New York Times Company. Reprinted by permission.

Page 200: Reprinted with permission of Four Winds Press, an imprint of Macmillan Publishing Company from COATA INDIAN FAMILY: Children of the Incas by David Mangurian. Copyright © 1979 by David Mangurian.

Continued on page 753

6 7 8 9 10 – RRD – 06 05 04 03

ISBN 0-382-32725-X

CONTENTS

UNIT 2 THE COUNTRIES OF NORTH AMERICA

UNIT 3
THE COUNTRIES OF SOUTH AMERICA

UNIT 4
EUROPE AND THE FORMER SOVIET UNION

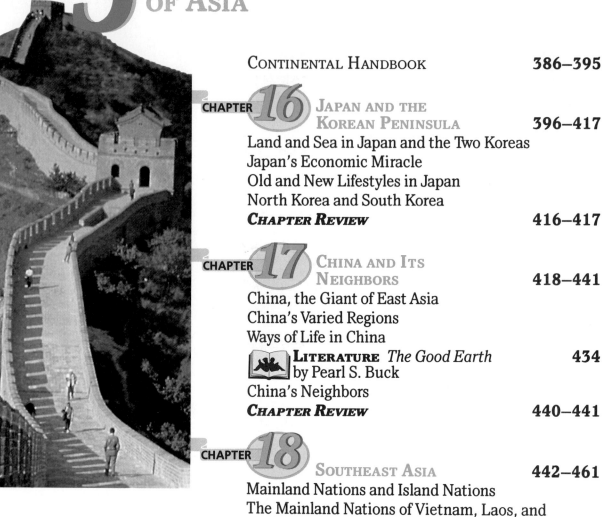

UNIT 5 THE COUNTRIES OF ASIA

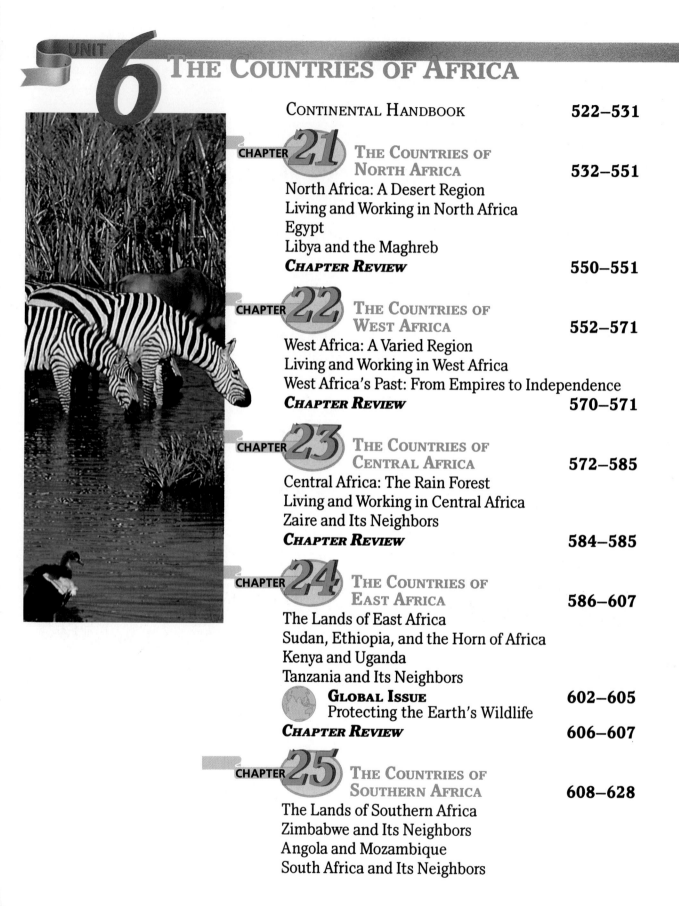

UNIT 6 THE COUNTRIES OF AFRICA

Understanding a Cartogram
Evaluating Facts and Opinions

RESOURCE SECTION

MAPS

ATLAS

TIME LINES

GRAPHS

TABLE OF COUNTRIES

TABLES

CHARTS

DIAGRAMS

Special Features

Using Source Material

Literature

Growing Up In

Global Issues

Skillbuilders

Social Studies

Language Arts

Graph Appendix

MAP SKILLS HANDBOOK

Knowing how to work with maps is a skill that everyone should have. You cannot thoroughly learn about geography without being able to read maps. Maps also have uses that go beyond what you learn in school.

Watch the nightly news on television. How many times are maps used during the broadcast? The next time you are in a library, look at a newspaper or weekly news magazine. How many times are maps used to help explain the subject of articles? Are maps used in any advertisements on television or in magazines?

If you kept track of how many times you saw maps on television and in newspapers and magazines during one week, you would see that maps are an important source of information. You would also see how important it is to be able to understand maps.

As you study geography, you will use map skills that you have already learned. You will also learn some new map skills. This Map Skills Handbook presents many of the map skills you will need to get the most out of your textbook — and many of the map skills that you can use to understand the world around you.

LESSON 1

Map Essentials

SPAIN: POLITICAL

Bay of Biscay	FRANCE	
Bilbao	PYRENEES	ANDORRA
Valladolid	Saragossa	Barcelona
PORTUGAL	Ebro River	
Douro River		
Madrid	Tagus River	40° N
SPAIN		BALEARIC
Guadiana River	Valencia	ISLANDS
Córdoba		Mediterranean
Seville		Sea
ATLANTIC OCEAN	Málaga	
Strait of Gibraltar	4° W	0°

⊕ National capital
• Other cities

0   150   300 miles
0   150   300 kilometers

8° W   4° E

Showing the Earth on a Map

NEW YORK CITY: CENTRAL PARK

Manhattan

Hudson River

Henry Hudson Pkwy.

Broadway

Central Park

Park Ave.

FDR Dr.

0   1/2   1

Scale: 1 inch stands for 1 mile

From Round Earth to Flat Paper

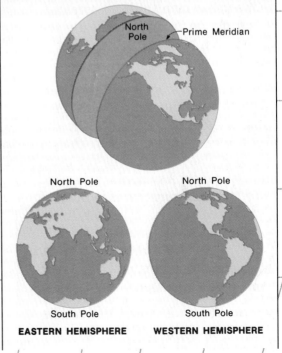

EASTERN AND WESTERN HEMISPHERES

North Pole

Prime Meridian

North Pole

North Pole

South Pole

South Pole

EASTERN HEMISPHERE

WESTERN HEMISPHERE

Map Essentials

CONNECTIONS

To read a map you must know the elements, or parts, of a map. Look at the map on this page. Name the parts of the map that you recognize. Now point out the parts you don't recognize.

TERMS

key, compass rose, grid system, latitude, longitude, scale, kilometer

FOCUS

What are the elements and symbols that are found on a map?

A. The Parts of A Map

Finding a City Almost 11,000 athletes represented 172 countries at the 1992 Summer Olympics in Barcelona (bahr suh LOH nuh), Spain. "Barcelona, Spain?" you ask yourself. Where is that?

No doubt, some of you do know where Barcelona is. But how would you describe its location to someone who doesn't? You probably already know the answer: By using a map.

So let's use a map to find Barcelona. Since it is a city in Spain, we will use the map of that country like the one that is shown on this page.

The Key Before we start looking for Barcelona, let's take a moment to review some of the map's essential elements. At the bottom of the map is a small box that is the map's **key**. The key explains the symbols used on the map. A symbol is a drawing that stands for something that is in the real world. Symbols can be points or dots, lines, shaded areas, or little pictures. On this map, a dot is used to indicate a city. A circle with a star means a capital city. What is the name of Spain's capital city?

The Compass Rose In about the middle of the map is the **compass rose**, or direction

marker. This shows where the cardinal directions are on the map. As you know, the cardinal directions are north, south, east, and west. The compass rose also shows the intermediate directions: northeast, northwest, southeast, and southwest.

Cartographers, the people who draw maps, have used these directions for centuries. The cardinal directions were originally determined by where the sun appears to rise, which is the east, and where the sun appears to set, which is the west. If you stand with your right arm to the east and your left arm to the west, then you are facing north, and south is the direction directly behind you.

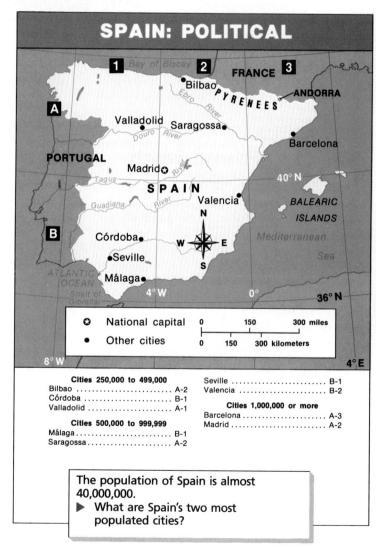

SPAIN: POLITICAL

| ☉ National capital | ● Other cities |

0   150   300 miles
0   150   300 kilometers

Cities 250,000 to 499,000
Bilbao A-2
Córdoba B-1
Valladolid A-1

Cities 500,000 to 999,999
Málaga B-1
Saragossa A-2

Seville B-1
Valencia B-2

Cities 1,000,000 or more
Barcelona A-3
Madrid A-2

The population of Spain is almost 40,000,000.
▶ What are Spain's two most populated cities?

Barcelona hosted the 1992 Summer Olympics. The inset shows the Olympic torch being lit during the dramatic opening ceremonies.
▶ In what country is Barcelona located?

B. The Grid System

The Gazetteer On a small map like this one, it is easy enough to pick out Barcelona. And you can use the key and the compass rose for help in describing exactly where Barcelona is—to the northeast of Madrid, the capital city of Spain. In this book the important places mentioned in a chapter are listed in a section called the Gazetteer. Turn to the Gazetteer, on pages 707–720. You can see that each city has an important fact reported about it. After that fact are the **latitude** and **longitude** of the city.

What are latitude and longitude? They are part of the **grid system** that cartographers have created to help us find places on maps. The horizontal lines on this grid system are lines of latitude, and the vertical lines are lines of longitude.

Latitude Lines of latitude are called parallels. They circle the earth in an east-west direction and are parallel to the Equator. Parallels measure distance north and south of the Equator. You can see from the map on page 6 that each line of latitude has a measurement in degrees. The Equator is at

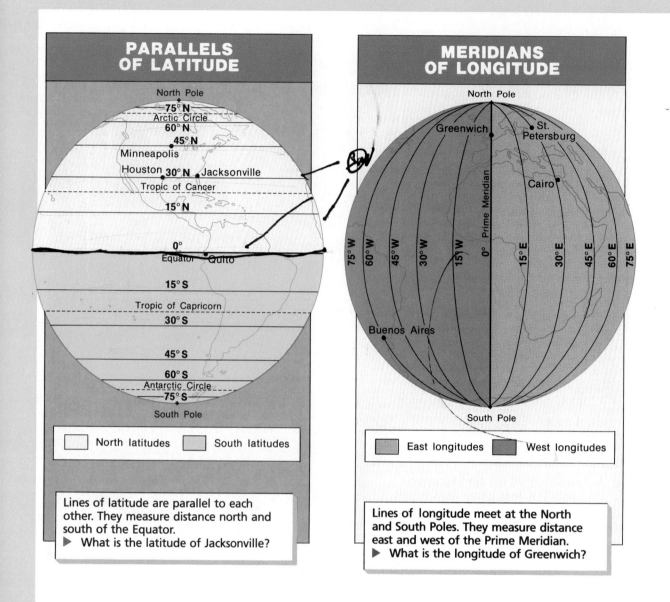

PARALLELS OF LATITUDE

North Pole
75°N
Arctic Circle
60°N
45°N
Minneapolis
Houston 30°N Jacksonville
Tropic of Cancer
15°N
0°
Equator   Quito
15°S
Tropic of Capricorn
30°S
45°S
60°S
Antarctic Circle
75°S
South Pole

☐ North latitudes   ☐ South latitudes

Lines of latitude are parallel to each other. They measure distance north and south of the Equator.
▶ What is the latitude of Jacksonville?

MERIDIANS OF LONGITUDE

North Pole
Greenwich   St. Petersburg
Cairo
Prime Meridian
75°W 60°W 45°W 30°W 15°W 0° 15°E 30°E 45°E 60°E 75°E
Buenos Aires
South Pole

☐ East longitudes   ☐ West longitudes

Lines of longitude meet at the North and South Poles. They measure distance east and west of the Prime Meridian.
▶ What is the longitude of Greenwich?

0° latitude. Lines of latitude north of the Equator are called lines of north latitude. On a map, they are shown as 20°N, 30°N, and so on. The latitude for the North Pole is 90°N.

Lines of latitude south of the Equator are called lines of south latitude. On a map they are shown as 20°S, 30°S, and so on. The South Pole is 90°S.

Longitude   The lines of longitude in the grid system are called meridians. Meridians run from the North Pole to the South Pole. They are used to measure distance east and

west of the starting point, called the Prime Meridian. The Prime Meridian passes through Greenwich, England. Greenwich is a town located near London. Sometimes the Prime Meridian is called the Greenwich Meridian because of its location. Find the Prime Meridian on the map above.

Longitude is also measured in degrees. The Prime Meridian is the starting point, so it is numbered 0°. Lines of longitude to the west of the Prime Meridian are called west longitude. Lines of longitude to the east are called east longitude.

The lines of longitude are numbered east

6

and west to 180° from the Prime Meridian. The meridian of 180° lies on the opposite side of the earth from the Prime Meridian.

Coordinates If you look up Barcelona in the Gazetteer, you will find that its latitude and longitude are listed there as 41°N/2°E. This set of numbers, or *coordinates*, locate the city precisely.

Suppose you had to find Barcelona on a world map, such as the one below. Unless you already knew where Spain was, you would have a hard time looking through all the countries on the map to first find Spain and then Barcelona. You can see how useful the coordinates are.

Another Grid System If you look again at the map of Spain on page 4, you will see at the top the numbers 1, 2, and 3. Along the left-hand side of the map you will see the letters *A* and *B*. These letters and numbers identify the boxes that the lines of latitude and longitude form.

Look at the listing of cities under the map. This *city index* lists all the cities shown on the map. The name of each city is followed by the letter and the number of the box in which the city is located. For example, the city index for this map tells us that Barcelona is in box A-3, which is where row *A* and column 3 meet. Once you find the box, you can scan it and locate Barcelona. The city index and the grid system allow us to easily find places on this or any other map.

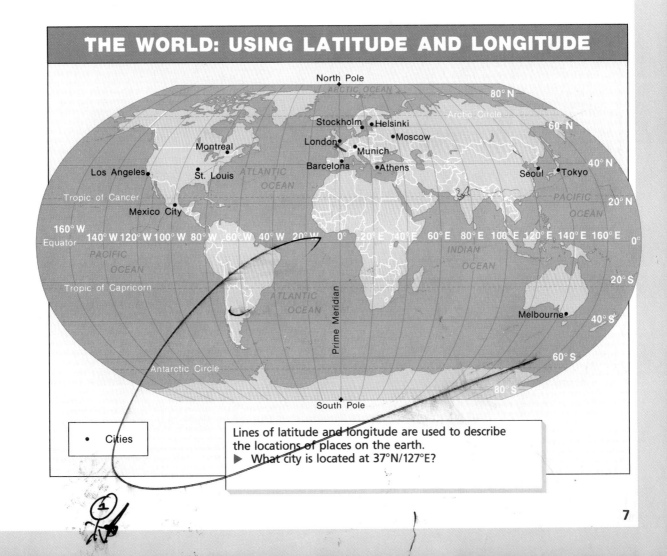

THE WORLD: USING LATITUDE AND LONGITUDE

• Cities

Lines of latitude and longitude are used to describe the locations of places on the earth.
► What city is located at 37°N/127°E?

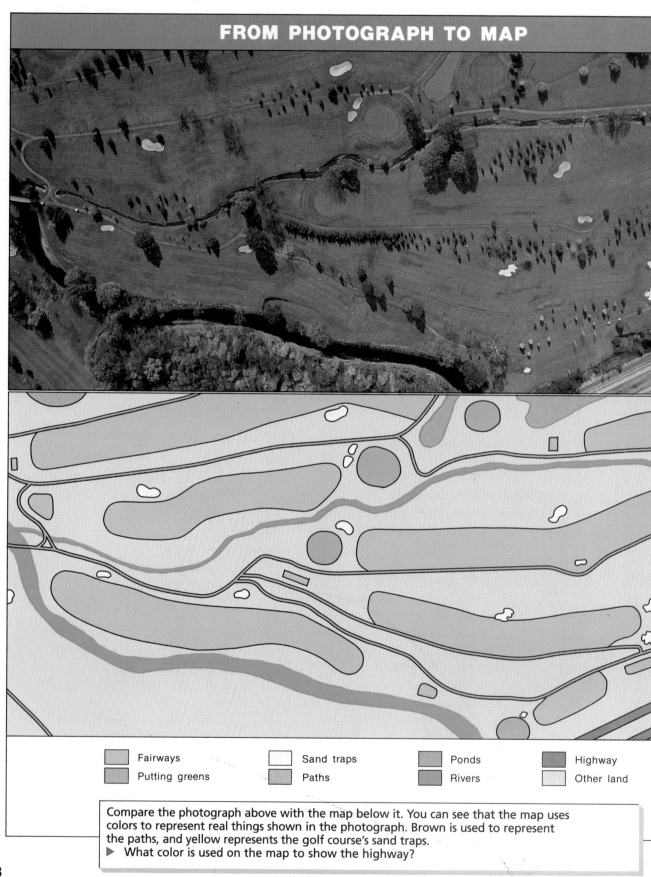

	Fairways		Sand traps		Ponds		Highway
	Putting greens		Paths		Rivers		Other land

Compare the photograph above with the map below it. You can see that the map uses colors to represent real things shown in the photograph. Brown is used to represent the paths, and yellow represents the golf course's sand traps.
▶ What color is used on the map to show the highway?

The Metric System of Measurement

If you turn to the scale bar shown on the map of Spain on page 4, you will see that measurement is given in both miles and **kilometers**. A kilometer is a measure of distance in the metric system.

This system is used for measuring distance. It is also used for measuring weight, capacity, and temperature. The metric system is in use or is being introduced in all the major countries of the world except the United States. Thus, it is important that we become familiar with this system.

To help you become familiar with the metric system, we have used both customary measurements, which are in general use in the United States, and metric measurements in this book. When a customary measurement appears, it is followed in parentheses ( ) by the metric measurement that is about equal to it.

As you read this book, you will see that inches are followed by centimeters (cm), feet and yards by meters (m), miles by kilometers (km), and acres by hectares (ha). Pounds are followed by kilograms (kg), and quarts by liters (l). Degrees Fahrenheit (°F) are followed by degrees Celsius (°C).

C. Drawing a Map to Scale

From Photo to Map All maps are drawings of parts of the earth. But maps do not show everything that exists on the part of the earth being mapped. The photograph and the map on page 8 illustrate how maps show only some details of the earth. The photograph shows details not shown on the map, such as the grass and the trees of the golf course. The map uses colors to show the parts of the golf course that the cartographer wanted on the map.

Scale All maps are drawn to a certain **scale**. Scale means that a certain number of inches on the map represents or stands for a certain number of feet or miles on the earth's surface. The scale bars found on maps give you this relationship.

Scale can be shown in three different ways. On some maps, the scale is shown as "One inch equals 200 feet." Scale is also shown a second way, by a fraction or ratio. For example, the ratio scale, or fraction on a map might read "1:2,400." This means that one unit of measurement on the map equals 2,400 units of the same length in the real world.

The third way to show scale is by a bar scale. If you turn back to the map of Spain on page 4, you can see that the bar scale is the straight line in the key with the distances marked off on it. All three of these scales show the relationship between the actual distance on the earth's surface and the distance shown on the map.

LESSON 1

Review

REVIEWING MAIN IDEAS
A. How is the key on a map used?
B. Why is the grid system useful for locating places?
C. What are the three ways of showing scale on a map?

SKILLS CHECK

MAP SKILL

Turn to the Gazetteer on pages 707–720. Find the coordinates of the following cities.

Athens	Mexico City
Los Angeles	London

Showing the Earth on a Map

CONNECTIONS

Suppose you were going on a trip across the United States. What kinds of maps would you need for your trip?

TERMS

landform, physical map, contour line, distribution map

FOCUS

What are some of the different kinds of maps that can be used to describe an area?

A. Different Maps for Different Purposes

One of the projects you might be assigned this year is to write a report on one of the world's countries. An important part of any country report is a map of the country you are writing about. But what kind of map should you draw? One map of a country can show only a limited amount of information about the country. For example, an outline map of the country would show only the country's shape and its boundaries with other countries.

One way to avoid this problem is to include several different kinds of maps of the country. You could show a map of the continent the country is located on. You could also draw a map showing the country's major **landforms**. Landforms are features of the earth's surface that are made by nature. They include mountains, hills, rivers, lakes, and oceans.

B. Maps Have Different Scales

You might run into a problem when you begin to draw the maps. How can you fit a map of a continent and a map of a country on pages that are the same size? For example, a map of Asia would have to be larger than the size of the notebook

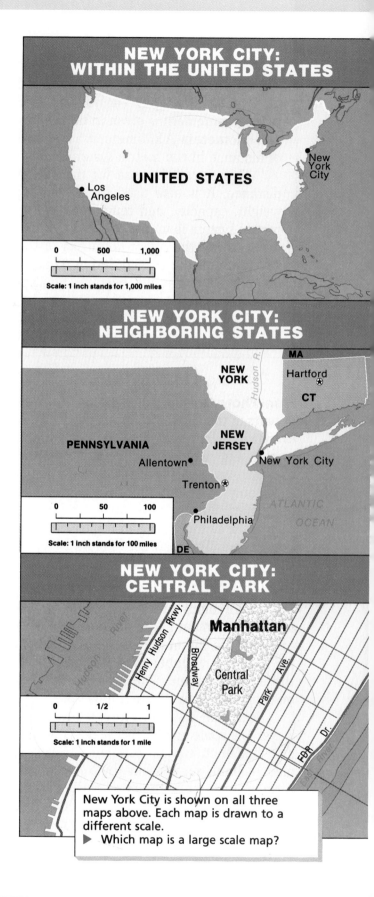

NEW YORK CITY: WITHIN THE UNITED STATES

UNITED STATES

Los Angeles

New York City

0   500   1,000

Scale: 1 inch stands for 1,000 miles

NEW YORK CITY: NEIGHBORING STATES

MA

NEW YORK

Hartford

CT

Hudson R.

PENNSYLVANIA

NEW JERSEY

Allentown

New York City

Trenton

Philadelphia

ATLANTIC OCEAN

DE

0   50   100

Scale: 1 inch stands for 100 miles

NEW YORK CITY: CENTRAL PARK

Manhattan

Hudson River

Henry Hudson Pkwy.

Broadway

Central Park

Park Ave.

FDR Dr.

0   1/2   1

Scale: 1 inch stands for 1 mile

New York City is shown on all three maps above. Each map is drawn to a different scale.
▶ Which map is a large scale map?

10

People enjoy a view from one of the many fields in New York City's Central Park.
▶ Why are parks important to people who live in cities?

paper if a map of China, which is located in Asia, is drawn to fill the entire page.

To fit all the maps on pages of the same size, you would have to use different scales for the different-size areas. As you learned in Lesson 1, maps are scale drawings of the real world. The maps you include in your country report would have to be drawn at different scales in order to fit on same-sized pages.

For example, on page 10 the maps showing New York City are drawn to three different scales. The bottom map shows part of New York City. With this map, we are able to find some of New York's landmarks, such as Central Park and Broadway. This is called a large-scale map. To show more detail of an area, a cartographer uses a large-scale map.

The middle and top maps show New York City's neighboring states and its location in the United States. These maps show much less detail about New York City, but they do show more of the area that surrounds New York. These maps are called small-scale maps. Small-scale maps show large parts of the earth's surface; large-scale maps show small parts of the earth.

Here's another example of how scale works. If you drew a map of your classroom, you would have a large-scale map. Then, if you mapped the neighborhood around the school, you would show more area in less detail. This map of the neighborhood would be a small-scale map. If you went on to map the whole town, you would be using a still smaller scale. And a map of even smaller scale would be needed for the state.

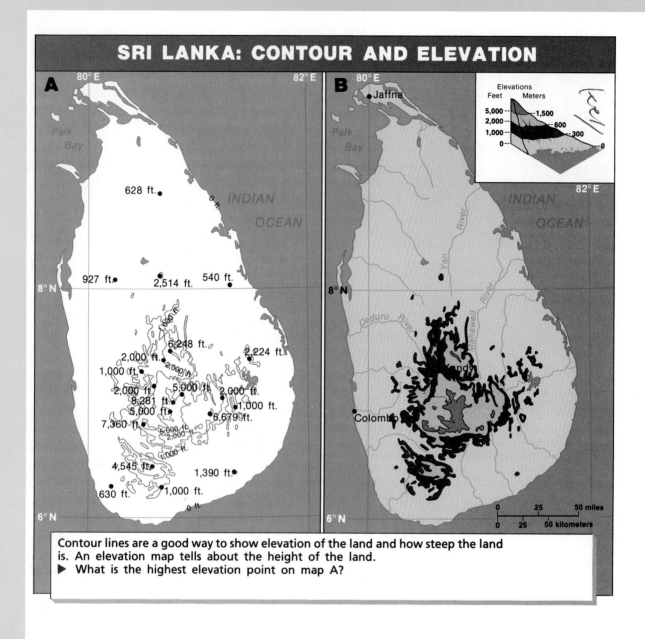

SRI LANKA: CONTOUR AND ELEVATION

A

80°E   82°E

Palk Bay

628 ft.

INDIAN OCEAN

8°N

927 ft.
2,514 ft.
540 ft.

6,248 ft.
2,224 ft.
2,000 ft.
1,000 ft.
2,000 ft.
5,000 ft.
2,000 ft.
8,281 ft.
5,000 ft.
1,000 ft.
6,679 ft.
7,360 ft.
2,000 ft.
5,000 ft.
1,000 ft.
4,545 ft.
1,390 ft.
630 ft.
1,000 ft.
0 ft.

6°N

B

80°E
Jaffna

Palk Bay

INDIAN OCEAN

82°E

8°N

Yan River
Deduru River
Mahaweli River

Kandy

Colombo

6°N

Elevations
Feet   Meters
5,000 --   -1,500
2,000 --   --600
1,000 --   --300
0 --   --0

0   25   50 miles
0   25   50 kilometers

Contour lines are a good way to show elevation of the land and how steep the land is. An elevation map tells about the height of the land.
▶ What is the highest elevation point on map A?

C. Showing the Earth's Relief on Maps

Physical Maps One map that should be in your report is a **physical map** of the country. A physical map shows the earth's features, such as mountains and plains. It also shows what the elevation, or height, of the land is.

The best way to get an accurate picture of the earth's surface on a map is to use **contour lines**. A contour line is a line drawn on a map that connects all points of land that are the same height above sea level.

Sea level is considered to be 0 feet (0 m). Map A on this page shows how the contour lines connect elevations at 1,000 feet (305 m), 2,000 feet (610 m), and 5,000 feet (1,524 m).

You can learn many things about the land from contour maps. If the contour lines are close together, the slope of the hill or mountain is steep. The slope is more gentle the farther apart the lines are. If a contour map has very few contour lines, it means the land is almost level. Look at the contour map of Sri Lanka on the opposite page. Which part of the island has the steepest slope? What is the elevation of Colombo and Jaffna? What is the elevation of Kandy? What is the average height of the island's highest point?

Showing Elevation   On the physical maps you will use this year, the areas between the contour lines are colored. These colored areas show the different elevations. Compare the contour map of Sri Lanka on the opposite page with the elevation map of the same area. The key on map B indicates that green is used to show elevations between sea level and 1,000 feet (300 m). Then different shades of orange and purple are used to show higher elevations.

Physical maps have a variety of uses. People who build roads and railroads need to know where the most level land is, so they use physical maps. They are also useful for determining where to build houses.

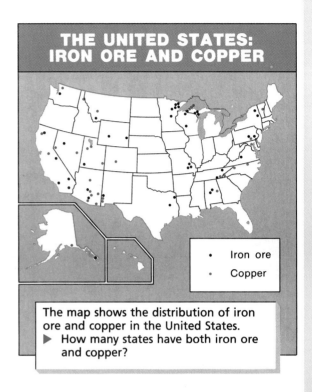

THE UNITED STATES: IRON ORE AND COPPER

- Iron ore
- Copper

The map shows the distribution of iron ore and copper in the United States.
▶ How many states have both iron ore and copper?

D. Other Kinds of Maps

There are several other kinds of maps that you could use in your country report. A daily weather map would show the weather patterns across the country. Another interesting kind of map to include is a **distribution map** of the country's resources. A distribution map shows the range of people, crops, or resources in a country or region.

The map at the top of this page shows the distribution of iron ore and copper deposits in the United States. Distribution maps help us understand why some industries develop in certain parts of the country. For example, in which part of the country do you think copper mining is the major industry? In which part of the country is iron-ore mining important?

Look at the distribution map of oil and natural gas fields. Which part of the country has the largest oil fields? Is it the same part of the country that has a large number of natural gas fields?

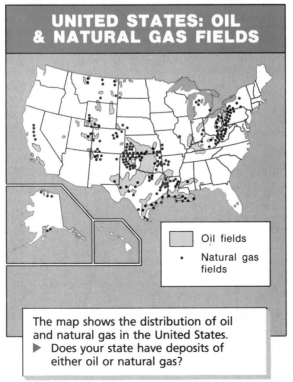

UNITED STATES: OIL & NATURAL GAS FIELDS

Oil fields

- Natural gas fields

The map shows the distribution of oil and natural gas in the United States.
▶ Does your state have deposits of either oil or natural gas?

13

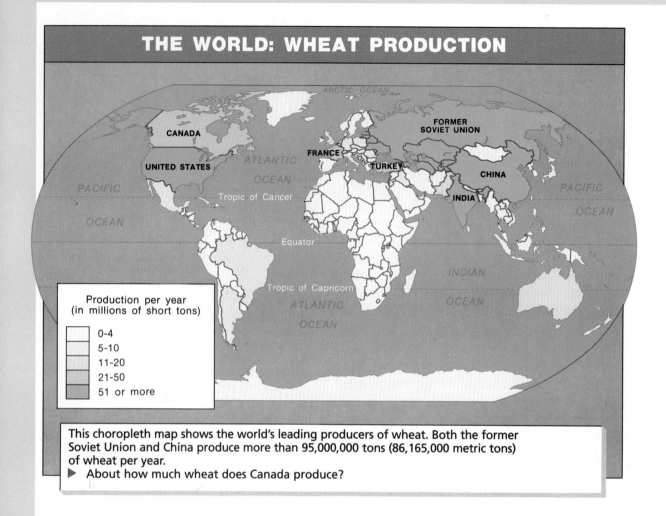

THE WORLD: WHEAT PRODUCTION

Production per year (in millions of short tons)

- 0–4
- 5–10
- 11–20
- 21–50
- 51 or more

This choropleth map shows the world's leading producers of wheat. Both the former Soviet Union and China produce more than 95,000,000 tons (86,165,000 metric tons) of wheat per year.

▶ About how much wheat does Canada produce?

Another map that shows distribution is a *choropleth* (KOR uh pleth) map. A choropleth map uses different colors to show the distribution of a product in a region or in the world. The colors also show how much of the product is produced by the countries.

The map on this page is a choropleth map of wheat production. The map key explains what each color means on the map. For example, on this map, you can see that the darkest green means that a country produces 51 million tons or more of wheat. Yellow means that a country produces between 0 and 4 million tons of wheat. You can use the choropleth map to find the world's largest and smallest producers of wheat.

LESSON 2

Review

REVIEWING MAIN IDEAS

A. What is a landform?
B. What is the difference between small-scale maps and large-scale maps?
C. How do physical maps show elevation?
D. Name three kinds of special-purpose maps.

SKILLS CHECK

MAP SKILL

Turn to the Atlas, on pages 688–706, and name the kinds of maps you find there for each continent. Choose one of the continents and explain how you would use the maps to describe that continent.

From Round Earth to Flat Paper

CONNECTIONS

If someone said to you that the earth was flat, how would you prove to him or her that it is round?

TERMS

cartography, distortion, projection, great circle, hemisphere

FOCUS

What are map projections and how are different projections used?

The cartographer in the above photograph is tracing the outline of a country for a map.
▶ How is she tracing the outline?

A. Measuring the Round Earth

Long ago in Egypt, there lived a wise man named Eratosthenes (er uh TAHS thuh-neez). Eratosthenes had a revolutionary idea—he believed that the earth was round. Most people in Eratosthenes' time thought the earth was flat and that if they went too far in any direction, they would fall off the edge into everlasting darkness.

Eratosthenes set out to prove that these people were wrong. Some scientists before Eratosthenes had also believed that the earth was round. Eratosthenes used these scientists' arguments and took them one step further—he showed how large the round earth really was.

Eratosthenes knew that at the beginning of summer, the sun would shine directly down into a deep well at a place called Syene (now Aswan) on the Nile River. This told him that the sun was directly overhead at that point. Eratosthenes also had observed that the sun was never directly overhead at Alexandria, which was about 500 miles (800 km) north of Syene.

These observations about the sun's rays led Eratosthenes to calculate that the distance around the earth must be 25,000 miles (40,225 km). He was very close to being absolutely correct. With modern instruments, scientists have found that the distance around the earth is actually 24,860 miles (40,000 km). Amazingly, Eratosthenes was not that far off!

Even after Eratosthenes' discovery, some people continued to believe that the earth was flat. Gradually, however, most people came to believe that the earth really was round. Of course, today almost everyone has seen photographs showing the earth from space. From these photographs, we know that the earth is a sphere revolving in space around the sun.

B. Making a Map of a Globe

Mapping the Earth The perfect model of the earth is a globe. Like the earth, a globe is round in shape, and it shows the earth's continents and oceans. But what are maps? Maps, too, are representations of the earth. The difference is that a map is drawn on a flat piece of paper, not on a round ball. Why do we need maps? One answer is simple. Maps are easy to fold or roll up and carry along with us everywhere we go. Imagine trying to carry a large globe along as you travel.

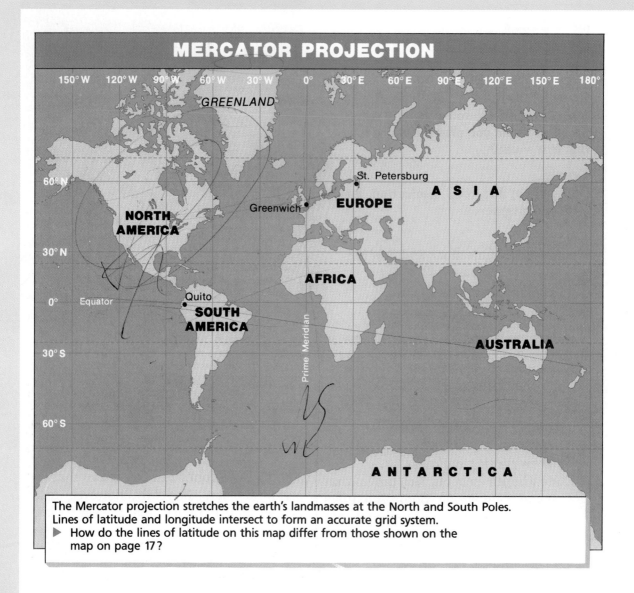

MERCATOR PROJECTION

150° W 120° W 90° W 60° W 30° W 0° 30° E 60° E 90° E 120° E 150° E 180°

GREENLAND

60° N

NORTH
AMERICA

ASIA

St. Petersburg

EUROPE

Greenwich

30° N

AFRICA

0° Equator Quito

SOUTH
AMERICA

Prime Meridian

AUSTRALIA

30° S

60° S

A N T A R C T I C A

The Mercator projection stretches the earth's landmasses at the North and South Poles. Lines of latitude and longitude intersect to form an accurate grid system.
▶ How do the lines of latitude on this map differ from those shown on the map on page 17?

The early explorers knew that maps were more practical to use than globes. One of the main fields of geography during the Age of Exploration was **cartography**, or map making. Cartographers drew maps of all the new places being discovered.

The Distorted Earth But the cartographers found that showing the round earth on a flat map was not so easy. Why? Because when cartographers transfer the round globe to a flat surface, some changes occur in the earth's directions, shapes, sizes, and distances. These changes are **distortions**, or errors in the way the earth actually looks.

Through the years cartographers have developed many ways to draw the round earth on flat surfaces. Each of these different ways is called a **projection**. All projections, however, distort the way the earth looks on a globe. Some projections distort the sizes of continents; some distort the shapes; and others distort distances and directions.

C. The Mercator Projection and Navigation

A Navigator's Map One of the most famous map projections is called the Mer-

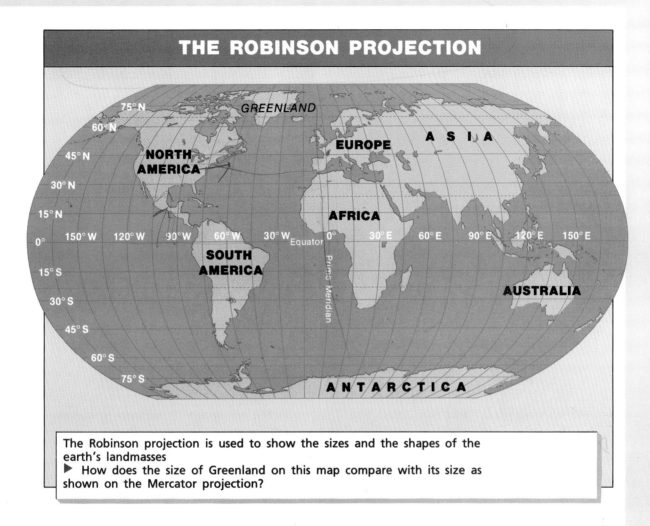

THE ROBINSON PROJECTION

The Robinson projection is used to show the sizes and the shapes of the earth's landmasses
▶ How does the size of Greenland on this map compare with its size as shown on the Mercator projection?

cator (mur KAYT ur) projection. In the 1500s, explorers and sailors needed a map that would allow them to find their way around the oceans of the world. A cartographer named Gerardus (juh RAHR dus) Mercator developed a new projection, which was named for him. Mercator's projection showed the positions of places on the map exactly as they appear on a globe. Ships could easily find their destinations with a compass and Mercator's map.

The Mercator projection was great for the sea captains and sailors navigating the world's oceans. But Mercator's map was not good at all for showing the correct shapes and sizes of lands near the poles.

You can see this is true if you compare a Mercator map with a globe. Look at the Mercator map on page 16 and compare the size of Greenland with that of South America. Now look at the same two areas on the globe in your classroom. You will see from the globe that Greenland is only about one-eighth the size of South America. On the Mercator map, however, Greenland is much larger than South America. The Mercator projection stretches lands near the North and South Poles to much bigger sizes than they actually are.

Robinson Projection   If you want to show the correct sizes and shapes of the continents, you must use another projection. In this book, we have chosen the Robinson projection. You can see what this kind of map looks like above. The Robinson pro-

NORTHERN AND SOUTHERN HEMISPHERES

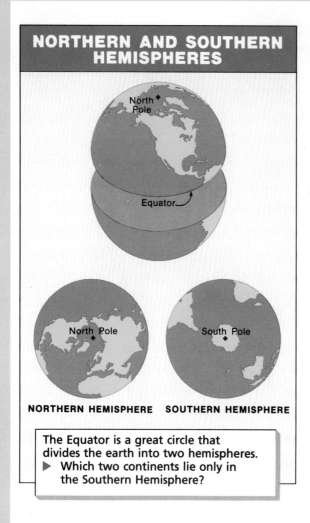

NORTHERN HEMISPHERE   **SOUTHERN HEMISPHERE**

The Equator is a great circle that divides the earth into two hemispheres.
▶ Which two continents lie only in the Southern Hemisphere?

EASTERN AND WESTERN HEMISPHERES

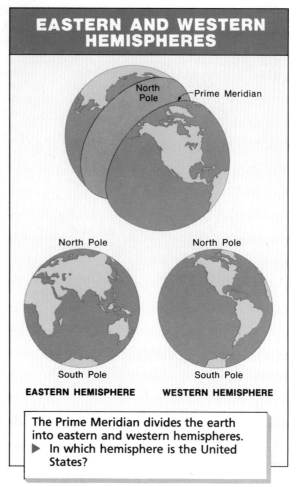

EASTERN HEMISPHERE   **WESTERN HEMISPHERE**

The Prime Meridian divides the earth into eastern and western hemispheres.
▶ In which hemisphere is the United States?

---

jection shows the size and shape of the continents with little distortion. Compare the size of Greenland and South America on this map. You can see that Greenland is much smaller. This is closer to the actual size and shape of Greenland on a globe.

D. Great Circles and Straight Lines

The Hemispheres The Mercator projection shows that ships and planes can travel in a straight line from, say, London, England, to New York. But on the globe, a straight line is not the shortest or the quickest way to travel. Instead, a **great circle** is the shortest possible distance between any two places on the surface of the earth.

A great circle is any circle you can draw on a globe that divides it into equal parts. If you were to cut a globe along a great circle, the knife would pass through the center of the globe and divide it into **hemispheres**, or two equal parts.

The Equator is a great circle because it divides the earth into northern and southern hemispheres. The Prime Meridian is also a great circle. As you can see from the map above, it divides the earth into eastern and western hemispheres.

Great Circle Routes Ships and airplanes often follow the curve of a great circle. By following great circle routes, ships and airplanes use less fuel, and passengers and cargo reach their destinations sooner.

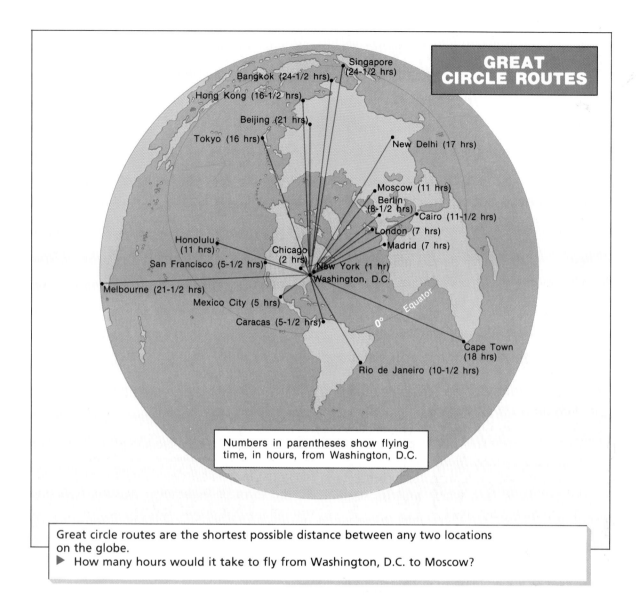

GREAT CIRCLE ROUTES

Singapore (24-1/2 hrs)
Bangkok (24-1/2 hrs)
Hong Kong (16-1/2 hrs)
Beijing (21 hrs)
Tokyo (16 hrs)
New Delhi (17 hrs)
Moscow (11 hrs)
Berlin (8-1/2 hrs)
Cairo (11-1/2 hrs)
London (7 hrs)
Madrid (7 hrs)
Honolulu (11 hrs)
Chicago (2 hrs)
San Francisco (5-1/2 hrs)
New York (1 hr)
Washington, D.C.
Melbourne (21-1/2 hrs)
Mexico City (5 hrs)
Caracas (5-1/2 hrs)
Equator
0°
Cape Town (18 hrs)
Rio de Janeiro (10-1/2 hrs)

Numbers in parentheses show flying time, in hours, from Washington, D.C.

Great circle routes are the shortest possible distance between any two locations on the globe.
▶ How many hours would it take to fly from Washington, D.C. to Moscow?

Great circle routes are best shown on maps that we sometimes call polar projections. A polar projection puts the North Pole or South Pole at the center of the map. Two of the maps on page 18 are polar projections. Can you tell which ones they are? The map on page 675 is another example. Polar projections allow great circle routes to be drawn in straight lines across the map.

Look at the map above. It is similar to a polar projection. The red lines shown on this map are parts of great circle routes.

LESSON 3

Review

REVIEWING MAIN IDEAS
A. What is the size of the earth?
B. How do maps distort the earth?
C. Why was the Mercator projection useful to navigators?
D. What is a polar projection?

SKILLS CHECK

MAP SKILL
What projection is used to show Antarctica on page 675?

MAP SKILLS HANDBOOK REVIEW

REVIEWING TERMS

On a separate sheet of paper, write the letter of the term that best matches each numbered statement.

a. key
b. compass rose
c. latitude
d. longitude
e. physical map
f. contour line
g. cartography
h. distortion
i. projection
j. hemisphere

1. An error in the way the earth actually looks
2. A marker that shows where the cardinal directions are on a map
3. A way to draw the earth on a flat surface
4. Distance, measured in degrees, east and west of the Prime Meridian
5. A line drawn on a map that connects all points of land which are the same height above sea level
6. Distance, measured in degrees, north and south of the Equator
7. The work of making maps
8. The part of a map that explains the symbols used on the map
9. A map that shows the earth's relief, or physical features, and land elevations
10. Half the earth or the globe

❖❖❖❖

REVIEWING THE FACTS

On a separate sheet of paper, answer the following questions in complete sentences.

1. What are the four cardinal directions?
2. What is the starting point of longitude called?
3. What relationship does scale show?
4. What kind of map would a cartographer use to show more detail of an area?
5. How can you tell which land forms are represented by contour lines?
6. How are physical maps used?
7. Why do different map projections have distortions?
8. What distortion is found in a Mercator projection?
9. Why is the Robinson projection used in this book?
10. How are great circle routes best shown on a map?

❖❖❖❖

WRITING ABOUT GEOGRAPHY

Imagine that you are designing a new ski area for the town of Innsbruck, Austria. Explain what maps you would find useful to help you select the best location.

❖❖❖❖

THINKING CRITICALLY

On a separate sheet of paper, answer the following questions in complete sentences.

1. How does the grid system help to locate places on a map?
2. Why do maps have different scales?
3. What map would you use to compare the resources of the United States with those of Canada?
4. Why, do you think, might Eratosthenes' discovery have encouraged explorers to seek new lands?
5. Why is it important to develop accurate maps?

On a separate sheet of paper, draw a graphic organizer that is like the one shown here. Copy the information from this graphic organizer to the one you have drawn. Under the main idea for each lesson, write three statements that you think best support the main idea.

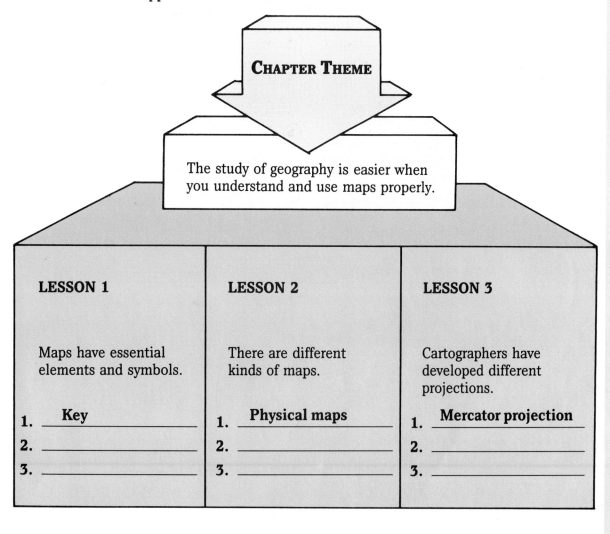

CHAPTER THEME

The study of geography is easier when you understand and use maps properly.

LESSON 1

Maps have essential elements and symbols.

1. _____Key_____
2. _____
3. _____

LESSON 2

There are different kinds of maps.

1. __Physical maps__
2. _____
3. _____

LESSON 3

Cartographers have developed different projections.

1. __Mercator projection__
2. _____
3. _____

UNIT **1**

LEARNING ABOUT THE EARTH

STUDYING THE WORLD AND ITS PEOPLE

Robinson Crusoe's Life on a Deserted Island

CONNECTIONS

Imagine you are on a deserted tropical island and have only a hammer and an axe. With a partner, list the ways you would use these tools to gather food and build a shelter on the island.

TERMS

plantation, geography, natural resource, atmosphere, weather, climate, domesticate

FOCUS

In what ways do we use our physical environment to live?

A. Robinson Crusoe and His Island Home

September 30, 1659—I, poor miserable Robinson Crusoe, being shipwrecked during a dreadful storm, came on shore this dismal unfortunate island, . . . all the rest of the ship's company being drowned, and myself almost dead. . . .

I had neither food, house, clothes, weapon nor place to fly [flee] to; and in despair of any relief saw nothing but death before me; either that I should be devoured by wild beasts, murdered by savages, or starved to death for want of food. At the approach of night I slept in a tree for fear of wild creatures. . . .

This is the first entry from a journal kept by Robinson Crusoe. Crusoe was the hero of a fictional adventure story called *Robinson Crusoe,* which was written in 1719 by a British writer named Daniel Defoe. *Robinson Crusoe* tells the story of young Crusoe's adventures after he decided to become a sailor and leave England. Crusoe eventually sailed to Brazil, the largest country in South America, and became the owner of a **plantation**, which is a large, commercial farm that grows only one crop.

Some fellow plantation owners asked Crusoe to join them in a trip to the west coast of Africa. There the owners would buy slaves and bring them back to Brazil to work on their sugar and tobacco plantations.

Crusoe agreed to take the long and dangerous trip across the Atlantic Ocean. Unfortunately, this was to be a journey filled with incredible misfortune and adventure for both Crusoe and the ship's crew. A few days after the start of the journey, Crusoe's ship ran straight into the path of a powerful hurricane. This huge ocean wave capsized the ship, drowning the ship's crew and sweeping Crusoe onto the beach of a deserted island.

B. Crusoe and the Geography of His Deserted Island

To survive, Crusoe had to learn the **geography** of his new island home. Geography is the study of the earth and how people use the earth. Geography may not seem as exciting as the adventure story about Crusoe. You probably think geography is only the memorization of the names of important mountain ranges and rivers, and learning the products of countries. It is true that you will be expected to learn many facts about the world. Knowing the names and locations of countries, cities, mountains, and rivers is the foundation of geography. After all, you can't talk about skiing in the Rocky Mountains unless you know what and where they are.

But geography is much more than memorizing facts. Geography explains the world around us. It answers questions such as why is it cold at the North Pole, why is Florida just right for swimming in January, and why do palm trees grow in California but not in Kansas? Most important, geography shows us how people use the earth and change it to produce the food we eat, to make the clothes we wear, and to build the homes in which we live.

▶ Workers hurry to their jobs on Wall Street in New York City.

Crusoe built a raft to carry the many supplies he retrieved from the wrecked ship.
With the supplies, he was able to build a shelter, hunt, and farm.
▶ What kinds of supplies did Crusoe find on the ship?

C. Crusoe's Exploration of the Island

Crusoe decided that the beach, which was swampy and wet, was not a good spot to stay and build a shelter. He thought over what a good location should offer him.

I consulted several things in my situation, which I found would be proper for [my new home]. Firstly, health and fresh water. . . . Secondly, shelter from the heat of the sun. Thirdly, security from ravenous [starving] creatures, whether men or beasts. Fourthly, a view to the sea, that if God sent any ship in sight I might not lose any advantage for my deliverance, of which I was not willing to banish all my expectation yet.

Crusoe studied the landscape of the island, hoping to find a proper site for a new home. Near a small stream he found a flat, grassy plain beside a rising hill. Crusoe decided that this should be the site of his new home.

Crusoe now set to work building a permanent shelter. Fortunately, Crusoe had retrieved some tools, guns, and other supplies from the ship, which lay wrecked near the island. With these he dug a small cave in the side of the hill. In the front of the cave mouth, he pitched his tent, which was made from the sails of the wrecked ship. Crusoe felt he needed protection, so with great effort he cut down several trees and built a log wall around his tent and cave.

D. From Hunting to Farming

Hunting "I went out [once a day]," Crusoe wrote in his journal, "with my gun . . . to see if I could kill anything fit for food." At first, Crusoe hunted the wild goats he found on the island. He also fished in the surrounding ocean waters and dug for turtle eggs hidden in the beach sands.

As time passed, Crusoe continued to explore his island and found other foods to eat. Looking through a tangle of vines one day, he found bunches of grapes. Near the grapes he discovered a grove of lemon trees and other fruit trees.

Crusoe also discovered a few barley plants and rice plants on the island. Instead of immediately cooking and eating the plants, Crusoe allowed them to bear seeds. He then planted these seeds after heavy rains occurred. Crusoe's first crop of barley failed to grow.

> *Finding my first seed did not grow, which I easily imagined was by the drought, I sought for a moister piece of ground. . . . I dug up a piece of ground near my new bower [home], and sowed the rest of my seed in February, a little before the vernal equinox. And this having the rainy months of March and April to water it, sprung up very pleasantly, and yielded a good crop. . . .*

Even though he planted after the rains, a drought, or dry period without rain, killed the plants. It was only after Crusoe understood when the rainy season occurred that his crops of barley and rice grew.

By Crusoe's second year on the island, he had a steady supply of food from his garden. Later, he caught some young goats and **domesticated** them. *Domesticate* means to "tame wild animals to live with humans." The goat herd provided Crusoe with meat, which freed him from having to worry about hunting every day.

Natural Resources Crusoe could build a home and grow food because he learned to

The island's abundant rainfall allowed Crusoe to grow a large wheat crop.
▶ How did Crusoe harvest his crop of wheat?

27

Wilmington Institute Library, photo
courtesy of Brandywine River Museum.

Crusoe built his home inside a cave opening. It was here that he began his journal.
▶ How did Crusoe build the table and chair he is using?

Crusoe also had to learn about the island's seasons and the changes in the island's temperature in order to grow his crops. The temperature, the amount of sunshine, and the amount of rainfall are all conditions of the **atmosphere**. The atmosphere is the blanket of air that covers the earth. If the earth had no atmosphere, there could be no life.

We use two words to describe the atmosphere. One word that we use all the time is **weather**. Weather is how the atmosphere is at a certain time and place. A weather report on television or a weather forecast in the newspaper describes what the weather is today or predicts what it will be tomorrow. Another word we use to describe the atmosphere is **climate**. Climate is the pattern of weather that a place has over a period of time. Crusoe's island had a climate that was warm all year, and it had rainy seasons and dry seasons.

E. Crusoe's Story and Our Life Today

Learning from Crusoe Crusoe survived on his island for almost 30 years, until he was finally rescued by the crew of a passing ship. During those 30 years, the resources of the earth and Crusoe's hard labor provided Crusoe with abundant food and adequate clothing and shelter.

You will probably never be lost on an island without food, shelter, and clothing. And if you ever are, you will have learned a few lessons from Crusoe about how to survive. But there is a more important lesson to learn from Robinson Crusoe that we can apply to our everyday lives. Today it seems that humans can do almost anything with their tools and imagination. We have flown to the moon and are exploring the frontiers of the universe. Television gives us instant information about almost any part of the world. We can microwave our dinners in a few minutes and we can

use the island's **natural resources**. Natural resources are materials made by nature that people can use. What were the natural resources Crusoe used? He used the soil to grow crops and trees to build the fort. The animals living on the island provided him with what he needed for food and to make clothing.

The natural resources we find on the earth are the source of our food, clothing, and shelter. But these natural resources require the labor, or work, of people to make them useful products. These products are usually processed, or changed into different forms. This is exactly what Crusoe had to do. He used the barley he grew to make bread. He took the skin from his goats and cut and sewed them into a vest and pants.

FROM: **The Sea Around Us**

Rachel Carson

Crusoe came upon an island that was well stocked with natural resources. But at one time, the island—like all islands—was nothing more than a barren, rocky, empty piece of land surrounded by the ocean. How did it come to be covered with trees, grasses, birds, and animals? In her book, *The Sea Around Us*, Rachel Carson wrote about how newly born islands come to be alive with so many different forms of life.

We can only guess how long after its emergence from the sea an oceanic island may lie uninhabited. Certainly in its original state it is a land bare, harsh, and repelling [disgusting] beyond human experience. No living thing moves over the slopes of its volcanic hills; no plants cover its naked lava fields. But little by little, riding on the winds, drifting on the currents, or rafting in on logs, floating brush, or trees, the plants and animals that are to colonize it arrive from the distant continents.

So deliberate, so unhurried . . . are the ways of nature that the stocking of an island may require thousands or millions of years. It may be that no more than half a dozen times in all these eons [years] does a particular form, such as a tortoise, make a successful landing on its shores. To wonder impatiently why man is not a constant witness of such arrivals is to fail to understand the majestic pace of the process. . . .

The wide-ranging birds that visit islands of the ocean in migration may . . . have a good deal to do with the distribution of plants, and perhaps even some of the insects and minute [small] land shells. . . .

A lawyer uses a computer to help her research a legal issue.
▶ How else might the lawyer use the computer?

program computers to solve math problems that would take a person several years to figure out.

Using the Earth Crusoe's struggle for food, shelter, and clothing seems very distant and removed from these modern-day accomplishments. Yet, like Crusoe, we still use the earth's resources—even to make tools like computers and microwaves. Knowing what these resources are and how we use them will give us a fuller understanding of the world we live in.

Robinson Crusoe was an explorer, an observer, and a learner. He investigated his island, he examined the island's landscape, and he learned how to live on the island. You, too, can follow in his footsteps this year as you explore the world, observe its people and places, and learn how these people and places affect you.

LESSON 1

Review

REVIEWING MAIN IDEAS
A. Why did Crusoe decide to sail to Africa?
B. Why is the study of geography important?
C. Name the four things Crusoe wanted his home to have.
D. How did Crusoe obtain food on his deserted island?
E. What message does the story of Robinson Crusoe have for people today?

SKILLS CHECK
WRITING SKILL
Reread Crusoe's first journal entry, on page 25. Imagine that you have landed on a deserted island. Write a journal entry that describes how you would feel and what your plans would be to find food, clothing, and shelter.

People Have Many Different Ways of Life

CONNECTIONS

Have you ever eaten any foods that tasted different from what you normally eat? Describe what you liked or disliked about the food.

TERMS

culture, language family, mosque

FOCUS

How does culture shape the way we live?

A. Culture and Crusoe's Island Life

Robinson Crusoe survived on a deserted island by using the island's natural resources. The way Crusoe used these resources was based on his **culture**. Culture is the way a person or people live. The language we speak, our religion, and our beliefs about what is good and bad are all parts of our culture. Culture also includes the clothes we wear, the music we listen to, and almost everything else that makes up our way of life.

Crusoe's way of life on the island was based on the English culture in which he was raised. Crusoe could have lived perfectly well by hunting goats and other wild animals on his island and by picking wild fruits and berries. But he immediately set to work trying to tame the wild goats and trying to grow grain to make bread. If someone from a different culture had landed on the island, he or she would have found different ways of surviving, because that person would have used the island's resources differently.

B. Language and Our Thoughts

Learning Language Robinson Crusoe lived alone on his island for 25 years before he rescued a man from some cannibals who had landed on the island. The rescued man, whom Crusoe named Friday, was a South American Indian who had been brought to the island for sacrifice by the cannibals. Crusoe described his first encounter with Friday after the rescue.

He spoke some words to me, and though I could not understand them, yet I thought they were pleasant to hear, for they were the first sound of a man's voice that I had heard, my own excepted, for about twenty-five years. . . . I was greatly delighted with him, and made it my business to teach him everything . . . but especially to make him speak and understand me. . . .

Until Friday and Crusoe could speak the same language, they could only communicate by pointing at objects and by making signs with their hands. Once Friday learned English, the men could talk to each other and Friday could begin to learn about Crusoe's culture.

Language is one of the most important parts of culture. Thousands of languages are spoken today by the nearly 6 billion people who live on the earth. Most people in the United States speak English, which comes to us from England, the European country that once controlled our country.

At one time, England had the largest empire in the world, and the English language spread with England's empire. Today the lands England once controlled are independent countries, but English is still spoken by many people in these countries. In fact, English is one of the most widely spoken languages in the world.

Language Family English is a Germanic language, which means that it is related to languages spoken in northern Europe. Germanic is a **language family**. A language family is a group of languages that all come from one common ancestor language. The other important European language families are the Romance languages of southern Europe and the Slavic languages that are used in Eastern Europe.

31

Many important languages are not related to the European language families. Arabic is spoken by millions of people in northern Africa and the Middle East. In Asia, Chinese and Japanese are the most important languages. Swahili is an important language in Africa, and Quechua (KECH wah) is still spoken by Indians in some parts of the Andes mountains of South America. These are only a few of the thousands of languages used by the different peoples on the earth.

C. Religion: An Important Part of Culture

Different Religions Robinson Crusoe was English. His religion was Protestant, one of the Christian religions that was the religion of most people in England during the time the story was written. Do you remember that Crusoe lived in Brazil for a time? Brazil was controlled by people from Portugal, who were Roman Catholics, another Christian religion. In an earlier adventure in the book, Crusoe was captured by pirates off the coast of Africa. The pirates were Muslims, which is the name for the followers of the Islamic religion.

These are only a few of the many religions practiced by people around the world. Not all religions share the same beliefs. For example, most Christians believe that Sunday is a day of worship. This belief shapes the work schedule of most Christians, who work from Monday through Friday or Saturday. For Muslims, Friday is a day of rest, and for Jews, Saturday is the day of worship.

Religion affects more than just work schedules. People who belong to the Hindu religion in India do not eat meat. Muslims do not eat pork, and Jewish dietary laws place restrictions on the preparation and kinds of foods Jews can eat.

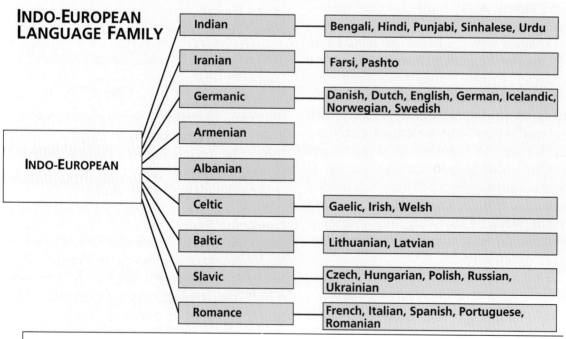

INDO-EUROPEAN LANGUAGE FAMILY

Indian	Bengali, Hindi, Punjabi, Sinhalese, Urdu
Iranian	Farsi, Pashto
Germanic	Danish, Dutch, English, German, Icelandic, Norwegian, Swedish
Armenian	
Albanian	
Celtic	Gaelic, Irish, Welsh
Baltic	Lithuanian, Latvian
Slavic	Czech, Hungarian, Polish, Russian, Ukrainian
Romance	French, Italian, Spanish, Portuguese, Romanian

The table shows the 9 major branches of the Indo-European language family. Each branch is made up of one or more spoken languages.

► What branch does the Spanish language belong to?

32

Michelangelo's important religious works of art include this section from his painting on the ceiling of the Sistine Chapel. This scene shows God reaching out to touch the finger of Adam.
▶ What are the figures that surround God?

Religious Art Much of the greatest art in the world is religious art. Michelangelo was a great artist who lived in Italy in the sixteenth century. His best-known paintings and sculptures are of scenes from famous Bible stories. In fact, much of the great European art in the centuries before and after Michelangelo has religion as its subject matter.

Art works from other parts of the world also have religious roots. Statues of Buddha, the founder of the Buddhist religion, are important artworks from China, India, and Southeast Asia. Sculptures of Hindu gods from India are found in art museums around the world. Art museums also have collections of African masks and wood carvings. Most of these were originally made for religious ceremonies or for other religious purposes.

Each religion also has its own special kind of church or temple architecture. Because of this, we can easily identify a Christian cathedral in France; an Islamic **mosque**, or Islamic place of worship, in Turkey; or a Buddhist shrine in Burma. Other religions around the world also have their own special style of art and their own way of building places of worship.

D. Culture and the Way We Eat

If you were invited to eat dinner in the home of an Arab Bedouin, what would you eat? Bedouins are wandering herders who live in the deserts of the Middle East and North Africa. You begin by washing your hands. Then the men are invited into the tent where your host lives. Because men and women eat separately, the women will eat after the men have finished.

33

A group of Arab men sit cross-legged around their meal. The pieces of bread are eaten with the dinner.
▶ Which hand is used to eat with?

All the men sit on rugs around a huge platter. On the platter is a large, flat wheat bread that looks like a giant pancake. Rice is mounded on top of the bread. Then pieces of boiled lamb are put on top of the rice, and a seasoned butter sauce is poured over the rice and lamb.

You won't be given any silverware. Instead, you will be expected to pick the rice and lamb from the platter with your right hand. After the men have eaten, they relax and enjoy cups of strong Arab coffee.

This is only one example of the many different foods and the customs for preparing and eating food that you can find in the countries of the world. We can also find different foods in our own country. Perhaps you have eaten in a Chinese restaurant. Unless you learned to use chopsticks as a child, you would find that eating with chopsticks is very different from using silverware.

Certainly the foods we eat are partly influenced by the places where we live. An Arab living in the interior of a desert is not likely to eat seafood, which would not be easy to get so far from the ocean. However, the ways in which foods are prepared are largely determined by the unique culture or customs practiced by the people who live in a region.

LESSON 2

Review

REVIEWING MAIN IDEAS
A. What do we mean when we use the term *culture*?
B. Why is English so widely spoken throughout the world?
C. Name two ways in which culture is influenced by religion.
D. Give an example of how the way people eat is influenced by their culture.

SKILLS CHECK
THINKING SKILL
Describe how music, clothing, or food is an important part of our culture today.

34

Making a Living in the World

CONNECTIONS

Describe a career you might want to pursue when you finish your education. Explain why that career appeals to you.

TERMS

subsistence, ore, pastoralism, alloy, nomad

FOCUS

How have people used the earth's resources to make a living?

A. People as Resources

Subsistence Economy You have learned how Robinson Crusoe had to use the natural resources of his environment to survive. There are other resources that are as important as natural resources. You may be surprised to learn that people, too, are a resource. In fact, it is human resources, that is, people, who do the work to make natural resources useful.

Like Crusoe, our ancestors had to learn about natural resources and use their human resources to make them into useful products. Like Crusoe, early humans survived by hunting animals and gathering any edible plants they could find. Edible plants are the fruit, leaves, roots, or other plant parts that are good to eat. Unlike Crusoe, these early people did not have guns. Instead, they hunted with weapons such as traps, slingshots, and spears.

People who live from hunting and gathering have a **subsistence** economy. A subsistence economy is one in which the people collect only enough food to feed themselves.

When Crusoe first arrived on his island, he had a subsistence economy. He hunted when he needed meat, and he gathered grapes and other plants. As you may remember from Lesson 1, Crusoe domesti-

cated some wild goats, which gave him a more secure food supply.

Pastoralism Early humans also tamed animals to make them pets or to use their meat, milk, and hides. Larger animals could be used for pulling carts or for riding. Eventually, people who lived in the great grasslands of Asia and the semidesert regions of Africa learned to herd animals for a living. Herding animals for a living is called **pastoralism.**

The pastoralists had to move their herds of animals to find enough good grasses for the animals to graze on. They became **nomads**, people who have no permanent home. Nomads move from place to place, living in tents or other movable shelters.

An African boy herds his family's cattle and sheep. Pastoralism is still practiced in many parts of the world.
▶ Why is the boy carrying sticks?

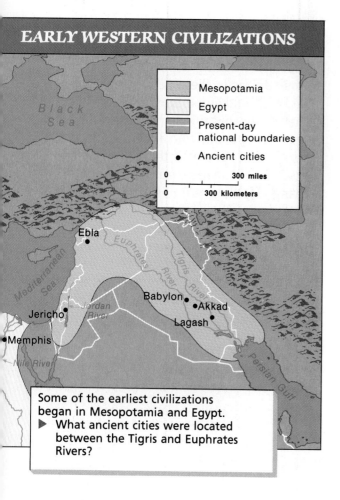

EARLY WESTERN CIVILIZATIONS

Mesopotamia

Egypt

Present-day national boundaries

• Ancient cities

0   300 miles

0   300 kilometers

Black Sea

Mediterranean Sea

Ebla

Euphrates River

Tigris River

Babylon• •Akkad

Jericho•

Jordan River

Lagash•

•Memphis

Nile River

Persian Gulf

Some of the earliest civilizations began in Mesopotamia and Egypt.
▶ What ancient cities were located between the Tigris and Euphrates Rivers?

B. Farming and the Rise of Cities

Growth of Farming When Robinson Crusoe began planting grain, he changed his economy, or way of making a living, from hunting and gathering to farming. Early humans also went through a similar change. They realized that certain plants could be grown in one area where they could be protected and where they might be more easily harvested than in the wild. This new way of growing crops was the beginning of agriculture, or farming.

The change from hunting and gathering to farming is one of the most important events in human history. Farming made it possible for people to produce a surplus of food. When they had a surplus, they could store it for times when crops failed. But

surplus food also meant that not everyone had to spend time hunting and gathering or farming. Some people could spend their time doing other kinds of work. These people became specialists, or people who do only one kind of job. Some people made weapons and tools, and others made baskets or pottery.

The number of people living in one place also started to grow. Camps became villages and villages became towns. Eventually, the first cities began to develop. These cities required a government to keep everything running smoothly. Since many goods were gathered in the cities, armies were created to provide protection.

Growth of Trade Trade began to develop between cities when people realized that goods produced in one city could be traded for different goods produced in another city. Trade routes sprang up between cities as merchant caravans carried loads of goods for trading.

The people living in the cities developed a way of life known as civilization. Civilizations have productive farms, governments, armies, a system of writing, large ornate buildings, and great works of art. Civilizations began to grow in many parts of the world.

One early center of civilization was Mesopotamia, the area between the Tigris and Euphrates rivers in what is today the country of Iraq. Great cities were built here between 5,000 and 6,000 years ago. About the same time, another important Western civilization began along the banks of the Nile River in Egypt.

C. The Rise of Manufacturing

Using Resources The people living in cities learned new ways to use natural resources. They melted **ores**, or rocks that contain minerals, to make metals such as copper and iron. Later they improved these

36

A worker in protective clothing tends a huge vat of molten steel.
▶ Why is the worker wearing protective clothing?

metals by mixing them in **alloys** such as bronze and steel. Alloys are mixtures of metals that are harder or stronger than the individual metals from which they are made. Both of these processes allowed people to make stronger weapons and tools.

About 200 years ago a revolutionary advance was made in our ability to use energy. In England, James Watt made the first steam engine. Steam engines could be used to run machines in factories. They could also be mounted on carts that ran on rails; these became the first railroads. About the same time, steam engines were put on ships. Now ships could sail under their own power rather than depend on wind to move them.

These inventions and others made it possible to build large factories. The first factories made cloth for clothing and other uses. Soon, more factories were built to manufacture tools, guns, transportation equipment, and thousands of other goods for people to use.

D. Work Today and in the Future

Manufacturing is still an important part of the economy of most countries. But as in the past, the way people make a living is again changing. Today some major countries are moving from manufacturing to information and service industries as their most important economic activities. Information industries gather, process, and store information in computers. Service industries provide services for other people. Service industry jobs include work in education, health, restaurants, and tourism.

Some experts believe that in the future most people will work in these kinds of jobs. These experts also believe that by using computers and other new electronic tools, more and more people will be able to work from their homes. Today, many companies have given workers computers to use at home. The home computers are linked to other computers at the company's office. The workers send the work they have done on their home computers to the main company computer.

LESSON 3

Review

REVIEWING MAIN IDEAS
A. What early human activity is part of a subsistence economy?
B. What effects did surplus food have on people's lives?
C. How did the invention of the steam engine change the way in which people produced goods?
D. How might the industries of the future affect the way people work?

SKILLS CHECK

MAP SKILL
Turn to the map of South America on page 696. Crusoe's ship may have wrecked near 7°N/50°W. Name the countries that are near this coordinate.

REVIEWING TERMS

Match each term with the correct definition. Write your answers in sentence form.

atmosphere   geography
nomad   natural resource
culture   pastoralism
weather   service industry
climate   language family

1. A material made by nature that people can use
2. The way a person or people live
3. A person with no permanent home
4. The blanket of air that covers the earth
5. A group of languages from one common ancestor language
6. An economy based on the herding of animals
7. Work that provides services rather than goods
8. The condition of the atmosphere at a certain time or place
9. The pattern of weather a place has over a period of time
10. The study of the earth and how people use the earth

REVIEWING THE FACTS

On a separate sheet of paper, answer the questions in complete sentences.

1. What were the natural resources that Crusoe used to survive on his island?
2. What do weather and climate describe?
3. How did English become one of the most widely spoken languages in the world?
4. Name three religions that help shape the culture of people around the world.

5. Why can we say that Crusoe had a subsistence economy?
6. Why did pastoralists become nomads?
7. Why did trade develop between ancient cities?
8. What was the result of creating alloys such as bronze and steel?
9. What were wind and water used to power?
10. What are service industries?

WRITING ABOUT GEOGRAPHY

When Crusoe met Friday, they could not understand each other's language. Write a paragraph explaining how you would teach someone from another country how to speak a few sentences in English.

THINKING CRITICALLY

On a separate sheet of paper, answer the following in complete sentences.

1. How can the study of geography help you plan a vacation to a foreign country?
2. How could the lessons of Crusoe's survival have been applied to man's first landing on the moon?
3. In what ways does culture influence the way people live?
4. How did the beginning of agriculture allow the development of civilization?
5. Why was the steam engine a revolutionary advance in technology?

Summarizing the Chapter

On a separate sheet of paper, draw a graphic organizer like the one shown here. Copy the information from this graphic organizer to the one you have drawn. Next to each main idea, write three statements that you think best support it. The first statement has been done for you.

Chapter Theme

Geography is the study of the earth and the way people live on the earth.

Lesson 1 People use the physical environment in many different ways.	1. To grow food 2. ____________ 3. ____________
Lesson 2 Culture shapes the way we live.	1. The language we speak 2. ____________ 3. ____________
Lesson 3 There are many ways of using the earth's resources to make a living.	1. Hunting and gathering 2. ____________ 3. ____________

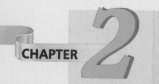

CHAPTER **2**

THE FIVE THEMES OF GEOGRAPHY

1. The Earth and Its Regions

2. Location and Place

3. Human Changes to the Earth

4. The Importance of Movement

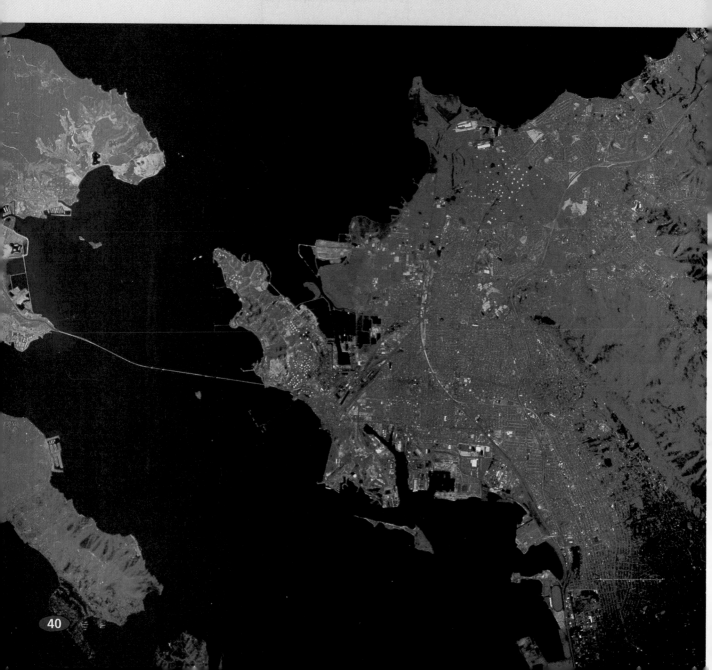

The Earth and Its Regions

CONNECTIONS

Imagine that you are an astronaut standing on the moon. Describe what the earth would look like to you.

TERMS

region, relief, glacier

FOCUS

Why do we divide the earth into regions?

A. Viewing the Earth from Space

This was it. We were 100 miles up and going at a velocity of 25,730 feet per second. Now for the first time, I could look out the window and see back along the flight path. I could not help exclaiming over the radio about what I saw. "Oh," I said, "that view is tremendous!" It really was. I could see for hundreds of miles in every direction—the sun on white clouds, patches of blue water beneath, and great chunks of Florida and the southeastern U.S.

I saw the Canary Islands through the periscope and then saw them through the window. They were partially hidden by clouds. While I was reporting in by radio to the Canary Islands tracking station, I had my first glimpse of the coast of Africa. The Atlas Mountains were clearly visible through the window. Inland, I could see huge dust storms blowing across the desert, as well as clouds of smoke from brush fires raging along the edge of the desert. One of the things that surprised me most about the flight was the percentage of the earth that was covered by clouds. They were nearly solid over central Africa and extended out over most of the Indian Ocean and clear across the Pacific.

These words were written by John Glenn, the first American to orbit the earth. Glenn made his historic trip on Tuesday, February 20, 1962, in the spacecraft named *Friendship 7.* The fascinating scenes that unfolded beneath *Friendship 7* as it moved through space gave John Glenn a new and different view of the earth. You, too, will see the earth in a special way when you study geography. But unlike Glenn, one of the ways you will view the earth is by looking at its different **regions**. A region is a part of the earth that has one or more common characteristics.

The Five Themes Region is one of the five themes, or main ideas, of geography. The other four themes are absolute and relative location, place, relationships within places, and movement.

The themes are like telescopes, since each theme gives us a special way of looking at the earth. In this chapter you will learn how the themes work, and how you can use them to understand the world around you.

This satellite photo of the earth, which was taken from space, shows Africa.
▶ What other continents are visible in the photograph?

▶ A Landsat photograph taken from a satellite shows part of San Francisco Bay.

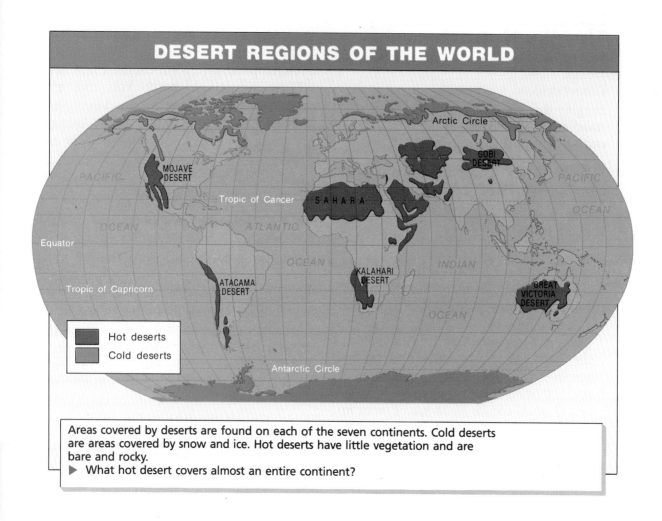

DESERT REGIONS OF THE WORLD

Arctic Circle

GOBI DESERT

MOJAVE DESERT

PACIFIC

OCEAN

Tropic of Cancer

S A H A R A

ATLANTIC

PACIFIC

OCEAN

Equator

OCEAN

INDIAN

ATACAMA DESERT

KALAHARI DESERT

OCEAN

GREAT VICTORIA DESERT

Tropic of Capricorn

Hot deserts

Cold deserts

Antarctic Circle

Areas covered by deserts are found on each of the seven continents. Cold deserts are areas covered by snow and ice. Hot deserts have little vegetation and are bare and rocky.

▶ What hot desert covers almost an entire continent?

B. Defining Different Regions

Regions vary according to the characteristics, or qualities, that we use to identify them. One example of this is the climate regions of the world. These are areas that have similar climates that often cover a large part of a continent. The map on this page shows the regions of the world that are covered by desert climates. What other characteristics might these regions have in common?

Regions can also be defined according to economic activities, such as farming and manufacturing. Cultural traits, such as language, religion, and food, can also be used to identify a region. Political divisions, such as the boundaries between countries or states, also identify regions. During a news

program on radio or television, you may have heard the announcer say, "Today in Southeast Asia . . ." or "Yesterday in Western Europe. . . ." You may have read a newspaper story about Southern Africa, Eastern Europe, the Middle East, or Central America. These names refer to geographical regions of the earth that are made up of many countries.

An area can also be part of more than one region. The city of Philadelphia, Pennsylvania, for example, is in the mid-Atlantic region of the United States. It is also part of a region known as Megalopolis, an area of large cities and many people in the eastern part of the country. This Megalopolis stretches from Boston, Massachusetts, to Washington, D.C.

C. The Many Forms of the Land

O beautiful for spacious skies,
For amber waves of grain,
For purple mountain majesties
Above the fruited plain.

Do you recognize these lines? They are from the first verse of the song "America the Beautiful," which was written in 1893 by Katharine Lee Bates. In the summer of that year, Bates made a trip from Massachusetts to Colorado. From the top of Pikes Peak, she could see the Rocky Mountains stretching off to the west. Turning to the east, she could see the Great Plains fading off into the distance. This view so impressed Bates that she later composed her song. The purple mountains are the Rocky Mountains, and the fruited plain is covered by the Great Plains.

Landforms The Great Plains and the Rocky Mountains are landform regions of the United States. Landforms are the forms or shapes of the earth. Plains, plateaus, hills, and mountains are the four main kinds of landforms. Each of these landforms is different from the others because of its **relief**.

Relief is the difference in the elevation or height of the land.

A plain is an almost flat area, with little difference in elevation between the high parts and the low parts. This is why we say plains have low relief. There are many different kinds of plains. Coastal plains are areas near the ocean coast that were once underwater. Lake plains were once the bottoms of lakes that were exposed when the lakes dried up.

A plateau is a plain that has been raised up by pressures inside the earth so that it stands high above the areas around it. Plateaus often have canyons that cross them. The canyons were formed by many rivers that cut into the surface of the plateau. The Grand Canyon is an example of such a canyon. Sometimes the surface of the plateau may be broken by hills or mountains, too.

Hills are areas of moderate relief. This means that the difference in elevation between the tops of hills and the bottoms of the valleys is between 300 feet (91 m) and 1,000 feet (305 m). Hills may have either steep or gentle slopes.

The snow-covered top of Pikes Peak looks down over pine forests and grass-covered plains.
▶ Where is Pikes Peak located?

FOUR KINDS OF LAND RELIEF

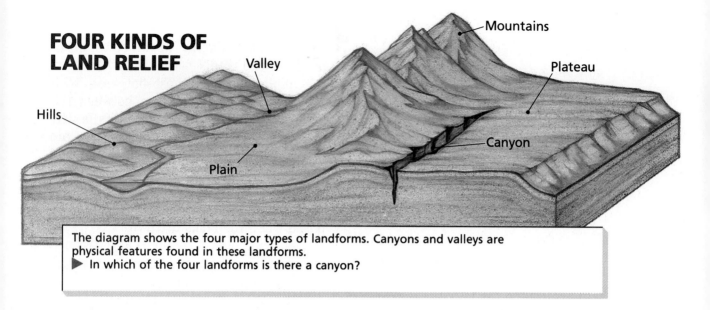

Hills

Valley

Mountains

Plateau

Plain

Canyon

The diagram shows the four major types of landforms. Canyons and valleys are physical features found in these landforms.
▶ In which of the four landforms is there a canyon?

Hills often form in an area where there was once a plateau. The hills occur when rivers that flowed across the plateau cut so many canyons and valleys in the plateau that there is little or none of the original flat plateau surface left. The Allegheny Plateau in the eastern United States is an example of a plateau that has worn down so much that it is really a region of hills. However, geographers continue to call it a plateau.

High Relief Mountains are the most spectacular landforms. Mountains have high relief, which means that a mountain's peak is at least 1,000 feet (305 m) above the land around them. Many mountains are so tall that they have snow on them all year round. The snow can harden into ice and form **glaciers**, large wide rivers of ice that slowly flow down the sides of a mountain, carving the mountain into a sharp, pointed peak. Many of the peaks in the Rocky Mountains and the Sierra Nevada Mountains of the United States were once covered by glaciers.

Mountains often form in long rows that are called mountain ranges. The tallest mountain range in the world is the Himalaya Mountains in Asia. Mount Everest, the highest mountain in the world at over 29,000 feet (8,840 m), is found in the Himalayas.

The longest mountain range in the world is the Andes in South America. The Andes extend all the way down the western side of South America. They are over 4,000 miles (6,436 km) long, which is greater than the distance between New York and Los Angeles.

An important thing to remember about all these landforms is the fact that each can change. The Allegheny Plateau is only one example of how weather and rivers can wear down and slowly change a landform.

LESSON 1
Review

REVIEWING MAIN IDEAS
A. What is meant by a region?
B. Name three different ways in which a region can be defined?
C. What are the four major landform regions?

SKILLS CHECK

MAP SKILL
Using the climate map on page 42, name the continents on which a desert climate is found.

44

Location and Place

CONNECTIONS

Name the landmarks you would use if you wanted to direct a friend from your school to your home.

TERMS

navigator, meteorologist, absolute location, relative location

FOCUS

How do we use location and place?

A. John Glenn's Return to Earth

Navigation You read about what John Glenn saw from space. Now let's see what happened when he came back to the earth. Glenn's spacecraft was pulled to the earth by gravity. Gravity is the force that attracts objects toward the earth. Friction with the atmosphere slowed the spacecraft down a little, but giant parachutes were used before the craft landed. These kept the ship from hitting the earth so hard that Glenn would be injured. The impact of landing was also reduced by aiming the spacecraft at the Atlantic Ocean.

Unlike the pilots of today's space shuttles, Glenn could not steer his spacecraft. As a result, no one was sure exactly where he would land in the Atlantic. How could the United States Navy's ships find Glenn? There were no landmarks on the ocean to guide people who had the job of finding Glenn and his spacecraft.

Fortunately, we have invented a way of telling where anything is on the earth, even if there aren't any landmarks to go by. **Navigators** are people who are responsible for locating ships and planes. These same people were also responsible for finding Glenn's spacecraft after it splashed down. Navigators have created a system of imaginary lines that divide up the earth. This system is called the grid system, which you learned about in the Map Handbook.

The longitude and latitude numbers that make up the grid system allow us to locate a country or object anywhere on earth. If we know the latitude and longitude of a place, we can find its location, no matter where it is.

Absolute Location The latitude and longitude of a place is called **absolute location**. Using sophisticated computers and maps, the navigators on the ships that were to pick up John Glenn were able to determine the absolute location where Glenn had landed. They had no trouble finding the spacecraft when it landed.

Knowing how to find the absolute location of a place is a basic skill in geography, since it is the quickest way to find a place on a map. Throughout this year, you will often be asked to find the absolute location of the earth's cities, towns, lakes, and rivers.

The space shuttle *Columbia* lands in the desert at Edwards Air Force Base in California.
▶ How did the shuttle's navigator find Edwards Air Force Base?

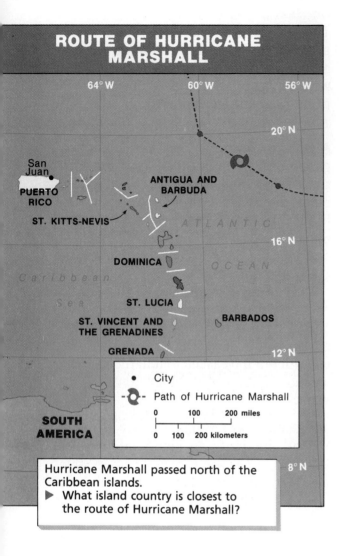

ROUTE OF HURRICANE MARSHALL

City
Path of Hurricane Marshall

0   100   200 miles
0   100   200 kilometers

Hurricane Marshall passed north of the Caribbean islands.
▶ What island country is closest to the route of Hurricane Marshall?

B. Finding Our Way by Relative Location

At 6 P.M. Central Daylight Time, Hurricane Marshall was centered near the latitude 18°N and longitude 57°W, or about 600 miles (965 km) east of San Juan, Puerto Rico. The storm is traveling northwest at about 12 miles per hour (19 km per hour), and is expected to be centered at about 20°N latitude and 60°W longitude by 6 A.M. This would put Marshall about 200 miles (322 km) northeast of the island of Barbuda. Hurricane Marshall is not believed to be an immediate threat to any land area.

How is the location of the hurricane given in this newspaper report? Perhaps you noticed that the article gives the absolute location of the hurricane. The storm was 18°N and 57°W at 6 P.M., and it was expected to move to 20°N and 60°W by the next morning. These locations are very useful for **meteorologists**, the scientists who study the weather, because the locations allow them to follow the storm's exact progress. But absolute location is not very useful to people who don't have maps showing latitude and longitude lines.

Relative Location The newspaper also tells you that the hurricane is located 600 miles (965 km) east of San Juan, Puerto Rico. If you know where the city of San Juan is, or if you have a map that shows it, you can estimate how far 600 miles (965 km) is and know just about where the hurricane is. When we find the location of a place by telling how far and in what direction it is from somewhere else, we are using **relative location**. Relative location gives the location of a place relative to some known landmark.

Imagine that you had to tell someone how to find your school. You might say, "My school is one block north of the Greengate Shopping Center, which is on Elm Street." When you give these kinds of directions, you are using relative location. You have told the person the distance and direction of the school from the shopping center, and you have told him or her what street the school is on. If you were telling a person where your town is located, you would probably begin by noting its relative location to the nearest large city, or some significant landform.

Most of us use relative location every day to find the places where we need to go. Absolute location is used by navigators, meteorologists, and others who need to find exact locations without having to depend on landmarks.

C. Natural and Human Features of Places

Almost heaven, West Virginia,
Blue Ridge Mountains, Shenandoah River.
Life is old there,
Older than the trees,
Younger than the mountains
Blowin' like a breeze.

Country Roads, take me home
To the place I belong:
West Virginia,
Mountain Momma
Take me home,
Country Roads.

All my mem'ries gather round her,
Miner's lady, stranger to blue water.
Dark and dusty, painted on the sky,
Misty taste of moonshine,
Teardrop in my eye.

Describing the Land These words are from a popular song, "Take Me Home, Country Roads," which was written and recorded by John Denver. What impressions do you get from this song? You may think of West Virginia as a state with mountains and rivers. Maybe the lines "Miner's lady, stranger to blue water. / Dark and dusty, painted on the sky" made you think that mining is an important part of West Virginia's economy. Of course, the "miner's lady" is West Virginia, and "stranger to blue water" and "dark and dusty" are references to how coal mining has changed the land and water of the state.

Many popular songs, poems, novels, and paintings have a theme similar to the one in "Take Me Home, Country Roads." They show in words or pictures what some part of the earth is like. Most of these works of art also show how both nature and human beings have shaped the character of a place. Nearly every place on the earth is the way it is because of the way people have used and changed the natural environment.

Think about the place where you live. The natural environment of your area includes the kind of climate it has. For example, in the southeastern United States summers are long, hot, and humid, and winters are short and mild. Vegetation such

Deep inside a mine, a coal miner uses a machine to cut away coal from a tunnel wall. The coal is then gathered and sent to the surface.
▶ What do you think it is like to work in a coal mine?

as forests, grasslands, and deserts is part of the natural environment. Landforms such as mountains, plateaus, plains, and hills are also considered to be parts of the natural environment.

Human Characteristics of a Place You can see how people shape the character of a place by looking at the diagram below. Each section of the diagram shows the changes that have occurred in a particular area. In the first section, the land is untouched by humans. But this does not mean changes do not occur. Even in nature, the land constantly changes. Trees die, rivers change course, and new weather patterns can create deserts where there was once forest.

In the second section, people have moved onto the land and have begun to farm it. A few houses built from the area's natural resources are scattered about. Some of the forest has been cleared to grow crops for the individual families.

In the third section, the individual farms have started to disappear as a village begins to grow. A road has been built to connect the farms to the village. The fields are no longer just small patches in the forests. Notice also that the village is located on the stream that flows through the section. Can you guess what uses the village might make of the stream?

The fourth and the fifth sections show how the farming village slowly changes into a community that is no longer based on farming. These two sections show the effects of a new way of making a living. This is especially clear from the fifth section. Factories have been built, the stream has been covered over, and the paths have become paved roads.

In the sixth section, a modern city has grown from the factory town. Freeways have replaced the one-lane roads. Office buildings stretch into the sky, allowing thousands of people to work together in a small area. Most of the land is covered by buildings and highways; now only a few of the forest's trees are left.

The human and natural characteristics of a place change over time. As you can see from this diagram, the modern city, such as this one in Europe, began as a few scattered houses. These became farming villages that slowly grew into trading towns. Beginning in the eighteenth century, towns developed factories and business

As you can see from section six, some of the past changes to the land continue to exist in the modern city. But few of the earlier buildings and roads remain in the modern city. And it is hard to see what the natural environment of the land used to be. Both the human characteristics and the natural features of this place have changed.

Changing the Land Now think about the different ways in which people have changed the natural environment in the community where you live. You would want to note whether there is farming where you live, what kind of transportation moves people and goods into and out of the community, and where the transportation routes go.

You would also want to think about the cities and towns that have been built in your area. How many people live in them, and what are their major economic activities? For example, are there factories, farms, mines, ports, rail yards, or other evidence of how people earn a living? You might also want to look at the kinds of houses and other buildings people have built. These are only a few of the many ways that human activities can change the characteristics of the places in which people live.

LESSON 2

Review

REVIEWING MAIN IDEAS
A. How was Glenn's spacecraft located when it landed?

B. How is relative location different from absolute location?

C. What shapes the character of a place?

SKILLS CHECK
WRITING SKILL

Write a paragraph in which you describe the natural and human features of your community. Include landforms, other towns or cities, and states.

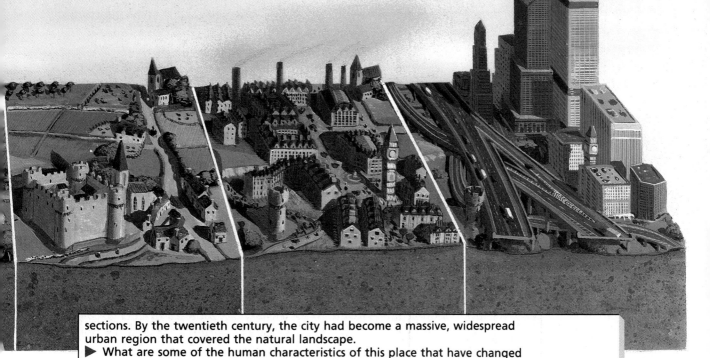

sections. By the twentieth century, the city had become a massive, widespread urban region that covered the natural landscape.
► What are some of the human characteristics of this place that have changed over the centuries?

49

Human Changes to the Earth

CONNECTIONS

Imagine that you are a geographer who is studying the area where you live. How would you describe the landscape of this area?

TERMS

technology, irrigation, reservoir, ground water

FOCUS

How do people change the land?

A. The Great Plains 200 Years Ago

Imagine that you had a time machine and could go back to the Great Plains as it was 200 years ago. The land that now covers the middle part of North America from Texas to Canada and from the Rocky Mountains to the centers of Kansas, Nebraska, and South Dakota, was once covered by this vast grassy plain.

Herds of buffalo sent huge columns of dust up into the sky as they thundered across the Great Plains. The only human inhabitants were Indians, or Native Americans. These nomadic people lived in temporary camps in which they set up teepees, or cone-shaped tents made of buffalo hides. The Indians didn't farm, living instead from hunting buffalo and gathering the few useful plants that grew on the plains. If the Indians had disappeared, they would have left little evidence that they had ever lived on the Great Plains.

B. The Great Plains Today

What is the Great Plains like today? The Indians now live on reservations, public lands that have been set aside by the government for Native Americans. The vast herds of buffalo that roamed the Great Plains are now gone. The buffalo survive only in parks or on a few ranches.

The grasslands that stretched from horizon to horizon have been plowed up and the land is now used for growing wheat and other grains or as pasture for cattle. Many rivers that cross the plains have been dammed to control floods, to provide water for crops, to generate electricity, and to make lakes for recreation. The Indian trails that led across the grassy plains are now railroads, roads, and freeways for trains, trucks, and cars. In the towns and cities of the Great Plains, there are stores, schools, churches, and a thousand other things that the Indians never knew. And, unlike the Indian camps, the settlements are permanent, not temporary.

The Indians lived much the same way for hundreds of years. What has caused the rapid change on the Great Plains? The answer is that different people with a different culture and a more advanced **technology** came to the Great Plains. Technology is the knowledge and skill people use to make things. With their new technology, the people who took over the Indians' lands were able to make great changes.

C. The Interaction of Humans with the Environment

Interaction The way the earth is today is the result of the ways in which people have interacted with the environment. The Indians of the Great Plains had a very simple technology. They adapted to the environment by learning to make tools from stone, bone, and other natural materials. If they couldn't find buffalo to hunt, they would go hungry. In the winter they kept warm by building fires from dry buffalo dung, or excrement, called buffalo chips, because there were no trees to use for wood.

Many of the Indians who lived in North America farmed for at least part of their food. Why didn't the Indians of the Great Plains do the same? Agriculture would have given them an extra food supply and made

Huge irrigation machines spread ground water in a circular pattern on the dry Great Plains. Irrigation has made it possible to grow a variety of crops.
▶ What is ground water?

their lives more secure. The Plains Indians were unable to farm because the plains are too dry for dependable farming. For the Plains Indians, hunting was the most dependable way to get food.

Why are there farms in the Great Plains today? Part of the answer is in the kinds of plants that are grown. Wheat and other grains that are grown in the Great Plains can grow with small amounts of water. The Indians did not have these crops.

Irrigation Another answer is **irrigation**. Irrigation is the watering of crops or other plants by pipes, canals, or ditches. To irrigate their crops, modern farmers in the Great Plains use **reservoirs**, or lakes and other areas where water is stored for use. Another source of irrigation is **ground water**, which is rainwater that collects in underground rocks. Farmers can drill wells to bring the ground water to the surface.

These are but two examples of the hundreds of different ways that people have learned to adapt to and change the world's environments in order to survive. This year, you will learn about the many different ways that the world's people have learned to make the environment yield the things they need to survive and improve their lives.

LESSON 3

Review

REVIEWING MAIN IDEAS
A. Why did the Indians of the Great Plains live in temporary camps?
B. How did technology change life on the Great Plains?
C. Why is farming possible on the Great Plains today?

SKILLS CHECK

THINKING SKILL
Irrigation and other forms of technology changed the Great Plains. How, do you think, might the same technology be used to change a desert region?

51

The Importance of Movement

CONNECTIONS
List the different ways you could send a message to a friend who lives in another neighborhood.

TERMS
import, consumer

FOCUS
How are transportation and communication important to our lives?

A. Transportation and Trade

Commuting How far do members of your family travel to work each day? If you live in or near a large city, they may travel as few as 5 miles (8 km) or as many as 30 miles (48 km) or more to get from your home to their workplace. The people of the United States and other industrialized countries are highly mobile. Our society is dependent on transportation. Many of us travel long distances each day to go to work, to go shopping, or for entertainment. We may travel hundreds or even thousands of miles for vacations or to visit relatives. Each year, millions of people move from one city to another, to another part of the United States, or even to a foreign country. These people move to attend school, to get a new job, or to find a place that they think is better to live in.

But this isn't the only way in which we might think of our society as being mobile. Even if you never moved from the home where you live now, never took a vacation, and worked in your home, you would still be dependent on transportation for most of the things you need to live.

For example, look at the labels on the clothes you are wearing. Most likely, at least one piece of your clothing was made outside the United States. If you have a television, a videocassette recorder, or a stereo, it was probably **imported**, or brought into the country from another country.

Even when goods are not imported, movement is essential to getting them to the **consumers** who will buy and use them. Consumers are people who buy and use many types of goods. The food you ate this morning was probably bought in a nearby store. Have you ever thought how that food got to the store?

Moving Goods Let's take the example of breakfast cereal. Cereal is made of grain that may have been grown on a farm in Kansas or Nebraska. The farmer took the harvested grain to a grain elevator, where it was stored until it was shipped by railroad to a mill perhaps in Kansas City, Missouri. From there the processed grain was sent to another city, such as Minneapolis, Minnesota, where the cereal company made it into cereal and put it into boxes.

The boxes were sent to a warehouse, where they were stored before they were shipped to grocery stores throughout the country. Even if you live in one of the states where the grain in your breakfast cereal was grown, it probably traveled hundreds or even thousands of miles before it finally got to the store where you bought it.

A similar story could be told for nearly everything you buy. Unlike the Plains Indians, we grow and make very little of what we need to survive. Instead, we depend on a complex system that moves the things we need from the places where they are produced to stores near where we live.

B. The Movement of Information

Electronic Information Communication is another kind of movement—the movement of information. The way information is moved is quite different from the way goods are moved. Why? Information can be moved through wires as electronic impulses. It can also be moved through the air as radio waves.

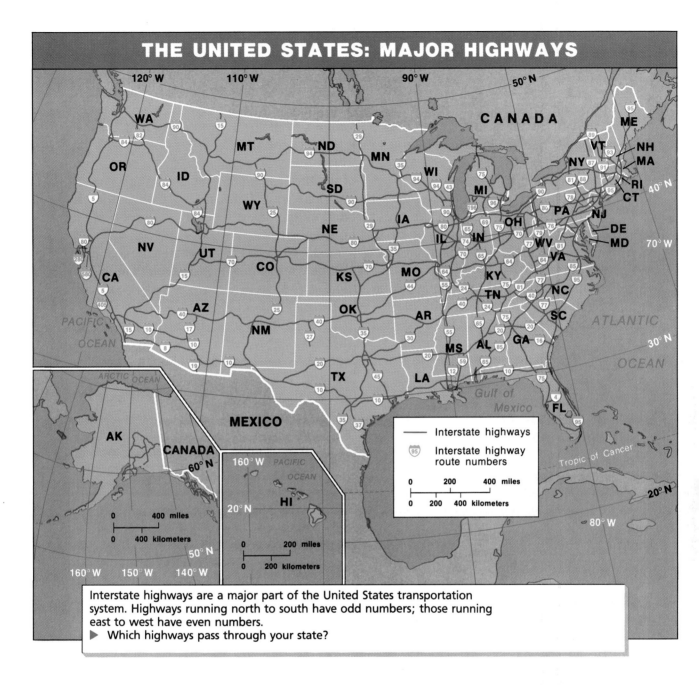

THE UNITED STATES: MAJOR HIGHWAYS

Interstate highways
Interstate highway route numbers

| 0 | 200 | 400 miles |
| 0 | 200 | 400 kilometers |

Interstate highways are a major part of the United States transportation system. Highways running north to south have odd numbers; those running east to west have even numbers.
▶ Which highways pass through your state?

Think about how communication has changed our lives. Do you have relatives or friends who live in another town? If you want to talk with them, all you have to do is pick up the telephone and dial their number. We can call nearly any city in the world by telephone. We take this convenience for granted, but before that, there was no way to send voice messages farther than the loudest shout.

Communicating Today Now we can use radio, television, computers, and satellites to send information almost instantly to any part of the world and to space. You can watch live sporting events on television from anyplace in the world, and you can learn about important events almost at the same time that they occur.

Rapid communications have changed business even more than our private lives.

53

Important papers can be delivered overnight by air express services. If overnight isn't fast enough, computers can send large amounts of information to each other by telephone. Drawings and other documents can be sent by fax, or facsimile, machines. These machines transform the drawings or words into electronic signals. The signals are sent by telephone in a few minutes to other fax machines, where they are printed out immediately on paper. In fact, you could send a copy of this book to any place in the world where there is a telephone and a fax machine.

Transportation and communication provide important links between places. They make it possible for you to buy goods from all parts of the world. And they make it possible for businesses to have offices or factories in different cities or countries.

C. Putting the Five Themes of Geography Together

This chapter has introduced you to the five important themes of geography. In the first lesson you learned about the theme of regions. In the second lesson you read about the theme of absolute location and relative location. You also learned a third theme— that every place has distinct characteristics or features. In the third lesson, you read about the way humans interact with and change their environment. Environment is the fourth theme. In this lesson you learned about the importance of movement in connecting different places on the earth. This is the fifth theme.

These five themes all fit together. Every place has a location on the earth. The combination of natural environment and human activities gives each place a special quality. The way people live in a place shows us how they have adapted to the environment. Technology allows people to make great changes in the natural environment of a place and to develop productive economies. Movement connects places and allows products, people, and ideas to travel from place to place. Similar kinds of places can be grouped into regions. Each region has a location and a special character that comes from the environment and the way of life of the people who live there. As you read the chapters that follow, you will see how the five themes of geography help to explain why there are so many different and unique lands, peoples, and ways of life on the earth.

In 1873, a French writer named Jules Verne wrote a novel titled *Around the World in Eighty Days*. The hero of this book made a bet that he could travel all the way around the world in 80 days. In those days no one had ever traveled around the world so quickly. This book will take you on a trip around the world, too. It will take you longer than 80 days to make your tour, but by the time you return you will have learned many useful and interesting things about the fascinating world in which we live.

LESSON 4

Review

REVIEWING MAIN IDEAS
A. Why is transportation so important in our society?
B. How has the movement of information changed in recent years?
C. What are the five themes of geography?

SKILLS CHECK

MAP SKILL

A box of cereal can travel a long way before it gets to the grocery shelf. Use the scale on the map of the United States on page 692 to find the distance in miles between the following cities. Add the distances between the cities to find the total distance the cereal traveled.
1. Kansas City, MO
2. Minneapolis, MN
3. Sacramento, CA

REVIEWING TERMS

region
relief
glacier
absolute
  location
relative
  location

technology
irrigation
reservoir
import
consumer

On a separate sheet of paper, write the word or words from the list above that best complete the sentences.

1. Southeast Asia is a political _____ of the earth that is made up of countries.

2. "The supermarket is two blocks from my home." This statement gives the supermarket's _____ .

3. For more variety, a jeweler may want to _____ gems from another country.

4. The _____ of Detroit, Michigan is 42°N/83°W.

5. The movement of a _____ can create pointed mountain peaks.

6. An advanced _____ can change a landscape.

7. Desert farming is possible because of _____ .

8. Melting winter snow and heavy spring rains help to keep up water levels in a _____ .

9. Some people will argue that a good _____ carefully checks prices.

10. Across North America one finds a varied _____ of mountains, hills, valleys, and canyons.

REVIEWING THE FACTS

On a separate sheet of paper, answer the questions in complete sentences.

1. What are the five themes of geography?

2. What are some of the characteristics of a region?

3. What is the major difference between plains, hills, and mountains?

4. What are the tallest and longest mountain ranges?

5. What is the job of a navigator?

6. How are locations useful for meteorologists?

7. How does life on the Great Plains today compare with life on the Great Plains two hundred years ago?

8. What changed life on the Great Plains?

9. Why do we say that the people of the United States live in a mobile society?

10. What forms of movement provide the links between places?

WRITING ABOUT GEOGRAPHY

Absolute location and relative location are two ways of describing where a place is located. Absolute location is used less frequently in our daily lives. Most people use relative location, especially when giving directions. Write a paragraph that gives the relative location of your school. Write another paragraph that gives the relative location of your state capital.

THINKING CRITICALLY

Answer the following questions in complete sentences.

1. What are the characteristics of your natural environment?
2. Look at the diagram on pages 48–49. At what stage of change would you place the community in which you live? Give examples to defend your choice.
3. How have rapid means of communication changed our lives?
4. "The Five Themes of Geography" is the title of this chapter. Which of the five themes would apply to viewing another planet?
5. The two songs in this chapter relate to the natural environment and to humans changing the environment. Write a song, poem, or paragraph that shows how you feel about the natural environment you described in answer to question 1.

SUMMARIZING THE CHAPTER

On a separate sheet of paper, draw a graphic organizer like the one shown here. Copy the information from this graphic organizer to the one you have drawn. Below each main idea, write two statements that you think best support it. The first statement for each main idea has been done for you.

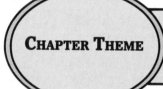

CHAPTER THEME

We can use the five themes of geography to study the earth and the way people live on the earth.

LESSON 1 Regions are defined by the characteristics we use to identify them.

1. By climate
2. _____
3. _____

LESSON 2 Finding location is important to many people.

1. Navigators need to locate planes and ships.
2. _____
3. _____
   _____

LESSON 3 People change the land.

1. Forests are cleared to grow crops.
2. _____
3. _____

LESSON 4 Movement is important in connecting different places on the earth.

1. Goods can be imported into a country.
2. _____
   _____
3. _____

COOPERATIVE LEARNING

In Unit 1 you learned how people survive in the world by using the natural resources around them. It is important for us to understand how to use these resources.

Robinson Crusoe needed to learn the geography of his new island home to survive. He learned to hunt and farm and use the natural resources wisely. He investigated his island, he examined the island's landscape, and he learned how to live on the island.

PROJECT

Your group will work together to create a board game about Robinson Crusoe's life on a deserted island. You may decide that your game will contain facts about the geography of his island home. Or perhaps it may contain facts about Crusoe's way of life. Or the group may decide to design a game that includes a variety of ideas about geography and living conditions on the island.

Work together to design a game board. Think about other games you have played and about how the boards are designed. Also decide how the pieces in your game will advance. Many games use spinners, cards, or dice to determine how the player will move. Sometimes, bonus cards give players extra turns and chances to move ahead. Penalty cards make players lose a turn or move backward. The cards could include topics such as geography, hunting, farming, natural resources, and other details about Crusoe's way of life.

Once your group has discussed and chosen a design, each group member should work to construct part of the game. One person should sketch the board on butcher paper. The others should make the game pieces, dice, cards, or spinner. Each group member could write three bonus cards and three penalty cards.

Finally, your group should meet to put the game together. Don't forget to give it a name.

PRESENTATION AND REVIEW

Your group should test your game by playing it together. By testing the game, you will be able to find and fix any problems. When the group is pleased with the way the game works, present it to the rest of the class.

Then trade games with other groups in your class. Ask them to tell you how they liked your game. Ask if they have any suggestions that would improve the game.

Your group should meet again to discuss how well you worked together. Did everyone have a chance to speak? Did everyone take part in making the game? List the advantages of working with a group. How could you improve the group activity?

REMEMBER TO:
- Give your ideas.
- Listen to others' ideas.
- Plan your work with the group.
- Present your project.
- Discuss how your group worked.

SKILLBUILDER

UNDERSTANDING CLIMOGRAPHS

WHY DO I NEED THIS SKILL?

Your geography textbook is a study of the many different regions of the world. An important part of this study is the influence of climate on the people and land of these regions. As you have learned, climate is the pattern of weather in a particular place over a period of time. Climate can vary from region to region and can help explain many of the differences in how people around the world live.

The two major elements of climate are temperature and precipitation. By looking at temperature and precipitation data for a particular place, you can determine what type of climate that place has. A **climograph** combines a line graph with a bar graph to provide temperature data and precipitation data.

LEARNING THE SKILL

As you know, temperature is the amount of heat in the atmosphere, or air, and precipitation is the amount of moisture that falls to the earth as rain, snow, sleet, hail, or mist. The climographs in this textbook show the average monthly temperature and the average monthly precipitation for certain cities over the course of a year.

For example, the climograph on this page shows the annual temperature and precipitation data for New York City, New York. On the bottom of the climograph are abbreviations for the 12 months of the year. The scales on the left side of the climograph show average monthly temperature in two ways: in degrees Fahrenheit (°F) and in degrees Celsius (°C). The scales on the right show average monthly precipitation both in inches (in.) and in centimeters (cm).

The average temperature for each month is shown by a dot on the graph, and all 12 dots are connected by a line. By looking at this line graph, you can see how the city's temperature may vary from month to month. You can also determine the annual temperature range by finding the difference between the highest and lowest temperatures that occur during the year. For example, the annual temperature range for New York City is about 43°F (24°C).

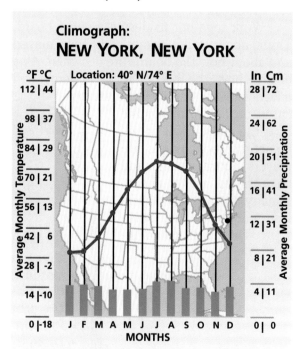

Climograph: **NEW YORK, NEW YORK**

58

The average precipitation for each month is shown by a bar rising from the bottom of the graph. By looking at the bar graph, you can see how the city's precipitation varies during the year. For example, the climograph for New York shows that the amount of precipitation the city receives from month to month is fairly constant. What is the difference between the lowest and highest amounts of precipitation that New York receives?

You can see from the climograph that on the average, New York receives the most precipitation in July and August. You can also see that these are the warmest months, with temperatures over 70°F (21°C). What are the two coldest months of the year in New York City?

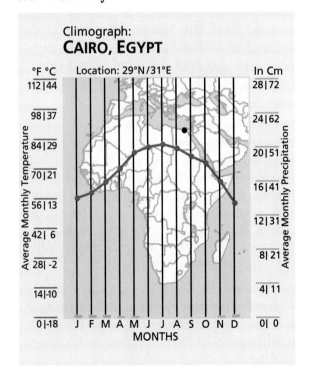

Climograph:
CAIRO, EGYPT

Location: 29°N/31°E

°F °C
112|44
98|37
84|29
70|21
56|13
42|6
28|-2
14|-10
0|-18

In Cm
28|72
24|62
20|51
16|41
12|31
8|21
4|11
0|0

Average Monthly Temperature

Average Monthly Precipitation

J F M A M J J A S O N D
MONTHS

PRACTICING THE SKILL

Use the climograph for New York and the climograph for Cairo, Egypt, shown on this page, to answer the following questions.

1. During which month does Cairo have its highest average temperature?
2. What is the coldest month in Cairo, and what is the average temperature during that month?
3. In which city is the average temperature lower during May—New York or Cairo?
4. What is the average precipitation in New York during October?
5. What is the average precipitation in Cairo during October?
6. Which city receives more precipitation in a year?
7. Which of these two cities do you think might be located on or near a desert?
8. What problems would the climate of each city create for someone who wanted to grow and maintain a flower garden in the city?

APPLYING THE SKILL

As you study the different regions of the world, you can use the climographs in your geography textbook to understand the climate of particular cities in these regions. The climate data will help you understand the relationship between climate and how people in different regions live. In addition, by comparing climograph data with climate data presented in other ways for other places in the world, you will be able to predict or infer what type of climate these other places may have.

SKILLBUILDER

USING SQR

WHY DO I NEED THIS SKILL?

Your social studies book contains abundant amounts of information about people, places, and events. Therefore, you must try to learn and remember many facts and ideas. In this Skillbuilder you will learn to use a strategy, or plan of action, for reading a social studies lesson. The strategy is called **SQR.** These letters stand for *Survey, Question,* and *Read.* Using **SQR** will help you learn and remember the important ideas found in this book and in the other textbooks that you use.

LEARNING THE SKILL

There are three steps in the **SQR** strategy. They are as follows:

Step 1: Survey the lesson. *Survey* means "look over what you will read to get a general idea of what the lesson is about." Begin your survey by reading the lesson title. Ask yourself if you already know some things about the topic of the lesson. Then read the list of terms and the headings in the lesson. The headings are the boldface statements that have the letters *A, B, C,* and so on in front of them. As you read the headings, try to make some guesses or predictions about what will be in the lesson.

Be sure to look at any pictures, photographs, maps, charts, or other visuals in the lesson. This will also help you get a general idea of what the lesson is about. After surveying the lesson, you will be prepared to read and understand it.

Step 2: Ask questions. Think of any questions you may have about the lesson from the survey you just did. Use the words *who, where, when, why, what,* and *how* to help you think of questions. Then read the questions asked by the author of your book. Read the focus question, which is found at the beginning of the lesson and which asks about the main idea of the lesson. Also read the questions that ask about the photographs and other visuals. Finally, read the questions in the lesson review box.

Now fold a sheet of paper lengthwise. On the left-hand side, write down the questions that you plan to answer as you read the lesson. Select five to seven questions that you think deal with important ideas.

Step 3: Read the lesson. As you read the lesson, look for the answers to your questions. Write the answers on the right-hand side of your paper. Add to your list any other questions that come to mind as you read.

PRACTICING THE SKILL

Practice using **SQR** for the first part of Lesson 3 in Chapter 2, on page 50. Refer to the "Using SQR" table if you need help in remembering the steps in the strategy. After you finish, answer these questions.

1. How are the Great Plains today different from what they were like 200 years ago?
2. How has technology played a role in the changes that have occurred in the Great Plains?

APPLYING THE SKILL

The **SQR** strategy helps you learn and remember important ideas. It is also helpful when you study for a test. Save your **SQR** questions and answers, and use them to review the materials before a test.

Use **SQR** as you read the next chapter, which is about Canada. See if using **SQR** helps you to learn, understand, and remember the ideas in the lessons in that chapter. Try using **SQR** when you read the textbooks for all of your classes.

USING SQR			
Survey	• Look at headings, questions, vocabulary words, and visuals.	• Think about what you already know about the topic.	• Make predictions about the lesson topic.
Question	• Think about the questions already in the lesson.	• Use vocabulary words, headings, and other lesson features to prepare your own questions.	• Make predictions about the lesson content.
Read	• Read to answer your questions.	• Write down the answers or say them to yourself.	• Ask and answer any other questions that come to mind as you read.

61

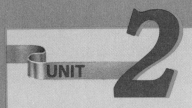

UNIT 2

THE COUNTRIES OF NORTH AMERICA

CONTINENTAL HANDBOOK

TABLE OF COUNTRIES

CONNECTIONS

What are some of the reasons why the United States works with other countries?

TERMS

foreign policy, harbor, volcano, magma, lava

FOCUS

How have the geography and climates of North America helped the United States?

Free Trade Accord for North America Is Expected Today
By Keith Bradsher

WASHINGTON, Aug. 11, 1992—The United States, Canada, and Mexico tentatively agreed today to create a free-trade area covering all of North America, eliminating customs, duties, and other restrictions.

The agreement will allow companies to do business the length of the continent with few barriers.

A. Trade Among the Countries of North America

The North American Free Trade Agreement (NAFTA) is a trade agreement between Canada, the United States, and Mexico. Leaders of these three nations agreed in 1992 to eliminate many barriers that restricted trade between their countries. The agreement encourages companies to build factories, ship raw materials, and sell their products freely among the three countries.

NAFTA is one of many economic, political, and cultural agreements that the United States has with other countries. These agreements make up part of our **foreign policy.** Foreign policy is the decisions a country makes about how it will work with other nations.

NAFTA caused much debate. Many experts believed that the United States would benefit greatly from the agreement. For example, they believed Mexico would buy more products made in the United States. That would help provide more jobs for American workers.

Other experts disagreed. They predicted that many companies would close their factories in the United States and open new factories in Mexico. As a result, there would be fewer factory jobs for workers in the United States. They also pointed out that the pollution laws in Mexico were less strict than those in the United States and Canada. Opening more factories in Mexico, they claimed, would eventually cause more damage to the environment of North America.

Mountain ranges extend along the west coast of North America. The eastern coast is mainly a region of low-lying plains.
▶ What are the three elevations of the Great Plains?

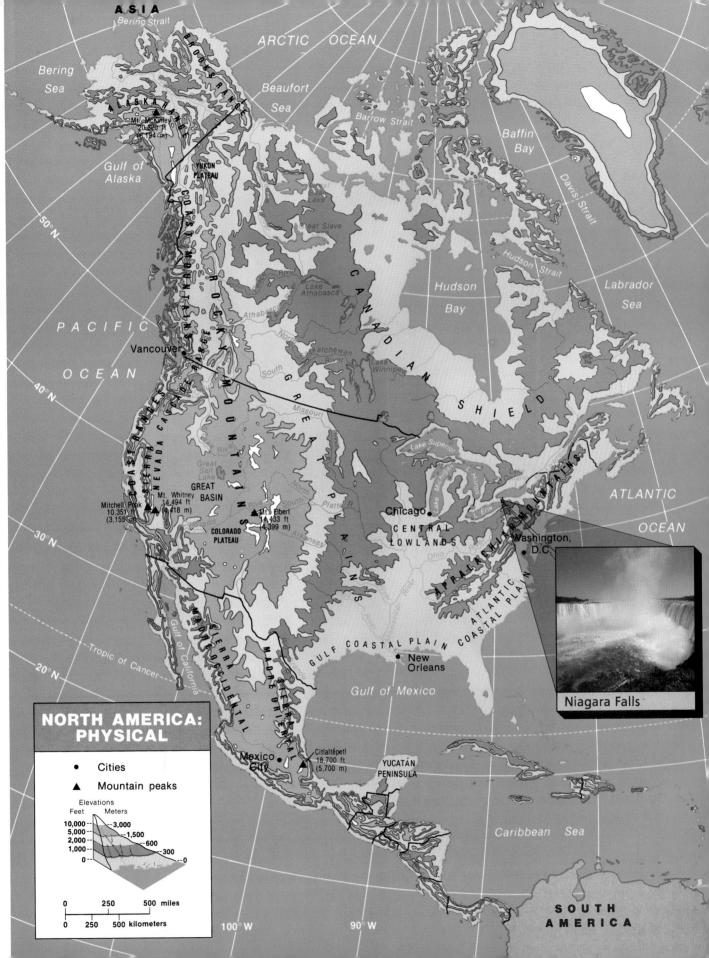

ASIA

ARCTIC OCEAN

Bering Strait

Bering Sea

Beaufort Sea

Barrow Strait

Baffin Bay

BROOKS RANGE

ALASKA RANGE

▲ Mt. McKinley
20,320 ft
(6,194 m)

Gulf of Alaska

YUKON PLATEAU

COAST MOUNTAINS

Davis Strait

Great Slave Lake

CANADIAN SHIELD

Hudson Strait

Labrador Sea

50°N

PACIFIC OCEAN

Lake Athabasca

Athabasca R.

ROCKY MOUNTAINS

North Saskatchewan River

Hudson Bay

Vancouver ●

Lake Winnipeg

40°N

GREAT PLAINS

Missouri River

COAST RANGES

CASCADE RANGE

SIERRA NEVADA

Columbia River

North Platte R.

South Platte R.

Great Salt Lake

GREAT BASIN

Mt. Whitney
14,494 ft
(4,418 m) ▲

Mitchell Peak
10,351 ft
(3,155 m) ▲

▲ Mt. Elbert
14,433 ft
(4,399 m)

COLORADO PLATEAU

Colorado River

Arkansas River

Lake Superior

Lake Michigan

Lake Huron

Lake Erie

Lake Ontario

Chicago ●

CENTRAL LOWLANDS

APPALACHIAN MOUNTAINS

ATLANTIC OCEAN

Washington, D.C. ●

30°N

Ohio River

Mississippi River

Tennessee R.

Red River

ATLANTIC COASTAL PLAIN

Tropic of Cancer

20°N

Gulf of California

SIERRA MADRE OCCIDENTAL

SIERRA MADRE ORIENTAL

GULF COASTAL PLAIN

New Orleans ●

Gulf of Mexico

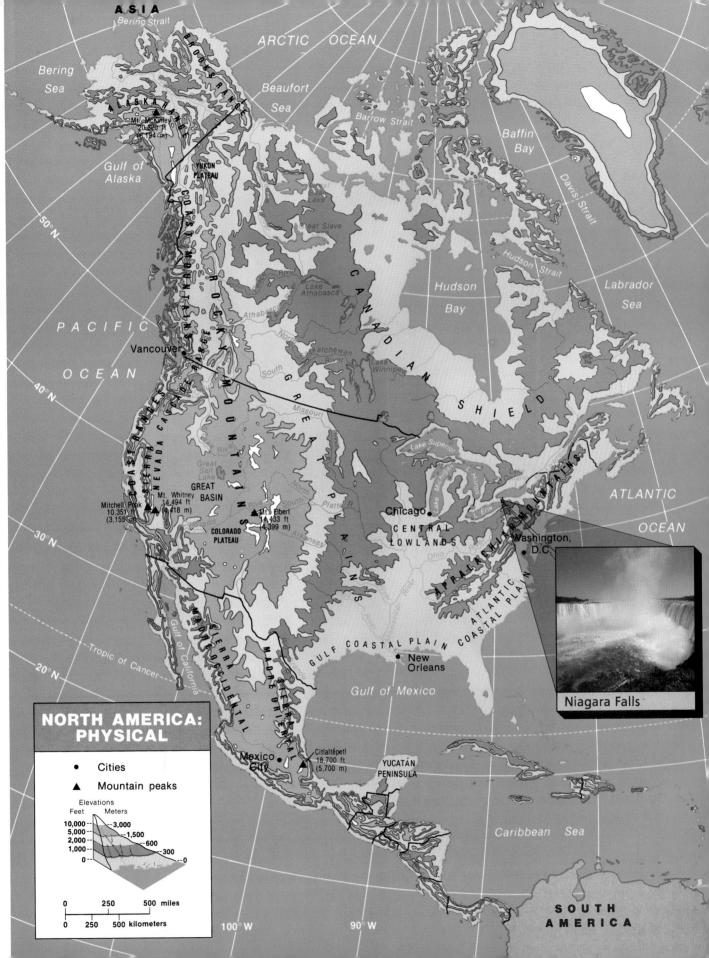

Niagara Falls

Mexico City ●

▲ Citlaltépetl
18,700 ft
(5,700 m)

YUCATÁN PENINSULA

Caribbean Sea

NORTH AMERICA: PHYSICAL

- ● Cities
- ▲ Mountain peaks

Elevations

Feet	Meters
10,000	3,000
5,000	1,500
2,000	600
1,000	300
0	0

0   250   500 miles

0   250   500 kilometers

100°W   90°W

SOUTH AMERICA

The Rio Grande forms the border of the United States and Mexico.
▶ How would you describe the river and the surrounding area?

B. A Central Location

One reason that the United States has been able to become a major world power is because of its enormous resources. But another, more important reason is its central location on the continent of North America.

To the west and to the east of North America are the world's largest oceans: the Atlantic and the Pacific. The United States has coastlines with good **harbors** on both these oceans. A harbor is a protected area. These harbors allow the United States to ship goods to and receive goods from Europe and Asia.

The Atlantic and Pacific oceans also separate the United States from other countries. The United States has borders with only two other countries in North America—Canada and Mexico. Both borders are undefended, and the United States is friendly with each of these countries. The United States also has good relations with most of the island nations off its southern coast.

C. The Continent of North America

These island nations, Canada, Mexico, the United States, and the countries of Central America make up the continent of North America. North America is the third largest landmass in the world; only Africa and Asia are larger.

If you look at the map on page 65, you can see that North America has several major landforms. The largest and most prominent landform is the chain of mountains that runs down the western edge of the continent. The longest range is the Rocky Mountains. It begins in Canada and stretches into Mexico.

To the west of the Rockies are a series of mountains that make up the coastal ranges. These mountains are the scene of earthquakes and eruptions of **volcanoes.** A volcano is an opening in the ground out of which melted rock and other materials pour. The diagram on page 68 shows how these materials are forced to the earth's surface. **Magma,** the melted rock inside the earth, is under great pressure from the weight of the solid rock around it. This pressure causes the magma to push through a weak spot in the earth's surface. When the magma reaches the surface, it is called **lava.** The lava flows out of the volcano, cools, and becomes rock.

Three large nations and several small nations occupy the continent of North America.
▶ Where are the national capitals of most of the small nations located?

Bering Strait

ARCTIC OCEAN

Bering
Sea

ALASKA
(U.S.)

Beaufort
Sea

Barrow Strait

Yukon River

Gulf of
Alaska

50°N

Mackenzie River

Great Bear
Lake

Great Slave
Lake

Baffin
Bay

GREENLAND
(DENMARK)

Davis Strait

C A N A D A

Hudson
Bay

Hudson Strait

Labrador
Sea

PACIFIC

OCEAN

40°N

Edmonton

Calgary

North Saskatchewan River

South Saskatchewan River

Lake
Winnipeg

Winnipeg

Columbia River

Great
Salt
Lake

Missouri River

Great Lakes

St. Lawrence River

Montreal

Ottawa

San Francisco
San Jose

Denver

Colorado River

River

Milwaukee
Chicago

North York
Toronto
Detroit
Columbus
Cleveland

Boston

New York
Philadelphia

30°N

Los Angeles

San Diego

Phoenix

UNITED STATES OF AMERICA

Indianapolis

Arkansas River

Ohio River

Baltimore
Washington, D.C.

ATLANTIC

Ciudad Juárez

Dallas

Memphis

OCEAN

Tropic of Cancer

Rio Grande

San
Antonio

Houston

New Orleans

Jacksonville

20°N

Monterrey

MEXICO

Gulf of Mexico

FR.   —FRANCE
NETH. —NETHERLANDS
U.K. —UNITED KINGDOM
U.S. —UNITED STATES

Gulf of California

León

Guadalajara

110°W

Mexico City

Netzahualcóyatl

Nassau

Havana

BAHAMAS

PUERTO RICO
(U.S.)

CUBA

VIRGIN ISLANDS
(U.S.) (U.K.)

DOMINICAN
REPUBLIC

ANTIGUA
AND BARBUDA

NORTH AMERICA:
POLITICAL

Belmopan

BELIZE

GUATEMALA

Guatemala City

San Salvador

EL SALVADOR

Tegucigalpa

HONDURAS

NICARAGUA

Managua

JAMAICA

Kingston

HAITI

Port-au-
Prince

Santo
Domingo

ST. CHRISTOPHER–NEVIS

GUADELOUPE (FR.)

DOMINICA

MARTINIQUE (FR.)

ST. LUCIA

NETH. ANTILLES

ST. VINCENT AND
THE GRENADINES

GRENADA

✪ National capitals

• Other cities

0   250   500 miles
0   250   500 kilometers

COSTA RICA

San Jose

Panama Canal

Panama

PANAMA

Caribbean   *Sea*

TRINIDAD
AND TOBAGO

SOUTH
AMERICA

0°

Equator

100°W

90°W

THE ERUPTION OF A VOLCANO

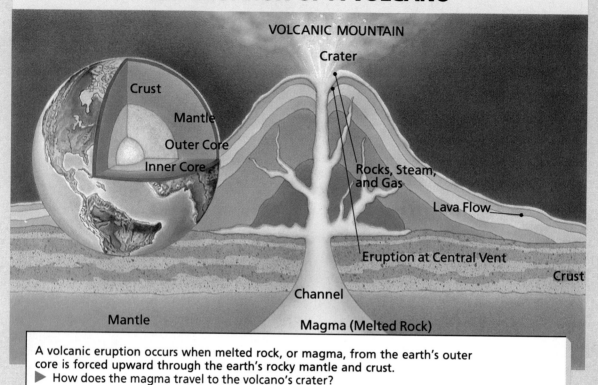

VOLCANIC MOUNTAIN

Crater

Crust

Mantle

Outer Core

Inner Core

Rocks, Steam, and Gas

Lava Flow

Eruption at Central Vent

Crust

Channel

Mantle

Magma (Melted Rock)

A volcanic eruption occurs when melted rock, or magma, from the earth's outer core is forced upward through the earth's rocky mantle and crust.
▶ How does the magma travel to the volcano's crater?

East of the Rockies the land begins to gradually decrease in elevation. This great expanse of gradually sloping land is called the Great Plains. The Great Plains gradually becomes a region of low elevation that is called the Interior Lowlands. You can see from the physical map on page 65 that the Interior Lowlands covers a large part of North America.

Many of the major bodies of water of North America are in the Interior Lowlands. In the north are the five Great Lakes: Superior, Michigan, Huron, Erie, and Ontario. These lakes form a great inland ocean, which forms part of the United States—Canada border.

The Interior Lowlands is bounded by a relatively low chain of mountains that stretches southward from Canada into the United States. This is the Appalachian (ap uh LAY chun) mountain chain.

Review

REVIEWING MAIN IDEAS

A. How did the North American Free Trade Agreement link Canada, the United States, and Mexico?

B. How have the harbors found along the Atlantic and Pacific coasts benefited the United States?

C. What are the major landforms of North America?

SKILLS CHECK

MAP SKILL

Turn to the maps of North America on pages 65 and 67. What is the elevation of each capital city?

Ottawa, Canada
Washington, D.C.
Mexico City, Mexico

NORTH AMERICA

| | FLAG AND PRINCIPAL LANGUAGE(S) | POPULATION AND LANDMASS | PRINCIPAL PRODUCTS EXPORT | IMPORT |

ANTIGUA AND BARBUDA

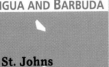
St. Johns

English

POPULATION
66,000
386 per sq mi/149 per sq km

LANDMASS
171 sq mi/443 sq km

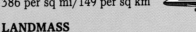
Aircraft Parts

Machinery

BAHAMAS

★Nassau

English

POPULATION
257,000
48 per sq mi/19 per sq km

LANDMASS
5,386 sq mi/13,950 sq km

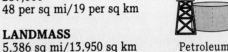
Petroleum   Crude Oil

BARBADOS

★Bridgetown

English

POPULATION
256,000
1,542 per sq mi/596 per sq km

LANDMASS
166 sq mi/430 sq km

Electrical Parts   Machinery

BELIZE

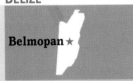
Belmopan ★

English, Spanish

POPULATION
214,000
24 per sq mi/9 per sq km

LANDMASS
8,867 sq mi/22,966 sq km

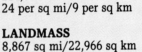
Sugar

Food

CANADA

Ottawa ★

English, French

POPULATION
28,400,000
7 per sq mi/3 per sq km

LANDMASS
3,851,809 sq mi/9,976,185 sq km

Vehicles   Vehicles

COSTA RICA

★San José

Spanish

POPULATION
3,419,000
174 per sq mi/67 per sq km

LANDMASS
19,652 sq mi/50,899 sq km

Coffee

Chemicals

CUBA

★Havana

Spanish

POPULATION
10,938,000
256 per sq mi/99 per sq km

LANDMASS
42,804 sq mi/110,820 sq km

Sugar

Crude Oil

DOMINICA

★Roseau

English

POPULATION
82,600
286 per sq mi/110 per sq km

LANDMASS
289 sq mi/749 sq km

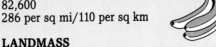

Bananas

Food

69

NORTH AMERICA

	FLAG AND PRINCIPAL LANGUAGE(S)	POPULATION AND LANDMASS	PRINCIPAL PRODUCTS EXPORT	IMPORT
DOMINICAN REPUBLIC  Santo Domingo	Spanish	**POPULATION** 7,948,000 426 per sq mi/165 per sq km **LANDMASS** 18,657 sq mi/48,332 sq km	Sugar	Crude Oil
EL SALVADOR San Salvador	Spanish	**POPULATION** 5,870,000 711 per sq mi/275 per sq km **LANDMASS** 8,260 sq mi/21,393 sq km	Coffee	Chemicals
GRENADA ★St. George's 	English	**POPULATION** 94,000 707 per sq mi/273 per sq km **LANDMASS** 133 sq mi/344 sq km	Cocoa	Food
GUATEMALA  Guatemala	Spanish, various Indian dialects	**POPULATION** 10,999,000 262 per sq mi/101 per sq km **LANDMASS** 42,042 sq mi/108,889 sq km	Coffee	Crude Oil
HAITI Port-au-Prince	French, Creole	**POPULATION** 6,518,000 608 per sq mi/235 per sq km **LANDMASS** 10,714 sq mi/27,749 sq km	Coffee	Food
HONDURAS  ★Tegucigalpa	Spanish	**POPULATION** 5,460,000 126 per sq mi/49 per sq km **LANDMASS** 43,277 sq mi/112,087 sq km	Bananas	Crude Oil
JAMAICA  Kingston	English, Creole	**POPULATION** 2,574,000 576 per sq mi/222 per sq km **LANDMASS** 4,471 sq mi/11,580 sq km	Alumina	Crude Oil
MEXICO  Mexico City	Spanish	**POPULATION** 93,986,000 123 per sq mi/48 per sq km **LANDMASS** 761,600 sq mi/1,972,544 sq km	Crude Oil	Machinery

	FLAG AND PRINCIPAL LANGUAGE(S)	POPULATION AND LANDMASS	PRINCIPAL PRODUCTS EXPORT	IMPORT

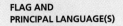

NICARAGUA

★ Managua

 Spanish

POPULATION
4,206,000
85 per sq mi/33 per sq km

LANDMASS
49,579 sq mi/128,410 sq km

 Coffee — Crude Oil

PANAMA

Panama City

 Spanish, English

POPULATION
2,681,000
92 per sq mi/36 per sq km

LANDMASS
29,157 sq mi/75,487 sq km

  Bananas — Crude Oil

PUERTO RICO

★ San Juan

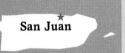

 Spanish, English

POPULATION
3,622,000
1,054 per sq mi/407 per sq km

LANDMASS
3,435 sq mi/8,897 sq km

    Chemicals — Crude Oil

ST. KITTS-NEVIS

★ Basseterre

 English

POPULATION
41,000
347 per sq mi/134 per sq km

LANDMASS
118 sq mi/306 sq km

    Sugar — Food

ST. LUCIA

★Castries

 English

POPULATION
156,000
655 per sq mi/253 per sq km

LANDMASS
238 sq mi/616 sq km

     Bananas — Food

ST. VINCENT & THE GRENADINES

Kingstown

 English

POPULATION
118,000
787 per sq mi/304 per sq km

LANDMASS
150 sq mi/389 sq km

    Bananas — Food

TRINIDAD AND TOBAGO

★ Port-of-Spain

 English

POPULATION
1,271,000
642 per sq mi/248 per sq km

LANDMASS
1,980 sq mi/5,128 sq km

  Crude Oil — Machinery

UNITED STATES

Washington D.C.

 English

POPULATION
264,000,000
73 per sq mi/28 per sq km

LANDMASS
3,615,123 sq mi/9,363,169 sq km

  Machinery — Vehicles

CHAPTER **3**

CANADA

Canada: A Varied Country

CONNECTIONS

With a partner, list what you already know about Canada. Make another list of what you would like to know about Canada.

TERMS

tundra, permafrost, population density, land bridge, federation, constitutional monarchy

FOCUS

What are some similarities between Canada and the United States?

A. From Kanata to Canada

What's in a Name? Canada. We all know that country's name. But did you know that a misunderstanding of the Native American word for "village" led to the name of this huge nation? Here is how it happened.

In 1534 the French explorer Jacques Cartier (zhahk kahr tee AY) sailed from France to North America. Traveling up the St. Lawrence River, he landed at a Native American village that was inhabited by people of the powerful Iroquoian (ihr uh KWOI un) nation. Cartier asked the Iroquoians what they called the place where he had landed. Using the Iroquoian word meaning "settlement" or "village," the Native Americans answered, "Kanata." So Cartier and his fellow explorers started calling that location, which was where Quebec City is today, by the name *Kanata*.

The name *Kanata* soon began to appear on the maps Europeans drew of North America. On some of the maps, *Kanata* was spelled Canada, and it became widely used to refer to the whole region, not just the one Native American settlement. The name *Canada* was first used as an official name in 1791, and by 1867 it was applied to the entire region to the north of the United States. Cartier's simple misunderstanding of the Iroquoian word for village eventually led to a new name for this huge nation to our north.

The Giant Neighbor Canada is the second largest country in the world. Only Russia is larger. In fact, Canada covers almost one half of the continent of North America. Unlike most countries of the world, Canada has oceans on three of its borders. The Atlantic Ocean is on the east, the Pacific Ocean is on the west, and the Arctic Ocean is on the north. Because of these ocean borders, Canada shares a land boundary in two locations with only one other country: the United States.

Canada and the United States are friendly, and each nation likes and respects the other. Because they have such good relations, Canada and the United States share the longest undefended border in the world. Millions of Canadians and Americans cross the border every year. Sometimes, firefighters from the United States race across the border to help fight Canadian fires. Families from both countries often attend services in the same church or temple.

Canada and the United States are alike in many ways. Both countries share many of the same major landforms, such as the Rocky Mountains. People in both countries speak English, although French is also an official language in Canada. And each nation is divided into smaller political units. We call ours states, and Canadians call their political divisions provinces. It is these similarities and close ties that make Canada a special neighbor.

B. A Country of the Far North

Above the Arctic Circle From the map on page 74, you can see that Canada's southernmost point is in Lake Erie. The northernmost point is on Ellesmere Island

▶ Toronto's most famous landmark is the Canadian National Railways Tower.

CANADA: PHYSICAL

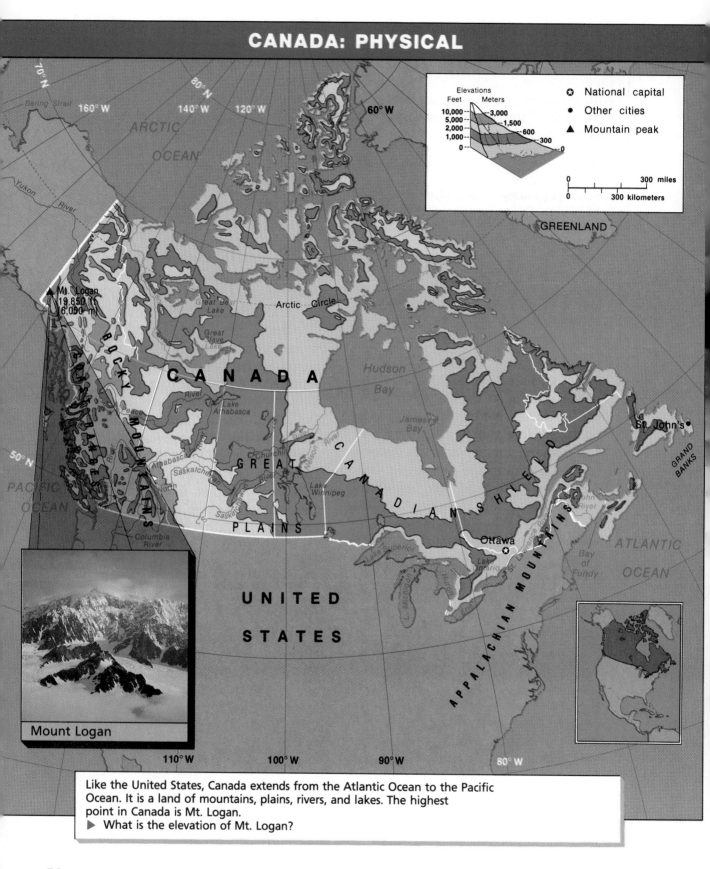

Elevations

Feet	Meters
10,000	3,000
5,000	1,500
2,000	600
1,000	300
0	0

⊛ National capital
● Other cities
▲ Mountain peak

300 miles
300 kilometers

GREENLAND

ARCTIC OCEAN

Bering Strait

Yukon River

Mt. Logan
19,850 ft
(6,050 m)

Great Bear Lake

Arctic Circle

Great Slave Lake

ROCKY MOUNTAINS

COAST RANGES

CANADA

Hudson Bay

River

Lake Athabasca

Peace River

River

Athabasca River

Saskatchewan River

North Saskatchewan River

South Saskatchewan River

Churchill River

Nelson River

GREAT

PLAINS

Lake Winnipeg

James Bay

CANADIAN SHIELD

PACIFIC OCEAN

Columbia River

UNITED

STATES

Lake Superior

Lake Michigan

Lake Huron

Lake Erie

Lake Ontario

Ottawa

St. Lawrence River

St. John River

St. John's

GRAND BANKS

ATLANTIC OCEAN

Bay of Fundy

APPALACHIAN MOUNTAINS

Mount Logan

Like the United States, Canada extends from the Atlantic Ocean to the Pacific Ocean. It is a land of mountains, plains, rivers, and lakes. The highest point in Canada is Mt. Logan.
▶ What is the elevation of Mt. Logan?

in the Arctic Ocean. A large part of Canada stretches far beyond the Arctic Circle. This northerly location means that most of Canada lies within climate regions where it is cool or cold for much of the year. The growing season is short, limiting the kinds of crops that can be grown.

Permafrost In the extreme northern region of Canada, it is too cold for trees to grow. The line where trees stop growing is called the *timberline*. North of the timberline lies the **tundra**. The tundra is a region where only a few plants, like mosses and lichens, can grow. These plants grow in the short summer, when the top layer of the ground thaws out. Below this top layer, all the soil is permanently frozen. This frozen soil is called **permafrost**.

Because of the permafrost, special construction techniques must be used to build houses and other buildings in the tundra. If houses were built directly on the frozen ground, the heat from the houses would cause the ground to thaw. If this happened, the buildings would slowly settle into large mud puddles. To avoid this problem, buildings are set on stilts, or posts, to keep them off the ground. The area below the buildings is insulated so that the heat from the buildings cannot melt the permafrost.

Boreal Forest South of the timberline is a broad belt of *coniferous*, or evergreen, trees that extends from the Atlantic Ocean to the Alaskan border. Because the climate here is not as harsh as in the tundra, pine and fir trees can survive. This broad expanse of evergreen trees is called a boreal (BOR ee ul) forest. Boreal forests are one of Canada's most valuable natural resources.

Only along the southern edge of Canada is the climate warm enough to allow farming. Here are found Canada's wheat farms and important manufacturing centers. This southern region is also where most Canadians live.

Many different animals live on the tundra, including the snowy owl, the arctic fox, and the caribou.
▶ Do trees grow on the tundra?

Population Density Because of Canada's northern location, much of the country is uninhabited. Even though it contains about 46 percent of the land area of North America, Canada has only about 6 percent of the total population of the continent. There are only 7 people per square mile (3 people per sq km). In the United States, there are 73 people per square mile (28 people per sq km). The average number of people who live in a square mile or square kilometer of a country is called the **population density.** To find the population density of a country, you divide the total number of people who live in a country by that country's total land area. The map on page 91 shows Canada's population density.

C. The People of Canada

Native Americans Thousands of years ago, the first people to settle in Canada traveled across the Bering Strait from Asia to what is now Alaska. They made their trip over the Bering Strait **land bridge** that connected the continents of Asia and North America. A land bridge is a narrow piece of land that connects two larger landmasses.

The people who crossed the Bering Strait are called Native Americans. Over several thousand years, they spread throughout North and South America. In Canada some Native Americans settled and built fishing villages along the coast of the Pacific Ocean. Other Native Americans lived on the grasslands of south central Canada and in the northern forests and around the Great Lakes.

The Inuit One Native American group that is known as the Inuit, or Eskimos, settled on the tundra along the Arctic coast. The Inuit survived by hunting seals, walruses, caribou, and whales. The hunters lived in igloos—temporary shelters built out of blocks of ice. Today the Inuit's traditional way of life has changed. Most now live in modern-style wooden houses. Some still hunt and fish for a living, but others work for companies that are developing Canada's natural resources.

Some of the Inuit who live on the tundra along the Arctic coast still hunt and fish for a living.
▶ What modern means of transportation do the Inuit use when they hunt and fish?

Only about 2 percent of Canada's population is Native American. About 40 percent of the people are of British descent. British sailors visited the coast of Canada as early as the 1400s. By 1500, England had claimed the northeastern coast of North America. More than a century later, English people began settling in the regions along the Atlantic Coast.

Immigrants Some of Canada's English-speaking settlers were from the United States. During the American Revolution, many people in the American colonies remained loyal to Great Britain. They were called the Loyalists. After the American colonies gained their independence, many of the Loyalists fled to Canada.

The French Canadians are the second largest group of people in Canada. Like the English in the 1500s, French explorers claimed parts of northeastern North America. French settlers moved to Canada in the early 1600s and built farms and villages in the St. Lawrence River valley. Today about 27 percent of Canada's population is of French descent. Most live in the large province of Quebec (kwee BEK).

During the late 1800s, people from other European countries, such as Russia, began moving to Canada. Most of these people settled in the cities where industries had begun to grow. Others settled on the prairies and began to build wheat and cattle farms.

Between 1940 and 1960, more immigrants came to Canada from Europe. Many came from European countries such as Germany, the Netherlands, Italy, Poland, and Sweden. Recently, immigrants from the Caribbean islands and from Asia have contributed to the growth and variety of Canada's population.

D. The Government of Canada

Federation The political map on page 81 shows that Canada is made up of ten provinces and two territories. These provinces and territories are joined together in a **federation**. A federation is a government in which the national government and the governments of the provinces share certain powers. The national government has the power to conduct foreign policy, but the provinces and territories do not.

The head of state of Canada is the queen of England. This is a result of the long period during which Canada was a colony of England. When Canada became an independent country, it retained some ties with England. Today the queen does not rule the country directly. Instead, Canada is a **constitutional monarchy**. In a constitutional monarchy, the king or queen does not actually rule the country. Laws are made by a governing body.

Queen Elizabeth of England is the constitutional monarch of Canada.
▶ Does the Queen make the laws that govern Canada's people?

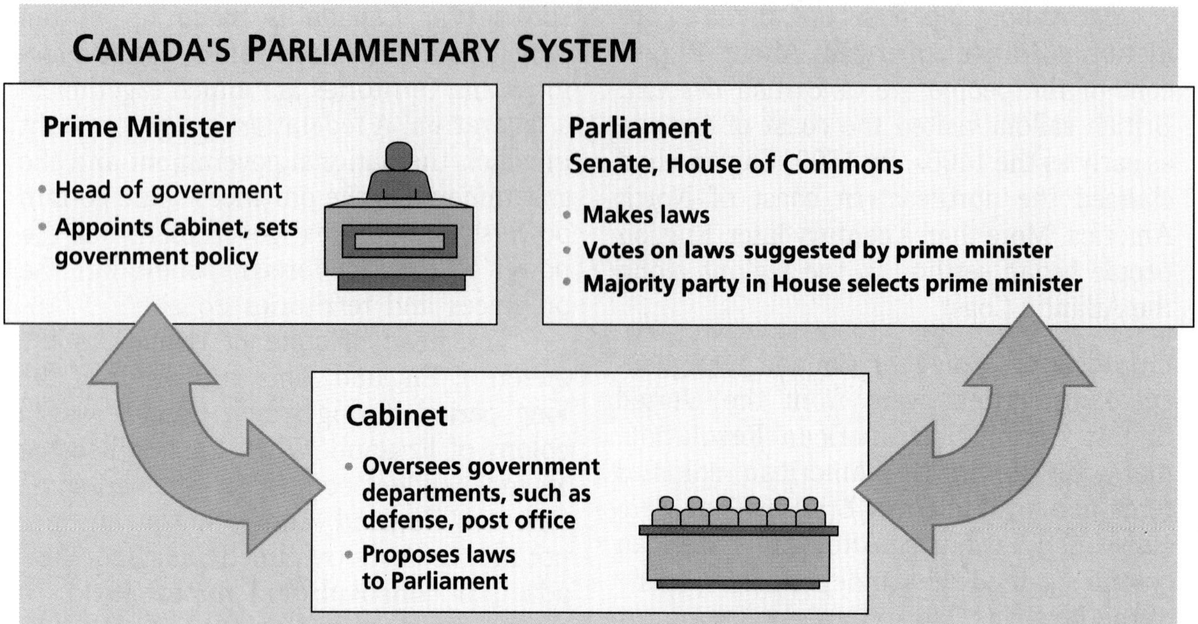

CANADA'S PARLIAMENTARY SYSTEM

Prime Minister

- Head of government
- Appoints Cabinet, sets government policy

Parliament
Senate, House of Commons

- Makes laws
- Votes on laws suggested by prime minister
- Majority party in House selects prime minister

Cabinet

- Oversees government departments, such as defense, post office
- Proposes laws to Parliament

Canada has a parliamentary system of government. The Parliament is divided into two parts. Only the members of the House of Commons are elected by voters; the prime minister appoints the members of the Senate.
► Who selects the prime minister?

Parliament In Canada the governing body is called Parliament. As you can see from the diagram above, Parliament is made up of two parts—the Senate and the House of Commons. Only members of the House are elected. The head of the Parliament is the prime minister. The prime minister suggests laws and programs to Parliament. The members of Parliament vote on the prime minister's suggestions.

Canada's ten provinces are somewhat like the states in the United States. They have the power to make laws about local matters. Each province has a one-house parliament. The provincial parliaments have no Senate, only a Legislative Assembly. Each provincial government is led by a premier. The national government controls the affairs of the two sparsely populated territories.

LESSON 1

Review

REVIEWING MAIN IDEAS

A. What are the oceans and countries that form Canada's borders?

B. How does Canada's location affect the country's soils and vegetation?

C. What are the largest ethnic groups in Canada?

D. What form of government does Canada have?

SKILLS CHECK

MAP SKILL

Look at the map of the world on pages 688–689. Name five countries of the world besides Canada that extend above the Arctic Circle.

Canada's Regions: A Journey of Discovery

CONNECTIONS

Each section of this lesson covers a part of Canada. Looking at the photographs in each section, name the kinds of vegetation or landforms you find in the photographs.

TERMS

fjord, bilingual, lock, prairie, hydroelectricity

FOCUS

What are the main geographical regions of Canada?

A. The Provinces by the Sea

Atlantic Provinces St. John's, Newfoundland, is where you first see the sun rise in North America. This part of Canada stretches far out into the waters of the Atlantic Ocean. Signal Hill, at the entrance to the harbor of St. John's, is only 1,900 miles (3,057 km) from Europe. In fact, someone standing on Signal Hill is actually closer to Ireland than he or she is to the Mississippi River, in the United States.

Once the sun rises over the water, you can see the old town of St. John's. Many of the houses are painted blue, pink, red, yellow, turquoise, and white. These brightly painted houses are typical of houses in the small towns

and villages in this part of eastern Canada. Because of the cold, wet climate and the rocky, bleak landscape, many of the people who live here paint their houses like this to brighten up their landscape.

Four Provinces Four provinces make up this southeastern corner of Canada. Two are islands—Newfoundland (NOO fund land) and Prince Edward Island. The other two—Nova Scotia (noh vuh SKOH shuh) and New Brunswick—are peninsulas. These provinces are called the Atlantic provinces, since the entire region has its border on the Atlantic Ocean.

Most people in the Atlantic provinces live close to the coast, where hundreds of bays and inlets provide good harbors for fishing boats. Some of these arms of the sea are called **fjords** (fyords). A fjord is a deep valley with steep cliffs on each side. Fjords were carved out by glaciers. Glaciers are large masses of ice that were formed from snow. They move very slowly down a mountainside or along a valley. The deep valleys carved by the glaciers along the coast were later filled in by the ocean.

This photograph shows the town of St. John's Newfoundland, the easternmost point in North America.
► How far is St. John's from Europe?

Newfoundland St. John's is at the eastern end of the Trans-Canada Highway. This highway goes all the way across Canada from the Atlantic Ocean to the Pacific Ocean. The map on page 81 shows the route through southern Canada followed by the Trans-Canada Highway.

A seagoing ferry carries cars from Newfoundland across Cabot Strait to the northern tip of Nova Scotia. Here, on Cape Breton Island, are high mountains with very steep slopes that drop right into the ocean. These mountains are part of the Appalachian Mountain range of North America. The Appalachians begin in the United States and extend northward through the Atlantic provinces. Here they are mainly low hills of about 1,500 feet (457 m).

Nova Scotia Most of the people who live in Nova Scotia today are descendants of early settlers from Great Britain. But the British were not the only settlers on this peninsular province. French farmers and fur trappers also settled in the region in the seventeenth century. The French settlers called the region Acadia. The descendants of these French settlers in Nova Scotia are still called Acadians.

Halifax Halifax, Nova Scotia, is the largest city in the Atlantic provinces. Halifax is an important port city in Canada. In the winter the St. Lawrence River freezes, preventing ships from reaching other Canadian cities like Montreal and Quebec. The harbor at Halifax, however, remains free of ice throughout the winter.

Just north of Halifax is the Annapolis River valley, one of the most fertile farming regions in the Atlantic provinces. The Annapolis River valley is a region known for its productive apple orchards. Farmers here and throughout Nova Scotia also grow potatoes and blueberries, and raise dairy cattle and beef cattle.

In many places in Canada, the steep slopes of the Appalachian Mountains drop straight into the Atlantic Ocean.
▶ Where do the Appalachians begin?

CANADA: POLITICAL

Legend

- ✪ National capital
- ✪ Provincial/Territorial capitals
- • Other cities
- — Trans-Canada Highway

0   200   400 miles
0   200   400 kilometers

GREENLAND

ARCTIC OCEAN

ALASKA

A

YUKON TERRITORY

Whitehorse

VICTORIA ISLAND

BAFFIN ISLAND

Designated Inuit Area (Nunavut)

Arctic Circle

NORTHWEST

TERRITORIES

Yellowknife

Great Bear Lake

Great Slave Lake

C A N A D A

ATLANTIC OCEAN

Labrador

B

BRITISH COLUMBIA

ALBERTA

Lake Athabasca

SASKATCHEWAN

MANITOBA

Hudson Bay

James Bay

NEW FOUNDLAND

Edmonton

Lake Winnipeg

QUEBEC

PRINCE EDWARD ISLAND

St. John's

Charlottetown

NEW BRUNSWICK

Victoria

Vancouver

Calgary

Dauphin

Regina

Winnipeg

ONTARIO

Sault Ste. Marie

Quebec

Montreal

Ottawa

Fredericton

Parrsboro

Halifax

NOVA SCOTIA

Bay of Fundy

PACIFIC OCEAN

C

Lake Superior

Lake Huron

Lake Michigan

Toronto

Lake Ontario

UNITED STATES

Lake Erie

1 2 3 4 5 6 7 8 9

120°W   110°W   100°W   90°W   80°W   70°W

70°N   80°N   50°N   40°N

Cities less than 100,000

Charlottetown C-8
Dauphin B-4
Fredericton C-8
Parrsboro C-8
St. John's C-9
Sault Ste. Marie C-6
Victoria C-2
Whitehorse A-1
Yellowknife A-3

Cities 100,000 to 499,999

Halifax C-8
Ottawa C-7
Quebec C-7
Regina B-4
Vancouver C-2

Cities 500,000 to 999,999

Calgary B-3
Edmonton B-3
Toronto C-7
Winnipeg C-5

Cities 1,000,000 or more

Montreal C-7

Canada is made up of ten provinces and two territories. Most of its largest cities are found along the southern border.
▶ Through how many provincial capitals does the Trans-Canada Highway pass?

81

Bay of Fundy The Bay of Fundy separates the peninsula of Nova Scotia from New Brunswick. The bay holds the world's record for high tides and low tides. At low tide near Parrsboro, a town on the bay, all the boats, even large freighters, rest on dry ground in the harbor. As the time for the next high tide approaches, a long ripple of water moves in from the open sea and within minutes arrives at the Parrsboro dock. This *tidal bore* marks the beginning of the incoming high tide. Soon the boats in the harbor are afloat in deep water.

Prince Edward Island From Nova Scotia a ferry carries the Trans-Canada Highway traffic over to Prince Edward Island, the smallest Canadian province. The island is protected from ocean storms and has a warm climate and sandy soils. The main crops grown here are potatoes and tobacco.

New Brunswick The fourth Atlantic province is New Brunswick. It is also connected by ferry to Prince Edward Island. About 80 percent of New Brunswick is forest. The main crop grown in this province is potatoes, an important crop in all the Atlantic provinces. In fact, this region produces 60 percent of the potatoes grown in Canada.

B. Traveling Across French Canada

Quebec If you were to travel through the province of Quebec, you would soon notice that the road signs are in French. Quebec province is home to most French-speaking Canadians. However, many of the citizens here also speak English, the main language spoken in the other parts of Canada. Canada is a **bilingual,** or two-language, country. French and English are Canada's two official languages.

Tides on the Bay of Fundy sometimes rise to over 50 feet (15 m) high.
▶ What problems do you think the high and low tides create for boats on the bay?

This photograph shows a section of one of the first cities the French established in Canada.
► What is the name of the city shown?

Canadian Shield Quebec is the largest Canadian province, covering about one sixth of the country. It reaches northward from the United States border all the way to 62°N. That's as far as the distance from Florida to Maine. About 90 percent of the province is part of the Canadian Shield. The Canadian Shield is a huge horseshoe-shaped region that curves around either side of Hudson Bay. The Shield also covers parts of Newfoundland, Ontario, Manitoba, and the Northwest Territories.

Thousands of years ago, large glaciers slowly moved down from northern Canada. As they moved across the land, the glaciers scraped away soil and exposed the shield of rock underneath. Rivers were dammed, forming many lakes. Because of its thin, rocky soil, the Shield is of little use for farming. But it contains vast regions of trees, many rivers for water power, and enormous amounts of important minerals. What was once considered a useless region has helped to make Canada a rich nation.

One of the first cities the French established in Canada was Quebec City. The old section of Quebec City near the river has become a tourist center. Many people visit the city because its old buildings look as if they belong in Europe rather than in North America. As in much of Quebec, French is the main language spoken here, though most people also speak English.

Montreal Montreal, which is also in the province of Quebec, is the second-largest French-speaking city in the world. Its name means "Mount Royal." It comes from the high hill in the center of the island in the St. Lawrence River where the city is built. Montreal began as a city located at the *head of navigation* on the St. Lawrence River. The head of navigation is the place where ships cannot go any farther upstream because of rapids or waterfalls.

On some maps of Canada, you will find the words *Lachine Rapids* (luh SHEEN RAP ihdz) near Montreal. *Lachine* is French for "China." Some early French explorers thought that if they could only get past these rapids at Montreal, they could follow the St. Lawrence River through North America to get to China.

St. Lawrence Seaway Of course, we all know now that you can't get to China by sailing up the St. Lawrence River. However, the river has become an important transportation route. In 1959, Canada and the United States joined together to build the St. Lawrence Seaway from Montreal to Lake Ontario. The seaway is part of the Great Lakes-St. Lawrence Waterway. This waterway allows ships to travel from the Great Lakes to the Atlantic Ocean.

Building the seaway was a difficult task. The Atlantic Ocean is at sea level. Lake Superior is 600 feet (183 m) above sea level. To make up for the changes in water level, the waterway has a number of **locks**. A lock is an enclosed area with gates at each end. Pumps raise or lower the water level in each lock. This allows ships to be raised or lowered from one water level to another. The locks allow ships to move from the Great Lakes to the Atlantic Ocean. They also allow ships to carry the resources of eastern Canada to industrial areas of the United States and Canada around the Great Lakes. Because of its location on the seaway, Montreal has become Canada's chief transportation center.

C. The Shining Waters of Ontario

British Canada Just a few miles west of Montreal is the province of Ontario. *Ontario* is a Native American word for "the shining waters." The name is appropriate, because the province of Ontario borders four of the five Great Lakes. It also contains thousands of smaller lakes and rivers.

Quebec is "French" Canada; Ontario is "British" Canada. Ontario was settled mainly by people of British descent. English is the predominant language in this part of the Canadian Shield.

Lakes Peninsula Several large cities are found in southern Ontario. This part of Ontario is called the Lakes Peninsula. It is

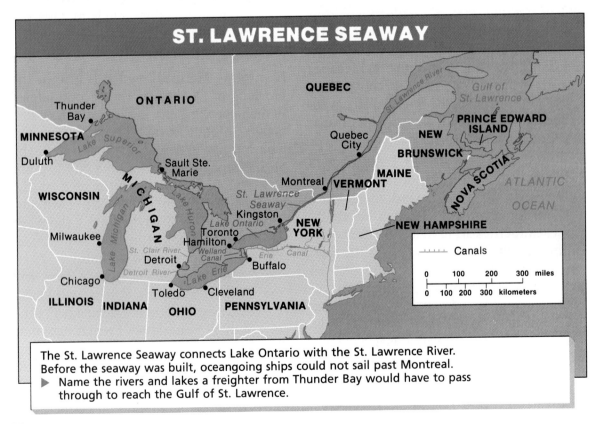

The St. Lawrence Seaway connects Lake Ontario with the St. Lawrence River. Before the seaway was built, oceangoing ships could not sail past Montreal.
▶ Name the rivers and lakes a freighter from Thunder Bay would have to pass through to reach the Gulf of St. Lawrence.

The landscape of the Prairie provinces is dotted with tall grain elevators.
▶ Canada is one of the world's leading producers of what type of grain?

plunges over a high rocky ledge and forms the famous Niagara Falls. The ledge over which the river falls runs for many miles around the Great Lakes. Lake Ontario is 326 feet (99 m) below the level of Lake Erie. For ships to get past the falls, the Welland Canal, with seven locks, had to be built.

The Soo Another canal with a system of locks is located in the rocky, hilly wooded part of the Canadian Shield in western Ontario. This is the "Soo." The Soo is what Canadians call the Sault Ste. Marie (soo saynt muh REE) canal and locks. The locks allow large ships carrying iron ore or other cargo to travel along the St. Marys River between Lake Superior and Lake Huron.

West of Lake Superior the landscape of Canada changes dramatically. Rainfall decreases, and the climate gradually becomes drier. The dark, green woods of the Canadian Shield gradually give way to a gently rolling, open grassland region.

D. The Prairie Provinces

The Prairies When the first settlers moved into the **prairies** of Canada, many of them called their wagons prairie schooners, for they were like ships crossing the endless sea of grass. A prairie is a large area of level or rolling land that is covered by tall grass and has fertile soil.

Manitoba, Saskatchewan, and Alberta are called the Prairie provinces. The land in these provinces is an extension of the Great Plains of the United States. Much of the Canadian prairie is used for wheat farming. Canada is one of the world's leading producers of wheat. Other crops you will see growing here are corn, flax, and lentils, which are a kind of pea.

Manitoba Winnipeg is the capital of the province of Manitoba. Not far north of Winnipeg is an area with old farmhouses

located between Lake Huron and Lake Erie, and contains about one third of all the people in Canada. The national capital is Ottawa, which is in the southeastern corner of the province.

Toronto The largest city in Ontario is Toronto, located on the northwestern shore of Lake Ontario. With a metropolitan area population of over 4 million, Toronto is a large, modern city and is Canada's chief manufacturing center. Food processing and printing are the city's major industries.

Toronto is also the location of the world's tallest free-standing structure, the Canadian National Railways Tower. This tower, with a height of 1,815 feet (553 m), has a revolving restaurant at its top that can be reached by an exciting ride up one of the tower's glass-walled elevators.

South from Toronto, across Lake Ontario, is the Niagara River. Along the 30-mile (48 km) route that this river flows between Lake Erie and Lake Ontario, it

that have walls of mud and thatched roofs. These farmhouses were built by people who moved here from a part of Europe that is called the Ukraine. About half a million Ukrainians live in Canada, mostly in the Prairie provinces.

Saskatchewan West of Manitoba is the province of Saskatchewan. All through Saskatchewan are towns with names like Moose Jaw, Swift Current, and Gull Lake. Many of these towns are located along the railroads, and most have grain elevators with tall towers, a symbol of life on the prairie.

Alberta The largest city in the Prairie provinces is Calgary, in the province of Alberta. The city is the headquarters of over 600 oil companies, which have moved here to pump oil from beneath the surrounding prairie.

North of Calgary is another oil-rich town—the capital city of Edmonton. In 1987, Edmonton became the home of the world's largest shopping mall. Covering many acres, this huge indoor mall even has an amusement park that is called Canada Fantasyland.

E. Across the Cordillera to the Pacific

The Cordillera West of Calgary and Edmonton, the Rocky Mountains sharply rise above the Canadian prairies. The Rockies form the western border of the province of British Columbia.

Most of British Columbia is mountainous. The region is called the Cordillera, meaning "a system of mountain ranges." As you can see from the map on page 74, The Rocky Mountains and the Coast Ranges stretch along the western edge of Canada

Edmonton's huge shopping mall has over 800 stores, 110 eating places, a hotel, and an amusement park.
▶ What part of the mall is shown here?

southward into the United States. The Coast Ranges rise steeply from the ocean, and the coastline is cut by fjords similar to the ones seen in Newfoundland. The Canadian Rockies are among the most rugged mountains in the world.

A Forested Region The climate along the Pacific Ocean coast is fairly mild, and abundant rainfall here has created lush, dense forests. As you might expect, lumbering is an important industry in the region. The mountains of British Columbia also contain minerals such as coal and gold. But perhaps more important to the region are the rivers that flow from the mountains. These rivers are used to make **hydroelectricity**, electricity made from the force of flowing water. Three of Canada's major rivers have their source in the mountains of British Columbia—the Columbia, Yukon, and Fraser rivers. Canada's longest river, the Mackenzie, has its source in the Northwest Territories. The Mackenzie River flows northwest from the Great Slave Lake for about 1,000 miles (1,600 km) to the Arctic Ocean.

The Northwest Territories makes up more than one third of Canada's land area, but less than 1 percent of Canada's people live there. Many who live in the cold climate of the Territories are Inuit. Most of the Northwest Territories is in the Canadian Shield. Minerals have been found in this area, and a few mining towns have been built here.

The other territory in northern Canada is the Yukon Territory. This territory is largely mountainous and is part of the Cordillera region.

Vancouver Vancouver, at the southwestern tip of British Columbia, is Canada's third largest city and its most important Pacific port. From Vancouver, Canada exports products such as wheat, coal, and lumber. It is Canada's main port for its growing trade with the nations of Asia.

Vancouver's excellent harbor has helped make this city Canada's most important port.
▶ Which mountains are in the background?

LESSON 2

Review

REVIEWING MAIN IDEAS

A. How does the Atlantic Ocean affect the climate of the Atlantic provinces?
B. How has the Great Lakes–St. Lawrence Waterway contributed to Montreal's growth?
C. How do the cities of Ontario make use of the Great Lakes?
D. How have wheat and oil changed life in the Prairie provinces?
E. What important resources are found in the Cordillera?

SKILLS CHECK

WRITING SKILL
Canada has two official languages, English and French. Write a paragraph explaining how you would feel if the United States had two official languages.

Living and Working in Canada

CONNECTIONS

Think about the regions of Canada that you have just read about. What do you think are some of the ways people make a living in each of these regions?

TERMS

renewable resource, wood pulp, smelting, glacial till

FOCUS

How do the people of Canada make their living?

A. Harvesting the Riches from the Sea

Grand Banks Fishing has long been an important economic activity in Canada. Even before the first settlers arrived in the 1600s, ships from England were sailing along the coast of Newfoundland and fishing the Grand Banks. A *bank* is a shallow area of the ocean where sunlight can penetrate deep into the water. The sunlight helps to produce an abundant supply of foods for schools of fish. Several of these banks are found in the Atlantic Ocean along the coast of the Atlantic provinces.

The Grand Banks are still an important source of fish. In fact, from New Brunswick northward along the coast of Newfoundland is a coastline almost 5,000 miles (8,000 km) long that is excellent for fishing. Cod, haddock, herring, halibut, and mackerel are found in abundance.

B. Forests: Furs, Lumber, and Recreation

Furs One of the most important natural resources in Canada is the country's forests. Early in Canada's history, French explorers began a profitable fur trade in the eastern forests. Furs were in great demand in Europe and in the cities along the eastern coast of the United States. Beaver pelts, or furs, were especially wanted because they were used to make tall beaver top hats.

Today only a few trappers crisscross the Canadian north country and set out their beaver traps. Most furs now come from fur farms.

Renewable Resource Forests provide one of Canada's greatest **renewable resources**. A renewable resource is a resource that can be replaced once it has been used. For example, although the trees are cut down, new trees are planted to replace them. Forests extend across Canada in an unbroken belt some 500 to 1,300 miles (805 to 2091 km) wide. They provide the raw material for the great lumber industry.

The Rocky Mountains that stretch across eastern British Columbia are covered with coniferous forests. The climate of the region is mild and wet, which is ideal for tree growth. Quebec and Ontario also have huge stands of timber. The forests here are located on the Canadian Shield.

Pulp and Paper The trees that grow on the Canadian Shield are not as large as those growing in the Rocky Mountains.

These men are fishing the Grand Banks, one of Canada's major fishing regions.
▶ Why is this a good area for fishing?

This is one of the thousands of lumber mills found throughout Canada. The worker in the photograph to the right is sawing a log into boards.
▶ What other product comes from Canada's forests?

Because of the size of the trees, they are harvested, or cut, to make **wood pulp**. Wood pulp is a wet, soggy mass of ground-up wood chips. The pulp is used to manufacture paper. Pulp and paper production is helped by the cheap electricity generated from dams on the many rivers on the Shield.

The United States is Canada's best customer for wood pulp and newsprint. It buys about one half of all Canada's exports of pulpwood and about four fifths of the exports of newsprint, the paper used for newspapers.

C. Wealth from Mineral Resources

Gold Canada is extremely rich in mineral resources. Across the vast Canadian Shield are large deposits of important minerals. One of the more exciting minerals found in this region is gold. Most of the gold mined on the Shield today comes from a belt that stretches from central Ontario eastward into Quebec. This region is some-times called the Valley of Gold. Canada ranks fourth in the world in the production of gold.

Smelting Nickel and Copper Nickel and copper are the most important minerals found in the Shield. Nickel is used to make steel harder and stronger. It is also used to make coins. Canada ranks second in the world in the production of nickel. The largest nickel deposits are located at Sudbury, Ontario. Here, at a large plant, the nickel is extracted, or removed, from the rocks containing it. This extraction process is called **smelting**, which is a method of separating ore from rock.

Zinc is also mined from the Shield in Ontario. Canada is the world's leading producer of this bluish-white metal. Zinc is used to coat steel to prevent the steel from rusting.

Zinc Production The bar graph on this page shows the world's leading producers of zinc. Each bar on a bar graph stands for a fact. The bars are arranged to make it easy to compare these facts. This bar graph compares the amounts of zinc produced by the five largest producers of zinc in the world. The names of the countries are shown at the bottom of the graph. There is a bar to represent the amount of zinc each country produces. Each side of the graph has a scale. The scales measure the amount of zinc produced. From the bar graph we can see that Canada produces over 1,300,000 short tons of zinc per year.

Other Minerals Ontario's neighboring province of Quebec is the source of Canada's extensive deposits of asbestos. This mineral is processed from rock into long threadlike fibers that do not burn or conduct heat. However, asbestos is also dangerous because it has been found to cause cancer. As a result, asbestos insulation has been removed from many public buildings.

Canada is the world's second largest producer of uranium, a mineral used to power nuclear reactors. It is found in the rocks of the Canadian Shield and in northern Saskatchewan. Beneath the prairies of southern Saskatchewan are huge reserves of potash. Potash is used in plant fertilizers.

Iron Ore Newfoundland, Quebec, and Ontario hold Canada's iron ore deposits. Today, Canada is a leading world producer of iron ore, which is used to make steel. The high quality of the iron ore of Newfoundland and eastern Quebec makes Canadian iron ore especially valuable.

D. Farming in Canada

The Prairies' Products In Canada there are two areas that are the most important farming regions. You may have guessed that

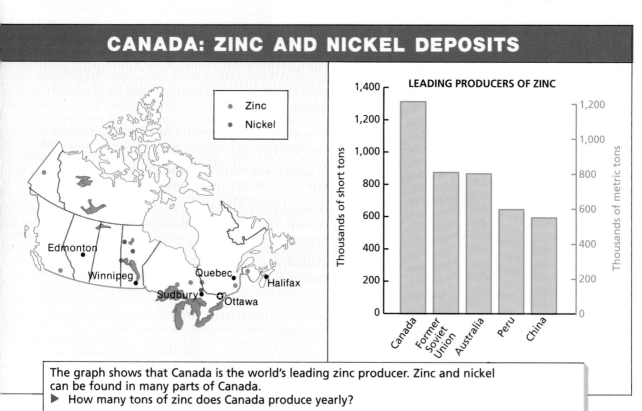

CANADA: ZINC AND NICKEL DEPOSITS

The graph shows that Canada is the world's leading zinc producer. Zinc and nickel can be found in many parts of Canada.
▶ How many tons of zinc does Canada produce yearly?

CANADA: POPULATION DENSITY

National capital ✪
Other cities •

Persons per
square mile	square kilometer
0	0
2	1
25	10
125	50
250	100

0   200   400 miles
0   200   400 kilometers

THE 25 LARGEST CITIES OF CANADA

City	Population	City	Population	City	Population
Montreal	1,018,000	Hull	319,000	Saskatoon	186,000
Calgary	711,000	Hamilton	318,000	Regina	179,000
Toronto	635,000	Laval	314,000	Quebec	168,000
Edmonton	617,000	Ottawa	314,000	Kitchener	168,000
Winnipeg	617,000	Etobicoke	310,000	Burnaby	159,000
North York	563,000	London	303,000	Markham	154,000
Scarborough	525,000	Surrey	245,000	Longueuil	154,000
Vancouver	472,000	Brampton	234,000		
Mississauga	463,000	Windsor	191,000		

Much of Canada has less than 2 people per square mile. The highest population
density and the largest number of cities are located along the southern border.
▶ Which cities are located in the highest population density region?

91

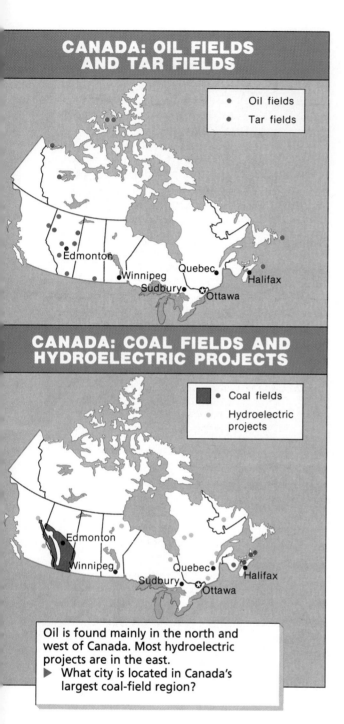

CANADA: OIL FIELDS AND TAR FIELDS

- Oil fields
- Tar fields

Edmonton
Winnipeg
Quebec
Sudbury
Halifax
Ottawa

CANADA: COAL FIELDS AND HYDROELECTRIC PROJECTS

- Coal fields
- Hydroelectric projects

Edmonton
Winnipeg
Quebec
Sudbury
Halifax
Ottawa

Oil is found mainly in the north and west of Canada. Most hydroelectric projects are in the east.
▶ What city is located in Canada's largest coal-field region?

Ontario Peninsula The second important farming area is around the lower Great Lakes and St. Lawrence River valley. The map on page 91 shows the Ontario peninsula, a region of southern Ontario between Lake Huron and Lake Erie. This peninsula, along with the upper part of the St. Lawrence River valley, is sometimes called Canada's heartland. This region is less than one tenth of Canada's total area. Yet it is home to more than two thirds of Canada's population, and over half of Canada's farm products are raised there.

The land of this region is level and easily cultivated. These level areas of soil are called **glacial till**. Glacial till is the soil and silt deposited by glacial ice sheets as they melted and retreated northward.

In the heartland farming region, hay and oats are grown. During the summer months, thousands of dairy cattle can be seen grazing in the pasture lands. However, because of the harsh, snowy winters, the cattle have to be sheltered and fed inside large dairy barns.

Niagara Fruit Belt One section of the Ontario peninsula is famous for its fruit orchards. This is known as the Niagara Fruit Belt. Because of its location between Lake Ontario and Lake Erie, this section has winters that are not quite so harsh. The milder climate and good soil allow farmers to grow fruits such as peaches, grapes, apples, and sweet cherries.

E. Canada's Energy Resources

Oil and Gas Canada is a country rich in energy resources. Most of Canada's petroleum and natural gas is found in Alberta and Saskatchewan. So far, the petroleum deposits have been enough to meet the needs of Canada's population. But there is concern that Canada may have to begin to import oil if demand continues to grow.

the one region is the prairies in southern Manitoba, Saskatchewan, and Alberta. The rich soils of the prairies are ideal for growing wheat and hay for livestock. Many prairie farmers also raise beef cattle, barley, and sugar beets.

The government is exploring for oil in the northern reaches of the country near the Arctic Ocean. Areas along the Atlantic coast are also being explored for oil deposits. Canada's huge natural gas deposits are large enough to meet the country's needs and leave enough for Canada to export to the United States.

In addition to its oil and gas fields, Alberta has large supplies of tar sands. These sands, which are saturated, or filled, with oil, are in the central part of the province. It is expensive to remove the oil from the sands. However, if the oil fields ever run dry, these tar sands may become an important source of oil.

Hydroelectricity Canada's chief source of power is its thousands of lakes and rivers, especially those in the Canadian Shield. The lakes are the source of many rivers. Within the Shield and at its edge, these rivers break into waterfalls and rapids. The waterfalls and rapids are used to produce hydroelectric power for many of Canada's industries.

The pie graph on this page shows the large amount of electricity produced by water power. A pie graph is a graph used to show the parts of a whole. The whole pie graph stands for the total amount of electricity produced in Canada. Each slice of the pie graph stands for part of the total amount of electricity produced. Hydropower produces 57.5 percent of the total amount of electricity. You can also compare the amount of electricity produced by each source. In this pie graph, you can see that more hydropower than nuclear power is used to produce electricity. According to the graph, what is the second largest source of Canada's electricity?

Canada's future is promising. The resources of its provinces and territories have made it a wealthy nation. This prosperity will undoubtedly continue as Canada enters the twenty-first century.

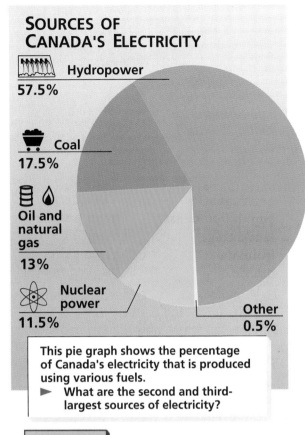

SOURCES OF CANADA'S ELECTRICITY

Hydropower
57.5%

Coal
17.5%

Oil and natural gas
13%

Nuclear power
11.5%

Other
0.5%

This pie graph shows the percentage of Canada's electricity that is produced using various fuels.
► What are the second and third-largest sources of electricity?

LESSON 3

Review

REVIEWING MAIN IDEAS
A. Why is the Grand Banks a good fishing area?
B. What products are made from Canada's extensive forests?
C. What are three important natural resources that are found in the Canadian Shield?
D. Why is it difficult to grow crops in most of Canada?
E. Why is Canada considered to be rich in energy resources?

SKILLS CHECK

THINKING SKILL
Look at the pie graph above. Use the information from the pie graph to construct a bar graph showing the amount of electricity produced by each method. Use the example of a bar graph on page 90 to help guide you.

REVIEWING TERMS

Match each term with the correct definition. Write your answer in sentence form.

tundra   renewable
permafrost   resource
population density   wood pulp
land bridge   smelting
bilingual   glacial till
prairie

1. A narrow piece of land that connects two larger land masses
2. A region where only lichens and mosses grow
3. The layer of soil that is permanently frozen
4. The average number of people who live in a given area
5. A country with two official languages
6. The process of extracting ore from rock
7. A wet, soggy mass of ground-up wood chips that is used to manufacture paper
8. A resource that can be replaced once it has been used
9. Soil and silt that have been deposited by glacial ice sheets as they melted and retreated northward
10. A large area of level or rolling land with tall grass and fertile soil

REVIEWING THE FACTS

On a separate sheet of paper, answer the questions in complete sentences.

1. Who was the French explorer who traveled the St. Lawrence River?
2. How does Canada compare in size with other countries in the world?
3. What is the timberline?
4. How has the Inuit's way of life changed?
5. What are the political units that make up Canada's federation?
6. Who makes the laws in a constitutional monarchy?
7. Which Atlantic province produces 60 percent of the potatoes grown in Canada?
8. Which province is home to the most French-speaking Canadians?
9. What mineral resources are found in the Canadian Shield?
10. Which three major rivers have their source in the mountains of British Columbia?

WRITING ABOUT GOVERNMENT

Write a paragraph explaining how the political systems of Canada and the United States are similar and different.

THINKING CRITICALLY

On a separate sheet of paper, answer the following in complete sentences.

1. What effect has climate had on Canada's population?
2. In what way does Quebec differ from the other provinces of Canada?
3. What are the advantages and disadvantages of the Canadian Shield?
4. Why, do you think, does Canada export a large part of its natural resources?
5. Why are there good relations between Canada and the United States?

Summarizing the Chapter

On a separate sheet of paper, draw a graphic organizer like the one shown here. Copy the information from this graphic organizer to the one you have drawn. Complete the chart by writing in the correct information for each region. The first region has been done for you.

Chapter Theme

Canada's location and natural resources have made Canada a wealthy country with a high standard of living.

Regions	Provinces and Territories	Resources	Economic Activities
Atlantic Provinces	Newfoundland Prince Edward Island Nova Scotia New Brunswick	fish, iron ore	fishing, farming
Canadian Shield			
Prairie Provinces			
Cordillera			

CHAPTER 4

THE UNITED STATES

Describing the United States

CONNECTIONS

If you were to take a trip in the United States, what part of the country would you go to and why?

TERMS

navigable, coastal plain, immigrant, Hispanic

FOCUS

What are the major physical features of the United States?

A. An Imaginary Journey

Our Huge Country The United States is the country that most of us know best. It is a very large country, and few of us are likely to know more than a small part of it. But just how large is the United States? Imagine that you live near New York City and that you are driving with your family to California during your summer vacation. How long will the trip take? You can travel between 400 and 500 miles (644 and 805 km) a day unless you stop to visit places along the route, as you probably will.

The first day's journey takes you across the Appalachians and into Ohio. At the end of the second day, you may reach the Mississippi River, still not halfway across the country. On the third, you will be traveling across a wide area of level land that gently rises as you drive westward. On the fourth, you will be crossing the Rocky Mountains. On the fifth, as you travel beyond the Rocky Mountains, you will notice that the land is broken by many short hills and mountain ridges. On the sixth, you will drive into San Francisco.

Your trip has taken you across the middle of the continent of North America, nearly 3,000 miles (4,827 km), or about an eighth of the distance around the earth. Yet you have not seen all 50 states. Their total area of 3,615,123 square miles (9,363,169 sq km), makes the United States the fourth largest country in the world. Only Russia, Canada, and China are larger.

Connecting the Country Transportation and communication are often difficult in countries with vast amounts of territory. The United States is different because it possesses a varied and efficient transportation system. There are excellent harbors along the coastlines of the Atlantic and Pacific oceans and the Gulf of Mexico. Long, deep, **navigable** rivers, such as the Mississippi and the Delaware, connect large manufacturing cities with the country's mineral and agricultural resources. *Navigable* means that a river or lake is large and deep enough to allow the passage of ships. Railway lines also crisscross the nation.

Superhighways The most dramatic symbols of the excellent transportation system

Barges filled with goods pass by St. Louis as they make their way down the Mississippi River.
▶ Is the Mississippi a navigable river?

▶ El Capitan rises more than 3,000 feet (1,000 m) above Yosemite National Park.

are the roads and highways that cross our country. The largest and most important highway system is the Interstate Highway System. This project was started in the mid-1950s and is scheduled for completion in the 1990s. Because of the Interstate Highway System, people and goods can move across the country quickly, cheaply, and efficiently.

B. The Eastern Regions of the United States

Studying the United States There are many ways to study our country's geography. Most often, it is done by looking at the regions of the United States. As you read in Chapter 2, a region is an area that has one or more features that make it special. Since the United States has five major landforms, we can divide it into five landform regions. Use the map on page 99 as you read about the five landform regions—the Coastal Plain, the Appalachian region, the Interior Plains, the Rocky Mountains, and the Pacific region.

The Coastal Plain If you look again at the map of the United States, you can see that a plain stretches from Maine along the Atlantic seaboard to Florida and then turns westward along the coasts of Alabama, Mississippi, Louisiana, and Texas. We call this landform the Coastal Plain. A **coastal plain** is an area of flat land that borders a coast.

The Coastal Plain changes in width from only a few miles in New Jersey to more than 500 miles (805 km) in Mississippi. Numerous rivers wind slowly across the plain and flow into the Atlantic Ocean or the Gulf of Mexico. Bays cut into the plain in some areas, creating natural harbors. These harbors have helped to make several coastal cities in the eastern part of the United States large and important shipping centers.

The Appalachian Region To the west of the Coastal Plain is the Appalachian region. In the last chapter, you read that the Appalachian Mountains almost drop off into the sea in eastern Canada. This long mountain range continues southward into the United States. The Appalachians are not high—the average elevation is less than 6,000 feet (1,829 m). High ridges, steep slopes, and many valleys are a part of the region.

Today it is easy for people to cross the Appalachian Mountains. They can drive along well-engineered roads, and they have maps to indicate what lies ahead. But for the early settlers of the United States as they pushed west, the Appalachians presented a difficult challenge. The settlers had no roads and no maps to help them, and they had to find the easiest way to travel with their wagons. The routes included the valleys and narrow openings in the Appalachians.

The John F. Kennedy Expressway is one of the three expressways that provide transportation routes for Chicago.
▶ What other forms of transportation does a large city usually have?

THE UNITED STATES: PHYSICAL

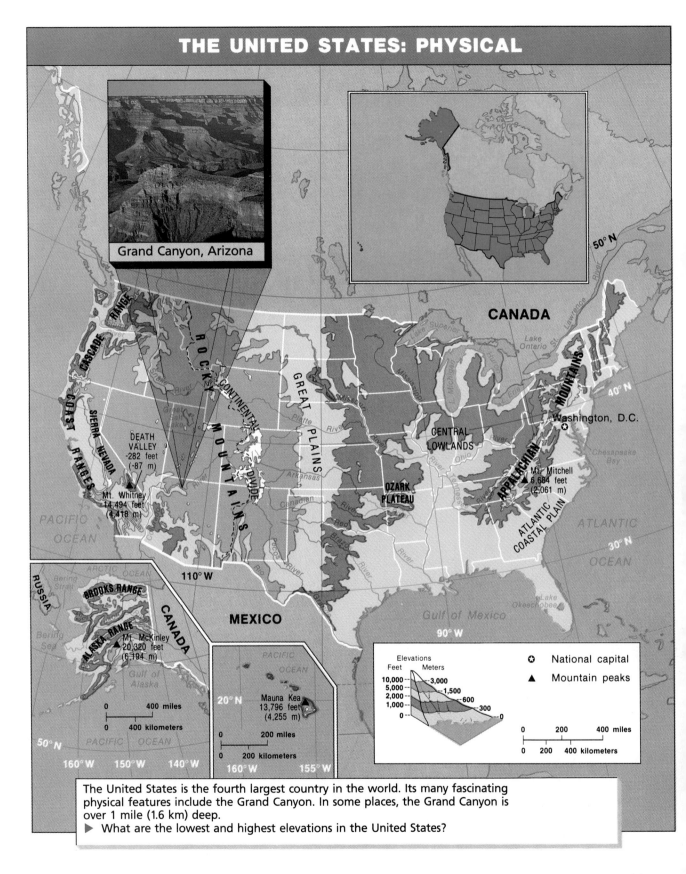

Grand Canyon, Arizona

CANADA

RUSSIA

MEXICO

CASCADE RANGE

COAST RANGES

SIERRA NEVADA

ROCKY MOUNTAINS

CONTINENTAL DIVIDE

GREAT PLAINS

CENTRAL LOWLANDS

OZARK PLATEAU

APPALACHIAN MOUNTAINS

ATLANTIC COASTAL PLAIN

DEATH VALLEY
-282 feet
(-87 m)

Mt. Whitney
14,494 feet
(4,418 m)

Washington, D.C.

Mt. Mitchell
6,684 feet
(2,061 m)

PACIFIC OCEAN

ATLANTIC OCEAN

Gulf of Mexico

Lake Okeechobee

Chesapeake Bay

110° W
90° W
50° N
40° N
30° N

BROOKS RANGE

ALASKA RANGE

CANADA

Mt. McKinley
20,320 feet
(6,194 m)

Bering Strait

Bering Sea

Gulf of Alaska

ARCTIC OCEAN

PACIFIC OCEAN

0   400 miles
0   400 kilometers

50° N
160° W   150° W   140° W

PACIFIC OCEAN

Mauna Kea
13,796 feet
(4,255 m)

20° N

0   200 miles
0   200 kilometers

160° W   155° W

Elevations	
Feet	Meters
10,000	3,000
5,000	1,500
2,000	600
1,000	300
0	0

✪ National capital
▲ Mountain peaks

0   200   400 miles
0   200   400 kilometers

The United States is the fourth largest country in the world. Its many fascinating physical features include the Grand Canyon. In some places, the Grand Canyon is over 1 mile (1.6 km) deep.

▶ What are the lowest and highest elevations in the United States?

99

The Interior Plains A vast area stretches from the Appalachian Mountains in the east to the Rocky Mountains in the west. We sometimes think of it as a huge level plain from one side to the other. But in fact, it is far from level. Here and on this vast plain there are many hilly areas that break its surface.

As you can see from the map on page 99, the area to the west of the Appalachians is the Central Lowlands. This area gradually rises to become the grass-covered Great Plains. Few trees grow on the Great Plains. The most populated city on the Great Plains is Denver, Colorado.

The entire region is divided in half by the Mississippi River. The Mississippi rises among the forests and lakes of northern Minnesota, just west of Lake Superior. It winds generally southward through the Plains for nearly 2,350 miles (3,781 km) and empties into the Gulf of Mexico.

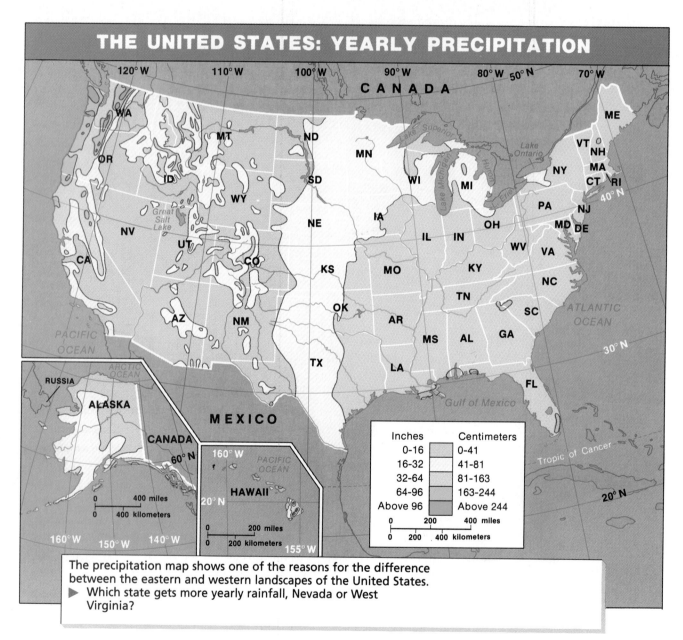

THE UNITED STATES: YEARLY PRECIPITATION

Inches	Centimeters
0-16	0-41
16-32	41-81
32-64	81-163
64-96	163-244
Above 96	Above 244

The precipitation map shows one of the reasons for the difference between the eastern and western landscapes of the United States.
▶ Which state gets more yearly rainfall, Nevada or West Virginia?

A group of backpackers enjoy the natural beauty of the Kaibab Trail, in the Grand Canyon. Many national parks in the mountain west allow camping.
▶ Have you ever gone backpacking?

C. The Western Regions of the United States

The Mountain West The western one third of the United States is made up of a vast system of mountains and high plateaus. The Rocky Mountains, which are the broadest chain of mountains in our country, rise steeply from the Great Plains. Like the Appalachians, the Rockies are made up of many separate ranges, but they are much higher than any mountains in the eastern United States. Their tops are snow-capped—all year in some cases—and the scenery is more spectacular than any to be seen in the East.

The Colorado River rises in the Rocky Mountains of Colorado, where it is fed by the melting snow. In its course southwestward to the Gulf of California, the Colorado has cut a huge gorge known as the Grand Canyon. Located in northern Arizona, the canyon is 277 miles (446 km) long, up to 18 miles (29 km) wide, and up to a mile (1.6 km) deep. An American adventurer and writer named Richard Halliburton once visited the Grand Canyon. The Grand Canyon so impressed him that he wrote about this natural wonder in a collection of essays. You can read part of his description of the Grand Canyon on page 102.

The Pacific Region West of the Rocky Mountains are several other mountain ranges—the Sierra Nevada, the Coast Ranges, and the Cascade Range. In the Sierra Nevada is Mount Whitney, which rises 14,494 feet (4,418 m) above sea level. In the Cascade Range is Mount Rainier, which is only a few feet lower. As you read on page 66 in the Continental Handbook, these mountain ranges are part of a region that is often affected by volcanic action and earthquakes.

Between these mountain ranges are fertile valleys. The Central Valley in California and the Willamette (wih LAM iht) Valley in Oregon are two of the most important farming regions in the United States.

West of the valleys, the Coast Ranges stretch along the Pacific coast. In many places the Coast Ranges drop straight into

LITERATURE

FROM:

Richard Halliburton's Complete Book of Marvels

by Richard Halliburton

When Richard Halliburton was a boy, his favorite schoolbook contained pictures of many of the earth's natural wonders. Although the book carried him away in his imagination to strange and wonderful lands, he yearned to see these wonders for himself.

As an adult, Halliburton did visit many parts of the world and wrote several books about his travels. The following selection is a part of his description of the Grand Canyon.

All of us have read stories and seen pictures of the Grand Canyon. These do not help us understand what the Canyon is really like. It's as if we tried to understand music just from reading about it, or from seeing pictures of a piano and a violin. The Canyon may even look rather dull in photographs. When you see the real thing with your own eyes, the sight strikes you speechless—that mile drop to the river—that ten-mile void across to the other brink—those color-splashed temples and towers and pyramids of rock that swell up from the terraced walls—that yawning sea of painted splendor falling away into bottomless mysteries.

The Grand Canyon is too huge for most of us to measure by any scale we know. I'm sure it must have been intended originally for the great planet Jupiter, or for Saturn, and got shipped to our little globe by mistake. By whatever chance it came to be here, the first sight of the Canyon, when the sunset is filling it with burning glory, or the moon with dark enchantment, is enough to overwhelm the most hardened traveler that ever lived.

the Pacific Ocean and form spectacular cliffs along the water's edge. In other places the mountains lie behind flat coastal land.

D. The American People

A Nation of Immigrants The United States is one of the few countries of the world in which the many different people who make up the country feel that they are all united as one people. This country is unique because the majority of its people have their roots in other lands. Only a small percentage of the country's total population is made up of descendants of the original inhabitants, the Native Americans.

In the early years of America's history, most of the **immigrants** who came to this country were from Europe. An immigrant is a person who comes into one country from another country to settle permanently. The pie graph on this page shows that as late as 1900–1910 more immigrants came from Europe than from any other place.

Asian Americans Europe was not the only source of immigrants. Asia, too, provided America with many people. The parents, grandparents, and great-grandparents of today's Asian Americans came from China, Japan, and, in recent years, from the war-torn countries of Southeast Asia.

African Americans The ancestors of today's African Americans also came from other countries—but they did not come as immigrants. African Americans are descendants of African people who were brought to the United States as slaves. Even though they now share the same rights as all other Americans, they have faced obstacles, including discrimination, over the years.

Hispanic Americans Another growing ethnic group is made up of **Hispanics**, or Spanish-speaking Americans. Hispanic Americans include people from Mexico and other places in the Americas.

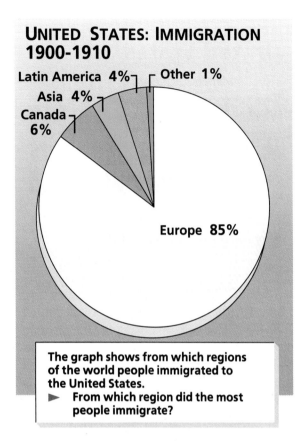

UNITED STATES: IMMIGRATION 1900-1910

Latin America 4%
Other 1%
Asia 4%
Canada 6%
Europe 85%

The graph shows from which regions of the world people immigrated to the United States.
► From which region did the most people immigrate?

LESSON 1

Review

REVIEWING MAIN IDEAS

A. How does the transportation system of the United States allow the swift movement of people and goods?
B. What are the landforms that make up the eastern regions of the United States?
C. What are the landforms that make up the western regions of the United States?
D. What do we mean when we say the United States is a nation of immigrants?

SKILLS CHECK

THINKING SKILL

Turn to the map on page 99. On a separate sheet of paper, list the highest elevation for each of the five landform regions of the United States.

The Climate of the United States

CONNECTIONS

What is your favorite season of the year? Why?

TERMS

axis, solstice, equinox, humid continental, humid subtropical, west coast marine

FOCUS

Why are there different climates?

A. The Four Seasons

Many Kinds of Weather You learned in Chapter 1 that climate means the pattern of weather a certain part of the earth has over a long period of time. In the United States, there are a great many different kinds of weather. There are also great contrasts in weather conditions. Alaska has weather that is bitter cold almost all year. Hawaii and southern Florida have weather that is warm all year long.

Most parts of the country, however, have weather that changes according to the season. Spring is pleasant and warm. Summer can be hot and rather wet. Autumn is cool and windy, and winter is often cold with ice and snow.

The Changing Seasons If you look at the diagram on page 105, you can see why the weather changes according to the season. The revolution of the earth around the sun and the tilt of the earth's **axis** cause the change of seasons. The earth's axis is a line through the earth between the North Pole and the South Pole. The earth turns around on this line. Because the axis is tilted, the North Pole is sometimes slanted toward the sun. At other times of the year it is slanted away from the sun.

Notice the position of the earth on June 21 or 22. The North Pole is tilted toward the sun, so that the sun appears overhead at the parallel of latitude called the Tropic of Cancer. On June 21 or 22 the sun is in the sky for 24 hours everywhere north of the Arctic Circle. In the Northern Hemisphere, the summer **solstice** occurs on June 21 or 22. The solstice marks the farthest advance of the overhead sun north and south from the Equator during the year.

In the Southern Hemisphere, however, this solstice is the beginning of winter and is called the winter solstice. At the time the South Pole is tilted as far from the sun as it ever gets, so the sun's rays reach the Southern Hemisphere at a slant.

After 6 months of revolving, on December 21 or 22, the position of the earth is the opposite of its position on June 21 or 22. Now the sun's rays reach the Northern Hemisphere at a slant. It is winter in the northern parts of this hemisphere. In the Southern Hemisphere, however, it is summertime.

The **equinox** marks the beginning of spring on March 20 or 21 and of autumn on September 22 or 23. An equinox is a time of the year when the sun's rays are overhead at the Equator. Then there are 12 hours of daylight and 12 hours of darkness everywhere on the earth.

B. The Climates of the United States

Humid Continental Climate If you look at the world climate map in the Atlas, you can see that most of the northeastern and midwestern United States has a **humid continental** climate. A humid continental climate has a wide range of temperatures, with warm to unpleasantly hot summers and cold to very cold winters. Precipitation also varies considerably in this climate.

Humid Subtropical The southeastern part of the United States has a climate that is

THE SEASONS

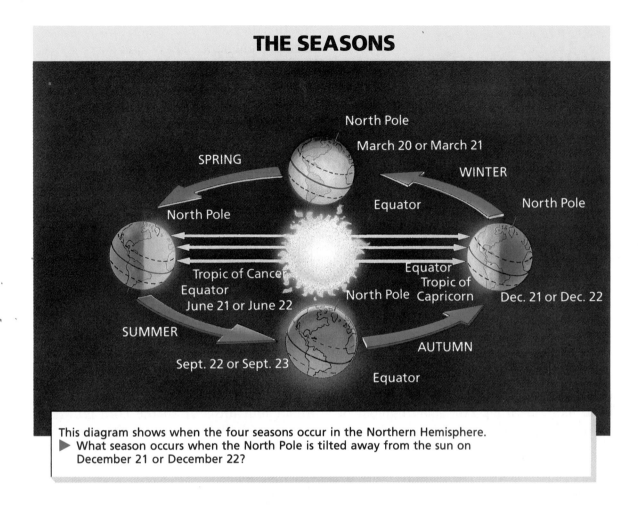

This diagram shows when the four seasons occur in the Northern Hemisphere.
► What season occurs when the North Pole is tilted away from the sun on December 21 or December 22?

similar to the humid continental climate. However, here the temperatures are hotter in summer and milder in winter. There is plenty of rain all year round, but very little snow. This is called a **humid subtropical** climate.

West Coast Marine The western half of the United States receives, on average, much less precipitation than the eastern half. The climates in this part of the country are mostly semiarid or dry climates. However, the coasts of northern California, Oregon, Washington, and Alaska have a **west coast marine** climate.

Areas with this climate lie directly in the path of winds blowing over warm ocean water. The ocean has a great influence on this type of climate. Temperatures are warm in the summer and cool in the winter. There is precipitation all year round, but it is heavier in the winter than in the summer.

LESSON 2

Review

REVIEWING MAIN IDEAS
A. What is the difference between a solstice and an equinox?
B. Which climates cover the largest parts of the United States?

SKILLS CHECK

THINKING SKILL
Turn to the Graph Appendix on pages 732-739. Use the Climate Data table to prepare a climograph of the west coast marine climate.

Agriculture in the United States

CONNECTIONS

Name five of your favorite foods. What is each of them made from?

TERMS

crop rotation, aqueduct, regional specialization

FOCUS

What are the major agricultural activities of the United States?

A. The Farm Belts

Much from Few In the United States today, less than three percent of the people make their living from farming. But these farmers, many of whom live in the midwestern part of the country, produce enough food to feed all 264 million of our citizens. Even more amazing, this small number of people also produces enough to feed many other people in the world. They are able to do this because American farms are extremely efficient. They make use of the most sophisticated farm machinery and the newest fertilizers and pesticides. Pesticides are chemicals used to keep insects from destroying crops.

Wheat Belt The three most important farming regions in the Midwest are called the Wheat Belt, the Corn Belt, and the Dairy Belt.

North and South Dakota, along with the drier western halves of Nebraska and Kansas, make up the Wheat Belt. Here huge wheat fields stretch as far as the eye can see. Only a few towns and cities are scattered throughout this region. When there is a small town, it is usually dominated by tall grain elevators.

Corn Belt The eastern and southern parts of the Midwest make up the Corn Belt. About four fifths of all the corn grown in the United States comes from the Corn Belt states.

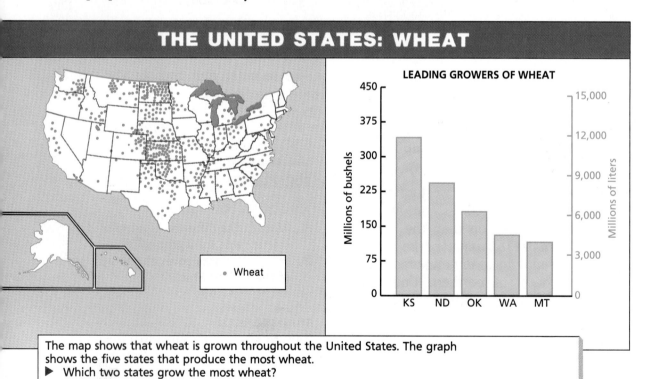

THE UNITED STATES: WHEAT

Wheat

LEADING GROWERS OF WHEAT

Millions of bushels / Millions of liters

KS ND OK WA MT

The map shows that wheat is grown throughout the United States. The graph shows the five states that produce the most wheat.
▶ Which two states grow the most wheat?

106

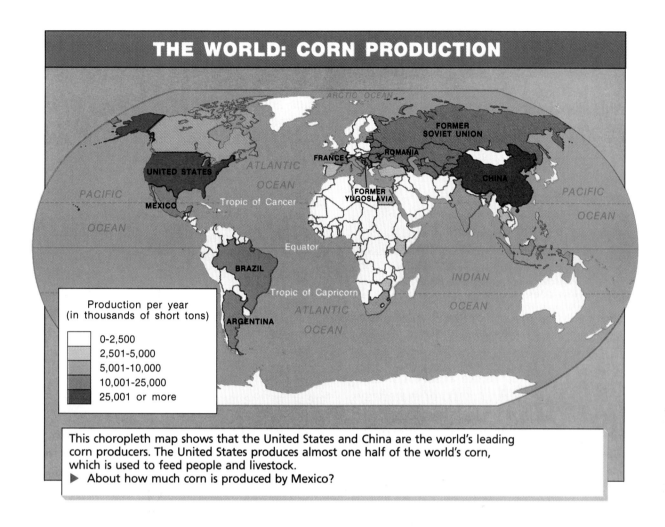

THE WORLD: CORN PRODUCTION

**Production per year
(in thousands of short tons)**

- 0-2,500
- 2,501-5,000
- 5,001-10,000
- 10,001-25,000
- 25,001 or more

This choropleth map shows that the United States and China are the world's leading corn producers. The United States produces almost one half of the world's corn, which is used to feed people and livestock.
▶ About how much corn is produced by Mexico?

Corn, however, is not the only crop grown in the Corn Belt. From year to year, farmers plant their fields with soybeans instead of corn. Soybeans provide feed for livestock and also help to rebuild the nutrients or chemicals in the soil that are used up by the corn crop. Planting fields with different crops each year is a practice that is called **crop rotation**.

Dairy Belt Just north of the Corn Belt is the Dairy Belt. This region produces much of our milk, butter, and cheese. Huge dairy barns are found across the dairy states of Michigan, Wisconsin, and Minnesota. Wisconsin is the leading dairy state. One of its main products is cheese. Scattered around the state are cheese-making plants.

B. The Productive West

The Midwest has the largest number of farmers and is the largest producer of wheat and corn. But it is in the West, and in only one state—California—that most of the nation's vegetables are grown.

At first glance, however, it would seem that this is an unlikely place to grow crops. Although land here, especially in the Central Valley, is extremely fertile, most of the area is extremely dry. To grow vegetables and fruit in this area, farmers irrigate their fields with water from nearby rivers. The Sierra Nevada usually receive quite a bit of snow, and some of the rivers that begin in the mountains flow across dry areas on their way to the Pacific Ocean.

A fisher in Maine looks over his catch of lobsters.
▶ How does the fishing industry help Maine's economy?

Large dams have been built across some of these rivers that flow down from the mountains to make reservoirs. Long **aqueducts** (AK wuh dukts), or waterways, have been dug from these reservoirs to carry water to the fields and orchards of the region. The crops grown on this irrigated farmland include lettuce, garlic, olives, artichokes, plums, prunes, almonds, walnuts, and all kinds of citrus fruit.

C. Regional Specialties

Fishing   When a certain economic activity is the specialty of a particular region, this is what geographers call **regional specialization**. Fishing has always been a very important regional specialization in the New England region of the Coastal Plain. For hundreds of years the Georges Bank, off the coast of Massachusetts, has been an important fishing ground.

Along the rocky coastline of Maine are small fishing villages with weathered old wooden houses and docks crowded with colorful fishing boats. Lobster pots, or traps in which lobsters are caught, are piled on the docks, and fish nets are hanging up to dry. Some of the best lobsters in the United States come from off the coast of Maine.

Forestry   Other parts of the United States have developed regional specialization in tree crops. The area around Orlando, in central Florida, is an excellent example. Miles and miles of orange trees cover the countryside. Although oranges grow in other states besides Florida, this state produces about 80 percent of the country's entire orange crop.

Lumber   Trees are also grown for lumber and for wood pulp. The United States is the second greatest lumber-producing country in the world. There are over 750 million acres (300 million ha) of forests in our country. The largest forests are located in the Rocky Mountains and in the southeast and south central parts of the United States.

The states bordering the Pacific Ocean form part of one of the largest lumbering areas in the world. Oregon, Washington, and California are our leading lumbering states. Alaska is also part of this huge forest area. So far, however, it has been too costly to send lumber from Alaska all the way to markets in the rest of the country.

LESSON 3

Review

REVIEWING MAIN IDEAS

A. Name the major crop belts of the United States.
B. Why is irrigation necessary for farming to take place in the West?
C. What are three regional specialties found in the United States?

SKILLS CHECK

THINKING SKILL

Turn to the Graph Appendix, on pages 732-739. What is the ranking of the United States for the production of the following crops?

Cotton   Potatoes   Soybeans

A Nation Built on Industry

CONNECTIONS

What are some of the products you use that are made in the United States?

TERMS

industry, nonrenewable resource, high-technology industries

FOCUS

How has the United States used its resources to become an industrial power?

A. A Leader in Industry

Riches of the Earth The United States is a world leader in **industry**. One of the meanings of *industry* is the manufacturing, or making, of goods. Fish canning and lumber milling are two big industries that grew because of the right supplies of fish and lumber. The United States also has many other valuable resources.

Metals are one great resource, and iron is one of the most important. Steel, an iron product, is used to make tools, machinery, and girders for bridges and buildings. It is also used to make rails, locomotives, ships, automobile bodies, and many other products that need a hard, strong metal. Steelmaking is one of the most important industries in the United States.

Steelmaking Steel is made by refining iron and mixing it with other metals. Iron is found in a kind of rock called iron ore. By using heat from burning coal, the iron can be melted out of the rock.

An important center for the mining of iron ore is the Mesabi Range in Minnesota. Minnesota produces more iron ore than any other state does. Much of the iron ore is transported by rail to ports on Lake Superior. The Soo Canals between Lake Superior and Lake Huron allow ore boats to travel to the lower Great Lakes. Steel mills were built at Buffalo, New York; Cleveland, Ohio;

Steel workers tend a huge vat of molten iron at a steel plant. The iron must first be melted before it is processed into steel.
▶ What fuel supplies heat for this process?

THE STEELMAKING PROCESS AND ITS PRODUCTS

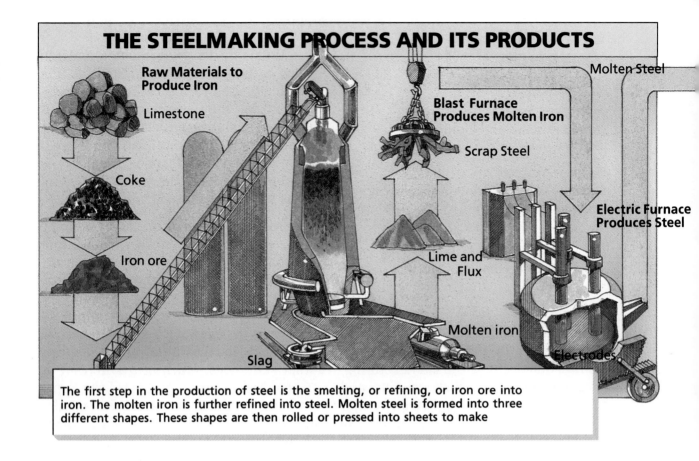

Raw Materials to Produce Iron

Limestone

Coke

Iron ore

Slag

Blast Furnace Produces Molten Iron

Scrap Steel

Lime and Flux

Molten iron

Molten Steel

Electric Furnace Produces Steel

Electrodes

The first step in the production of steel is the smelting, or refining, or iron ore into iron. The molten iron is further refined into steel. Molten steel is formed into three different shapes. These shapes are then rolled or pressed into sheets to make

---

Detroit, Michigan; Gary, Indiana; and other cities on the lake.

Coke is another ingredient of steel. Coke is made by placing coal in an oven and heating it until the gases have been removed. The United States has abundant coal deposits, especially in Kentucky, West Virginia, Wyoming, Pennsylvania, and Illinois. Pittsburgh, Pennsylvania; Birmingham, Alabama; and Gary, Indiana, are three leading steelmaking cities located near coal fields.

In recent years the steel industry has come upon hard times. One reason is that other metals and plastics have been substituted for steel in many products. Car manufacturers, for instance, have reduced the amount of steel in automobiles and have produced lighter cars that do not use as much gasoline. Another reason for the hard times in the steel industry is that many countries that once bought American

steel now have their own steel mills. A third reason is that Americans began to buy more foreign cars. This affected the American automobile industry and the steel mills that supply steel to make cars. Many people in the automobile and steel industries have lost their jobs.

B. Immense Mineral Resources

Other Metals The United States also has large amounts of other metals, including gold, silver, copper, lead, aluminum, and uranium.

Aluminum is a lightweight, silver-colored metal that can be formed into many different shapes. It is used to make aircraft parts, pots and pans, and drink cans. Aluminum is made from a claylike ore called bauxite. Most of the bauxite in the United States comes from Arkansas. The process of manufacturing aluminum requires large amounts of hydroelectric power.

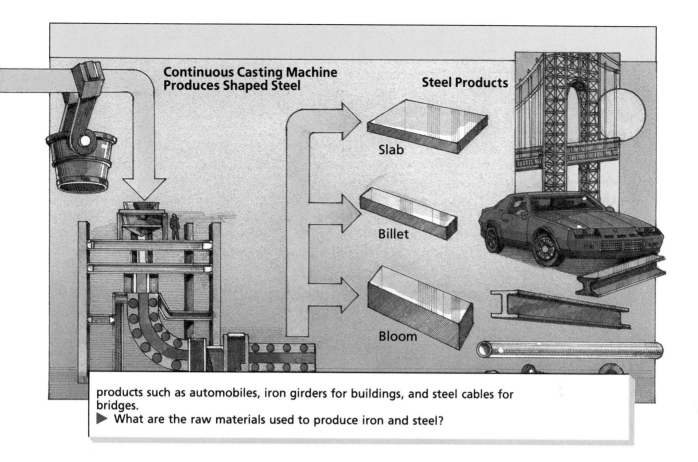

Continuous Casting Machine Produces Shaped Steel

Steel Products

Slab

Billet

Bloom

products such as automobiles, iron girders for buildings, and steel cables for bridges.
▶ What are the raw materials used to produce iron and steel?

The major aluminum-producing areas in the United States are in the Tennessee River Valley and along the Columbia River in Washington.

Copper is a reddish-orange metal that is mainly used in the making of electric wire. This metal was mined on the Upper Peninsula of Michigan as early as 1845. Large amounts of copper ore have also been dug at Butte, Montana, and Bingham Canyon, Utah. Arizona and New Mexico are also important copper-producing sites.

The United States has been fortunate to have abundant supplies of basic metal ores. The richest and most accessible ores are the first to be used. When these are gone, then the lower grade and less accessible ores are used. In time the mines are worked out, and it becomes necessary to look elsewhere for the ores. Once the ores have been used, they are gone from the earth. Since they cannot be replaced, they are called **nonrenewable resources**. However, some metal products, such as aluminum cans, can be recycled, and the metal is used again.

Petroleum The ability to make gasoline and other fuels for use in motors has brought about a great change in the way people have lived in this century. The Wright brothers made the first airplane flight at Kitty Hawk, North Carolina, in 1903. About the same time, Henry Ford began to mass-produce his Model T automobile in Detroit, Michigan. Since that time, automobiles and air travel have become available to almost everyone in the United States. The automobile and the airplane industries are closely linked to the petroleum industry.

The petroleum that provides the energy to run motors first came from wells in western Pennsylvania. The neighboring states of West Virginia, Ohio, Indiana, and

Illinois also developed oil fields. Then, huge oil fields were discovered in Oklahoma, Texas, and Louisiana. California also shared in the wealth that came with oil discoveries. Today the United States is the second largest oil-producing country in the world. Twenty-seven states produce oil. Some states also produce natural gas, which is another important fuel.

The newest oil fields in the United States were discovered in northern Alaska in 1968. Ice in the Arctic Ocean hindered the shipment of oil by tanker. So a pipeline was built across the state from north to south. The pipeline ends at Valdez, a city on the Gulf of Alaska.

The Valdez Oil Spill For many years environmentalists have been concerned about the dangers of a possible oil spill in Alaska. In the spring of 1989, their worst nightmares came true. A huge supertanker, the *Exxon Valdez*, ran aground in Prince William Sound. The resulting oil spill cov-

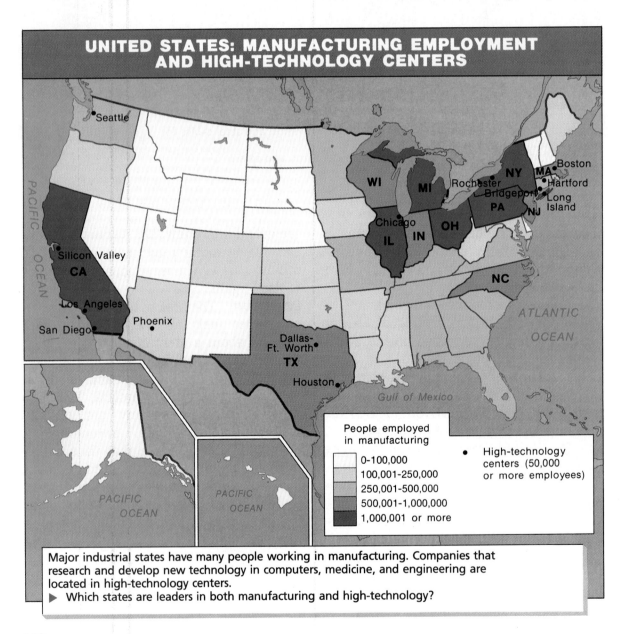

UNITED STATES: MANUFACTURING EMPLOYMENT AND HIGH-TECHNOLOGY CENTERS

People employed in manufacturing

0-100,000
100,001-250,000
250,001-500,000
500,001-1,000,000
1,000,001 or more

• High-technology centers (50,000 or more employees)

Major industrial states have many people working in manufacturing. Companies that research and develop new technology in computers, medicine, and engineering are located in high-technology centers.
▶ Which states are leaders in both manufacturing and high-technology?

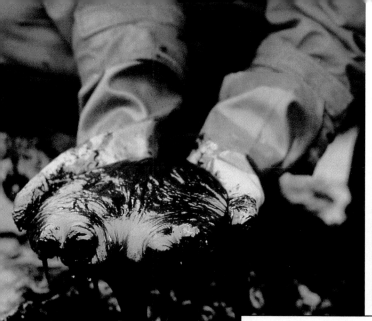

The photograph on the left shows the oil that workers struggled to remove from the shores of Prince William Sound.
▶ What damage does an oil spill cause?

ered hundreds of miles of clean, rocky shorelines with thick, black, gooey oil. Even though oil company officials and workers, and local fishermen and hundreds of volunteers worked hard to clean up the spill, it was a major disaster. It has taken years for the shorelines to become clean again, and for the fish and other wildlife to again live safely in the area.

C. The New Industries of America

High Tech   Many of the older industries in the United States have been replaced by new, **high-technology industries**. These are industries that produce electronics, computers, and other goods that are extremely complex and specialized. Because they require special kinds of laboratories and expert scientific knowledge, high-technology industries are usually located close to a major university. The university provides not only research knowledge but also the highly educated scientists and engineers needed to work in such industries. One of these areas is located near the Massachusetts Institute of Technology (MIT), in Cambridge, Massachusetts.

Silicon Valley   California also has a leading high-technology area. It is south of San Francisco near Stanford University. This area is known for the microchips and other computer parts designed and manufactured there. Because microchips are made of the material called silicon, this area has become known throughout the world by the name Silicon Valley.

LESSON 4

Review

REVIEWING MAIN IDEAS
A. What mineral resources are required for the production of steel?
B. Why are metal ores called nonrenewable resources?
C. Why are high-technology industries usually located near universities?

SKILLS CHECK

MAP SKILL
Turn to the map of manufacturing and high-tech centers on page 112. Use the map key to find the six-leading industrial states.

The Cities of the United States

CONNECTIONS

If you could live in any city in the United States, which one would you choose?

TERMS

metropolitan area, petrochemical

FOCUS

What are the major population centers in the United States?

A. An Urban Nation

New York About 75 percent of the people in the United States live in or near a city. New York is the most populated city in the country. More than 7 million people make their home there. And many more millions of people live in the New York **metropolitan area**. This area includes all the cities and towns around New York. New York is one of the most important business, banking, trading, and manufacturing centers in the world. Two of its largest industries are clothing manufacturing and book publishing. New York is also one of the world's greatest ports. Many ships enter the harbor each year, and millions of tons of cargo are handled.

Port Cities Another of the country's largest cities is Chicago. Nearly 3 million people live in the city, and another 5 million live in the Chicago metropolitan area. Chicago is on Lake Michigan. This location has helped the city grow into a major center of business, industry, and transportation. Its port, on Lake Michigan, is one of the nation's busiest. Chicago's factories produce iron and steel, electrical equipment, machinery, and many other products.

Los Angeles has nearly 3.5 million people. It is by far the largest city on the Pacific coast. The rich farmland in the area and nearby oil deposits have helped Los Angeles become a most important trade and manufacturing center. Los Angeles is also famous for its motion picture industry. The port for Los Angeles is in the nearby city of Long Beach.

This photograph shows New York's financial district along the Hudson River.
▶ What is the population of New York?

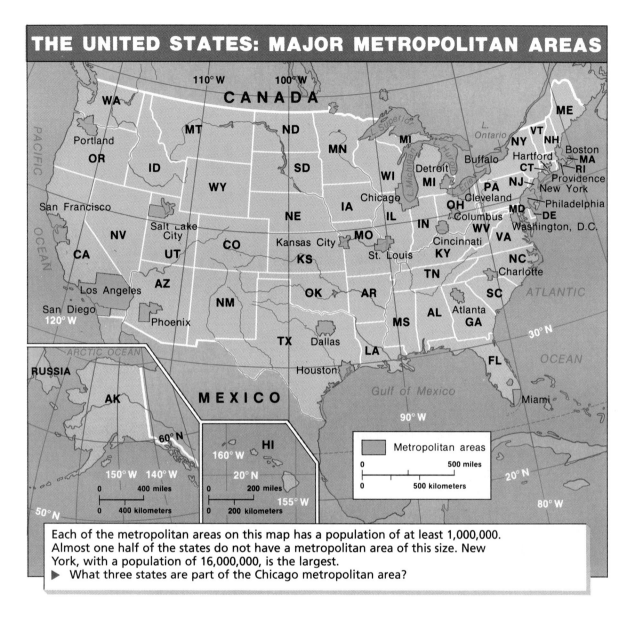

THE UNITED STATES: MAJOR METROPOLITAN AREAS

Each of the metropolitan areas on this map has a population of at least 1,000,000. Almost one half of the states do not have a metropolitan area of this size. New York, with a population of 16,000,000, is the largest.
▶ What three states are part of the Chicago metropolitan area?

Philadelphia is the largest city in Pennsylvania. Its location on the Delaware River makes it a busy port. This city is famous as the home of the Liberty Bell and Independence Hall, where the Declaration of Independence was signed in 1776.

Houston is the largest city in Texas. It is a leader in oil refining, in the manufacturing of parts for oil wells, and pipelines, and in **petrochemicals.** A petrochemical is a chemical or synthetic material made from petroleum or natural gas. Like New York, Chicago, and Philadelphia, Houston is an

important port city. To reach the port of Houston, ships have to travel through a deepwater channel. The channel connects Houston to the Gulf of Mexico, 50 miles (80 km) away.

Detroit is the largest city in Michigan, with a population of over 1 million. It is on the Detroit River, between Lake Huron and Lake Erie. Important industries include the making of machine tools, iron products, hardware, chemicals, drugs, paint, and wire products. Of course, its most famous products are automobiles and trucks.

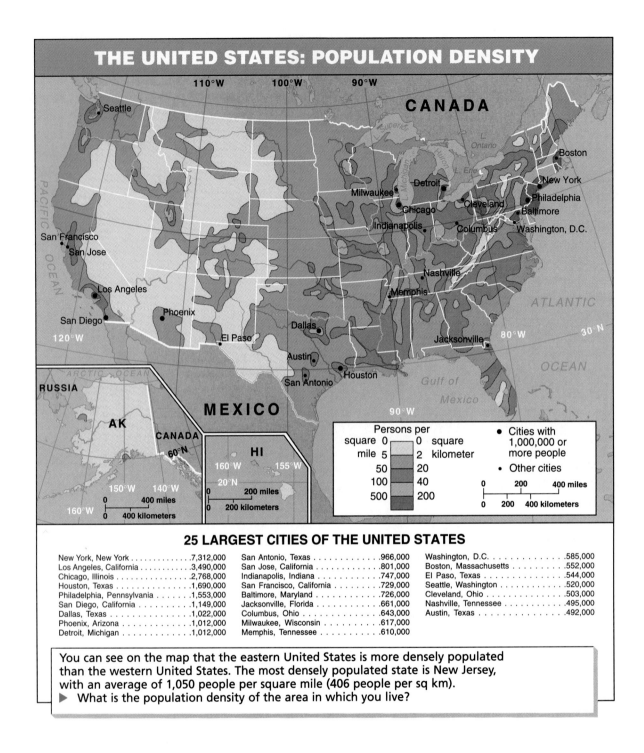

THE UNITED STATES: POPULATION DENSITY

Persons per

square	0	0	square
mile	5	2	kilometer
	50	20	
	100	40	
	500	200	

• Cities with 1,000,000 or more people

• Other cities

25 LARGEST CITIES OF THE UNITED STATES

New York, New York 7,312,000	San Antonio, Texas 966,000	Washington, D.C. 585,000
Los Angeles, California 3,490,000	San Jose, California 801,000	Boston, Massachusetts 552,000
Chicago, Illinois 2,768,000	Indianapolis, Indiana 747,000	El Paso, Texas 544,000
Houston, Texas 1,690,000	San Francisco, California 729,000	Seattle, Washington 520,000
Philadelphia, Pennsylvania 1,553,000	Baltimore, Maryland 726,000	Cleveland, Ohio 503,000
San Diego, California 1,149,000	Jacksonville, Florida 661,000	Nashville, Tennessee 495,000
Dallas, Texas 1,022,000	Columbus, Ohio 643,000	Austin, Texas 492,000
Phoenix, Arizona 1,012,000	Milwaukee, Wisconsin 617,000	
Detroit, Michigan 1,012,000	Memphis, Tennessee 610,000	

You can see on the map that the eastern United States is more densely populated than the western United States. The most densely populated state is New Jersey, with an average of 1,050 people per square mile (406 people per sq km).

▶ What is the population density of the area in which you live?

B. The Nation's Capital

Washington, D.C., the nation's capital, is a very different city from those you have just read about. Although it ranks nine-teenth in size, with 585,000 people, it is not an industrial city. There are no factories and few big companies with offices in Washington.

The city is on the Potomac River, but it is not an important port. It is, however, one of the country's most important cities. The main business of Washington is the government of the United States. More people in and around Washington work at government jobs than at any other kind. Every year, millions of Americans visit their country's capital. Around the city is the pleasant countryside of Maryland and Virginia.

C. Population Patterns

The Rust Belt Since about 1970, thousands of people have moved from the industrial states of the northeast to states in the southern and southwestern parts of the country. They have made the decision to change their homes for two important reasons. One is because many factories in the Northeast have closed, leaving people without jobs. Another reason they have decided to move is the warm and sunny climate of the South and the southwestern parts of the United States.

As a result, the populations of many states in the Northeast have grown very slowly. Some states even have decreasing populations. The declining populations and closed industries have led some people to call the Northeast the "Rust Belt."

The Sunbelt States like Florida, California, and Arizona have been increasing rapidly in population. These states are part of what is called the Sunbelt region. As you read above, this area has a warm, sunny climate. Many older, retired people from the northeast states have moved here. Workers from the northeast have also moved to this region because of the new industries that have grown here. The nation's rocket-launching center is at Cape Canaveral, in Florida.

There are large research centers where new products are developed. Technology Crescent, in the Atlanta, Georgia, area is a rapidly growing center. Research Triangle

Members of Congress meet at the United States Capitol in Washington, D.C., to debate and vote on legislation.
▶ Is Washington, D.C., a port city?

Park, near Raleigh-Durham and Chapel Hill, North Carolina, is one of the largest research centers in the United States.

LESSON 5

Review

REVIEWING MAIN IDEAS
A. What is a metropolitan area?
B. How is Washington, D.C., different from Chicago or Detroit?
C. Why have people moved from the Rust Belt to the Sunbelt?

SKILLS CHECK

WRITING SKILL
Write a paragraph advertising the city you chose at the beginning of this lesson.

IRRIGATING THE LAND:
THE QUEST FOR WATER

In the 1800s an explorer and United States Army officer, Major Stephen Long, described the area west of the Mississippi River as the "Great American Desert." He said the West was "almost wholly unfit for cultivation [farming] and of course uninhabitable." Long was not the only person to describe the region this way. Other explorers who traveled through the West said they saw nothing but arid plains covered by tough grasses, empty deserts, and dry stream beds that turned into raging rivers during rainstorms.

Today the area west of the Mississippi produces much of this country's agricultural products. Huge cities—such as Los Angeles, California; Denver, Colorado; and Phoenix, Arizona—spread out over the landscape. What has allowed the

building of great cities and profitable farms in the Great American Desert? The answer is water. But many people are concerned that there may not be enough water to supply the West's growing population and extensive irrigated farmlands.

The Arid West

As you have learned in this chapter, the western half of the United States is an arid region. In the area that makes up the Great Plains, average annual precipitation is generally adequate for farming. But the weather pattern may abruptly change, and a cycle of dry years may occur. In the 1870s, for example, there was an extended period of heavier than usual precipitation. Thousands of families

Much of the Great Plains is still grass covered, but irrigation now allows farming.
▶ Which landscape is irrigated?

ern Colorado. Then the "Dust Bowl" drought of the 1930s hit, and thousands of people were forced to give up their farms and move to other states.

In the mid-1940s, geologists—scientists who study the earth's structure—made a discovery in the Great Plains. There, beneath the earth's surface, was one of the world's largest reservoirs of ground water: the Ogallala aquifer (oh guh LAHL uh AK wuh fur). An aquifer is an underground rock cavern that contains water. The Ogallala aquifer holds water that began to seep down from the surface during the Ice Age. This vast reservoir holds the equivalent of all the water in Lake Huron.

Farmers in the eight Great Plains states that are located on the Ogallala aquifer quickly took advantage of this new source of water. From North Dakota to Texas, wells were dug to tap the ground water, and powerful pumps pulled the water to the surface. The water then was used to irrigate the surrounding dry land. The brown land soon turned green, as crops of sorghum, corn, alfalfa, wheat, and cotton filled huge areas of the Great Plains.

Making the Deserts Bloom

The areas west of the Rocky Mountains that cover Nevada, Utah, Arizona, and southwestern California are true deserts. Sand, gravel, and rock support mainly cactuses and thorny bushes. Yet rivers cross through or near the deserts. It is these rivers that have allowed Americans to make the deserts bloom. Of all the rivers in the West, the Colorado has been one of the most important sources of water for irrigation.

The Colorado River, almost 1,450

On the Great Plains, windmills like the one shown above are used to pump water from beneath the ground.
▶ How is the water stored?

moved to the plains, believing that the rainfall would continue and that they would prosper as farmers. By the 1880s, however, drought hit the region, forcing many settlers to leave.

This same cycle repeated itself in the early 1900s. Again, thousands of people moved into seemingly "wet" areas of western Kansas and Oklahoma and east-

miles (2,334 km) long, is an example of what geographers call an *exotic stream*. An exotic stream begins in an area that receives extensive precipitation, and then flows through an extremely dry region.

When joined by its main tributaries—the Green, Gunnison, and San Juan rivers—the Colorado becomes a raging river. Over the years, it has carved out of the desert some of the most spectacular canyons on earth, including the Grand Canyon. Along its course, the Colorado has been harnessed by a series of huge dams, such as Hoover Dam. These dams provide hydroelectric power for large areas of Utah, Arizona, Nevada, and California. The lakes created by the dams provide water for such agricultural regions as the Imperial Valley of California. The water is moved by huge canals and aqueducts.

An Area at Risk

By the mid-1980s, about 45 million acres (18 million ha) of land in the United States was being irrigated. Land irrigated in the West alone is equal to an area the size of Massachusetts and Connecticut. The land made fertile by irrigation has brought enormous economic benefits to the region, especially California. This state alone provides much of the nation's vegetable and fruit crop.

Relying on irrigation has its consequences, however. In the Great Plains, for example, farmers have pumped enormous amounts of water from the Ogallala aquifer. They have pumped so much, in fact, that some experts predict that this huge reservoir of water will be depleted in the next 40 years.

In the lands west of the Great Plains, the same water that makes the desert soils fertile may be destroying them. The problem comes from salt that is left on the farmland after the irrigation water has

evaporated or been absorbed by the plants. All fresh water contains salt, and all irrigated lands face the danger of becoming contaminated with too much salt. One of the worst problem areas in the United States is found in the lands irrigated with water from the Colorado River. Almost 11 million tons (10 million metric tons) of salt has been deposited on croplands irrigated with Colorado River water.

A third problem affecting water in the west is the continuing growth of the

In California, water from lakes in the Sierra Nevadas (above) is transported by aqueducts (left) to the state's farms and cities.
▶ What is an aqueduct?

North Africa and the Middle East face growing populations and limited water supplies.

There are some possible solutions to the water problems the United States and other countries face. In many countries of the world, large amounts of water are flooded on a field to irrigate crops. This method is wasteful, since most of the water evaporates. It also allows larger amounts of salt to be deposited on the soil. Scientists believe that improved irrigation methods may decrease the amount of salt deposited on soils. One of these methods is called drip irrigation. This system keeps the soil moist without using large amounts of water.

One way for cities to balance the problem of growing population and limited water is to require conservation measures. These might include higher prices for water, and bans on using water to wash cars or to water lawns.

Any solutions to the water problems facing the western United States will require the cooperation of farmers, businesses, and government. These three groups working together can ensure that the western United States will continue to be a productive part of the country.

region's population. Los Angeles and Phoenix, as well as Tucson, Arizona, are among the cities whose populations continue to grow. An increasing population means increasing water needs. Already, experts predict that California will face a critical water shortage by 2020 because of continued population growth. Tucson has required mandatory water conservation measures to help deal with the city's growing population and increasing water needs.

Managing Water Needs

These problems are not unique to the United States. Throughout the world other countries face similar problems. Egypt, Syria, Iran, and the Soviet Union all suffer from excessively salty soils because of irrigation. And countries in

THINKING CRITICALLY

1. How has irrigation allowed farming in the arid western United States?
2. What are some of the reasons for not irrigating larger areas of arid land? What are some of the reasons for continuing to make arid land productive cropland?
3. Imagine that you are the mayor of a large city in the western United States. Your city is growing in size, and more water will be required to supply the growing population. What are some water conservation practices that you could propose?

121

REVIEWING TERMS

On a separate sheet of paper, write the term that best completes each sentence.

coastal plain   pesticide
immigrant   crop rotation
Hispanic   regional specialization
axis   metropolitan area
equinox   petrochemical

1. A _____ is composed of a large city or several large cities and the surrounding towns, smaller cities, and other communities.
2. The earth's _____ is a line through the earth between the North Pole and the South Pole.
3. A _____ is an area of flat land that borders a coast.
4. A chemical or synthetic material made from petroleum or natural gas is called a _____.
5. The _____ marks the beginning of spring on March 20 or 21 and of autumn on September 22 or 23.
6. _____ occurs when a certain economic activity is the specialty of a particular region.
7. Farmers often use a _____ to keep insects from destroying crops.
8. A person who leaves one country to move permanently to a new country is called an _____.
9. Planting fields with different crops each year is called _____.
10. A _____ is a Spanish-speaking American.

REVIEWING THE FACTS

On a separate sheet of paper, answer the following questions in complete sentences.

1. What are the five landform regions that make up the United States?
2. What region of the United States does the Mississippi River cut in half?
3. Where are two of the most important farming areas in the United States located?
4. How is a humid subtropical climate different from a humid continental climate?
5. What are some major agricultural products of the United States?
6. What area in Minnesota is the source for most of the iron ore produced in the United States?
7. Why is the area in California that produces microchips and computer parts known worldwide as *Silicon Valley*?
8. Why is New York an important city?
9. What are two large industries of New York?
10. What resources have helped Los Angeles become an important trade and manufacturing center?

WRITING ABOUT GEOGRAPHY

What region of the United States do you live in? Is it a farming or industrial area? Does it have a regional specialization? Describe the region where you live and tell about its economic activities.

THINKING CRITICALLY

On a separate sheet of paper, answer the following questions in complete sentences.

1. How could a trip across the United States benefit a writer?
2. Why are the Rocky Mountains so much higher than the Appalachian Mountains?
3. Why do farmers practice crop rotation?

4. How would you explain the fact that the major aluminum-producing areas in the United States are located in the Tennessee Valley and along the Columbia River in the state of Washington?
5. Why is the automobile industry so closely linked to the petroleum industry?

SUMMARIZING THE CHAPTER

On a separate sheet of paper, draw a graphic organizer like the one shown. Copy the information from this graphic organizer to the one you have drawn. Under the main idea for each lesson, write three statements that you think support the main idea.

CHAPTER THEME

The United States is an industralized country with much land, many resources, and a variety of economic activities.

Lesson 1 The United States is divided into five landform regions.

1. _____
2. _____
3. _____
4. _____
5. _____

Lesson 2 The United States has different climates.

1. _____
2. _____
3. _____

Lesson 3 The United States has varied agricultural activities.

1. _____
2. _____
3. _____

Lesson 4 The United States has used its resources to become an industrial power.

1. _____
2. _____
3. _____

Lesson 5 The United States has major population centers located across the nation.

1. _____
2. _____
3. _____

CHAPTER 5

MEXICO

The Land of Mexico

Make a list of the words that you think of when you hear the name Mexico.

basin, sand dune

What are Mexico's main physical features?

A. Mexico: A Land of Contrasts

Describing Mexico A story is told about Hernando Cortés, the leader of the Spanish army that conquered the Aztec Indians and made Mexico a Spanish colony nearly 500 years ago. When Cortés returned to Spain and appeared at the court of King Carlos V, the king asked the great conqueror to describe the land of Mexico. Cortés answered by taking a paper he found lying on a table and crumpling it in his hand. He tossed the crumpled paper back on the table, saying, "This, your majesty, is the land of Mexico."

Of course, Cortés was showing the king that Mexico is a very rugged, mountainous land. But it is also a country of flat plains along the coasts and high plateaus. In fact, Mexico is a land of contrasts in both geography and climate. Hot, dry deserts in the north slowly give way to the almost always rainy, forested lands of the south of Mexico.

Mexico is about one fifth the size of the United States. Still, that makes Mexico the third largest country in North America. In population, Mexico is the second largest North American country. Over 94 million people live in Mexico.

Mexico shares a 2,500-mile (4,023 km) border with the United States. This border, like the one between Canada and the United States, is undefended. Every day, thousands of people and goods cross this border. Both Mexico and the United States work together on many issues, and they are also important trading partners.

B. A Mountainous Land

Mountain Ranges If you look at the map on page 126, you can see that Cortés did accurately describe much of Mexico. Mexico does, indeed, have lots of mountains. Northern Mexico is largely covered by a high desertlike plateau called the Mexican Plateau. Steep and rugged mountains border the plateau on its eastern and western sides. The eastern mountain range is called the Sierra Madre Oriental (see er uh mah dray or ee ENT ul), or Eastern Sierre Madre. The western range is called the Sierra Madre Occidental (ahk suh DENT ul), or Western Sierra Madre. In between these two mountain ranges are many smaller mountain ranges separated by dry desert **basins**. A basin is a broad, flat valley that has mountains all around it.

A railroad winds its way through a canyon in northern Mexico.
► What are Mexico's two main mountain ranges?

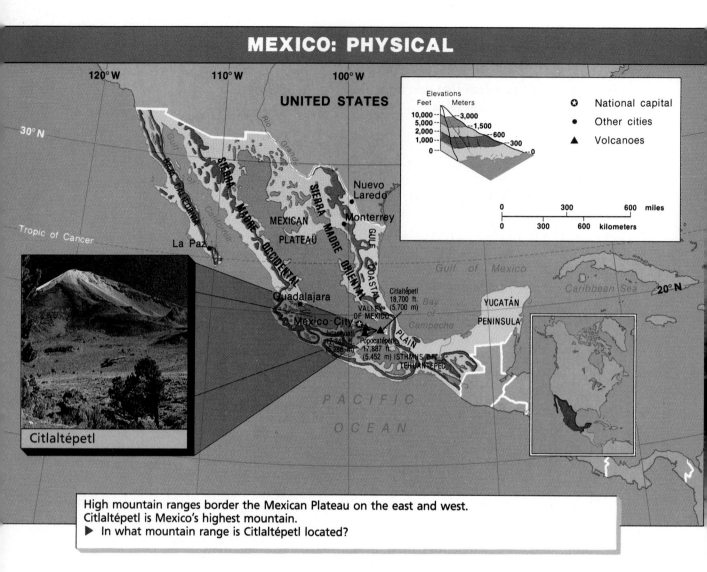

MEXICO: PHYSICAL

UNITED STATES

120° W · 110° W · 100° W

30° N

Tropic of Cancer

Elevations
Feet   Meters
10,000 -- -3,000
5,000 -- -1,500
2,000 -- -600
1,000 -- -300
0 -- -0

⊕ National capital
● Other cities
▲ Volcanoes

0   300   600 miles
0   300   600 kilometers

SIERRA MADRE OCCIDENTAL

SIERRA MADRE ORIENTAL

BAJA CALIFORNIA

Gulf of California

Rio Grande

Nuevo Laredo

Monterrey

MEXICAN PLATEAU

La Paz

Guadalajara

GULF COASTAL PLAIN

Gulf of Mexico

Citlaltépetl 18,700 ft. (5,700 m)

Bay of Campeche

VALLEY OF MEXICO

Mexico City

Iztaccihuatl 17,343 ft. (5,286 m)

Popocatépetl 17,887 ft. (5,452 m)

ISTHMUS OF TEHUANTEPEC

YUCATÁN PENINSULA

Caribbean Sea

20° N

PACIFIC OCEAN

Citlaltépetl

High mountain ranges border the Mexican Plateau on the east and west.
Citlaltépetl is Mexico's highest mountain.
▶ In what mountain range is Citlaltépetl located?

The southern end of the Mexican Plateau ends in a series of basins. The largest one is called the Valley of Mexico. Mexico City, the capital of Mexico, is located in the Valley of Mexico. This valley is over 7,000 feet (2,134 m) high.

Much of the area south of the Mexican Plateau is also mountainous. The mountains of southern Mexico are even more rugged and are harder to cross than those of the north. As a result, the small villages found throughout most of the south are isolated from one another. Many of those areas are the home of American Indians.

These Native Americans still speak the same language and observe many of the customs they had when the Spaniards conquered Mexico.

C. The Lowlands and Peninsulas of Mexico

Gulf Coastal Plain By now you may be thinking that Mexico is all mountains, but that isn't true. Mexico has some large areas of flat land. One of these areas is a part of the Gulf Coastal Plain. The Gulf Coastal Plain is an extension of the coastal plain that stretches along the eastern part of the

United States. If you look at the map on page 126, you can see that the plain ends in southern Mexico, just about where the coast begins to bend to the east.

Where the Gulf Coastal Plain ends, a large flat peninsula juts out into the Gulf of Mexico. This peninsula is called the Yucatán Peninsula. It separates the Gulf of Mexico and the Caribbean Sea. The soils of the Yucatán Peninsula are thin and rocky. Yet the Indians who live here have farmed this harsh land for thousands of years.

Baja California The map on page 126 shows that there is another peninsula in Mexico. That is the peninsula of Baja (BAH hah) California, on the Pacific coast. *Baja California* means "lower California" in Spanish. This peninsula is quite different from the Yucatán Peninsula. Baja California is quite mountainous. Even more important, it is a very dry desert that is mainly covered by bare rock and gravel.

D. The Deserts and Forests of Mexico

Northern Deserts Like Baja California, much of northern Mexico is also desert country. Some areas are covered with **sand dunes**, or mountains of sand that have been formed by the wind. Most of the deserts of northern Mexico have a covering of scattered grass and desert plants, similar to the deserts of Baja California.

In the mountains in the western part of Mexico, there is enough rain for forests to grow. There, at elevations above 6,000 to 7,000 feet (1,830 to 2,134 m), are thick forests of pine trees.

Forested Slopes Southern Mexico gets more rain than northern Mexico. There you would find lush forests on the lower slopes of the mountains and in the lowlands. The higher mountains have pine forests. Now, many of those forests have been cut down to clear land for farms.

Thick forests are found in southern Mexico.
▶ Why, do you think, is southern Mexico thickly forested?

LESSON 1
Review

REVIEWING MAIN IDEAS

A. Why was Hernando Cortés's description of Mexico inaccurate?
B. What are the principal physical features of the Mexican Plateau?
C. In what ways are Mexico's two peninsulas different from each other?
D. How does northern Mexico differ from southern Mexico?

SKILLS CHECK

MAP SKILL
Look at the map of Mexico on page 126 and find the important bodies of water that border Mexico. Write the names of these bodies of water on a separate sheet of paper.

Mexico's Three Regions

CONNECTIONS

Name some ways in which one part of a country can be different from other parts of the country.

TERMS

hacienda, adobe, ejido, cinder cone, mestizo, subsistence agriculture, reserve

FOCUS

What are the important differences among the three regions of Mexico?

A. The North: Mexico's Largest Region

A Semidesert Region Mexico is a large and varied country. To better understand this variety, we can divide the country into three large regions: the north, the central region, and the south.

Most people in rural Mexico still depend on wells for water for cooking and cleaning.
▶ How is the water taken from the well?

The northern region begins at the border with the United States and continues south nearly to Mexico City. It includes most of the Mexican Plateau and the Gulf Coastal Plain. The peninsula of Baja California and part of the Pacific coast are also in this region.

Most of the north is desert or semi-desert country that is covered by mountains. But the north is more than a barren, empty desert. When the Spaniards came to Mexico in the 1500s, they found valuable deposits of silver in the mountains of the Mexican Plateau. Soon mining became an important industry.

As the mining industry grew, so did ranching and farming. Ranches were needed to produce the animals, such as horses, mules, and oxen, that were used in the mines to haul rocks and to do other heavy work. Farms were needed to produce crops to feed the many workers that the mines required.

As the number of workers in the mines increased, towns were built. In these towns, miners could rent rooms and buy meals. Skilled workers who provided services for the miners also lived in the towns. Cooks, blacksmiths, and barbers are some of the people who set up businesses that earned money from the miners. Over the years, the population increased. Many of those towns are now important cities of the north, such as San Luis Potosí, Zacatecas, Hermosillo (er moh SEE yoh), and Chihuahua. You can find these cities on the map on page 132.

Many other minerals besides silver are also mined in the north. The mountains there hold valuable deposits of copper, zinc, lead, and iron. The iron is made into steel in factories in the cities of Monterrey and Monclova. Coal and oil are also found in the north. Most of Mexico's oil deposits are found in the Gulf Coastal Plain near the city of Tampico.

A HACIENDA IN MEXICO

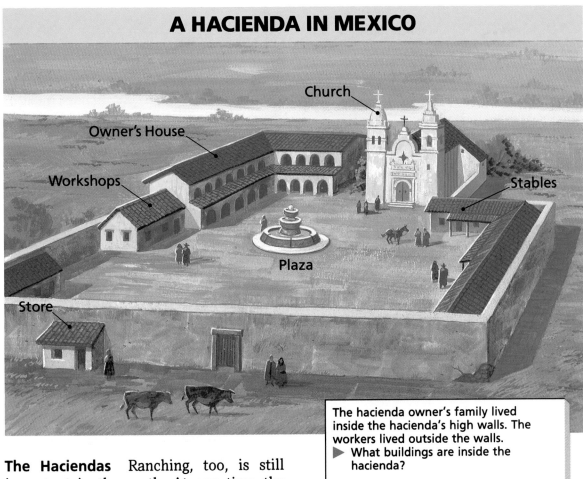

Church

Owner's House

Workshops

Stables

Plaza

Store

The hacienda owner's family lived inside the hacienda's high walls. The workers lived outside the walls.
▶ What buildings are inside the hacienda?

The Haciendas Ranching, too, is still important in the north. At one time the north was a land of huge estates called **haciendas** (hah see EN duz). During the 1800s, one family alone had a hacienda in Chihuahua that had over 1 million acres (405,000 ha) of land. This is over 1,560 square miles (4,040 sq km), or an area larger than the entire state of Rhode Island!

Not all haciendas included as much land, but most were very large. The hacienda owners lived in large, beautiful **adobe** houses. Adobe is sun-dried mud bricks. The adobe was covered with plaster and painted white. The houses had red-tile roofs and were sometimes two-stories tall.

In the center of most haciendas was a large open area called a plaza. In the center of the plaza was a large fountain. Across the plaza from the owner's house there were adobe storage buildings and stables. A church that was used by the hacienda owners was also on the estate.

Ejidos Today almost all the haciendas and their grand houses have been abandoned. Why? Between 1910 and 1920, Mexico went through a violent and bloody revolution. After the revolution, the new Mexican government divided the haciendas into smaller properties called **ejidos** (ay HEE dohz). The ejidos were given to the people who had worked for the owners of the haciendas. Today, most of Mexico's farmland is still in the form of ejidos. An ejido is owned by all the farmers who work the land, not by individuals. Lands that are owned by a community or group of people are called *communal* lands.

B. Central Mexico's Rich Lands

Volcanoes In the southern part of the Mexican Plateau, there are many **cinder cones.** Cinder cones are small volcanoes that look like cone-shaped hills. They are scattered throughout central Mexico. The smaller cinder cones aren't the only volcanoes in central Mexico. On a bright, sunny day in Mexico City, you can see Popocatépetl (poh poh kah TAY pet ul) and Ixtacihuatl (ess tah SEE waht ul). These two giant snowcapped volcanoes stand like sentinels guarding the city. Both are over 17,000 feet (5,180 m) tall. An even taller volcano in central Mexico is Citlaltépetl (see tlahl TAY pet ul).

Most of central Mexico is made up of the large basins that cover the southern part of the Mexican Plateau. These basins are the home of some of Mexico's largest cities, including Mexico City, its largest city, and Guadalajara (gwah dul uh HAHR uh), the second largest city.

Mexico City is the largest city in the Western Hemisphere. It has a population of nearly 10 million people, and the metropolitan area has nearly 20 million. Mexico City's metropolitan area spreads out as far as the eye can see in every direction.

With such large cities, you might think that there is not much land for farming in central Mexico, but that is not so. Central Mexico has some of the best farmland in Mexico. Farms in the Valley of Mexico, near Mexico City, produce grain, vegetables, fruit, milk, cheese, and other products for the large city markets.

Like the north, central Mexico has mineral wealth. The Spaniards found the Aztec Indians mining silver from rich mines near the present-day city of Pachuca. Those mines are still yielding up their precious treasure of silver ore. Silver was also mined at Guanajuato, at the northern edge of central Mexico.

Popocatépetl, a towering snow-capped volcano, stands east of Mexico City.
▶ Is this volcano a cinder cone?

In Lesson 1 you read that before the Spaniards arrived in Mexico, the north was the home of small groups of American Indians. Central Mexico was also the home of Indians, but these Indians differed greatly from those of the north.

In the 1500s the Aztecs ruled much of central Mexico and the south. They had one of the greatest Indian civilizations ever known. They lived in a valley on a high plateau in the center of Mexico. Today the Aztecs have vanished, but other Indians still live in central Mexico. They farm small plots of land in the high basins where their ancestors once lived. But they make up an increasingly smaller part of the population. Today most Mexicans in the north and in central Mexico are **mestizos**. A mestizo of Mexico is a person of mixed European and American Indian ancestry.

C. The South: An Indian World

Landforms The south includes nearly all of Mexico south of the Mexican Plateau. Much of this land is made up of two large mountain ranges that are separated by the Isthmus of Tehuantepec (tu WAHNT uh pek). Mexico narrows to about 150 miles (240 km) at the Isthmus of Tehuantepec. The south also includes part of the Gulf Coastal Plain and all of the Yucatán Peninsula.

The south lacks the rich mineral resources that attracted the Spaniards to the north and to the central region of Mexico. Since fewer Spaniards went to the southern part of Mexico, the Indians were better able to survive and keep their traditional ways. Today the south is the home of most of Mexico's Indian population.

Indian Life Most of the Indians farm small plots of land in the southern highlands and in the Yucatán Peninsula. Their main crops are corn, beans, squash, and chili peppers, which they grow mainly for their own use. A family that grows food chiefly for itself is said to practice **subsistence agriculture**.

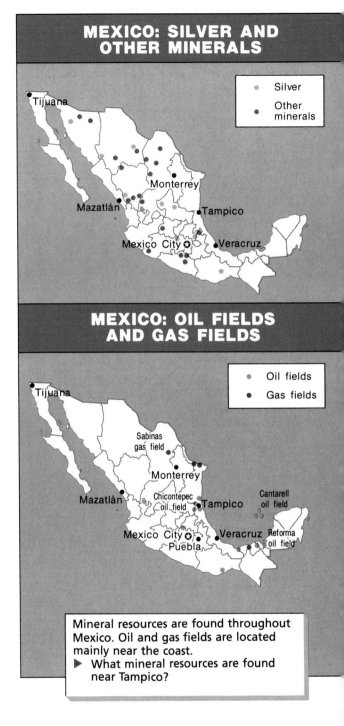

MEXICO: SILVER AND OTHER MINERALS

- Silver
- Other minerals

Tijuana
Monterrey
Mazatlán
Tampico
Mexico City
Veracruz

MEXICO: OIL FIELDS AND GAS FIELDS

- Oil fields
- Gas fields

Tijuana
Sabinas gas field
Monterrey
Mazatlán
Chicontepec oil field
Cantarell oil field
Tampico
Mexico City
Veracruz
Reforma oil field
Puebla

Mineral resources are found throughout Mexico. Oil and gas fields are located mainly near the coast.
▶ What mineral resources are found near Tampico?

Most of Mexico's Indians are poor. They live mainly on their small farms or in small villages or towns that are within walking distance of their farms. Some speak only an Indian language and do not understand Spanish, Mexico's official language.

131

Many Indians speak Mayan or Nahuatl, the ancient language of the Aztecs.

In the past, the Mexican government did not pay much attention to the Indians. Now the government wants the Indians to learn Spanish and receive an education so that they can improve their living conditions. The government's efforts have paid off, and each year there are more Indians who can read and write Spanish.

D. Changes in the South

Discovering Oil You have already read that oil is one of the important resources of the north. In the 1970s vast oil and natural gas deposits were discovered on the Gulf Coastal Plain and under the waters of the Gulf of Mexico. These oil reserves have made Mexico one of the world's most important oil-producing nations. Oil **reserves** are the supplies of oil that can be taken from the ground.

The United States imports much of Mexico's oil and nearly all of its natural gas. Pipelines have been built to move the natural gas from Mexico to the United States. The map on page 131 shows the location of these oil and gas fields.

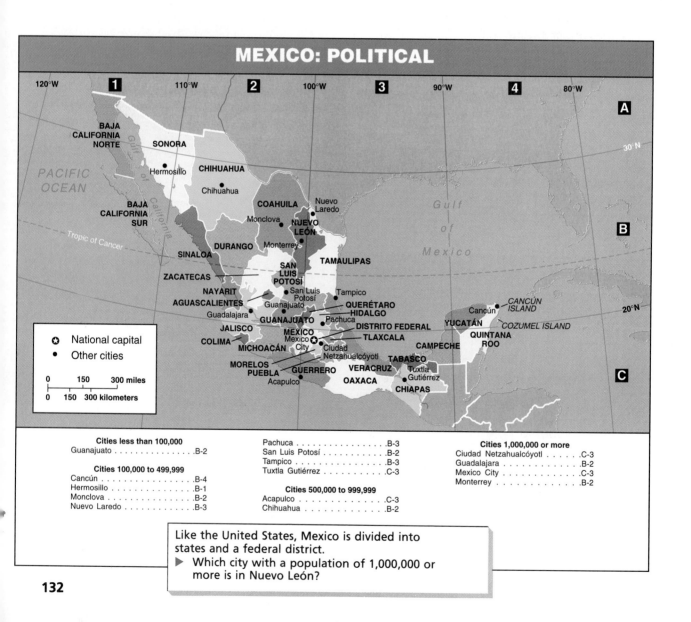

MEXICO: POLITICAL

Cities less than 100,000
Guanajuato B-2

Cities 100,000 to 499,999
Cancún B-4
Hermosillo B-1
Monclova B-2
Nuevo Laredo B-3

Pachuca B-3
San Luis Potosí B-2
Tampico B-3
Tuxtla Gutiérrez C-3

Cities 500,000 to 999,999
Acapulco C-3
Chihuahua B-2

Cities 1,000,000 or more
Ciudad Netzahualcóyotl C-3
Guadalajara B-2
Mexico City C-3
Monterrey B-2

Like the United States, Mexico is divided into states and a federal district.
▶ Which city with a population of 1,000,000 or more is in Nuevo León?

Tourists come to Mexico from the United States, Canada, and Europe. This resort is in Cancún on the Yucatán Peninsula.
► Find Cancún on the map on the opposite page. What body of water is shown in this photograph?

Tourist Resorts The Yucatán Peninsula is the site of another kind of development. In the late 1960s, construction began on a large tourist resort at Cancún (kan KOON), on the northeastern part of the peninsula. Today the city of Cancún has grown from only a few people to over 160,000 people. There are dozens of luxury hotels in the city. An international airport serves tourists who come from as far away as Japan.

Other resorts have been built on the Pacific coast. Acapulco was once a port through which goods to and from Spain passed. In recent years it has become the largest tourist center in Mexico. Now other Pacific coast towns are developing as tourist resorts to compete with Acapulco. These resorts are popular with Mexicans who live in the cool highlands. They also attract people from the United States and Canada who are looking for warm places to take a winter vacation.

LESSON 2

Review

REVIEWING MAIN IDEAS

A. How did mining and ranching begin in the northern region of Mexico?

B. What are the two major economic activities of the central region of Mexico?

C. Why do many Indians live in the southern region of Mexico?

D. Why is the south the most rapidly changing region of Mexico?

SKILLS CHECK

MAP SKILL

Look at the map of Mexico on page 126. Which of the following cities has the lowest elevation?

a. Mexico City
b. Monterrey
c. Guadalajara
d. Nuevo Laredo

133

Mexico City

CONNECTIONS

Imagine that you are planning to visit a large city for the first time. What would you be most interested in knowing about the city before your visit?

TERMS

causeway, mural

FOCUS

What are some of the points of interest in Mexico City?

A. Mexico City in the Past

Mexico City was once the capital city of the Aztec Empire. The Aztecs called the city Tenochtitlán (te nawch tee TLAHN). Tenochtitlán was built on an island in the middle of a shallow lake. The city was connected to the mainland by a system of **causeways**, or raised earthen roads, built across the lake. Bridges on the causeways allowed canoes to go from one part of the lake to another.

The Spanish conquistadores, or conquerors, who came to Mexico with Cortés were astounded when they saw such a marvelous city. Bernal Díaz del Castillo (kahs TEEL yoh), one of the Spaniards, described Tenochtitlán as he looked down upon the city from an Aztec temple. Here is what Bernal Díaz wrote.

We saw the fresh water that came from Chapultepec [chuh POOL tuh pek], which supplied the city, and the bridges on the three causeways, built at certain intervals so the water could go from one part of the lake to another, and a multitude of canoes, some arriving with provisions and others leaving with merchandise. We saw that every house in this great city and in the others built on the water could be

Life in the Aztec city of Tenochtitlán is shown in this painting. Goods were traded on a terrace overlooking the city.
▶ What is the name of Tenochtitlán today?

GROWING UP IN MEXICO

Ramon and Alex go to a private school in Mexico City. Ramon is in the sixth grade and Alex, his brother, is in the eighth grade. At their school, both boys learn Spanish, as well as English.

Many children in Mexico City attend private schools. Parents believe that their children will learn more than if they were in a public school.

Alex is on the football team at his school. But the football he plays is different from the sport of football in the United States. Football in Mexico is similar to soccer. Ramon is on his school's baseball and basketball teams.

The girls who attend private schools also enjoy sports. Many participate in volleyball. Both boys and girls belong to swimming teams.

Children who attend a private school in Mexico City are required to wear a uniform. The boys wear a white shirt with a brown tie, a brown jacket, and tan pants. The girls wear a white shirt and tan skirt.

During their free time, Ramon and Alex visit many of Mexico City's famous attractions. They spend time at Chapultepec Park, which is one of the most popular city parks in the world. On Sundays, they go to see the horsemen who ride in the park and wear colorful, national costumes. The boys also go to this park to visit the zoo, to go on the amusement park rides, and to watch the acrobats and other entertainers perform under the trees. Chapultepec Castle sits high on a hill in the park. This is where the rulers of Mexico City once lived. It is now the National Museum of History.

Before the summer is over, Alex wants to visit the Plaza of Three Cultures. In this plaza you can see buildings that show the three cultures of Mexico. The steps that lead up to the plaza were built by the Aztecs. There is an old church that was built by the Spaniards. There are also new buildings that have been built by the people of modern day Mexico City.

reached only by wooden drawbridges or by canoe. We saw temples built like towers and fortresses . . . all whitewashed; it was a sight to see. We could look down on the flat-roofed houses and other little towers and temples like fortresses along the causeways.

B. Modern Mexico City

The Heart of Mexico Today, Mexico City is the heart of Mexico. What would it be like to visit this giant city? If you came by car or bus, you would first see many different kinds of factories. Most of Mexico's industry is located near Mexico City.

As your car or bus neared the center of the city, traffic would become very heavy. Mexico City has grown quickly in recent years, and it is now crowded with thousands of buses and cars. The automobiles that clog the city have also given Mexico City a serious pollution problem. On some days, pollution is so bad that young children and older people are warned not to go outside.

A View of Mexico City Bernal Díaz stood on the steps of an Aztec temple to observe the glories of Tenochtitlán. Today only the base of the temple is left. However, it is possible to survey the city from the Latin American Tower. This 44-story building offers a fantastic view of Mexico City.

One of the most impressive sights in the city is formally called Constitution Plaza, but Mexicans call it the Zócalo (SOH kah loh). The Zócalo is a great place for people to gather. On holidays, hundreds of thousands of people crowd into the Zócalo to be part of the celebrations that take place there.

On one side of the Zócalo is the largest and oldest cathedral in Latin America. On another side is the National Palace, a government building that is the office of the president of Mexico. There also is a museum on the Zócalo. Many people visit the museum to see **murals** by Diego Rivera,

Mexico City's wide avenues are crowded with traffic.
▶ What problems are created by the heavy traffic?

a famous Mexican painter. One of his murals is shown on page 134. A mural is a painting drawn on a wall or ceiling.

LESSON 3

Review

REVIEWING MAIN IDEAS

A. What did Bernal Díaz see when he looked at Tenochtitlán from the temple?

B. What problems have been caused by Mexico City's rapid growth?

SKILLS CHECK

WRITING SKILL

Write a paragraph explaining how Mexico City's government could persuade people not to drive their cars into the city to work.

Rural Life in Mexico

CONNECTIONS

Describe some ways in which life in a rural area is different from life in a city.

TERMS

commercial farm, cooperative, inflation

FOCUS

What are two main problems that farmers in southern Mexico face?

A. Farms in the Southern Region

Southern Mexico is very different from northern and central Mexico. South of Mexico City are forested mountains. Farther south is a lowland valley where there are many **commercial farms**. A commercial farm is a farm on which crops are raised for sale rather than for home use. Sugarcane is the main crop grown on the commercial farms in the south. The stalk of the sugarcane is processed to make sugar.

Some sugarcane is grown on ejidos that are run as **cooperatives**. A cooperative is a plantation or other business that is owned by its workers. The workers all share the profits that come from the sale of the cooperative's crops or products.

Sugarcane is also grown on large private farms. These farms were originally much larger. After the revolution of 1910–1920, large landowners were allowed to keep part of their land. And a few of the large haciendas were not taken over by the government. As a result, there are still some private farms that are large enough to grow sugarcane, bananas, coffee, and other tropical crops.

B. Problems Caused by Lack of Land

Causes In many parts of Mexico, the land has been badly eroded, or worn down. This is an especially serious problem in the mountains and hills of southern Mexico. Only a limited amount of good land is available for farming.

In the hilly areas of southern Mexico, farmers plow their land with simple ox-drawn plows. Most of the farmers are Indians who practice subsistence agriculture.

Many farmers in Mexico practice subsistence farming. These farmers still use ox-drawn plows because they cannot afford tractors and other farm machinery.
▶ What other types of farms are in Mexico?

137

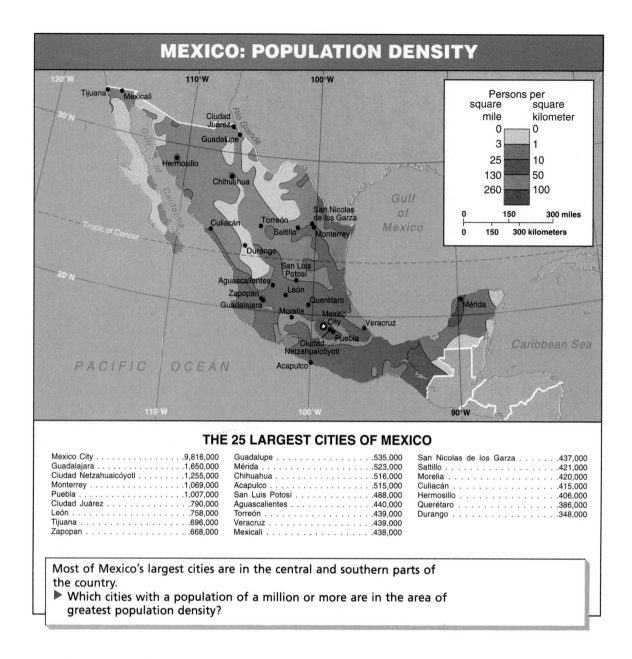

MEXICO: POPULATION DENSITY

Persons per	
square mile	square kilometer
0	0
3	1
25	10
130	50
260	100

0   150   300 miles

0   150   300 kilometers

THE 25 LARGEST CITIES OF MEXICO

Mexico City 9,816,000	Guadalupe 535,000	San Nicolas de los Garza 437,000
Guadalajara 1,650,000	Mérida .523,000	Saltillo .421,000
Ciudad Netzahualcóyotl 1,255,000	Chihuahua 516,000	Morelia .420,000
Monterrey 1,069,000	Acapulco 515,000	Culiacán 415,000
Puebla .1,007,000	San Luis Potosí 488,000	Hermosillo 406,000
Ciudad Juárez 790,000	Aguascalientes 440,000	Querétaro 386,000
León 758,000	Torreón .439,000	Durango 348,000
Tijuana .696,000	Veracruz 439,000	
Zapopan 668,000	Mexicali 438,000	

Most of Mexico's largest cities are in the central and southern parts of the country.
▶ Which cities with a population of a million or more are in the area of greatest population density?

Why do the farmers have only small plots of land to grow crops on? The main reason is that there simply isn't enough farmland in Mexico for all the people who need it. Another problem is that most of the farmers have large families. Imagine that a farmer who has eight children has been given 25 acres (10 ha) of land by the village committee that divides up the ejidos. If he has four sons and he wants to divide his land into four equal shares when they grow up, each son will get only 5 acres (2 ha). That is not enough land to support a family. Daughters do not usually receive land.

The shortage of land is the cause of two major problems for Mexico. One problem is the growing number of people who move to Mexico City from areas where there is not enough land to farm. That is why Mexico City is one of the world's largest and fastest-growing cities. It is predicted that its metropolitan population will be 30 million by the year 2000.

Illegal Migration The shortage of farmland also encourages many Mexicans to migrate to the United States. Most of the people do not want to leave their homes and families, but they have to find some way to survive. Most poor Mexicans who enter the United States do so illegally, or without proper permission from the United States. The number of Mexicans who illegally enter the United States has increased in recent years. The United States has reacted to this by closely watching the Mexican border.

C. Market Towns

The Marketplace Most Mexican towns have a market day. This is the day when the towns bustle with activity. Open markets in the plaza were once common throughout Mexico. Today things have changed. Most markets are now held in large buildings constructed for that purpose. Market vendors sell everything imaginable—beef and pork, vegetables, fruits, cheese, clothing, farm tools, and blankets.

Even though there are supermarkets in cities and large towns, many people still prefer to buy the things they need in markets. In larger towns and cities, the market is open every day. In most small towns the market is the only place to buy food or other things found in a supermarket in the United States. The market may be open only one or two days a week.

D. A Troubled Future

Oil and Debt Mexico is a country with many valuable resources. It has great mineral wealth, some modern farms, and factories. Unfortunately, Mexico has not succeeded in using its resources to help all its people. Although some Mexicans have prospered, many Mexicans are very poor.

Now Mexico faces a new problem. As you have already read, large deposits of oil

A variety of fresh fruits and vegetables are sold in the marketplace.
▶ How often is a small-town market open?

"Tropic Nocturns"

by Ruben M. Campos

Ruben M. Campos, the author of the poem "Tropic Nocturns," vividly describes a thunderstorm in a Mexican countryside.

Dim murmurs from the distant mountains drift
    Toward the lonely vale [valley] below,
The while a cloud gigantic grows and
    grows. . . .

The livid [raging] lightning twists a
    snakelike way
    Slashing back distances
While thunder sends its frightful roar
and loud
    Through caverns which roar back with
    echoes harsh.

The hunger-hunting howl of jaguars
    Hurls fresh horror forth,
Protected by the black terror of night
    They creep like cowards down to the
    ranchos.

The herded cattle in their shelter hear,
    Bellowing resoundingly [roaring with
    repeated sound],
They shake their heavy-hanging heads
in fear
    To plunge then rear, close-gathering
for defense.

Huge drops of rain fall wildly now
    From clouds that hang too low,
Flinging their shattered crystals that
    vibrate
    To ring against the barren rock's hard
    slopes.

The floodgates of heaven soon are opened
    wide,
    Powerfully great waters sweep

Uplifted by the winds, break barriers
    Then surge fantastic flinging waves afar.

The penetrating deep floods with wild
    sound,
    Funeral wail sends out;
A *danse macabre* [dance of death] of the
    witches sways!
    The lone wolf louder to his lone self
    cries!

Amid this symphony of terror night,
    A strange chant rises slow,
From narrow gorges tenebrous [gloomy]
    and dim
    The cactus-organ thunders forth its
    hymn.

Platform oil rigs like the one shown above are a common sight off the coast of Mexico.
▶ What are the men in the photo doing?

were discovered in Mexico in the 1970s. The sale of the oil allowed the Mexican government to develop Mexico's economy. The money from the sale of oil was not enough, however, to pay for the government's projects. As a result, the government also borrowed billions of dollars from banks in foreign countries to build new office buildings, factories, refineries, hotels, dams, and many other projects. The loans were to be paid with the profits from the oil Mexico would sell.

Inflation In 1981 the price of oil began to fall. By 1986 the money earned from the sale of oil was not enough to pay Mexico's debts. That caused the value of Mexico's money to go down. The decrease in value meant that Mexican money did not buy as many goods as it had before. This caused the cost of food and all kinds of goods to go up. The decline in the value of money combined with increasing costs is called **inflation.**

In the mid-1990s, the Mexican government took action to improve the economy. Among other things, it cut spending and

began to repay its debts to foreign countries. These actions caused great hardships for the Mexican people. However, the economy gained strength, and Mexico's future seemed brighter.

LESSON 4

Review

REVIEWING MAIN IDEAS

A. What is an advantage to farm workers in creating a cooperative?

B. Why is there a lack of land for farming in many parts of the southern region of Mexico?

C. How do markets in small towns in Mexico differ from markets in larger towns or cities?

D. What did Mexico do to improve its economy in the mid-1990s?

SKILLS CHECK

THINKING SKILL

Reread section B. List the two causes of land shortages in Mexico. Now list the problems land shortages have caused in Mexico.

141

REVIEWING TERMS

On a separate sheet of paper, write the term that best completes each sentence.

basin
sand dune
adobe
metropolitan
  area
mestizo
subsistence agriculture
causeway

mural
cooperative
inflation

1. A _____ is a person of mixed European and American Indian ancestry.
2. A _____ is a raised earthen road.
3. A broad, flat valley that has mountains all around it is called a _____.
4. _____, or sun-dried mud bricks, is used to build haciendas.
5. A family that grows food chiefly for itself is said to practice _____.
6. A _____ is a mountain of sand that has been formed by the wind.
7. A large city and the cities and communities around it are referred to as a _____.
8. A plantation or other business that is owned by its workers is called a _____.
9. A _____ is a painting that is drawn on a wall or ceiling.
10. A decline in the value of money combined with increasing costs is called _____.

REVIEWING THE FACTS

On a separate sheet of paper, answer the following questions in complete sentences.

1. Why is Mexico referred to as a land of contrasts?
2. What two bodies of water are separated by the Yucatán Peninsula?
3. What are some natural resources of the northern region of Mexico?
4. What products come from the rich farmlands of central Mexico?
5. What great Indian civilization developed in Mexico in the 1500s?
6. In which region of Mexico do most Indians live today?
7. In what city are most of Mexico's industries located?
8. What is the main crop grown on commercial farms in the south of Mexico?
9. Why do many Mexicans migrate to the United States?
10. Why does Mexico have such large debts?

WRITING ABOUT ECONOMICS

If you were a Mexican farmer, would you rather work on an ejido run as a cooperative or on a private farm? Explain your answer.

THINKING CRITICALLY

On a separate sheet of paper, answer the following questions in complete sentences.

1. Why is it important that Mexico and the United States continue to be good neighbors and remain on friendly terms?

2. Why were the haciendas of northern Mexico built of adobe instead of other materials, such as stone or wood?

3. What reasons can you think of that might have caused the revolution to occur in Mexico?

4. Why are the cities of Cancún and Acapulco important sources of income to the Mexican economy?

5. What problems might exist in Mexico City because of the large numbers of people who have moved there from the country?

SUMMARIZING THE CHAPTER

On a separate sheet of paper, draw a graphic organizer like the one shown here. Copy the information from this graphic organizer to the one you have drawn. Complete the chart by writing in the appropriate items for each box.

CHAPTER THEME Mexico is a land of contrasts in both geography and climate.

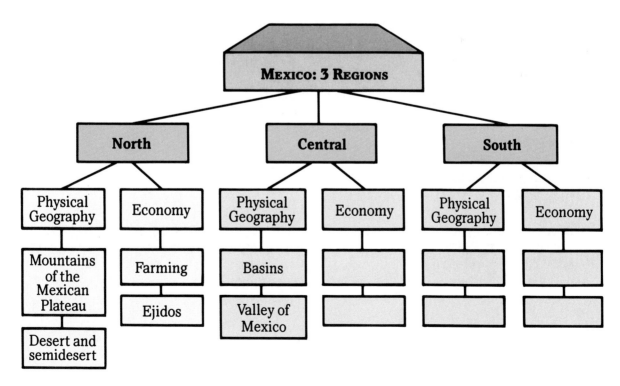

CENTRAL AMERICA AND THE WEST INDIES

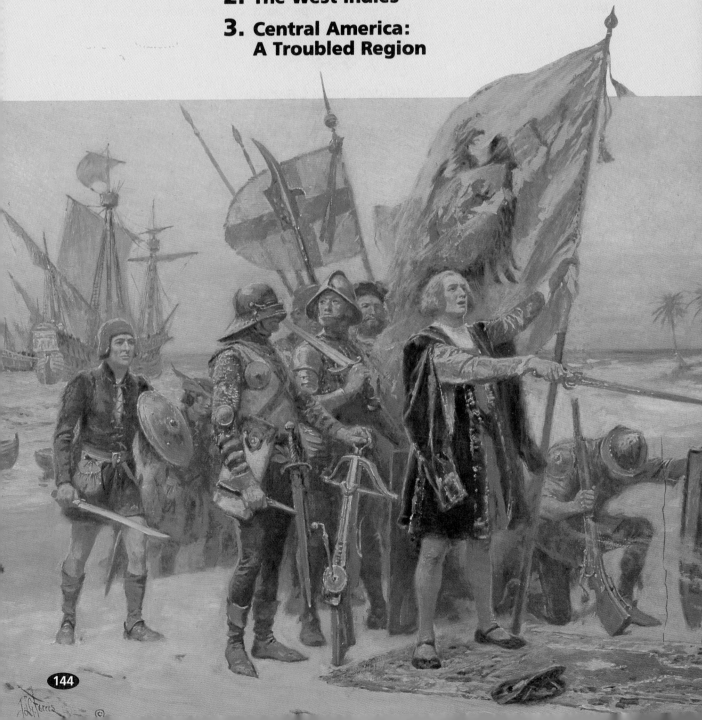

Locating Central America and the West Indies

CONNECTIONS

Turn to the map on page 146. If you had to travel between North America and South America, would it be easier to travel by land or by sea? Give the reason for your answer.

TERMS

archipelago, mulatto, isthmus

FOCUS

Why are there so many different countries in Central America and the West Indies?

A. A Voyage That Changed the World

A Frightening Voyage It is almost two o'clock in the morning on October 12, 1492. Three tiny ships roll in the choppy waters of the Atlantic Ocean. The nighttime sky is clear, and the moon shines on the water ahead.

More than two months have passed since the ships left Spain in search of the rich Indies islands of Asia, and it has been more than a month since the ships' crews last saw land. But in the last few days, tree branches have been seen floating in the water, and birds have flown by the ships— all signs that land must be near.

Before they had seen signs of land, the sailors had threatened to mutiny and turn back for Spain. But Christopher Columbus, the admiral of the fleet, persuaded them to continue the voyage. He promised to turn back if land was not sighted within three days.

Suddenly the voice of the lookout rings out in the night. *"Tierra! Tierra!"* At this call of "Land! Land!" in Spanish, the crews crowd the rails. There they wait for the light of dawn, anxiously peering at the dim shadow of land. Would the first light shine on the palace of the ruler of China, or perhaps reveal a Japanese city?

Dawn brought no oriental palaces, for this was not Asia. The land that Columbus's fleet had come upon was a tiny island in the Bahamas, a group of islands southeast of Florida. Columbus named the island San Salvador.

In his log, or journal, Columbus described the first meeting with the inhabitants of the island, whom he called Indians.

No sooner had we concluded the formalities of taking possession of the island than people began to come to the beach, all as naked as their mothers bore them. . . .

The people here called this island Guanahani in their language, and their speech is very fluent, although I do not understand any of it. They are friendly and well-dispositioned people who bear no arms except for small spears, and they have no iron. I showed one my sword, and through ignorance he grabbed it by the blade and cut himself. Their spears are made of wood, to which they attach a fish tooth at one end, or some other sharp thing.

The Arawaks The friendly people whom Columbus met were the Arawaks. They lived in the Bahamas and on the large islands to the south of the Bahamas. Columbus would have encountered a different reception if he had landed farther south on the small islands that lie between Puerto Rico and South America. Here lived the Caribs, a people who were fierce warriors and conquerors.

Neither Columbus nor the Indians knew it, but their meeting was the beginning of one of the greatest changes in the history of the world. Within just a few years, Spain and other European countries would colonize this region and the lands to the north and south, creating a "New World."

▶ This is an artist's version of Christopher Columbus claiming the West Indies for Spain.

145

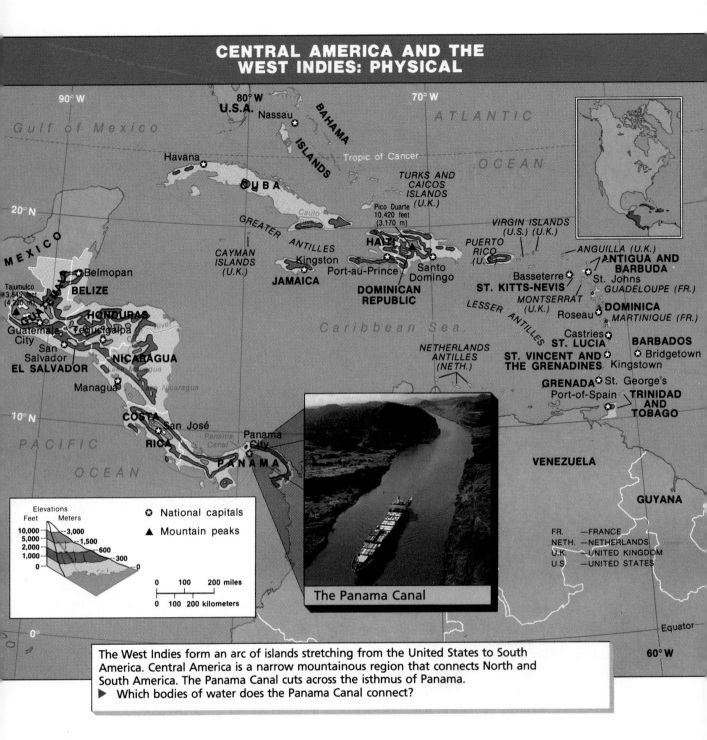

CENTRAL AMERICA AND THE WEST INDIES: PHYSICAL

90° W
80° W
70° W

Gulf of Mexico

U.S.A. Nassau

ATLANTIC

BAHAMA ISLANDS

Tropic of Cancer

OCEAN

Havana

CUBA

TURKS AND CAICOS ISLANDS (U.K.)

20° N

GREATER

Pico Duarte 10,420 feet (3,170 m)

VIRGIN ISLANDS (U.S.) (U.K.)

MEXICO

ANTILLES

HAITI

PUERTO RICO (U.S.)

ANGUILLA (U.K.)

ANTIGUA AND BARBUDA

CAYMAN ISLANDS (U.K.)

Kingston

Cauto

Belmopan

BELIZE

JAMAICA

Port-au-Prince

Santo Domingo

Basseterre

St. Johns

ST. KITTS-NEVIS

GUADELOUPE (FR.)

Tajumulco 13,845 feet (4,220 m)

DOMINICAN REPUBLIC

MONTSERRAT (U.K.)

DOMINICA

HONDURAS

Tegucigalpa

LESSER

Roseau

MARTINIQUE (FR.)

Guatemala City

Caribbean Sea

ANTILLES

Castries

San Salvador

ST. LUCIA

BARBADOS

EL SALVADOR

NICARAGUA

NETHERLANDS ANTILLES (NETH.)

ST. VINCENT AND THE GRENADINES

Bridgetown

Managua

Kingstown

Lake Nicaragua

GRENADA

St. George's

10° N

COSTA RICA

San José

Port-of-Spain

TRINIDAD AND TOBAGO

PACIFIC

Panama Canal

Panama City

OCEAN

PANAMA

VENEZUELA

Elevations

Feet	Meters
10,000	3,000
5,000	1,500
2,000	600
1,000	300
0	0

⊛ National capitals
▲ Mountain peaks

GUYANA

FR. —FRANCE
NETH. —NETHERLANDS
U.K. —UNITED KINGDOM
U.S. —UNITED STATES

0   100   200 miles
0   100 200 kilometers

The Panama Canal

Equator

60° W

The West Indies form an arc of islands stretching from the United States to South America. Central America is a narrow mountainous region that connects North and South America. The Panama Canal cuts across the isthmus of Panama.

▶ Which bodies of water does the Panama Canal connect?

B. The West Indies, an Island World

The Wrong Route Columbus sailed back to Spain and told all who would listen that he had found the fabled Indies of Asia.

Columbus made more trips to the Indies and Central America, always looking for the wealth and riches of the East. But by 1500 it was clear to most Europeans that these new lands across the sea were not Asia. They were named America in honor of an Italian navigator, Amerigo Vespucci (ves POOT chee), who sailed along the coast of South America in 1499.

If America wasn't Asia, then the islands where Columbus landed weren't the Indies. Still, the name stuck. So, even today, the islands that lie between North America and South America are called the West Indies.

The West Indies If you look at the map on page 146, you can see that the West Indies form a chain between the United States and South America. The Bahamas, where Columbus first landed, are the northernmost islands in the chain. Four large islands lie south and east of the Bahamas. These islands are Cuba, Jamaica, Puerto Rico, and Hispaniola (hihs pun YOH luh), which is divided into two countries, Haiti (HAYT ee) and the Dominican Republic. Because of their large size, these islands are called the Greater Antilles (an TIHL eez). The chain of small islands between the Greater Antilles and South America is called the Lesser Antilles. The Greater Antilles and the Lesser Antilles make up a large **archipelago** (ahr kuh PEL uh goh) that separates the Caribbean (kar uh BEE un) Sea from the Atlantic Ocean. An archipelago is a group or chain of islands.

Two Kinds of Islands The islands of the West Indies share a variety of landscapes and climates. The Greater Antilles are mainly hilly and mountainous, although they also have flat land. The islands of the Lesser Antilles have fewer mountains than the Greater Antilles.

Many of the islands in the Lesser Antilles were formed by volcanoes that have risen up above the sea. Other islands in the Lesser Antilles are made of limestone. Limestone is a type of rock that forms on the floor of the sea. Forces deep inside the earth forced parts of the limestone to rise above sea level to form islands. Limestone islands are generally flat and do not reach elevations over 1,500 feet (450 m).

The volcanic islands generally have more fertile soil and receive more rainfall than do the limestone islands. The volcanic islands are also more dangerous, because some of the volcanoes are *active*. As you read in Chapter 5, this means that they may erupt and spew out hot, poisonous gases and lava.

Hurricanes The biggest danger in all the West Indies, however, comes from hurricanes. These powerful storms form near the Equator during the summer and fall.

Examples of the two kinds of islands found in the West Indies are shown here. On the left is St. Lucia, one of the volcanic islands of the Lesser Antilles. A tourist resort on one of the Bahamas is pictured on the right.
▶ What type of islands are the Bahamas?

They often sweep northward toward the Caribbean Sea and the Gulf of Mexico.

What is a hurricane like? Some people have said the wind from a hurricane is like a giant fist that can flatten houses, people, and fruit trees. The high winds are accompanied by heavy rains that can wash away farmers' fields. The hurricane's winds also create huge waves on the sea, which can batter the shoreline of lands that are near the hurricane.

C. The Peoples of the Caribbean

Mulattoes When Columbus first saw the West Indies, they were populated by millions of Indians. If you went today to the same places Columbus visited, you would not see any Indians. Instead, you would see whites, blacks, and **mulattoes**. Mulattoes are people who are born of one black parent and one white parent.

A busy market in Port-au-Prince, Haiti.
▶ What different kinds of peoples would you find in this Caribbean market?

What happened to all the Indians who lived in the West Indies? Most disappeared a few years after Columbus's arrival. Many died from diseases that were carried by the colonists from Europe.

Slavery Spain soon began to bring large numbers of slaves into its colonies in the West Indies, Mexico, and Peru. However, most slaves were brought to the West Indies by sugar planters from England, France, and the Netherlands. These countries began to settle the islands of the West Indies in the 1600s and 1700s.

The colonists from these countries built huge plantations to grow sugarcane. The sugar that is processed from the cane was in great demand in Europe. The plantation owners needed large numbers of workers, so they brought in thousands of African slaves to work the plantations.

Today the results of past colonialism are seen in the cultures, languages, and governments of the West Indies. People of African descent make up the largest part of the population. Spanish, Dutch, French, and English are some of the languages that are spoken in the islands. And some of the islands are still territories of France, Great Britain, and the Netherlands.

D. The Isthmus of Central America

Seven Countries If you look at the map on page 146, you can see that Central America is the long, narrow strip of land that connects the continents of North America and South America. A small strip of land that connects two larger land areas is called an **isthmus**.

The isthmus that is Central America is about the size of California. It extends for more than 1,100 miles (1,770 km) from Mexico to Colombia. But at its widest point, Central America is only about 350 miles (563 km) across. In one place, only 30 miles (48 km) separate the Caribbean Sea and the Pacific Ocean. Along this narrow

Workers place a net around the bananas to protect them from insects.
▶ In which direction do bananas grow?

isthmus there are seven countries—Costa Rica, Guatemala, El Salvador, Belize, Honduras, Nicaragua, and Panama.

It is not easy to explain why an area as small as Central America should be divided into so many different countries. Two reasons are the differences in people and the results of Spain's colonization of Central America.

Different Histories The differences in people are a result of the history of the region. Like many of the islands in the West Indies, each country in Central America grew up around a different settlement. The settlements had their own people and their own ways of life. As a result, each country differs in many ways from its neighbors. Guatemala, for example, was part of the ancient Maya civilization, so many Indian people lived there. In contrast, Costa Rica never had a large native Indian population. Most of the citizens of Costa Rica are the descendants of the people who settled there after Spain colonized the Central American region.

Spain's Policies A second reason for the different countries is that Spain never built good roads to connect its Central American colonies. The Spanish kings wanted the Central American colonies to trade only with Spain. The lack of good roads continues. Even today, just one land route extends through Central America. This is the Pan-American Highway, which will eventually link all the countries of the Americas.

The countries of Central America do have some similarities. Spanish is spoken by most people, and the predominant religion in each country is Roman Catholicism. The similar language and religion are the result of Spanish colonization.

Coffee and Bananas In the nineteenth century, farmers in Central America began to plant coffee and bananas. The climate and soil were just right for growing these crops. They have become the largest sources of income for most of the Central American nations. The largest customer for these products is the United States.

LESSON 1

Review

REVIEWING MAIN IDEAS

A. What Indian groups lived in the region where Columbus landed?
B. Why are the Greater and Lesser Antilles called an archipelago?
C. Why were Africans imported as slaves to the West Indies?
D. Why are there many countries in Central America?

SKILLS CHECK

MAP SKILL

Look at the map of Central America and the West Indies on page 146. Name the capital city of each country listed below.

Belize   Cuba
Honduras   El Salvador
Nicaragua   Jamaica

The West Indies

CONNECTIONS

Look at the photographs in this lesson. How would you advertise the West Indies as an ideal place to go for a vacation when it is winter in the United States?

TERMS

expropriate, per capita income

FOCUS

How have the islands of the West Indies developed their economies?

A. Cuba and Puerto Rico: Two Paths to Change

Cuba Cuba is the largest country in the West Indies. With 42,804 square miles (110,820 sq km) of territory, it is about the size of Ohio. Cuba's 10 million people also make it the most populous nation among the countries of the West Indies.

Cuba has some of the best soils in the West Indies. It also has a moderate temperature of between 70°F (20°C) and 85°F (30°C), and adequate rainfall. All these combine to make this island a paradise of more than 8,000 different plants and trees. These conditions also make Cuba an ideal location to grow sugarcane. However, the early Spanish settlers did not grow sugarcane on the island. Instead, Cuba was used as a supply base for Spanish ships carrying gold and silver from Spain's other colonies.

Sugar Plantations In the nineteenth century, American businesspersons realized that Cuba would provide a good location for growing sugarcane for the large American market. Cuba is only 90 miles (145 km) from the United States. This short distance meant that sugar could be quickly and cheaply transported to the United States.

The businesspersons bought land to grow sugarcane. They built railroads to transport the cane to sugar mills, where it was processed into sugar for export.

United States sugar companies controlled the sugar business in Cuba until 1959. In that year the government was overthrown in a revolution led by Fidel (fee DEL) Castro. Castro **expropriated** the land owned by the Americans. *Expropriate* means "to take over the property of another." The government became the owner of all the land in Cuba.

Castro wanted to make Cuba less dependent on sugarcane, so he tried to grow other crops on the island. These did not provide as much income as sugarcane, however. As a result, sugarcane is still grown on over one half of Cuba's farmland. Other important crops include tobacco, coffee, and rice.

Cuba and the United States Since the revolution, the United States and Cuba have been enemies. Castro turned to the Soviet Union for aid and support. The Soviet Union bought most of Cuba's sugar.

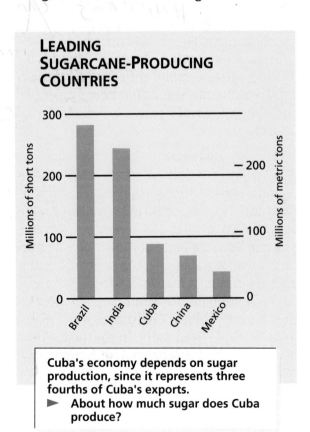

LEADING SUGARCANE-PRODUCING COUNTRIES

Cuba's economy depends on sugar production, since it represents three fourths of Cuba's exports.
► About how much sugar does Cuba produce?

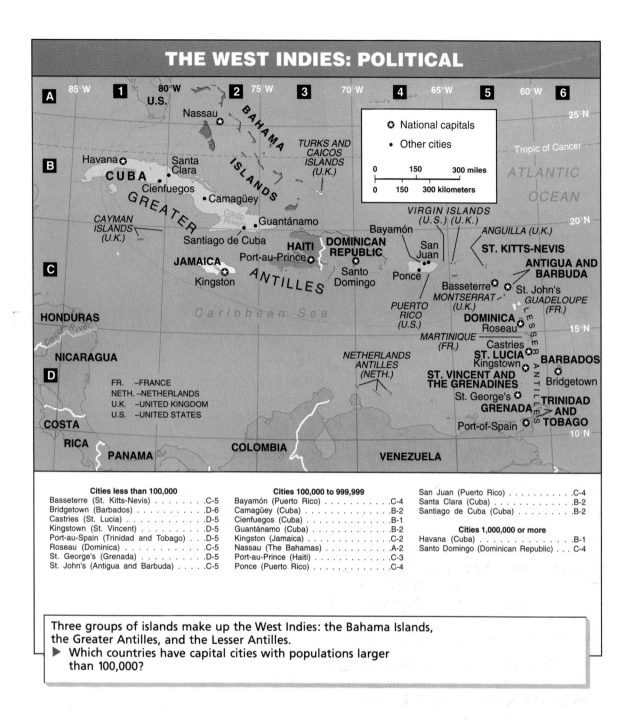

THE WEST INDIES: POLITICAL

A · 85°W · 1 · 80°W · 2 · 75°W · 3 · 70°W · 4 · 65°W · 5 · 60°W · 6

U.S.

Nassau

BAHAMA ISLANDS

TURKS AND CAICOS ISLANDS (U.K.)

25°N

Tropic of Cancer

ATLANTIC OCEAN

- ⊕ National capitals
- • Other cities

0 — 150 — 300 miles
0 — 150 — 300 kilometers

Havana ⊕
Santa Clara
CUBA
Cienfuegos
• Camagüey
Cauto River
CAYMAN ISLANDS (U.K.)
GREATER
Santiago de Cuba
• Guantánamo
JAMAICA ⊕
Kingston
Port-au-Prince ⊕
HAITI
ANTILLES
DOMINICAN REPUBLIC
Santo Domingo
Bayamón
San Juan
Ponce
PUERTO RICO (U.S.)
VIRGIN ISLANDS (U.S.) (U.K.)
ANGUILLA (U.K.)
ST. KITTS-NEVIS
ANTIGUA AND BARBUDA
Basseterre ⊕ St. John's
MONTSERRAT (U.K.)
GUADELOUPE (FR.)
DOMINICA ⊕
Roseau
20°N

15°N

Caribbean Sea

HONDURAS
Coco River
NICARAGUA

FR. –FRANCE
NETH. –NETHERLANDS
U.K. –UNITED KINGDOM
U.S. –UNITED STATES

COSTA RICA
PANAMA

NETHERLANDS ANTILLES (NETH.)

COLOMBIA

MARTINIQUE (FR.)
ST. LUCIA ⊕
Castries
Kingstown
ST. VINCENT AND THE GRENADINES
St. George's ⊕
GRENADA
Port-of-Spain ⊕
BARBADOS
Bridgetown
LESSER ANTILLES
TRINIDAD AND TOBAGO
10°N

VENEZUELA

Cities less than 100,000
Basseterre (St. Kitts-Nevis) C-5
Bridgetown (Barbados) D-6
Castries (St. Lucia) D-5
Kingstown (St. Vincent) D-5
Port-au-Spain (Trinidad and Tobago) . .D-5
Roseau (Dominica) C-5
St. George's (Grenada) D-5
St. John's (Antigua and Barbuda) C-5

Cities 100,000 to 999,999
Bayamón (Puerto Rico) C-4
Camagüey (Cuba) B-2
Cienfuegos (Cuba) B-1
Guantánamo (Cuba) B-2
Kingston (Jamaica) C-2
Nassau (The Bahamas) A-2
Port-au-Prince (Haiti) C-3
Ponce (Puerto Rico) C-4

San Juan (Puerto Rico) C-4
Santa Clara (Cuba) B-2
Santiago de Cuba (Cuba) B-2

Cities 1,000,000 or more
Havana (Cuba) B-1
Santo Domingo (Dominican Republic) . . . C-4

Three groups of islands make up the West Indies: the Bahama Islands, the Greater Antilles, and the Lesser Antilles.
▶ Which countries have capital cities with populations larger than 100,000?

After Castro took control of Cuba's government, more than 1 million Cubans left. Most of them came to the United States. In 1980 a new wave of Cubans left their country. Packed into small boats, they, too, came to the United States. Like the earlier Cuban immigrants, many have settled in Florida.

Puerto Rico Cuba was a colony of Spain's until 1898, when the United States took control of it after the Spanish-American War. Cuba became independent in 1902. Puerto Rico, another Spanish colony, also came under United States control after the war. Puerto Rico, however, has remained a part of the United States.

Puerto Rico is a *commonwealth* of the United States. This means that Puerto Rico can make its own laws and that its people are citizens of the United States. However, Puerto Ricans cannot vote in United States presidential elections.

Not all Puerto Ricans want to continue Puerto Rico's close relationship with the United States. Instead, they would like to make Puerto Rico an independent nation.

Economic Success Until 1940, Puerto Rico was one of the poorest lands in Latin America. Between 1940 and 1970 it became one of the wealthiest Latin American states. Puerto Rico's economy prospered because it succeeded in bringing industries that produce electronic equipment, appliances, textiles, and clothing.

These industries have helped to give Puerto Rico one of the highest **per capita incomes** in Latin America. Per capita income is the total amount of money that a nation's people earn in a year divided by the total population.

Even though Puerto Rico has a high per capita income, many Puerto Ricans

Computer assembly is one of the electronic equipment industries that have helped Puerto Rico's economy.
▶ What other industries have helped?

remain poor. Some have moved to the United States, where they hope to improve their lives by finding higher paying jobs.

B. Haiti and the Dominican Republic: Life on a Divided Island

Dominican Republic Between Cuba and Puerto Rico lies Hispaniola, the second largest island in the West Indies. This mountainous island is home to the Dominican Republic and Haiti—two countries with different languages, cultures, and histories.

The Dominican Republic occupies the eastern two thirds of Hispaniola. Santo Domingo, the capital city of this former Spanish colony, was founded in 1496 by Bartholomew Columbus, the brother of Christopher Columbus. It is the oldest city founded by Europeans in the Americas.

Between the mountain ranges that cross the Dominican Republic are plains and valleys that hold some of the most fertile farmland in the West Indies. As in Cuba, the most important crop grown here is sugarcane. Sugar from the Dominican Republic is exported to the United States, Canada, and the nations of Europe.

A Diverse Economy The leading manufacturing industry in the Dominican Republic is the refining of sugarcane. The government would like to *diversify* its economy so that it is not so dependent on sugar. To diversify an economy means to produce different kinds of goods. The government, like that of Puerto Rico, has concentrated on developing industries that produce goods such as electronics and clothing.

Tourism is another important part of the Dominican economy. Large tourist resorts have been built on the northern coast, which has the country's best beaches.

Haiti The western one third of Hispaniola is a predominantly hilly, mountainous area that is home to Haiti. Haiti was the second

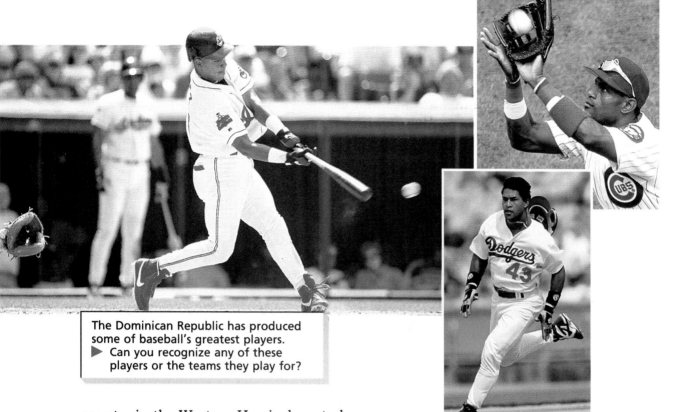

The Dominican Republic has produced some of baseball's greatest players.
► Can you recognize any of these players or the teams they play for?

country in the Western Hemisphere to become independent. In 1791 a former black slave named Toussaint L'Ouverture (too SAN loo ver TOOR) led groups of escaped slaves in an uprising against the French, who had colonized Haiti. L'Ouverture was captured by the French and died in prison. However, the revolution he had begun ended in 1804 with the final defeat of the French army and the independence of Haiti.

Haiti is the poorest country in the Western Hemisphere. The reason for this poverty can be partly traced to colonial rule and what has happened since then. The French colonists had built large sugarcane plantations on the country's few level plains and in the rugged mountains. After independence, former slaves wanted farms of their own. The plantations were divided into small farms. As the population grew, new farms were also built on the hillsides.

Over the years, the soil on the hillsides and mountains has washed away in heavy rains. Only poor soil and rock are left, and the farmers are not able to grow as many crops. Most of the farmers grow crops of manioc and other food for their families.

The few commercial farms grow sugarcane and coffee for export.

C. Jamaica: Independence with a British Accent

An English Colony Jamaica is the third largest island in the West Indies. Slightly smaller than the state of Connecticut, it lies about 90 miles (145 km) south of Cuba.

Jamaica was originally a Spanish colony, but it was captured by the English in 1655. The English grew coffee and sugarcane on huge plantations, and brought thousands of Africans to Jamaica to work as slaves on the plantations.

Bauxite and Tourism Jamaica has some of the most important bauxite deposits in the world. The bauxite is exported to the United States and Canada, where it is processed into aluminum.

Tourism has become an increasingly important part of the Jamaican economy. Well over half a million people, many from the United States, visit Jamaica each year.

D. The Many Small Islands of the Lesser Antilles

Many Cultures Like the Greater Antilles, the Lesser Antilles are a patchwork of European, African, and Native American cultures. During the seventeenth century, England, France, the Netherlands, and Spain fought over and colonized the tiny islands in this region.

Until recently, many of the Lesser Antilles were territories of the European powers. In the last 30 years, however, many of these islands have become independent, democratic nations.

Trinidad and Tobago Trinidad and Tobago is the largest country in the Lesser Antilles. This country is made up of two main islands. Trinidad, the larger of the two, is slightly smaller than Delaware. Trinidad and Tobago is also one of the richest countries in the Lesser Antilles, because it has valuable deposits of oil and natural gas. Trinidad and Tobago has used some of the money it receives from selling oil to develop steel, automobile, and fertilizer industries

The people of Trinidad and Tobago are different from the people in the rest of the West Indies. In the 1830s, England abolished slavery in all its colonies. The plantation owners on Trinidad and Tobago still needed workers, so they turned to India, another English colony. Many of the East Indians, as these workers came to be called, chose to stay in Trinidad and Tobago. Today they make up over 40 percent of the country's population.

Few Resources Trinidad and Tobago is unique among the smaller islands of the Lesser Antilles. Most do not have mineral resources. They also are very small. The island of Grenada (gruh NAYD uh), for example, is only about 133 square miles (344 sq km). This makes it about the same area as Philadelphia, Pennsylvania.

The small size of the islands means that there isn't enough land for people to make a living from farming. And there is not enough industry to provide jobs in the cities. Many of the islands have found tourism to be profitable, but there is never enough work for all the people.

Tourism is an important part of the economy of many of the islands in the Lesser Antilles.

▶ What in this photograph would attract tourists to this island?

LESSON 2

Review

REVIEWING MAIN IDEAS

A. Why does the United States have different relationships with Cuba and Puerto Rico?

B. How are the economies of Haiti and the Dominican Republic different?

C. What changes did the English bring to Jamaica?

D. Why is Trinidad and Tobago different from most countries in the Lesser Antilles?

SKILLS CHECK

WRITING SKILL

Write a short letter to a friend explaining why you chose the West Indies for a vacation.

Central America: A Troubled Region

CONNECTIONS

Look at the map on page 159. If you were traveling through Central America from Mexico to Colombia, would you be going north to south, or east to west?

TERMS

tropics, guerrilla, literacy rate

FOCUS

Why do many Central American countries have political problems?

A. Central America's Mountains Influence Climate

A Spine of Mountains Lay a piece of notebook paper flat on your desk. Now slowly push two opposite sides of the paper toward each other. The center of the paper will buckle upward, leaving the two flat sides on the table. This is how the landscape of Central America looks. Flat plains stretch along both coasts, and mountains bulge upward in the middle.

The whole length of Central America has a spine made up of hills and mountains, many of which are over 10,000 feet (3,048 m) high. The highest mountains are in Guatemala. Tajumulco (tah hoo MOOL koh), a volcano in Guatemala, is the highest point in Central America. It stands 13,845 feet (4,220 m) high.

Many of Central America's mountains are volcanoes. They form a chain that stretches parallel to the Pacific coast from southern Mexico to Panama. Several of the volcanoes are active, and eruptions are common in this region.

Three Climate Zones The mountains create three climate zones for Central America. You can travel through each of these climate zones in a day's trip across the mountains. Enrique Vázquez, a young boy who lives in Costa Rica, often makes such a trip when he visits his grandmother. Enrique lives in San José, the capital city of Costa Rica. His grandmother lives in a small town that is located on the Pacific Ocean coast of Costa Rica.

When he visits his grandmother, Enrique takes a bus that leaves San José and climbs high into the mountains to a place called *Cerro de la Muerte* (SER oh day lah MWAIR tay). This means "Death Mountain" in Spanish. Death Mountain got its name because crossing the mountain was so hard before there were good roads.

Tierra Fría At Death Mountain, Enrique's bus crosses a pass, or a low place in the mountains, that is over 12,000 feet (3,658 m) high. It becomes very cold, and Enrique has to put on his coat. The plants here seem strange. The trees are gnarled and stunted and hung with moss. And there are lots of small wildflowers and mosses growing on the ground.

Tajumulco in Guatemala rises above the clouds.
▶ What is the elevation of this volcano?

Enrique is in what is called the *tierra fría*, which means "cold land" in Spanish. You can see where the tierra fría is on the diagram on page 157. The tierra fría has a cool highland climate, just like the highlands of Mexico. In the higher parts of the mountains in Guatemala and Costa Rica, farmers grow crops such as cabbage, cauliflower, carrots, beets, strawberries, apples, and peaches.

These crops are not usually found in the **tropics**. The tropics is the part of the earth near the Equator. Sometimes this area is called the low latitudes, because it is near or at the Equator, which is at 0° latitude. In most of this part of the world, it is warm all year. There is no cold season or winter. Temperatures change very little from month to month during the year. All of Central America and the Caribbean are in the tropics.

Tierra Templada   Enrique's bus soon begins to descend the other side of Death Mountain. Enrique has to take off his coat because it has become warmer again. The

Cattle ranches are found along the lowlands of the Pacific coast.
▶ In what climate zone are the lowlands found?

vegetation has also changed; for example, the trees alongside the road are bigger and leafier.

Enrique is now in the middle elevation of the mountain. This is called the *tierra templada*, which means "temperate land" in Spanish. The temperatures here are warmer than in the tierra fría. In fact, some people say the tierra templada temperatures are like the temperatures on a spring day in the United States. Coffee is grown on many of the farms of the tierra templada. Enrique's home city, San José, and the capital cities of Guatemala and Honduras are also located in the tierra templada.

Tierra Caliente   Enrique's grandmother lives in the *tierra caliente*, which is Spanish for "hot land." The tierra caliente is hot and summerlike all year round. The lowlands along each coast are in the tierra caliente. The lowlands along the Caribbean Sea are rainy the entire year. Dense rain forests and areas with tall grasses are found along this coast. Banana plantations are also found here. They are the most important crop in the Caribbean lowlands.

The coastal lowlands along the Pacific Ocean have a long season of no rain. This is called the dry season. The most important crops in the Pacific lowlands are sugarcane and cotton. Cattle are also raised here.

B. Farming in Central America

Plantation Agriculture   The Spanish colonists who settled in Central America lived mainly in the highlands of the tierra templada. Those were the areas where most of the Indians lived, and they were cool and pleasant places. The Spanish colonists took the best lands from the Indians and made them into large haciendas, or farms, just as they had done in Mexico.

Even today, in most of Central America the best land is still held in large farms and plantations that grow bananas and

CENTRAL AMERICA'S CLIMATE ZONES

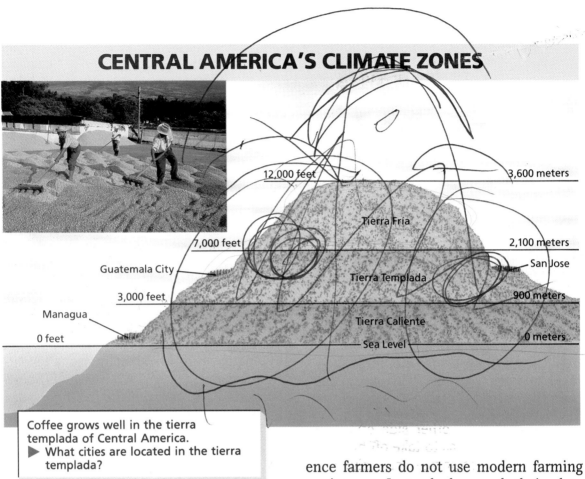

12,000 feet	3,600 meters
	Tierra Fría
7,000 feet	2,100 meters
Guatemala City	San José
3,000 feet	Tierra Templada
	900 meters
Managua	Tierra Caliente
0 feet	0 meters
	Sea Level

Coffee grows well in the tierra templada of Central America.
► What cities are located in the tierra templada?

coffee, and raise cattle. The products from these farms and plantations are exported to other countries.

The most important export crop from Central America is coffee. Coffee is grown in every Central American country except Belize. The largest coffee-producing countries are Costa Rica, El Salvador, and Guatemala. The second most important crop in Central America is bananas.

Subsistence Farming Plantations produce most of the export crops in Central America, but most Central American farmers do not work on plantations. Most farmers are subsistence farmers. On their small plots of land, they grow corn, beans, manioc, and other crops to feed their families. Unlike the plantation workers, the subsist-

ence farmers do not use modern farming equipment. Instead, they work their plots with hoes or animal-drawn plows.

Farmers who can no longer make a living from their farms move to the cities, where they hope to find work. This has happened quite often in the last few decades. As a result, the cities have grown very fast. Guatemala City, the capital of Guatemala, has grown from about 175,000 people in 1940 to over 1.2 million in 1994. During the same period, Managua, the capital of Nicaragua, grew from just under 85,000 in 1940 to nearly 1 million people.

Unfortunately, moving to the city does not mean the former farmers will find jobs. Most of the industries in Central America make goods such as food products, beverages, textiles, and clothing. These industries do not require a large number of workers, so many farmers that have moved to the city remain unemployed.

In 1990, democracy returned to Nicaragua when Violeta Chamorro was inaugurated president of the country.
▶ Who did Chamorro defeat in the election?

Many Central Americans have come to the United States, where they hope to find good jobs. Others flee to the United States to escape from violence and war. Many enter the country illegally. This means that they have not received permission to become residents of the United States.

C. Nicaragua and El Salvador: Fighting Revolutions

Revolution in Nicaragua Most of the Central American countries became independent countries in the 1830s. Since then, Guatemala, El Salvador, Honduras, Nicaragua, and Panama have suffered from dictators at some time in their histories.

In 1979, **guerrillas** called Sandinistas led a revolution that ended a dictatorship in Nicaragua. Guerrillas are people who fight against a government. As many as 50,000 Nicaraguans were killed, and many towns were destroyed in the revolution.

The Contras Some of the people who had been in the dictator's army escaped after the revolution into neighboring Honduras. There they planned to overthrow, or end the rule of, the Sandinistas. Since these former soldiers and other Nicaraguans who supported them were against the revolu-

tion, they were called counterrevolutionaries. In Spanish the word for "counter-" is *contra*. The rebels became known as contras because they fought against the revolution.

In 1989, a peace plan signed by the Central American nations called for a peaceful end to the fighting between the contras and the Sandinistas. The following year, an election was held that let the people of Nicaragua decide who should rule. Daniel Ortega (DAN yul awr TAY guh), leader of the Sandinistas, was defeated in the election by Violeta Chamorro (vee oh LET tuh chah MAWR roh). Mrs. Chamorro was supported by the contras and fourteen political parties that worked together to win the election.

El Salvador In El Salvador also, a revolution began in 1979. The United States supported the government in El Salvador and sent millions of dollars in military equipment. The United States also supplied money to help build El Salvador's struggling economy. About 75,000 people died during the civil war which raged for 12 years. In early 1992 a peace treaty was signed between the government and the rebels. It took 21 months for the United Nations to negotiate the treaty with the help of Mexico, Spain, Venezuela, and Colombia.

D. Guatemala, Honduras, and Panama

Guatemala Guatemala faces many of the same problems found in neighboring El Salvador. Guatemala has the largest Indian population in Central America. Most of the Indians live on small plots of land, where they practice subsistence farming. The largest and best farmlands are controlled by only a few families.

For many years, Guatemala was ruled by the military. Then in the mid-1980s, a civilian president was elected. Guatemala's slow progress to democracy has not been easy, however. A guerrilla war in the countryside continued into the 1990s.

Honduras Honduras is the second-poorest country in the Western Hemisphere. It has little industry and most of its farmland is very poor. Honduras produces little, except tropical fruits and other agricultural products that can be sold for export.

Honduras, too, has suffered from the wars in Central America. The contras used bases in Honduras to store their supplies during their war with the Sandinistas. Many times it seemed as if Honduras and Nicaragua would go to war because of the bases.

Panama Panama occupies an important location in Central America because the Panama Canal runs through the country. The United States built the canal across the country of Panama between 1904 and 1914. Before the canal was built, ships in the Caribbean Sea had to travel thousands of miles around South America to reach the Pacific Ocean. The canal shortened the trip to only 50 miles (80 km).

Today many large ships, such as aircraft carriers and oil tankers, cannot fit through the narrow locks of the canal. Because ships are again forced to sail around South America, there is growing interest in

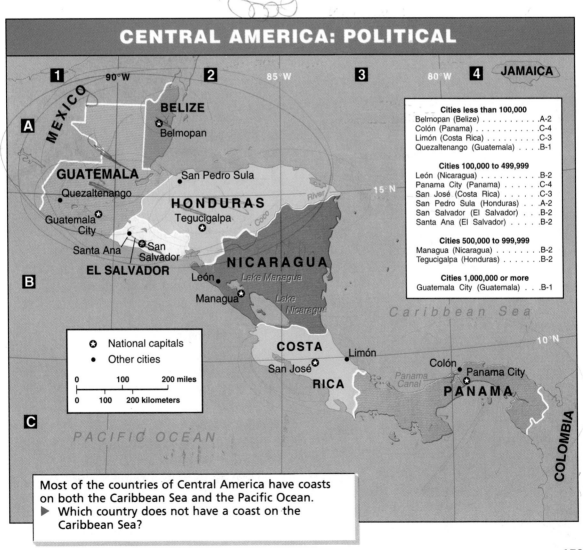

CENTRAL AMERICA: POLITICAL

Cities less than 100,000
Belmopan (Belize) A-2
Colón (Panama) C-4
Limón (Costa Rica) C-3
Quezaltenango (Guatemala) . . .B-1

Cities 100,000 to 499,999
León (Nicaragua) B-2
Panama City (Panama) C-4
San José (Costa Rica) C-3
San Pedro Sula (Honduras) . . .A-2
San Salvador (El Salvador) . . .B-2
Santa Ana (El Salvador) B-2

Cities 500,000 to 999,999
Managua (Nicaragua) B-2
Tegucigalpa (Honduras) B-2

Cities 1,000,000 or more
Guatemala City (Guatemala) . . .B-1

⊛ National capitals
• Other cities

0   100   200 miles
0 100   200 kilometers

Most of the countries of Central America have coasts on both the Caribbean Sea and the Pacific Ocean.
▶ Which country does not have a coast on the Caribbean Sea?

building a new canal. A Japanese company has begun looking into building an entirely new canal across Nicaragua.

The Panama Canal will face another change in the year 2000. In that year it will become the property of the country of Panama. The United States and Panama signed treaties in 1977 that have gradually given control of the canal back to Panama.

E. Costa Rica, a Central American Democracy

A Peaceful Country Nicaragua and El Salvador have enormous problems. One country in Central America, however, is at peace. This is Costa Rica. Here there is no fighting between guerrillas and the army. In fact, there is no army in Costa Rica!

Costa Rica *abolished* its army in 1948. Abolish means "to do away with something." Why would a country do away with its army? The Costa Ricans have elected their presidents democratically for years. They decided that they didn't need to have an army because they weren't likely to fight a war against their neighboring countries.

High Literacy The money that would have gone to pay for the army was used instead to build schools, hospitals, and roads. Now Costa Rica has one of the highest **literacy rates** in the world. The literacy rate is the percentage of people who know how to read and write. The pictograph on this page shows the literacy rates of the Central American countries.

Costa Ricans are also much better off economically than other Central Americans. Few of Costa Rica's people are extremely poor or extremely rich. The land is held in small farms rather than in large farms or plantations. The democratic government and strong economy have helped Costa Rica remain a strong, stable country.

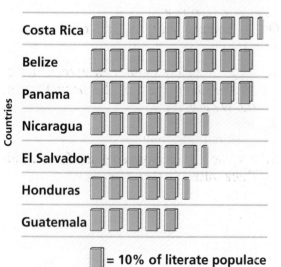

CENTRAL AMERICA: LITERACY RATES

Countries

Costa Rica
Belize
Panama
Nicaragua
El Salvador
Honduras
Guatemala

⬜ = 10% of literate populace

This pictograph uses symbols to show the percentage of a country's population that can read and write.
▶ Which country has the lowest rate?

LESSON 3

Review

REVIEWING MAIN IDEAS
A. How do the mountains of Central America affect the region's climate?
B. Why is it difficult for subsistence farmers to make a living?
C. Why do you think the United States was interested in the revolutions in Nicaragua and El Salvador?
D. What are some of the problems shared by Guatemala and Honduras?
E. What are the ways in which Costa Rica is different from the other Central American countries?

SKILLS CHECK

THINKING SKILL
Look at the Table of Countries for North America, on pages 69–71. Identify the largest and smallest countries of Central America. Which Central American country has the largest population? Which one has the highest population density?

REVIEWING TERMS

On a separate sheet of paper, write the letter of the term that best matches each numbered statement.

a. archipelago
b. mulatto
c. expropriate
d. per capita income
e. literacy rate

1. A person who is born of one black and one white parent
2. The total amount of money that a nation's people earn in a year divided by the total population
3. A group or chain of islands
4. The percentage of a country's population that knows how to read and write
5. A word that means "to take over the property of another"

REVIEWING THE FACTS

On a separate sheet of paper, answer the following questions in complete sentences.

1. What part of the world did Columbus think he had discovered when he reached San Salvador?
2. Which European countries brought the most slaves to the West Indies?
3. What results of past colonialism can be seen in the West Indies today?
4. What country buys the most coffee and bananas from Central America?
5. Why did American business people view Cuba as a good location for growing sugarcane?

6. What happened to Cuba in 1959?
7. Why is Haiti the poorest country in the Western Hemisphere?
8. What countries in Central America have suffered from dictators at some time in their history?
9. Why is Honduras the second poorest country in the Western Hemisphere?
10. Why did Costa Rica abolish its army in 1948?

WRITING ABOUT GEOGRAPHY

Take a trip back in time. Imagine you are a European sugar planter in the "New World." You are keeping a daily journal about your life in the West Indies. Write one or two journal entries that tell about the geography and climate of your new home.

THINKING CRITICALLY

On a separate sheet of paper, answer the following questions in complete sentences.

1. Why do people of African descent make up the largest part of the population of the West Indies?
2. Who do you think should own the sugar business in Cuba?
3. Why do you suppose so many Cubans left Cuba after Castro took control of the country?
4. What are some reasons you could give to support the position that Puerto Rico should become an independent nation?
5. What effects can a revolution have on a country's economy?

On a separate sheet of paper, draw a graphic organizer that is like the one shown here. Copy the information from the graphic organizer to the one you have drawn. Under the main idea for each lesson, write three statements that you think best support the main idea.

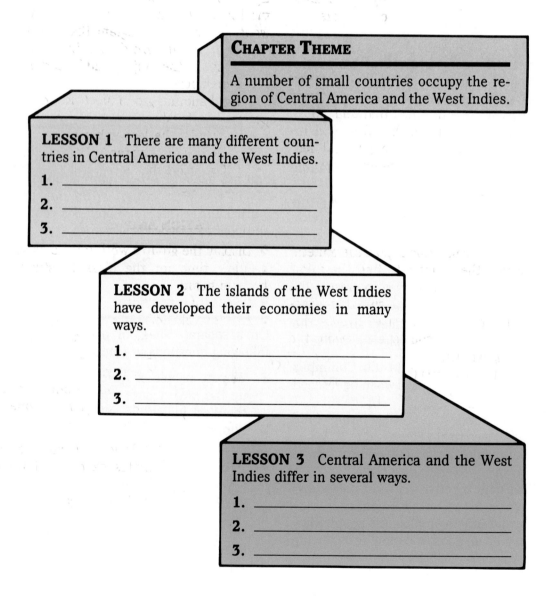

CHAPTER THEME

A number of small countries occupy the region of Central America and the West Indies.

LESSON 1 There are many different countries in Central America and the West Indies.

1. _____
2. _____
3. _____

LESSON 2 The islands of the West Indies have developed their economies in many ways.

1. _____
2. _____
3. _____

LESSON 3 Central America and the West Indies differ in several ways.

1. _____
2. _____
3. _____

COOPERATIVE LEARNING

In this unit you learned about Canada, the United States, Mexico, Central America and the West Indies. There are many varied landforms and climates in these countries.

PROJECT

Your teacher will assign one of the countries you studied to your group. Your group project is to create a bulletin board that tells about the country. The bulletin board should include information about the physical features, the climate, the natural resources, the largest cities, and unusual facts about the country. In addition, it will show how many people live in the country and how they earn their living.

Hold a group meeting to plan the bulletin board. Study the chapter to find the information you need. Decide how to present the information. At this point, be sure that everyone in your group is encouraged to share his or her ideas. Choose someone to record the group's suggestions.

Divide tasks among the group members. Your group might decide to assign the following tasks.

- Draw a map of the country that shows important physical features and major cities.
- Make signs and labels for the bulletin board.
- Look through old magazines for pictures of natural resources.

- Create a variety of charts, tables, and graphs that show information about the country's climate, population, industries, agricultural products, and minerals. You may also want to include a diagram that shows the ways that people earn their living.
- Coordinate the project and help the other group members.

Hold another group meeting when each person has finished his or her part of the project. Under the leadership of the coordinator, discuss the way the bulletin board will look. What colors should be used? How should the material be arranged?

PRESENTATION AND REVIEW

- Display the group's work for the class.
- Allow time for the class to study the bulletin board.
- Answer any questions.
- Ask your classmates to evaluate how well the group has presented the information about the country.

The group should meet for a final time to evaluate its work.

- How did your classmates react to the bulletin board?
- What things would you do differently the next time you had to do a bulletin board?
- How well did you work together?

REMEMBER TO:
- Give your ideas.
- Listen to others' ideas.
- Plan your work with the group.
- Present your project.
- Discuss how your group worked.

SKILLBUILDER

USING A RESOURCE MAP

WHY DO I NEED THIS SKILL?

As you study the different countries of the world, you will learn how natural resources influence the way people live. Natural resources are especially important to the economy of a country. A *resource map* shows how natural resources are distributed around the world or in a particular country, state, or region. By looking at a resource map, you can see what resources are available or produced in a particular area.

LEARNING THE SKILL

The resource map on page 165 shows the mineral resources and hydroelectric projects found in the provinces and territories of Canada. Notice that a number of different symbols and colors appear on the map. If you look at the key below the map, you will see that the symbols stand for specific resources. A black dot stands for a deposit of coal, a brown diamond stands for copper, an orange triangle stands for gold, a gray diamond stands for iron, and so on. What symbol is used to represent hydroelectric projects?

By looking at this map, you can tell what natural resources Canada has and how they are distributed throughout the country. You can see that some resources are concentrated in certain areas of Canada and that other areas do not have as many resources. For example, many of Canada's mineral resources, including lead, copper, and silver, are found in abundance in the country's southwestern corner.

This map shows most of Canada's resources. Some resource maps show only one resource of an area and how that resource is distributed. These maps are useful for comparing the availability of one resource in the different countries or regions shown on the map. Resource maps can also be used to make inferences about the type of industries that a particular area might have. A country like Canada, for example, would probably have oil refineries and well-developed transportation systems for processing and transferring the oil. A country with large agricultural areas would probably have factories to process its crops or other farm products. You can also infer from a resource map what kinds of products a particular country might export or import.

PRACTICING THE SKILL

Use the resource map of Canada to answer the following questions.

1. In how many places are tar sands found in Canada?
2. Near what lake are deposits of oil, silver, and copper found?
3. What resource is found in the northernmost part of Canada?
4. Along which Canadian rivers are there hydroelectric projects?
5. Which resources are not found in land that is part of the Canadian Shield?

APPLYING THE SKILL

The ability to use resource maps and other types of maps will help you understand and remember many of the details your geography textbook contains. Use these map skills as you read your book and whenever you study.

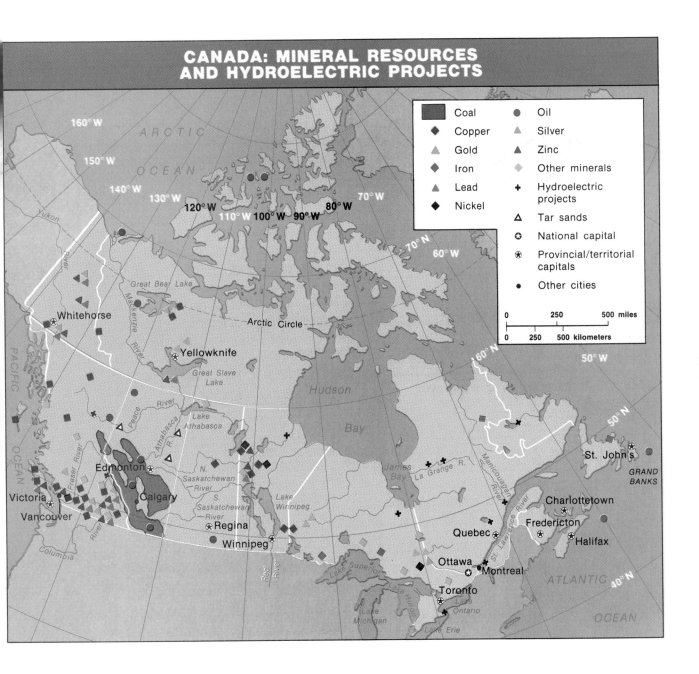

CANADA: MINERAL RESOURCES AND HYDROELECTRIC PROJECTS

Legend	
Coal	Oil
Copper	Silver
Gold	Zinc
Iron	Other minerals
Lead	Hydroelectric projects
Nickel	Tar sands
	National capital
	Provincial/territorial capitals
	Other cities

0   250   500 miles
0   250   500 kilometers

SKILLBUILDER

CLASSIFYING INFORMATION

WHY DO I NEED THIS SKILL?

Your social studies book contains many facts and ideas. If you are able to organize the material in a logical manner, it will be easier for you to learn and remember those facts and ideas.

One way to organize facts or ideas is to classify them. When you *classify* information, you group together ideas that are alike in some way. Classifying also lets you examine how various facts or ideas are different from one another.

LEARNING THE SKILL

One way to classify facts or ideas is to place them in *overlapping circles*. To make an overlapping circle diagram, follow these steps.

1. Select an important topic from a social studies chapter that has two or three categories. For example, in Chapter 5 you learned about the three areas of Mexico: the northern, central, and southern regions. The three regions would be your three categories.

2. Draw and label overlapping circles for each category. Follow the example shown on the next page.

3. Think of the unique characteristics, or features, that describe each category and write them within the appropriate circle. For example, the region of northern Mexico is desert or semidesert. You would write *desert or semidesert* in the circle for this region.

4. In the overlapping portions of the circles, write characteristics that apply to two or three categories. For example, farming occurs in all three regions of Mexico, so you would write *farming* where all three circles overlap. Silver mining occurs in the northern and central regions, so you would write these words where the circles for these two regions overlap.

PRACTICING THE SKILL

On a separate sheet of paper, draw a large overlapping circle diagram for the three regions of Mexico. Include the characteristics shown in the diagram in this Skillbuilder. Then add the following characteristics.

> Baja California
> coal
> oil
> cinder cones
> best farmland
> mestizos
> ranching
> large Indian population
> San Luis Potosí
> Mexico City
> subsistence farms
> large tourist industry

Finally, think of other characteristics of the three regions and add the information to the diagram. Try to think of at least one additional characteristic for each overlapping section. You may need to reread Chapter 5 to refresh your memory about the three regions of Mexico.

APPLYING THE SKILL

Use overlapping circle diagrams to help you classify facts and ideas in Chapter 7, which is about northern South America. Draw three circles and label them *Colombia, Venezuela,* and *The Guianas,* the areas you will study.

As you read the lessons, take notes about the important characteristics of each area. Look for characteristics that apply to two or all three areas. Then complete the overlapping circle diagram for the region of northern South America.

REGIONS OF MEXICO

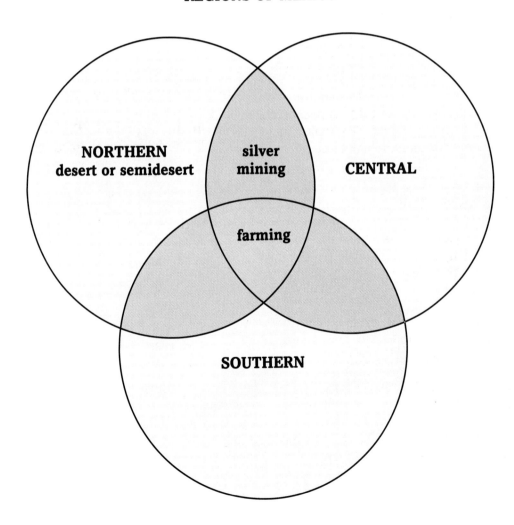

NORTHERN
desert or semidesert

silver
mining

CENTRAL

farming

SOUTHERN

UNIT 3

THE COUNTRIES OF SOUTH AMERICA

CONTINENTAL HANDBOOK

TABLE OF COUNTRIES

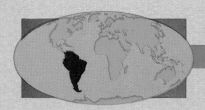
CONNECTIONS

Look at the map of South America on the next page. What landforms do you find in South America that are also found in North America?

TERMS

Pampas

FOCUS

What are the landforms of South America?

Pan Am Games Begin
By Michael Janofsky

INDIANAPOLIS, Aug. 8—After two and a half years of preparation, an unusually short time for such a massive event, the 10th Pan American Games began today with opening ceremonies at the Indianapolis Motor Speedway. . . .

The athletes from 38 Western hemisphere nations paraded and waved to a wildly enthusiastic crowd of 80,000 spectators.

A. The United States and South America

Once every four years, 38 nations from the Western Hemisphere gather to compete in the Pan American Games. These games, which began in 1951, demonstrate the friendship between the United States and South America.

For much of its history, the United States has worked to have good relations with the countries of South America. This large continent of many nations is close to the United States. The United States has felt that its security required good relations with these countries.

B. The Map of South America

If you have ever looked at a map of the continent of South America, you might have noticed that it looks a little like a giant ice-cream cone. The top of the continent looks like the scoop of ice cream, and the somewhat pointed bottom is shaped like a cone. The countries in the cone-shaped, southern part of South America are Argentina, Chile, Paraguay, and Uruguay. These countries are sometimes called the southern-cone countries.

The southern cone has two prominent features: the Andes Mountains and a large area of flat land called the **Pampas.** If you look at the map on page 171, you can see that the Andes stretch from the island of Tierra del Fuego all the way to Venezuela. It is the longest mountain range in the world, and it is the second

The continent of South America is about 4,500 miles (7,241 km) long and 3,200 miles (5,149 km) wide.
▶ Does most of South America lie above or below the Equator?

Caribbean Sea
Caracas

ATLANTIC
OCEAN

10° N

Lake Maracaibo

Orinoco

LLANOS

GUIANA HIGHLANDS

Mt. Tolima
18,425 ft.
(5,616 m)

ANDES MOUNTAINS

Amazon River
Delta

Equator

0°

A M A Z O N

Amazon   River

Mt. Cotopaxi
19,347 ft.
(5,897 m)

Mt. Chimborazo
20,561 ft.
(6,267 m)

B A S I N

Mt. Huascarán
22,205 ft.
(6,768 m)

10° S

ANDES

São Francisco

Lake
Titicaca

Mt. Ancohuma
20,958 ft.
(6,388 m)

La Paz

Brasília
(Federal District)

BRAZILIAN

Lake
Poopó

M O U N T A I N S

HIGHLANDS

SOUTH AMERICA: PHYSICAL

- Cities
▲ Mountain peaks

Elevations
Feet   Meters
10,000 —   — 3,000
5,000 —
2,000 —   — 1,500
1,000 —   — 600
0 —   — 300
            — 0

0   250   500 miles

0   250   500 kilometers

GRAN CHACO

Rio Salado

Paraná River

Uruguay River

20° S

Tropic of Capricorn

Mt. Aconcagua
22,834 ft.
(6,960 m)

Buenos Aires

PAMPAS

Rio de la Plata

PACIFIC

River

40° S

OCEAN

PATAGONIA

Amazon Rain Forest

FALKLAND ISLANDS (U.K.)
(MALVINAS ISLANDS)

Strait of Magellan

50° S

Tierra del Fuego

80° W   60° W   50° W   40° W   30° W

highest, after the Himalayas of Asia. The peaks of some Andean mountains reach heights of almost 23,000 feet (7,010 m).

The Pampas region was once covered by a vast sea of grass. Today, most of the Pampas region is planted with a variety of crops.

North of the southern-cone countries is Brazil, the largest country in South America. More than half of Brazil is covered by the Brazilian Highlands. This is really a huge plateau that has been carved into hills and valleys over many years by the rivers that cross the area.

C. The Amazon

The heart of Brazil is the large area of forested lowland called the Amazon Basin. This area covers about 1 million square miles (2.6 million sq km). The Amazon River flows through this basin. The Amazon is the longest navigable river in the world. Ships can sail from the mouth of the river all the way to its source, at Iquitos, Peru. Along the 2,300 miles (3,700 km) there is not a single dam, bridge, rapid, waterfall, or other obstacle to navigation.

The Amazon is also the largest river in the world. This means that it carries more water than any other river.

D. The Climates of South America

South America has all types of climates. Except for the highland areas, most places near the Equator—which passes through the northern part of the continent—are warm or even hot during the entire year. In these areas near the Equator, the climate and temperature vary with elevation, much as they do in Central America.

In fact, the three temperature zones found in Central America are also found in South America. As you may remember, these are the tierra caliente, or hot land; the tierra templada, or mild land; and the tierra fría, or cold land. However, in South America, the tierra fría is much colder than it is in Central America. This is because the Andes are much higher than the mountains of Central America. Toward the higher parts of the tierra fría, it is so cold that it is hard to find crops that grow well. Farmers are most likely to grow potatoes or raise sheep.

Review

REVIEWING MAIN IDEAS

A. Why has the United States been interested in the countries of South America?

B. What are the two prominent features of the southern cone?

C. Why are ships able to travel along almost the entire length of the Amazon River?

D. Why is the tierra fría in South America much colder than the tierra fría in Central America?

SKILLS CHECK

MAP SKILL

Turn to the map on page 171. Find the elevations of the following mountains that are located in the Andes.

Mount Aconcagua
Mount Huascarán
Mount Ancohuma

South America is a continent of many nations and many cultures. More than 308 million people live in South America.
▶ What two countries do not have a coastline?

Barranquilla

Maracaibo Caracas
Barquisimeto Valencia

10° N

Medellín

Bogotá

VENEZUELA

Georgetown
Paramaribo
GUYANA
Cayenne

MALPELO I.
(COLOMBIA)

Cali

COLOMBIA

SURINAME

**French
Guiana
(FR.)**

U.K. —UNITED KINGDOM
FR. —FRANCE

Quito

Equator

0°

ECUADOR

Belém

Guayaquil

Manaus

Amazon

River

B R A Z I L

Fortaleza

10° S

Callao Lima

Recife

PERU

Lake
Titicaca

Arequipa

La Paz

Brasília

BOLIVIA

(Federal
District)

Salvador

20° S

Sucre

Goiânia

PACIFIC

OCEAN

PARAGUAY

Belo
Horizonte

SAN FÉLIX I.
(CHILE)

SAN AMBROSIO I.
(CHILE)

Tropic of Capricorn

Asuncion

Campinas
São Paulo
Santo
André

Rio de Janeiro

Curitiba

River

Paraná

Pôrto Alegre

30° S

San
Justo

CHILE

Cordoba

JUAN FERNÁNDEZ IS.
(CHILE)

Rosario

URUGUAY

ATLANTIC

Buenos Aires

Santiago

Morón
Lomas
de Zamora

Montevideo

Rio de la Plata

OCEAN

ARGENTINA

40° S

40° W

30° W

**SOUTH AMERICA:
POLITICAL**

⊛   National capitals

●   Other cities

50° S

FALKLAND IS. (U.K.)
(MALVINAS IS.)

Strait of
Magellan

0   500 miles

0   500 kilometers

90° W   80° W   70° W   60° W   50° W

SOUTH AMERICA

	FLAG AND PRINCIPAL LANGUAGE(S)	POPULATION AND LANDMASS	PRINCIPAL PRODUCTS EXPORT	IMPORT

TABLE OF COUNTRIES

ARGENTINA

Buenos Aires

Spanish

POPULATION
34,293,000
32 per sq mi/12 per sq km

LANDMASS
1,072,156 sq mi/2,774,884 sq km

Wheat

Machinery

BOLIVIA

★La Paz

Spanish

POPULATION
7,896,000
19 per sq mi/7 per sq km

LANDMASS
424,162 sq mi/1,098,580 sq km

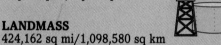
Natural Gas

Machinery

BRAZIL

★Brasília

Portuguese

POPULATION
160,737,000
49 per sq mi/19 per sq km

LANDMASS
3,284,426 sq mi/8,506,663 sq km

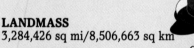
Coffee

Crude Oil

CHILE

★Santiago

Spanish

POPULATION
14,161,000
48 per sq mi/19 per sq km

LANDMASS
292,257 sq mi/756,946 sq km

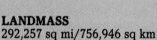
Copper

Vehicles

COLOMBIA

★Bogota

Spanish

POPULATION
36,200,000
82 per sq mi/32 per sq km

LANDMASS
439,735 sq mi/1,138,914 sq km

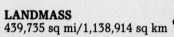
Coffee

Machinery

ECUADOR

★Quito

Spanish

POPULATION
10,981,000
100 per sq mi/39 per sq km

LANDMASS
109,483 sq mi/283,561 sq km

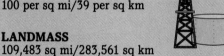
Crude Oil

Machinery

FRENCH GUIANA

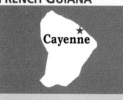
Cayenne

French

POPULATION
145,000
4 per sq mi/2 per sq km

LANDMASS
33,135 sq mi/91,000 sq km

Shellfish

N/A

	FLAG AND PRINCIPAL LANGUAGE(S)	POPULATION AND LANDMASS	PRINCIPAL PRODUCTS EXPORT	IMPORT

GUYANA

Georgetown

English

POPULATION
724,000
9 per sq mi/3 per sq km

LANDMASS
83,000 sq mi/214,970 sq km

Bauxite   Petroleum

PARAGUAY

★Asunción

Spanish, Guaraní

POPULATION
5,358,000
34 per sq mi/13 per sq km

LANDMASS
157,043 sq mi/406,741 sq km

Cotton   Crude Oil

PERU

Lima★

Spanish, Quechua

POPULATION
24,087,000
49 per sq mi/19 per sq km

LANDMASS
496,222 sq mi/1,285,215 sq km

Copper   Machinery

SURINAME

Paramaribo ★

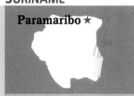

Dutch, English

POPULATION
430,000
7 per sq mi/3 per sq km

LANDMASS
63,251 sq mi/163,820 sq km

Alumina   Petroleum

URUGUAY

Montevideo
★

Spanish

POPULATION
3,223,000
47 per sq mi/18 sq km

LANDMASS
68,536 sq mi/177,508 sq km

Meat   Crude Oil

VENEZUELA

Caracas

Spanish

POPULATION
21,005,000
60 per sq mi/23 per sq km

LANDMASS
352,143 sq mi/912,050 sq km

Crude Oil   Machinery

NORTHERN SOUTH AMERICA

The Countries of Northern South America

CONNECTIONS

If you could live in the mountains or on a plain, which would you choose? Why?

TERMS

mesa, rain forest, deforestation

FOCUS

How are Venezuela and Colombia different from the Guianas?

A. Five Lands on the Northern Coast

Angel Falls The small airplane took off from the dirt runway and headed south. The year was 1933, and the person at the plane's controls was Jimmy Angel. Angel was an American pilot who had come to South America looking for gold. He was fascinated with stories he had heard about piles of gold that could be found in the **mesas** that tower above the jungles of southern Venezuela. A mesa is a large, flat-topped mountain with steep sides.

Angel flew over the largest mesa he could see. Because the mesa had such steep sides, no one had ever been able to climb to the top to see what was there. As he angled the plane above the mesa, Angel looked down. There was no pile of gold waiting to be discovered. But he did find something no one else had seen before: the world's highest waterfall. Today that waterfall bears his name, Angel Falls. The water in Angel Falls drops 3,212 feet (979 m) from the mesa top to the river at the jungle bottom below.

Unique Lands If you look at the map on page 178, you can see that Angel Falls is in the region called northern South America. This region is made up of four independent countries: Colombia, Venezuela, Guyana, and Suriname. The land to the east of Suriname, French Guiana (french gee AN uh), is a territory of France. French Guiana is the only area of South America that is not an independent country. Sometimes Guyana, Suriname, and French Guiana are called the Guianas. This is because Suriname was once called Dutch Guiana, and Guyana was once called British Guiana.

Guyana, Suriname, and French Guiana are unique because they are the only lands in South America that were not colonized by Spain or Portugal. Guyana was a colony of Britain, and Suriname was held by the Dutch. The most common languages of all other South American countries are Spanish or Portuguese. But in Guyana, the official language is English. Suriname's official language is Dutch. As you have probably guessed, French Guiana was a French colony and, as a part of France, has French as its official language.

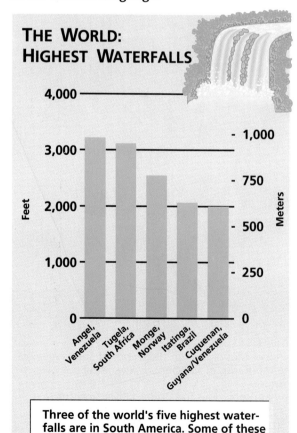

THE WORLD: HIGHEST WATERFALLS

Three of the world's five highest waterfalls are in South America. Some of these waterfalls have multiple falls.
► On which continent is Tugela Falls?

► The waters of Angel Falls cascade down the side of a mesa.

Two Spanish Colonies   Colombia and Venezuela are quite different from the Guianas. Both of these countries were Spanish colonies, and their official language is Spanish.

These two countries are considerably larger than Suriname, Guyana, and French Guiana. Venezuela, with 352,143 sq mi (912,050 sq km) of territory, is about twice the size of California. Part of the coast of Venezuela faces the Atlantic Ocean, but most of it is on the Caribbean Sea. Colombia is the only country in South America that has a coastline on the Caribbean Sea and the Pacific Ocean.

B. A Region of Mountains, Plains, and Rain Forest

The Northernmost Andes   Northern South America has three regions: the Andes, the lowlands, and the Guiana Highlands. If you look at the map on this page, you can see that the Andes begin in northern Venezuela. They then spread southward into Colombia. Most cities of Colombia and Venezuela are found in the Andes' valleys.

The Andes pose problems for Venezuela and Colombia. In Venezuela, they form a barrier between the coast and the interior. In Colombia, the mountain ranges

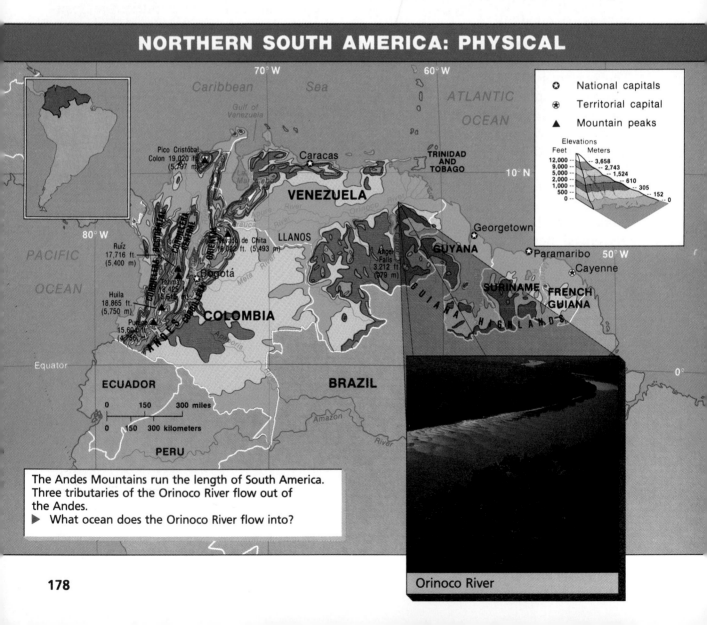

NORTHERN SOUTH AMERICA: PHYSICAL

National capitals
Territorial capital
Mountain peaks

Elevations
Feet	Meters
12,000	3,658
9,000	2,743
5,000	1,524
2,000	610
1,000	305
500	152
0	0

The Andes Mountains run the length of South America. Three tributaries of the Orinoco River flow out of the Andes.
▶ What ocean does the Orinoco River flow into?

Orinoco River

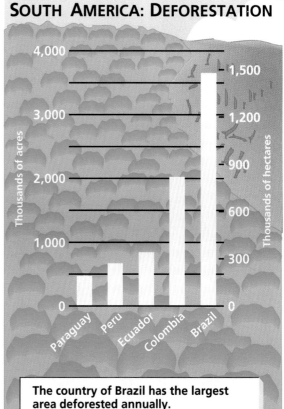

SOUTH AMERICA: DEFORESTATION

Thousands of acres

4,000
3,000
2,000
1,000
0

Thousands of hectares

1,500
1,200
900
600
300
0

Paraguay · Peru · Ecuador · Colombia · Brazil

The country of Brazil has the largest area deforested annually.
► Which northern South American country has the most deforestation?

make transportation difficult between western and eastern Colombia.

The Lowlands The lowlands are a region of plains and thick forest that spread eastward from the Andes. Much of Colombia and Venezuela lie in the lowlands, but only a few people live there. This sparsely populated area's climate is similar to the tierra caliente, or hot land, that you read about in Chapter 6.

The lowlands are divided into the Orinoco (or uh NAH koh) Plain and the rain forest. The Orinoco Plain is a flat, almost treeless grassland that has both a long dry season and a long rainy season. During the dry season, the grasses on the plain die and streams may dry up. In the rainy season, the grasses return and floods submerge, or

cover large areas of the plain. As you can see from the map on page 178, large rivers from the Andes flow across this broad plain.

The other half of the eastern lowlands is covered with a dense **rain forest** that is part of the Amazon rain forest. A rain forest is a very thick growth of tall trees that usually have large, broad leaves.

In Colombia and other South American countries, the Amazon rain forest is called the *selva*. For hundreds of years, the selva was home to small tribes of Indians. In the last 30 years, however, thousands of people have moved to the selva, clearing the forest and building farms. This large-scale clearing of the rain forest is called **deforestation.**

The Guiana Highlands The Guiana High-

The Dutch built this fort in Suriname in the late 1600s. Some people in Suriname today are of Dutch descent.
► The descendants of what other groups also live in Suriname today?

lands are the third region of northern South America. This is the region where Jimmy Angel saw the tall mesas that rise out of the forest like huge castles. The Guiana Highlands is a vast, sparsely populated land of forests and grasslands. They begin in eastern Venezuela and continue into the Guianas. Gold and diamonds are found in the Guiana Highlands, and adventurers like Jimmy Angel continue to travel into the jungle looking for them.

C. The People of Northern South America

The majority of the people who live in Colombia and Venezuela are mestizos. As you have learned, mestizos are people who have both Indian and European ancestors. People descended from Europeans make up the second largest part of the population. Most mestizos and Europeans live in the large cities and towns in the Andes. A small population of Indians lives in the rain forests of all the northern South American countries.

Blacks make up a small part of the population of Colombia and Venezuela. They live mainly in the coastal regions of these two countries. The blacks are the descendants of slaves who were brought to South America by the Spanish.

Blacks make up a larger part of the population of the Guianas. They were brought from Africa in the 1700s to work as slaves on the sugar plantations of these countries.

After slavery was abolished in the mid-1800s, workers from the Asian countries of India and Indonesia were brought to Guyana and Suriname to work on the plantations. India was a British colony and Indonesia was a colony of the Netherlands. The Indians and Indonesians came to South America as *indentured servants*. Indentured servants agreed to work on the plantations until they had paid back the owner the amount it cost for their journey to the Guianas. Once the owner was paid back, the workers were free to leave the plantations and find work elsewhere. Today, the populations of Guyana and Suriname include many people of African and Asian descent.

LESSON 1

Review

REVIEWING MAIN IDEAS
A. What make Guyana, Suriname, and French Guiana unique territories?
B. Where do most of Colombia's people live?
C. Why are people of African and Asian descent found in the Guianas?

SKILLS CHECK

MAP SKILL
Turn to the map on page 178. List the highest elevation for the Andes, the Orinoco Plain, and the Guiana Highlands.

Colombia's Productive Use of the Andes

CONNECTIONS

Based on what you have learned about mountains in Canada, the United States, and Mexico, what are some of the natural resources usually found in or near mountainous regions?

TERMS

cash crop, smuggling

FOCUS

How does Colombia use the resources of the Andes?

This pouch for cocoa beans is an example of the finely crafted gold objects the Inca made.
▶ What shape does the pouch resemble?

A. Colombia's Mineral Resources

When the Spanish came to Colombia in the 1500s, they heard a legend about an Indian king who covered his body with gold dust and dived into a sacred lake to wash it off once each year. The Spanish called this mythical king El Dorado. For years the Spanish searched for El Dorado, but they never found him.

Even though the Spaniards never found El Dorado, they did find gold. When it was a Spanish colony, Colombia's mines produced more gold than any other colony held by Spain. Colombia is still a gold producer, but another precious mineral, emeralds, is a more important mineral export. Colombia produces about 90 percent of the world's supply of these valuable green stones.

Colombia produces other important minerals. Iron is mined in the Andes. And Colombia has the largest supply of coal in South America. Some of the coal is used for Colombia's steel industry, but much of it is exported.

Oil is another important mineral in Colombia. At one time, most of Colombia's oil came from oil fields in different parts of northern Colombia. Now, most of Colombia's oil comes from the new oil fields in the selvas of southern Colombia.

B. Farming in Colombia

Coffee Coffee has been Colombia's main **cash crop** for about 50 years, and it makes up about half of Colombia's exports. A cash crop is a crop that is sold, usually for export.

Coffee grows best in a mild climate, with cool nights, warm days, and lots of rain. Many parts of the Andes have climate and soils that are perfect for growing coffee. Colombian coffee is famous for its mild flavor, and it can be sold for a high price.

Most Colombian coffee is grown on farms that are smaller than 125 acres (51 ha). The coffee farms are small because most of the coffee is grown on the steep slopes of the Andes. Large machines cannot be used on the steep slopes. As a result, most of the farm labor is done by the farmer, his family, and hired workers.

If you visited Colombia during the coffee harvest, you would see workers in the fields filling big burlap bags with ripe, red coffee berries. The bags of coffee berries

181

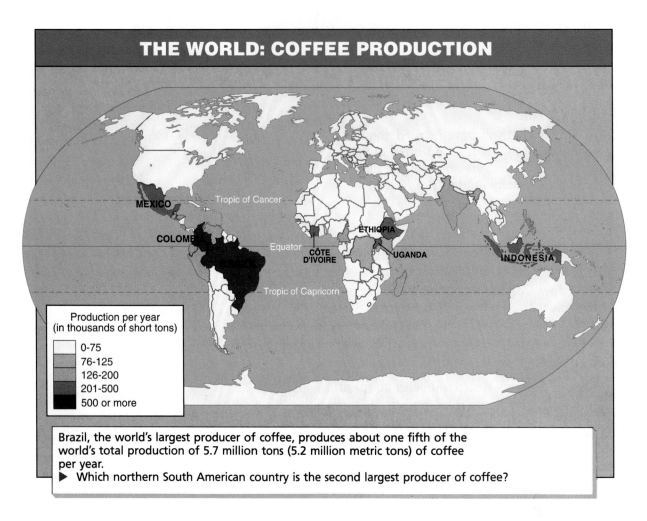

THE WORLD: COFFEE PRODUCTION

Production per year
(in thousands of short tons)

- 0-75
- 76-125
- 126-200
- 201-500
- 500 or more

Brazil, the world's largest producer of coffee, produces about one fifth of the world's total production of 5.7 million tons (5.2 million metric tons) of coffee per year.
▶ Which northern South American country is the second largest producer of coffee?

are carried to factories called *beneficios* (ben uh FEE see ohs). There the fruity pulp is taken off the berries, leaving the seeds, which look like beans. The coffee seeds, or beans as they are called, are dried and cleaned before they are exported to countries all over the world.

Coffee is not the only commercial crop grown in Colombia. Bananas are also grown on large plantations in the northern lowlands of the country. Sugarcane is grown in many parts of Colombia. Cotton is grown in the lowlands along the Caribbean Sea. Most of this cotton is used in Colombia to make cloth.

Colombia's Drug Problem In the past 20 years, Colombia has become a center for **smuggling**, or illegally shipping drugs to

the United States and other countries. The two most important drugs that come from Colombia are marijuana and cocaine.

Marijuana comes from a plant that grows throughout Colombia. Drug traffickers from Colombia began shipping marijuana to the United States in the 1970s. Later, Colombians in the city of Medellín (may day YEEN) began to process cocaine and ship it to cities in the United States. Cocaine comes from the leaves of the *coca* (KOH kuh) plant. Coca grows mainly on the lower slopes of the Andes in Peru and Bolivia.

Drug dealers from Medellín buy coca leaves from farmers in Peru, Bolivia, and other Andean countries and process the leaves to make cocaine. Many of the cocaine laboratories are in Colombia. The processed cocaine is then shipped from Colombia into the United States.

The Colombian drug dealers have become very rich and powerful from their illegal trade. In 1989, when the Colombian government tried to stop the export of drugs, the drug dealers declared war on the government. They set off bombs in public buildings and killed soldiers, judges, and political leaders.

The United States government has been helping the Colombian government try to control the illegal drug trade. The United States wants to stop the flow of cocaine into the United States because of the enormous problems it causes. In many cities throughout the United States, murders and robberies have increased because of the growing number of people addicted to a form of cocaine called crack. Families suffer when one or both parents become addicted, and hospitals struggle to treat those who seek help from their addiction.

C. The Cities of Colombia

The People of Colombia Colombia has a population of about 36 million people. That makes it the third most populous country in South America, after Argentina and giant Brazil. Most Colombians live in the Andes or along the Caribbean coast.

About 60 percent of Colombians are mestizos. Most mestizos live in the Andean region of the country. The 20 percent of Colombia's population descended from Europeans also live in the Andes, especially the large cities found there. Blacks live on the Caribbean and Pacific coasts, and a few Indians still live in the eastern rain forest.

Colombia's Capital Bogotá (boh guh TAH) Colombia's capital, is located 8,500 feet (2,590 m) high on a plateau in the Andes. The population of Bogotá, like that of Mexico City and most other large cities in Latin America, is growing quickly. Bogotá grew from about 2.8 million people in 1972

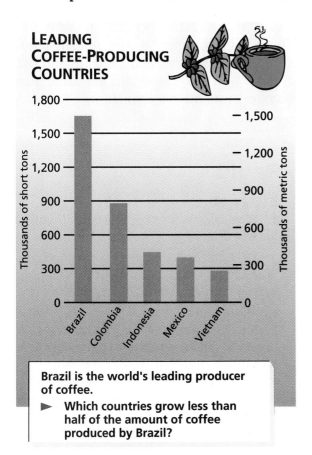

LEADING COFFEE-PRODUCING COUNTRIES

Thousands of short tons: 0, 300, 600, 900, 1,200, 1,500, 1,800

Thousands of metric tons: 0, 300, 600, 900, 1,200, 1,500

Brazil, Colombia, Indonesia, Mexico, Vietnam

Brazil is the world's leading producer of coffee.

► Which countries grow less than half of the amount of coffee produced by Brazil?

A worker picks by hand the bright red berries of coffee that grow on a mountainside in Colombia.
► Why must the berries be picked by hand?

183

This is the view of Bogotá as seen from a cable car ride to Monserrate.
▶ Why are cable cars used to travel up and down mountains?

to over 5.1 million in 1994!

Visitors to Bogotá often take a cable car ride to Monserrate (mahn sur RAT). A cable car is a vehicle suspended from cable that is used for transportation in mountain areas. Monserrate is a monastery high on a mountainside overlooking the city. From Monserrate, tourists can look down upon Bogotá and see the bullfight ring and the city's tall skyscrapers.

From Monserrate, visitors can also see many small white houses with red tile roofs. This is the older part of the city. The newer parts of the city include many poor areas where more than half of the people of Bogotá live. These areas lack water, electricity, and other vital services. The city government has been unable to supply these services because Bogotá has grown so quickly.

Medellín Medellín, with over 1.5 million people, is Colombia's second largest city. When Colombia was a Spanish colony, Medellín was the center of the richest gold-mining area in Colombia. Later, the area around Medellín became an important coffee-growing center.

Railroads and highways were built to transport the coffee to ports on the coast. These transportation routes helped Medellín move resources and goods in and out of the city. Today, Medellín has industries such as iron and steel mills.

LESSON 2

Review

REVIEWING MAIN IDEAS

A. What minerals are found in Colombia?
B. Why are drugs a problem for Colombia?
C. What are Colombia's major cities?

SKILLS CHECK

THINKING SKILL

Turn to the Table of Countries on pages 174-175. Find the population density for each of the northern South American countries. Make a bar graph that ranks the population densities from highest to lowest.

Venezuela and the Guianas

CONNECTIONS

Imagine that you are the leader of a country that has just discovered oil. On what kinds of projects would you spend the money the country will earn from the sale of the oil?

TERMS

shifting agriculture, fallow, dike

FOCUS

In what ways is Venezuela different from the Guianas?

A. Venezuela, South America's Largest Oil Producer

Venezuela's Spanish Heritage You might think Venezuela would share the culture of the Caribbean countries because it is on the Caribbean Sea. But because Venezuela was a colony of Spain for nearly 300 years, the people of Venezuela have many Spanish characteristics. Venezuela is more like Mexico, Central America, and most of the other South American countries.

A Mestizo Country Venezuela's population is about 21 million. This makes Venezuela the fourth most populous country in South America.

About 70 percent of Venezuela's people are mestizos. The coastal regions of Venezuela once had plantations that were worked by black slaves from Africa. Blacks still make up nearly 10 percent of the population. Most continue to live along the coast. Only a few Indians are left in Venezuela, and they live mainly in the rain forests of the Guiana Highlands. As in Colombia, many Europeans live in the large cities.

The Benefits of Oil Venezuela is the world's fifth largest producer of oil, and the largest oil producer in South America. Petroleum and petroleum products make up about 90 percent of Venezuela's exports.

Part of Venezuela's oil deposits are found on the Orinoco Plain. The largest deposits are located at the Orinoco River's *mouth* on the Caribbean Sea. The mouth of a river is where it empties into a larger body of water.

The lowlands surrounding Lake Maracaibo (layk mar uh KYE boh) in northwest Venezuela also hold large deposits of oil. Maracaibo, Venezuela's second largest city, is located on the western side of Lake Maracaibo. A large bridge crosses the wide part of the lake where it empties out into the Caribbean. This bridge connects the city of Maracaibo with the rest of Venezuela.

Venezuela's government has used the money from oil sales to improve the country's social services. It has developed new industries and it has built houses, schools, and hospitals.

The Orinoco River and Plain hold most of Venezuela's oil deposits.
▶ What country is South America's largest oil producer?

185

A Modern City Caracas, the capital of Venezuela, has also benefited from money earned from oil. It is a large, prosperous city of skyscrapers and modern freeways. The freeways make some people think of Los Angeles, California, when they see Caracas. But Caracas is very different from Los Angeles in other ways.

Caracas is located in a deep valley between two ranges of the Andes. It stretches through the valley for about 15 miles (24 km). Because the valley is so narrow, there is little space to build apartments and houses for people to live in. As a result, many families live in tall apartment buildings in the center of Caracas.

Because it is stretched out along the valley, Caracas is an ideal city to have a subway system. One line can connect nearly all parts of the city. The Venezuelan government built a modern subway that was finished in the mid-1980s. Now, people can zip along under the streets and avoid traffic jams on the freeways.

Caracas is a modern city, but it also has many poor neighborhoods, called *barrios* (BAHR ee ohs). Many of the barrios are on the hills outside the center of Caracas. About 35 percent of the population of Caracas lives in barrios.

B. Industry and Agriculture in Venezuela

Building an Industrial Center In 1960 it was only a small river port where the Caroní River flows into the Orinoco River. Today this small port has grown into Ciudad Guayana, with a population of over 750,000 people. This new city was built by the Venezuelan government to help develop the Orinoco Plains and the resources of the Guiana Highlands.

One of the trains on Caracas's new subway emerges from a tunnel.
▶ Why does Caracas need only one rail line for its subway system?

A Venezuelan farmer struggles to guide his ox-drawn plow.
▶ Why are Venezuela's farmers unable to produce enough food for the country?

A large dam was built on the Caroní River to provide electricity for industry and businesses. Large iron mines are located near Ciudad Guayana. This has made it possible for Ciudad Guayana to become Venezuela's most important iron- and steel-producing center.

Problems With Agriculture Venezuela is one of the most industrialized countries in South America, but it has been unable to develop its agriculture. Many of Venezuela's farms are tiny subsistence farms. Many subsistence farmers practice **shifting agriculture**. Farmers clear plots of forest land to plant crops. After only two or three years of cultivation, the land becomes infertile, or worn out. The land is then abandoned and the farmer clears another patch of forest. The old plot is allowed to lay **fallow**, or unused. In time its fertility returns and it can then be used for growing crops again.

Shifting agriculture is used by farmers in many parts of the tropics. As long as there isn't too much demand for land, it is a good way to farm in the tropics. However, when the land is not allowed to remain fallow long enough, it can lose all its vegetation and become badly eroded. Soon the land will not support farming or natural vegetation. This has happened to many of the subsistence farms in Venezuela.

The Venezuelan government has tried to open up more fertile areas for farming, especially in the Orinoco Plain. This region has traditionally been used to graze cattle that belong to large haciendas. The government has spent millions of dollars on irrigation projects so small farms can grow crops on the Orinoco Plain during the long dry season.

These efforts to increase the amount of land available for farming are still not enough. Venezuela must import much of the food it needs, and many farmers leave the land each year to move into the crowded cities and find new jobs.

C. Guyana, a Wet, Fertile Land

Coastal Lands Guyana has the largest population of the Guianas. Most of the country's 724,000 people live near the coast. Because the coastal lands are swampy, the people have built drainage canals to

187

keep the water off the land. They have also built **dikes** to keep the sea from flooding the land. A dike is a wall built to protect the land from the sea.

Sugarcane and Rice About one fifth of the farmland in Guyana is owned by 12 giant sugar plantations that are over 1,000 acres (400 ha) in size. Most of the rest of the farms in Guyana are only about 10 acres (4 ha) in size.

The plantations are *mechanized*, which means that machines are used to do much of the farming. Because so many machines are used, the sugarcane plantations don't need as many workers as plantations in other countries. The large plantations export most of the sugar they produce.

The small farms mainly grow rice. The rice was once grown to feed the farmers' families. Now, Guyana is an important exporter of rice. Farmers also grow citrus

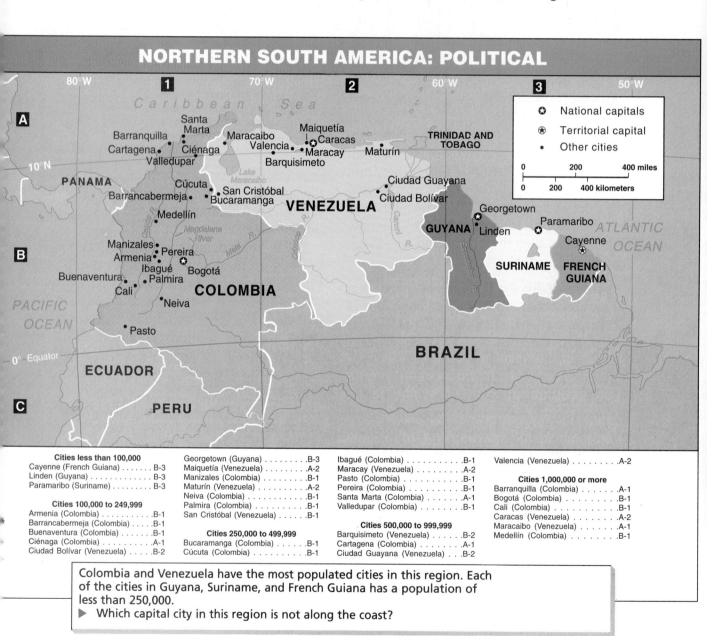

NORTHERN SOUTH AMERICA: POLITICAL

Legend:
- ✪ National capitals
- ✸ Territorial capital
- • Other cities

Scale: 0 — 200 — 400 miles / 0 — 200 — 400 kilometers

Cities less than 100,000
Cayenne (French Guiana) B-3
Linden (Guyana) B-3
Paramaribo (Suriname) B-3

Cities 100,000 to 249,999
Armenia (Colombia) B-1
Barrancabermeja (Colombia) B-1
Buenaventura (Colombia) B-1
Ciénaga (Colombia) A-1
Ciudad Bolívar (Venezuela) B-2

Georgetown (Guyana) B-3
Maiquetía (Venezuela) A-2
Manizales (Colombia) B-1
Maturín (Venezuela) A-2
Neiva (Colombia) B-1
Palmira (Colombia) B-1
San Cristóbal (Venezuela) B-1

Cities 250,000 to 499,999
Bucaramanga (Colombia) B-1
Cúcuta (Colombia) B-1

Ibagué (Colombia) B-1
Maracay (Venezuela) A-2
Pasto (Colombia) B-1
Pereira (Colombia) B-1
Santa Marta (Colombia) A-1
Valledupar (Colombia) B-1

Cities 500,000 to 999,999
Barquisimeto (Venezuela) B-2
Cartagena (Colombia) A-1
Ciudad Guayana (Venezuela) . . .B-2

Valencia (Venezuela) A-2

Cities 1,000,000 or more
Barranquilla (Colombia) A-1
Bogotá (Colombia) B-1
Cali (Colombia) B-1
Caracas (Venezuela) A-2
Maracaibo (Venezuela) A-1
Medellín (Colombia) B-1

Colombia and Venezuela have the most populated cities in this region. Each of the cities in Guyana, Suriname, and French Guiana has a population of less than 250,000.
▶ Which capital city in this region is not along the coast?

A technician performs tests on a rocket part at France's space center in French Guiana.
▶ How is the space center of economic benefit to French Guiana?

fruit, bananas, and other fruits that they can eat and sell.

Few Industries   Logging and mining are the most important industries in Guyana. The large rain forests produce rare and valuable wood, such as mahogany. Bauxite is the country's most important mineral.

D. Suriname and French Guiana

Suriname and French Guiana are like Guyana in many ways. Most of the people live in the hot, swampy lowlands near the coast. In Suriname the lowlands are protected by dikes and drained, just as they are in Guyana. Rice is the main crop.

Mining is even more important to the economy of Suriname than it is to Guyana. Bauxite and aluminum account for over 70 percent of Suriname's exports . Most of the country is still forested, and large parts of it are unexplored.

In French Guiana, there is little farming and only a small part of the mineral wealth of the territory is mined. The most important economic activity is the Guiana Space Center. This is the French government's main base for launching space satellites. The base is near the coastal town of Kourou.

LESSON 3

Review

REVIEWING MAIN IDEAS

A. How has Venezuela used the profits from the sale of oil?

B. Why does Venezuela have to import food?

C. How has Guyana made its coastal lands usable?

D. How are Suriname and French Guiana similar to Guyana?

SKILLS CHECK

WRITING SKILL

Write a paragraph describing what you think it would be like to explore the rain forest lands of Suriname and French Guiana.

REVIEWING TERMS

From the list below, choose a term that could be used in place of the underlined words in each sentence. Rewrite the sentences on a separate sheet of paper.

mesa   smuggling
rain forest   fallow
cash crop

1. A very thick growth of tall trees with large, broad leaves covers half of the eastern lowlands of northern South America.
2. Colombia has become a center for illegally shipping drugs to the United States and other countries.
3. Colombia's main crop that is sold, usually for export, is coffee.
4. More than one large, flat-topped mountain with steep sides can be seen rising out of the forests of the Guiana Highlands.
5. If land is allowed to lay unused for a long time, eventually it becomes fertile again and able to support crops.

REVIEWING THE FACTS

On a separate sheet of paper, answer the following questions in complete sentences.

1. What countries make up the region of northern South America?
2. How are Colombia and Venezuela different from the Guianas?
3. What are the three regions of northern South America?
4. What problem does the Andes create for Colombia?
5. What two valuable resources are found in the Guiana Highlands?

6. Why is the climate of Colombia perfect for growing coffee?
7. Why is the United States helping the Colombian government try to control the illegal drug trade?
8. What has the government of Venezuela done to try to develop its agriculture?
9. What are some crops grown in Guyana?
10. What are the most important industries in Guyana?

WRITING ABOUT CULTURE

Should the rain forests be cleared and the land used to grow much-needed food, or should the forests be preserved for the Indians who have lived there for hundreds of years? Write several paragraphs explaining your answer and the reasons for it.

THINKING CRITICALLY

On a separate sheet of paper, answer the following questions in complete sentences.

1. How does the growing of coffee in Colombia differ from the growing of sugarcane in Guyana?
2. What can the United States do to help the Colombian government control the illegal drug trade?
3. How did the railroads and highways that were built to transport coffee in Colombia help the city of Medellín become an industrial center?
4. What countries besides Venezuela have benefitted from money earned from oil?
5. Why, do you think, did the government of Venezuela choose to develop the small port city of Ciudad Guayana into a major industrial city?

On a separate sheet of paper, draw a graphic organizer like the one shown here. Copy the information from this graphic organizer to the one you have drawn. Fill in the blanks for each country with important facts. Answers may include the country's language, main physical features, mineral resources, agricultural products, and major ethnic groups. Some of the blanks have been done for you.

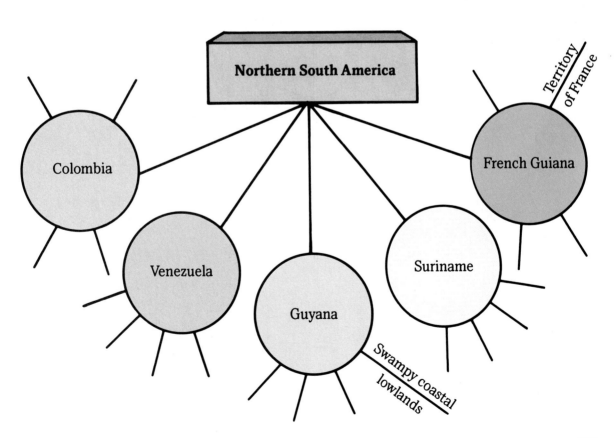

CHAPTER THEME

The countries of northern South America vary in size, economy, and geography.

Northern South America

Colombia

French Guiana

Territory of France

Venezuela

Guyana

Suriname

Swampy coastal lowlands

CHAPTER **8** **THE CENTRAL ANDES**

Locating the Central Andean Countries

CONNECTIONS

Imagine that you are a farmer who needs to sell your harvest of corn. Where are some of the places you could sell the corn?

TERMS

landlocked, geologic hazard, avalanche

FOCUS

What are the physical regions of the central Andean countries?

A. Three Mountainous Countries

The Market in Otavalo It was Saturday morning, and the sun had not yet risen when Tomás (toh MAHS) and his family awakened. Saturday was market day in Otavalo. After a hurried breakfast, Tomás and his parents set out on the narrow dirt road that led to Otavalo. They carried sacks of potatoes, beans, and onions. These were the chief crops that the family grew on their small farm in the Andes.

As the family approached Otavalo, Tomás thought about the people he would see at the market. There would be other farmers from mountain villages, bringing corn, potatoes, beans, and other vegetables to be sold in the market. Farmers from the lowlands would bring vegetables that grow in a hot climate and many kinds of fruit, such as pineapples, bananas, and plantains, which are similar to bananas but are eaten cooked.

For Tomás, the special section of the market where animals were bought and sold was the most exciting place of all. There were so many sounds—the voices of buyers and sellers arguing over prices, the shrieks of pigs, the mooing of cows, and the thump of a horse's hoof on the ground.

Otavalo, the village Tomás lives in, is high in the Andes of Ecuador (EK wuh dor).

Peru, Bolivia, and Ecuador are the three countries that make up the region known as the central Andes. If you were to go to almost any town or village in one of these countries on a market day, you would find a market much like the one in Otavalo.

An Indian Heritage The central Andean countries have other things in common besides village markets. Like Tomás and his family, many of the people of Ecuador, Peru, and Bolivia are Indians. In Ecuador more than 4 million people, or one fourth of the population, are Indians. Over half the people of Bolivia, which has a population of nearly 8 million, are Indians. Nearly half of all Peruvians, or about 12 million people, are descendants of the Incas, whose civilization was conquered by the Spaniards in 1533.

The Inca Empire extended from the northern part of present-day Ecuador through

The market at Otavalo offers a wide variety of goods for sale.
▶ In which country is Otavalo located?

▶ The ruins of the ancient Inca city of Machu Picchu in Peru

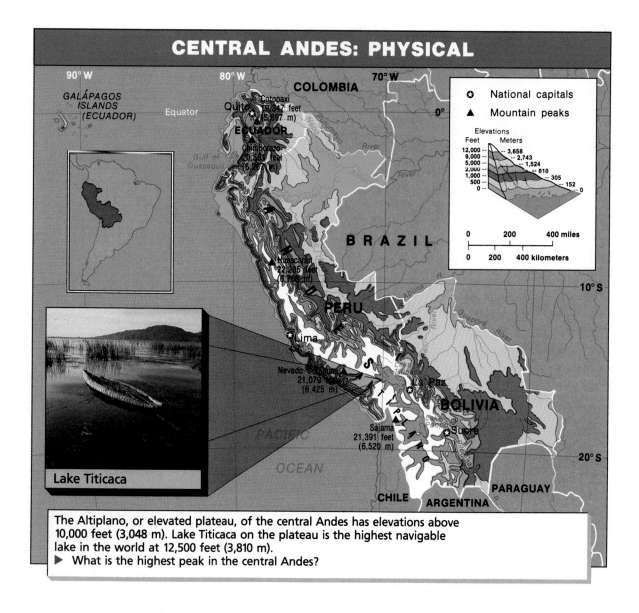

CENTRAL ANDES: PHYSICAL

- ⊙ National capitals
- ▲ Mountain peaks

Elevations
Feet	Meters
12,000	3,658
9,000	2,743
5,000	1,524
2,000	610
1,000	305
500	152
0	0

0   200   400 miles
0   200   400 kilometers

GALÁPAGOS ISLANDS (ECUADOR)
Equator
COLOMBIA
Cotopaxi 19,347 feet (5,897 m)
Quito
ECUADOR
Chimborazo 20,561 feet (6,267 m)
Gulf of Guayaquil
BRAZIL
Huascarán 22,205 feet (6,768 m)
PERU
Lima
Nevado Coropuna 21,079 feet (6,425 m)
La Paz
BOLIVIA
Sucre
Sajama 21,391 feet (6,520 m)
PACIFIC OCEAN
Lake Titicaca
PARAGUAY
CHILE
ARGENTINA

Lake Titicaca

The Altiplano, or elevated plateau, of the central Andes has elevations above 10,000 feet (3,048 m). Lake Titicaca on the plateau is the highest navigable lake in the world at 12,500 feet (3,810 m).
▶ What is the highest peak in the central Andes?

Bolivia to the mountains of northern Chile and Argentina. The capital of the Inca Empire was Cuzco (KOOS koh), a city in a broad, flat valley nearly 12,000 feet (3,658 m) high in the Andes.

Other Ethnic Groups Only a small percentage of the people of the central Andean countries are of European descent. They live mainly in the cities and towns. Most of the remaining people are mestizos.

About one tenth of Ecuador's population is black. The blacks are descendants of slaves who were brought to South Amer-

ica by the Spaniards. Most blacks live in the northern part of the country along the coast and in nearby mountain valleys.

B. The Regions of the Central Andean Countries

We can divide the central Andean countries into regions. In Ecuador and Peru the main regions are the coast, the highlands, and the eastern lowlands. The coast is the narrow strip of land between the Pacific Ocean and the Andes. The northern coast of Ecuador receives between 60 and 80 inches (152 and 203 cm) of rain.

The entire coast of Peru is a dry desert. The only farmland is in small valleys where rivers flowing down from the mountains provide water for irrigation. These irrigated valleys are Peru's most important commercial farming lands.

At one time, Bolivia reached to the Pacific coast and, like Ecuador and Peru, was made up of three regions. In 1884, Bolivia lost its only coastal lands in a war with Chile. As a result, Bolivia is now one of only two countries in South America that is **landlocked**, or without a coast. Look at the map on page 173 to find the other landlocked country.

C. Cool and Fertile Highlands

The Sierra   In the central Andean countries, the highlands are called the sierra. In Spanish the word *sierra* means "mountains." The Andes, which pass through Ecuador, Peru, and Bolivia, unite these countries into a region. The Andes give these three countries many advantages, such as rich mineral resources and cool climates. But the mountains also create many problems that make it difficult for these countries to use their resources.

One major problem is transportation. The great height of the Andes and their many jagged peaks make highways and railroads difficult and expensive to build. But despite the difficulty and cost, one of the highest railroads in the world was built in the Andes. It connects Lima (LEE muh), near the coast, and Huancavelica (wahn kuh vuh LEE kuh), in a valley high in the Andes. At its highest point, the railroad reaches an elevation of over 16,000 feet (4,900 m).

Geologic Hazards   Another serious problem in the central Andean countries is

Most people in the central Andes live in the valleys and plateaus of the mountains. Many villages are isolated since travel is difficult in the Andes.
▶ What is shown in the top photograph?

geologic hazards. A geologic hazard is a natural event involving the land, such as an earthquake, volcanic eruption, landslide, or flood, that causes problems for people. In 1962 a huge **avalanche** roared down the side of Mount Huascarán (wahs kah RAHN), a snowcapped peak in the Peruvian Andes that reaches a height of 22,200 feet (6,767 m). An avalanche is a giant snowslide that occurs in high mountain areas when too much snow builds up on steep slopes. The avalanche from Huascarán wiped out several villages in a valley below and killed thousands of people.

The Altiplano Despite these hazards, more than half the people of Bolivia and Peru and nearly half the Ecuadorians live in high plateaus and valleys of the Andes. One of these plateaus near the border between Peru and Bolivia is called the Altiplano. The Altiplano is high, cold, and barren, but it has been the home of Indian farmers and herders for more than 2,000 years.

Lake Titicaca, which is the world's highest navigable lake, is in the Altiplano. Navigable means that a lake or river is large and deep enough to allow the passage of ships. Titicaca is 12,500 feet (3,810 m) high and more than 130 miles (208 km) long.

D. The Forested Lowlands

The eastern edges of the Andes decline into the vast valley of the Amazon River. This area is called the eastern lowlands. For centuries the eastern lowlands have been lands of mystery and legend. Few people lived here except for the forest Indians. These Indians were never conquered by either the Incas or the Spaniards. Today, however, their lands are rapidly being taken over by people from the highlands and coast.

The eastern lowlands of Ecuador and Peru are covered by a vast rain forest. The

A family stands outside its thatch home in the eastern lowlands.
▶ Why is the house built above ground?

rain forest extends south into Bolivia. It ends in southern Bolivia, where the climate becomes drier. Here the rain forest is replaced by the *Gran Chaco* (grahn CHAH koh), a semiarid region of grassy plains and short, thorny shrubs and cacti.

LESSON 1

Review

REVIEWING MAIN IDEAS

A. What different ethnic groups live in the central Andean countries?

B. How are the regions found in Bolivia different from those found in Ecuador and Peru?

C. How do the Andes make transportation difficult?

D. Why have the eastern lowlands been lands of mystery and legend?

SKILLS CHECK

MAP SKILL

Using the map on page 194, find the length of the coastal lands of Ecuador and Peru. Which has the longer coastline?

Peru's Varied Economy

CONNECTIONS

What reasons might people have for wanting to move from their homes in rural areas to large cities?

TERMS

squatter settlement, primate city, coup d'état, terrace

FOCUS

What are the major sources of income for Peru's economy?

A. Lima, Peru's Primate City

Beginning a New Life About 10 years ago, Anna and Ronaldo Porras moved to Lima from their village in the Andes. The Porrases left their village because they had no land to farm and there was no other work for them. In Lima, they hoped to find jobs and begin a new life.

At first, Anna and Ronaldo lived in a one-room apartment with friends who had moved to Lima several years earlier. Then Ronaldo learned of an empty area in the desert outside Lima where people could build houses. The land belonged to the government and was not being used. A group of people had decided that if they could get enough people to move into the empty area and build houses there, the government would not make them leave the land.

This is the way most of the poor people of Lima find a place to live. People who take over land they do not own are called *squatters*. Because settlements like the one Ronaldo and Anna's friends were planning are filled with squatters, they are called **squatter settlements**.

The Porrases decided to join the group. They packed their few belongings and traveled to the desert at the edge of Lima. When they arrived, they built a house. The walls were made from cardboard cartons that Ronaldo had found in the city. He nailed the cardboard to poles that held up the roof, which was made of boards and

The one-room houses of a squatter settlement are in strong contrast to the busy downtown of Lima, Peru.
▶ Describe what you think life might be like in a squatter settlement.

197

pieces of tin. Since Lima is in the desert, the Porrases did not have to worry about rain. But the house wouldn't keep them warm during the cool desert nights. Since there are no clouds in the desert sky at night, the warm desert air rises and quickly cools down after the sun goes down.

Ronaldo found a job as a construction worker in Lima. Within a few years, he and Anna and a few other families in the settlement were able to build sturdier houses. The settlement even had a school, a church, and small stores. Eventually the government allowed the settlement to have running water and electricity.

A Primate City Ronaldo and Anna's story is similar to that of thousands of people who have left their villages and moved to Lima. The movement of all these people

Fishing is an important part of the Peruvian economy.
▶ Why are fish so plentiful in the waters off Peru's coast?

into Lima has made it the largest city in Peru. Over 6 million people, or 25 percent of all Peruvians, live in Lima. In fact, Lima has about ten times more people than Arequipa (ah ruh KEE puh), the second largest city in Peru.

Lima has the largest number of schools, hospitals, businesses, industries, and jobs in Peru. Lima also forms the country's *transportation hub*. The map on page 194 shows that Lima is near the sea but not on the seacoast. However, Peru's chief seaport is Callao (kuh YAH oh), which is located only 8 miles (13 km) west of the city. Lima is an example of a **primate city**, or a city that is far more important than any other city in a country.

B. Farming and Fishing on the Peruvian Coast

The Desert Coast If you look at the map on page 194, you can see that Lima is near the middle of the country's coastline. As you have already read, the Peruvian coast is a desert. Rivers cross parts of the coastal desert. At one time, large plantations were built near the rivers. The rivers provided irrigation water to grow fields of sugarcane, cotton, and rice.

Until 1968, companies from the United States and other countries owned the plantations. Then the Peruvian army staged a **coup d'état** (koo day TAH) and took control of the government of Peru. A coup d'état is the removal of a country's leader by force instead of by election. After the coup d'état, the military government took over the foreign-owned plantations and made them into cooperatives that were run by the workers.

The Peru Current Fishing has long been an important part of the economy of the Peruvian coast. The abundance of fish in this region is the result of the Peru Current. As you can see from the map on page 199, the Peru Current is a current of cool water

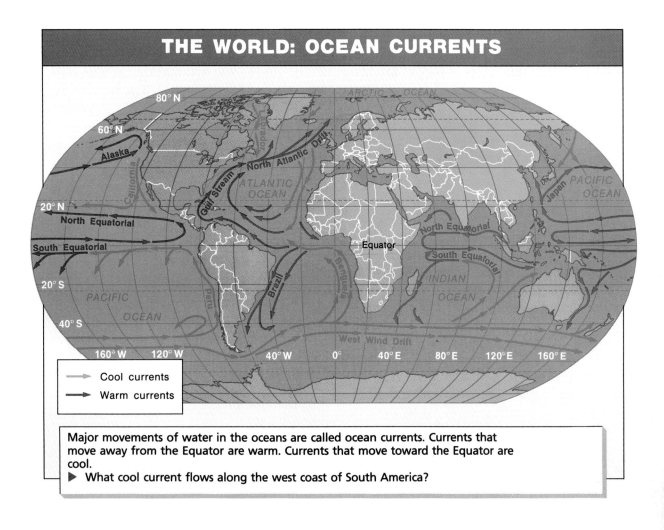

THE WORLD: OCEAN CURRENTS

Major movements of water in the oceans are called ocean currents. Currents that move away from the Equator are warm. Currents that move toward the Equator are cool.

▶ What cool current flows along the west coast of South America?

that flows along the coast of South America from about the middle of Chile to Ecuador. The cold waters of the Peru Current carry enormous amounts of small sea plants and other foods that fish eat.

During the 1950s and 1960s, the Peruvian fishing industry was one of the largest in the world. But in the early 1970s, the number of fish decreased and Peru's fishing industry almost ended. The problem was caused by overfishing, or catching fish faster than they can reproduce. It was also caused by a change in the Peru Current. About 1970 the Peru Current moved away from the coast, taking its rich food with it. The current has since returned to its normal location, and the fish population has started to grow again.

Today the fishing industry in Peru is owned by the government. The government regulates, or controls, the amount of fish that can be caught each year. The main fish caught off Peru is the anchovy, a small, sardinelike fish that is used to make fish meal, a rich fertilizer. Anchovies are caught by the millions in nets. Peruvians also catch larger fish, such as tuna and sea bass.

C. Farming and Mining in the Highlands

Highland Farming Several years ago David Mangurian, an American photographer and writer, went to a village on the Altiplano near Lake Titicaca in southern Peru. There he lived with an Indian family who had a 13-year-old son named Modesto. David

199

Mangurian later wrote a book called *Children of the Incas* in which Modesto tells what his life is like. Here is part of Modesto's story.

> *We don't eat meat very often because we don't own many animals. Most of our sheep belong to a woman from the city.*
>
> *She and her brothers own all the pastureland around here. We're her caretakers. My grandfather has served her for years.*
>
> *She comes and has us slaughter one or two sheep and takes the meat away to market. She leaves us the intestines. Same with the cows. In return for taking care of the animals, the woman lets us graze our own animals on her land. We don't have any other place for them to feed.*
>
> *We also farm on her land. The woman brings the seed. We do the work. Half the harvest is ours. The other half belongs to her.*

The hard life that Modesto describes is like that of many highland Indian farmers. They have little or no land to farm, and they raise only a few animals, such as cattle, sheep, llamas, or alpacas. Llamas and alpacas are relatives of the camel. They live in the Andes and are mainly used as pack animals and for their wool. The wool of the llama is used to make blankets, rugs, and clothing. Dyes made from plants are used to create beautifully bright patterns on these wool products.

Crops The main crop grown in the highlands is potatoes, which grow well in the cool climate. Grains such as wheat, barley, and corn are also grown.

As you might guess, much of the land in the mountains is too steep for the kind of farming practiced on the flatter coastal lands. Farmers would be unable to grow crops here if they did not take advantage of the **terraces** the Incas and previous farmers have built on the mountainsides. Terraces are flat areas cut into the side of mountains so that

A Peruvian Indian family with its pack of llamas stands on a hillside that overlooks an Inca ruin.
► What are some of the uses of the llamas' wool?

crops can be planted there. Many of the Inca terraces are still used for farming today.

Mineral Resources Peru has long been known for its mineral riches. The Spaniards found immense deposits of silver in Peru; in the 1600s their ships sailed back to Spain loaded with silver.

Peru is still a major world producer of silver, but other minerals are also important export products. Copper is mined in the central Andes of Peru. Iron ore is another important mineral mined in this region.

D. Peru's Lowlands

The Montaña The eastern slopes of the Peruvian Andes make up the *montaña* (mohn TAHN yah), or forest region. The montaña is a land of forests and farms. The government has encouraged people from the highlands to move into the valleys of the montaña. The new settlers have cleared parts of the forests and have used the land to grow crops such as coffee, tea, and sugarcane.

The most important crop grown in the montaña is coca. The montaña farmers have grown coca for centuries. As you learned in the last chapter, a chemical in the coca leaves can be processed to make the powerful and illegal drug called cocaine. The montaña farmers have found it profitable to grow coca to supply the illegal drug trade. Because of the terrible problems cocaine causes, the Peruvian government has tried to convince the farmers to stop growing coca.

Oil Peru's most valuable export is oil. The largest oil deposits are in the rain forest of the eastern lowlands. The city of Iquitos (ee KEE tohs), on the Amazon River, is the main center for the oil industry. A large pipeline carries the oil from the lowlands across the mountains to the port of Bayovar on the Pacific coast. There it is loaded on ships for export.

The Indians of Peru and the central Andean countries have practiced terrace farming for centuries.
▶ What is a terrace?

LESSON 2

Review

REVIEWING MAIN IDEAS

A. Why has Lima become Peru's largest city?

B. How did a change in the Peru Current affect Peru's fishing industry?

C. How do farmers grow crops in Peru's highlands?

D. What important resource comes from the eastern lowlands?

SKILLS CHECK

THINKING SKILL

Imagine that you are a government official trying to convince a farmer to stop growing coca. Write a paragraph stating the reasons why the farmer should not grow coca.

201

Living and Working in Ecuador and Bolivia

CONNECTIONS

If you could live in a hot, humid climate or in a cool climate, which would you choose? Why?

TERMS

antimony, capital

FOCUS

What are Ecuador's and Bolivia's main resources?

A. The Cool Highlands on the Equator

The City on the Equator *Ecuador* is Spanish for "Equator." It is an appropriate name, since the Equator cuts across the northern third of the country. Much of Ecuador, however, is nothing like the other lands that are crossed by the Equator. In fact, the capital city, Quito—which is almost directly on the Equator—has pleasant, springlike temperatures year round.

Why does part of Ecuador not have the hot, rainy climate we expect to find near the Equator? The reason is the Andes. As you learned in Chapter 6, elevation affects climate. Even though Quito is on the Equator, its height of over 9,000 feet (2,743 m) keeps it cool.

A Tale of Two Cities Quito has a population of about 1.1 million. But Quito is not the most populated city in Ecuador. Instead, the country's most populated city is Guayaquil (gwye ah KEEL), a city in the Pacific coastal lowlands. Guayaquil has 1.5 million people. The lowlands around Guayaquil are hot and humid throughout the year. Mosquitoes and other insects that carry deadly diseases such as malaria and yellow fever once flourished in the lowlands. Why, then, did Guayaquil, which has a much less pleasant climate, become the country's most populated city?

Quito was once the most populated city in Ecuador. Its size and importance were the result of its location. Both the Incas and the Spaniards settled in the cool highlands, so Quito was near the majority of the country's population. Crops such as potatoes and corn grew well in the fertile soils of the highlands.

Quito is the second largest city in Ecuador. It sits in a green valley high in a range of the Andes. It began as the northern capital of the Inca Empire.
▶ Why was Quito once the largest city in Ecuador?

Guayaquil is Ecuador's port city and the largest city in the country.
▶ On what ocean is the port at Guayaquil located?

Guayaquil's Growth Guayaquil started to grow once the dreaded diseases found in the lowlands were brought under control. People then moved into the lowlands to clear the lands around Guayaquil. In the nineteenth century, the lumber from the trees that were cut down was shipped from Guayaquil's port to Europe or North America. The cleared land was then planted with bananas, rice, sugarcane, coffee, and cacao. All of these became important export crops, which were shipped from Guayaquil. The city soon became the country's most important industrial and business center.

Quito was unable to compete economically with Guayaquil, and it became an isolated, highland capital. It still has less business and industry than the lowlands. For the first time in Ecuador's history, more people live in the coastal lowlands than live in the highlands.

B. The Discovery of Oil in the Eastern Lowlands

Ecuador's eastern lowlands were once the least populated part of the country. In 1970, oil deposits were discovered in the lowlands near the Colombian border. People began to move into the lowlands to work for the oil companies.

The discovery of oil brought another important change to the lowlands. The oil companies built roads to move their equipment through the lowland rain forest. Ecuadorians eager for new land to farm followed the new roads. The settlers cleared the forest and planted coffee, cacao, and other crops that grow well in the lowlands.

Because of the oil and new settlers, the population of the eastern lowlands is growing quickly. In 1970, only a few thousand people lived there. Today there are over 200,000 people, and more arrive daily.

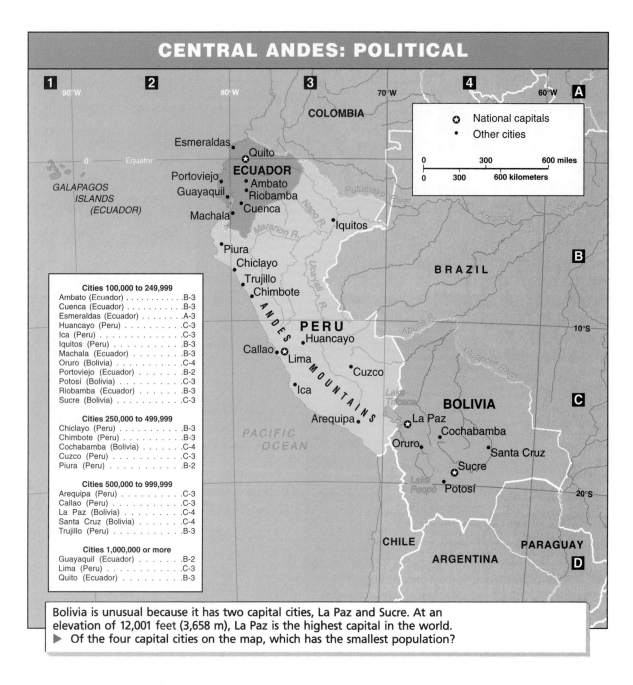

CENTRAL ANDES: POLITICAL

1 90°W **2** 80°W **3** 70°W **4** 60°W **A**

COLOMBIA

◎ National capitals
• Other cities

| 0 | 300 | 600 miles |
| 0 | 300 | 600 kilometers |

Esmeraldas•
Equator 0
•Quito
ECUADOR
GALAPAGOS
ISLANDS
(ECUADOR)
Portoviejo•
• Ambato
Guayaquil•
•Riobamba
Machala•
•Cuenca

•Iquitos

B

Putumayo River

•Piura
Chiclayo

BRAZIL

Marañón R.

Napo R.

Ucayali R.

Amazon River

•Trujillo
•Chimbote

ANDES

PERU
•Huancayo

10°S

Abuña R.

Guaporé River

Callao•◎
Lima

•Cuzco

MOUNTAINS

•Ica

Lake
Titicaca

BOLIVIA

C

PACIFIC
OCEAN

Arequipa•

•La Paz
•Cochabamba
Oruro•
•Santa Cruz

Lake
Poopó
◎Sucre
•Potosí

20°S

CHILE

D

PARAGUAY
ARGENTINA

Cities 100,000 to 249,999
Ambato (Ecuador) B-3
Cuenca (Ecuador) B-3
Esmeraldas (Ecuador) A-3
Huancayo (Peru) C-3
Ica (Peru) C-3
Iquitos (Peru) B-3
Machala (Ecuador) B-3
Oruro (Bolivia) C-4
Portoviejo (Ecuador) B-2
Potosí (Bolivia) C-3
Riobamba (Ecuador) B-3
Sucre (Bolivia) C-3

Cities 250,000 to 499,999
Chiclayo (Peru) B-3
Chimbote (Peru) B-3
Cochabamba (Bolivia) C-4
Cuzco (Peru) C-3
Piura (Peru) B-2

Cities 500,000 to 999,999
Arequipa (Peru) C-3
Callao (Peru) C-3
La Paz (Bolivia) C-4
Santa Cruz (Bolivia) C-4
Trujillo (Peru) B-3

Cities 1,000,000 or more
Guayaquil (Ecuador) B-2
Lima (Peru) C-3
Quito (Ecuador) B-3

Bolivia is unusual because it has two capital cities, La Paz and Sucre. At an elevation of 12,001 feet (3,658 m), La Paz is the highest capital in the world.
▶ Of the four capital cities on the map, which has the smallest population?

Thousands of acres of forest have been cleared for farms; roads crisscross the forest; and there are now cities of 25,000 people and more where no one lived in 1970.

C. Bolivia: South America's Highest Country

City in the Clouds The airport outside La Paz (lah PAHS), Bolivia, is called Aeropuerto El Alto (ah er oh PWER toh el AHL toh) in Spanish. This translates to "the high airport." The La Paz airport is the highest commercial airport in the world. It is in the Altiplano, at an elevation of nearly 13,200 feet (4,023 m).

The city of La Paz is in a canyon about 1,000 feet (305 m) below the Altiplano. Still, La Paz is the highest national capital in the world. Mount Illimani (ee yee MAH nee), a beautiful snow-covered mountain, looms over the city. Mount Illimani, which is one of the highest mountains in the Andes, rises more than 21,000 feet (6,400 m) skyward.

The sides of the narrow valley that surrounds La Paz are eroded into fantastic shapes that look as if they belong to another world. Some people think that the landscape of Bolivia's Altiplano resembles the surface of the moon. There are no trees, only short grasses and occasional cacti.

Travelers who have not been to La Paz before find walking around the city difficult at first. The city's altitude is so high there is little oxygen in the air. People who are unaccustomed to the thin air often suffer from *soroche* (suh ROH chee), or altitude sickness.

Why would people build a capital city so high in the mountains?

And why would anyone want to live in La Paz? Part of the answer is that La Paz is on the part of the Altiplano near Lake Titicaca. Here it is warm enough to grow crops such as potatoes, which have adapted to the area's climate.

Gold is another reason for the city's location. The Spaniards decided to build a city here after they discovered gold and other valuable minerals nearby. Once a small mining town, La Paz now has a population of more than 700,000.

Two Capitals Bolivia actually has two capital cities; it and the Netherlands are the only countries in the world with this distinction. The legal capital is the city of Sucre (soo kray). Sucre is a city of about 130,000 people that is located in a valley in the southern part of the highlands.

It was the first capital of Bolivia. Toward the end of the 1800's, La Paz became more important than Sucre because

La Paz sits in a rugged valley that is watched over by the snowcapped volcano Mount Illimani.
▶ Do you think it is difficult to travel to and from La Paz?

205

A Bolivian tin miner processes tin. Tin has a variety
of uses, since it is easy to shape and bend.
▶ Why has Bolivia's tin production decreased?

valuable deposits of tin were found nearby.
Wealthy tin mine owners convinced a Bolivian president to move the government to
La Paz, where it has been ever since. The
law was never changed to make La Paz the
legal capital, but nearly all the government
offices are in La Paz.

A Mineral-Rich Country Bolivia was once
the world's most important producer of tin,
and this was the country's largest export.
Since 1979, however, Bolivia's tin production has dropped sharply. Many of the
mines have been depleted, and it is difficult
to reach the remaining tin in other mines.

Bolivia's tin mines were once the source
of the country's wealth; they have also been
the source of many of its problems. For
much of Bolivia's history, only a few
people owned the country's tin mines. These
wealthy mine owners cared little for the

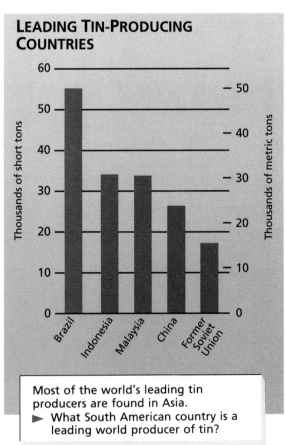

LEADING TIN-PRODUCING COUNTRIES

Most of the world's leading tin
producers are found in Asia.
▶ What South American country is a
leading world producer of tin?

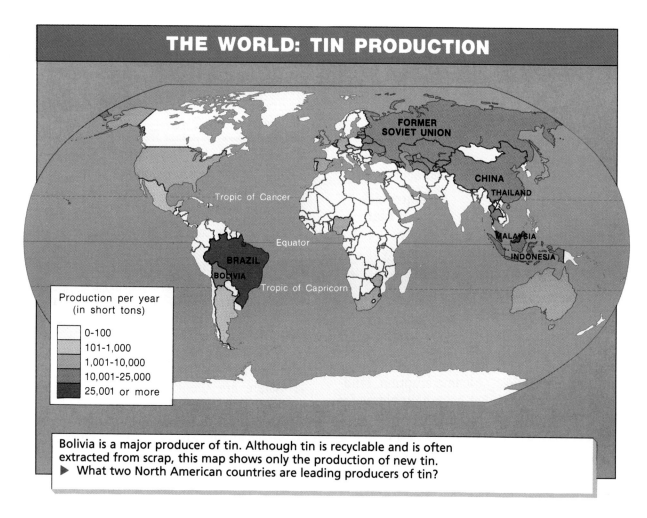

THE WORLD: TIN PRODUCTION

Production per year (in short tons)
- 0-100
- 101-1,000
- 1,001-10,000
- 10,001-25,000
- 25,001 or more

Bolivia is a major producer of tin. Although tin is recyclable and is often extracted from scrap, this map shows only the production of new tin.
▶ What two North American countries are leading producers of tin?

workers who mined the tin. The workers lived in villages near the mines. The houses and the stores in the village were often owned by the mine owners.

In 1952, the government took over the mines. However, conditions at the mines have not improved much since then. Workers still face the problems of poor housing and low wages.

Bolivia is rich in other minerals, such as copper, silver, gold, and **antimony**. Antimony is a mineral used to make metal harder. Unfortunately, Bolivia lacks the **capital** to take advantage of these resources. Capital is money put to a productive use, such as building roads, farms, and businesses. A government usually receives the capital it needs for economic projects from taxes. Since Bolivia's population is so poor, it has been unable to raise enough capital through taxes.

LESSON 3

Review

REVIEWING MAIN IDEAS

A. Why does Guayaquil have a larger population than Quito?

B. How did the discovery of oil affect the eastern lowlands?

C. Why does Bolivia have two capitals?

SKILLS CHECK

WRITING SKILL

Look back at the photographs of Guayaquil and Quito on pages 202–203. Then write a paragraph that describes the differences in the way the two cities look.

207

REVIEWING TERMS

On a separate sheet of paper, write the term that best completes each sentence.

landlocked	primate city
geologic hazard	coup d'état
avalanche	terrace
navigable	antimony
squatter settlement	capital

1. A settlement, or community of houses, built by poor people on government land is called a _____.
2. A_____ is a natural event involving the land, such as an earthquake, volcanic eruption, landslide, or flood that causes problems for people.
3. Bolivia is one of two countries in South America that is _____.
4. A _____ is the removal of a country's leader by force instead of by election.
5. _____ means that a lake or river is large and deep enough to allow the passage of ships.
6. _____ is money put to a productive use, such as building roads, farms, and businesses.
7. A _____ is a flat area cut into the side of a mountain where crops can be planted.
8. An _____ can occur in high mountain areas when too much snow builds up on steep slopes.
9. A city that is far more important than any other city in a country is called a _____.
10. _____ is a mineral used to make metal harder.

REVIEWING THE FACTS

On a separate sheet of paper, answer the following questions in complete sentences.

1. What three countries make up the central Andes?
2. What advantages do the Andes give to countries they unite?
3. What are the three main regions of Ecuador and Peru?
4. Who owns the fishing industry in Peru?
5. Why is life difficult for the highland Indians of Peru?
6. What are three important minerals found in Peru?
7. Where are the largest oil deposits in Peru located?
8. What changes have occurred in the eastern lowlands of Ecuador since the discovery of oil?
9. Why was the city of La Paz built?
10. Why doesn't Bolivia take advantage of its mineral resources?

WRITING ABOUT GEOGRAPHY

Imagine you are on a scientific expedition traveling through the three regions of Ecuador. Your job is to record your observations of the physical features and climate of each region. Write three paragraphs showing what you would record.

THINKING CRITICALLY

On a separate sheet of paper, answer the following questions in complete sentences.

1. What, do you think, are some disadvantages of being a landlocked country such as Bolivia?
2. What problems could arise from many people moving into a city or unpopulated area over a short period of time?
3. How could squatter settlements benefit a city?
4. What are some characteristics of a primate city?
5. What other areas of the world have problems with geologic hazards?

❖❖❖

SUMMARIZING THE CHAPTER

On a separate sheet of paper, draw a graphic organizer like the one shown here. Copy the information from this graphic organizer to the one you have drawn. Under the main idea for each lesson, write three statements that you think best support it.

CHAPTER THEME → The three regions of the central Andean countries have distinctive physical and ethnic characteristics.

LESSON 1	LESSON 2	LESSON 3
The central Andean countries have three distinct regions.	The major sources of income for Peru's economy are varied.	Equador's and Bolivia's main resources differ.
1. _____	1. _____	1. _____
2. _____	2. _____	2. _____
3. _____	3. _____	3. _____

CHAPTER **9**

THE SOUTHERN CONE

1. Lands of Plains and Mountains

2. Argentina and the Pampas

3. Uruguay and Paraguay

4. Chile: The Coastal Nation

Lands of Plains and Mountains

CONNECTIONS
What kinds of boats can be used as transportation on rivers?

TERMS
estuary, confluence

FOCUS
How are the lands and the peoples of the southern cone countries different from one another?

A. A Great River System

The Río de la Plata   The silver boat shone in the afternoon sun as the group of tourists walked onto the dock. The boat looked like an ordinary ferry, with rows of windows and a cabin for the captain. But this ferry was a hydrofoil. A hydrofoil is a type of boat with foils, or wings, attached to the bottom that help the boat move quickly over the water. The tourists were taking the hydrofoil from Montevideo (mahnt uh vuh DAY oh), the capital of Uruguay, to Buenos Aires (BWAY nus er eez), the capital of Argentina. The 125-mile (200-km) long trip would take four hours.

Everyone boarded the hydrofoil, which soon was moving at over 55 miles (88 km) an hour up the wide Río de la Plata (REE oh de lah PLAH tah) **estuary**. An estuary is the mouth of a river into which ocean water flows, mixing freshwater and sea water. The Río de la Plata, which separates Argentina and Uruguay, is one of the largest estuaries in the world.

The tourists looked back and saw the lighthouse that stands on the small hill near Montevideo's harbor become smaller and smaller as the hydrofoil continued up the estuary. The dark, muddy brown waters of the Río de la Plata spread out so far that it was hard to see land on either side.

Buenos Aires finally came into view, a jumble of tall skyscrapers and factories. The hydrofoil slowed to dock, passing by huge freighters loaded with the products of Argentina's vast plains and farmlands.

Buenos Aires is located on the Río de la Plata. It has grown from a small town of only 24,000 in 1778 to a metropolitan area of 10 million today.
▶ How can you tell this is a port city?

▶ Gauchos and cattle cross the green fields of the Pampas.

211

SOUTHERN SOUTH AMERICA: PHYSICAL

BOLIVIA

20° S

PACIFIC OCEAN

ATACAMA DESERT

ANDES

CHILE

PARAGUAY

Asunción

Tropic of Capricorn

GRAN CHACO

30° S

ARGENTINA

Aconcagua
22,834 ft
(6,960 m)

Santiago

BRAZIL

URUGUAY

Montevideo

Buenos Aires

PAMPAS

40° S

Gulf of San Matias

ATLANTIC

PATAGONIA

OCEAN

50° S

Strait of Magellan

FALKLAND IS.
(U.K.)

50° W

TIERRA DEL FUEGO

Cape Horn

Drake Passage

70° W   60° W

✪ National capitals

▲ Mountain peaks

Elevations
Feet   Meters
10,000 — —3,000
5,000 — —1,500
2,000 — —600
1,000 — —300
0 — —0

Land below sea level

0   250   500 miles

0   250   500 kilometers

The Pampas is a region of plains that extends almost 1,000 miles (1,609 km) through Argentina.
▶ In what countries is the Gran Chaco?

Mount Aconcagua

Important Waterways As you can see from the map on this page, the Río de la Plata is formed by the **confluence** of the Uruguay and Paraná rivers. A confluence is where two or more streams or rivers join. It is possible to travel by boat for 1,000 miles (1,609 km) up the Paraná River and the Paraguay River to Asunción (ah soon SYOHN), the capital of Paraguay.

B. Regions of the Southern Cone

Dramatic Contrasts As you learned in the Continental Handbook, the southern cone is the narrow, cone-shaped southern part of South America. This part of South America is a land of dramatic contrasts. Towering mountain peaks in the west descend into dry flatlands in the east. Humid rain forests are found in the northern section of the region. In the south, the rocky, barren tips of Chile and Argentina are only about 1,000 miles (1,609 km) from the frozen land of Antarctica.

The Andes The most prominent landform in the southern cone is the Andes. Chile

212

and Argentina share this mountain range for more than 2,000 miles (3,218 km). The Andes spread across the northern part of Chile and Bolivia. Toward the south they narrow into a spine of high peaks. Mount Aconcagua (ah kawn KAH gwuh) in Chile, is the tallest peak along this spine and the highest mountain in the Western Hemisphere. It is 22,831 feet (6,959 m) high.

Isolated Chile The Andes cut Chile off from the rest of the southern cone nations. This western coastal land includes incredibly dry deserts as well as productive farmlands. These farmlands depend on irrigation water from the rivers that flow out of the Andes to the Pacific Ocean.

A Shared Geography The landscape on the eastern side of the Andes is made up mainly of plains and plateaus. The three largest regions are the Gran Chaco, the Pampas, and Patagonia.

As you read in the last chapter, the Chaco is the large semiarid land that extends eastward from the Andes in Bolivia. The Chaco covers northern Argentina and western Paraguay. Most of the Chaco is too dry for farming, but cattle and sheep can graze on the grasses that grow in this region.

The Pampas The Pampas is a large, grassy plain that covers the part of Argentina around Buenos Aires and extends north into Uruguay, Paraguay, and Brazil.

The Pampas makes up one of the richest farming and cattle-raising areas in all of South America. It forms the economic heartland of Argentina. Most of Argentina's industry is in the Pampas, and about two thirds of Argentina's people live there. All of Uruguay is in the Pampas, but the land there is hillier than in most of the Argentine Pampas.

The Pampas, like the Great Plains of the United States, was once open range. Open range is land that has no fences, so cattle can wander freely to find grass to graze on. Gauchos, the legendary cowboys of Argentina, herded the cattle.

Patagonia The southern third of Argentina forms a large region called Patagonia. It is a cold, dry, treeless plateau that stretches south along the eastern side of the Andes to the island of Tierra del Fuego (tee ER uh del FWAY goh), at the far southern tip of South America. Because it is so cold and dry, few people live there. Most of this grass-covered land is used to graze sheep.

C. Europeans and Mestizos in the Southern Cone

During the late nineteenth and early twentieth centuries, thousands of Europeans immigrated to Argentina. These immigrants came to take advantage of the land available for farms in the Pampas. Most of the immigrants came from Spain and Italy, but there were also people from England, Ireland, Germany, and many other European countries. Because of the large number of immigrants, the people of Argentina today are mainly European.

Gauchos are still found herding cattle on the Pampas of the southern cone countries.
▶ Describe the gaucho's clothing.

213

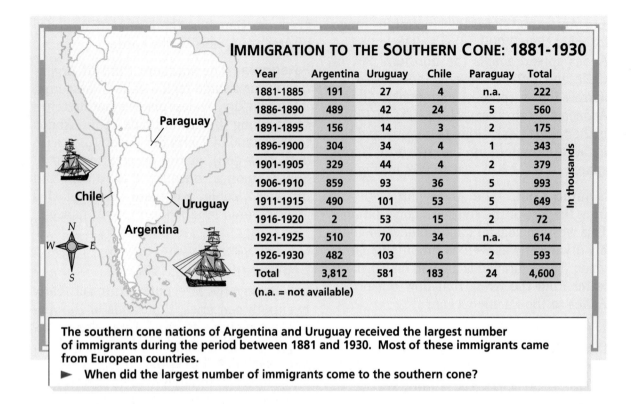

IMMIGRATION TO THE SOUTHERN CONE: 1881-1930

Year	Argentina	Uruguay	Chile	Paraguay	Total
1881-1885	191	27	4	n.a.	222
1886-1890	489	42	24	5	560
1891-1895	156	14	3	2	175
1896-1900	304	34	4	1	343
1901-1905	329	44	4	2	379
1906-1910	859	93	36	5	993
1911-1915	490	101	53	5	649
1916-1920	2	53	15	2	72
1921-1925	510	70	34	n.a.	614
1926-1930	482	103	6	2	593
Total	3,812	581	183	24	4,600

In thousands

(n.a. = not available)

The southern cone nations of Argentina and Uruguay received the largest number of immigrants during the period between 1881 and 1930. Most of these immigrants came from European countries.

► When did the largest number of immigrants come to the southern cone?

Most of the immigrants settled in Buenos Aires, the capital. Today, Buenos Aires, with a metropolitan area population of over 10 million, has about 35 percent of all the people who live in Argentina.

Like Argentina, Uruguay received many immigrants from Italy, Spain, and Germany. Uruguay's population is also mainly of European ancestry.

Paraguay is different from Argentina and Uruguay in an important way. Paraguay was the home of the Guaraní (gwah ruh NEE) Indians. These Indians eventually mixed with the small Spanish population, so that today Paraguay is a mestizo nation. The Guaraní language is still spoken by many people in Paraguay; in fact, Paraguay is the only truly bilingual nation in South America.

Chile is a mestizo country too, even though it received many immigrants from Europe during the last century. The number of Europeans, however, never was larger than the Indian population. That is why, today, about two thirds of Chile's people are mestizo. Another one third are European.

LESSON 1

Review

REVIEWING MAIN IDEAS

A. How do rivers connect Argentina, Paraguay, and Uruguay?

B. What region is shared by Argentina, Paraguay, and Uruguay?

C. Why are Paraguay's and Chile's populations different from Argentina's and Uruguay's?

SKILLS CHECK

MAP SKILL

Turn to the map on page 212. Find the elevations of the four capital cities of the southern cone.

Argentina and the Pampas

CONNECTIONS

In Chapter 4, you learned about the products of the Great Plains. What are some of the products and industries you might expect to find on Argentina's plains?

TERMS

tannin, rain shadow

FOCUS

Why is the Pampas the most important region in Argentina?

A. Argentina's Heartland

Immense Plains To the Spanish settlers who saw them for the first time, the Pampas looked like an immense sea of grass. For miles, as far as they could see, there was nothing but the tops of green, lush grasses moving slowly back and forth in the wind.

Four hundred years later, it is still possible to see endless grasslands. But in most of the Pampas, there are now also groves of trees, huge fields of wheat and corn, and, of course, large herds of cattle. The products of the Pampas—wheat, corn, and cattle—have long been central to Argentina's economy. They continue to be three of the country's largest exports.

Although it makes up only one fifth of Argentina's total area, the Pampas has been the most important region in the country. This region of warm, well-watered plains is the country's most intensively cultivated, or farmed, area. It is also the most densely populated part of Argentina. More than 70 percent of the Argentine people live in the cities, towns, and ranches of the Pampas.

Argentina's Urban Center Buenos Aires is the largest city in the Pampas and the largest city in Argentina. It is the country's political and industrial center.

Buenos Aires is nicknamed the Paris of South America. Many of the older buildings are based on French architecture, and there are sidewalk cafes like those found in Paris. Like Paris also, this is a city of buildings that contain the offices of banks, export companies, and thousands of different businesses. Subways rumble beneath the city, and cars, trucks, and buses clog the streets. At night, people go the city's opera house, theaters, restaurants, and cafes.

Trains loaded with cattle and grain from the Pampas roll into Buenos Aires warehouses along the Río de la Plata. At the docks, which are always busy, workers load beef and grain onto waiting freighters.

Ninth of July Avenue in Buenos Aires is one of the world's widest streets.
▶ How many lanes of traffic can you count in this street?

215

Córdoba Buenos Aires is not the only large city in the Pampas. Córdoba (KOR duh buh), the second largest city in Argentina, has a population of about 1.2 million. Córdoba is located on the western edge of the Pampas, about 400 miles (644 km) northwest of the capital. Many transportation industries, such as automobile and bus manufacturing, are located in Córdoba.

B. The Northwestern Region

A Dry Land Argentina's northwestern region includes the lands that stretch from the eastern part of the Andes. As in the Chaco, the land is dry and desertlike. However, rivers that flow out of the Andes provide water for crops and for people in the several large cities found in this region.

In the north it is warm enough for farmers to grow crops such as sugarcane and cotton. Farther south it is cooler in the winter. Here farmers grow vegetables, nuts, and fruits, including grapes.

Mendoza Mendoza is the most important city in the northwest. Grapes from the surrounding area are processed in the city's famous wineries. Mendoza is also an important industrial center. Hydroelectricity from dams on rivers in the nearby Andes, as well as oil from oilfields along the eastern side of the mountains, provide energy for the city's factories.

USES FOR CATTLE

FOOD PRODUCTS   NON-FOOD PRODUCTS

SOUR CREAM

YOGURT

BUTTER

MILK MILK

DOG

Cattle are used for both food and non-food products. Food products include meats and dairy products, made from milk. The main use for cattle around the world is as draft animals, which pull carts and plows.
▶ Name three of the food products and three of the non-food products.

THE RAIN SHADOW EFFECT

Moist Wind

Dry Wind

Moist air forced upward by a mountain falls as rain. The winds, now empty of moisture, create a dry climate on the opposite side of the mountain. The photo shows Patagonia, which is in the rain shadow of the Andes.
▶ Which side of the diagram is in the rain shadow?

C. The Chaco and Patagonia

The Chaco The Chaco covers northern Argentina. The more humid eastern parts of the Chaco are covered with trees, such as the quebracho (que BRAH choh) and the yerba mate (yer buh MAH te). The quebracho tree is valuable because it contains a chemical called **tannin**. Tannin is used to cure leather. The leaves of the yerba mate are used to make a drink similar to tea that is popular in the southern cone countries of Argentina, Paraguay, and Uruguay.

The Rain Shadow Patagonia, the southern part of Argentina, is a cold, dry, windswept region. Patagonia is dry because it is in the **rain shadow** of the Andes. The diagram on this page shows how mountains such as the Andes create the dry lands found in the rain shadow.

Sheep are herded on a few scattered ranches in Patagonia. The sheep are sheared for their wool, which is then exported.

LESSON 2

Review

REVIEWING MAIN IDEAS
A. Why is the Pampas called Argentina's heartland?
B. What crops are grown in Argentina's northwestern region?
C. How does the rain shadow affect Patagonia?

SKILLS CHECK
WRITING SKILL
Imagine that you are an airplane pilot flying over the Pampas. In a paragraph, describe what you see below you as you fly over the Pampas.

Uruguay and Paraguay

CONNECTIONS

What are some of the ways a landlocked country can import and export products?

TERMS

urban population, rural population

FOCUS

What are the main exports of Uruguay and Paraguay?

A. Uruguay: A Nation of Ranches

An Urban Population Uruguay is the second smallest independent country in South America; only Suriname is smaller. Its total area of 63,251 sq mi (163,820 sq km) makes it about the size of the state of Wisconsin.

Uruguay, like Argentina, has a large **urban population**. An urban population is one that is in or near cities or towns. Over 40 percent of the Uruguayan people live in one city: Montevideo, the capital. Another 50 percent live in the country's smaller cities and towns. The rest of the population lives on the farms and ranches found throughout the country. This is called the **rural population.**

Land for Grazing The fertile Pampas covers almost all of Uruguay. About 90 percent of the land is used to graze sheep and cattle. As in Argentina, most of Uruguay's land was once held in large estancias and worked by gauchos. The estancias have now been broken up into smaller ranches.

Uruguay's main exports are wool and woolen cloth, meat, and leather; all are products of the cattle and sheep industry. Only a small part of the Pampas is used to grow crops. Wheat is the main crop, and it is an important export. Because so much of the land is used for cattle and sheep

Uruguay provides free public education to all its citizens. Shown here is a university in Montevideo.
▶ What is a university?

218

ranching, Uruguay must import much of the food that it needs.

Few Mineral Resources Unlike most South American countries, Uruguay has few mineral resources. It has no coal, oil, or important minerals. Minerals for industries and for energy must be imported.

Developing the Economy At one time, most of Uruguay's exports went to European countries. Now, the most important markets for Uruguayan products are the neighboring countries of Brazil and Argentina. Uruguay hopes to take advantage of its location between these two large countries to develop manufactured products to sell to them.

B. Paraguay: Between Two Rivers

A Divided Nation Like Uruguay, Paraguay is a small country. Its total area of 157,043 sq mi (406,741 sq km) makes it about the size of California. If you look at the map on this page, you can see that the country is nearly cut in half by the Paraguay River. The eastern side of the river is a humid land covered by forests and grasslands. The area to the west of the river is covered by the dry Chaco grasslands and deserts.

Although western Paraguay contains almost 60 percent of the country's land, it has only a small part of the population. Almost all of Paraguay's people live in the eastern part of the country. The forest has been cleared for farmland, and there are also grasslands for grazing cattle. Asunción, the capital of Paraguay, is located on the east bank of the Paraguay River.

A Mystery Country Paraguay is one of the mystery countries of South America. Few people from other countries know much about this nation. In part, this is because Paraguay is landlocked. Most people and goods must enter the country by using the Paraná and Paraguay rivers.

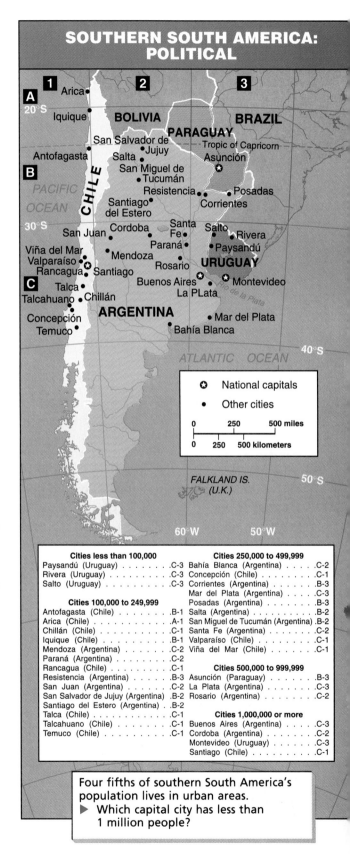

SOUTHERN SOUTH AMERICA: POLITICAL

Legend:
- ✪ National capitals
- • Other cities

Scale:
0 — 250 — 500 miles
0 — 250 — 500 kilometers

FALKLAND IS. (U.K.)

Cities less than 100,000	
Paysandú (Uruguay)	C-3
Rivera (Uruguay)	C-3
Salto (Uruguay)	C-3

Cities 100,000 to 249,999	
Antofagasta (Chile)	B-1
Arica (Chile)	A-1
Chillán (Chile)	C-1
Iquique (Chile)	B-1
Mendoza (Argentina)	C-2
Paraná (Argentina)	C-2
Rancagua (Chile)	C-1
Resistencia (Argentina)	B-3
San Juan (Argentina)	C-2
San Salvador de Jujuy (Argentina)	B-2
Santiago del Estero (Argentina)	B-2
Talca (Chile)	C-1
Talcahuano (Chile)	C-1
Temuco (Chile)	C-1

Cities 250,000 to 499,999	
Bahía Blanca (Argentina)	C-2
Concepción (Chile)	C-1
Corrientes (Argentina)	B-3
Mar del Plata (Argentina)	C-3
Posadas (Argentina)	B-3
Salta (Argentina)	B-2
San Miguel de Tucumán (Argentina)	B-2
Santa Fe (Argentina)	C-2
Valparaíso (Chile)	C-1
Viña del Mar (Chile)	C-1

Cities 500,000 to 999,999	
Asunción (Paraguay)	B-3
La Plata (Argentina)	C-3
Rosario (Argentina)	C-2

Cities 1,000,000 or more	
Buenos Aires (Argentina)	C-3
Cordoba (Argentina)	C-2
Montevideo (Uruguay)	C-3
Santiago (Chile)	C-1

Four fifths of southern South America's population lives in urban areas.
▶ Which capital city has less than 1 million people?

219

The Itaipu Dam is one of the world's largest producers of hydroelectricity. It was built between 1975 and 1982.
▶ Which countries built the dam?

Paraguay's Rivers Paraguay's most valuable resource is its rivers. The two most important rivers are the Paraguay and the Paraná rivers.

Almost all of Paraguay's trade is along the Paraguay River. Goods and people travel by riverboats to and from Buenos Aires and other ports on the Río de la Plata. Recently, Paraguay's dependence on the river has decreased somewhat. An agreement with Brazil allows Paraguay to use the port of Paranaguá (pah rah nah GWAH) on Brazil's Atlantic coast to ship goods in and out. A highway connects the port with Asunción.

The Itaipu Dam Paraguay's other important river is the mighty Paraná, which forms Paraguay's border with Argentina and Brazil. The Paraná has great hydroelectric potential. However, since Paraguay shares the Paraná River in different locations with Brazil and Argentina, these countries must agree to a project before it can be built.

The first of these projects was the Itaipu (ee TYE poo) Dam, which was built by Paraguay and Brazil. The Itaipu Dam is the world's largest dam. It is 600 feet (183 m) high and 5 miles (8 km) wide. The dam produces far more electricity than Paraguay can use, so most of Paraguay's share of the power is sold to Brazil, which needs additional electricity for its growing economy.

LESSON 3

Review

REVIEWING MAIN IDEAS
A. How is most of Uruguay's land used?
B. Why are rivers important to Paraguay?

SKILLS CHECK

MAP SKILL
Turn to the map on page 212. Name the rivers that form Argentina's borders with Uruguay and Paraguay.

Chile: The Coastal Nation

CONNECTIONS

Find Chile on the map on page 219. What are some of the advantages and disadvantages of having a long coastline?

TERMS

nitrate, commodity

FOCUS

What are Chile's three regions?

A. Chile's Three Regions

An Isolated Country On a map, Chile looks like a giant rope that has been stretched out its full length alongside the Andes. This long country extends more than 2,000 miles (3,218 km) along South America's coast. But its widest point is only 250 miles (402 km). It would take someone a week to drive

The Atacama Desert is one of the driest places on earth. Pictured above is an area of it called the "Valley of the Moon."
▶ How is this area like the moon?

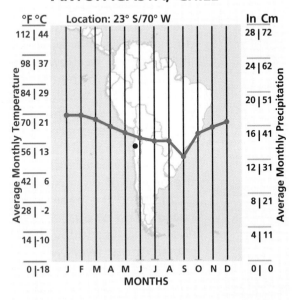

Climograph:
ANTOFAGASTA, CHILE

Location: 23° S/70° W

°F °C — Average Monthly Temperature
In Cm — Average Monthly Precipitation

°F	°C	In	Cm
112	44	28	72
98	37	24	62
84	29	20	51
70	21	16	41
56	13	12	31
42	6	8	21
28	-2	4	11
14	-10		
0	-18	0	0

MONTHS: J F M A M J J A S O N D

Although Antofagasta is on the Pacific coast of Chile, it receives less than 1 inch (2.54 cm) of rain per year.
▶ During which months does precipitation fall in Antofagasta?

the full length of Chile, but only about four and one half hours to cross it.

If you did cross Chile, you would discover two barriers on either side of the country. To the west are the cold, deep-blue waters of the Pacific Ocean. To the east are the snow-topped Andes. These two natural barriers have isolated Chile from the rest of South America.

The Atacama Desert Northern Chile is covered by the Atacama Desert. This desert, which is an extension of the desert in Peru, covers about one third of Chile. The Atacama Desert is one of the driest areas in the world; in some parts of the Atacama, not a drop of rain has ever been recorded!

In Peru, rivers flowing out of the Andes cross the coastal desert, allowing some farming. But there are no rivers in the Atacama Desert, so there is practically no farming. The few people who live in the

221

FROM:

The Green Continent

by German Arciniegas

Mighty rivers flow through much of the varied landscape of South America—through the world's largest rain forest, through vast, rolling grasslands, and even through a large desert region. In this selection, the Colombian author, German Arciniegas describes the important role these rivers have played in South America's history.

The map of South America seems to rest on a tree of rivers. There are rivers that shatter their waters against the mountain crags [cliffs], or run deep and quiet beneath the foliage of the jungle, or hurl themselves down in monstrous cataracts [falls], or spread out over the defenseless plains. Transparent rivers, red rivers, black rivers, honey-colored rivers. On the plains the valiant [bold] cut across them swimming; in the mountains the Indians cross them on swaying bridges of withes [twigs]. Along these rivers the conquistadors made their way, and at times they swallowed up whole armies in their seething [boiling], wool-like waters. They were the route that missionaries, scientists, and bandits followed; they have traced the profile of our history and formed the bewitched background of our legends. Whoever follows the course of our rivers will penetrate to the heart of our life, the depths of our valleys, our mountains aloof.

Santiago, located in central Chile, is known for its magnificent view of the Andes and its pleasant climate.
▶ Why is central Chile the heart of the country?

Atacama are miners or residents of cities like Antofagasta and Arica. These are port cities from which minerals that have been mined in the Atacama are loaded on ocean-going ships for export.

Central Chile About 75 percent of Chile's people live in central Chile. This is the heart of the country. Santiago, the capital city, is a metropolitan area of nearly 5 million. It is nestled in a broad valley at the foot of the Andes. On a clear day, the snowy peaks can be seen from the city.

The valley where Santiago is located has rich soils, mild temperatures, and enough rainfall to grow a variety of crops. It is one of the best farming areas in all of the continent of South America.

Southern Chile Along the coast of southern Chile are many islands, and large and small inlets of the sea. Much of this region has forests and a cool, rainy climate. Near the southern tip of this region, however, it becomes much colder. Here glaciers from the mountains reach clear to the sea, dropping icebergs into the waters of the Pacific Ocean. Few people live in this cold, forbidding land.

B. Chile's Productive Farms

As you have read, Chile's richest farmland is in the central region of the country. Farms here grow wheat, olives, vegetables, and a variety of fruits, such as apples, pears, and peaches. This area is also known for its grapes and for the wines that are produced from them.

Some Chilean farms now produce fruit and vegetables for export. If you go to a grocery store in the United States in the winter, you may find grapes, peaches, and other fruit and vegetables that have been imported from Chile.

The emphasis on exporting food has

Over half of the copper mined in Chile comes from this open pit copper mine at Chuquicamata.
▶ What is an open pit mine?

are found in the Atacama Desert. Large mines in the Atacama produced nitrates that were exported to Europe and many other parts of the world. About 70 years ago, however, scientists found a way to produce nitrates inexpensively from chemicals. As a result, nitrates are now only a small part of Chile's mineral exports.

Depending on Copper Chile's main export today is copper. If you look at the chart below showing world copper production, you can see that Chile is the world's largest producer of copper. Chile also has the world's largest *open-pit* copper mine. An open-pit mine is a large hole or pit that has been dug to take the minerals from the ground.

Like many nations, Chile depends mainly on the export of one product. Depending on one **commodity** for export can cause problems for a country. A commodity

created a problem for Chile. This country must now import some kinds of food, such as wheat, that it once grew enough of to export to other countries.

C. A Mineral-Rich Country

Minerals for Industry The Andes in Chile have rich mineral deposits of copper and other metals. Chile also has large deposits of coal, petroleum, iron ore, and other minerals that are necessary for industry.

Chile is also a source of **nitrates**. Nitrates are minerals that can be used to make fertilizers, explosives, and other products. The largest deposits of Chile's nitrates

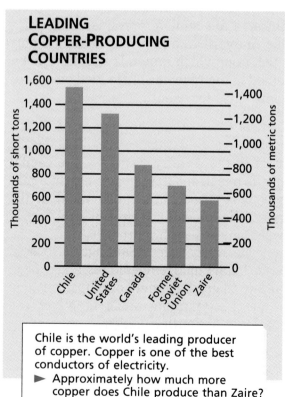

LEADING COPPER-PRODUCING COUNTRIES

Chile is the world's leading producer of copper. Copper is one of the best conductors of electricity.
▶ Approximately how much more copper does Chile produce than Zaire?

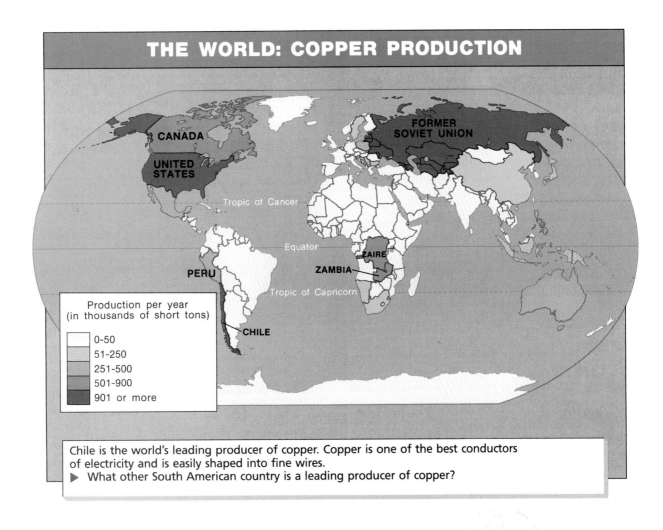

THE WORLD: COPPER PRODUCTION

CANADA

UNITED STATES

FORMER SOVIET UNION

Tropic of Cancer

Equator

ZAIRE

PERU

ZAMBIA

Tropic of Capricorn

CHILE

Production per year
(in thousands of short tons)

0-50
51-250
251-500
501-900
901 or more

Chile is the world's leading producer of copper. Copper is one of the best conductors of electricity and is easily shaped into fine wires.
► What other South American country is a leading producer of copper?

is a product that is bought or sold. One problem is that the price for which the commodity is sold at can go up or down very rapidly. For example, when the price of copper is high, Chile receives more money from its export sales and the copper mines produce more copper. But when the price of copper is low, as it was during the 1980s, the mines slow down production and the amount of money the government receives from the sale of copper decreases.

A country that exports a variety of products does not face the same problem. Even if a drop occurs in the price of one commodity, the country can still rely on its export of other commodities.

LESSON 4

Review

REVIEWING MAIN IDEAS

A. What are the climates in Chile's three regions?
B. Why does Chile need to import food?
C. Explain how depending on one export can cause problems in Chile's economy.

SKILLS CHECK

MAP SKILL

Look at the map on this page. What countries are the five leading producers of copper in the Western Hemisphere?

REVIEWING TERMS

On a separate sheet of paper, write the letter of the term that best matches each numbered statement.

a. estuary
b. confluence
c. urban population
d. nitrate
e. commodity

1. The people who live in or near cities or towns
2. A mineral that is used to make fertilizers, explosives, and other products
3. The mouth of a river into which ocean water flows, mixing freshwater and sea water
4. A product that is bought or sold
5. The joining together of two or more streams or rivers

REVIEWING THE FACTS

On a separate sheet of paper, answer the following questions in complete sentences.

1. What rivers make up the southern cone's most important transportation system?
2. What is the most prominent landform in the southern cone?
3. Why do so few people live in Patagonia?
4. How is the Pampas different today than when the Spanish explorers first saw it?
5. What are Uruguay's main exports?

6. What are the two languages spoken in Paraguay today?
7. How do the countries of Uruguay, Paraguay, and Brazil produce electricity?
8. What two natural barriers have isolated Chile from the rest of South America?
9. Where is Chile's richest farmland located?
10. What minerals do the Andes provide for Chile?

WRITING ABOUT GEOGRAPHY

Write a paragraph that explains why you would choose to live either in an urban area or in a rural area.

THINKING CRITICALLY

On a separate sheet of paper, answer the following questions in complete sentences.

1. What are the geographic features of the southern cone that cause it to be a land of striking contrast?
2. How would you explain the term *land-locked*?
3. Why does the Pampas form the economic heartland of Argentina?
4. Why do almost all of Paraguay's people live in the eastern part of the country?
5. What could Uruguay do to decrease the amount of food that it needs to import?

SUMMARIZING THE CHAPTER

On a separate sheet of paper, draw a graphic organizer that is like the one shown here. Copy the information from this graphic organizer to the one you have drawn. Next to the main idea for each lesson, write three statements that you think best support the main idea.

CHAPTER THEME

The southern cone countries of South America vary in size, economy, and environment.

Lesson 1 The lands and peoples of the southern cone countries are different from one another.

1. _____
2. _____
3. _____

Lesson 2 The Pampas is the most important region in Argentina.

1. _____
2. _____
3. _____

Lesson 3 Uruguay and Paraguay are developing their economies.

1. _____
2. _____
3. _____

BRAZIL

228

South America's Largest Country

CONNECTIONS

Like the United States, Brazil is a large country with many natural resources. What are some of the problems that a large country might encounter as it tries to use its resources?

TERMS

scrub forest

FOCUS

How is Brazil's population density related to the country's geography?

A. South America's Giant

The Easter Discovery It was the Wednesday of Easter week in the year A.D. 1500 when the men sighted land. The fleet of 12 ships had left Portugal a month and a half earlier on a voyage to India to buy spices and other valuable goods. Their trip was to take them around the continent of Africa on their way to India, but they had drifted far to the west—all the way across the Atlantic Ocean to this new land.

The commander of the fleet, Pedro Álvares Cabral (PAY droh AHL vuh rihsh kuh BRAHL), must have been surprised to hear the lookout shout that he had sighted land—a mountain. Cabral had some of the best maps available at the time, yet the land he had come upon was not on them.

Cabral claimed the new land for the king of Portugal. He named the mountain the lookout had seen Easter Mountain, because of the week during which it had been found.

Of course, when Pedro Álvares Cabral claimed this area for Portugal, he didn't know it was part of a continent. And he could not have dreamed that the land he claimed for Portugal would one day be the largest country in South America and the fifth-largest country in the world.

Cabral would have been amazed to learn that Brazil would grow to have a population of more than 160 million, making it the sixth most populated country in the world. And Cabral would have been truly astounded to learn that Brazil has the largest Portuguese-speaking population in the world—much larger than Cabral's homeland, Portugal.

Brazil's Landscapes With 3,284,426 square miles (8,506,663 sq km) of territory, Brazil is nearly the same size as the continental United States. But unlike the United States, which stretches across all of North America, Brazil does not extend across South America. Its only seacoast is on the Atlantic Ocean. To the west, vast rain forests mark the country's border with the Pacific coast nations of South America.

Although Brazil is a large country, its landscape does not vary tremendously. Most of the country has relatively low elevation; the only significant mountain range is no more than 9,000 feet (2,743 m) in height. As you can see from the map on page 230, this range of mountains extends along the eastern coast. To the north it flattens out into a broad plain along the Atlantic coast. To the south it descends gradually into grasslands like those found in Uruguay.

West of the mountains is the vast interior of Brazil. The largest area in the interior, the Amazon Basin, receives over 80 inches (203 cm) of rain a year. Much of the area is covered by rain forest.

The southern parts of the interior receive less rain and are covered mainly by grasslands and **scrub forest.** Scrub forest consists of trees that do not grow very high because of a dry climate. This drier region extends into an area of higher elevation that is called the Brazilian Highlands. You can find the highlands on the map on page 230. The slightly higher elevation makes this area cool, even though it is in the tropics.

▶ An evening view of Sugar Loaf Mountain in Rio de Janeiro

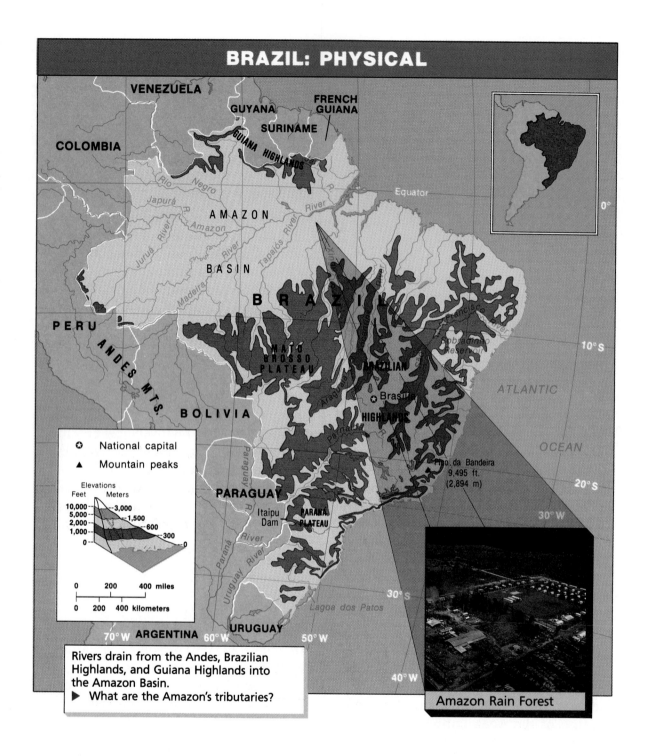

BRAZIL: PHYSICAL

VENEZUELA

GUYANA
FRENCH GUIANA
SURINAME

COLOMBIA

GUIANA HIGHLANDS

Rio Negro
Japurá
Equator
0°

AMAZON

Amazon River
Juruá River
Tapajós River

BASIN

B R A Z I L

Madeira

PERU

ANDES MTS.

MATO GROSSO PLATEAU

BRAZILIAN

Araguaia

São Francisco

Sobradinho Reservoir

10°S

BOLIVIA

Brasília

HIGHLANDS

ATLANTIC

Paraná

National capital

Mountain peaks

Elevations
Feet   Meters
10,000 -- 3,000
5,000 -- 1,500
2,000 -- 600
1,000 -- 300
0 -- 0

PARAGUAY

Paraguay River

Pico da Bandeira
9,495 ft.
(2,894 m)

OCEAN

20°S

Itaipu Dam

PARANÁ PLATEAU

30°W

0   200   400 miles
0   200   400 kilometers

Paraná River

Uruguay River

30°S

Lagoa dos Patos

40°W

70°W   ARGENTINA   60°W   URUGUAY   50°W

Rivers drain from the Andes, Brazilian Highlands, and Guiana Highlands into the Amazon Basin.
▶ What are the Amazon's tributaries?

Amazon Rain Forest

B. The Empty Interior, the Crowded Coast

The Amazon When people think of Brazil, they often think also of the Amazon River. The Amazon and the 500 rivers that flow into it form a huge web that drains the Amazon Basin. The Amazon slowly weaves through this basin for 4,000 miles (6,436 km) and into the Atlantic Ocean.

The Amazon is navigable for most of its length. But unlike the Mississippi River, the Amazon connects few major cities and prosperous farmlands. During most of its long, curving journey from the interior to the sea, the Amazon passes mainly through wilderness and scattered settlements.

For most of Brazil's history, the Amazon Basin and other parts of the interior passes have been only sparsely populated. In the last 30 to 40 years, Brazil's government has tried to encourage people to move into the empty center of their giant country. To do this, it built a new capital city, Brasília, south of the Amazon Basin in the interior in the 1960s.

The government has also built many roads into the interior. One of the largest road-building projects was the Trans-Amazon Highway. This highway connects coastal Brazil with the Peruvian border, in the far west. New dams are also being built on Brazil's many rivers. Electricity from the dams will be used to power new factories in the western and southern parts of the country.

The Atlantic Coast The map on page 235 shows that all of Brazil's large cities are located on the Atlantic coast. These coastal cities are Brazil's manufacturing and transportation centers. If you look at the map again, you can see that this is also Brazil's most populated region.

C. The People of Brazil

Brazil has the most diverse population of any country in South America. Indians, Africans, Europeans, and mulattoes all have descendants in Brazil. As you have learned, a mulatto is a person who has one white and one black parent. Immigrants from many countries have also come to Brazil. One of the largest groups of immigrants is the Japanese. There are also Italians, Germans, Syrians, Lebanese, and Russians.

Many of the people from Japan, as well as those from European countries,

These Indian huts have been built to form a central area in which village ceremonies can be held.
▶ Where do Brazil's Indians live?

settled in the southern highlands of Brazil, where the climate is cooler.

Only a few thousand Indians survive in Brazil; most of them live in the Amazon rain forests. Blacks and mulattoes live mainly in the northeast.

LESSON 1

Review

REVIEWING MAIN IDEAS

A. What vegetation dominates the Amazon Basin?
B. Why do the interior and coastal regions of Brazil have different population densities?
C. Why does Brazil have such a varied population?

SKILLS CHECK

MAP SKILL

Look at the map on page 230. What is the average elevation in most of the Amazon Basin?

The Regions of Brazil

CONNECTIONS

What are some of the obstacles you would have to deal with if you planned to build a city in the rain forests of Brazil's interior?

TERMS

gasohol, planned city

FOCUS

Which of Brazil's three regions is most important, and why?

A. The Wealthy Southeast

An Urban Region Brazil is an enormous country, but it can be easily divided into three regions: the southeast, the northeast, and the interior.

The southeastern region of Brazil includes the southern one third of the Brazilian coast and the lands that stretch inland from the coast. The southeast has the most industry, the largest cities, and the most productive farms in Brazil.

Five of Brazil's largest cities are in the southeast. The largest city in that region, and the largest city in Brazil, is São Paulo (soun POU loo). São Paulo's metropolitan area population is over 15 million people. After São Paulo, the largest and most important city in Brazil is Rio de Janeiro (REE oh day zhuh NER oh). Rio has nearly 10 million people. Another large city, Belo Horizonte, is also located in the southeast region.

Industry and Agriculture Brazil's lands hold the world's largest reserves of iron ore. The largest deposits are in the southeast. Factories in and near the region's large cities use the iron ore to produce steel, ships, cars and trucks, and many other goods. Other industries produce a variety of goods. Many are exported to other countries. For example, Brazil exports tires, shoes, and car parts to the United States; it exports automobiles to other countries

in South America and even to countries in Africa.

The southeast also has rich farmlands. Here, farmers grow corn, coffee, rice, oranges, and soybeans. Brazil is the world's largest coffee producer, and nearly all the crop is grown on the rich lands of the southeast. The southeast also includes extensive grasslands, where large herds of cattle graze.

B. The Northeast

A Wealthy Past The northeast is very different from the southeast. The map on page 235 shows that this region extends from French Guiana to the city of Fortaleza.

Most of the northeastern coast has a rainy, hot climate. Crops such as sugarcane and cacao grow especially well here. The Portuguese colonists took advantage of the climate and the region's fertile soils to

Brazil's growing industries include the manufacture of computers.
▶ What kind of training do you think might be required for this work?

PROCESSING SUGARCANE INTO REFINED SUGAR

1. The stalk of the sugarcane plant contains a large amount of sugary juice.

2. Before harvesting, the dried leaves of the plant are burned off.

3. Most of the harvesting is done by hand, using a large steel knife to cut the cane close to the ground.

4. Excess leaves and the top of the cane are cut off, and the cut cane is transported to the sugar mill.

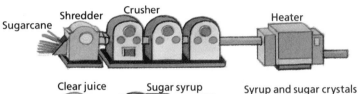

Sugarcane Shredder Crusher Heater

Clear juice Sugar syrup Syrup and sugar crystals

Clarifier Evaporator Vacuum pan Centrifuge Raw sugar

5. The stalks of the cut sugarcane are washed, shredded, and crushed into cane juice. This juice is then processed into yellowish-brown crystals, called raw sugar.

6. The raw sugar is shipped to a refinery to be made into white sugar.

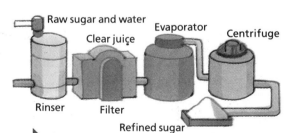

Raw sugar and water Evaporator Centrifuge
Clear juice
Rinser Filter
Refined sugar

7. Raw sugar is mixed with water and filtered until it becomes a clear liquid. This liquid is then evaporated into refined white sugar.

8. Packaged refined sugar is now ready for sale.

Sugarcane requires an immense amount of processing before it is ready for sale. Much of the initial work requires human labor. The actual processing of the cane juice into the refined, white sugar bought in grocery stores is a two-step process.
▶ What is the difference between raw sugar and refined sugar?

build huge sugarcane plantations. The sugarcane was harvested and processed into sugar, which was exported to Europe. The profits from the sale of sugarcane made the northeast Brazil's wealthiest region.

Today there are still massive fields of sugarcane in the northeast. But this region is no longer the wealthiest part of the country. Brazil has concentrated on exporting other commodities and no longer relies on sugarcane as an important export.

Sugarcane, however, continues to be an important crop in the northeast. Why? Because it is now used to produce **gasohol**. Gasohol is gasoline that has been mixed with alcohol that is made from sugarcane. It can then be used as a fuel for cars and trucks.

Brazil became interested in using gasohol because the country has only small deposits of petroleum. Instead of importing expensive petroleum, it found a way to make car motors run efficiently on the sugarcane-based gasohol. Thousands of Brazilian cars now fill up with gasohol.

An African Population Sugar helps to explain why such a large number of Africans live in the northeast. The Portuguese brought millions of African slaves to the northeast to work on the sugar plantations. The Africans brought with them many customs that are now a part of life in this region. For example, many of the foods of northeastern Brazil, such as palm oil, okra, and peanuts, originally came from Africa.

The Dry Northeast The inland areas of the northeast receive much less rain than does the coast. One part of the region is so dry that when the sky is cloudy, people greet each other with the expression ''What a beautiful day!''

In some years, such as those between 1981 and 1985, drought occurs. When that happens, the land dries up; even the rivers stop flowing. People living in the regions affected by drought usually migrate to cities

Sugarcane plantations continue to be an important part of Brazil's economy.
▶ What is one use of sugarcane?

and towns along the coast. Some travel to Rio de Janeiro or São Paulo, hoping to find work until rains come again to their region.

C. The Interior, Brazil's Frontier

Developing the Interior The interior region of Brazil represents about two thirds of the country. This vast land is made up of the Amazon Basin and a large area of forests and grasslands. As you learned in Lesson 1, for centuries few people lived in the interior except for the Indians. Today it is Brazil's most rapidly growing region.

Brasília In the 1950s, Brazil's government decided that it was time to settle the interior. One of its first steps was to move the capital city from Rio de Janeiro to a new site in the interior. This new **planned city** is called Brasília. A planned city is one that has been built according to a plan.

Brasília was designed in the shape of a giant airplane. Government buildings make up the body of the plane. On either side of the body, stretching out like wings, are rows of superblocks. A superblock is a large apartment building that houses several hundred families. Each superblock has a

BRAZIL: POLITICAL

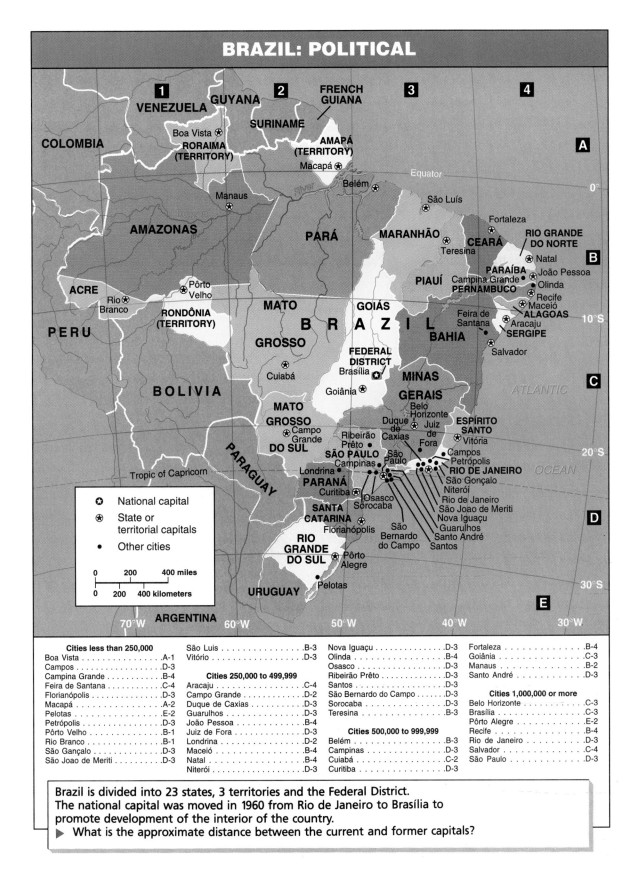

1 VENEZUELA GUYANA **2** FRENCH GUIANA **3** **4**

COLOMBIA
Boa Vista ⊛
RORAIMA (TERRITORY)
SURINAME
AMAPÁ (TERRITORY)
Macapá ⊛
A

Equator 0°

Belém
Manaus ⊛
São Luís ⊛
Fortaleza ⊛
RIO GRANDE DO NORTE
Natal ⊛
B

AMAZONAS PARÁ MARANHÃO CEARÁ
Teresina
PARAÍBA João Pessoa
Campina Grande • Olinda
PERNAMBUCO Recife
Maceió
ALAGOAS
SERGIPE Aracaju ⊛

ACRE Pôrto Velho ⊛
Rio ⊛ Branco
RONDÔNIA (TERRITORY)
MATO GOIÁS
PIAUÍ
Feira de Santana
10°S

PERU
B R A Z I L
GROSSO BAHIA
FEDERAL DISTRICT Brasília ⊛
Salvador
C ATLANTIC

BOLIVIA
Cuiabá ⊛
Goiânia ⊛
MINAS GERAIS
Belo Horizonte
MATO GROSSO Campo ⊛ Grande
DO SUL
Ribeirão Prêto •
Duque de Caxias Juiz de Fora
ESPÍRITO SANTO Vitória ⊛
Campos
Petrópolis
20°S OCEAN

PARAGUAY
Tropic of Capricorn
SÃO PAULO São Paulo
Campinas
Londrina •
PARANÁ
Curitiba ⊛
RIO DE JANEIRO
São Gonçalo
Niterói
Rio de Janeiro
São Joao de Meriti
Nova Iguaçu
D

Osasco
Sorocaba
SANTA CATARINA ⊛
Florianópolis
São Bernardo do Campo
Guarulhos
Santo André
Santos

RIO GRANDE DO SUL ⊛
Pôrto Alegre
Pelotas
30°S
E

URUGUAY

Legend
- ⊛ National capital
- ⊛ State or territorial capitals
- • Other cities

0   200   400 miles
0   200   400 kilometers

70°W ARGENTINA 60°W 50°W 40°W 30°W

Cities less than 250,000		
Boa Vista	. . . .	A-1
Campos	. . . .	D-3
Campina Grande	. . . .	B-4
Feira de Santana	. . . .	C-4
Florianópolis	. . . .	D-3
Macapá	. . . .	A-2
Pelotas	. . . .	E-2
Petrópolis	. . . .	D-3
Pôrto Velho	. . . .	B-1
Rio Branco	. . . .	B-1
São Gançalo	. . . .	D-3
São Joao de Meriti	. . . .	D-3

São Luis	. . . .	B-3
Vitório	. . . .	D-3

Cities 250,000 to 499,999

Aracaju	. . . .	C-4
Campo Grande	. . . .	D-2
Duque de Caxias	. . . .	D-3
Guarulhos	. . . .	D-3
João Pessoa	. . . .	B-4
Juiz de Fora	. . . .	D-3
Londrina	. . . .	D-2
Maceió	. . . .	B-4
Natal	. . . .	B-4
Niterói	. . . .	D-3

Nova Iguaçu	. . . .	D-3
Olinda	. . . .	B-4
Osasco	. . . .	D-3
Ribeirão Prêto	. . . .	D-3
Santos	. . . .	D-3
São Bernardo do Campo	. . . . . .	D-3
Sorocaba	. . . .	D-3
Teresina	. . . .	B-3

Cities 500,000 to 999,999

Belém	. . . .	B-3
Campinas	. . . .	D-3
Cuiabá	. . . .	C-2
Curitiba	. . . .	D-3

Fortaleza	. . . .	B-4
Goiânia	. . . .	C-3
Manaus	. . . .	B-2
Santo André	. . . .	D-3

Cities 1,000,000 or more

Belo Horizonte	. . . .	C-3
Brasília	. . . .	C-3
Pôrto Alegre	. . . .	E-2
Recife	. . . .	B-4
Rio de Janeiro	. . . .	D-3
Salvador	. . . .	C-4
São Paulo	. . . .	D-3

Brazil is divided into 23 states, 3 territories and the Federal District. The national capital was moved in 1960 from Rio de Janeiro to Brasília to promote development of the interior of the country.
▶ What is the approximate distance between the current and former capitals?

Brasília is noted for its modern architecture. The Chamber of Deputies meets in the bowl-shaped structure, and the Senate meets in the domed building.
▶ Why was the capital moved to Brasília?

school, a supermarket, a playground, a health clinic, and even a swimming pool.

Environmental Problems The interior region is now crisscrossed by a network of new highways and roads. Hydroelectric projects, mines, and factories now exist where only a short time ago there was nothing but forest. Thousands of people have moved to the interior to begin new lives as farmers and ranchers.

Rapid growth in the interior has brought with it many problems. One of the biggest problems is the change that is happening to Indians who live in the interior. Many lived much as they had for thousands of years. They hunted animals and cleared small patches of forest to grow crops. The building of new roads and the construction of dams has forced many Indians to move from their traditional homelands. The government has given them reservations to live on, but they dislike moving from their homes and changing their old ways of life.

Another problem is the rapid deforestation of the Amazon rain forest. The Amazon Basin has the largest area of rain forest in the world. It covers an area of about 1 million square miles (2.6 million sq km). This is equal to almost one third of the area of the United States. The forest is an important source of plants that might be useful for making medicines or for other uses. Also, many rare and unique animals live in the rain forest. Scientists are concerned that they will never be able to explore and use the valuable plants and animals of the rain forest if development continues so quickly. You can explore the problems of the destruction of the Amazon rain forest in the Global Issues feature at the end of this chapter.

LESSON 2

Review

REVIEWING MAIN IDEAS
A. Why is the southeast Brazil's wealthiest region?
B. How has the use of sugarcane changed in the northeast?
C. What changes are occurring in Brazil's interior?

SKILLS CHECK
WRITING SKILL

Imagine that you and your family have just moved to an undeveloped area of the interior of Brazil. In a paragraph, describe what it is like to be living in an area without running water, hospitals, roads, or schools.

Brazil's Growing Economy

CONNECTIONS

Brazil is a nation with an enormous supply of natural resources. What are some of the ways in which a country can develop its resources?

TERMS

foreign debt

FOCUS

How has Brazil developed its economy?

A. South America's Industrial Center

An Economic Power You know that Brazil is the largest country in South America. But did you know that Brazil is South America's largest industrial power? Only 50 years ago most people would have been surprised to learn that Brazil had become such an important economic power.

Brazil's government has worked hard to develop the country's resources and turn Brazil into an industrial power. It did this by pouring money into new industries. As a result, Brazil's economy has grown enormously, and the country no longer depends on the export of agricultural commodities for much of its export income.

Since the 1960s, Brazil has transformed itself. Once it was an importer of steel, heavy machinery, petrochemicals, weapons, and many other industrial products. Now it makes these same products and exports many of them. Today you might see Brazilian-made airplanes flying between cities in the United States. Brazilian computers are used by the Chinese government and by businesses in China.

Foreign Debt Brazil's remarkable economic growth has not been without problems. The biggest problem is the huge **foreign debt**. Foreign debt is money a government owes to banks in another country. When Brazil's government decided to develop new industries, it needed money to build them. Since it did not have enough money, the government borrowed large amounts from banks in the United States and other countries.

Unfortunately, Brazil has been unable to pay back the loans. Money that is earned from the export of goods must be used to pay off the loans, which now total more than $44 billion. This has made it extremely difficult for Brazil to continue to develop its economy.

B. Brazil's Busy Cities

The Economic Triangle Almost all of Brazil's industries are located in three cities: São Paulo, Rio de Janeiro, and Belo Horizonte. As you learned in Lesson 2, these cities are located in the southeastern region. Because they could be connected by lines on a map to form a triangle and because they have so much industry, these

São Paulo has grown to become Brazil's largest and busiest city.
▶ How would you describe São Paulo from this photograph?

GROWING UP IN BRAZIL

Heitor is a 12-year-old boy who lives with his mother and father and five brothers and sisters in the city of Salvador. Salvador was the capital of Brazil for over 200 years. It is still one of the country's most beautiful places. The city is located north of Rio de Janeiro on a narrow stretch of land between the Atlantic Ocean and a bay named All Saints Bay. Many tourists visit Salvador to see the churches, forts, and other old buildings that were built while the city was Brazil's capital.

Heitor's father works in the port loading and unloading ships. Heitor's mother sells vegetables in the city's marketplace. Like many people in Brazil, Heitor's parents barely make enough money to pay for food and housing.

Heitor attends school, but many of his friends do not. Like many other poor Brazilians, their families cannot afford school supplies for their children.

Every day after school, Heitor goes to the beach near his house to help the fishers mend their nets. The fishers go out daily in their small boats called *jangadas* (jan GA das). These boats are made of logs or boards that are tied together with rope or nailed. They have big triangle-shaped sails that help them move over the waves. Jangadas are hardly any bigger than surf boards with sails, and fishers sometimes drown when their tiny crafts are upset by large waves.

Heitor helps the sailors drag their jangadas up onto the beach when they come back with their catch of fish. At the end of the day Heitor likes to buy cooked fish or fruit from one of the Bahians on the street. Bahians are women who set up little stands on the streets to sell food to people who pass by.

When he is not at the beach, Heitor likes to go to the market in the lower part of Salvador where his mother works. Sometimes he takes the elevator that carries people from the lower part of town to the higher part, which is about 230 feet (70 m) above the market. The higher part of the city contains many of Salvador's older buildings. This part of the city looks much as it did two centuries ago. Great efforts have been put into preserving this historical section of Salvador.

Heitor also likes to practice *capoeira* (kah poo E rah) dancing with his friends in the streets. Capoeira began as a form of karate that was brought to Brazil from Africa by slaves. The fighting gradually changed into a kind of dance that men and boys do to the beat of drums.

cities are called Brazil's economic triangle. If you look at the map on page 235, you can also see that these are the three most populated cities in Brazil.

São Paulo In population, São Paulo towers above all the other cities in Brazil. Its metropolitan area population of over 15 million makes it the largest city in Brazil and one of the largest cities in the world.

Skyscrapers crowd the city's center and spread out in almost every direction. At lunch time, businesspeople pour out into the streets to eat in small restaurants or browse in the city's fashionable shops. Cars, trucks, and buses honk their horns continuously as they slowly move through the city's crowded streets.

São Paulo's enormous size is partly the result of its location near the productive farmlands and mines of the southeast. Trucks and trains carry coffee and soybeans harvested from huge plantations to the city's port at Santos. They also carry tons of oranges to processing plants in the city. The plants squeeze the oranges to make orange juice concentrate. The concentrate is then loaded onto specially designed freighters. The orange juice you drank this morning might have come from Brazil, since the United States is the largest importer of Brazilian orange juice concentrate.

Hydroelectricity generated from nearby rivers and from the Itaipu Dam powers São Paulo's many factories. Steel, motor vehicles, tools, and a wide range of textiles, household appliances, and other consumer goods are produced in these factories.

Rio No more than 200 miles (322 km) north of São Paulo is Brazil's second most important city. Rio de Janeiro—or Rio, as it is usually called—is often said to be one of the world's most beautiful cities. The warm crystal-blue waters of the Atlantic Ocean and the brilliant white sandy beaches have made this city a top vacation spot.

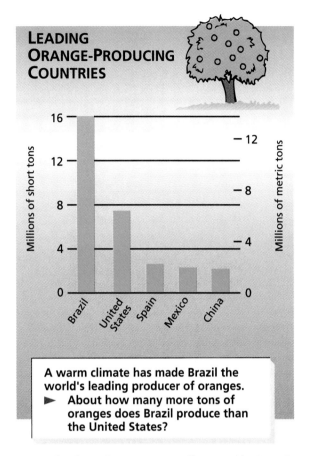

LEADING ORANGE-PRODUCING COUNTRIES

Millions of short tons

Millions of metric tons

Brazil, United States, Spain, Mexico, China

A warm climate has made Brazil the world's leading producer of oranges.
► About how many more tons of oranges does Brazil produce than the United States?

The beaches are usually crowded with thousands of sunbathers. Behind the beaches and sunbathers stretch miles of apartment buildings. And behind the buildings are the towering skyscrapers that show Rio to be an important business center.

This huge city spreads up and down the valleys formed by mountains that seem to slip right into the Atlantic. The valley sides are covered with the tin-roofed homes of the many poor people who live in Rio. The poor have come to the city hoping to find jobs that will give them a better life than did the farms they have abandoned in the interior.

Belo Horizonte The third city in the economic triangle, Belo Horizonte, is very different from Rio and São Paulo. Those two cities spread out in all directions. In their older sections, narrow streets glide crazily into one another, and shops and factories are found throughout the city.

Soccer is Brazil's most popular sport.
▶ What are some other countries where soccer is popular?

In Belo Horizonte the streets are wide. Each street has been carefully planned to follow the pattern of the streets in Washington, D.C. Government buildings, houses, and factories have also been built according to a plan. In fact, Belo Horizonte was Brazil's first planned city. Like Brasília, it was designed to draw people from the coastal regions into the country's interior.

The city has grown rapidly in the last 100 years. Steel is the major industry. The city's steel plants work continuously, turning the rich iron ore of the neighboring region into steel and steel products.

C. The Rural Settlements

Brazil's agriculture is a mixture of plantations, large family-owned farms, and small subsistence farms. The south is the most prosperous farming region in Brazil. As you have read, the huge farms in southern Brazil grow many crops such as soybeans and corn.

Along the coastal areas of the northeast, there are huge sugar and cacao plantations. Large cattle ranches are found inland. This part of the northeast also has many small subsistence farms.

The subsistence farmers in the northeast are poor. Most of the people here are unable to find a doctor when they are sick; most cannot read or write; and most do not get enough to eat. Roads are poor, and there are few if any telephones. The difficulty of rural life in the northeast is one reason why people continue to migrate to the cities on the eastern coast of Brazil.

The government continues to encourage people to move into rural Brazil. But because of its interest in developing new industries, the government has not had enough money to provide services in the newly opened lands. Improving the lives of the people in rural Brazil is one problem that the country needs to solve as it continues to grow.

LESSON 3

Review

REVIEWING MAIN IDEAS

A. Why does Brazil have a problem with foreign debt?
B. What are the major economic activities of the cities in the economic triangle?
C. What kinds of agriculture are found in Brazil?

SKILLS CHECK

THINKING SKILL

Write a paragraph that discusses some of the ways that the government can improve the lives of people who live in Brazil's rural areas.

THE VANISHING RAIN FOREST

In the vast interior of Brazil, huge fires burn night and day during the dry season. The thick, puffy gray clouds of smoke that drift upward mark one of the twentieth century's greatest environmental problems: the clearing of the Amazon rain forest.

The fires are set by ranchers and farmers, who have found this the quickest way to clear land for new farms and ranches. Lumber companies have also cut down large areas of forest. The logs are then sent to port cities and are exported.

The cutting and burning is having an enormous impact on the Amazon rain forest. Scientists estimate that the forest is being cleared at a rate of about 100 acres (40 ha) a minute. This means that an area the size of the state of Nebraska is stripped of trees every year. If this continues, the vast Amazon rain forest will be gone in about 20 years. And with it will disappear one of the earth's unique environmental treasures.

The Rain Forest Environment

Rain forests are found in the tropical lands of Asia, Africa, Oceania, South America, and North America. The Amazon rain forest of South America is the world's largest. This huge sea of trees covers over 2 million square miles (5 million sq km), an area equal to the United States west of the Mississippi River.

The rain forest is different from other kinds of forests. In the rain forest the giant trees grow so close together that their leaves and branches entangle one another. This mass of leaves and branches is called the rain forest's *canopy*. The canopy makes it difficult for sunlight to reach the forest floor, so few plants grow here.

The canopy is home to the rain forest's bird life. The air is alive with the sounds of hundreds of different kinds of birds whistling and chirping. The birds range in size from the giant red, blue, and yellow macaw—a kind of parrot—to the tiny hummingbird. The canopy is also home to many different kinds of monkeys and other animals, such as the sloth. This creature spends its life hanging upside

A worker sets fire to brush and trees in a section of the Amazon rain forest in Brazil.
▶ Why is the forest being burned?

RAIN FOREST CANOPY AND WILDLIFE

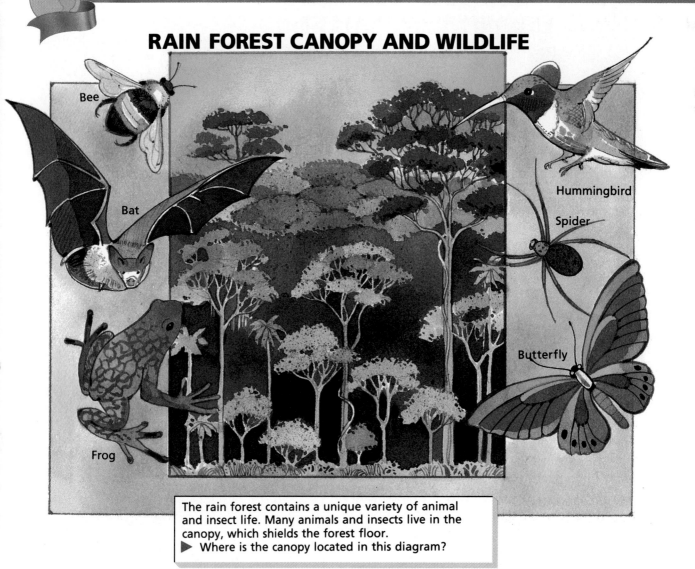

Bee

Bat

Hummingbird

Spider

Butterfly

Frog

The rain forest contains a unique variety of animal and insect life. Many animals and insects live in the canopy, which shields the forest floor.
▶ Where is the canopy located in this diagram?

down from the limbs of the giant rain forest trees.

A few large animals live on the rain forest floor. These include jaguars, tapirs, and giant anacondas. The anaconda is the world's largest snake. A huge variety of insects make up the largest population. The forest floor crawls with hundreds of thousands of different kinds of ants, termites, beetles, butterflies, flies, and mosquitoes. Large numbers of lizards, salamanders, frogs, toads, and alligators also live here.

An almost unbelievable variety of plants grow in the rain forest. Over 100

different kinds of trees may be found in a single acre. No one knows how many thousands of different trees and smaller plants grow nowhere in the world except in the Amazon rain forest.

The Amazon rain forest is valuable. Many of the plants discovered in the Amazon and other rain forests have important uses. The many different kinds of plants found here can be used for food and for insecticides, which are chemicals used to kill insects. Some plants are useful for medicines. In fact, one fourth of the medicines sold by prescription in the United States come from rain forest plants. Scientists believe that rain forest plants may contain chemicals that could cure cancer or prevent malaria. The rain forest may be more valuable standing than it is cut down.

Progress or Destruction?

The rumble of bulldozers pushing over trees and the roar of chain saws cutting timber are the sounds of progress to South American countries that have rain forests. This is especially true in Brazil. The Brazilian government has built roads, airports, dams and cities, and cleared millions of acres of rain forest. Many poor people without land have followed the new highways to claim former rain forest land for farming.

Large companies are also moving into the rain forest. About 25 years ago an American businessman named Daniel Ludwig bought a huge piece of land on the Jari River in northern Brazil. He hoped to clear the land of rain forest and grow a special kind of tree on the land to make wood pulp and paper. In what Ludwig called the Jari Project, workers cleared thousands of acres of rain forest and built a complete paper mill and power plant.

Other companies have cleared thousands of acres of forest to grow pasture grasses for cattle. Unfortunately, the soils of the rain forest are not very fertile. The grasses planted by the ranchers do not grow well in the rain forest soil, so within a few years the pastures have to be abandoned. Farmers face the same problem that ranchers face. Crops planted in the

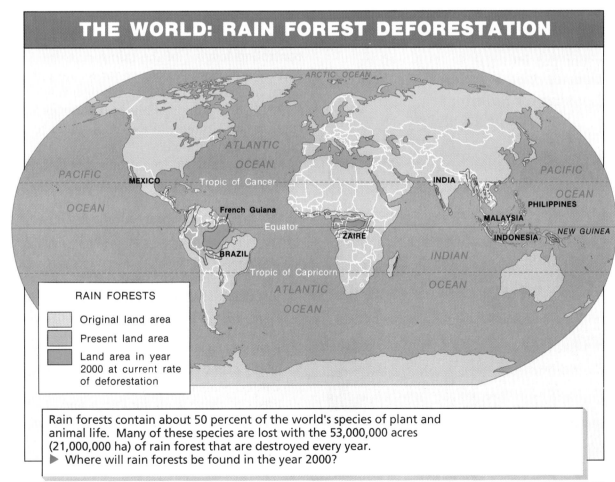

THE WORLD: RAIN FOREST DEFORESTATION

RAIN FORESTS

Original land area

Present land area

Land area in year 2000 at current rate of deforestation

Rain forests contain about 50 percent of the world's species of plant and animal life. Many of these species are lost with the 53,000,000 acres (21,000,000 ha) of rain forest that are destroyed every year.
▶ Where will rain forests be found in the year 2000?

cleared rain forest soil require expensive fertilizers to grow. This is why many poor farmers have given up on farming in the Amazon region.

A Global Problem

Why should people in other countries be concerned about the destruction of rain forest in the Amazon Basin? The answer is that the loss of the Amazon rain forest may cause worldwide changes.

The Amazon rain forest is thought to have a major influence on the world's climates. This is because the rain forest acts like a giant water pump. The roots of the trees suck in water from the rivers and soils. The leaves of the trees then release this water into the atmosphere as water vapor. Winds carry the water vapor around the world, where it falls as precipitation in the form of rain, snow, sleet, and hail. Clearing the forests would reduce the amount of water vapor put into the air, thus making climates drier.

Looking for Solutions

The Brazilian government has re-sponded to the world's criticisms of its development of the rain forest. Burning and deforestation has started to decrease because of changes in government policy. Farmers in some parts of the country are now fined for burning sections of forest. Landowners no longer have to pay a tax for leaving rain forest lands undeveloped.

The Brazilian government has also established a number of ecological stations throughout the Amazon rain forest. These stations include large areas of rain forest that cannot be cut down. Groups of scientists live at the stations, where they study and classify the plants, animals, and insects of the rain forest.

Other countries have taken action to protect their rain forests. Peru recently created a rain forest nature reserve that is the size of the state of Connecticut. Indonesia has banned the export of logs from its rain forest. Many countries have begun controlled logging of the rain forest. In controlled logging, areas of forest are cut down and then replanted with new trees. Controlled logging has allowed countries such as the United States and Canada to maintain their forests.

These changes do not mean that the deforestation of the rain forest is under control. They do mean that one of the earth's greatest environmental problems has become a subject of worldwide concern.

A vast section of the Brazil's rain forest was cleared to provide housing for the Jari Project workers.
▶ What was the Jari Project?

THINKING CRITICALLY

1. What are some of the ways the rain forest affects the global environment?
2. How could other countries help Brazil use its rain forests without destroying them?
3. Many other countries, including the United States, have deforested large areas of their lands for farms and ranches. Why should Brazil and other Amazonian countries not have the same right to develop their lands?

REVIEWING TERMS

On a separate sheet of paper, write the term that best completes each sentence.

> scrub forest
> gasohol
> planned city
> foreign debt

1. Brasília is a _____, or one that has been built according to a plan.
2. _____, gasoline mixed with alcohol that is made from sugarcane, is used in Brazil as fuel for cars and trucks.
3. A _____ is an area covered mainly by trees that do not grow very high because of a dry climate.
4. The money that a government owes to banks in another country is called _____.

REVIEWING THE FACTS

On a separate sheet of paper, answer the following questions.

1. Where are grasslands found in Brazil?
2. How is the Amazon River different from the Mississippi River?
3. Where are the major manufacturing and transportation centers of Brazil located?
4. What natural resource does Brazil have that allows it to produce steel, ships, cars and trucks, and many other goods?
5. Why do large numbers of blacks live in northeastern Brazil?
6. What problems are occurring as a result of rapid growth in the interior of Brazil?

7. What three cities form Brazil's economic triangle?
8. How has São Paulo's location helped it to become the largest city in Brazil?
9. How does the city of Belo Horizonte differ from the cities of Rio de Janeiro and São Paulo?
10. What crops are raised on the plantations and farms of Brazil?

WRITING ABOUT GEOGRAPHY

Plan a city. Write several paragraphs describing how your planned city would be organized. Tell where you would locate roads, industries, office buildings, homes, parks, and other features you think should be part of a city. Draw a map to accompany your description.

THINKING CRITICALLY

On a separate sheet of paper, answer the following questions in complete sentences.

1. How do the landscapes of Brazil differ from the landscapes of the United States?
2. Why, do you think, were the Amazon Basin and other parts of the interior of Brazil sparsely populated for so long?
3. What are some advantages to building a planned city?
4. How does the southeast region of Brazil differ from the northeast region?
5. What are some of the services the Brazilian government could provide to people who live in Brazil's poor rural areas?

SUMMARIZING THE CHAPTER

On a separate sheet of paper, draw a graphic organizer like the one shown here. Copy the information from this graphic organizer to the one you have drawn. Under the main idea for each lesson, write three statements that you think best support the main idea.

CHAPTER THEME

Brazil is a rapidly
developing nation with a
diverse population and many resources.

Lesson 1 Brazil's population density is related to its geography.

1. _____
2. _____
3. _____

Lesson 2 Brazil can be divided into three geographic regions.

1. _____
2. _____
3. _____

Lesson 3 Brazil has developed its economy in many ways.

1. _____
2. _____
3. _____

COOPERATIVE LEARNING

When travelers prepare for a visit to a foreign country, they may read guidebooks. Guidebooks describe the geography and interesting places of various regions. They also describe the customs of the people who live there. How would you go about writing a guidebook?

PROJECT

Each group will be assigned one of the countries discussed in Unit 3. Hold a group meeting to decide what information your guidebook will include. Be sure to share ideas and record group members' suggestions.

Divide tasks among group members. Depending on the number of students in the group and the information your guidebook will include, your group might divide tasks as follows.

● A mapmaker to make and label a map of the country

● An illustrator to draw pictures
● A book designer to make a cover and put the book together
● Researchers to locate information and share it with other members
● A writer to organize the information and write it in the guidebook

PRESENTATION AND REVIEW

After your group members have met and put all the information together, present your guidebook to the rest of the class. Work together to answer any questions the other students may have about the country your guidebook describes.

After your group has made its presentation, meet again to evaluate your project. How well did your group's members work together? How could your guidebook have been improved?

REMEMBER TO:
● Give your ideas.
● Listen to others' ideas.
● Plan your work with the group.
● Present your project.
● Discuss how your group worked.

SKILLBUILDER

UNDERSTANDING A HISTORICAL MAP

WHY DO I NEED THIS SKILL?

Based on their content, maps can be classified into different categories, such as political maps, physical maps, resource maps, population density maps, and historical maps. Historical maps help us understand things as they were or as they happened in the past.

LEARNING THE SKILL

The world map to the right was drawn by the Greek historian Herodotus in about 450 B.C. It is a historical map because it shows the world as it was known at that time. How much did the ancient Greeks and the people in other ancient civilizations know about the physical geography of the earth? You can find out by comparing Herodotus' map with the current world map on pages 688–689.

Herodotus' map is incomplete and inaccurate because it is based on the limited travel experiences of the people at that time. The contemporary map is complete and accurate. It is based on actual observations of the earth from airplanes and satellites.

Another type of historical map is one that shows something that happened long ago. The map on the next page shows the voyages made by Christopher Columbus about 2,000 years after Herodotus drew his map. As you can see, Columbus made four voyages between Spain and the New World. Columbus's four voyages took him to the Caribbean Islands and to the coasts of Central and South America.

Each of Columbus's voyages is marked with a different color line showing the route that Columbus traveled. The years in which each voyage took place are shown in the map key. By looking at the map, you can see that Columbus reached various islands of the Caribbean during his first two voyages. He reached Central America and South America during the later voyages.

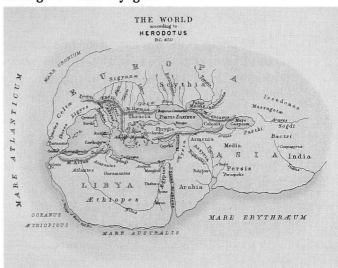

The Granger Collection

PRACTICING THE SKILL

Use the map showing Columbus's voyages to answer the following questions.

1. What was the first island that Columbus reached?
2. During which voyage did Columbus reach the coast of South America?
3. Use the scale on the map to calculate the distances Columbus sailed in each of his voyages. Which voyage was the longest?
4. In what year did Columbus visit the Cape Verde Islands?
5. From what port city did Columbus set sail in 1493?

248

Another explorer who reached South America was Sir Francis Drake, the first Englishman to sail around the world. In December 1577 he set sail from England for the easternmost coast of South America, to what is now the country of Brazil. From there Drake continued down the Atlantic coast of South America and around the southern tip of the continent. He sailed up the Pacific coasts of both South and North America until he reached an area just south of what is now San Francisco, California. Then he sailed west through the Pacific Ocean and Indian Ocean, around the southern tip of Africa, and north through the Atlantic. He arrived back in England in 1580.

Based on this information, you can make a historical map showing Francis Drake's voyage around the world. Trace a world map, such as the one found on pages 688–689 of this book, or get an outline map from your teacher. Use other maps in your book or in an atlas to find the places where Drake traveled and draw his route on your historical map. Then look in an encyclopedia or other reference book to find other historical maps showing Drake's voyage, and compare them with your map. How could you have made your map more accurate?

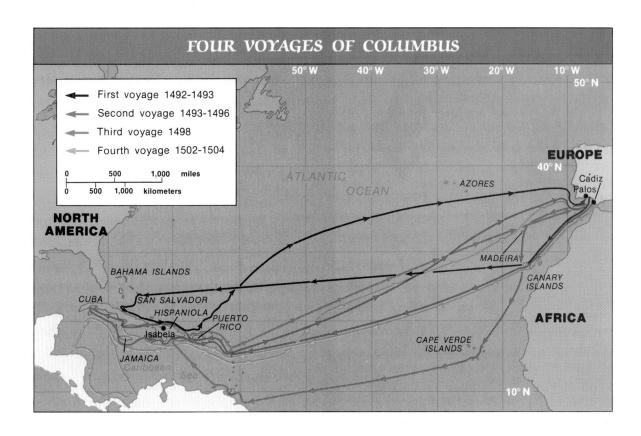

FOUR VOYAGES OF COLUMBUS

First voyage 1492-1493
Second voyage 1493-1496
Third voyage 1498
Fourth voyage 1502-1504

WRITING A SUMMARY

WHY DO I NEED THIS SKILL?

Lessons in your social studies book contain a tremendous amount of information. It is impossible to remember all of it, so you must be able to identify and remember the main ideas. One way to do this is to write a summary of each lesson. A *summary* is a short way of recording the important ideas of the lesson in your own words.

LEARNING THE SKILL

The lessons in your text are organized by main ideas. The lesson title tells the central subject. The sections within the lesson, beginning with the letters *A, B, C,* and so on, each tell about a main idea.

These main ideas can be used to help you write a summary for an entire lesson. To do this, you can construct a "summary ladder," like the one shown on the next page. Write the lesson title above the top step of the ladder. On each step of the ladder, write a heading that begins with a letter. Under the heading, write the important details that were included in that section of the lesson.

PRACTICING THE SKILL

Construct a summary ladder for Lesson 2 of Chapter 9, which is about Argentina and the Pampas. On a sheet of paper, copy the summary ladder shown on the next page. Then reread each section of the lesson, thinking about main ideas and details as you read. Write each section heading in sequence, on a step of the ladder. Then fill in the important details from each section.

As you reread and look for important details, ask yourself, "What are the major points in this section?" The boldface subheadings might help you identify important details. Remember to write the important details in your own words. Do not copy sentences directly from the book.

What are the important details in the first three paragraphs of section A, "Argentina's Heartland"?

Immense Plains   To the Spanish settlers who saw them for the first time, the Pampas looked like an immense sea of grass. For miles, as far as they could see, there was nothing but the tops of green, lush grasses moving slowly back and forth in the wind.

Four hundred years later, it is still possible to see endless grasslands. But in most of the Pampas, there are now also groves of trees, huge fields of wheat and corn, and, of course, large herds of cattle. The products of the Pampas—wheat, corn, and cattle—have long been central to Argentina's economy. They continue to be three of the country's largest exports.

Although it makes up only one fifth of Argentina's total area, the Pampas has been the most important region in

ARGENTINA AND THE PAMPAS

A. Argentina's Heartland

♦ Argentina's lush green plains, called the Pampas, are used to produce three important exports: cattle, corn, and wheat.

♦ Buenos Aires, the largest city in Argentina, is the country's political, commercial, and industrial center. It is nicknamed the Paris of South America.

♦ Córdoba, Argentina's second largest city, is also located in the Pampas. It supports many transportation industries.

B. The Northwestern Region

C. The Chaco and Patagonia

the country. This region of warm, well-watered plains is the country's most intensively cultivated, or farmed, area. It is also the most densely populated part of Argentina. More than 70 percent of the Argentine people live in the cities, towns, and ranches of the Pampas.

The important details in these paragraphs are shown in the summary ladder. The other important details in section A are about Buenos Aires, Argentina's major urban center, and Córdoba, Argentina's second largest city.

Complete the summary ladder by filling in the remaining headings and by writing important details for sections B and C in Lesson 2. Then construct summary ladders for Lessons 3 and 4 of Chapter 9.

APPLYING THE SKILL

Summary ladders can help you identify and remember the most important information in the lessons. You can use the ladders to help you prepare for tests and when you read and study textbooks in other subjects, such as science.

You can even use a summary ladder when writing a report. Complete your research and then organize your report by constructing a ladder. Then write your report, using the main ideas and important details from your ladder. Fill in additional details from the resources you collected when you did your research.

UNIT 4

EUROPE AND THE FORMER SOVIET UNION

CONTINENTAL HANDBOOK

TABLE OF COUNTRIES

CONNECTIONS

Study the map of Europe on page 255 to find two ways in which the continent of Europe is different from the continents of North America and South America.

TERMS

Eurasia

FOCUS

What natural features make agriculture and trade possible in Europe?

Gorbachev, Last Soviet Leader, Resigns; U.S. Recognizes Republics' Independence
By Francis X. Clines

MOSCOW, December 25, 1991— Mikhail S. Gorbachev, the trailblazer of the Soviet Union's retreat from the cold war and the spark for the democratic reforms that ended 70 years of Communist tyranny, told a weary, anxious nation tonight that he was resigning as President and closing out the union. . . .

Within hours of Mr. Gorbachev's resignation, Western and other nations began recognition of Russia and the other former republics.

A. A New Europe in the Making

The resignation of Mikhail Gorbachev (mee kah EEL gor buh CHAWF) and the division of the Soviet Union continued the dramatic changes in Europe which began in 1989. In that year, the Communists lost control of Eastern Europe, and new governments that were not tied to the Soviet Union came to power. Beginning early in 1990 the republics of the Soviet Union began to announce their desire for independence from Communist control. This desire became a reality as 15 independent nations were created from the former Soviet Union.

With the collapse of communism in Eastern Europe and the breakup of the Soviet Union, the division between the democracies of Western Europe and the Communist countries of Eastern Europe ceased to exist. A new spirit of cooperation has been growing between all the nations of Europe.

B. Defining the Boundaries of Europe

In Unit 1 you learned that most continents are separate landmasses surrounded by water, but Europe does not fit this description. It is difficult to see where Europe ends and Asia begins. In fact, Europe and Asia are sometimes considered to make up one giant landmass called **Eurasia.**

Oceans and seas clearly show where Europe ends in certain places. The map on page 255 can help you name two oceans that form Europe's boundaries.

The continent of Europe includes the European region of the former Soviet Union. The North European Plain is a low-lying fertile region that stretches across most of Europe.
▶ What is the average elevation of the North European Plain?

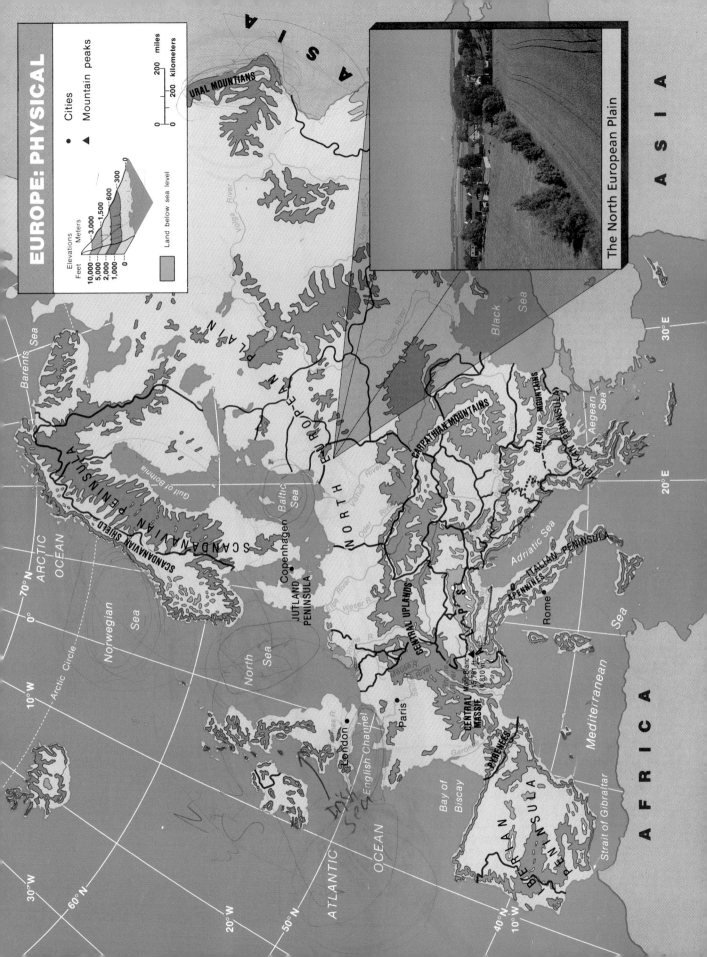

EUROPE: PHYSICAL

Cities •
Mountain peaks ▲

Elevations
Feet	Meters
10,000	3,000
5,000	1,500
2,000	600
1,000	300
0	0

Land below sea level

200 miles
200 kilometers

The North European Plain

ASIA

URAL MOUNTIANS

ASIA

AFRICA

Barents Sea

ARCTIC OCEAN

Arctic Circle

Norwegian Sea

ATLANTIC OCEAN

North Sea

Irish Sea

English Channel

Bay of Biscay

Strait of Gibraltar

Mediterranean Sea

Adriatic Sea

Aegean Sea

Black Sea

Baltic Sea

Gulf of Bothnia

SCANDINAVIAN PENINSULA

SCANDINAVIAN SHIELD

JUTLAND PENINSULA

NORTH EUROPEAN PLAIN

CARPATHIAN MOUNTAINS

BALKAN MOUNTAINS

BALKAN PENINSULA

ITALIAN PENINSULA

APENNINES

IBERIAN PENINSULA

PYRENEES

CENTRAL UPLANDS

CENTRAL MASSIF

ALPS

Mont Blanc 15,781 ft. (4,810 m)

Volga River

Dnieper River

Vistula River

Oder River

Elbe River

Weser R.

Rhine R.

Meuse R.

Seine River

Loire R.

Garonne

Rhône R.

Po R.

Danube River

Copenhagen

Paris

London

Rome

30°W
20°W
10°W
0°
10°E
20°E
30°E

70°N
60°N
50°N
40°N

Marking other edges of Europe are smaller bodies of water, such as the Mediterranean Sea, the North Sea, and the Baltic Sea. Along the southern edge of the Soviet Union, there are only two small bodies of water—the Black Sea and the Caspian Sea. The rest of this border does not have clear markers. Usually we say that the Ural Mountains separate the eastern edge of Europe from Asia.

C. The Population of Europe

Parts of Europe, such as northern Sweden and Norway, have few people. But Europe's entire population of 821 million people is large. This total population does not include the Soviet people who live east of the Ural Mountains. By comparison, North America has only about 453 million people.

Many places in Europe are crowded and have a high population density. For example, in the Netherlands the population density is 1,093 people per square mile (422 people per sq km). The Netherlands is 15 times as crowded as the United States. In the United States the average population density is 73 people per square mile (28 people per sq km).

Even though Europe has a high population density, most Europeans have a high standard of living. They have homes and jobs like those found in the United States. They have healthy diets and good schools and hospitals. How did Europeans achieve a high standard of living even though they have such crowded living conditions? One reason is that they have developed strong economic ties with other countries. Other reasons for Europe's wealth relate to the physical geography of the continent.

D. The Major Landforms and Economic Activities of Europe

Nature has given Europe warm or hot summers, mild winters, and plentiful rainfall for food crops. Europe also has flat land with rich soils. The largest area of flat land in Europe is the North European Plain, where the temperatures and rainfall are suitable for growing wheat, potatoes, and other vegetables. This vast plain stretches about 1,400 miles (2,253 km) across Europe from France to Russia.

On the map on page 255, you may also notice the Alps and other rugged areas in central Europe. High, snowy peaks are found throughout the Alps, but even in this mountainous area, there is land that can be used for farming. Wide, flat river valleys, like those made by the Po River and Danube River, cut through the Alps.

Review

REVIEWING MAIN IDEAS
A. What political changes have taken place in Europe since 1989?
B. Why is it difficult to determine where Europe ends and Asia begins?
C. What are some examples of Europeans' high standard of living?
D. What are the major landforms of Europe?

SKILLS CHECK

MAP SKILL
Use the Gazetteer to find an important fact about the following places. Write a sentence about each place.

Alps   Danube River   Ural Mountains

The many nations of Europe have different governments, languages, and tradition. The borders of these nations have changed many times in their history.
▶ What countries on this map border the Mediterranean Sea?

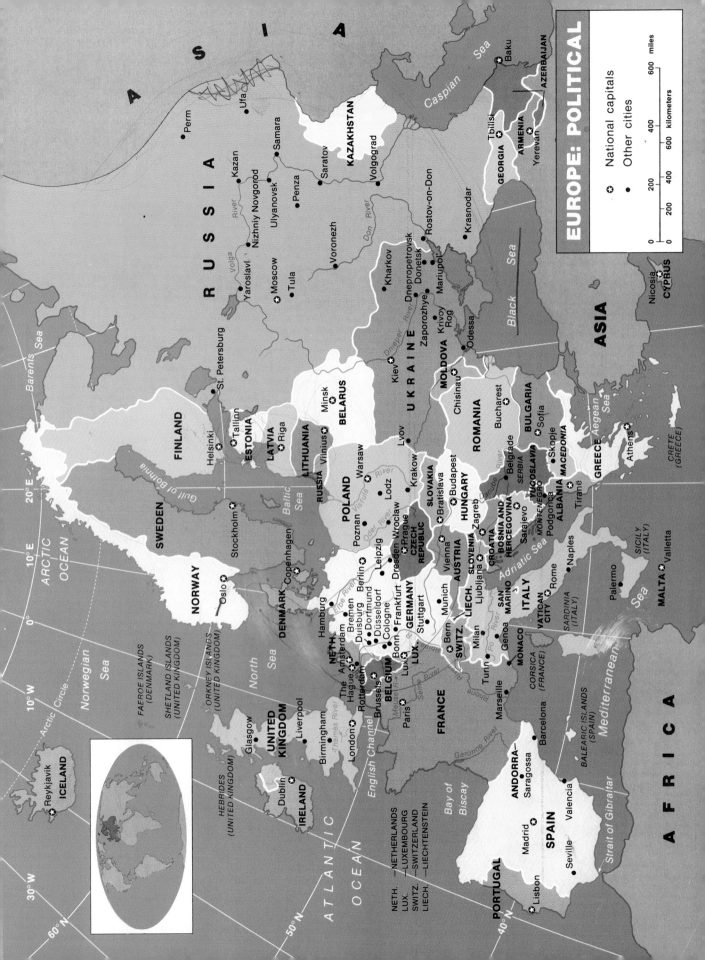

EUROPE: POLITICAL

⊗ National capitals
• Other cities

0 200 400 600 miles
0 200 400 600 kilometers

EUROPE &
THE FORMER SOVIET UNION

	FLAG AND PRINCIPAL LANGUAGE(S)	POPULATION AND LANDMASS	PRINCIPAL PRODUCTS EXPORT	IMPORT
ALBANIA 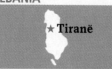 ★ Tiranë	Albanian	**POPULATION** 3,414,000 308 per sq mi/119 per sq km **LANDMASS** 11,100 sq mi/28,749 sq km	Crude Oil	Iron and Steel
ANDORRA  Andorra la Vella ★	Catalan, French, Spanish	**POPULATION** 66,000 367 per sq mi/142 per sq km **LANDMASS** 180 sq mi/466 sq km	N/A	N/A
AUSTRIA  Vienna ★	German, Serbo-Croatian, Magyar	**POPULATION** 7,987,000 247 per sq mi/95 per sq km **LANDMASS** 32,375 sq mi/83,851 sq km	Machinery	Chemicals
BELGIUM  Brussels ★	Dutch, French	**POPULATION** 10,082,000 856 per sq mi/331 per sq km **LANDMASS** 11,781 sq mi/30,513 sq km	Chemicals	Vehicles
BULGARIA  ★ Sofia	Bulgarian	**POPULATION** 8,775,000 205 per sq mi/79 per sq km **LANDMASS** 42,823 sq mi/110,912 sq km	Machinery	Machinery
CYPRUS  ★ Nicosia	Greek, Turkish, English	**POPULATION** 737,000 206 per sq mi/80 per sq km **LANDMASS** 3,572 sq mi/9,251 sq km	Clothing	Crude Oil
FORMER CZECHOSLOVAKIA*  ★ Prague	Czech, Slovak, Hungarian	**POPULATION** 15,800,000 320 per sq mi/ 124 per sq km **LANDMASS** 49,371 sq mi/127,871 sq km	Machinery	Machinery
DENMARK  Copenhagen	Danish	**POPULATION** 5,199,000 313 per sq mi/121 per sq km **LANDMASS** 16,629 sq mi/43,069 sq km	Food	Crude Oil
ESTONIA  ★ Tallinn	Estonian, Russian	**POPULATION** 1,600,000 92 per sq mi/36 per sq km **LANDMASS** 17,413 sq mi/45,082 sq km	N/A	N/A

TABLE OF COUNTRIES

* The dissolution of Czechoslovakia into the Czech Republic and Slovakia is discussed on page 345.

	FLAG AND PRINCIPAL LANGUAGE(S)	POPULATION AND LANDMASS	PRINCIPAL PRODUCTS EXPORT	IMPORT
FINLAND Helsinki	 Finnish, Swedish	**POPULATION** 5,085,000 39 per sq mi/15 per sq km **LANDMASS** 130,128 sq mi/337,032 sq km	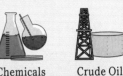 Paper	Crude Oil
FRANCE ★Paris	French	**POPULATION** 58,109,000 273 per sq mi/105 per sq km **LANDMASS** 212,918 sq mi/551,458 sq km	 Chemicals	Crude Oil
GERMANY ★Berlin	German	**POPULATION** 81,338,000 593 per sq mi/229 per sq km **LANDMASS** 137,162 sq mi/355,250 sq km	 Machinery	Machinery
GREECE ★Athens	Greek	**POPULATION** 10,648,000 209 per sq mi/81 per sq km **LANDMASS** 50,944 sq mi/131,945 sq km	 Fruits	Crude Oil
HUNGARY ★Budapest	Hungarian	**POPULATION** 10,319,000 287 per sq mi/111 per sq km **LANDMASS** 35,919 sq mi/93,030 sq km	 Machinery	Machinery
ICELAND  ★Reykjavik	Icelandic	**POPULATION** 266,000 7 per sq mi/3 per sq km **LANDMASS** 39,702 sq mi/102,828 sq km	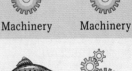 Fish	Machinery
IRELAND  ★Dublin	English, Irish (Gaelic)	**POPULATION** 3,550,000 133 per sq mi/51 per sq km **LANDMASS** 26,600 sq mi/68,894 sq km	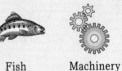 Machinery	Machinery
ITALY  ★Rome	Italian, German, French, Slovene	**POPULATION** 58,262,000 501 per sq mi/194 per sq km **LANDMASS** 116,313 sq mi/301,251 sq km	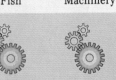 Machinery	Crude Oil
LATVIA  ★Riga	Latvian, Russian	**POPULATION** 2,763,000 109 per sq mi/42 per sq km **LANDMASS** 25,400 sq mi/65,786 sq km	N/A	N/A

EUROPE &
THE FORMER SOVIET UNION

TABLE OF COUNTRIES

	FLAG AND PRINCIPAL LANGUAGE(S)	POPULATION AND LANDMASS	PRINCIPAL PRODUCTS EXPORT	IMPORT
LIECHTENSTEIN  ★Vaduz	German	**POPULATION** 31,000 500 per sq mi/193 per sq km **LANDMASS** 62 sq mi/161 sq km	Machinery	N/A
LITHUANIA  Vilnius ★	Lithuanian, Russian	**POPULATION** 3,876,000 148 per sq mi/57 per sq km **LANDMASS** 26,173 sq mi/67,788 sq km	N/A	N/A
LUXEMBOURG Luxembourg ★	French, German, Letzburgesch	**POPULATION** 405,000 405 per sq mi/157 per sq km **LANDMASS** 999 sq mi/2,587 sq km	Steel	Crude Oil
MALTA ★Valletta	Maltese, English	**POPULATION** 370,000 3,033 per sq mi/1,171 per sq km **LANDMASS** 122 sq mi/316 sq km	Clothing	Machinery
MONACO  Monaco ★	French	**POPULATION** 32,000 43,836 per sq mi/16,932 per sq km **LANDMASS** 0.73 sq mi/2 sq km	N/A	N/A
NETHERLANDS Amsterdam ★	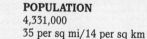 Dutch	**POPULATION** 15,453,000 1,093 per sq mi/422 per sq km **LANDMASS** 14,140 sq mi/36,623 sq km	Chemicals	Crude Oil
NORWAY ★Oslo	Norwegian, Lapp Dialect	**POPULATION** 4,331,000 35 per sq mi/14 per sq km **LANDMASS** 125,049 sq mi/323,877 sq km	Crude Oil	Machinery
POLAND  ★Warsaw	Polish	**POPULATION** 38,792,000 321 per sq mi/124 per sq km **LANDMASS** 120,756 sq mi/312,758 sq km	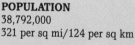 Machinery	Machinery
PORTUGAL ★Lisbon	Portuguese	**POPULATION** 10,562,000 299 per sq mi/115 per sq km **LANDMASS** 35,383 sq mi/91,642 sq km	Clothing	Crude Oil

	FLAG AND PRINCIPAL LANGUAGE(S)	POPULATION AND LANDMASS	PRINCIPAL PRODUCTS EXPORT	IMPORT
▶ **ROMANIA**  Bucharest ★	Romanian	**POPULATION** 23,198,000 253 per sq mi/98 per sq km **LANDMASS** 91,699 sq mi/237,500 sq km	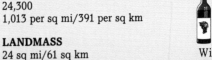 Machinery	Crude Oil
▶ **SAN MARINO**  ★ San Marino	Italian	**POPULATION** 24,300 1,013 per sq mi/391 per sq km **LANDMASS** 24 sq mi/61 sq km	Wine	N/A
▶ **FORMER SOVIET UNION** [1]  ★ Moscow	Russian	**POPULATION** 302,700,000 35 per sq mi/14 per sq km **LANDMASS** 8,649,512 sq mi/22,402,236 sq km	Crude Oil	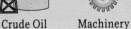 Machinery
▶ **SPAIN** ★ Madrid 	Spanish, Castilian, Basque	**POPULATION** 39,404,000 202 per sq mi/78 per sq km **LANDMASS** 194,881 sq mi/504,742 sq km	Vehicles	Crude Oil
▶ **SWEDEN** Stockholm	Swedish	**POPULATION** 8,822,000 51 per sq mi/19 per sq km **LANDMASS** 173,665 sq mi/449,792 sq km	Machinery	Machinery
▶ **SWITZERLAND** ★ Bern 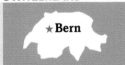	German, French, Italian	**POPULATION** 7,085,000 444 per sq mi/171 per sq km **LANDMASS** 15,941 sq mi/41,287 sq km	Chemicals	Chemicals
▶ **UNITED KINGDOM** ★ London 	English, Welsh, Scottish, Gaelic	**POPULATION** 58,295,000 616 per sq mi/238 per sq km **LANDMASS** 94,598 sq mi/245,009 sq km	Crude Oil	Electrical Machinery
▶ **VATICAN CITY** 	Italian, Latin	**POPULATION** 811 4,771 per sq mi/1,843 per sq km **LANDMASS** 0.17 sq mi/0.44 sq km	N/A	N/A
▶ **FORMER YUGOSLAVIA** [2] Belgrade ★	 Serbo-Croatian, Slovenian, Macedonian	**POPULATION** 23,200,000 235 per sq mi/91 per sq km **LANDMASS** 98,766 sq mi/255,804 sq km	Chemicals	Crude Oil

[1] See pp. 360–361 for the new nations created from the breakup of the former Soviet Union.
[2] See p. 349 for the new nations created from the breakup of the former Yugoslavia.

THE BRITISH ISLES AND SCANDINAVIA

Getting to Know the British Isles and Scandinavia

CONNECTIONS
Name an advantage and a disadvantage that an island country has over a country that is part of a large landmass.

TERMS
channel, maritime, Commonwealth of Nations

FOCUS
What are the similarities between the British Isles and Scandinavia?

A. A Region of Islands and Peninsulas

The Influence of the Sea For almost three centuries, Great Britain was one of the world's most powerful countries. This small island nation established colonies on almost all the world's continents. The sailors who sailed on the British ships that traveled between Great Britain and its colonies often chanted this poem.

> *Old England is our home, and Englishmen are we;*
> *Our tongue is known in every clime,*
> *Our flag in every sea.*

The location of the British Isles and Scandinavia is perfect for sailing, trading, and exploring, because the countries of this region are almost completely surrounded by seas and oceans. But these waters are often rough, making it difficult to travel through them. Yet the oceans and seas have given the people of this region the keys to build prosperous economies.

British Isles It might seem that the British Isles are the most important area in Europe, because we hear and read so much about them in our country. As you can see on the map on page 264, however, the British Isles have a small land area.

The islands that make up the British Isles do not all belong to the same country. There are two main islands. The larger one is named Great Britain, and the smaller island is named Ireland. There are also about 5,000 very small islands scattered around Great Britain and Ireland. The total area of the British Isles is about 94,598 square miles (245,009 sq km), which is about the size of New York, Pennsylvania, and West Virginia combined.

The larger island, Great Britain, includes the regions called England, Scotland, and Wales. Together with the part of the island of Ireland that is called Northern Ireland, they make up the country of the United Kingdom. The capital of the United Kingdom is London. The rest of the island of Ireland is an independent country called the Republic of Ireland, or Eire (ayr). The capital city of Ireland is Dublin.

In the late eighteenth century, Britain had the world's largest navy.
▶ What provided the ship's power?

▶ The Tower Bridge is a historical landmark on the Thames River in London, England.

40°W 70°N 30°W 20°E 30°E 40°E

ARCTIC
OCEAN   Barents
          Sea

20°W

Reykjavik ICELAND   10°W Arctic   0°   10°E   RUSSIA
                                Circle
                        Namsen River

60°N   Norwegian Sea

          FAEROE
          ISLANDS   NORWAY   FINLAND
          (DEN.)
ATLANTIC SHETLAND   Helsinki
          ISLANDS   ESTONIA
OCEAN   (U.K.)   ORKNEY   SCANDINAVIAN Stockholm
     HEBRIDES   ISLANDS   PENINSULA
     (U.K.)   (U.K.)   Oslo   SWEDEN
     Ben Nevis   LATVIA
          UNITED   Copenhagen
                      JUTLAND   LITHUANIA
     Dublin   PENINSULA   RUSSIA
                      KINGDOM   DENMARK
IRELAND   NETH.
     Irish Sea   POLAND
50°N   Thames
                     River   London
          English Channel BELGIUM GERMANY

          FRANCE

Elevations
Feet   Meters
5,000 1,500   0   200   400 miles
2,000   600   0   200   400 kilometers
1,000   300
   0   0   National capitals
                   ▲ Mountain peak

Geiranger Fjord, Norway

Peninsulas and islands are the major landforms in the British Isles and Scandinavia.
▶ What two countries are found on the Scandinavian Peninsula?

Scandinavia Scandinavia is a region made up of five countries. It includes the island nation of Iceland, as well as the peninsular countries of Norway, Sweden, Finland, and Denmark. If you look at the map above, you can see that Norway and Sweden share the Scandinavian Peninsula. Finland and Denmark are located on separate peninsulas. Sweden is the largest Scandinavian country, and Denmark is the smallest. Iceland is about 600 miles (965 km) from the Scandinavian Peninsula. The Norwegian Sea separates it from the peninsula.

B. Links Across the Sea

A Few Short Rivers Because the British Isles and Scandinavia are so dependent on the seas for trade and transportation, they are different from the European regions near them. Unlike the long rivers found in most of Europe, the rivers in the British Isles and Scandinavia are short. These rivers do not connect many different cities or regions, as do the rivers found elsewhere in Europe. For example, the Thames (temz) River in the United Kingdom links the city of London with the North Sea, which is about 40 miles (64 km) away. But the Thames does not connect London to any other major cities of the United Kingdom.

Transportation Routes The **channels**, or water passages, of the British Isles and Scandinavia are the main transportation routes for this region, and they are always busy with activity. The largest body of water in this region is the Atlantic Ocean. The part of the Atlantic Ocean called the North Sea surrounds the British Isles, the Scandinavian countries, and the mainland of Europe. The English Channel forms a narrow body of water separating the southern edge of the island of Great Britain from France. Farther to the east, the Baltic Sea separates the peninsular Scandinavian countries from Germany, Poland, Russia, and the Baltic nations.

Few people in the British Isles live more than 50 miles (80 km) from the sea.

In Scandinavia, most people live within 150 miles (240 km) of the coast. Because of their closeness to the sea, the British Isles and Scandinavia are known as **maritime** nations. Many people in these regions have become excellent sailors and navigators. As far back as the 900s, Scandinavian sailors traveled throughout the northern part of the Atlantic Ocean, exploring parts of Greenland and North America. Scandinavian sailors and traders brought to their lands many goods, ideas, and customs from other countries. And they introduced their languages and their culture throughout the British Isles and other lands bordering on the western edge of the Atlantic Ocean.

The British built the world's largest and most powerful navy in the 1700s, and they explored lands all over the earth's surface. British trading ships visited port cities in North America, South America, Africa, and Asia. The British established colonies on each of these continents. After

London is an important port city and the capital of the United Kingdom.
▶ What river links London with the North Sea?

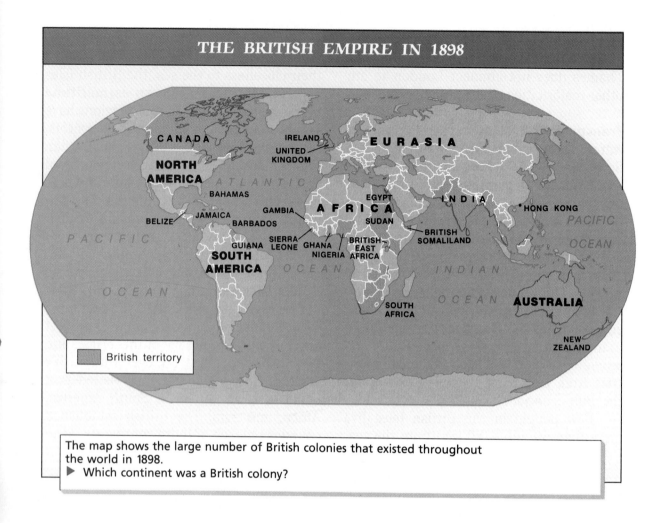

THE BRITISH EMPIRE IN 1898

British territory

The map shows the large number of British colonies that existed throughout the world in 1898.
▶ Which continent was a British colony?

World War II, many of these colonies became independent countries. The map above shows the borders of the countries that were created from the colonies. Canada is the largest of the former British colonies.

British leaders brought the new nations into a **Commonwealth of Nations**. The countries that belong to the Commonwealth help defend each other against attack. The member nations also have special tax and trade agreements that make it easier for the members to trade with one another. There are 48 member nations in the British Commonwealth.

C. Peaks, Plains, and Climate

The Kjølen and Pennines Rugged mountains rise from the peninsulas and islands of the British Isles and Scandinavia. The highest are the Kjølen (CHUHL un) Mountains in Norway. The Kjølen are about 8,000 feet (2,438 m) high. They are much higher and steeper than the Pennine Mountains, which form a spine from north to south through Great Britain.

The Pennine Mountains of Great Britain are only about 4,000 feet (1,219 m) high. The Pennines give this part of Great Britain a rugged and stark landscape, since they are practically bare. These mountains are covered with only a few trees. Few people live in or near the Pennine Mountain range.

If you could stand on the highest mountain peak in the Kjølen Mountains and looked toward the east or the south, you would see that the land slowly flattens and eventually becomes a plain in the southern tip of Sweden and all of Denmark. If you stood on a peak in the Pennine Mountains and looked toward the east, you would see something similar. Hills gradually give way to a flat plain that stretches out across southeastern Great Britain. If you had superhuman vision, you could look to the west and see the frozen peaks rising from Iceland.

Climate and Resources All of the British Isles and Scandinavia receive sufficient precipitation for agriculture and for growing pasture grasses. However, only the British Isles, the southern edge of Iceland, and the lowlands of the peninsular Scandinavian countries have the mild climate needed for agriculture. Farming and raising livestock are important economic activities in these southern areas.

Farmland is limited by the rugged mountain terrain. All of these countries need to import food. At the same time they export certain kinds of food that they have in abundance. For instance, fish account for two thirds of Iceland's exports. One fourth of Ireland's exports are meat and dairy products.

Temperatures are quite cold during most of the year in the north, especially in the lands near the Arctic Circle. In the coldest areas, only short grasses and mosses grow. The climate here is similar to that of Canada's tundra. Most of southern Sweden and Finland, however, is warmer, and evergreen trees, such as pines and firs, grow well. Forests have been important to the people of this region for centuries. In the British Isles, many forests have been cut down to make room for farms, towns, and industries. But in Scandinavia, extensive forests are still found. The forests have been a profitable resource for these countries. The lumber is used for construction and for making paper.

Logs harvested from Sweden's vast forests are floated down a river to a lumber mill.
► How are the logs moved on the river?

LESSON 1

Review

REVIEWING MAIN IDEAS
A. What are the two main islands that make up the British Isles?
B. Why are the waters around the British Isles and Scandinavia so important to these two regions?
C. Which areas of the British Isles and Scandinavia have mild climates?

SKILLS CHECK

THINKING SKILL

Use the Table of Countries on pages 258–261 to find the populations of the following countries. Make a bar graph showing the populations.

United Kingdom	**Norway**
Ireland	**Denmark**
Iceland	**Sweden**

The British Isles

CONNECTIONS

Look at the photographs in this lesson. Describe what you think the climate is like in the British Isles.

TERMS

peat, bog

FOCUS

How has the geography of the British Isles helped trade, industry, and agriculture develop?

A. Exploring the British Isles

Green Fields If you had to choose a color that best represents the British Isles, it would probably be green. This is the color of the meadows, trees, and grassy fields that cover the islands like green velvet blankets. This is why Ireland has often been called the "Emerald Isle."

Vegetation is lush and thick all year because rainshowers and fogs from the moist ocean winds seem to continue endlessly. Here is how the British author Charles Dickens described the fogginess of the British Isles.

Fog everywhere. Fog up the river, where it flows among the aits [river islands] and meadows; fog down the river . . . . Fog all around them . . . and hanging in the misty clouds.

The precipitation rarely turns into snow because temperatures are mild all year. Dublin's average temperature in January is about 41°F (5°C). This is slightly warmer than the temperature of Nashville, Tennessee, which is much farther south and closer to the Equator. The warm temperatures and frequent rainfall combine to make a very fertile area for growing corn, wheat, potatoes, and many other crops. Livestock graze on the green grasses in pastures like the one in western England pictured on this page.

North Atlantic Drift How can the British Isles be so warm in winter when they are farther from the Equator than the United States? If you look at the map on page 199, you can see where the North Atlantic Drift flows as an ocean current. It begins near the Equator in the warm waters of the Atlantic Ocean. It then moves toward the north. Along the east coast of the United States, it is called the Gulf Stream. This current brings warm water across the Atlantic Ocean all the way to the British Isles. It warms the air above, keeping the islands warm in winter.

You might think that the North Atlantic Drift would also make the summers hot, but that is not the case. During the summer, land heats up faster than water. This means that the ocean winds are cooler than the warm air above the land. Since the North Atlantic Drift is relatively cool in the summertime, it keeps the British Isles fresh

Lush green scenery is common in the British Isles.
► What animals are grazing in this pasture in western England?

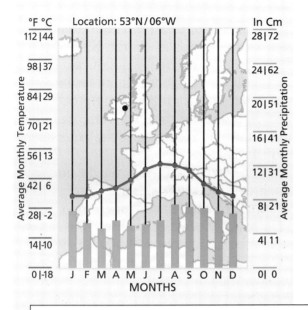

Climograph:
DUBLIN, IRELAND

Location: 53°N / 06°W

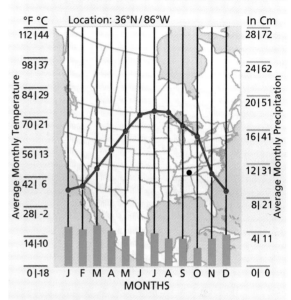

Climograph:
NASHVILLE, TENNESSEE

Location: 36°N / 86°W

The climographs above show the average monthly temperature and the average monthly precipitation in Nashville, Tennessee, and Dublin, Ireland.

► What is the average December temperature in each city?

and cool. London's average summer temperature is about 60°F (16°C), which is similar to southern Alaska's summer temperature. For most Americans, that would be a cold summer.

B. The High Road or the Low Road?

Oh! ye'll take the high road,
And I'll take the low road,
And I'll be in Scotland afore ye.

The Highlands The two roads in this song pass through the two physical regions of the British Isles—the highlands and the lowlands. The highlands are a rugged, bleak region of low, desolate mountains. They are found in the northern and western parts of Great Britain, covering most of Wales and Scotland.

The center of the highlands runs along the Pennine Mountains. The highest peak in this low mountain range is Ben Nevis, which is 4,406 feet (1,343 m) high. The Pennines hold significant deposits of coal and iron ore. This highland area also has many beautiful lakes that attract tourists and vacationers.

The Lowlands The low road through the British Isles leads through the flatter lands on either side of the highlands. To the east of the highlands are the gently rolling hills and valleys of England. To the west of the highlands is the island of Ireland. Ireland's farms, villages, and cities are on the island's broad lowland. The lowlands of the British Isles have been used for farmland and pastures. Most of the population of the British Isles lives in the lowland regions.

269

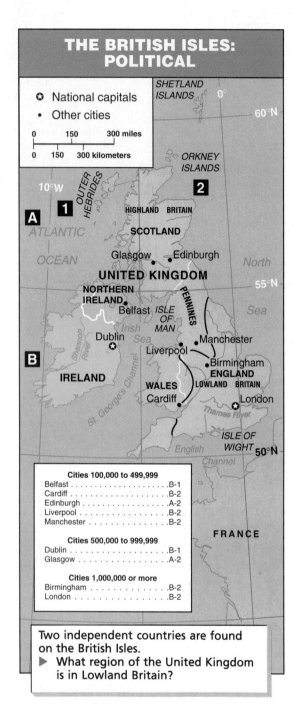

THE BRITISH ISLES: POLITICAL

- ⊕ National capitals
- • Other cities

0   150   300 miles
0   150   300 kilometers

Cities 100,000 to 499,999
Belfast .B-1
Cardiff .B-2
Edinburgh A-2
Liverpool B-2
Manchester B-2

Cities 500,000 to 999,999
Dublin .B-1
Glasgow A-2

Cities 1,000,000 or more
Birmingham B-2
London B-2

Two independent countries are found on the British Isles.
▶ What region of the United Kingdom is in Lowland Britain?

C. The Importance of Coal and Iron

Fueling Industry Coal and iron ore, which are found mostly in the highlands of Wales and Scotland, became vitally important to the economy of the United Kingdom in the 1700s. This was when people first learned to use these resources for modern industry.

The coal was used to fuel factories, and the iron ore was manufactured into steel.

Steel production and coal mining are still an important part of the United Kingdom's economy. The United Kingdom exports some of the steel it produces. It uses the rest for making machinery for factories and mines, and for railway equipment. The steel is also used to make cars, including luxury automobiles such as the Rolls Royce and the Jaguar.

The lowlands in Ireland do not have much coal, so the Irish have used another resource for fuel, called **peat**. Peat is the remains of decaying plants. The brown substance is dug out of **bogs**, or swamps, and dried before it is burned. Peat is much cheaper than oil, but it produces less heat. Today peat is burned to help produce electricity and to heat homes.

Coketown With abundant fuel and mineral resources, the young industries of the nineteenth century grew rapidly. This rapid growth worried many people, including Dickens, the British novelist. In his novel about a city called Coketown, he described how things looked as industry grew.

> *Coketown was a town of red brick, or of brick that would have been red if the smoke and ashes had allowed it. . . . It was a town of machinery and tall chimneys, out of which interminable [endless] serpents of smoke trailed themselves for ever and ever, and never got uncoiled. It had a black canal in it, and a river that ran purple with ill-smelling dye, and vast piles of buildings full of windows where there was a ratling and a trembling all day long. . . .*

Dickens and others saw that industry was polluting the waters of rivers and coasts. Perhaps this pollution was the price that the United Kingdom had to pay to build modern industries. Other countries have also encountered the same problem of pollution as they have industrialized.

Industrial cities in the 1800s were overcrowded and polluted with the smoke from coal-fueled factories.
▶ How does the artist's drawing of this city agree with Dickens's description of Coketown?

North Sea Oil Just as coal was the United Kingdom's greatest treasure in the past, oil and natural gas are its newfound fuels. Vast fields of oil and natural gas were discovered under the North Sea in 1974. The United Kingdom and other countries bordering the sea divided up the fields. Each country can use or sell the oil it finds in the area. By 1980, the United Kingdom was producing enough oil to supply its own need and to export. In fact, oil is now the United Kingdom's largest export. Always looking outward across the oceans, this country has again become a supplier of a precious fuel.

Agriculture New British industries created jobs for many people. Today only about one worker out of every fifty is involved with farming. But the British produce very little food. A lot of the food people eat has to be imported from other countries. Why is so much food imported? The answer is simple. Most of the farmland in Britain is pasture that is used to raise grasses for livestock. The sheep and cattle that graze in these pastures produce some of the world's most famous wools and dairy products. Two British specialties are cheddar cheese and Shetland wool, which is made into warm sweaters.

LESSON 2

Review

REVIEWING MAIN IDEAS

A. How does the North Atlantic Drift affect the climate of the British Isles?
B. How do the two main physical regions of the British Isles differ?
C. How is peat used?

SKILLS CHECK

WRITING SKILL

Reread the passage about Coketown on page 270. Write a short paragraph about how you think Dickens felt about factories and pollution.

271

Living and Working in the British Isles

CONNECTIONS

The following is a list of British words. See if you can guess what they mean.

sweets	crisps
flat	mum
tyre	petrol

TERMS

refuge, Gaelic, Parliament, famine

FOCUS

What are the leading economic activities of the four regions of the United Kingdom?

A. The Center of the United Kingdom

England England, Scotland, Wales, and Northern Ireland are the four regions of the United Kingdom. Many citizens of the United Kingdom call themselves Welsh, English, Scottish, or Irish, depending on where they are from. Even so, they are all British citizens, except for those who live in the Republic of Ireland.

We could say that England is the heartland, or center, of the United Kingdom. Over 80 percent of the United Kingdom's population lives in England. England is also home to London, one of the most important cities in the world.

London London is the United Kingdom's principal urban center and the country's seat of government. Over 11 million people reside in London and its suburbs along the Thames River. Some manufacturing is done here, but most Londoners are employed in government offices, banking, international businesses, or tourism.

London is a city of historic buildings. Among the sites that attract tourists is Buckingham Palace, the home of the Queen of England. Westminster Abbey, the most famous church in the United Kingdom, is another attraction. Here have been held the *coronations* or crownings of the kings and queens of England.

Birmingham and Liverpool Birmingham and Liverpool are large industrial cities. The factories in these cities manufacture steel and steel products, using iron ore and coal mined from the highlands. Today, industries throughout the United Kingdom also produce aerospace equipment, electronic equipment, and space satellites.

B. Scotland and Wales

Refuges Scotland and Wales have some similarities and some differences. Both are

separated from England by highlands. When the Romans invaded the British Isles, these regions became **refuges**, or safe places, for the Celtic tribes. People in some of these regions still speak Celtic languages along with the English language. In Wales the Celtic language is called Welsh. In Scotland it is called **Gaelic**.

People in Scotland and Wales are worried that their languages might die out. Many of the children do not want to speak the old languages, since English is more important in schools and jobs. But some people in Wales and Scotland are trying to keep some of the old languages and customs. In folk festivals, traditional music

The Romans built Hadrian's Wall to keep out Celtic warriors.
▶ Do you think the wall was an effective barrier to invaders?

and dances are performed. One television station in Wales broadcasts only in Welsh.

Scotland and Wales have different economies. Scotland has always had shipbuilding and manufacturing, especially the manufacturing of textiles. These industries are mainly found in the area between Glasgow and Edinburgh (ED un bur uh). These two important Scottish cities benefit from their location in the Scottish lowlands. Edinburgh, Scotland's cultural and historical center, is located at the eastern end of the Scottish lowlands. Glasgow grew into a major city at the western end of the Scottish lowlands. It began as a major port and trading center. Glasgow's shipyards built many of the British navy's powerful ships.

The Scottish towns on the North Sea coast are booming with industry because of the North Sea oil fields. The coastal towns are crowded with people and oil-drilling equipment.

Wales The economy of Wales is not booming like Scotland's economy. Wales is a problem area for the United Kingdom. Unemployment is high. Many Welsh people have left to find jobs in other countries. **Parliament**, the governing body of the United Kingdom, is trying to improve the Welsh economy.

C. The Divided Island of Ireland

Terrorism Along with the problem of Wales, Parliament faces another problem. Northern Ireland, the fourth region of the United Kingdom, has become a place of war and conflict. Geography and religion have made this a troubled region.

Before 1921, the entire island of Ireland was under the rule of England. It was a lush, green land. Belfast was an important shipbuilding city. Linen, an expensive and fragile textile, was made there and sold around the world. Most of the people who lived in Ireland were members of the Cath-

Dublin is the busy capital of the Republic of Ireland. The city was founded more than 800 years ago.
▶ Describe the buses shown.

conflict in Northern Ireland. Irish leaders supported the mid-1990s peace efforts.

Ireland has always depended on agriculture to survive. Its mild, rainy climate is favorable to farming, which is the country's main economic activity. For several years in the 1840s, there was too much rain. Potatoes, the main food crop of the Irish, rotted in the ground. There was a **famine**, or terrible shortage of food. As a result, about 2 million people emigrated to other countries. Many of the Irish came to the United States. They settled in cities such as Boston, New York, Philadelphia, and San Francisco.

Today, life is much better in the Republic of Ireland. Farming is still an important economic activity, but industry employs a growing number of people. Dublin, Ireland's largest city, has industries that produce textiles, chemicals, processed foods, and machine parts.

Businesses from other countries have also built factories in Ireland. The government hopes these new factories will increase employment and make the country less dependent on farming.

olic religion. But over the years, many people from Scotland and England moved to the northern part of the island. They were mostly Protestants. The Scots and the English stayed in the northern area and soon they began to outnumber the Catholics there.

In 1921 the southern two thirds of the island became the independent country of Ireland. Northern Ireland remained part of the United Kingdom. This seemed sensible because the people of Northern Ireland were mostly Protestants, as were the people who live in England, Scotland, and Wales.

Today about one third of the people in Northern Ireland are Catholics. They have felt that the Protestants discriminate against them. Conflicts between Catholics and Protestants have often erupted. In the mid-1990s, leaders on both sides tried to end the violence. However, their efforts to solve their differences peacefully were undermined by acts of terrorism.

The Irish Republic The Republic of Ireland also has been very concerned about the

LESSON 3

Review

REVIEWING MAIN IDEAS

A. Why is England called the heartland of the United Kingdom?
B. What are the differences in the economies of Scotland and Wales?
C. How is Northern Ireland different from the Republic of Ireland?

SKILLS CHECK

MAP SKILL

Use the Gazetteer on pages 707–720 to find the latitude and longitude for the following cities.

London	Birmingham
Liverpool	Glasgow
Belfast	Dublin

The Scandinavian Countries

CONNECTIONS
Describe how the length of daylight in summer and winter affects people's daily lives.

TERMS
Lapps, geyser

FOCUS
What are the chief characteristics of the physical features of Scandinavia?

A. Land of the Midnight Sun

Daylight at Night When the sun rises early in mid-April, the people in the far northern islands of Scandinavia know that it will be months before the sun will set again. In fact, there will be daylight until the beginning of August. Because there is daylight even at night, this region is called the Land of the Midnight Sun.

Of course, this does not happen everywhere in Scandinavia, the area that includes five countries shown on the map on page 276. In the northern regions of these countries, there are long summers with no darkness and long winters with no light. Midnight sun occurs in places north of the Arctic Circle, or above 66°N latitude. You can see from the map on page 276 that most of the region of Scandinavia is south of the Arctic Circle.

The Tilted Earth Why is there daylight even at night in northern Scandinavia? You already know that the earth is tilted on its axis. In December the North Pole is tipped away from the sun. The lands near the North Pole are in shadow all the time. By June the earth has revolved to the other side of the sun, and the North Pole is then tipped toward the sun. When that occurs, the sun does not set. This is just one way that daily life is affected by location.

B. The Scandinavian Coasts

A Rugged Coastline As you can see from the map on page 276, Scandinavia includes scattered islands and long coastlines with many harbors. In this way it is similar to the British Isles. On the map find the two oceans and four seas that touch the Scandinavian countries.

Even though it is late at night, the sun still shines behind the City Hall of Stockholm, Sweden.
▶ Where does midnight sun occur?

You can see on the map that the coastline of Scandinavia looks rough, not smooth. This is because of its many long, narrow harbors. If you were to travel by airplane along the Atlantic coast of Norway following a straight line, your trip would be 2,100 miles (3,379 km). Now imagine walking along the entire coast of Norway, in and out of all the bays and harbors. If you carried a rope and unrolled it along the ground as you walked, and then gathered and measured the rope at the end of your journey, it would be 15,000 miles (24,135 km). The rope could stretch more than halfway around the earth at the Equa-tor. That is because so many bays cut into the land from the sea.

Fjords Norwegians call these narrow, deep bays fjords. As you read in Chapter 3, a fjord is a long, narrow, often deep inlet of the sea, lying between steep cliffs. Fjords were carved out of mountains thousands of years ago by huge ice sheets called glaciers. These glaciers moved down from the North Pole across much of the Northern Hemisphere more than one million years ago. As the glaciers advanced south, they moved large blocks of earth and huge rocks. In places where rocks were soft, glaciers

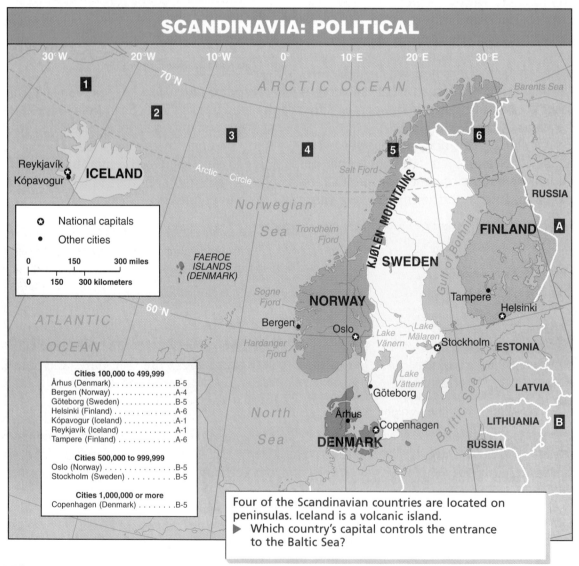

SCANDINAVIA: POLITICAL

Cities 100,000 to 499,999
Århus (Denmark) B-5
Bergen (Norway) A-4
Göteborg (Sweden) B-5
Helsinki (Finland) A-6
Kópavogur (Iceland) A-1
Reykjavík (Iceland) A-1
Tampere (Finland) A-6

Cities 500,000 to 999,999
Oslo (Norway) B-5
Stockholm (Sweden) B-5

Cities 1,000,000 or more
Copenhagen (Denmark) B-5

Four of the Scandinavian countries are located on peninsulas. Iceland is a volcanic island.
▶ Which country's capital controls the entrance to the Baltic Sea?

carved out valleys, lakes, and bays. When the ice melted and seawater entered these hollowed out areas, fjords were formed. Along the shores of the fjords are towering cliffs and mountains, not sandy beaches. Cruise ships often sail into the fjords, which offer breathtaking views to many tourists who travel to the area each year.

C. Mountains, Shields, and Plains

According to Norwegian fairy tales, boys and girls were always on the lookout when traveling in the mountains. The children had to watch out for trolls, which are Scandinavian elves of ancient fairy tales. According to these stories, mountain trolls are horrible looking creatures with many heads. The legends say that long ago trolls captured children and carried them off to their mountain hideaways.

It would be easy to believe these tales if you saw Norway's mountains. The mountains extend from north to south where Norway borders Sweden. The largest mountains are more than 8,000 feet (2,438 m) high, and their snow-covered peaks reach into the clouds. Norway's mountains are one of the major landforms of Scandinavia, and they are important to Scandinavia's climate. The warm waters of the North Atlantic Drift bring a mild, rainy climate to the Atlantic coast of Norway and to Denmark and southern Sweden. For that reason, there are many small farms in the valleys and coasts of western Norway.

But the mountain wall that forms part of the border between the countries of Norway and Sweden traps the rain and warmth. It does not allow the warm, moist air to reach northern Norway, Sweden, or Finland. These areas are dry and cold, making agriculture more difficult there. Farmers grow wheat and potatoes, and raise goats on the stony hillsides.

The forest trolls of Scandinavian folk stories are even more horrible than the

Steep roads wind their way through the mountains of Scandinavia.
▶ How do mountains affect Scandinavia's climate?

mountain trolls. Elvajean Hall, an American librarian who often traveled in Norway, described a forest troll found in a Scandinavian legend.

Sometimes a troll would lose his eye. Then you never heard such thrashing and banging in the forest. . . . The racket was actually caused by a blind troll hunting for his eye and banging into trees and stumps.

Scandinavian Shield The forests of Finland and Sweden are vast, dark, and dense. These forests are found mostly on a huge flat plateau called the Scandinavian Shield. Thousands of years ago, glaciers changed the landscape here as they did in Norway's fjords. On the Scandinavian Shield, they scraped soil and stones off the land's surface, and the glaciers left a hard rock core, called a shield, with just a thin layer of soil on top. There was enough soil for trees to grow into thick forests.

In the far north of the Scandinavian Shield, near the Arctic Ocean, live a sturdy people known as **Lapps**. For centuries, the Lapps followed reindeer herds, eating the reindeer meat and using reindeer milk to make cheese. They were nomadic, that is, they moved about rather than have permanent homes. In summer they moved to the cool, moss-covered mountain fields. Later they followed the reindeer herds to lower flat land to spend the winter. To help them move from one place to another, they trained some of their reindeer to pull large sleds packed with their clothes, tools, and other belongings. Today the majority of Lapps no longer migrate with their herds. They remain in permanent settlements and are a part of Scandinavian society.

North European Plain Denmark and the southern parts of Norway, Sweden, and Finland are quite different from the mountainous and shield areas. The North European Plain, another major landform of Scandinavia, stretches across Denmark and the three neighboring countries. Only a small part of this huge flat lowland covers Scandinavia, but it holds an important natural resource, fertile soil.

The North European Plain has many areas of rich soil and fertile land for dairy farms. The soils of the North European Plain were deposited by rivers and streams carrying sand and gravel that the glaciers scraped away from the Scandinavian Shield. When these soils are fertilized, they provide good farmland.

This part of Scandinavia is heavily populated. Most people of Norway, Sweden, Denmark, and Finland live along the seacoasts of the North Sea and the Baltic Sea. The capital cities of all four countries are located here. Find these capital cities on the map on page 276.

The roundup of reindeer at the end of summer is an annual event among the Lapps of Scandinavia. The Lapps depend on the reindeer for clothing and food, but they no longer follow the reindeer herds during migrations.
▶ What is the boy using to capture the reindeer?

D. Iceland: A Place of Fire and Ice

Volcanoes and Lava Poking up out of the cold ocean waters of the North Atlantic is a huge chunk of rock named Iceland. This island nation has several different landscapes, because not all of the island is covered with ice, despite its name. Some areas have lakes, volcanoes, hot fields of lava, or melted rock, and **geysers** (GY zurs). A geyser is a fountain of steam and water that has been heated by hot lava and forced above ground by volcanic gases.

Volcanoes actually formed this island nation. Over many centuries, volcanoes erupted on the ocean floor. The lava and rock they created cooled and slowly hardened, layer by layer. Eventually these layers reached the ocean's surface, forming an island just above the ocean waters. This process is still continuing today in Iceland. Every once in a while, a river of hot lava flows down the side of a volcano and extends into the sea. In this way, Iceland gets a small amount of new territory. But for many years this new land is useless rock and ash.

Beautiful rivers and fields are found along the southern coast of Iceland. Daytime temperatures only occasionally fall below freezing, allowing farmers to raise pasture grasses and hay to feed herds of sheep and cattle. Meat and dairy products, together with vegetables, are Iceland's important agricultural products. Most of these products are used in Iceland.

The southern coast is home to nearly three fourths of Iceland's population. The buildings in the cities and towns of the south are usually heated with steam or hot water from Iceland's many hot springs. Iceland has almost no coal or oil, but the rivers that rush into the sea along the southern coast produce hydroelectricity for Iceland's industries. Cement, fertilizers, and fish products are Iceland's principal manufactured products.

Volcanic eruptions are a frequent occurrence in Iceland. Lava flows add new territory to the country.
► What is lava?

LESSON 4

Review

REVIEWING MAIN IDEAS
A. Why is the northern part of Scandinavia called the Land of the Midnight Sun?
B. How do fjords affect the coastline of Norway?
C. What are the important natural resources of the Scandinavian Shield?
D. How was Iceland formed?

SKILLS CHECK

THINKING SKILL

Turn to the Index on pages 740-752 and find the term *Canadian Shield*. Scan the pages that refer to the Canadian Shield to find how the Canadian Shield and the Scandinavian Shield are alike. Make a chart on which you list the ways they are alike.

Living and Working in Scandinavia

CONNECTIONS

List some changes that you might have to make in your life if you were to move to one of the Scandinavian countries.

TERMS

smorgasbord, neutral

FOCUS

How do the people of each Scandinavian country use their natural resources?

A. Similarities and Differences

High Incomes Although the five Scandinavian countries are separate, the lives of Scandinavians are bound together in several ways. Most Scandinavians believe in the Lutheran religion. They have shared this Protestant religion for four centuries. Scandinavians enjoy a high standard of living. The average family has an income that is higher than the average family income in most European countries. Schools, child-care centers, and healthcare programs are of high quality. Travelers to the Scandinavian countries often remark how clean and well-kept the streets are.

Different Languages One way that the Scandinavian countries differ is in their language. Each country has its own language. The languages of Scandinavia are Norwegian, Swedish, Danish, Icelandic, and Finnish. The first four of these languages belong to the same parent language of the ancient Germanic peoples.

Norwegians, Swedes, and Danes are usually able to communicate with one another, because their languages have many words in common. Icelandic has preserved, or saved, many of the ways Scandinavians spoke centuries ago. Today Icelandic is not easily understood by other Scandinavians.

Finnish, the language of Finland, belongs to another language family. Some Finns also speak Swedish. At one time Finland was united with Sweden. Swedish continues to be one of the official languages of Finland. That makes Finland a bilingual, or two-language, nation.

Daily Life In Scandinavian cities, people live much as people live in the United States. Children attend school and parents work. Most Scandinavians enjoy outdoor sports, especially skating, skiing, and water sports. Many like to spend weekends and vacations in the mountains or forest regions of Scandinavia.

The ancient glaciers left a useful gift behind for Finland's city dwellers. Finland is dotted with more than 55,000 small lakes. Most are huge pits that glaciers carved in the surface of the earth. Later, these pits filled with water. Now the lakes are popular vacation spots. On weekends many families rush from Helsinki, the capital city, to enjoy these lakes. People who live in large cities in Sweden and Norway also take advantage of their many lakes.

Cottages like these are found throughout the Scandinavian countryside.
▶ What outdoor activities could people enjoy here?

The Vikings explored and raided many lands traveling the open sea in open and light ships.
▶ What new, unexplored land did the Vikings reach years before Christopher Columbus?

All over Scandinavia, fish is a main ingredient of many meals. Scandinavians eat more fish than do British or Irish people because Scandinavia has less flat land for farming and more coastline than the British Isles. Scandinavians especially like cod, herring, and salmon. These are often eaten with other foods, such as salads, meats, and sliced bread. This variety of foods is known as a **smorgasbord**. A smorgasbord is served on a long table where you can eat all the food you want.

B. The Importance of the Sea to Iceland and Norway

Different Resources The natural resources of the Scandinavian countries are different from place to place. But Scandinavians have learned to use their natural resources well to build strong economies.

For example, Iceland has almost no farmland, forests, or minerals, so its people look toward the sea for survival. Over 75 percent of Iceland's exports are fish products. Fish caught from the sea is frozen, canned, dried, or salted. Some of the fish is processed into fertilizer or fish oil. Icelanders do well with their economy and so they have a high standard of living and good schools.

In Norway, people also have learned to use the sea. Norwegians never took over other lands or ruled an empire as the British did. But during the ninth and tenth centuries, explorers called Vikings traveled far over the Atlantic Ocean.

One of the most famous Vikings was Leif Ericson. He was probably the first European to arrive at the shores of North America. This occurred about A.D. 1000, several centuries before Columbus arrived in the Americas.

Finland's forests provide lumber.
► How can the Finnish people
continue to use their forests
without destroying this resource?

that huge amounts of petroleum and natural gas were found under the North Sea in 1974. Today Norway shares with the United Kingdom some of these petroleum and natural gas fields.

Mountains and Forests Norwegians and Swedes take advantage of their mountains. The rivers that tumble out of the mountains to the coast are ideal for producing hydroelectric power. With this electricity, Norwegian companies have built factories to produce aluminum, metal products, and machinery. So many factories have been built in recent years that the need for workers has greatly increased. With the growth in population in manufacturing centers, people jokingly say that Oslo, the capital city of Norway, now reaches all the way to the Arctic Circle.

In Sweden, hydroelectric power is brought from northern mountains to the southern cities by long electric power lines. The electricity helps power Sweden's factories, which manufacture products such as paper, steel, machinery, and electronics such as computers.

About 75 percent of Finland's land is covered with forest. In the winter, birch, pine, and fir trees shiver in the frosty Scandinavian air. Lumber companies cut the forests to get lumber for ships and furniture, or to grind some of the lumber in pulp, which is a soft, thick liquid used to make paper. Finland's forests make up the country's most important natural resource, and they are so valuable that they are sometimes called "green gold."

C. Guardians of the Baltic Sea

Denmark is the smallest Scandinavian country, with about 16,600 square miles (42,994 sq km). It is about the same size as Massachusetts, Connecticut, and Rhode Island together. It does not have vast empty areas like the countries of Norway, Sweden, and Finland.

Today there are no more Viking explorers, but the sea is still important to most Scandinavians because it provides numerous trade routes. Each of the Scandinavian countries has valuable natural resources and manufactured goods to sell. Each also needs to import many essential products. Iceland and Finland, for example, need to import fruits, vegetables, and other foods because they have little farmland. None of the Scandinavian countries except Sweden has many minerals, so they must import metals and other raw materials for manufacturing.

Norwegian shipping companies have become experts in the trading business. They send ships all over the world to trade. Norway carries out more shipping than any other country of the world. The Vikings would be proud of this success.

Recently the sea gave Norway another valuable gift. You read earlier in this chapter

Nature has given Denmark a climate especially suited for growing pasture grasses. The Danish people have learned how to use this resource carefully. As a result, butter and cheese are at the top of Denmark's list of exports. These products come from the cattle that graze on the grasses of the North European Plain.

The largest country in Scandinavia is Sweden. Its land area is about 173,700 square miles (449,883 sq km), which is more than ten times the size of Denmark. The Scandinavian Shield covers much of Sweden's territory. Shields contain the world's oldest rocks and valuable minerals. The Scandinavian Shield has given Sweden a large, rich iron ore field called Kiruna (KIHR aw nah). Swedish industries manufacture this iron ore into steel and products such as automobiles, tools, and precision instruments. Sweden's steel products are of high quality and are among Sweden's most valuable exports.

Two Peninsulas Denmark and Sweden share one important feature. If you look closely at the map of Scandinavia on page 276, you will see that Scandinavia is made up of two peninsulas. On the large peninsula are Norway, Sweden, and a small part of Finland. The small peninsula, called Jutland, contains Denmark. These two peninsulas almost touch at Copenhagen, the capital city of Denmark. Ships leaving or entering the Baltic Sea must pass by the narrow channel in view of Copenhagen.

The country that controls both sides of this entry has a great deal of power. Partly for this reason Denmark ruled Sweden from 1397 until 1523. Denmark also formed a union with Norway from 1381 until 1814. This gave the Danes control over important coasts around the Baltic Sea and its entry. When Sweden became an independent country in 1523, it started to take over lands all around the Baltic Sea. Its capital city, Stockholm, was built on a

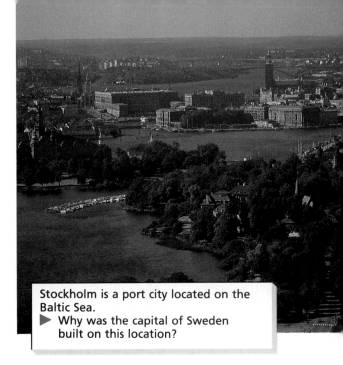

Stockholm is a port city located on the Baltic Sea.
▶ Why was the capital of Sweden built on this location?

strategic location near the Baltic Sea.

Perhaps conflicts over the entrance to the Baltic Sea made Scandinavians realize the importance of peace. Both Finland and Sweden are **neutral** countries. Neutral means "not taking sides in conflicts." Norway, too, works for world peace. Each year a committee of Norwegians helps select the winner of the Nobel Peace Prize.

LESSON 5

Review

REVIEWING MAIN IDEAS
A. Name two things that Scandinavians have in common.
B. How does the sea help the economies of Iceland and Norway?
C. Why is the Baltic Sea so important to Denmark and Sweden?

SKILLS CHECK

MAP SKILL
Look on the map on page 276 to find the capital cities of the five Scandinavian countries. On a separate sheet of paper, list the capital cities that border on the Baltic Sea.

283

11 REVIEW

REVIEWING TERMS

Match each term with the correct definition. Write your answer in sentence form.

channel   fjord
maritime   Lapps
peat   lava
Parliament   geyser
famine   neutral

1. A great shortage of food
2. A long, narrow, often deep inlet of the sea lying between steep cliffs
3. Melted rock
4. Decayed plant matter used as fuel
5. Associated with the sea
6. A fountain of water and steam that has been heated by hot lava and forced above ground by volcanic gases
7. The governing body of the United Kingdom
8. A nomadic group that lives in Scandinavia
9. A nation that does not take sides in a conflict
10. A water passage

REVIEWING THE FACTS

On a separate sheet of paper, answer the questions in complete sentences.

1. What are the four regions of the United Kingdom?
2. Why do the countries of the British Isles and Scandinavia have a marine climate?
3. What natural resources have contributed to the growth of British industry?
4. Why does the United Kingdom import food?
5. In what ways is Scotland's economy booming?

6. Conflict occurs in Northern Ireland between which two groups?
7. How did glaciers affect the Scandinavian Shield?
8. What landform crosses southern Scandinavia?
9. What languages are spoken in the Scandinavian countries?
10. How do the Norwegians and Swedes take advantage of their mountains and forests?

WRITING ABOUT GEOGRAPHY

Charles Dickens described the imaginary Coketown. It was based on his observation and feelings toward industry in Britain. Create your own imaginary town in the British Isles or Scandinavia and describe what you see, hear, and feel.

THINKING CRITICALLY

On a separate sheet of paper, answer the following in complete sentences.

1. How has the economy of the United Kingdom been influenced by its island geography?
2. What are some of the advantages and disadvantages of belonging to a commonwealth of nations?
3. Why is hydroelectricity not a commonly used source of energy in the British Isles?
4. Is the use of terrorism an effective form of protest?
5. What locations in the Southern Hemisphere could also have the label Land of the Midnight Sun?

SUMMARIZING THE CHAPTER

On a separate sheet of paper, draw a graphic organizer like the one shown here. Copy the information from this graphic organizer to the one you have drawn. Under each column, fill in a plus (+) if the country has the characteristic listed. Fill in a minus (−) if the country does not have the characteristic.

CHAPTER THEME

The location and natural resources of the nations of the British Isles and Scandinavia have helped these nations develop high standards of living.

Characteristic	United Kingdom	Ireland	Sweden	Norway	Iceland	Finland	Denmark
Peninsula nation							
Island nation							
Maritime nation							
Pennine Mountains							
Kjølen Mountains							
Fjords							
Jutland Peninsula							
Thames River							
North Sea							
Baltic Sea							
English Channel							
British Isles							
Geysers							
Scandinavian Shield							
Midnight Sun							

THE HEARTLAND OF WESTERN EUROPE

Looking at the Heartland

CONNECTIONS

You often hear about Western Europe on the news. What are some Western European countries that are often mentioned?

TERMS

summit, pass

FOCUS

How are the major landforms of Western Europe helpful to the people of the region?

A. Sharing Geography and History

Connecting Western Europe The car left London headed for France at more than 60 miles per hour (96 km per hour). When it came to the English Channel, the car slowed for a moment and then quickly descended into the lamplit interior of a tunnel. The car and its passengers were doing what had only been dreamed about for centuries—crossing the English Channel from the United Kingdom to the continent of Europe quickly and easily.

No one can do this yet. But in 1994 a railway tunnel was opened beneath the English Channel. It made possible train trips between the United Kingdom and France. Special tunnel trains now carry cars, buses, and trucks. A tunnel for use only by motor vehicles may be built in the early 2000s.

The railway tunnel was built by both the United Kingdom and France. It is an example of the cooperation that has led to strong economic and political ties between the United Kingdom and the countries of Western Europe.

The Heartland If you look at the map of Western Europe on page 288, you can see that seven countries occupy a central position in Western Europe. These countries form the heartland of Western Europe.

The heartland countries are separated from other regions of Europe. The North Sea and the Baltic Sea separate the British Isles and Scandinavia from the heartland. The Pyrenees (PIHR uh neez) cut off Spain, and the Alps separate Italy from the heartland. The countries to the east of the heartland form their own region because of their ties with the former Soviet Union. For these reasons we say that the countries of the heartland of Western Europe form a region of their own.

Rivers of the Heartland The heartland countries share several important rivers that crisscross the region's mountains and plains and connect its countries and cities. The Danube (DAN yoob) River, which is 1,770 miles (2,848 km) long, is the longest of these rivers. It is much shorter than the Mississippi River, which is 2,348 miles (3,778 km) long and the longest river in the United States. The Danube River flows toward the east, along the northern edge of the Alps. It passes through Austria, where it forms the Danube Valley, an area known for its rich soils. The Danube empties into a large body of water farther east. Turn to the physical map on page 255 and identify that body of water.

The Rhine (ryn) River is much shorter than the Danube. But the heartland countries all along its 820-mile (1,319 km) length depend on the Rhine for trade and transportation. The Rhine flows in a northerly direction through Germany and then flows west through the Netherlands. It empties into the North Sea at Rotterdam, one of the world's most important port cities.

The Rhine, the Danube, and other rivers cut across the three main regions of the heartland: the Alps, the Central Uplands, and the North European Plain. If you look carefully at the map on page 288, you can see that the Alps and the plain curve across western Europe's heartland. The Alps are in the southeast corner. The Cen-

▶ Castles are a common sight along the rivers of southern Germany.

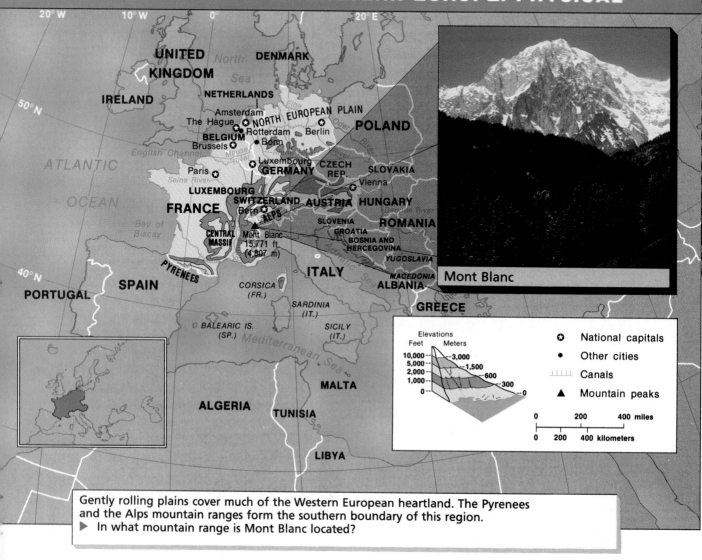

Mont Blanc

Gently rolling plains cover much of the Western European heartland. The Pyrenees and the Alps mountain ranges form the southern boundary of this region.
▶ In what mountain range is Mont Blanc located?

tral Uplands arch around the Alps, and the North European Plain spreads out in an even greater curve to the north.

B. The Towering Peaks of the Alps

Rugged Peaks An adventurer traveling in the Alps once wrote,

The Alps! . . . For more than twenty centuries, this glorious group of dazzling peaks and glaciers, of deepset mountain lakes and tumbling streams, of pine forests and flowering glades, has stirred the imagination of the world.

The Alps form a knot of rugged peaks that fill most of Switzerland. They spread out into France, Germany, and Austria, covering a distance of about 600 miles (965 km). The peaks of the Alps are spectacular. The highest peak is Mont Blanc (mohn BLAHN), in France. Mont Blanc is 15,771 feet (4,807 m) high. It is not quite as high as Mount McKinley, which, at 20,320 feet (6,194 m), is the highest mountain peak in the United States. *Mont Blanc* means "white mountain" in French. Like other peaks in the Alps, Mont Blanc is so high that the snow never melts from its **summit**. The summit of a mountain is its highest point. Some of Europe's mightiest rivers begin in the Alps as tiny trickles of water high on a mountainside and flow down the mountains and out to sea. The Rhine and Danube are examples of rivers that make this long journey.

Crossing the Alps The Alps are so rugged and so high that you may think of them as a wall. Actually, the Alps have many river valleys and mountain **passes** that allow people to cross through. A pass is a low place in a mountain range.

Perhaps the most famous example of travel through the Alps occurred in 218 B.C. In the spring of that year, Hannibal, a military leader of Carthage, in northern Africa, and one of Rome's fiercest enemies,

put together a daring plan. In the land now called Spain, which Carthage partly controlled, Hannibal organized and trained an army. Then he set out for Italy to attack Rome. But he did not take his large army of 30,000 men, hundreds of horses, and 37 elephants to Italy by crossing the Mediterranean Sea. Instead, he marched from Spain through the Alps toward Italy, where he surprised the Roman army.

C. The Hilly Central Uplands

Central Massif Extending along the northern and western edges of the Alps is a wide, curved region of hills, valleys, and plateaus called the Central Uplands. This large and varied region includes several important physical features. An extensive hilly plateau called the Central Massif covers much of central and southern France. Its highest elevations reach approximately 6,000 feet (1,829 m), which is much lower than the peaks of the Alps. The Jura Mountains, on the eastern edge of the Central

Many tourists from across the world travel to the Alps to ski.
▶ Where is it possible to ski in your area?

VINCENT VAN GOGH AND FRANCE'S GEOGRAPHY

Vincent van Gogh Foundation/
National Museum
Vincent van Gogh, Amsterdam

Vincent Van Gogh (VIHN sunt van GOH) was a famous painter whose work influenced the development of modern art. Van Gogh was born in the Netherlands in 1853. He explored several careers before becoming a painter. In 1888 he moved to Arles (ahrl), a town in southern France. Van Gogh was impressed by the scenery and people of Arles.

The changing light and color of the countryside of Arles fascinated Van Gogh. As a result, his landscapes of southern France are filled with brilliant light and color. He especially liked to paint rural subjects. His painting "The Harvest" is an autumn scene that shows peasants harvesting crops.

1. What colors might Van Gogh have used if he had painted the same landscape in the spring?

2. What features of the landscape of southern France, do you think, impressed Van Gogh?

3. How can you tell that the farmland in the painting is near the foothills of the Alps?

Uplands, form the border between France and Switzerland. And to the north is the Ardennes (ahr DEN), a flat plateau in southern Belgium.

The Central Uplands are important to the heartland's economy. The Central Uplands are lower and less rugged than the Alps, so farming and herding can be practiced on this region's many slopes and in its valleys. The farmers here raise sheep and goats and cultivate fruit orchards and grapes. Most of the farms found in the Central Uplands are small but prosperous.

D. The North European Plain

The Outside Curve You have already read about the North European Plain in Chapter 11 when you studied the Scandinavian countries. But the North European Plain is not found just in Scandinavia and the United Kingdom. This flat area runs in a wide curve along the coasts of the Atlantic Ocean, the North Sea, and the Baltic Sea. It begins at the southern border of France, near the Pyrenees. It curves through Belgium, the Netherlands, Germany, and Poland, and then widens and stretches out across the Baltic nations, Belarus, Ukraine, and Western Russia. Because it is so flat, the North European Plain has been crossed and recrossed many times by invaders and conquerors throughout history.

Many rivers that rise in the Alps and in the Central Uplands cut through the North European Plain. These rivers help to make the soils of the region rich for agriculture. As they cross the plain, the rivers sometimes flood their banks. When this happens, the soil and sand they have carried from the mountains are spread across the land. This flooding produces fertile soil. Dairy cattle are able to graze on the grasses that grow here. Large amounts of cheese and butter are produced on the dairy farms of this region.

The rivers that cross the North European Plain are also excellent transportation routes. Many of them are connected by canals. Barges and ships carry farm products; raw materials, such as coal and minerals; and manufactured goods, such as textiles and paper. Traffic is heavy on most rivers of the North European Plain.

Climate Agriculture on the North European Plain is helped by a climate that is similar to the climate of the British Isles and southern Scandinavia. Winds from the Atlantic Ocean bring mild temperatures and moisture to the land, but the winds are useful in another way, too. People of this region learned to build windmills, which are machines that use the wind's power. The arms of the windmill are pushed around like a fan by the force of the wind. As the arms move they turn gears that can be used to drive a pump or a wheel for grinding wheat into flour. Europeans have used windmills for centuries. Of course, today the Europeans have electricity, too, to perform these tasks.

LESSON 1

Review

REVIEWING MAIN IDEAS

A. How are the heartland countries separated from the rest of Western Europe?
B. How are the Alps important to the heartland of Western Europe?
C. Why is farming possible in the Central Uplands?
D. How are rivers important in the North European Plain?

SKILLS CHECK

MAP SKILL
Vienna, Paris, and Rotterdam are three cities that share something in common. Use the Gazetteer, on pages 707–720, to find what that common item is and write a sentence telling what you have learned.

Old and New Meet in France

CONNECTIONS

Imagine that you are going to visit France for a vacation. Look at the photographs and maps on pages 292–295 of this lesson and list the places you might like to visit and the things you might do while in France.

TERMS

vineyard, modernize

FOCUS

How has France modernized its economy?

A. Touring France by Cable Car

High above the Alps, a group of tourists traveled from Italy into France by cable car, a vehicle that travels above the ground along a suspended cable. Fields of snow, rocky cliffs, and evergreen forests passed far below. Slowly the cable car made its way over a high ridge. When it descended into France, the tourists left the cable car, excited by this unique experience.

During their trip across the mountains and valleys, the tourists saw many ski resorts. The economy of the Alps region of France depends on tourism, but agriculture is important, too. Here and there the cable car passengers looked down on what appeared to be green ribbons winding around the mountains. These were valleys where corn, tobacco, and grapes grow well. The passengers could even see cows, goats, and sheep grazing on the grassy slopes of the valleys. The milk of the cows grazed here is used to make some of the world's most famous cheeses, which include Brie (bree), Camembert (KAM um ber), and Rocquefort (ROHK furt).

This spectacular area is just a small part of France, because the Alps fill only the southeastern corner of the country. There are many other regions in this large

Cable cars such as this one are used throughout the Alps to travel from valley floors to the peaks of the Alps.
▶ How is the cable car suspended?

country. The map on page 288 shows the Alps and the other regions of France. It is easy to find France on a map of Europe because France is the largest country in Europe except for Russia. France's total area is 212,918 square miles (551,458 sq km), making it about the same size as the state of Texas.

B. French Farming: Old and New

Varied Crops Most French farms are in the flat North European Plain or in the hilly Central Uplands region. Of course, mountain cable cars don't travel through these areas. But if they did, we could cross France in one and see below us land that appears to be divided into green, brown, and yellow squares. The color of each square depends on what is growing in the

292

square. Green comes from corn or other vegetables, ripe wheat creates a yellow color, and empty fields are brown. In southern and western France, the land is divided into small squares by hedges and fences. Farmers in this part of France grow a variety of crops, including wheat, fruit, herbs, tobacco, and vegetables such as corn, peas, onions, and tomatoes.

Some farmers in these regions grow special products. Near the city of Bordeaux (bor DOH), for example, the temperature, humidity, sunshine, and soils are just right for growing grapes. Farmers' **vineyards** (VIHN yurds), or fields of grape vines, produce some of the finest wines in the world. Vineyards are also common east of Paris, in the regions of Champagne (sham PAYNE) and Burgundy. The soil in Burgundy is said to be so valuable that farmers wipe it off their boots before leaving the fields.

In the south some farmers also plant flower gardens at the same time they plant food crops. They sell their flowers to factories that use them to create French perfumes, which are known throughout the world. In northern France we would see something different. In this area, the squares of crops are larger. This region is the breadbasket of France, where wheat, potatoes, and sugar beets are important crops. Wheat is France's leading crop, and much of it is grown in this northern region.

Past Influences Why do we see farms of small squares in the south and large farms in the north? In the north there are large farms because of the Franks, tribes who settled in northern France around the year 400. France's name comes from these people. The Franks settled in villages and farmed without putting hedges or fences between fields. Their fields were open, not separated into individual fields. People in northern France have kept this tradition and still live in villages that are surrounded by open fields.

The Franks gradually took over much of northern France, but in the south they ran into the descendants of the Romans, who had lived in southern France for almost five centuries.

The southern people had their own ways of farming. Each family had a small section of land here and there. The Franks could not change this method of farming, so even today southern French farms remain smaller than those that are found in the north.

Why is this difference between northern and southern farms important? After World War II the leaders of France began to **modernize**, or develop, the economy of their country. One project they carried out was to change the boundaries of the farms throughout France.

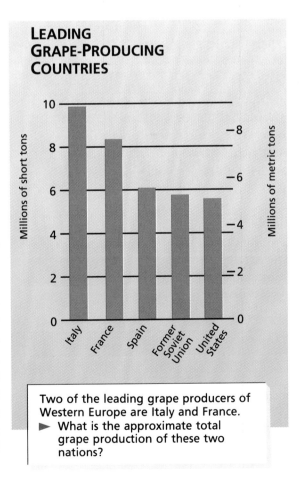

LEADING GRAPE-PRODUCING COUNTRIES

Two of the leading grape producers of Western Europe are Italy and France.
► What is the approximate total grape production of these two nations?

293

In order to do this, the government had to change the old farming traditions. Each farm family was given one large section of land to work on to replace the many small pieces of land. In this way, even farm families in the south could use large machines to produce more food. This project was successful, and France today is a major world exporter of foods such as apples, wheat, and sugar beets.

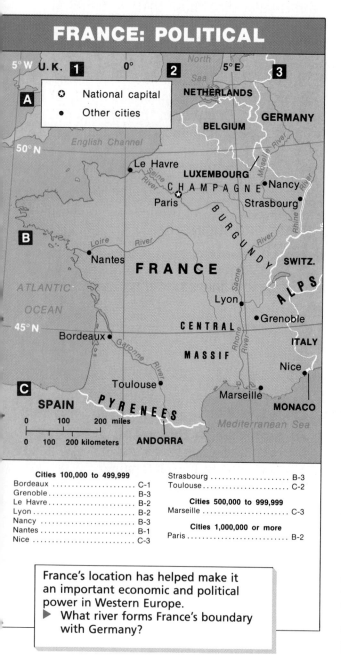

FRANCE: POLITICAL

○ National capital
• Other cities

Cities 100,000 to 499,999		
Bordeaux	C-1	
Grenoble	B-3	
Le Havre	B-2	
Lyon	B-2	
Nancy	B-3	
Nantes	B-1	
Nice	C-3	

Strasbourg	B-3
Toulouse	C-2

Cities 500,000 to 999,999
Marseille C-3

Cities 1,000,000 or more
Paris B-2

France's location has helped make it an important economic and political power in Western Europe.
▶ What river forms France's boundary with Germany?

C. Paris: The Center of a Star

Near the middle of northern France appears to be the center of a star, with arms radiating, or extending, in all directions. The center of the star is Paris, the capital city of France, and the arms are roads, canals, and railroads.

Paris, the largest city in France, has been an important city since it was founded in 300 B.C. It was first built on an island in the middle of the Seine River. The Seine River begins in eastern France and then flows westward through the middle of the country. After passing Paris, the Seine empties into the English Channel at Le Havre (luh HAHV ruh), which is one of France's major port cities.

Because it was built on an island, Paris was easy to defend. It also had direct river connections to the east and to the west. Even when it was a small town, Paris was the destination of many people looking for customers for their farm products. By road and river, they traveled to its markets.

Later, Napoleon Bonaparte (BOH nuh pahrt) also helped to make Paris the center of French life. After he became emperor of France in 1804, Napoleon ordered the construction of a famous monument, the Arch of Triumph, in Paris, with 12 roads leading from its center. Some of these roads are still beautiful boulevards today. The Eiffel Tower, stands 984 feet (300 m) tall. This is one of the world's most famous landmarks. From its soaring heights, tourists can view other treasures of Paris, such as the Notre Dame Cathedral, which was built in the thirteenth century. Paris is called the City of Light because its great cathedrals, museums, and universities are shining examples of human achievement.

D. France's Industrial Regions

Three Industrial Regions France is one of the world's most industrialized countries, producing a great variety of products that

Lights illuminate the Eiffel Tower at night. An elevator takes tourists to the top of the tower.
▶ What is the tower made of?

range from automobiles to delicate perfumes. French industries are concentrated in three areas. One region is near the city of Nancy, in northeastern France. Here are some of Europe's largest coal and iron ore deposits. Factories in and near Nancy produce steel, heavy machinery, and chemicals. The Rhine River forms the boundary between France and Germany here. Barges and ships carry many goods up and down the Rhine River.

A second industrial region is located near the city of Lyon (lee OHN). Factories in Lyon use the resources of the Central Massif. The most important resources of the Central Massif are its minerals and metals, which include iron ore, coal, copper, lead, tin, and bauxite. In the industrial city of Lyon and cities nearby, huge factories produce railroad equipment, airplane engines, tires, and household appliances.

Automobiles, such as the Renault (ruh NAWLT) are built in Lyon. In fact, France is the world's fourth largest automobile maker.

The Rhone The Rhone River begins in the Alps and journeys south through France, giving France a direct water route to the Mediterranean Sea. The Rhone empties into the Mediterranean at Marseille (mahr SAY), an important port city.

France has very little oil, so many of the country's factories use hydroelectric power from the rivers of the Alps. The French factories also use power from France's many nuclear power plants, which supply much of the electricity used in French homes and businesses. France has the largest number of nuclear power plants in all of Western Europe.

Just outside of Paris is a third industrial zone, with thousands of factories that make a great variety of products. There is little coal, iron ore, or other minerals near Paris. Most factories produce items such as jewelry, clothing, and food products. Clothing designers in Paris have made the French fashion industry world famous.

LESSON 2

Review

REVIEWING MAIN IDEAS

A. What are the two important economic activities in the French Alps region?
B. How did the Franks and the Romans affect modern French farming?
C. Why is Paris in a good location for trade?
D. Where are the three largest industrial centers in France?

SKILLS CHECK

MAP SKILL

Look at the map on page 294 and find Paris, Nancy, and Lyon. Using the scale on the map, find the distance in miles between these cities.

The Benelux Nations Work Together

CONNECTIONS

With two other students in your class, imagine the following situation. You are the leaders of three small countries that are surrounded by larger countries. Decide how your countries might cooperate.

TERMS

polder, flax, Fleming, Walloon, tariff, European Union

FOCUS

In what ways are the Benelux countries connected physically and economically?

A. The Importance of Rivers to the Benelux Countries

Benelux Belgium, the Netherlands, and Luxembourg are often called the Benelux countries. If you look at the beginning letters of each of these countries, you will know why. These three small countries are often grouped together by one name because they are closely linked by rivers. The principal rivers of the Benelux countries are the Rhine and three smaller rivers. These rivers are the Meuse (myooz) River and the Schelde (SKEL duh) River, which cross Belgium, and the Moselle River, which runs along the eastern border of Luxembourg and empties into the Rhine.

Trading Nations Barges, ships, and many other kinds of vessels travel constantly up and down these rivers. Some carry raw materials, such as coal, iron ore, and other minerals, from northern France and southern Germany. Some of these raw materials are loaded for export onto ocean-going ships in Rotterdam or other coastal port cities. Refined oil, chemicals, and other products are moved on the river from the coastal ports to markets in the countries of the heartland.

B. The Netherlands: A Prosperous Country

A Riddle If you looked at a list of the natural resources of the Netherlands, you might think it is a poor country. It has almost no forests or hydroelectric plants, little oil or coal, and no iron ore. It is a small country with not much land for farming. It has a high population density, with 1,093 people per square mile (422 people

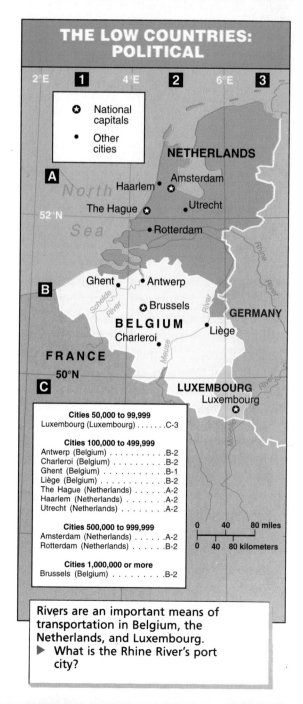

THE LOW COUNTRIES: POLITICAL

Legend:
- ⊛ National capitals
- • Other cities

Cities 50,000 to 99,999
Luxembourg (Luxembourg) C-3

Cities 100,000 to 499,999
Antwerp (Belgium) B-2
Charleroi (Belgium) B-2
Ghent (Belgium) B-1
Liège (Belgium) B-2
The Hague (Netherlands) A-2
Haarlem (Netherlands) A-2
Utrecht (Netherlands) A-2

Cities 500,000 to 999,999
Amsterdam (Netherlands) A-2
Rotterdam (Netherlands) B-2

Cities 1,000,000 or more
Brussels (Belgium) B-2

Rivers are an important means of transportation in Belgium, the Netherlands, and Luxembourg.
▶ What is the Rhine River's port city?

296

per sq km). Yet the people of the Netherlands have a high standard of living, comfortable homes, and healthy diets. How did the Dutch, the name for the people of the Netherlands, become so prosperous?

One reason for their wealth is the fact that they are energetic and hard working people. Another reason for the wealth of the Netherlands is the great city of Rotterdam, which is one of the busiest port cities in the world. Goods and raw materials arriving by sea from the Atlantic Ocean can be shipped from Rotterdam all the way to Basel, Switzerland, on rivers and canals.

Rotterdam is not only a busy port, but also a manufacturing city. Huge refineries turn imported oil into petroleum, and factories process imported chemicals. These products are then sold all over the world. Shipbuilding is another important industry in Rotterdam.

Amsterdam Amsterdam, the largest city in the Netherlands, also grew into an important city because of trade. Amsterdam is not directly on the Rhine River, but it is connected by a canal to the Rhine and by another canal to the North Sea.

In the eighteenth and nineteenth centuries, Amsterdam was a commercial center for the whole world, because important trading companies had their headquarters here. Two of Amsterdam's well-known products are cocoa and chocolate candy, which are made from cacao beans imported from Africa. Amsterdam is also known for diamonds, which are cut, or shaped, from raw stones imported from diamond mines in South Africa.

The Dutch have built great port cities and industrial centers, but their economy also depends on farming. Most of the Netherlands is in the North European Plain, with flat lands and plentiful rainfall. Much of the land is below sea level. This is why Belgium, the Netherlands, and Luxembourg are called the Low Countries.

A diamond cutter in Amsterdam uses a magnifying glass to examine a diamond he is cutting.
▶ What are some uses of diamonds?

C. Holding Back the Sea

Dikes and Polders There is only one thing standing between the farmlands of the Netherlands and the sea. That is the Dutch method of holding back the sea and drying out lands along the coast. Workers build dikes along the ridges of sand dunes on the shore. A dike is a wall built to protect land from the sea. The dikes hold the sea's waters away from the land. The water left on the land is pumped into canals that empty into the sea. The Dutch call such drained land a **polder**. The polder can be filled in with soil, and used for farming or for the construction of buildings.

The soil in the polders is especially good for raising tulip bulbs and for growing pasture grasses for dairy cattle. Flowers and flower seeds and bulbs are important Dutch exports, along with cheese and butter. Farther inland from the coast, where the land is higher and drier, farmers grow wheat, potatoes, and sugar beets.

Zuider Zee The largest area of polders is north of Amsterdam. Here an arm of the

FROM FLAX TO LINEN

1 Flax is planted close together to encourage the plants to grow straight and tall. This helps the plants develop long fibers.

2 Flax is harvested by being pulled straight from the ground. The pulling preserves the full length of the flax fibers.

3 The harvested flax is combed, spread out, and drafted several times until a sliver of flax fiber is formed.

4 The flax fiber is then spun into linen yarn.

5 The linen yarn is either woven or knitted before being bleached or dyed.

6 The finished linen is used for household textiles, fabrics, and clothing.

The flax plant has many uses. The seeds can be made into linseed oil, which is used in paint. The flowchart shows how the fiber is made into linen.
▶ What are some of the products made from linen?

North Sea called the Zuider Zee (ZYE dur ZEE) used to reach into the land for almost 50 miles (80 km). In 1925 the Dutch began to build a large dike to cut this saltwater body off from the sea. After the dike was built, some of the Zuider Zee's water was drained and polders were built. Thousands of acres of new land were created this way.

D. Cooperation and Disagreement in Belgium

Major Cities The Schelde River, which crosses Belgium and empties into the North Sea, is one of Belgium's most important rivers. Antwerp, a major industrial city, is located on the Schelde. Antwerp's shops and stores carry a variety of goods made in

Belgium. Belgium is known for high-quality products, such as fine carpets, soaps, glassware, and linens. Linen is a fabric made from **flax**, a plant with threadlike fibers that is widely grown in Belgium. Belgian linens are carefully made and sell for quite a high price.

Antwerp is also home to much of Belgium's industry. Oil refineries and chemical plants get their raw materials from barges that have traveled up the Rhine and Schelde rivers. They process these materials and ship them back out to be sold all over the world.

Brussels is the capital city of Belgium. Brussels is not on a major river, but it does have railroads and highways that connect it in every direction to the rest of Belgium. Trucks and trains bring in food from Belgian farms and steel and other metals for manufacturing tools and machinery. Brussels has the main offices of many international organizations. For example, the North Atlantic Treaty Organization (NATO) has its headquarters in Brussels. NATO is an alliance of the United States, Canada, and most countries of Western Europe. These countries have pledged to help one another in case of attack.

North and South Brussels is also important because it is near the center of Belgium, where an invisible line divides the country into two regions—the northern and southern. The Belgians who live in these two regions have serious differences. The people of Flanders, a region of northern Belgium, are called **Flemings**, and they speak Dutch. Flanders is part of the North European Plain, and many Flemish people are farmers who raise tulips and cattle.

The people of southern Belgium speak French and are called **Walloons**. Their region is hilly, with forests and abundant coal supplies. With iron ore that has been imported, the southern cities produce steel, tools, and heavy machinery for export.

How important are the differences between these two regions of Belgium? They are quite important to the Belgians themselves. The Flemings and the Walloons have often argued whether French or Dutch should be Belgium's official language. They have sometimes had difficulty working together in the national government. But to maintain peace and order, they have usually found solutions to their problems.

E. Luxembourg

A Tiny Country Luxembourg has beautiful forested hills and towns that attract tourists. This is especially true of northern Luxembourg, where the land and people are similar to the land and people across the border in southern Belgium.

Southern Luxembourg is slightly more level than the northern part of the country. It has rich soils, so that potatoes, oats, vegetables, and other foods grow well here. To the west of the farmland are iron ore mines. You may remember that Nancy, an industrial city in northern France, is near a large iron ore field. This same field reaches into southern Luxembourg. Until 1981 this field held large deposits of iron ore that accounted for Luxembourg's huge output of iron, steel, and manufactured goods. Now iron ore must be imported, because the iron ore field has been depleted. Coal from Belgium and Germany is also imported and used for fuel in many of Luxembourg's industries.

Luxembourg is similar to the Netherlands and Belgium in an important way. None of the Benelux countries has all the natural resources it needs for industry. Each country must import coal, iron ore, and other essential raw materials for industry. As a result, all three countries depend on trade with other countries for these raw materials. They also depend on each other to allow the transport of goods along the rivers that they share.

The flags of the European Union members fly outside the organization's headquarters in Brussels, Belgium.
▶ How many nations belong to the European Union?

Tariff Agreements The Benelux countries try to help each other through their **tariff** (TAR ihf) agreements. A tariff is a tax paid on an item when it is exported or imported. How does a tariff work? Let's say that a company in Luxembourg wanted to export steel to Ireland through the port of Rotterdam, in the Netherlands. The steel company would have to pay a tariff to the government of the Netherlands when the steel was shipped from the port. Because of the tariff, the company would have to charge Ireland's factories a high price in order to make a profit. The Irish factories might then look for cheaper steel from another country. Luxembourg's steel industry might not do very well.

European Community The Benelux countries have worked together to solve these kinds of problems. In 1948 they formed a special group that would charge low tariffs or no tariffs on each other's products. Farms and industries in all three countries benefited. Other European countries saw that this idea worked well. In 1957 they formed a group with similar trade arrangements called the European Economic Community, or the EEC. The Benelux nations were original members. In 1993 the organization also began dealing with noneconomic matters and became known as the **European Union**. By 1997, 15 Western European nations were members.

These nations hope to eliminate all tariffs on each other's products. They also plan to coordinate their agricultural policies, allow the free movement of people across their borders, and use a single type of currency. In spite of their differences, the Benelux countries have paved the way for economic cooperation among the nations of Western Europe.

LESSON 3

Review

REVIEWING MAIN IDEAS

A. Name the three rivers that are important trade routes for the Benelux countries.
B. What economic activities have helped the Netherlands become prosperous?
C. How have the Dutch reclaimed land in the Netherlands?
D. Who are the Walloons and the Flemings?
E. Why did the Benelux countries create a special trade group?

SKILLS CHECK

MAP SKILL

Look at the map on page 296 to find the national capitals of the Netherlands, Belgium, and Luxembourg. Using the scale on the map, find the distances in kilometers between the four cities.

Germany: An Industrial Giant

CONNECTIONS

Germany is known for high-quality products. Name a German product you might find for sale in the United States.

TERMS

autobahn, Slav, potash, lignite, tributary

FOCUS

Where are the most important industrial centers of Germany located?

A. A Nation United Again

Celebrating Freedom On the evening of November 9, 1989, thousands of jubilant East Germans and West Germans gathered at the Berlin Wall. Just a few hours earlier, the government of East Germany had announced that all citizens of the country were free to cross into West Germany through the East German crossing points.

The following day tens of thousands of East Germans poured into West Berlin on foot and by car and special shuttle buses. They were greeted by crowds of West Berliners. The sounds of ringing church bells, honking car horns, and singing filled the air. And all over the world people rejoiced as the wall that had separated East Germany from West Germany was torn down.

On October 3, 1990, eleven months after the fall of the Berlin Wall, East Germany ceased to exist. The citizens of East Germany and West Germany were united in a single Germany, the Federal Republic of Germany. The new democratic government declared that October 3 was to be established as a public holiday throughout Germany. It was to be known as the Day of German Unity.

Remembering the Past In 1945, when Germany was defeated at the end of World War II, that country was divided into four sections. Each of the Allies—France, the United Kingdom, the United States, and the Soviet Union—controlled a section. In 1949, the French, English, and American sections were combined to form the Federal Republic of Germany, or West Germany. Bonn became the capital of West Germany. The Soviet Union set up a separate Communist nation in its section, which became known as the German Democratic Republic, or East Germany.

Berlin was the capital of Germany before the country was divided. After World War II, Berlin was also divided into four sections by the Allies. The Soviet section of Berlin became the capital of East Germany. In 1961, the Communist East German government built a 26 mile (42 km) concrete and barbed-wire wall through Berlin to prevent people from East Germany from escaping into West Berlin and freedom.

THE DIVIDED CITY OF BERLIN 1961

In 1945, Berlin was divided into four sectors. In 1961, the Berlin Wall was built, separating the Soviet sector from the three other sectors.
▶ What country controlled East Berlin?

CENTRAL EUROPE: POLITICAL

Cities 100,000 to 499,999
Basel (Switzerland) B-1
Bern (Switzerland) B-1
Bonn (Germany) A-1
Geneva (Switzerland) B-1
Graz (Austria) B-3
Innsbruck (Austria) B-2
Mannheim (Germany) B-1
Rostock (Germany) A-2
Wolfsburg (Germany) A-2
Zurich (Switzerland) B-1

Cities 500,000 to 999,999
Bremen (Germany) A-1
Cologne (Germany) A-1
Dortmund (Germany) A-1
Dresden (Germany) A-2
Duisburg (Germany) A-1
Düsseldorf (Germany) A-1
Essen (Germany) A-1
Frankfurt (Germany) A-1
Hannover (Germany) A-1
Leipzig (Germany) A-2
Stuttgart (Germany) B-1

Cities 1,000,000 or more
Berlin (Germany) A-2
Hamburg (Germany) A-2
Munich (Germany) B-2
Vienna (Austria) B-3

Germany, Switzerland, and Austria form the heart of Europe. Both Austria
and Switzerland are landlocked countries.
▶ Which bodies of water border on Germany?

Looking Toward the Future Reunification presents a great challenge to Germany's government, economy, and people. Before reunification, the government of East Germany controlled that economy. East Germany's standard of living was higher than that of any other Eastern European country. But it was lower than West Germany's. Bringing the East German economic standard up to Western standards will require a huge investment of money by Germany.

Protecting the environment is another important concern for the people in Germany. Air and water pollution increased rapidly in both West Germany and East Germany with industrial growth after World War II. East Germany paid more attention to industrial growth than to environmental issues. West Germany was aware of environmental problems and tried to control them. Today, saving the environment is an economic problem as well as an environmental problem in Germany.

In spite of the problems that reunification presents, the people of Germany are working together. They are committed to the growth of their nation, which has as its foundation respect for human rights.

A Wealthy Country Germany has over 81 million people, more than any other European country except Russia. And it has more industry than any other country in Western Europe. Germany ranks fourth in the world, after the United States, Japan, and the former Soviet Union, in the amount of goods it produces.

Karl Heinrich is a German truck driver who spends many hours driving on the **autobahns** (AWT oh bahnz), Germany's superhighways. Cars zip along at high speed, sometimes as fast as 70 miles (113 km) per hour. One summer his teenage son Robert traveled with him to interview people he delivered goods to. Robert wanted to use the information he gathered to write a

A portion of Germany's autobahn passes through the beautiful evergreen forests near the Alps.
▶ What is the autobahn?

travel report for his school newspaper when he returned to classes in the fall. Robert's trip along the autobahns showed him how Germans have put their resources to work.

B. Industry and Farming in the North

Hamburg Robert and his father began their trip in Hamburg, Germany's second largest city and the main port for the entire country. Hamburg is on the Elbe (EL buh) River about 68 miles (109 km) from the North Sea. It is a city of docks, bridges, canals, and factories. There Robert met Heinz Brahms (hynz brahmz), a dock worker, who explained Hamburg's importance to Germany.

An amazing variety of goods passes through these sheds: for example, basketware from China, fertilizers, textiles, huge rolls of paper, copper wire, and sacks of rice. From Hamburg, goods can be transported by barge to the industrial areas. Goods are also taken down the Elbe River to other parts of Germany and Czechoslovakia.

Hamburg is Germany's second largest city and its most important industrial center. It is also one of Europe's major ports.
▶ Why are there so many cranes in the port of Hamburg?

The Elbe River is more than just a busy trade route. In the past it was also the border between Germanic tribes, such as the Franks in the west and the **Slavs** in the east. The Slavs were among the first people to live in the region that is called Eastern Europe.

As villages to the west of the Elbe developed, the Germanic people usually let their streets and buildings be built without plans for the villages. To outsiders, their villages looked disorganized. East of the Elbe River, the Slavs planned their villages to have straight streets, and they made rules for constructing the buildings. Today those differences remain in the older parts of towns on each side of the Elbe River.

Climate and Crops Even with all the traffic on the autobahns, there are quiet rural areas in northern Germany. This area is part of the North European Plain, which has a cool, damp climate like the climate of the British Isles and southern Scandinavia. This region also has areas that are like the dairy country of Denmark.

Potatoes, cabbages, and sugar beets are important crops in northern Germany, along with the grain crops barley and rye and other crops used for livestock feed. Most of these crops provide many traditional German foods, such as potato salad, rye bread, and sauerkraut, which is made from cabbage. Recipes for these foods, popular in the United States today, were brought to this country by German immigrants.

The only major industrial resource in northern Germany is **potash**, a type of mineral salt that is mined from deposits found below the earth's surface. It is especially useful in making soap, glass, and fertilizers. Germany is a major world producer of potash.

Berlin From Hamburg, Robert and his father traveled southeast to Berlin. Again the capital city of all of Germany, Berlin is located on the North European Plain. It is Germany's largest city, with a population of nearly 4 million people. The North European Plain's farmers send their crops to Berlin, where they are processed into foods such as flour, canned vegetables, and dairy products. Then the products are sold all over the country or exported for sale in other countries.

C. Industry in Central Germany

Ore Mountains To the south of Berlin are Germany's Ore Mountains. Coal, silver, uranium, and other minerals are mined in these mountains. Coal is especially important to Germany because the mines in the Ore Mountains produce more coal than those of any other European country except the former Soviet Union. However, the coal, which is called **lignite**, is of low quality. That means that much more lignite than hard coal must be burned to produce heat.

Leipzig One of Germany's major cities is near the mines of the Ore Mountains. Leipzig (LYP sihg) is the tenth most populated city in Germany. Its factories produce many kinds of manufactured goods, including scientific equipment, paper, and clothing. Leipzig grew up as a center for trade along a major road running between Berlin and Munich.

Leipzig is also famous for its Sports and Physical Education College. Students who attend the college become coaches and world-class Olympic athletes. Sports are an important part of the cultural life of Germany. Cities and towns throughout Germany maintain swimming pools and playing fields for public use. Many Germans are members of sports clubs and prefer playing soccer, tennis, and other sports rather than watching sports events.

The Ruhr River Valley Robert and his father gradually made their way to the western city of Cologne (kuh LOHN). Near Cologne is the Ruhr River, a **tributary** of

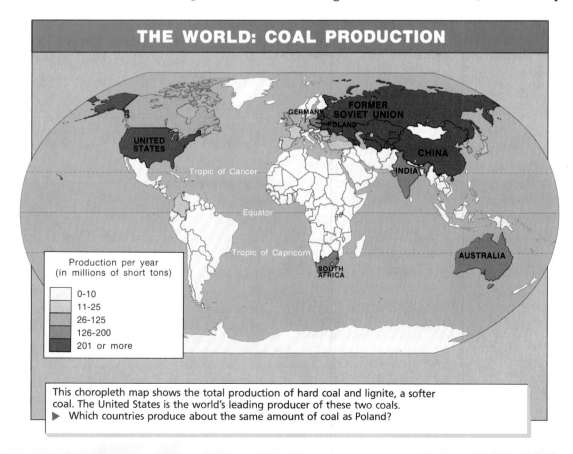

THE WORLD: COAL PRODUCTION

Production per year
(in millions of short tons)

0-10
11-25
26-125
126-200
201 or more

This choropleth map shows the total production of hard coal and lignite, a softer coal. The United States is the world's leading producer of these two coals.
▶ Which countries produce about the same amount of coal as Poland?

the Rhine River. A tributary is a river or stream that flows into a larger river or body of water. The Ruhr River valley holds the greatest concentration of industry in all of Europe. Robert's father introduced Robert to Joseph Olbrich (awl brihk), an engineer at a huge coal mine near Cologne. Robert asked about industries in the Ruhr and found out that the coal mines supply enough fuel for power plants to produce 25 percent of Germany's electricity. Mr. Olbrich happily summed up by saying that, "At our present annual output, this means that there are another 30 years of mining. So my future seems pretty secure!"

Along with the coal mines, the Ruhr has helped make Germany a leading world producer of cars, electrical goods, and chemicals. The famous Krupp steelworks are known for high-quality steel products, including kitchen knives.

But there are problems with all the industry in the Ruhr River valley. Eventually, the coal will be depleted. To prepare for this time, Germany has been building nuclear power plants that will enable it to continue producing electricity far in the future. Another problem that Mr. Olbrich pointed out was that coal mining

> has brought a lot of hardships to the people living in this area. Whole villages, farms, forests, and rivers have disappeared. Since 1945, 26,000 people in some 72 villages have had to move to make way for our [coal] excavators [digging equipment].

Rhine Valley   After leaving Cologne, Robert and his father drove a short distance south to Bonn. Bonn was just a small city on the Rhine River until the end of World War II. Then it became necessary for West Germans to choose a new capital because Berlin, the original capital city, was part of East Germany after the war.

Robert and his father toured a vineyard in the Rhine Valley near Bonn, and Robert interviewed Karin Schulz, the vineyard's owner. She pointed out that the climate is just right for wine grapes along the Rhine River almost as far north as Bonn. She explained that in the second century B.C., the ancient Romans brought grapes from the region around the Mediterranean Sea and began growing them along the Rhine. Mrs. Schulz described her vineyards.

> These vineyards have been owned by my family for over 200 years. My father and grandfather taught me the art and science of winemaking. It is hard work. The vines do best when they are planted on a south slope facing the sun. But machines cannot work well on steep slopes, so we have to do much of the work by hand.

D.   The Two Economies of Bavaria

Farming   Continuing south along the autobahn to Munich (MYOO nihk), which is near the southern border of Germany, Robert noticed beautiful rolling hills and forests. Robert and his father were traveling through the Central Uplands toward the Alps. In the foothills of the Alps of Germany, the region called Bavaria is the home of woodcarvers, who make many items from wood by hand. With wood from

Thousands of tourists visit Bavaria each year. In addition to beautiful scenery, there are wood carvings to see.
▶ How many faces have been carved in this tree trunk?

Loreley

by Heinrich Heine

The Rhine River flows through much of Germany and has been important in the nation's history. It has also influenced German art, music, and literature.

One of Germany's great poets was Heinrich Heine. In his poem "Loreley" (LOR uh lye) he describes the Rhine and its hidden dangers for those who sail on the river.

I do not know what haunts me,
What saddened my mind all day;
An age-old tale confounds me,
A spell I cannot allay [calm].

The air is cool and in twilight
The Rhine's dark waters flow;
The peak of the mountain in highlight
Reflects the evening glow.

There sits a lovely maiden
Above, so wondrous fair,
With shining jewels laden,
She combs her golden hair.

It falls through her comb in a shower,
And over the valley rings
A song of mysterious power
That lovely maiden sings.

The boatman in his small skiff is
Seized by turbulent love,
No longer he marks where the cliff is,
He looks to the mountain above.

I think the waves must fling him
Against the reefs nearby,
And that did with her singing
The lovely Loreley.

Bavaria's forests, these farmers carved valuable products and earned additional income. Today, farming and woodcarving are still important in Bavaria.

Munich and Industry Bavaria has much more than farms. When Robert arrived in Munich, Bavaria's principal city, he discovered that this city is the home of many international corporations. Siemens Corporation has a huge plant in Munich where computer systems and household appliances such as electric mixers are produced. Bavarian Motor Works (BMW), which produces high-quality cars sold all over the world, is also located in Munich. This city is especially famous for its breweries, where malts, or grains, are brewed. The ingredients for Munich's beers come from nearby farms. Optical equipment, clothes, and engineering supplies are also made here.

In Munich and other industrial cities, large numbers of foreign workers and their families are arriving to find factory jobs.

The tower of Munich's City Hall stands above the Marienplatz, or city square.
▶ What purpose, do you think, does the Marienplatz serve?

Jutta Weishaupl, a teacher in Munich, told Robert how this affected her classroom.

> *There are half a dozen foreign children—from Czechoslovakia, New Zealand, Italy, and Turkey. There are special classes for children who cannot speak German. Part of a lesson is held in German and part in their own language. When their German is good enough, they are integrated into the other classes. It's very tough on them, learning a new language as well as keeping up with all the other subjects.*

This mixing of people from different cultures has been going on for centuries in Germany. The ancient Germanic tribes in the west lived alongside the Slavic peoples in the east. The Romans dominated the southern part of Germany. Together these different peoples created the variety of cultures that Robert had observed along the autobahns.

LESSON 4

Review

REVIEWING MAIN IDEAS

A. Why is October 3, 1990 important in the history of Germany?
B. Why is the Elbe River important to Hamburg?
C. Why is coal an important resource in the Ruhr Valley?
D. Why could we say that Bavaria has a balanced combination of agriculture and industry?

SKILLS CHECK

WRITING SKILL

Choose information about one topic that you find especially interesting in this lesson. Present that information in a brief report similar to the quotations that you have read in the lesson.

Switzerland and Austria

CONNECTIONS

Name the ways in which people who live in a mountainous country could make a living.

TERMS

transhumance, confederation, canton

FOCUS

Why did Switzerland develop industries that are different from those of Austria?

A. Looking for Geographic Clues

Like most West European countries, Austria and Switzerland have high standards of living. Almost all their citizens are literate, or can read and write, and most adults have high-paying jobs. Both countries have prosperous farms and industries. Austria has some mineral resources, such as iron ore, but Switzerland has almost no mineral resources. How did Switzerland, with few mineral resources, become as prosperous as Austria? To find out, you would have to dig for geographical clues about these two countries.

Geographers often begin comparing two countries by first comparing their areas and their population. If you look at the Table of Countries on pages 258–261, you will see that Austria's area is 32,375 square miles (83,851 sq km), which is more than twice the size of Switzerland's area of 15,941 square miles (41,287 sq km). Austria also has a larger population, with nearly 8 million people; Switzerland has about 7 million.

The next step in searching for geographical clues about countries is to learn how people use their land and natural resources. This is what we will do as we further investigate the economies of Austria and Switzerland. What should we investigate? How people use the land, especially the resources that are available and the products that are made from them.

B. The Imaginative Use of Resources in Switzerland

Transhumance The highest of the Alps are in the southern half of Switzerland. In most places of the world, steep slopes and ice-cold winters make farming quite difficult. But Swiss farmers have adjusted to these conditions. Instead of planting crops, they practice a type of cattle herding called **transhumance**. Transhumance means that in the spring the Swiss farmers take their cattle up the mountainsides to graze in the cool, grassy meadows. In winter they bring the cattle back down to the valleys, where the cattle are safe from freezing winds and snow. Swiss farmers have been very successful with this kind of herding, and their cheese and dairy products are sold around the world. The Swiss prove that mountains can be put to good use.

Dairy cattle are a common sight in the high meadows of the Alps.
▶ When are the cattle brought down to the warmer valleys?

309

Tourism The Alps are also valuable because they attract thousands of tourists each year, including mountain climbers. Mont Blanc is the highest peak in the Alps, but it is Switzerland's Matterhorn that is most famous among mountain climbers. The Matterhorn is called the tiger of the Alps because its frozen, snow-covered peaks are a challenge to climbers.

Skilled Workers The Swiss have not been discouraged by their country's lack of minerals and fuels for industry. Ships and barges from other countries bring iron ore and other minerals, chemicals, and coal to the city of Basel, on the Rhine River. These raw materials are then transported to factories in other cities. Because it is expensive to import all these raw materials, the Swiss produce goods that require few raw materials and that sell for a high price. For example, in Zurich, Switzerland's largest city, workers use their education and skills to make fine watches, scientific instruments, medicines, and other specialized products. These products are known for their high quality, and people are willing to pay high prices for them. The profit earned from the sale of these products helps to pay for the raw materials that must be imported.

C. A Nation of Many States

In the thirteenth century, Switzerland was created as a **confederation**, or union, of many different states. The people of these states today have different languages, religions, and traditions, but they respect one another's customs. Each group has its own territory, called a **canton**. A canton is a small political unit similar to a state in the United States. Each canton has its own constitution, laws, and language. In fact, about three fourths of the Swiss people speak German, and the rest speak French, Italian, or an ancient language that is called Romansh.

Statues and shops surround an outdoor cafe in Vienna, Austria.
▶ What is Vienna famous for?

All cantons work together as a nation, with their capital city in Bern. The Swiss have enjoyed many centuries of peace and prosperity. Many international banks have their headquarters in Switzerland because they are confident that Switzerland will not have a civil war or revolution.

D. Finding Clues to Austria's Prosperity

Mountains and Forests The Swiss have built a country that is admired for its peace and prosperity. Has Austria been as successful as Switzerland? To answer this important question, we would have to find out more about Austria.

Austria shares part of the Alps with Switzerland. Snowy peaks over 12,000 feet (3,658 m) high curve through Austria's western region. Like the Swiss, Austrians

transportation route. Up and down the Danube, barges and ships carry raw materials, such as farm products, oil, minerals, and cotton. The factories of Austria's main city, Vienna, turn these raw materials into flour, canned and frozen foods, plastics, fuel oil, iron, steel, and clothing. These processed goods are then shipped from Vienna to other areas of Austria. You can now understand why the Danube is called Austria's lifeline.

The Danube Valley and the city of Vienna have long been the seat of power and wealth in Austria. Vienna is famous for its cultural attractions, such as opera houses, art galleries, and concert halls. But Vienna has not always ruled over a stable country. Austria was once part of a huge empire that included parts of Germany, France, and Hungary. After World War I, in 1918, this empire lost many territories. The independent republic of Austria was carved out of a part of this empire. In 1938, Austria was taken over by Germany. It became a free country again after World War II.

enjoy hiking, skiing, and mountain climbing. They have many mountain resorts, like the city of Innsbruck, with its hotels, gift shops, restaurants, and ski centers.

Where the Alps begin to flatten out, toward central Austria, they are covered with thick forests that provide lumber, one of Austria's most important resources. Lumber, paper, and paper products are major exports. Many of the mills and plants that process these materials use hydroelectric power that comes from the mountain rivers in western Austria. Near the Alps there are also deposits of minerals.

The Danube The Danube River, Austria's lifeline, runs through northern Austria. The river's wide valleys provide level land and rich soils. The Danube Valley's farms grow rye, potatoes, and sugar beets.

The Danube River is also an important

LESSON 5
Review

REVIEWING MAIN IDEAS
A. Name two ways in which Austria and Switzerland are different.
B. Why do the Swiss produce the kinds of products they do?
C. How do the cantons in Switzerland differ from one another?
D. Why is the Danube River Austria's lifeline?

SKILLS CHECK
THINKING SKILL
To compare Austria and Switzerland, make a chart, using the following categories: total area, population, mineral resources, economic activities, major exports.

BATTLING ACID RAIN

Germany's Black Forest is a land of deep valleys and high mountains. Tall, dark-green pine trees cover the sides of the mountains. The beauty and the darkness of the Black Forest have made it the setting for many fairy tales, including *Hansel and Gretel.*

In the early 1980s, German scientists noticed a growing number of unhealthy trees in the Black Forest. The needles on the pine trees, which were usually a bold, dark-green, had yellowed or had fallen off. In some areas of the forest, many acres of brownish-gray, dead trees stood starkly against the sky. The scientists said the Black Forest suffered from forest death.

However, not only trees were dying. In Sweden, lakes that had once been filled with fish were now lifeless. Swedish scientists tested the water in the lakes and found high amounts of acid.

The Causes of Acid Rain

Where did the acid come from? Scientists said it was the result of *acid rain.* Acid rain is the term used for rain, sleet, snow, mist, fog, and clouds containing acid. The acid results from the burning of fossil fuels, such as petroleum, coal, and natural gas. When the fuel is burned, sulfur or nitrogen gas is given off. These gases mix with oxygen in the air to form sulfur dioxide gas or nitrogen oxide gas. When the sulfur dioxide or nitrogen oxide mixes with moisture in the air, the precipitation becomes as acidic as vinegar.

Acid rain has only recently become a problem. Its origins, however, can be traced back over the last 90 years. During that time, the modern industrial countries of the world have burned increasingly larger amounts of fossil fuels, especially coal. These fuels have been used to power factories and electricity plants. As a result, more sulfur dioxide has been released into the air.

The Effects of Acid Rain

Acid rain falls on everything on the earth's surface—buildings, soil, rivers, and trees. A visitor walking through the wooded countryside of Germany said that the trees he saw in a forest

The destruction of the trees in the Black Forest was one of the first signs of acid rain.
▶ Where is the Black Forest?

THE ACID RAIN PROCESS

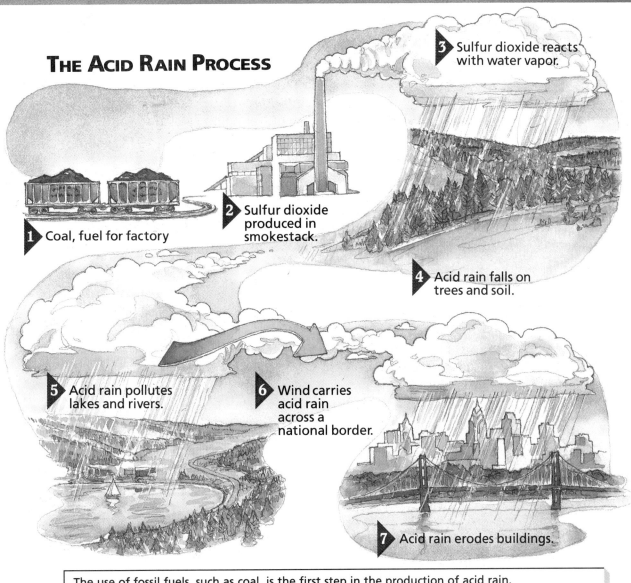

1 Coal, fuel for factory

2 Sulfur dioxide produced in smokestack.

3 Sulfur dioxide reacts with water vapor.

4 Acid rain falls on trees and soil.

5 Acid rain pollutes lakes and rivers.

6 Wind carries acid rain across a national border.

7 Acid rain erodes buildings.

The use of fossil fuels, such as coal, is the first step in the production of acid rain. The smoke from burning the coal reacts with rain-bearing clouds to produce acid rain. Winds then blow the clouds far from the source.
▶ At what stage would it be easiest to stop acid rain from forming?

damaged by acid rain were "completely dead as far as the eye could see."

The tragic loss of Germany's forests also has an economic cost. Each year the German lumber industry loses as much as $250 million worth of timber because of acid rain. This does not include the cost of jobs that have been lost in the lumber industry in Germany.

Germany is not the only country experiencing the tragedy of acid rain. In almost every country of the world where industries use oil or coal for fuel, acid rain causes some kind of damage. In Denmark, acid rain is eroding the brick, stone, and cement of buildings. A Danish architect has said that these buildings are melting away like sugar candy. In the 1990s, acid rain will probably eat away one tenth of the surfaces of buildings and sculptures in Krakow, Poland. Even the Statue of Liberty, in the harbor of New York City, has suffered damage from acid rain. In the mid-1980s, the statue had to be cleaned and repaired to protect its metal from further damage.

In the United States, trees are dying, and the water in many rivers and lakes has become so acidic that fish and plants cannot live in them. Anne LaBastille, a writer and nature guide, lives in a log cabin near a lake in New York's Adirondack Mts. She has noticed that "native trout are now scarce, as are loons, osprey, and otters. Bullfrogs are all but silent. As much as a third of the . . . red spruce around the lake have died."

Cleaning up Acid Rain Pollution

What are the solutions to the acid rain problem? Like many environmental problems, acid rain will be expensive and

Eastern Europe's forests have suffered greatly from acid rain. This "dead forest" on the border of northern Czechoslovakia once thrived with living trees.
▶ Describe what the forest now looks like.

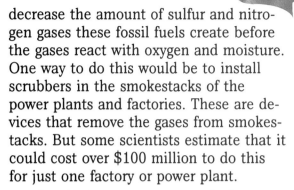

time-consuming to eliminate. Industries could burn less oil or coal, but they would then need to find other means of producing energy, such as nuclear power. Nuclear power also poses a problem, however, since there is no safe way to dispose of the radioactive waste generated by nuclear power plants.

Burning other kinds of coal is another possible solution. For example, anthracite coal has much less sulfur than lignite coal. However, anthracite is not as plentiful as lignite, and it is more expensive to mine.

Industries using coal or oil could also decrease the amount of sulfur and nitrogen gases these fossil fuels create before the gases react with oxygen and moisture. One way to do this would be to install scrubbers in the smokestacks of the power plants and factories. These are devices that remove the gases from smokestacks. But some scientists estimate that it could cost over $100 million to do this for just one factory or power plant.

Acid Rain Knows No Boundaries

Acid rain poses an important geographical problem because wind currents can carry it far from the factories that created it. A factory in Poland may produce acid rain that does not fall to earth until it reaches Germany or Sweden. European countries have met and have agreed to cooperate in finding a way to stop the spread of acid rain. The United States and Canadian governments have also met to try to work out a plan that will end acid rain.

Acid rain's destruction of forests, lakes, and buildings has drawn increasing concern from the public. In a public-opinion poll taken in Germany, German citizens said that acid rain is an even more urgent problem than having nuclear missiles in their country. Perhaps if a poll were taken in the United States, we would discover that Americans are just as concerned as Germans about acid rain.

THINKING CRITICALLY

1. What are the causes and the effects of acid rain?
2. What do you think might be some of the consequences of allowing the continued destruction of forests by acid rain?
3. Suppose you had the authority to require industries to install scrubbers in their smokestacks. Who would you ask to pay for installing the scrubbers—the government or business? Give two reasons for your choice.

REVIEWING TERMS

✓ **summit**	**tariff** ✓
✓ **vineyard**	**autobahn** ✓
✓ **canton**	**tributary** ✓
polder	**transhumance** ✓
✓ **Flemings**	**confederation** ✓
✓ **Walloons**	

From the list above, choose a term that can be used in place of the underlined word or phrase in each sentence. Rewrite the sentences on a separate sheet of paper.

1. *autobahn* Automobile speeds allowed on the <u>superhighway in Germany</u> are much higher than speeds allowed on roads in the United States.
2. The French-speaking <u>people of southern Belgium</u> *Walloon* sometimes have difficulty working in government with the Dutch-speaking <u>people of northern Belgium.</u> *Fleming*
3. Switzerland was created as a <u>union</u> of many states in the thirteenth century. *canton*
4. *vineyard* The <u>type of field of grape vines</u> found in Bordeaux and Burgundy is among the finest in the world.
5. The European Union decided to eliminate the <u>tax on imports and exports</u> between member nations. *tariff*
6. Each Swiss <u>state</u> has its own language, religion, and traditions. *confederation*
7. *summit* The <u>highest point</u> of the Matterhorn is 14,690 feet (4,478 m) above sea level.
8. For centuries the Swiss have been practicing <u>a type of herding cattle in which cattle are moved between the mountainsides and valleys, based on the season.</u> *transhumance*
9. Without the dike, the low-lying <u>drained land</u> would be flooded. *polder*
10. The Ruhr River is a <u>stream that flows into</u> the Rhine River. *tributary*

REVIEWING THE FACTS

On a separate sheet of paper, answer the questions in complete sentences.

1. Which countries does the tunnel under the English Channel connect?
2. How did Hannibal attack the Romans in Italy?
3. What is the climate of the North European Plain?
4. What are France's special crops used for?
5. Why is Paris called the City of Light?
6. What are the major products of each of France's three industrial regions?
7. What is the largest area of polders in the Netherlands?
8. What two international organizations have their headquarters in Brussels?
9. What problems has industry created in the Ruhr River valley?
10. Why do many international banks have their headquarters in Switzerland?

WRITING ABOUT GEOGRAPHY

Write an article about what you think happened the first day the tunnel beneath the English Channel was opened for use. You might include comments from people who used the tunnel.

THINKING CRITICALLY

On a separate sheet of paper, answer the following in complete sentences.

1. How, do you think, might the reunification of Germany affect the heartland of Western Europe?

2. What advantages and disadvantages are there for a country that puts a tariff on imported goods?

3. How can the Netherlands, which has few resources, have a high standard of living?

4. How would the economy of the heartland be different if there were no major rivers, such as the Danube, Seine, Rhine, and Ruhr rivers?

5. What imaginative uses of resources are found in the heartland?

SUMMARIZING THE CHAPTER

Copy this graphic organizer on a separate sheet of paper. Copy the information from this graphic organizer to the one you have drawn. Complete the chart by writing the appropriate items in each box.

CHAPTER THEME → The countries in the heartland of Western Europe have developed high standards of living through modern economies based on industry and trade.

	AGRICULTURAL PRODUCTS	MANUFACTURED PRODUCTS
FRANCE		
BENELUX NATIONS		
GERMANY		
SWITZERLAND		
AUSTRIA		

CHAPTER *13*

THE COUNTRIES OF SOUTHERN EUROPE

1. Southern Europe: A Land of Peninsulas and Islands

2. The Iberian Peninsula: Spain and Portugal

3. Italy: Modern Challenges in an Ancient Land

4. Greece and Cyprus: A Shared Culture

318

Southern Europe: A Land of Peninsulas and Islands

CONNECTIONS

Name the ways in which a country that borders an ocean or sea might be different from a landlocked country.

TERMS

Mediterranean climate, emigrate

FOCUS

How are the countries of Southern Europe alike?

A. Five Countries, Three Peninsulas, and Thousands of Islands

The Rock Jutting straight out of the waters of the Mediterranean Sea and reaching 1,400 feet (427 m) into the sky is a towering cliff called the Rock of Gibraltar. The Rock of Gibraltar, or the Rock, as it is often called, guards the Strait of Gibraltar, the narrow passageway connecting the Atlantic Ocean and the Mediterranean Sea. From the Rock, you can see two continents at once, Europe and Africa.

The Rock is at the southern tip of the Iberian Peninsula, one of the three peninsulas that are found in Southern Europe. The map on page 320 can help you name the three peninsulas that extend from Europe into the Mediterranean Sea. Four countries in Southern Europe are located on peninsulas. Italy occupies the peninsula that is shaped like a boot. Italy has over 57 million people, which is the largest population of any of the countries of Southern Europe.

Italy also includes two large islands. Sicily, the largest island in the Mediterranean Sea, is located just off the southern tip of Italy. It is 9,926 square miles (25,708 sq km) in area, which makes it somewhat larger than the state of Maryland. North-west of Sicily is Italy's second island, Sardinia, which is nearly as large as Sicily.

To the west, the Iberian Peninsula is shared by two countries—Spain and Portugal. Spain is the largest country of Southern Europe, with an area of 194,881 square miles (504,742 sq km). This makes it about the same size as the state of Oregon. Portugal is much smaller. Its area is 35,383 square miles (91,642 sq km), which is about the same size as the state of Maine. Finally, on the third peninsula we find Greece, a country that includes over 2,000 islands. To the east of Greece is a large island in the Mediterranean Sea, named Cyprus, the fifth country of Southern Europe.

The seas surrounding the peninsulas and islands of Southern Europe provide water routes between the peninsulas. The Mediterranean Sea separates the Iberian Peninsula from Italy. The beautiful blue Adriatic Sea separates Italy from Greece, and the Aegean Sea separates Greece from the island of Cyprus.

Cultural Influences The culture of Southern Europe has been influenced by North Africa and by other peoples living near the Mediterranean Sea. The narrow waterway allowed Arabs from North Africa to invade Southern Europe in the eighth century. Arab culture spread throughout the Iberian Peninsula until the fifteenth century. At that time, Christians from northern Spain pushed the Arabs out of the Iberian Peninsula and back to North Africa.

The ancient Romans also left lasting influences on Southern European cultures. The Roman Empire controlled most of the lands around the Mediterranean Sea from 27 B.C. until A.D. 476. One of the most important influences the Romans had was on the languages that are used in Southern Europe. Portuguese, Spanish, and Italian are called Romance languages because they are based on the Latin language used during the Roman Empire.

▶ The ruins of the Acropolis in Athens, Greece

319

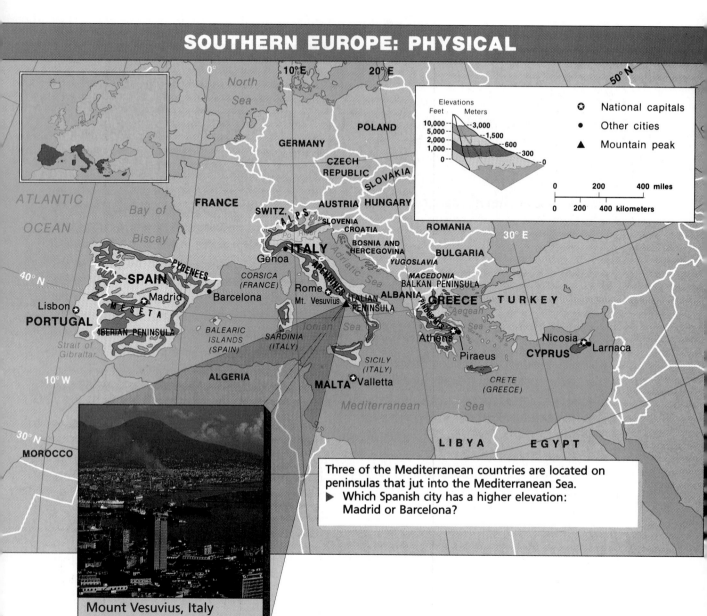

Three of the Mediterranean countries are located on peninsulas that jut into the Mediterranean Sea.
▶ Which Spanish city has a higher elevation: Madrid or Barcelona?

Mount Vesuvius, Italy

B. The Climate and Agriculture of Southern Europe

Mediterranean Climate The table on the next page gives the average temperatures of three cities in Europe for January and July and the average annual precipitation. The table shows that Athens, Greece, has a drier climate than Dublin, Ireland, or Vienna, Austria. This makes sense if you remember from Chapter 11 the gray fogs and mists of the British Isles. And all along the North European Plain there is quite a bit of moist air. In contrast, the region that borders the Mediterranean Sea has little rainfall. It has what is called a **Mediterranean climate**. A Mediterranean climate has hot, dry summers and cool, rainy winters.

The temperatures of Southern Europe are much warmer than those in other European regions. As you learned in Chapter 11, the countries of the British Isles and Scandinavia have a climate influenced by the North Atlantic Drift.

Mediterranean Crops Most Southern European farmers cannot grow the thick green pasture grasses that thrive in the marine climate of Western Europe, but they grow other products. They take advantage of the hot, dry summers to grow citrus fruits, such as oranges, lemons, and grapefruits. Olives and grapes also grow well in this climate, which helps to make Southern Europe the world's main supplier of olive oil and wine.

In the cooler winter months, the farmers raise wheat and vegetables such as potatoes, tomatoes, and beans. These foods as well as fish, which are plentiful along the coast, are essential items for traditional meals. Such meals include bread; stews; soups; and pasta, a dough made of flour, eggs, and water and shaped into forms we know as spaghetti and macaroni.

C. Major Cities of Southern Europe

Capital Cities You can find the capital cities of the southern countries of Europe on the map on page 320. In the capital cities are found some of the world's great cultural treasures. For example, in Athens, the capital city of Greece, there are the ruins of the Acropolis and other temples and buildings that are over 2,000 years old.

In Rome, the capital city of Italy, are the remains of ancient buildings, such as the famous sports stadium called the Coliseum. Madrid, the capital of Spain, is home to many beautiful buildings and the Prado, a famous art museum that holds masterpieces of European art and sculpture.

Several important port cities are in Southern Europe. They are Oporto, in Portugal; Barcelona, in Spain; Genoa (JEN uh wuh), in Italy; Piraeus (pye REE us), in Greece, and Larnaca, in Cyprus.

Today many raw materials essential for industry are imported into the Southern European countries through their coastal ports. For example, factories in northern Italy import huge amounts of coal, iron ore, and petroleum. These factories produce so many manufactured goods that Italy is a top European industrial power.

People, too, continue to move through the countries of Southern Europe. Many workers, especially those from Spain, Portugal, and Greece, **emigrate**, or leave their countries, to live permanently in other countries, including the United States. Some leave their towns and cities to work temporarily in factories in Western Europe's heartland. At the same time, millions of

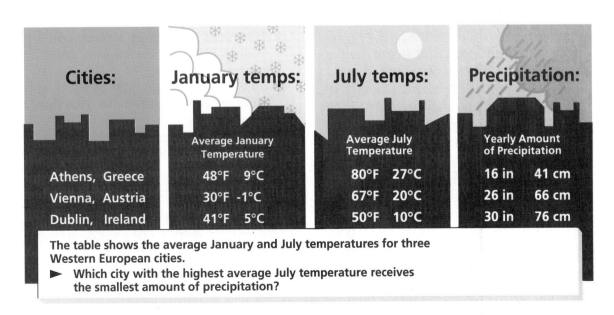

Cities:	January temps: Average January Temperature		July temps: Average July Temperature		Precipitation: Yearly Amount of Precipitation	
Athens, Greece	48°F	9°C	80°F	27°C	16 in	41 cm
Vienna, Austria	30°F	-1°C	67°F	20°C	26 in	66 cm
Dublin, Ireland	41°F	5°C	50°F	10°C	30 in	76 cm

The table shows the average January and July temperatures for three Western European cities.
► Which city with the highest average July temperature receives the smallest amount of precipitation?

321

A cruise ship prepares to dock at a harbor along the coastline of Greece.
▶ Do you think the climate of the Mediterranean region attracts tourists?

about one-half the size of New York City. For centuries, Andorra was isolated from outsiders because of its mountain location. Some of its citizens became famous for smuggling goods between France and Spain.

Today, thousands of tourists travel to Andorra each year to enjoy the country's scenery and ski resorts. They also come to shop. The main highway crossing Andorra is lined with many shops selling a fantastic variety of items.

The Apennines and Pindus Mountains Another group of Southern European mountains is the Apennines (AP uh nynz), which run north and south along the peninsula of Italy. The Apennines, which are not as high or as rugged as the Alps or the Pyrenees, include many volcanic mountains. The Pindus Mountains, which cover much of Greece, are dry, with poor soils and a small population.

tourists from all over the world arrive in the southern countries every year by plane and by cruise ship.

D. Southern Europe's Mountainous Peninsulas

The Pyrenees The Pyrenees, a rugged, hostile mountain range, form the border between the countries of Spain and France. The Pyrenees reach only about 11,000 feet (3,353 m) in height, so they are not as high as the Alps. But the Pyrenees are far more difficult to travel through. The Alps have many low passes and valleys, but the Pyrenees are very steep, with few level areas for highways or railway lines. As a result, the Pyrenees create a great barrier between Spain and France.

Andorra High in the Pyrenees is the tiny nation of Andorra. Andorra is only 180 square miles (466 sq km) in size, which is

LESSON 1

Review

REVIEWING MAIN IDEAS

A. What are the two major physical features of Southern Europe?

B. How does the climate of Southern Europe influence the kinds of crops grown in this region?

C. How has the geography of Southern Europe contributed to the growth of port cities?

D. How do the Alps of Southern Europe differ from the Pyrenees?

SKILLS CHECK

MAP SKILL

Imagine that you are taking a tour of the capital cities of Southern Europe. Make a list of the capitals. Then use the map on page 320 to find the straight-line distance traveled in going from Lisbon, Portugal, to Nicosia, Cyprus.

The Iberian Peninsula: Spain and Portugal

CONNECTIONS
List the countries in North and South America where Spanish or Portuguese is spoken.

TERMS
Moors, tungsten

FOCUS
How have climate and landforms influenced economic activities on the Iberian Peninsula?

A. The Regions of Spain's Meseta

Dialects and Regions The Spanish language has many dialects, each one slightly different from the others. For example, the Spanish spoken by the people living near Madrid is called Castilian Spanish. It is quite different from Catalan (KAT uh lan), the Spanish dialect spoken by people who live in the region near Barcelona.

To understand the people of Spain and their different dialects and cultures, it is important to learn about Spain's geography. Most of Spain is part of a 4,000-foot-high (1,219-m-high) plateau called the Meseta. Mountains crisscross the Meseta like fingers spread flat across a table. The mountains divide the Meseta into many separate regions and make travel between the regions difficult. Each region is surrounded by rugged mountains.

These individual regions were once separate kingdoms. Each kingdom had its own territory, its own culture, and sometimes, its own dialect of the Spanish language. Today these kingdoms have become states that are united into the nation of Spain, but, like the kingdoms, these states are quite different from one another. Among the differences are people's special customs and accents.

Madrid, the capital city of Spain, is located on the Meseta. The area around Madrid is called Castile, and the people call themselves Castilians. Barcelona, which borders on the Mediterranean Sea, is the second most important city in Spain. Barcelona has a population of nearly 2 million people. It is the home of Spain's major port and many industries. Nearby, one of Spain's most important rivers, the Ebro (AY broh), empties into the Mediterranean Sea.

The Basques The Basques, another group of Spain's citizens, feel that they are different. The Basques live near the Pyrenees and speak an ancient language called Basque in addition to Spanish. Their dress, diet, and customs are also different from those of other Spaniards.

Madrid has preserved many of its old, beautiful buildings with their unique architecture.
▶ What is the area around Madrid called?

323

Many Basques feel that their region should become an independent country, as it was before it became a part of Spain in 1939. Some Basques feel so strongly about this that they have carried out terrorist acts against the Spanish government. Only a few Basques are terrorists, but their desire for an independent country creates a complex problem for Spain's leaders.

If independence is given to the Basques, then other groups in Spain might also want to create their own countries. The nation of Spain would be broken into many small countries.

B. Climates and Agriculture in Spain

Two Climates People in different regions of Spain build their houses according to the climate of their area. Octavio Torres (ahk TAY vee oh TAWR rays), an architect in Madrid, has explained how he builds houses in the different regions in Spain. In the south of Spain, along the Mediterranean Sea, it is very hot and sunny.

My main problem is keeping the inside of a house cool. So, the houses I design are normally built round an interior patio, which very often has a fountain in the middle, surrounded by shrubs and trees. All of the rooms of the house look or open out on to the patio—which is shady and cool.

In the north, along the Atlantic Ocean coast, Mr. Torres designs houses a different way because of the area's climate.

Most of the time it is wet and cold. Houses have to be designed so that most things can be done inside. The rooms are larger and the windows are bigger in order to let in as much light as possible. The fireplace is a very important feature because people spend a lot of their time in front of it.

Flowering plants hang from the windows and walls that face the patio of this house in Southern Spain.
▶ Why does the house have a patio?

Only a small part of Spain has this marine climate. Most of Spain has the warm, dry Mediterranean climate. So most houses in Spain are built around patios or gardens.

Agriculture Spain's climate affects farming as well as architecture. Both the climate and farm products of Spain's Atlantic coast are similar to those of the North European Plain and the British Isles. Corn, wheat, and apples are grown in this coastal zone. But the soil is poor, and harvests of these crops are not abundant. The Atlantic coastal area is more important to Spain's economy because it supplies a large part of the cattle used for meat and leather. This region also supplies much of Spain's fish, especially sardines and tuna.

Most of Spain is too dry for growing crops without irrigation. For this reason, Spain's rivers are necessary for farming, since they provide water for crops during dry periods. Without irrigation water from the rivers, Spain's farmers would find it difficult to grow crops because of the dry, warm climate. A traveler passing through the Meseta in the dry summer heat wrote,

> *As far as I could see there were no towns, no villages, only the brassy, shimmering heat rising up from the plains and the implacable [merciless] sky without even a wisp of cloud.*

The map on this page shows that most of Spain's rivers flow west to the Atlantic Ocean, crossing through the country of Portugal. The Tagus, Spain's longest river, follows a westward route. The Tagus begins high on the Meseta and flows 625 miles (1,006 km) across the Iberian Peninsula before emptying into the Atlantic Ocean near the city of Lisbon, Portugal.

These rivers are very different from the more famous rivers of Europe, such as the Rhine and the Danube. Spain's rivers are not wide and deep enough for large ships to travel up from the ocean. And Spain's harbors are not large enough to allow much trade. However, Spain's farms, homes, and factories depend on these rivers for water for drinking, cleaning, manufacturing, and irrigation.

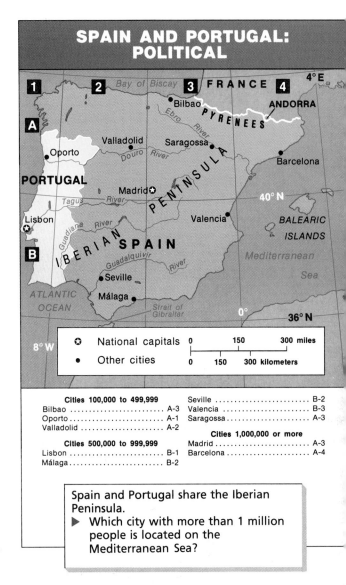

SPAIN AND PORTUGAL: POLITICAL

National capitals ✪
Other cities •

Cities 100,000 to 499,999		
Bilbao	A-3	
Oporto	A-1	
Valladolid	A-2	

Cities 500,000 to 999,999	
Lisbon	B-1
Málaga	B-2

Seville	B-2
Valencia	B-3
Saragossa	A-3

Cities 1,000,000 or more	
Madrid	A-3
Barcelona	A-4

Spain and Portugal share the Iberian Peninsula.
▶ Which city with more than 1 million people is located on the Mediterranean Sea?

On the Meseta, irrigation makes it possible for farmers to grow crops such as wheat and vegetables. Sheep and cattle are also grazed on the Meseta. This region has long been used for grazing. Shepherds herd their flocks in the region's valleys and hills. The shepherds eat cheese, meat from their sheep or goat herds, bread made from wheat flour, and wine. These are important products of the Meseta.

Closer to the Mediterranean Sea, olives, grapes, and citrus fruits, such as oranges, grapefruits, and lemons, are grown. One

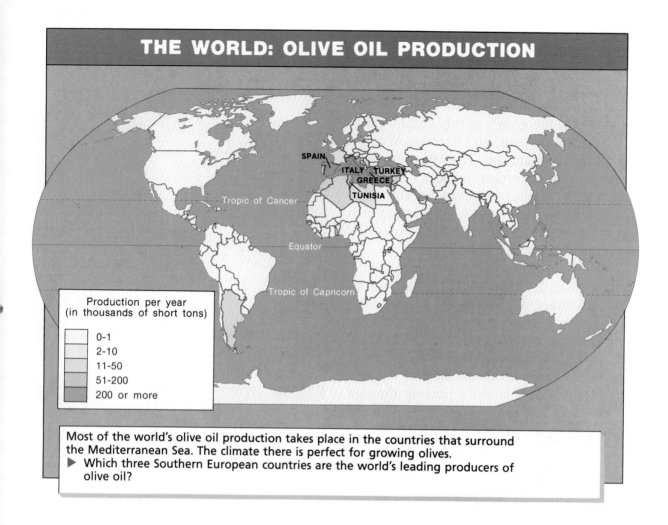

THE WORLD: OLIVE OIL PRODUCTION

SPAIN

ITALY TURKEY
GREECE
TUNISIA

Tropic of Cancer

Equator

Tropic of Capricorn

Production per year
(in thousands of short tons)

0-1
2-10
11-50
51-200
200 or more

Most of the world's olive oil production takes place in the countries that surround
the Mediterranean Sea. The climate there is perfect for growing olives.
▶ Which three Southern European countries are the world's leading producers of
  olive oil?

of Spain's main agricultural export is olive oil, which is made from many black ripe olives. As you can see from the map on this page, Spain is one of the world's major producers of olive oil.

C. Resources for Industry

Spain's Exports In 1986, Spain became a member of the European Union. This new membership made it easier for Spain to sell its products to other Western European countries. These products include fruits, vegetables, grains, and manufactured goods.

Spain has the world's largest supply of mercury, which is used in some types of thermometers, in some paints, and in medicines. Spain also has some iron ore and coal, but not enough for its own needs. Its few other minerals are mainly found in the northern mountains.

D. A Culture with Many Roots

The Moors Many different peoples contributed to Spain's culture and history. About 5,000 years ago, people from northern Africa called Iberians settled on the peninsula that is now named after them. Over time their culture became mixed with those of other people who moved into this region. The Romans, who occupied the Iberian Peninsula from the third century B.C. until the fifth century A.D., built hundreds of cities, roads, bridges, and irrigation canals. Today, tourists visit the ruins of these Roman structures.

In A.D. 711 the **Moors**, Islamic invaders from northern Africa, conquered the Iberian Peninsula. Spain's culture changed dramatically because of the influence of the Moors. Today the cultures of Spain and Portugal are quite different from other cultures of Europe because of the Moorish influence on their art, architecture, engineering, music, and literature.

The Spaniards' fight to take land back from the Moors was called the Reconquest, and it required long years of war with the Moors. By the late 1400s the Moors had been driven out of the Iberian Peninsula and the Reconquest was over. Then the Spanish began a different kind of conquest—the conquest of the Americas.

Exploration It must have been exciting to live in Spain and Portugal at this time. Many people caught the fever of adventure and exploration. Christopher Columbus, who received money and ships from Spain, was one such person. Columbus and the sailors and settlers who followed him braved the unknown to explore uncharted oceans. By the 1600s, Spain and Portugal had become major world powers with huge colonial empires.

Spain and Portugal ruled these great empires for almost three centuries. By the 1900s, Spain's and Portugal's colonies had become independent countries. Spain and Portugal are no longer as powerful and wealthy as they were in the past. But most Spaniards and Portuguese are still proud of their countries' achievements and successes in the arts, the sciences, literature, and conquest.

E. Portugal, a Farming Nation

Two Different Nations Portugal and Spain had similar experiences with Iberians, Romans, and Moors during their histories. Both Portugal and Spain had huge wealthy empires. Portugal controlled colonies in Africa and Asia as well as its gigantic colony

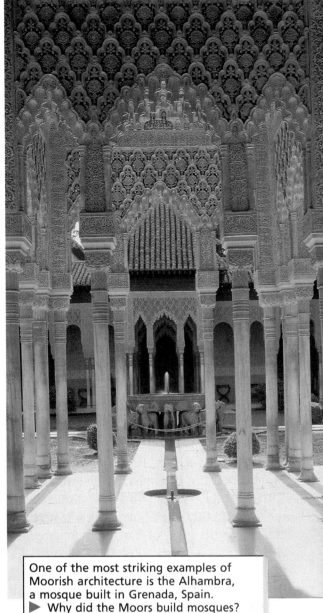

One of the most striking examples of Moorish architecture is the Alhambra, a mosque built in Grenada, Spain.
▶ Why did the Moors build mosques?

of Brazil in South America. Spain controlled most of the rest of South America and parts of North America. And both countries eventually lost their empires.

Today, Spain and Portugal are quite different. Their economies, however, are somewhat similar. In northern Portugal, wide valleys and flat areas between mountains hold many farms and vineyards. Wheat, corn, and potatoes are grown here. It is also the area where famous Portuguese wines, such as port, are produced and exported through the port city of Oporto.

Workers load cork bark onto a truck after cutting it from the cork oak trees.
▶ Do you think the cork is heavy?

make the filaments in light bulbs. With local and imported iron ore, factories produce steel instruments and tools such as knife blades and scissors. Manufacturing woolen textiles is the largest industry in Portugal. This industry depends on wool from sheep that graze on Portugal's dry, hilly lands. Shipbuilding, engineering, chemical industries, and fish canning are important economic activities around Lisbon and Oporto, the main cities of Portugal.

Like Spain, Portugal joined the European Union in 1986. Both countries have been slower to build industries than many other European countries. But Spain and Portugal are catching up, and their people are leading more comfortable lives. Every year more families are able to buy radios, household appliances, and automobiles. And people in these two countries are healthier and live longer than in the past.

Crops In southern Portugal the land is more level, but it is also drier and hotter. Citrus fruits, olives, and rice are raised, often with the aid of irrigation. Much of the southern part of Portugal is covered with forests of cork oak trees. Cork oak trees are shaped differently from other trees. One observer, traveling through a cork oak forest, wrote,

> I had never seen [such trees] before. They were low, extremely sturdy, with dark gray trunks and gnarled branches that reached wide . . . limbs twisting and turning in the hot air as if they were gasping for breath.

The bark of these trees is used to make cork tiles for walls and ceilings of houses and corks for bottles. Portugal is the world's leading producer of cork, and it is one of Portugal's main exports.

Tungsten Like Spain, Portugal has few mineral resources or fuels. Its principal mineral resource is **tungsten**, a mineral that is used to make steel harder and to

LESSON 2

Review

REVIEWING MAIN IDEAS
A. How has the geography of the Meseta created many separate regions in Spain?
B. How do the climates of Spain affect agriculture?
C. How has Spain benefited from being a member of the European Union?
D. What influence did the Moors have on Spain?
E. What does the economy of Portugal have in common with the economy of Spain?

SKILLS CHECK

WRITING SKILL
Reread the section about the Basques on pages 323–324. Write a paragraph describing what you think might be some of the positive and the negative results of giving special treatment to one group of people in a country.

328

Italy: Modern Challenges in an Ancient Land

CONNECTIONS

From what you already know about Southern Europe, describe what you think the climate of Italy is like.

TERMS

arid, in-migration

FOCUS

In what ways are the regions of Italy different from one another?

A. The Many Industries and Cities of Northern Italy

Three Regions Just as the Iberian Peninsula has a variety of cultures and economies, so do the three regions of Italy. Northern Italy, central Italy, and southern Italy differ in many ways. Modern industries are found in northern Italy. Southern Italy is a land of agriculture, with a hot, dry climate. Central Italy includes the great city of Rome, which once controlled the entire Mediterranean Sea.

Northern Italy The high peaks of the Alps spill out of Switzerland and across the northern border of Italy. Although southern Europe's climate is Mediterranean, northern Italy has many ski resorts tucked away in the snow-covered Alps.

Along the foothills of the Alps flows the Po River, a wide, fast-flowing river that is fed by many mountain streams rushing down from the Alps. Turin, one of the largest cities of the Po Valley, is an industrial center and home of Fiat automobiles. Other vehicles as well as many parts for trucks and motorcycles are also manufactured in Turin.

About 75 miles (120 km) to the northeast of Turin is Milan, Italy's most important manufacturing city. Milan is Italy's second largest city, with about 1.5 million people. Almost everything is made in Milan's factories, including tools, chemicals, appliances, textiles, and shoes. Milan has a variety of attractions along with all the industrial plants. Milan has beautiful old cathedrals and museums with great works of art and sculpture. For example, the opera house in Milan called La Scala is the most famous opera house in the world.

If you look at the map on page 330, you will see that Italy's two main industrial cities, Turin and Milan, are not port cities. Exports and imports must come through other cities on the coast. Genoa, which is to the south of these industrial cities, is the main port for northern Italy. With 700,000 people, Genoa is the fifth largest Italian city.

A conveyor belt moves automobile parts at Fiat's auto assembly plant in Turin.
▶ Which port city does Turin rely on for imports and exports?

329

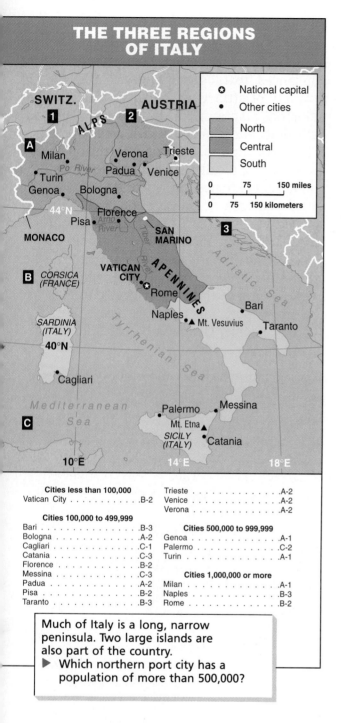

THE THREE REGIONS OF ITALY

⊘ National capital
• Other cities

North
Central
South

0   75   150 miles
0   75   150 kilometers

SWITZ. **1**
AUSTRIA **2**
ALPS
A
Milan
Verona   Trieste
Turin   Padua   Venice
Po River
Genoa   Bologna
44°N
Florence
Pisa   Arno River
SAN MARINO
MONACO
3
Adriatic Sea
B CORSICA (FRANCE)
VATICAN CITY
⊘ Rome
APENNINES
SARDINIA (ITALY)
Bari
40°N
Naples   ▲ Mt. Vesuvius
Taranto
Tyrrhenian Sea
Cagliari
Mediterranean Sea
C
Palermo   Messina
Mt. Etna ▲
SICILY (ITALY)   Catania
10°E   14°E   18°E

Cities less than 100,000		Trieste A-2
Vatican City B-2		Venice A-2
		Verona A-2
Cities 100,000 to 499,999		
Bari B-3		**Cities 500,000 to 999,999**
Bologna A-2		Genoa A-1
Cagliari C-1		Palermo C-2
Catania C-3		Turin A-1
Florence B-2		
Messina C-3		**Cities 1,000,000 or more**
Padua A-2		Milan A-1
Pisa B-2		Naples B-3
Taranto B-3		Rome B-2

Much of Italy is a long, narrow peninsula. Two large islands are also part of the country.
▶ Which northern port city has a population of more than 500,000?

B. Central Italy

A Giant T Italy is like a giant T with the Alps running across the top. The Apennine Mountains run down the middle of this T for over 700 miles (1,126 km). Orchards, vineyards, and livestock dot the valleys and areas of level land. Wheat, corn, and tomatoes grow well in central Italy. Vineyards are found everywhere. Wine is one of Italy's most important exports, and much of this wine is made from grapes grown on the sunny slopes of the Apennines.

San Marino The tiny country of San Marino is perched high in the northern Apennines of Italy. The people of San Marino believe that their country was founded in the fourth century A.D., making San Marino the oldest republic in the world.

San Marino has a total area of only 24 square miles (61 sq km) and fewer than 25,000 inhabitants. Most of San Marino's people speak Italian and make their living through tourism. Millions of tourists visit San Marino every year to see the country's many beautiful old churches, museums, and fortresses.

Rome, the Eternal City The city of Rome dominates central Italy. Rome, the largest city in Italy, is called the Eternal City because it has been the location of major civilizations and many historical events for centuries. It became the capital city of Italy soon after Italy became a modern nation, in 1870.

Rome was probably founded in 753 B.C. Until A.D. 500, it was the heart of the huge Roman Empire. This empire included many parts of Europe that you have already studied in this unit. A famous saying, "All roads lead to Rome," refers to the ancient network of roads, bridges, and tunnels that connected Rome with the many far-away places under its control.

Today the Italian people have wonderful opportunities to learn about both old and new Rome. The Tiber River runs through the city of Rome, and seven hills rise along one side of the river. On these seven hills are many ancient ruins. For example, a famous tourist site is the Roman Forum, which contained a marketplace and

Both old and new Rome are seen in this view of the Colosseum, a large stadium that was built by the Romans.
► What are examples of the new Rome?

public square. It also held the meeting place of the Roman Senate, the legislative body that helped govern the Roman Empire. Another popular site for visitors to Rome is the Trevi Fountain, built in 1762. Legend says that if you throw a coin into the Trevi Fountain, someday you will return to Rome.

On weekends, Roman families often stroll along the main street of Rome, which is called the Via de Corso. This busy route connects two piazzas, or open squares, that are about 1 mile (1.6 km) apart. Halfway between these two squares is the famous Piazza Colonna, which marks the heart of Rome. Here Romans stroll past elegant shops and international banks and hotels, perhaps with a stop at a sidewalk coffee shop for ice cream.

Rome is a modern, growing city with the same problems that other cities have. For example, Rome has very old, narrow streets that were built before automobiles were invented. Today the streets in Rome's older downtown areas quickly fill with traffic jams every morning as hundreds of cars, buses, and large trucks crowd into the city.

Vatican City Tourists also visit Rome to see Vatican City. Vatican City is the seat of the Roman Catholic Church and the home of the pope, the leader of the Roman Catholic Church. The most remarkable thing about Vatican City is that it is an independent state within the city of Rome. Vatican City is dominated by St. Peter's Cathedral, which was built in the sixteenth century. The ceiling of the cathedral's dome is 360 feet (110 m) high, which is as high as a 30-story skyscraper. Two of the greatest artists of the time, Raphael and Michelangelo, helped to construct St. Peter's.

The ruins of Pompeii have been dug out from beneath the lava and ash.
▶ What nearby volcano erupted and buried Pompeii?

ern Italy's active volcanoes. In the year A.D. 79, Mount Vesuvius erupted and nearly buried the nearby city of Pompeii (pom PAY) with sheets of ash and lava. From time to time, steam or ash showers towns and farmland for miles around Mount Vesuvius.

Volcanoes and earthquakes are not the only problems facing the people of southern Italy. Another problem is that the land is **arid**. This means the land is dry because of insufficient rainfall, especially during the summer. The government is building additional irrigation systems to store and distribute water more efficiently.

Farmers in southern Italy struggle to keep their small farms productive. If the farms fail, the farmers might have to emigrate to other parts of Italy to find work elsewhere. This movement into another region or community is called **in-migration**. And since there are fewer natural resources in southern Italy, not many industrial jobs are available.

C. The Landscape of Southern Italy

Landscape Southern Italy is very different from northern and central Italy. This region includes the city of Naples and the area to the south of it. It also includes the islands of Sardinia and Sicily, where the climate and economy are similar to those of the southern mainland. Southern Italy is a land of many small farms that produce grapes, olives, and citrus fruits. Italy is the world's second largest producer of olive oil. Only Spain produces more. Most of Italy's olive oil comes from this region.

Volcanic Activity The people of southern Italy live in a zone of earthquakes and volcanoes. Mount Vesuvius, which is about 3,900 feet (1,189 m) high, is one of south-

LESSON 3

Review

REVIEWING MAIN IDEAS

A. What are the main economic activities of northern Italy?
B. Why is Rome the most important city in central Italy?
C. Name two ways in which southern Italy is different from northern Italy.

SKILLS CHECK

THINKING SKILL

Place the following events in chronological order:
1. Italy becomes a modern nation
2. Rome is founded
3. Trevi fountain is built
4. Mount Vesuvius erupts
5. San Marino is founded
6. St. Peter's Cathedral is built

332

Greece and Cyprus: A Shared Culture

CONNECTIONS

Look at the photograph on this page. Why, do you think, do people come to Greece for vacations?

TERMS

overgrazing, erosion

FOCUS

What advantages and disadvantages do the people of Greece and Cyprus face in building modern economies?

A. Greece: A Land of Mountains and Islands

A Rocky Land Many people believe that the scenery of Greece is the most beautiful in the world. Hundreds of islands sparkle in the blue waters of the Mediterranean Sea. Most of these islands are uninhabited. The islands are popular among tourists because of their sunny beaches and clean, clear water.

The rocky Pindus Mountains rise from the land in many places, reaching 8,000 feet (2,438 m) in elevation. Mount Olympus, the highest peak in the Pindus Mountains, reaches 9,550 feet (2,911 m). The ancient Greeks believed that the gods they worshiped lived on Mount Olympus. On the hillsides, flocks of sheep and goats graze alongside vineyards and orchards of olive trees.

Greek farmers have been quite busy for many centuries on these peaceful hillsides. The climate of Greece is similar to the climate of most of Italy and Spain, with long, hot, dry summers. Farmers carefully use their water from irrigation systems in tending their crops. The natural vegetation, however, is not irrigated and struggles to survive. The sheep and goats that graze on the hillsides find only scrubby bushes and grasses to eat. With little rain, there is only scanty food for the animals, and they eat all the vegetation they can find.

Deforestation Allowing livestock to eat too much of the natural vegetation is called **overgrazing**. As a result of overgrazing, vegetation is unable to grow, and each year there is even less food than before for the animals. The farmers and townspeople who live in the Pindus Mountains have also cut down most of the trees on the hillsides to use for firewood and construction. Deforestation, the large-scale cutting down of forests, is a serious problem in Greece. Without forests, there is little wood to use to manufacture paper, lumber, or furniture. And without trees to hold the soil in place, **erosion** occurs. Erosion means that the soil blows away in the wind or washes down the slopes of the hills when it rains.

The hillsides of Greece are interesting to look at, but their inhabitants struggle to make an adequate living. With little rain, the Pindus Mountains do not have large rivers that can produce hydroelectric power. The mountains hold small amounts of lead, iron ore, and bauxite.

Small boats crowd the harbor of Mykonos, an island in Greece.
▶ Why are the Greek islands popular tourist spots?

333

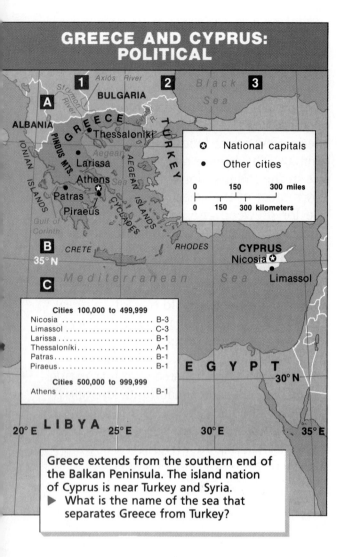

GREECE AND CYPRUS: POLITICAL

○ National capitals
• Other cities

0   150   300 miles
0   150   300 kilometers

Cities 100,000 to 499,999
Nicosia B-3
Limassol C-3
Larissa B-1
Thessaloníki A-1
Patras B-1
Piraeus B-1

Cities 500,000 to 999,999
Athens B-1

Greece extends from the southern end of the Balkan Peninsula. The island nation of Cyprus is near Turkey and Syria.
▶ What is the name of the sea that separates Greece from Turkey?

Greece must trade with the nations of the Middle East and the Soviet Union to get the petroleum and natural gas it needs. Recently, a pipeline was built to supply Greece and other nations with natural gas from the former Soviet Union.

B. Athens and Macedonia: Centers of Prosperity

Athens The Greek people face enormous obstacles in building productive farms and strong industries in the Pindus Mountains, but they have had great success in two areas—in the city of Athens and in the northern region called Macedonia. The city of Athens, the capital of Greece, is a living monument to the ancient Greeks. The Greeks developed the idea of democracy in Athens, and they introduced their ideas and ways of life to people all around the Mediterranean Sea. Athens itself is not directly on the coast, however. The nearby port city of Piraeus (pye REE us) has been the outlet for Greek exploration, trading expeditions, and conquests. You could say that Piraeus has been responsible for much of the fame of Athens. Today the ruins of ancient Greek temples, palaces, and other buildings are of great economic value. They bring thousands of tourists every year to Athens and nearby towns.

Macedonia Far in the northeast of Greece is the plain of Macedonia (mas uh DOH nee uh), which is a fertile farming zone. Tobacco and cotton are the main crops. Greece is one of Europe's principal exporters of tobacco. Much of the tobacco is sold to companies in the United States, where it is mixed with other tobacco to make cigars and cigarettes. Greek factories use the cotton to make textiles and clothing. Macedonia's farms also grow corn, rice, olives, and grapes. Along with Spain and Italy, Greece is a major producer of olive oil.

Many of these products are exported through Thessaloniki (thes uh LAHN ih kee), a busy port city on the Aegean Sea. Thessaloniki is Greece's second largest city. Only Athens is larger.

C. The Island Nation of Cyprus

Greek and Turkish Influence The island nation of Cyprus is east of the most southern point of Greece and only 40 miles (64 km) from Turkey. Both Greece and Turkey have had a strong influence on the history of Cyprus.

Greek people began to settle in Cyprus in 1500 B.C. The Greek language and Greek culture are still important on Cyprus. The island became part of the Roman Empire in 58 B.C. The Romans named the island Cyprus because of the copper deposits they found there. In the 1500s, Turkish conquerors gained control of the island. The British controlled the island from 1878 until Cyprus gained independence in 1960.

Because of the British influence, many Cypriots, or citizens of Cyprus, speak the English language. Greek and Turkish cultures, however, remain important. About one fifth of the Cypriots are Muslims who speak Turkish. The other four fifths are Greek-speaking Christians.

A Divided Island When Cyprus became an independent nation, most Greek Cypriots wanted to unite Cyprus with Greece. Turkish Cypriots wanted their own separate nation in the northern part of Cyprus. In 1974, Turkish soldiers invaded the northern part of the island, and they remain there today. The United Nations helped to prevent fighting and has tried to remove the troops. In 1983 the Turkish Cypriots seceded from the Republic of Cyprus and formed their own country in northern Cyprus, called the Turkish Republic of Northern Cyprus. Only Turkey recognizes this country.

Beaches of golden sand attract many tourists to Cyprus, but tourism is not the country's only economic activity. Across the northern and southern coasts of Cyprus are two long mountain ranges. Between these mountains spreads the flat and fertile Mesaoria Plain. Farmers in the Mesaoria Plain produce a variety of crops, including citrus fruits, potatoes, wheat, and barley. Some of the surplus fruits and vegetables are exported.

Cyprus is a crossroad between the Middle East and Europe. Its location between Europe, Asia, and Africa has given it contacts all over the Mediterranean. Business people, tourists, journalists, and diplomats bound for Asia and Europe travel through the international airport in the capital city of Nicosia.

Cyprus has many ruins that date from the time it was held by the Greeks.
▶ What other peoples have influenced Cyprus?

LESSON 4

Review

REVIEWING MAIN IDEAS
A. Describe why soil erosion has occurred in Greece.
B. Why are Athens and Macedonia important economic areas?
C. Why is Cyprus a center of political conflict?

SKILLS CHECK

MAP SKILL
Use the scale on the map on page 320 to find the distance between the following cities.
1. Athens and Rome
2. Athens and Nicosia

335

REVIEWING TERMS

On a separate piece of paper, write questions for the answers listed below. Use the following terms.

Mediterranean climate	arid
emigrate	in-migration
Moors	overgrazing
tungsten	erosion

1. A mineral that is used to make the filaments in light bulbs

2. The movement of people into a new community or region of the same country

3. Allowing animals to eat too much of the natural vegetation found in an area

4. The wind and rain carrying the soil away as a result of deforestation

5. When a person leaves his or her home country to live permanently in another country

6. A climate with hot, dry summers and cool, rainy winters

7. People who overran the Iberian Peninsula in A.D. 711

8. Dry because of insufficient rainfall

WRITING ABOUT GEOGRAPHY

Tourism is important to the economy of most European nations. Write a description of the countries of Southern Europe that would convince tourists to spend their vacations in that region.

REVIEWING THE FACTS

On a separate sheet of paper, answer the questions in complete sentences.

1. What are the three European peninsulas that extend into the Mediterranean Sea?

2. What two large islands in the Mediterranean Sea belong to Italy?

3. Why are Portuguese, Spanish, and Italian known as Romance languages?

4. Besides the winter crops of wheat and vegetables, what three crops grow well in the Mediterranean area?

5. What three mountain ranges are found on the peninsulas of Southern Europe?

6. Which group of people in Spain would like to become independent?

7. What are the main differences between the two climates of Spain?

8. What are some uses for mercury?

9. What is the bark of cork oak trees used for?

10. What is the largest industry in Portugal?

11. What is La Scala?

12. Why is Rome called the Eternal City?

13. What small state is found inside the city of Rome?

14. What attractions bring thousands of tourists to Athens every year?

15. How is Cyprus a divided island?

THINKING CRITICALLY

On a separate sheet of paper, answer the following questions in complete sentences.

1. Why is control of the Strait of Gibraltar important to Mediterranean nations?
2. Why are Southern European nations leaders in the production of olive oil?
3. Why do so many people from southern Italy leave their homes to live in other nations?
4. Why is northern Italy more industrialized than southern Italy?
5. Why is trade so important to Greece?

SUMMARIZING THE CHAPTER

Draw a graphic organizer like the one shown here. Copy the information from this graphic organizer to the one you have drawn. Next to each main idea, write three statements that you think best support it.

CHAPTER THEME

Southern Europe, a region of peninsulas and islands, has been influenced throughout its history by its Mediterranean location and its Mediterranean climate.

LESSON 1 The countries of Southern Europe are alike.

1. _____
2. _____
3. _____

LESSON 2 Mountains and a dry climate have influenced the way of life on the Iberian Peninsula.

1. _____
2. _____
3. _____

LESSON 3 The three regions of Italy are different from one another.

1. _____
2. _____
3. _____

LESSON 4 Both Greece and Cyprus face difficulties in building modern economies.

1. _____
2. _____
3. _____

EASTERN EUROPE

338

Between Western Europe and Asia

CONNECTIONS

Imagine that you have moved to a foreign land. What might you do to feel at home?

TERMS

censor

FOCUS

How have recent political changes affected the people of Eastern Europe?

A. The People of Eastern Europe

Slavic People Throughout history, many people have moved from Asia to the western edge of Europe by crossing through the flat lands of Eastern Europe. Greeks, Romans, Turks, and many other peoples have traveled through Eastern Europe. All of these groups influenced the region and helped to create the present-day culture of Eastern Europe.

Of all the peoples who crossed Eastern Europe, the Slavs have had the greatest impact on Eastern European culture. The first Slavs lived near the eastern border of modern Poland. The Slavs spread across Eastern Europe in the second and third centuries. Today most of the people of Eastern Europe are Slavs.

Languages The Slavs speak a group of closely related Slavic languages. Czech and Slovak are Slavic languages. The former Yugoslavia had several Slavic languages. Polish is also a Slavic language. Hungarian, Romanian, and Albanian are not Slavic, though they each contain words borrowed from the Slavic languages. These languages help to define the countries in Eastern Europe. Polish identifies Poland, Hungarian identifies Hungary, and so on.

Religion Most Eastern European people are members of Christian religions. The majority of Czechs, Slovaks, Hungarians,

The fall of the Berlin Wall is symbolic of the collapse of Communist governments in Eastern Europe.
▶ In what ways has Eastern Europe changed since 1989?

Croatians, and Poles are Roman Catholics. Most people in Bulgaria, Romania, and Serbia are Eastern Orthodox Christians. However, many Bosnians and most Albanians are Muslims. There is also a small Jewish population in Eastern Europe today.

B. Eastern Europe and the Soviet Union

Communist Rule After World War II, which ended in 1945, the Communist government of the Soviet Union controlled most of the present-day countries of Eastern Europe, including Bulgaria, Romania, Hungary, Poland, the Czech Republic, and Slovakia. Albania and the former Yugoslavia also had Communist governments, but they were not directly controlled by the Soviet Union.

Under the Communist system of government, the people did not truly choose those who governed them. The people had no opportunity to vote for anyone who opposed the Communists. They had very little chance to hear any ideas discussed except those approved by the Communists. The government **censored**, or controlled,

339

▶ Warsaw, Poland, was rebuilt with great pride after World War II.

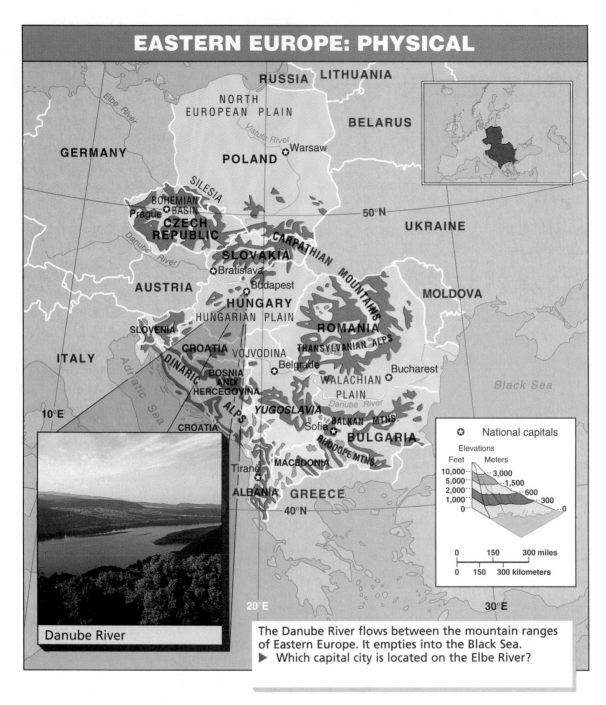

EASTERN EUROPE: PHYSICAL

RUSSIA
LITHUANIA
Elbe River
NORTH EUROPEAN PLAIN
BELARUS
Vistula River
Warsaw
GERMANY
POLAND
SILESIA
BOHEMIAN BASIN
Prague
CZECH REPUBLIC
50°N
UKRAINE
CARPATHIAN MOUNTAINS
Danube River
SLOVAKIA
Bratislava
AUSTRIA
Budapest
MOLDOVA
HUNGARY
HUNGARIAN PLAIN
SLOVENIA
ROMANIA
CROATIA
VOJVODINA
TRANSYLVANIAN ALPS
ITALY
DINARIC
Belgrade
Bucharest
Black Sea
BOSNIA AND HERCEGOVINA
10°E
Adriatic Sea
WALACHIAN PLAIN
Danube River
ALPS
YUGOSLAVIA
CROATIA
Sofia
BALKAN MTNS.
BULGARIA
RHODOPE MTNS.
Tiranë
MACEDONIA
ALBANIA
GREECE
40°N
20°E
30°E

National capitals

Elevations

Feet	Meters
10,000	3,000
5,000	1,500
2,000	600
1,000	300
0	0

0   150   300 miles
0   150   300 kilometers

Danube River

The Danube River flows between the mountain ranges of Eastern Europe. It empties into the Black Sea.
▶ Which capital city is located on the Elbe River?

newspapers, magazines, and radio and television broadcasts.

Communist Collapse In 1989 and 1990, however, a political revolution swept through Eastern Europe. Communist governments in almost all the Eastern European countries fell from power. The revolution was inspired by the political changes that were sweeping the Soviet Union. Because of the changes in the Soviet Union, the countries of Eastern Europe also began to allow more political and economic freedoms.

New Challenges The freedoms that the people of Eastern Europe have begun to enjoy have brought new challenges. Since many of the people in the region have lived from birth under Communist rule, they have no real experience with the responsibilities that people in a free society assume. Now they have to learn how to deal with the many problems that have resulted from the more than 40 years of Communist rule.

Solving economic problems is another challenge to the people of Eastern Europe. For years the people have struggled with high prices and shortages of food and consumer products. Plans for economic growth include moving away from the region's high level of dependence on the former Soviet Union. This means finding new markets where goods can be sold and bought. The move to economic independence depends to a great extent on how much support the Eastern European countries receive from other countries.

C. The Plains of Eastern Europe

Most Eastern European countries have important regions of level land called plains. The northern part of the region belongs to the North European Plain, which extends across Europe from northern France to Russia. Most plains in Eastern Europe are important agricultural and livestock regions. Large cities are found in these plains.

Major rivers run through most of Eastern Europe's plains. When the great Danube leaves Austria, it crosses the Hungarian Plain. It continues across Yugoslavia's Vojvodina (voi vuh DEE nuh) and Romania's Walachian Plain. The Elbe River rises in the northwestern part of the Czech Republic, flows through that country's rich Bohemian Basin, and empties into the North Sea. The Vistula (VIHS choo luh) River crosses Poland's North European Plain and flows into the Baltic Sea.

Some Bosnian villages, such as this one, have large Muslim populations.
► What other religions are practiced in Eastern Europe?

The rivers that flow through these plains are natural inland waterways for transporting harvests of crops from farms to food-processing factories in cities. An inland waterway is a river, lake, or sea that is used for transportation within a country.

LESSON 1

Review

REVIEWING MAIN IDEAS
A. What are two ways in which most people of Eastern Europe are alike?
B. What political changes have occurred in Eastern Europe in recent years?
C. Why are Eastern Europe's plains important to the region?

SKILLS CHECK

MAP SKILL
Use the map on page 340 to find the countries of Eastern Europe that are located entirely or partly between 40°N and 50°N and between 10°E and 20°E.

Poland

What have you already learned about Poland that might help you predict a major economic activity for this country?

TERMS
strike, Solidarity

FOCUS
What are the major economic activities of Poland?

A. The Agricultural and Industrial Strengths of Poland

Rebuilding a Nation During World War II, Poland was almost completely destroyed. Cities, factories, and farms were bombed and ruined. Near the end of World War II, Poland came under the control of the Soviet Union. Today, Poland is independent, and its people are proud of their progress in rebuilding their economy.

Farming Most of Poland lies in the North European Plain. The soil in the region is rich, the land is level, and there is ample rainfall. In the northern and central regions of Poland, there are many farms. Poland's farmers produce large harvests of potatoes, turnips, and flax. Poland is also a leading world producer of oats and rye.

The agricultural system in Poland is unusual in Eastern Europe because most of Poland's farms are privately owned. In most of the other Eastern European countries, the governments own and control the farms. Some of those state farms are quite large, and dozens of families work them together. There are few state farms in Poland.

Industrial Cities Northern Poland has an important port city on the Baltic Sea. It is Gdansk (guh DAHNSK), and it has a huge shipbuilding industry, docks, and storage facilities. Gdansk has an ideal location for trade because it is near the mouth of the Vistula River, Poland's most important river. The factories, forests, and mines of southern Poland send products down the Vistula River for export through Gdansk.

Coal comes from mines near Katowice (kah toh VEE tse), a city located near the great coal fields of Silesia, in southwestern Poland. The country is third in coal production in Europe, after Germany and the former Soviet Union. The industrial city of Katowice provides tools and equipment for these coal mines. Many coal miners live

Agriculture is the leading economic activity of Poland.
Rolling hills cover much of the southern part of the country.
▶ Why, do you think, are cattle and sheep raised in this part of Poland?

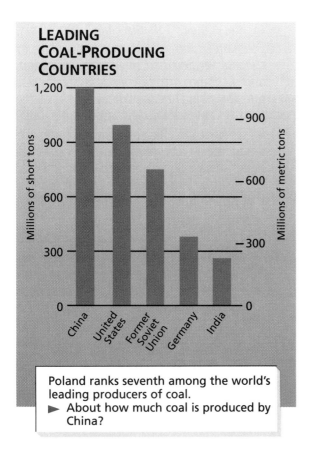

LEADING COAL-PRODUCING COUNTRIES

Millions of short tons / Millions of metric tons

Poland ranks seventh among the world's leading producers of coal.
► About how much coal is produced by China?

in Katowice, as do people who work in the factories and plants that process minerals such as copper and zinc.

Though Poland has large coal deposits that it can use for industry, it has little iron ore. Large amounts of iron ore are imported through the port of Gdansk and transported up the Vistula River to the cities of the south. For this reason, Kraków (KRA kou), located on the Vistula River near Silesia, is Poland's main industrial city. Some of the major steel mills in Europe are located in Kraków. The city also manufactures chemicals, leather, textiles, and processed food.

Solidarity Industrial workers are essential for building Poland's economy. In 1980, many workers joined together and went on **strike**. They refused to work until the government allowed them to form unions free of government control. Many workers joined an organization called **Solidarity**. Solidarity was a labor organization that was independent of the Communist party. This organization hoped to gain freedoms that the Communist government had prohibited.

As the number of members increased, government officials could not continue to ignore Solidarity's demands. In 1982, the government outlawed Solidarity. Many of the leaders of the Solidarity union were arrested and imprisoned. Eventually, however, the government was forced to take a less harsh position. In 1989, the government recognized Solidarity as a legal union. When elections were held for Parliament, Solidarity members were allowed to run for office. In an amazing victory, Solidarity won the most votes and formed the first non-Communist government in Eastern Europe since World War II.

Lech Walesa (lekh vah WEN sah) had been Solidarity's chairman from the time the union was founded. In 1983, he was awarded the Nobel Peace Prize for his efforts to gain rights for workers through peaceful means rather than by violence. In 1990, Walesa resigned as chairman of the Solidarity union and was elected president of Poland. He served as president until 1995, when he was defeated for reelection.

A Polluted Land After Solidarity came to power, the government began to report that Poland was suffering from enormous environmental problems. For years, the steel, chemical, and power plants have used coal for power. As you read earlier, the smoke from coal causes acid rain. In Poland, there were no regulations on how much coal smoke could be released. As a result, trees are dying from acid rain, and the air is heavy with coal dust. Other countries, such as Russia and Germany, are also suffering from air pollution. The governments of all these countries face the task of cleaning up their environments.

Warsaw, which is located on the Vistula River, is the capital of Poland.
▶ At what time of year do you think this photograph was taken?

B. Poland's Capital

A Modern City Warsaw is located almost in the center of Poland. It is Poland's capital and most populated city. Nearly 1.6 million people live in Warsaw. Many kinds of goods, including bicycles, textiles, and processed foods, are manufactured there. Goods that are to be exported are sent along the Vistula River, which flows through Warsaw, to the port of Gdansk. And thousands of Polish people work in the government offices in Warsaw, since it is the capital city.

Preserving the Past Warsaw, as well as many other cities of Poland, is old. It dates back hundreds of years. Beautiful buildings with ornate decorations crowd the streets of the city. Christine Hotchkiss is an American writer who was born in Poland and lived in Warsaw until World War II. In her book *Home to Poland,* she describes how the people of Warsaw have worked to preserve their city.

In the course of the last 300 years, [Warsaw] was destroyed many times by successive Swedish, German, Austrian, and Russian attacks; each time it was quickly rebuilt. In the fall of 1944, at the time of [World War II], the whole town was razed to the ground. German SS detachments [soldiers] went from street to street, dynamiting the houses which had escaped fire or artillery shelling. A town of over a million inhabitants became a desert of rubble and smoking ruins.

"This city will not rise again," said the German Commander von dem Bach.

He was wrong.

A great feeling of love bound the people of Warsaw close to their capital. . . . Reconstruction work was started immediately by people still living in cellars. . . . Slowly Warsaw began to rise from the ashes.

The energy and courage of the people of Poland allowed them to rebuild their city. Warsaw has risen from its own ashes and remains a source of pride to its citizens. It reminds the Polish people of their glorious past and gives promise to their hope-filled future.

LESSON 2

Review

REVIEWING MAIN IDEAS

A. Name an important difference between the northern region of Poland and the southern region.

B. Why is Warsaw a major city in Poland?

SKILLS CHECK

WRITING SKILL

Use the information in this lesson to write a paragraph in which you describe changes that a person who returned to Poland after a long absence might find in the country.

344

Czech Republic, Slovakia, and Hungary

CONNECTIONS
Name a problem that landlocked countries face.

TERMS
Czechs, Slovaks, Magyars

FOCUS
Why are rivers and plains so important in the Czech Republic, Slovakia, and Hungary?

A. The Czech Republic

A Country Divides When the Communist government in Czechoslovakia fell in 1989, a new government was formed. But in 1993 a remarkable event occurred. Czechoslovakia, a country that had existed for more than 70 years, divided without war or bloodshed into two new countries. The Czech Republic was created from the western part of the former Czechoslovakia, where most of the people are **Czechs.**

The second new nation, Slovakia, was formed from the eastern part of the former Czechoslovakia. Most people of this area are **Slovaks,** whose culture is different from that of the Czechs.

Bohemian Basin Over 10 million people live in the Czech Republic, mostly in and around the Bohemian Basin. The Bohemian Basin is a prosperous region. It has farms, orchards, and grazing land for dairy cattle. Its factories produce goods such as steel, cement, chemicals, shoes, and clothing.

Prague (prahg), the capital and largest city of the Czech Republic, is located in the Bohemian Basin. More than a million people live in Prague. It is a city of historic churches, castles, and museums. Prague was the only large city in Eastern Europe to escape extensive damage during World War II.

St. Vitus' Cathedral is one of many beautiful, old buildings in Prague.
▶ Why are there still many old buildings in Prague?

Ostrava (OHS trah vah), the main industrial city of the Czech Republic, is located near the border with Slovakia. Ostrava produces iron and steel, tanks, materials for building bridges, and railroad cars. Although the Czech Republic produces less steel than some countries of Western Europe, steel is a major export.

B. Slovakia: Land of the Slovaks

Slovakia, with about 5.5 million people, has a much smaller population than the Czech Republic. The Slovaks chose Bratislava as their capital city. It is located close to where Slovakia, Austria, and Hungary meet.

The Slovaks' land is much more rugged than the land of the Czech Republic. It is hemmed in by the Tatra Mountains, which have high and rugged peaks that rise in some places to over 8,000 feet (2,438 m). For this reason, Slovakia is sometimes called

Bridges that cross the Danube River connect the two sections of Budapest.
▶ What are the names of the two sections of this capital city?

the Switzerland of Eastern Europe. The Tatras make communication and travel between Slovak communities difficult. As a result, Slovak villages are somewhat isolated and not as modern as the towns of the Bohemian Basin. Many Slovaks still follow century-old practices in their daily life. Birthdays, weddings, and other family gatherings are celebrated with folk music, dancing, and traditional foods.

Many Slovaks are farmers or herders. Since the region lacks mineral resources, there are no large factories. Scattered throughout Slovakia are small workshops where people make clothing, shoes, and wood products, often by using hand tools.

C. Hungary: A Fertile, Flat Plain

Hungarian Plain Unlike Slovakia, Hungary is located in a large basin, called the Hungarian Plain. The mountains of Slovakia, Romania, Slovenia, Croatia, and Yugoslavia surround the Hungarian Plain, and the magnificent Danube River crosses the Plain from north to south.

Magyar ancestors The Hungarians trace their ancestry back to the ancient **Magyars** (MAG yahrz). In the ninth century, these invaders traveled on horseback from what is now a part of Russia and settled on the Hungarian Plain. They became farmers but never lost their interest in waging war on horseback. Their influence on Hungarian language and customs lasted many centuries. Even today the ancient Magyar art of fencing is a national sport in Hungary.

A United City Budapest was once two cities divided by the Danube River. Buda was a city on the west bank of the Danube. Bridges joined it to the city of Pest on the east bank. In 1873 the two cities merged and took the name *Budapest*. Today the capital has over 2 million people. The Buda section has parks, beautiful old homes, new apartment buildings, restaurants, and hotels. In the Pest section there are government offices, business offices, and some factories. It is the busier and more crowded part of the city.

346

Budapest is near the center of the fertile Hungarian Plain. The soils and climate here are ideal for raising corn, sugar beets, and potatoes. Summer temperatures are quite warm, generally reaching 80°F (27°C) during the day. There is ample rainfall during the growing season. Hungary is a major European exporter of apples, but its most famous product is the red pepper, which is used to make a spice called paprika. The Hungarian Plain supplies the flour mills and food-processing plants of Hungary with many products that are turned into foods for the Hungarian people.

Bauxite is Hungary's most important mineral resource. The deposits of bauxite are so plentiful that Hungary is Europe's principal producer of this mineral. Most industries in Hungary use bauxite in producing automobiles, airplanes, and such small articles as kitchen utensils.

D. Rivers That Provide Outlets to the Sea

Landlocked Countries The Czech Republic, Slovakia, and Hungary are landlocked and therefore have a disadvantage that other Eastern European countries do not have. Using the map on page 340, identify some of the bodies of water that touch the countries of Eastern Europe.

River Transportation The Czech Republic, Slovakia, and Hungary are not completely cut off from access to the sea. The Danube River flows along part of the border between Slovakia and Hungary and then winds through Hungary on its way to the Black Sea. The industries and cities in the Bohemian Basin of the Czech Republic also have an outlet to the sea.

The Bohemian Basin is connected to the North Sea by the Elbe River. You may recall from Chapter 12 that the Elbe River winds its way through Germany and finally empties into the North Sea at Hamburg, Germany.

The Danube and Elbe rivers provide access to seaports for Czechs, Slovaks, and Hungarians. But imports and exports must travel through other countries to reach the sea. This can be expensive for both consumers and businesses.

Students help with the potato harvest on a farm in the Czech Republic.
▶ In what area of Hungary do farmers raise potatoes?

LESSON 3

Review

REVIEWING MAIN IDEAS

A. Why is the Bohemian Basin important to the Czech Republic?

B. In what ways are the Slovaks different from the Czechs?

C. What are the main economic activities of the Hungarian Plain?

D. Why are rivers so important to the Czech Republic, Slovakia, and Hungary?

SKILLS CHECK

MAP SKILL

On a separate sheet of paper, write the following sets of coordinates: 44°N/26°E; 52°N/21°E; 50°N/14°E; 50°N/20°E. Use the map on page 350 to find the city at each location.

347

The Nations of the Balkan Peninsula

CONNECTIONS

The republics of the former Yugoslavia are often in the news. What changes have you heard about there? If you were a reporter, what questions would you ask the people there?

TERMS

chromium

FOCUS

What are the valuable resources and products of the Balkan Peninsula?

A. The Former Yugoslavia

The Balkan Peninsula The Balkan Peninsula lies between the Adriatic Sea and the Black Sea and stretches into the Mediterranean Sea. Yugoslavia was one of five nations that made up the Balkan Peninsula. However, today there are more than five nations in the Balkans because some of Yugoslavia's former republics broke away in the early 1990s and became independent nations. The other Balkan nations are Romania, Bulgaria, Albania, and Greece. Greece is at the southern tip of the Balkan Peninsula, but it is not considered part of Eastern Europe. In the past, Greece was the only country on the Balkan Peninsula that did not have a Communist form of government. Also, Greece's culture and economy are closely associated with Western Europe's.

Yugoslavia was originally divided into six republics. Each republic had its own government as well as representatives in the federal government. Within these six republics were almost a dozen different ethnic groups. The largest included Serbs, Croats, and Muslims. When the Communist government lost its control over Yugoslavia, conflicts arose between the different ethnic groups.

Each ethnic group in Yugoslavia considered itself a separate nationality. Several of these groups sought independence. In 1991, Croatia and Slovenia declared independence. Serbs living in Croatia opposed

The devastation of the war in the former republics of Yugoslavia left thousands of people homeless.
▶What caused the war in Yugoslavia?

NEW BALKAN NATIONS

SLOVENIA
In 1991, Slovenia became the first republic to secede from Yugoslavia. Slovenia is recognized as an independent country by the international community.

SERBIA
Serbia is the largest, most powerful republic, and it opposed the breakup of Yugoslavia. It sent troops to help the Bosnian Serbs fight in Bosnia, but Serbia eventually agreed to peace in 1995.

CROATIA
Croatia also seceded in 1991. Croatia is also recognized as an independent country by the international community.

MACEDONIA
Macedonia also seceded from Yugoslavia but was not recognized by many nations due to a dispute over its name. Greece objected to the name because there is a region in northern Greece with the same name. In 1993 the United Nations settled the dispute and recognized Macedonia's independence.

BOSNIA AND HERCEGOVINA
Bosnia and Hercegovina, often called Bosnia, suffered from civil war after it declared independence in 1992. A peace agreement that stopped the fighting was signed in 1995.

MONTENEGRO
Montenegro united with Serbia as the Federal Republic of Yugoslavia.

New Balkan nations were created from the breakup of the former Yugoslavia. Tensions remained high in the Balkans in the late 1990s.
▶ Which two republics make up the Federal Republic of Yugoslavia?

independence and civil war broke out. The war spread to another newly independent republic, Bosnia and Hercegovina, as Croats, Serbs, and Muslims fought each other.

The war in Bosnia cost many lives and destroyed dozens of towns. Thousands of people were forced to flee their homes. The peoples of the former Yugoslavia and other nations tried but failed to end the fighting. Finally, in 1995 the United States helped bring a truce and then sent troops to keep an uneasy peace. The table above explains the status of the former republics.

B. The Mountains and Plains of Romania

Mountains and Plains Romania is a land of great beauty and mystery. Many of its remote mountains and towns have not been visited by tourists. The heart of Romania is in the south, in the rich Walachian Plain. The Danube River rolls along the edge of the Walachian Plain and finally reaches its destination in eastern Romania, where it empties into the Black Sea. The prosperous farms in the Walachian Plain produce a variety of crops. Romania is a major world producer of corn and flax. Grapes, tobacco, and swine are also important agricultural products.

If you have ever read Bram Stoker's novel *Dracula* or seen a movie based on it, you have heard of the region of Romania that is known as Transylvania. The Transylvanian Alps cross the middle of Romania from east to west. Monasteries and old castles are hidden away in Transylvania's rugged mountain valleys. The Carpathian Mountains cross northern Romania. These mountains contain many valuable minerals, such as coal, iron ore, copper, lead, and silver.

Important Oil Fields Romania's most valuable resources are its petroleum and natural gas supplies. One of the world's most important oil fields is near the city of Ploieşti, in the Walachian Plain.

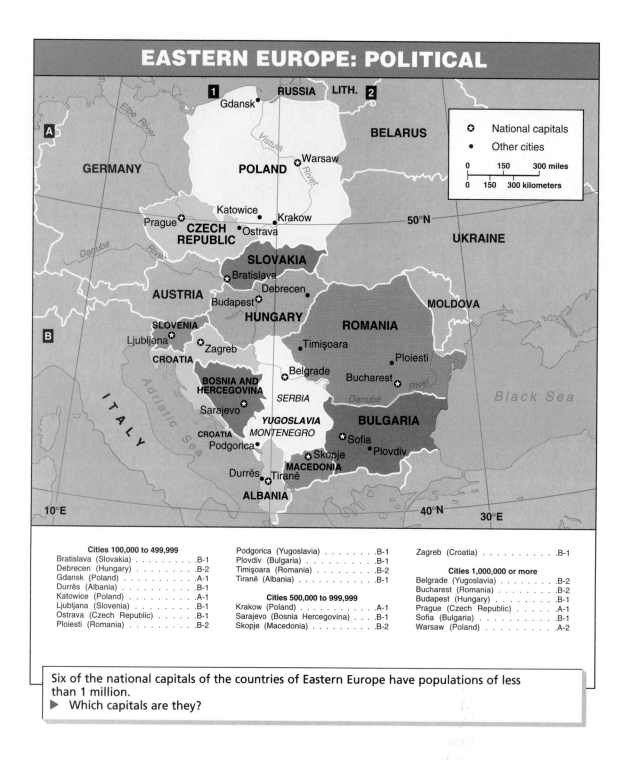

EASTERN EUROPE: POLITICAL

1   RUSSIA   LITH. **2**

Gdansk

BELARUS

GERMANY

Elbe River

POLAND

Vistula River

Warsaw

Katowice

Krakow

50°N

Prague   CZECH REPUBLIC   Ostrava

UKRAINE

Danube River

SLOVAKIA

Bratislava

Debrecen

AUSTRIA

Budapest

HUNGARY

SLOVENIA

Ljubljana

Zagreb

CROATIA

ROMANIA

Timişoara

MOLDOVA

Ploiesti

Belgrade

Bucharest

Danube River

Black Sea

BOSNIA AND HERCEGOVINA

SERBIA

Sarajevo

I T A L Y

Adriatic Sea

YUGOSLAVIA
MONTENEGRO

CROATIA

BULGARIA

Podgorica

Sofia

Plovdiv

Skopje

MACEDONIA

Durrës   Tiranë

ALBANIA

10°E

40°N

30°E

✪	National capitals
•	Other cities

0   150   300 miles
0   150   300 kilometers

Cities 100,000 to 499,999
Bratislava (Slovakia) B-1
Debrecen (Hungary) B-2
Gdansk (Poland) A-1
Durrës (Albania) B-1
Katowice (Poland) A-1
Ljubljana (Slovenia) B-1
Ostrava (Czech Republic) B-1
Ploiesti (Romania) B-2

Podgorica (Yugoslavia) B-1
Plovdiv (Bulgaria) B-1
Timişoara (Romania) B-2
Tiranë (Albania) B-1

Cities 500,000 to 999,999
Krakow (Poland) A-1
Sarajevo (Bosnia Hercegovina) B-1
Skopje (Macedonia) B-2

Zagreb (Croatia) B-1

Cities 1,000,000 or more
Belgrade (Yugoslavia) B-2
Bucharest (Romania) B-2
Budapest (Hungary) B-1
Prague (Czech Republic) A-1
Sofia (Bulgaria) B-1
Warsaw (Poland) A-2

Six of the national capitals of the countries of Eastern Europe have populations of less than 1 million.
▶ Which capitals are they?

Romania is also a land of cities and beaches. In Bucharest, the capital city, a wide variety of goods are manufactured, including textiles, shoes, and farm machinery. The people of Bucharest stroll along its avenues in their spare time, stopping at cafes and movie theaters. Many people who visit Bucharest travel east to the beautiful beaches of the Black Sea, where villas and hotels line the shore.

C. Bulgaria: Land of Mountains

Two Ranges Bulgaria has two ranges of mountains. The Balkan Mountains stretch across the middle of Bulgaria from east to west. The other range, called the Rhodope (RAHD uh pee), runs along the southern part of Bulgaria.

In this mountainous region is Sofia, the capital and largest city of Bulgaria. The city is filled with gardens, parks, and tree-lined streets. There are theaters, libraries, museums, beautiful old universities, and modern government buildings.

Maritsa Valley Between the Balkan Mountains and the Rhodope is the beautiful Maritsa Valley. The surrounding mountains protect the valley from severe winds, and so it is an ideal place for plum orchards and tobacco farms. Fields of roses, a common sight in this region, are cultivated for use in the perfume industry.

D. Albania: A Rural Landscape

A Narrow Land Albania occupies a narrow strip of land on the Balkan Peninsula. Its coastal region, which is washed by the Adriatic Sea, enjoys a Mediterranean climate with mild, rainy winters and warm summers. Nearly three quarters of Albania is mountainous. Some of the mountain areas are wind-swept and snow-covered in winter and cool in summer.

Most Albanians are farmers or herders, or they make a living by fishing. Hand-crafted items are produced on a small scale with simple tools and hand-operated machines. The mines of Albania produce large quantities of **chromium**, a mineral that is used to make steel harder. Albania is a leading producer of chromium.

Major Cities There are two main cities in Albania. One is Tiranë (tuh RAHN uh), the capital city, and the other is the port city of Durrës (DOOR us). Each is a small city,

Each year, Bulgarians in the Maritsa Valley gather in traditional dress to celebrate the Festival of the Roses.
▶ What is one use for the roses that are grown in the Maritsa Valley?

with populations of less than 250,000. These cities are free of pollution and noise because they have little industry.

LESSON 4

Review

REVIEWING MAIN IDEAS

A. How did ethnic differences in the former Yugoslavia lead to war in the newly independent republics?

B. What are the main resources of Romania?

C. Why are there orchards and farms located in the Maritsa Valley of mountainous Bulgaria?

D. How do the physical features of Albania influence the economy of that country?

SKILLS CHECK

THINKING SKILL

Read the chart on page 349 that compares the status of the former republics of Yugoslavia. What research would you need to do in order to update the chart?

351

REVIEWING TERMS

On a separate sheet of paper, write the term that best matches each numbered statement.

censor
Slovaks
strike
chromium
Magyars

1. The act of refusing to work until demands have been met
2. The people who recently broke away from the Czechs to form their own country
3. The ancestors of modern Hungarians
4. A blue-white mineral that is used to make steel harder
5. To control the content of publications and radio and television broadcasts

REVIEWING THE FACTS

On a separate sheet of paper, answer the following questions in complete sentences.

1. How does a Communist government differ from a democratic one?
2. Why will the years 1989 and 1990 remain important in the history of Eastern Europe?
3. Why are the rivers of the Eastern European plains important?
4. How has the location of Gdansk helped to make it an important city?
5. What are the dominant physical features of the Balkan Peninsula?
6. What is unusual about agriculture in Poland?

7. How does the geography of the Czech Republic differ from that of Slovakia?
8. What mineral is very important to Hungary's industries?
9. Which two bodies of water lie on the eastern and western borders of the Balkan Peninsula?
10. What climate does the coastal region of Albania have?

WRITING ABOUT CULTURE

Do you think the culture of a nation is affected by the amount of freedom given to the people of the nation? Write several paragraphs explaining your opinion.

THINKING CRITICALLY

On a separate sheet of paper, answer the following questions in complete sentences.

1. Why are people who challenge the people in power often later challenged themselves?
2. What freedoms, do you think, did the members of Solidarity hope to gain when they went on strike?
3. What actions could Eastern Europeans take to clean up their environment?
4. In what areas of the world besides Slovakia are communication and travel made more difficult because of mountains?
5. Why, do you think, do the countries of Eastern Europe need and deserve the support and encouragement of other nations?

SUMMARIZING THE CHAPTER

On a separate sheet of paper, draw a graphic organizer like the one shown here. Copy the information from this graphic organizer to the one you have drawn. Under the main idea for each lesson, write three statements that you think best support it.

CHAPTER THEME

Many Eastern European countries are undergoing great political changes. The countries share similar landscapes and resources.

Lesson 1 The countries of Eastern Europe are similar in many ways.

1. _____
2. _____
3. _____

Lesson 3 The Czech Republic, Slovakia, and Hungary have important rivers and plains.

1. _____
2. _____
3. _____

Lesson 2 The people of Poland have faced major challenges since 1939.

1. _____
2. _____
3. _____

Lesson 4 The Balkan Peninsula has valuable resources and products.

1. _____
2. _____
3. _____

The Former Soviet Union: 15 New Nations

CONNECTIONS

Sometimes, a country faces such serious problems that they threaten its existence. How do you think government leaders might react if their country was breaking apart?

TERMS

superpower

FOCUS

What caused the Soviet Union to break apart?

The Lithuanian basketball team won the Bronze medal at the 1992 Summer Olympics.
► Where is Lithuania located?

A. A Union Breaks Up

New Countries In the night's darkness, a flaming arrow shot high over the spectators to light a huge torch at the Olympic Stadium in Barcelona, Spain. It was quite a dramatic moment, and thousands of viewers caught their breath in surprise.

But for many of the athletes taking part in the Summer Olympic Games there were other reasons to be excited, too. These athletes came from countries that had only recently won their independence from the country formerly called the Soviet Union. Some of the gymnasts who won medals came from the countries of Ukraine (yoo KRAYN), Belarus (byel ah ROOS), and Russia. Others, such as members of the basketball team from Lithuania, proudly explained to reporters that they were the first athletes their country had sent to the Olympics for many decades. Until 1992, they had all competed together as members of one team from the Soviet Union.

The names of these newly independent countries were unfamiliar to many audiences watching the games on television or in Barcelona. Where did these new country names come from? The answer lies in the geography and the history of the former Soviet Union.

Union of Republics The Soviet Union, or the Union of Soviet Socialist Republics, was more than twice as large as the United States. From west to east the Soviet Union extended about the same length as a line stretching from the westernmost tip of Alaska, across the entire continent of North America, and beyond the Atlantic Ocean to Norway!

The words in the name *Union of Soviet Socialist Republics* can help to explain this country's large size. In a union, several states are united to form one country. Our country is a federation, or union, of 50 states. The Union of Soviet Socialist Republics was a union of 15 republics.

We need to know about the Soviet Union because for many decades it was one of the world's two **superpowers**. A superpower is a large and powerful country that plays a leading role in world affairs. The other superpower is the United States. The Soviet Union and the United States became superpowers after the end of World War

► Russia's national flag has replaced the red flag of the former Soviet Union.

355

II. For more than 50 years both nations played a major role in shaping world politics.

Then, in 1991, the Soviet Union broke up as its 15 republics declared themselves independent. It was a remarkable time in history, partly because there was little fighting about independence. Independence came quickly for these countries.

Because of these changes, the Soviet Union no longer exists, and the United States is the only superpower today. In fact, the United States and the countries of the former Soviet Union are now working together to reduce tension between countries around the world. These countries are also working to improve their economic and cultural ties.

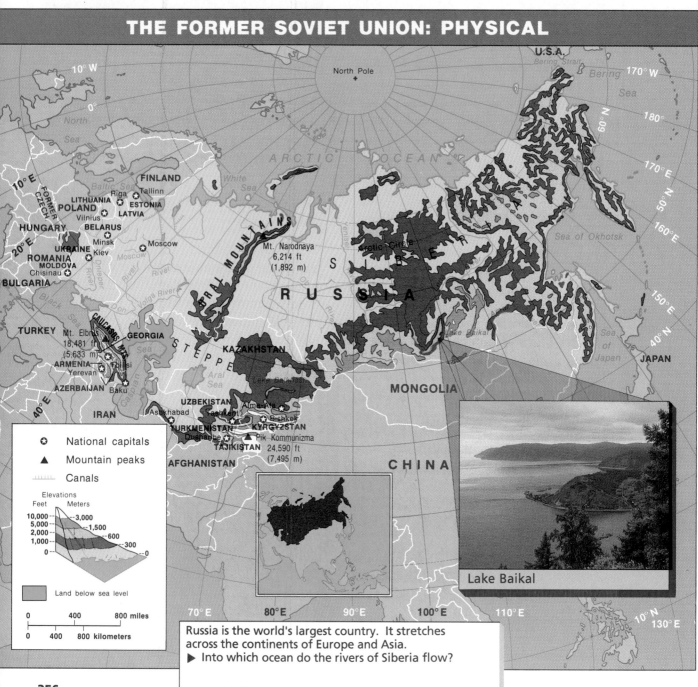

THE FORMER SOVIET UNION: PHYSICAL

North Pole

U.S.A.
Bering Strait
Bering Sea

ARCTIC OCEAN

FINLAND
Tallinn
Riga
ESTONIA
LITHUANIA
LATVIA
POLAND
Vilnius
FORMER CZECH.
HUNGARY
BELARUS
Minsk
Moscow
UKRAINE
Kiev
ROMANIA
MOLDOVA
Chisinau
BULGARIA

URAL MOUNTAINS
Mt. Narodnaya
6,214 ft
(1,892 m)

SIBERIA

RUSSIA

Arctic Circle

Sea of Okhotsk

Lake Baikal

Sea of Japan

JAPAN

TURKEY
Mt. Elbrus
18,481 ft
(5,633 m)
CAUCASUS MTS.
GEORGIA
Tbilisi
ARMENIA
Yerevan
AZERBAIJAN
Baku
IRAN

STEPPE
KAZAKHSTAN
Aral Sea
Lake Balkhash

MONGOLIA

UZBEKISTAN
Ashkhabad
Tashkent
Alma-Ata
Bishkek
TURKMENISTAN
Dushanbe
KYRGYZSTAN
Pik Kommunizma
24,590 ft
(7,495 m)
TAJIKISTAN
AFGHANISTAN

CHINA

◎ National capitals
▲ Mountain peaks
⸰⸰⸰ Canals

Elevations
Feet   Meters
10,000 -- --3,000
5,000 -- --1,500
2,000 -- --600
1,000 -- --300
0 -- --0

Land below sea level

0   400   800 miles
0   400   800 kilometers

Lake Baikal

70°E   80°E   90°E   100°E   110°E   130°E

Russia is the world's largest country. It stretches across the continents of Europe and Asia.
▶ Into which ocean do the rivers of Siberia flow?

356

B. Russia and Its Neighbors

Russia Russia is by far the largest new country to become independent from the breakup of the Soviet Union. The other newly independent countries of the former Soviet Union are located along the western and southern edges of Russia. Russia's area of 6,592,800 square miles (17,075,352 sq km) is nearly twice the size of the United States and spreads over two continents, Europe and Asia.

Russia has a population of nearly 150 million people. These millions of people are not spread out evenly over the land. Most of the people live to the west of the Ural Mountains; this is where the majority of the farms, industries, and transportation lines are located. In this region is Moscow—Russia's capital and the largest city in Europe. Moscow has a population of nearly 9 million. Another large Russian city is St. Petersburg, formerly Leningrad, with about 4.5 million people. Both of these cities offer an astonishing variety of museums, theaters, and universities.

Russia's Neighbors Six new countries to the west of Russia have locations near European countries. They include Estonia, Latvia, and Lithuania, which all have coasts along the Baltic Sea. For that reason they are called the Baltic Nations. Belarus, Ukraine, and Moldova (mawl DAW vuh)are the remaining countries in the European group. They are called the Interior Nations because they do not have coastlines on oceans or seas.

The people of the eight new countries to the south of Russia are similar to Asians in their cultures and histories. Georgia, Armenia, and Azerbaijan (az ur bye JAHN) are located between the Black Sea and the Caspian Sea. The Caspian Sea is easy to find on the map on page 356 because the sea is shaped like a giant S. These three countries are called the Caucasus (KAW kuh sus) Countries because they are located in the Caucasus Mountains. The five remaining countries of the former Soviet Union are Kazakhstan (kuh ZAK stan), Turkmenistan, Uzbekistan (ooz BEK ih stan), Tajikistan (tah JIHK ih stan), and Kyrgyzstan (KIHR geez stan). They are all located east of the Caspian Sea and are called the Central Asian Nations.

C. Transportation and Trade in a Giant Land

Transporting Resources A country with a vast territory usually has a large population, extensive mineral deposits, long navigable rivers, and sizable farmlands and forests. The former Soviet Union had all of these. Today, Russia has inherited these features. Unfortunately, the vast size and diverse climates of Russia also make it difficult to use the country's many natural resources. Most major manufacturing centers are located far away from these resources, making it expensive to transport them to factories.

A good transportation system—including many roads, railroads, airports, and navigable rivers—is found west of the Ural Mountains. However, to the east of the Ural Mountains, transportation facilities are poor. This region of deserts and frozen arctic lands has few transportation connections to the lands west of the Ural Mountains.

The longest railroad in the world, the 6,200-mile (9,976 km) Trans-Siberian Railway, is one of the few connections between the western and eastern parts of Russia. Many more railroads are still needed to settle and develop more of this huge land. In fact, near the eastern end of the Trans-Siberian Railway, there are many areas that are not yet inhabited.

Extreme Temperatures A problem with the territory of Russia is that most of it is quite far north. If you look at the map on page 356, you can see that most of Russia is north of 50°N latitude, which is farther north than the border between the United States and Canada. This cold and barren land is called Siberia.

Siberia, the largest region east of the Ural Mountains, is sparsely populated. It extends east across northern Russia, from the Ural Mountains to the Pacific Ocean. Siberia is well known for its cold climate. In the United States, we often say we feel like we're in Siberia when the weather turns icy. Across this vast region of Russia, winter temperatures often drop to −50°F (−46°C), and sometimes even as low as −90°F (−68°C). Surprisingly, summer days can reach 70°F (21°C) or even 80°F (27°C).

Siberia's natural environment makes it difficult to live there. In fact, its land is almost exactly like that of northern Canada, which you studied in Chapter 3. A region of tundra is found across the northern edge of Siberia, along the Arctic Ocean. There are just enough plants to feed reindeer, so herding is the main activity of the very few people who live on the Siberian tundra.

The soil of the Siberian tundra is frozen in winter and wet and marshy in summer. Beneath this top layer of soil is permafrost. When the top layer of soil thaws during the summer months, the melted water has nowhere to go, since the permafrost layer underneath it remains frozen. The water accumulates on the surface, making bogs or marshes. For people living in these northern lands, having a large territory does not necessarily mean that they can make all their resources and lands useful.

Frozen Coastline The coastline of Russia is the longest of any country in the world. But most of this 28,982-mile (46,632-km) coastline is along the Arctic Ocean, which is frozen solid for 8 to 10 months each year. Ships cannot pass through these iceblocked waters during the winter months.

Because of its long coastline on the Arctic Ocean, Russia has always been interested in acquiring lands with warm-water ports. These are ports and harbors that can be used the year round.

The city of St. Petersburg, on the Baltic Sea, is an important warm-water port. Ships leaving St. Petersburg travel west through the Baltic Sea, passing by the Danish city of Copenhagen on their way to the Atlantic Ocean. Far to the east is Vladivostok (vlad ih VAHS tahk), an important Russian port city on the Pacific Ocean. During the winter months, ships leaving this city have to travel southwest through three different seas to

Siberia's harsh winters make it difficult for workers to keep machinery running.
▶ What is the coldest temperature you have ever experienced?

reach the waters of the Pacific Ocean. Odessa is another important warm-water port. Odessa is located in Ukraine, far south of St. Petersburg, on the Black Sea. To reach the Mediterranean Sea from the Black Sea, ships must pass through the Bosporus, a narrow strait that extends past Istanbul, Turkey.

D. Sweeping Changes and Their Impact

Glasnost For most of the twentieth century, the government of the Soviet Union controlled almost every aspect of the Soviet people's lives. The government censored, or controlled, books, newspapers, movies, and television. Government officials made all the decisions about what farms, factories, and businesses could produce. This government control created economic and social problems including shortages of goods, poverty, unemployment, poor health care, and environmental problems.

In 1985, things began to change in the Soviet Union. In that year, Mikhail Gorbachev (mee kah EEL gor buh CHAWF) was named leader of the Soviet Union. Under his leadership, the Soviet government adopted a new policy called *glasnost* (GLAHS nust), or "openness." Under glasnost, the Soviet people were allowed more freedom to communicate with each other and with people living in other countries. Soviet citizens were allowed to travel to other countries, and some books and movies that had been banned were made available to the public. Gorbachev also wanted people to speak out about social problems so that the problems could be corrected.

One problem that people spoke out about was the Communist political system. So Gorbachev tried to give the Soviet people a larger voice in their government. In 1989, he allowed elections that did not require the candidates to be chosen by the Communist party. And in 1990, he proposed that

Boris Yeltsin became the first democratically elected president of Russia following the breakup of the Soviet Union.
▶ What was glasnost?

the Communist party would no longer be the country's only legal party.

The changes in the Soviet Union led to upheaval in Eastern Europe. One by one, the countries of Eastern Europe abandoned communism. After 40 years of Soviet control, the collapse of communism in Eastern Europe came with startling suddeness.

Independence Even more startling was the collapse of communism in the Soviet Union itself. Lithuania was the first Soviet republic to declare its independence. Other republics announced their intention to become independent over a period of time. In reaction to the changes that were taking place, a group of high-ranking Soviet leaders tried to overthrow Gorbachev's government. This coup attempt failed, and within a short time, all 15 republics had declared themselves independent countries.

FIFTEEN NEW NATIONS

These nations once belonged to the Union of Soviet Socialist Republics.

		TOTAL AREA	POPULATION	FLAG
ARMENIA ★Yerevan		11,306 sq mi 29,283 sq km	3,557,000 315 per sq mi 122 per sq km	
AZERBAIJAN ★Baku		33,400 sq mi 86,506 sq km	7,790,000 233 per sq mi 90 per sq km	
BELARUS [1] ★Minsk		80,200 sq mi 207,718 sq km	10,437,000 130 per sq mi 50 per sq km	
ESTONIA ★Tallinn		17,413 sq mi 45,100 sq km	1,625,000 93 per sq mi 36 per sq km	
GEORGIA ★Tbilisi		26,911 sq mi 69,699 sq km	5,726,000 213 per sq mi 82 per sq km	
KAZAKHSTAN ★Alma-Ata		1,049,200 sq mi 2,717,428 sq km	17,377,000 17 per sq mi 7 per sq km	
KYRGYZSTAN [2] ★Bishkek		76,642 sq mi 198,503 sq km	4,770,000 62 per sq mi 24 per sq km	
LATVIA ★Riga		24,695 sq mi 63,960 sq km	2,763,000 112 per sq mi 43 per sq km	
LITHUANIA ★Vilnius		26,173 sq mi 67,788 sq km	3,876,000 148 per sq mi 58 per sq km	
MOLDOVA [3] ★Chisinau		13,012 sq mi 33,701 sq km	4,490,000 345 per sq mi 133 per sq km	
RUSSIA ★Moscow		6,592,800 sq mi 17,075,352 sq km	149,909,000 23 per sq mi 9 per sq km	
TAJIKISTAN [4] ★Dushanbe		54,019 sq mi 139,909 sq km	6,155,000 114 per sq mi 44 per sq km	

[1] Formerly Byelorussia   [2] Formerly Kirghizia   [3] Formerly Moldovia   [4] Formerly Tadzhikistan

		TOTAL AREA	POPULATION	FLAG
TURKMENISTAN [5] ★Ashkhabad		188,417 sq mi 488,000 sq km	4,075,000 22 per sq mi 8 per sq km	
UKRAINE ★Kiev		233,100 sq mi 603,729 sq km	51,868,000 226 per sq mi 87 per sq km	
UZBEKISTAN ★Tashkent		172,700 sq mi 447,293 sq km	23,098,000 134 per sq mi 52 per sq km	

[5] Formerly Turkmenia

The Soviet Union's government fell from power. Gorbachev resigned as the last leader of the Union of Soviet Socialist Republics, and above the Kremlin, the Soviet flag was lowered for the last time. People were no longer Soviet citizens; they were citizens of new countries—such as Russia, Kazakhstan, or Estonia.

In December of 1991, an important treaty was signed by 11 of the new countries. This treaty created the Commonwealth of Independent States, an organization that loosely united the new countries. Only Georgia and the Baltic Nations—Estonia, Latvia, and Lithuania—did not join the commonwealth. Each member of the Commonwealth of Independent States maintained its freedom but agreed to work with other member countries on important economic and political problems.

Despite the goal of the Commonwealth of Independent States to encourage cooperation among its members, arguments soon arose. One of the aims of the organization was to have a single military force. But several members expressed the fear that Russia might dominate the organization because of its size and power. They wanted to form their own armed forces.

Some countries believed that the Commonwealth of Independent States was a temporary organization. By the mid-1990s the commonwealth had little real power. Instead, most of the new republics had become truly independent countries.

LESSON 1

Review

REVIEWING MAIN IDEAS

A. How many republics made up the former Soviet Union?

B. What are the four groups of countries that are Russia's neighbors?

C. Why are warm-water ports important to Russia?

D. What events led to the end of the Soviet Union?

SKILLS CHECK

WRITING SKILL

Write a paragraph describing what you think life is like in the former Soviet Union. Use the list of words you came up with at the beginning of the lesson.

The People and Places of Russia

CONNECTIONS
Imagine that you are going to Russia. Make a list of questions you would like to ask the Russian people.

TERMS
czar, communism, light industry, taiga, heavy industry, consumer goods

FOCUS
In what ways did communism affect Russia's economy?

A. Taking a Tour of Moscow

City of Churches Imagine that you could take a walking tour of Moscow, the capital city of Russia. What would you see? The towers and domed roofs of churches rise across the skyline, sandwiched between modern skyscrapers. Before the 1950s, when skyscrapers began to appear in Moscow, the spires and towers of churches were the highest points and the most impressive sights on the horizon. Moscow was known as the City of Forty Times Forty Churches. Today, onionshaped church domes still mark the landscape and remind us of the importance of religion in Russia's past.

Moscow began as a poor trading village in the twelfth century. From just a few houses at a crossroad, Moscow has grown into a major world city. Moscow is a transportation center for Russia and neighboring countries, and it is the center of Russia's government.

On your tour of Moscow, you would notice that most of Moscow's churches are no longer used for religious practice. Although the Russian people always attended

religious services, the former Soviet Union was officially an atheistic, or nonreligious, country. Today, the newly independent Russians are beginning to repair some of their churches and reopen them for religious services.

During your tour, you might decide to do what many Russian students do. They visit museums and monuments to learn about the culture of their country, much the way Americans visit Washington, D.C., to learn about their national heritage.

The Kremlin The heart of Moscow is the huge complex of buildings called the Kremlin, which is shown below. The Kremlin was originally a fortress, with palaces and churches inside for the ruling families of the Russian empire. Today these buildings are museums and government offices. Until very recently, the Kremlin was known around the world as the seat of power of the Soviet Union.

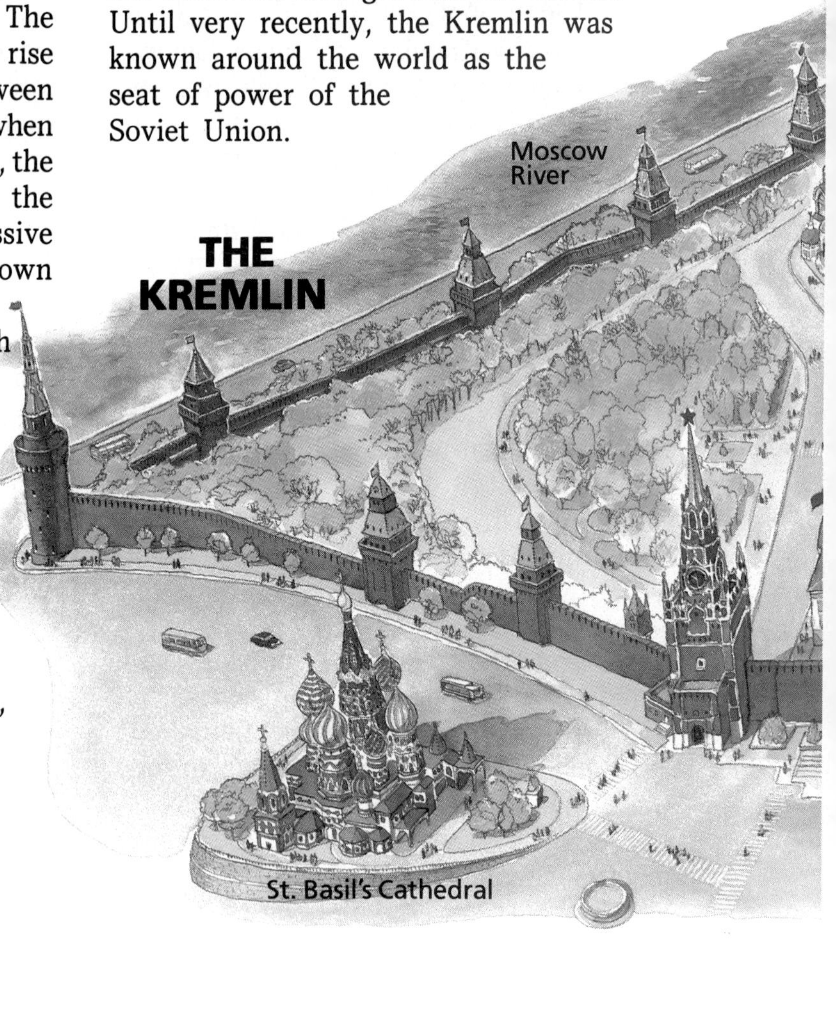

Moscow River

THE KREMLIN

St. Basil's Cathedral

People in the streets of Moscow look much like the people of other cities throughout the world. They rush along the city's sidewalks on their daily business, glancing at window displays and dashing into shops and offices. On your tour you would notice the many cars, trucks, and buses that crowd Moscow's busy streets. You would also notice that the streets are free from trash and newspapers. But according to a Moscow resident in a recent interview, the city is not as clean as it was in the past.

There was a time when anyone seeing someone throwing a cigarette stub or an apple core on the street would call the thoughtless citizen to account and make him pick it up and put it in a trash can. But now no one bats an eye. Just look at some of our streets, particularly around the Metro [subway] stations; it's a shame. Moscow's reputation for cleanliness is our pride.

On your tour, you would have to be sure to see the Bolshoi (BOHL shoi) Theater. It is the most important cultural center in Russia, presenting opera and ballet. Ballet is a respected art in Russia, and many children study it in their spare time. There is an old story

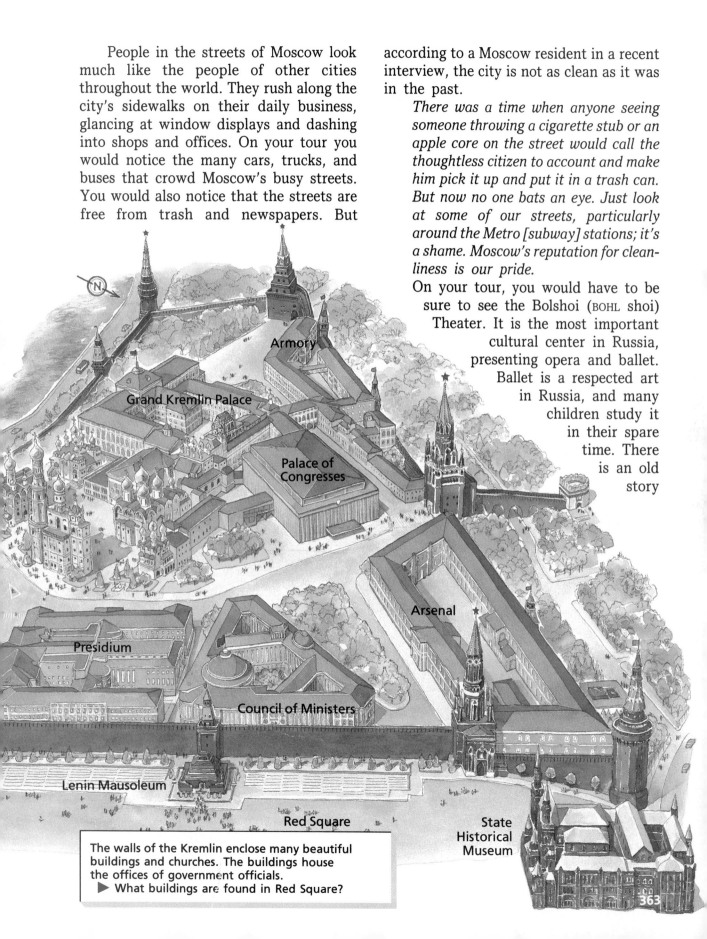

Armory

Grand Kremlin Palace

Palace of Congresses

Arsenal

Presidium

Council of Ministers

Lenin Mausoleum

Red Square

State Historical Museum

The walls of the Kremlin enclose many beautiful buildings and churches. The buildings house the offices of government officials.
▶ What buildings are found in Red Square?

363

about a young girl who was asked if she would like a new dress for Christmas. She looked through a catalog of clothing, but she pushed it away and said, "Couldn't you get me a ticket to the Bolshoi?"

B. The Russian Empire

Rise of Russia Modern Russia began as a small state of Slavic people called the Rus. The Rus traded with Scandinavian people to the north and Mediterranean people to the south.

In the 1200s, Tatars from Asia invaded and conquered most of the Rus. In the 1400s, Moscow, a Rus city, became the center of Rus, or Russian, culture. It was from here that Russian armies began to drive the Tatars out of Russia.

During the next three centuries, **czars (zahrz)**, the Russian word for "leader", expanded the power and territory of the Russians. Under the first czar, Ivan the Terrible, the Tatars were driven east of the Ural Mountains. Russian soldiers then

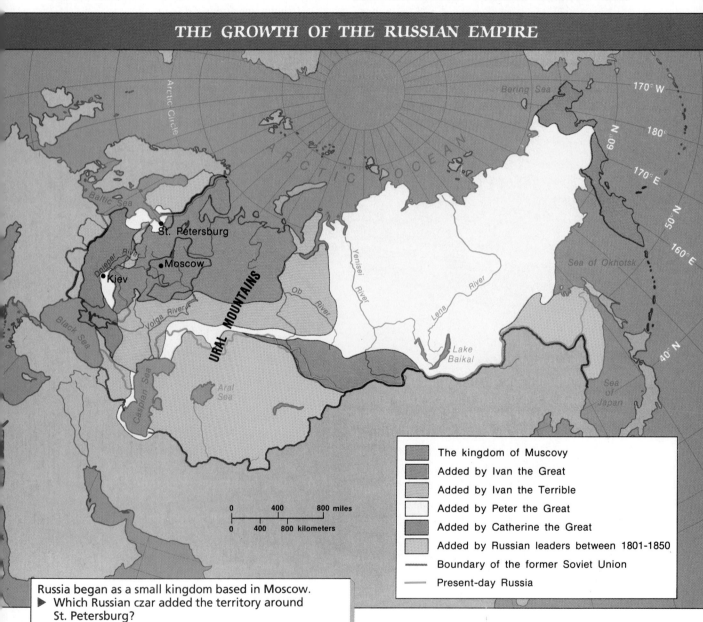

THE GROWTH OF THE RUSSIAN EMPIRE

	The kingdom of Muscovy
	Added by Ivan the Great
	Added by Ivan the Terrible
	Added by Peter the Great
	Added by Catherine the Great
	Added by Russian leaders between 1801-1850
-------	Boundary of the former Soviet Union
———	Present-day Russia

Russia began as a small kingdom based in Moscow.
▶ Which Russian czar added the territory around St. Petersburg?

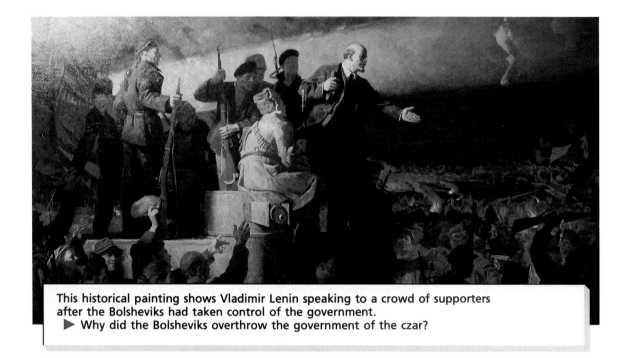

This historical painting shows Vladimir Lenin speaking to a crowd of supporters after the Bolsheviks had taken control of the government.
▶ Why did the Bolsheviks overthrow the government of the czar?

explored and conquered the lands from Siberia to the Pacific Ocean. Some Russian explorers and traders established settlements in North America, reaching present-day California in the early 1800s.

Under Czar Peter the Great, who ruled from 1682 to 1725, the capital city was moved from Moscow to St. Petersburg. St. Petersburg was closer to Russia's European neighbors than Moscow was and thus more convenient for trade and foreign relations. Catherine the Great, who ruled Russia from 1762 to 1796, expanded the Russian empire's territory toward the south.

Life was difficult for the Russian people during these centuries. Most people worked as serfs on the farmlands of wealthy landlords. The serfs were poor, illiterate, and usually hungry; many were treated like slaves. Czar Alexander II finally abolished serfdom in 1861, but by then new miseries had arisen for the Russian people. Hunger and poverty haunted the cities that had begun to grow as industry developed in Russia. People worked in factories for 12 hours a day, six days a week. Even women and young children worked long and hard at dangerous industrial jobs.

Revolution Both rural and city people grew dissatisfied with the Russian government. In 1917 a revolution occurred, led by the Communist party. The leader of the party was Vladimir Lenin. Lenin and his party believed in **communism**, which calls for the common ownership of land and industry by all the people of a country. In a Communist country, the government is controlled by the Communist party.

The Communist party remained in power in Russia for over 70 years after 1917. Why? Because for most of this period, only members of the Communist party were allowed to govern. In 1990, however, the government agreed to allow non-Communist party members to run for office. And since 1991, when Russia declared itself free and separate from the Soviet Union, the Communist party of Russia has encountered opposition from new political parties.

C. A Varied Land

The Russian Heartland The area west of the Ural Mountains is the heart of Russia. It was here, in the city of Moscow, that the old Russian empire had its center. One

LITERATURE

FROM: Dr. Zhivago

by Boris Pasternak

Boris Pasternak, a Russian poet and writer, wrote *Dr. Zhivago* in 1954. However, the Soviet government banned publication of *Dr. Zhivago* in the Soviet Union. The government did not like Pasternak's views on communism.

Dr. Zhivago was first published in Italy and then translated into English. In 1988, it was published in the Soviet Union for the first time.

Throughout the book, Pasternak describes the experiences of Dr. Zhivago. Zhivago, his family, friends, and enemies experience the many conflicts and consequences of the Russian Revolution. In this passage, Dr. Zhivago describes to his young friend, Misha Gordon, the landscape of the Carpathian Mountains just before a battle.

Once again they were lying on their bunks on either side of the long low window, it was night and they were talking.

Zhivago was telling Gordon how he had once seen the tsar at the front. He told his story well.

It was his first spring at the front. The headquarters of his regiment was in the Carpathians, in a deep valley, access to which from the Hungarian plain was blocked by this army unit. . . .

At the bottom of the valley was a railway station. Zhivago described the landscape, the mountains overgrown with mighty firs and pines, with tufts of clouds catching in their tops, and sheer cliffs of gray slate and graphite showing through the forest like worn patches in a thick fur. It was damp, dark April morning, as gray as the slate, locked in by the mountains on all sides and therefore still and sultry [humid]. Mist hung over the valley, and everything in it steamed, everything rose slowly—engine smoke from the railway station, gray vapors from the fields, the gray mountains, the dark woods, the dark clouds.

reason for this region's importance is the major river system that makes it possible to move goods easily north and south.

The Volga River is the most important river in Russia and the longest river in Europe. The map on page 356 shows that the Volga begins near the middle of the heartland of Russia and flows in a wide curve to the east and then south. There it empties into the Caspian Sea. Along the Volga River's 2,194 mile (3,530 km) length, many dams and reservoirs have been built. These have made the Volga useful for shipping, for irrigating farmlands, and for generating hydroelectric power.

The heartland of Russia has vast and valuable resources, making it an important manufacturing region. Moscow is a major manufacturing center for **light industry**, which is the production of goods such as textiles, clothing, furniture, and the processing of grains and vegetables.

The Russian Plain   The dominant physical feature of Russia's heartland is the Russian Plain. The Russian Plain is actually part of the North European Plain. The rolling hills of the Russian Plain have rich soils that have made this an important agricultural area. The region's continental climate offers warm summer months and sufficient rainfall for a variety of crops. The farms here help to make Russia one of the world's largest producers of barley, potatoes, rye, tobacco, butter, cheese, and hogs.

The Taiga   In the northern and coldest part of Siberia, the trees are short and stubby and useful only for grinding into pulp or for making into paper. The southern edge of Siberia is covered with a type of forest called **taiga (TYE guh)**, which means "evergreen forest" in Russian. The pine, spruce, and fir trees of the taiga are important natural resources to Russia. These trees are cut for lumber. Like the rest of Siberia, the taiga is only sparsely populated.

Siberia's Minerals   Siberia's climate and land are poor for farming, but many valuable resources lie underground. The Ural Mountains along the border between Siberia and the heartland of Russia hold important minerals, such as chromium, copper, and iron ore. These minerals are used in **heavy industry**—the production of goods such as railway cars, mining equipment, and farm machinery. Factories are powered by petroleum and natural gas from the nearby Ob River basin. This area has one of the world's largest natural gas fields and a tremendous amount of petroleum, too.

The Ural Mountains and the western edges of Siberia form the new zone of heavy industry in Russia. The industrial future of Russia will depend on the resources of western Siberia. However, it is difficult to extract, or remove, these minerals because of Siberia's harsh climate. As a result, the Soviet government has built large numbers of nuclear power plants to generate electricity in other parts of the country.

In 1986 one of these nuclear plants at Chernobyl (chur NOH bul), a city southwest of Moscow, caught fire and melted down. Over 30 people were killed immediately, and winds carried the radiation from the nuclear fuel across the countries of northern Europe.

Thousands of people from the Chernobyl area were relocated to escape the dangerous radiation. Scientists are still analyzing the long-term health risks and environmental damage caused by this accident.

D. New Challenges

Why Shortages?   In the 1980s the Soviet government realized that it had to solve the problem of shortages of goods and food. Today, Russia is still struggling to solve this problem. Goods that Americans take for granted, such as food, clothes, and automobiles, are in limited supply in Russia. Yet, as you have just read, Russia has abundant natural resources within its vast territory,

367

GROWING UP IN RUSSIA

Tatiana (tache YA nuh) is an ordinary Russian schoolgirl who lives in a rather extraordinary place. Her hometown is Verkhoyansk (ver kuh YANSK), a town located above the Arctic Circle in northern Siberia. Her hometown is known around the world for being the coldest city on earth. In winter, temperatures there often fall below -58°F (-33°C)!

Like all Russian children, Tatiana must attend school. If she decides to study for a profession such as medicine or law, she will prepare to enter a university. But many of her friends are thinking of going to a vocational high school. There they will learn industrial skills that will allow them to take factory jobs after they graduate. Russian law requires that jobs be provided for all graduates of vocational and trade schools.

Tatiana enjoys sports in her spare time, especially gymnastics. Her brother, Vladimir (VLAD uh mihr), is a member of an ice hockey team. Ice hockey is one of the most popular sports in Russia. Many young people also play soccer and basketball.

In the very cold northern areas of Russia, children become experts in skiing at a young age, since they must ski to school each day. In Verkhoyansk, it is especially difficult to drive cars in the winter. Automobiles cannot be operated in extremely cold weather unless they are kept in heated buildings. Sometimes people drain the engine's oil at night and heat it in the morning before returning it to the engine. But very few people own cars, and for Tatiana and her family it is easier to walk or ski when they go places.

Even with an automobile, Tatiana's family would not be able to go very far. There are no railroads or roads leaving Verkhoyansk. In winter, the only connection with the outside world is by air. In summer, boats and barges come up the Yana River from

the Laptev Sea to deliver goods and passengers.

But even in this isolated area, Tatiana keeps up with the latest fashions of the young people of Russia. She has a transistor radio, and her father has a shortwave radio. The shortwave radio allows them to hear news, music, and sports broadcasts from all over the world.

On their family vacations during the summer, Tatiana's family travels far from Siberia to visit friends and relatives in Moscow and St. Petersburg. Tatiana especially likes to visit the beaches along the Caspian Sea to warm up in the summer sun before returning to the coldest city on earth.

and its industries are among the largest in the world. This giant country also has the largest area of farmland in the world. How could there be shortages of so many goods in this country of rich resources?

In the former Soviet Union, the government controlled the country's economy and made decisions about what goods should be produced. The government decided to use natural resources mainly to produce machines, tools, heavy vehicles, and weapons instead of **consumer goods**, or goods that individuals buy for themselves or their households. This is why there were, and still are, shortages of consumer goods.

Economic Changes Because of these shortages, the Soviet government under Gorbachev adopted an economic policy called *perestroika* (per es TROI kuh). Perestroika allowed some small businesses, such as restaurants and shops, to make their own business decisions. The managers could decide what to produce and how much to charge for products. The businesses then kept the profits from their sales instead of returning all money earned to the government.

Gradually, the government began to sell its factories to individuals or to the workers who operated them. Some government-owned farms were turned over to the workers to manage for themselves.

At first few people took advantage of the new opportunities because they didn't have much money saved to start businesses or to rent farmland. Some families opened up tiny restaurants in their houses and began their own businesses that way.

These were exciting but frightening changes to many people. As long as the government controlled everything, people knew that they would always have jobs and houses. But without the government's control, they weren't sure what might happen to them in the future.

A Russian man talked about the plans he and his wife were making.

Many new small businesses have been created in the former Soviet Union.
▶ What change allowed the development of new businesses?

Olga and I have decided to start our own business as soon as we can. At last the country is doing something to encourage private enterprise. Many of my co-workers dream of owning their own businesses too. . . . I'm an optimist. I think that everything will be fine.

LESSON 2

Review

REVIEWING MAIN IDEAS

A. What landmarks would you visit on a tour of Moscow?
B. Why was the Communist party so important in Russia's past?
C. What are the main natural resources of Russia?
D. Why are there shortages of many goods in Russia?

SKILLS CHECK

MAP SKILL

Look at the map on page 356 to find the Lena, Ob, and Yenisei rivers. Into which body of water do they flow?

Russia's Neighbors

Imagine that the United States separated into independent countries. What problems would your state encounter as an independent country? What would be your new country's strength?

TERMS

steppes, chernozem

FOCUS

What difficulties lie ahead for the new countries formed from the former Soviet Union?

A. Ethnic Groups of the Soviet Union

When the Soviet Union broke up into 15 independent countries, it was not difficult to decide on borders for the new countries. Each of the original republics of the Soviet Union kept its borders as it gained independence. These borders made sense because they were drawn around the largest ethnic groups in order to give each group its own homeland.

Each ethnic group, including the Russians, is proud of its heritage and traditions. To help develop a sense of unity in their country, the government of the former Soviet Union decided that all its people should be able to speak, read, and write Russian. Today, many schools in places where Russian is not the native language teach Russian as a second language. This allows children to keep their native languages but also to understand a language that is understood by millions of people.

Even though each ethnic group, and each country, considers itself unique, we can group some countries together because their languages or cultures are somewhat similar. These groups are the Baltic Nations, the Interior Nations, the Caucasus Countries, and the Central Asian Nations. Russia is in a group by itself because it is so large and has so many people.

This Georgian man, Uzbeki woman, and Russian girl show the diversity of ethnic groups in the Soviet Union.
▶ What is the largest ethnic group?

B. The Baltic Nations

Renewed Independence Three ethnic groups—the Latvians, the Lithuanians and the Estonians—live in three small countries that border the Baltic Sea. The people of these countries feel a stronger relationship with the people of Western Europe than with those of the former Soviet Union. The Baltic Nations were the first three countries to formally declare their independence from the Soviet Union.

Estonia Estonia is the most northern of the three Baltic Nations and is closely tied to Scandinavia. The Estonian language is somewhat similar to Finnish, and Estonia was once part of the old kingdom of Sweden. Estonia's capital city, Tallinn, is only 25 miles (40 km) across the Baltic Sea from Helsinki, the capital city of Finland. This short distance made it possible for Estonians to receive television and radio broadcasts from Western Europe when the Soviet government censored such broadcasts in the rest of the Soviet Union.

Estonia has natural resources that make it possible to produce electricity and a variety of manufactured goods. Most of its goods were sold to other republics of the Soviet Union. This is one reason why it is important for Estonia to maintain good relationships with its neighbors.

Latvia In Latvia, the middle country of the three Baltic Nations, Russians make up about one third of the population. Why are there so many Russians in Latvia? The answer is in Latvia's prosperity.

When Latvia was a republic of the Soviet Union, many factories were built, and Latvia's standard of living rose steadily. The factory jobs that opened up attracted many people, including Russians. Eventually, so many Russians arrived in Latvia that some Latvian people resented them. Like Estonia, Latvia needs to maintain strong ties with its neighbors to ensure progress and peace.

Lithuanians march in their capital city to celebrate independence from the Soviet Union.
▶ What is the capital of Lithuania?

Lithuania The present-day country of Lithuania was once a powerful empire that extended far across Eastern Europe. Today, it is much smaller in size and has a very short coastline along the Baltic Sea. Lithuania has little industry, and its agriculture is modernizing only slowly.

In spite of their economic problems, Lithuanians have great pride in their country and in their culture. The capital city, Vilnius, was a scene of dramatic demonstrations and protests when Lithuania declared independence. The languages of Latvia and Lithuania are similar and are said to have Baltic roots, coming from the ancient Baltic people who had inhabited their territories. Today, Lithuanians are looking forward to strong economic ties with their neighbors.

THE FORMER SOVIET UNION: POLITICAL

⊕ National capitals	0 400 800 miles
• Other cities	0 400 800 kilometers

Cities 100,000 to 499,999
Ashkhabad (Turkmenistan) D-4
Chernobyl (Ukraine) B-2
Tallinn (Estonia) B-1
Verkhoyansk (Russia) A-12

Cities 500,000 to 999,999
Dushanbe (Tajikistan) D-5
Bishkek (Kyrgyzstan) C-6
Chisinau (Moldova) C-1
Krivoy Rog (Ukraine) C-2
Murmansk (Russia) A-2
Riga (Latvia) B-1
Vilnius (Lithuania) B-1
Vladivostok (Russia) C-12

Cities 1,000,000 or more
Alma-Ata (Kazakhstan) C-6
Baku (Azerbaijan) C-3
Donetsk (Ukraine) C-2
Kiev (Ukraine) C-2
Minsk (Belarus) B-1
Moscow (Russia) B-2
Odessa (Ukraine) C-1
St. Petersburg (Russia) B-1

Tashkent (Uzbekistan) C-5
Tbilisi (Georgia) C-3
Yerevan (Armenia) C-3

Fifteen independent countries have been created from the former Soviet Union.
The largest one is Russia. Armenia and Moldova are the smallest.
▶ Which cities in Russia have a population of 1,000,000 or more?

C. The Interior Nations

Ukraine The Ukrainians were second in population to the Russians in the former Soviet Union. Today their country, Ukraine, is a strong economic force in the region. The area called the **steppes** makes Ukraine one of the world's great breadbasket countries. This belt of grasslands begins in Ukraine and continues along the southern edge of Siberia. Because of the **chernozem** (chur NOH zem), the rich black soil of the steppes, Ukrainian farmers are major world producers of wheat, sugar beets, corn, and oats.

Adding to Ukraine's wealth is a rich industrial base and important raw materials. Just north of the Black Sea is the Donets (duh NETS) Basin, which is a major center of heavy industry. Factories in the Donets Basin produce such goods as tractors, mining equipment, and factory machinery.

372

The Donets Basin has one of the world's largest deposits of coal. The hard coal of the Donets Basin is the best kind for producing steel because it creates intense heat when it burns. Not far away from the Donets coal fields is the great iron ore field called Krivoy Rog. The iron and steel plants in the Donets Basin and Krivoy Rog are among the largest in the world. The steel is used to manufacture products such as farm equipment and supertankers.

Moldova Sandwiched between Ukraine and Romania is the tiny republic of Moldova. Its area is only about twice the size of New Jersey, and its total population is less than the population of a large city in the United States. Its location is not very desirable, because it is located between two large countries and is also landlocked.

But Moldovans are not especially worried about their future. Why not? Nearly two thirds of the people of Moldova have Romanian ancestors, speak Romanian, and feel strong cultural ties with their Romanian neighbors to the west. Moldova changed the name of its capital city from the Russian form, Kishinev, to the Romanian form, Chisinau. In fact, most Moldovans and many Romanians are hoping that someday Moldova can be reunited with Romania.

Belarus On a map, the country of Belarus seems to be in a central location, and throughout history, this country has been overrun from every direction by different invaders. Belarussian agriculture is not very productive, but it is modernizing slowly. The country's industrial base is expanding slowly as well, but it is almost entirely located in the capital city, Minsk. Perhaps Belarussians were happy to have their capital city chosen as the headquarters for the Commonwealth of Independent States. After all, they will need to have neighbors who can help them develop their economy and defend their borders.

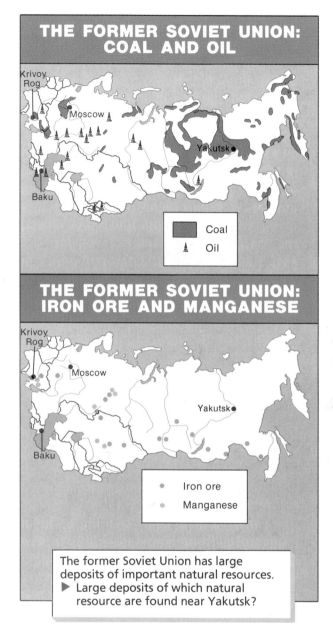

THE FORMER SOVIET UNION: COAL AND OIL

Coal
Oil

THE FORMER SOVIET UNION: IRON ORE AND MANGANESE

Iron ore
Manganese

The former Soviet Union has large deposits of important natural resources.
▶ Large deposits of which natural resource are found near Yakutsk?

D. The Caucasus Countries

A Mountainous Region The Caucasus Mountains are located south of the Russian Plain, between the Black Sea and the Caspian Sea. This mountainous region has many farms and small towns nestled in its valleys. In 1988, a devastating earthquake struck this region, killing nearly 25,000 people and leaving almost half a million people homeless. Many of the world's

Workers begin cleaning up debris after a devastating earthquake destroyed many Armenian cities in 1988.
▶ How did other nations help the earthquake victims?

nations—including the United States—sent clothing, blankets, and medical supplies to help the victims of this terrible tragedy.

Georgia A unique ethnic group lives in the country called Georgia, which is in the western part of the Caucasus Mountains. The Georgians, the name for the people who live here, are proud of their culture and are recognized as having a higher standard of living and more wealth than most other people in neighboring countries. In the fertile mountain valleys they produce tea, fruits, and tobacco, and their capital city, Tbilisi, is one of the oldest and most beautiful cities in this part of the world.

Georgia did not join the Commonwealth of Independent States upon becoming independent in 1991. In the early 1990s, Georgia suffered from civil war as some regions tried to secede. In 1993 Georgia joined the Commonwealth of Independent States. By the mid-1990s, the situation in Georgia was becoming more stable.

Armenia and Azerbaijan Some of the ethnic groups in the former Soviet Union felt that other ethnic groups discriminated against them. Usually the powerful military forces of the Soviet government prevented armed struggles between groups. But as the Soviet Union dissolved into independent countries, ethnic conflicts began to erupt, especially in the two Caucasus Countries of Armenia and Azerbaijan. To understand this ethnic conflict we must learn about these countries' economies and cultures.

Azerbaijan, the larger of the two countries, has a coastline on the Caspian Sea and a giant petroleum field near its capital city, Baku. The Baku petroleum field produces a large amount of oil, much of which is sold to Russia.

Armenia is much smaller than Georgia or Azerbaijan and is landlocked in the south central Caucasus Mountains. Its rugged mountains produce large amounts of hydroelectricity, and it produces substantial amounts of minerals and fruits.

In Armenia, industry is not nearly as modern or as productive as industry in Azerbaijan. Over many decades, Armenians left their country to work in the oil fields and factories in Baku and elsewhere in Azerbaijan. Another factor is that the Azerbaijanis are mainly Muslims, and most Armenians are Christians.

These two groups have not lived together peacefully in Azerbaijan. Occasionally fighting breaks out between the Azerbaijanis and the Armenians. Many Azerbaijanis believe that the Armenians should move back into Armenia. They have tried to force the Armenians to leave, but the Armenians resist. Many people of both groups have been killed during these struggles.

THE FORMER SOVIET UNION: VEGETATION

The area of the former Soviet Union has six major vegetation zones. Tundra covers much of the area north of the Arctic Circle.
▶ Which vegetation zone covers the largest area?

Legend:
- Tundra
- Taiga
- Steppe
- Desert
- Mountain vegetation
- Hardwood forest

E. The Central Asian Nations

Desert Climates Five nations located to the south of Russia—Kazakhstan, Kyrgyzstan, Turkmenistan, Uzbekistan, and Tajikistan—gained their independence from the Soviet Union. These Central Asian Nations share a desert climate. This desert region borders the eastern edge of the Caspian Sea and extends to the east past the Aral Sea and into China.

Fortunately for the people living in these five nations, there are high mountain ranges on the southern and eastern borders of Turkmenistan, Tajikistan, and Kyrgyzstan. Though these rugged mountains create problems for transportation, they also provide streams and rivers for the lower desert region. In recent years, great efforts have been made to use the water from these rivers to irrigate dry lands for agriculture. Uzbekistan has had much success with irrigated agriculture and is now a major cotton producer. In the other nations, smaller amounts of wheat, corn, pasture grasses, fruits, and vegetables are produced on irrigated lands.

375

Many ships have been left beached because the level of water in the Aral Sea varies from one year to the next.
▶ Which countries border on the Aral Sea?

In Tajikistan and Kyrgyzstan, many people continue to live as nomadic herders, like their ancestors. The wool and hides from their sheep, cattle, and yaks provide the raw materials for textile and food processing industries.

Modern Industry Kazakhstan, the northernmost of the Central Asian Nations, had close ties with Russia. In the northeastern area of Kazakhstan, major mineral deposits have been used to develop industries. And in the west, along the shores of the Caspian Sea, important petroleum and natural gas provide valuable raw materials. The northern half of Kazakhstan has good transportation links with Russia.

Culture Most residents in the Central Asian Nations are Muslims of Turkic ancestry, so their culture is quite different from the culture of people living in Russia, the Baltic Nations, or the Interior Nations.

But there are many minority groups in the Central Asian Nations, as well. Many Russians live in Kazakhstan, and there are also Russian residents in the other four nations. Ukrainians, Armenians, and others make up additional minority groups in the Central Asian Nations. Likewise, many Central Asian people live outside their nations, too.

These five neighboring nations have several major problems to solve in the coming decades. They need to create jobs and provide the basic goods needed by their rapidly growing populations. They need to depend less on irrigation water for agriculture, since this water is in limited supply. And like people in other parts of the world, they need to resolve tensions between the different religious and cultural groups in their populations in order to avoid conflict. Even though the people of these countries have little in common with Russians, Ukrainians, and others, they are working together with other countries of the former Soviet Union to make life better for all their people.

LESSON 3

Review

REVIEWING MAIN IDEAS

A. Why were there 15 republics in the former Soviet Union?
B. Which countries are called the Baltic Nations?
C. Why is Ukraine such an important country?
D. In what ways are Georgia, Armenia, and Azerbaijan different from each other?
E. What do the Central Asian Nations have in common?

SKILLS CHECK

THINKING SKILL
Write a paragraph explaining why people would prefer to have the kinds of freedoms found in democracies like the United States.

CHAPTER 15 REVIEW

REVIEWING TERMS

Match each term with the correct definition. Write your answers in sentence form.

steppes	taiga
superpower	chernozem
light industry	czar
heavy industry	communism
consumer goods	glasnost

1. An area of rich fertile grasslands

2. Goods people want for their homes or themselves

3. Sparsely populated evergreen forests

4. A nation powerful enough to influence world affairs

5. The policy of openness that began in Soviet society in the mid-1980s

6. The production of such goods as processed food, clothing, appliances, and furniture

7. A title that was given to Russian leaders

8. The common ownership of land and industry by all the people of a country

9. The production of such goods as factory equipment, heavy machinery, and farming and mining equipment

10. The rich, black soils of the steppes where wheat, corn, and oats are produced

REVIEWING THE FACTS

On a separate sheet of paper, answer the questions in complete sentences.

1. Why is it difficult for Russia to use its many resources?

2. What are Russia's main warm-water ports?

3. What are Russia's principal light and heavy industry centers?

4. How did perestroika try to reduce shortages of consumer goods?

5. Why is farming difficult in Siberia?

6. Why did the Soviet Union build many nuclear plants?

7. What are the major differences between the eastern and western parts of Russia?

8. Why did the Communist party remain in power for over 70 years?

9. In what ways did the Soviet government control people's lives before glasnost?

10. How many new nations were created from the breakup of the Soviet Union?

❖❖❖

WRITING ABOUT GOVERNMENT

In 1986, thousands of people were evacuated from the area around Chernobyl after a nuclear power plant accident. Imagine that you had lived close to the area and had to be evacuated and that your health would have to be monitored for many years. Write a letter to the editor of a newspaper to express your feelings on the events.

THINKING CRITICALLY

On a separate sheet of paper, answer the following in complete sentences.

1. Why is it important to learn about the world's superpowers?
2. What challenges face the newly independent nations created from the breakup of the Soviet Union?
3. Why is Moscow considered to be Russia's most important city?
4. Compare a Soviet citizen's life under communism before glasnost with a Russian's life under the rule of the czars.
5. Why are St. Petersburg and Vladivostok so important to Russia?

SUMMARIZING THE CHAPTER

On a separate sheet of paper, draw a graphic organizer like the one shown here. Copy the information from this graphic organizer to the one you have drawn. Under each main idea, write three statements that you think best support it.

CHAPTER THEME

Fifteen nations have been created from the breakup of the Soviet Union. All of these countries are still influenced by the years under Soviet control.

LESSON 1   The breakup of the Soviet Union created fifteen new nations.

1. _____
2. _____
3. _____

LESSON 2   Russia is the largest of the new nations created from the breakup of the Soviet Union.

1. _____
2. _____
3. _____

LESSON 3   Difficulties lie ahead for the countries formed from the former Soviet Union.

1. _____
2. _____
3. _____

UNIT 4 REVIEW

COOPERATIVE LEARNING

In Unit 4 you read about the countries of the British Isles, Scandinavia, Western Europe, Southern Europe, Eastern Europe, and the former Soviet Union.

Stories about these countries appear almost every day in a newspaper.

PROJECT

Your group will choose a country that was studied in Unit 4 and create a newspaper. The newspaper will consist of interesting facts and features about the chosen area. After your group has chosen a country, but before it begins to work on the newspaper, pick one member to be the group representative. The person will meet with the other group representatives in the class.

The purpose of this meeting is to see that each group works on a different country. The teacher will act as the mediator and make sure that each group has a different country. In the event that two groups choose the same place, the teacher will make the final decision.

Your newspaper should have headlines, articles, editorials, and pictures. You can also include advertisements, social notes, and local news. The newspaper should be two to three pages long. Remember to include an exciting headline on the front page.

Your newspaper will need the following workers.

- An editor to plan the articles and help the other group members
- Reporters to write the articles
- A headline writer
- An art designer to gather pictures

PRESENTATION AND REVIEW

The newspaper can be presented in a number of ways. Articles could be typed in two columns, cut out, and pasted on large sheets of butcher paper under headlines and around pictures. Or the material could be typed and set up according to your designer's and editor's request. When finished, display your newspaper in the classroom for everyone to see.

When your group has completed this project, each member should write an evaluation. Everyone should consider the following questions.

- How successful was the project?
- What did I contribute to this project?
- What improvements could be made in my work and in the way the group worked together?

Meet again as a group and discuss what everyone learned from working together.

REMEMBER TO:
- Give your ideas.
- Listen to others' ideas.
- Plan your work with the group.
- Present your project.
- Discuss how your group worked.

SKILLBUILDER

UNDERSTANDING POLITICAL CARTOONS

WHY DO I NEED THIS SKILL?

Political cartoons appear in newspapers and magazines just about every day. Political cartoons are never objective, that is, they always take sides. They are a quick and clever way of presenting a point of view. Understanding political cartoons is an important reading skill that everyone should develop.

© North America Syndicate, Inc.

LEARNING THE SKILL

A political cartoon is a drawing that makes a statement about a subject of public interest. It can be about a person, an event, or an important problem. The cartoonist, the person who draws the cartoon, tries to get people to see things in a certain way.

To understand a cartoon, the reader must first recognize the subject. What is the subject of a cartoon showing a lake with soda cans and plastic bottles floating in dirty water and one duck saying to another, "It wasn't this bad last year"? If you correctly answered "pollution," you knew enough about the background of the problem to understand the subject. You knew that cans and bottles contribute to the problem of polluted water and are easily recognizable symbols of the problem. You probably also knew that wildlife cannot live for very long in polluted areas. The caption for the cartoon tells you that the cartoonist thinks that the problem of water pollution is getting worse.

PRACTICING THE SKILL

As you read in the Continental Handbook for Europe and the former Soviet Union, the Berlin wall was erected in 1961 to stop East Germans from leaving their country. The wall came to symbolize the division of Europe that had occurred in 1945, at the end of the Second World War.

The cartoon to the left shows how one cartoonist, William Mauldin, felt when the Berlin wall was temporarily opened for Christmas in 1963. Relatives from West Germany were allowed to visit relatives in East Germany. At the time, Mauldin was an editorial cartoonist for a newspaper, the *Chicago Sun-Times*. He has won the Pulitzer Prize twice for his cartoons.

Study the cartoon on the previous page and answer the following questions.

1. What part of the cartoon symbolizes the Christmas holiday?
2. What part of the cartoon serves as a reminder that in 1963 the wall was still a barrier to freedom?
3. Can you picture people passing through the broken wall to visit their relatives? How does the cartoon make you feel?

    The cartoon to the right shows another cartoonist's reaction to the fall of the Berlin wall in 1989. The cartoon was created by Mike Luckovich and published in a newspaper, the *Atlanta Constitution*. You might remember watching the news on television and seeing the German people in East and West Berlin celebrate the fall of the Berlin wall. They were shown climbing over the wall and singing and dancing in the streets.

Study the cartoon on this page and answer the following questions.

1. What part of the cartoon symbolizes that the wall is down and that free travel is now allowed between East Germany and West Germany?
2. Who are the people in the cartoon who are remembering the wall?
3. Why is the cartoon from 1989 humorous and the cartoon from 1963 not humorous?

APPLYING THE SKILL

Look in a newspaper or magazine for a cartoon about some current problem. Tape it on a sheet of paper. On another sheet of paper, make a list identifying the various parts of the cartoon and telling what each means. Then in a short paragraph, explain the point that the cartoonist is trying to make.

    You may, instead, wish to draw a cartoon of your own. Pick a topic from current events or take a school situation or problem as your topic. Decide what symbols you can use to state your point of view quickly and clearly. Remember, a good cartoon makes its point without any extra explanation.

© Mike Luckovich and Creators Syndicate.

SKILLBUILDER

WRITING A REPORT

WHY DO I NEED THIS SKILL?

Report writing is hard work, but there are some tips in this Skillbuilder that can help you write a report. Knowing how to go about writing a report will help you learn more about social studies and also receive better grades on reports.

LEARNING THE SKILL

A *written report* is a detailed, factual paper on a specific topic. It can be both nonfictional and informative. Here are eight steps you can follow when you write reports. It is helpful to break down the process.

1. **Select a topic.** The *topic* is what the report is about. Sometimes your teacher will give you a topic. Other times, you may have to choose one yourself. Let's assume that your teacher has required everyone in your class to write a report on some geographical aspect of Italy, which you studied in Chapter 13.

2. **Narrow the topic.** The geography of Italy is a broad topic. You need to narrow the topic and decide what aspects you will write about. You could write about the land features of Italy, the people of Italy, Italian agriculture or industry, or a particular city, such as Milan or Rome. Let's suppose that the section in Chapter 13 on the volcano Mount Vesuvius interested you, so you have decided to report on the geography and history of Mount Vesuvius.

3. **Identify resources and do research.** Information for your report can be found in your school and public libraries. Books

are helpful resources. They can be located by using the *card catalog*. There are also articles on Italy, volcanoes, and Mount Vesuvius in *encyclopedias*. An *atlas* will give information about the geography of a specific part of Italy. More current information can be found by using the *Readers' Guide to Periodical Literature*, which will identify magazine articles on Mount Vesuvius, volcanoes, and Italy. Using these resources, you will be able to find information on your topic, read it, and take notes on important facts that you might want to include in your report.

4. **Organize information for your report.** The next step is to organize your ideas so you can begin to write. Decide what the subtopics (smaller ideas) are and how you will organize those topics in your report. Some students make an outline to help organize their writing. Others write ideas on index cards and organize the cards in a logical way.

5. **Write the first draft.** Now write a first draft of your report. Begin with a short introduction and then develop each idea and subtopic. Follow your organizational plan. For example, using index cards, you would first write the introduction and then present the rest of your ideas in the logical order that the cards reflect.

6. **Revise the report.** *Revise* means to "read over to correct or improve your writing." When you revise, decide whether your ideas are well organized. You might also look for information you could omit or areas where you need to add more information. For example, as you reread your report, you might recognize that you need

to explain more about the events of A.D. 79, when Mount Vesuvius erupted.

7. **Edit the report.** *Edit* means "prepare a piece of writing in its final form." It is important to check for correct grammar, spelling, punctuation, and capitalization. Then *proofread* the report to make sure you have corrected all errors.

8. **Write the final draft.** The last step is to write the final draft that you will give to your teacher. This should be in your neatest handwriting. If you use a typewriter or word processor, make sure that there are no typing errors.

PRACTICING THE SKILL

Now try out the eight steps for writing a report. Do the same assignment that was just described, but select a different country. Complete steps 1 through 4. Your teacher will then tell you whether you should complete steps 5 through 8.

APPLYING THE SKILL

Try using these eight steps when you have to write reports in social studies or any other subject area.

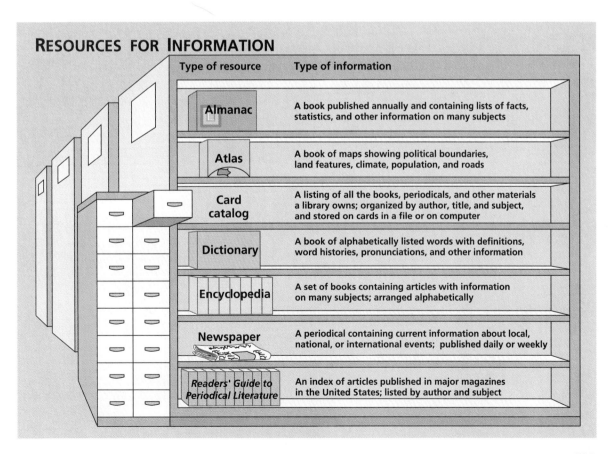

RESOURCES FOR INFORMATION

Type of resource	Type of information
Almanac	A book published annually and containing lists of facts, statistics, and other information on many subjects
Atlas	A book of maps showing political boundaries, land features, climate, population, and roads
Card catalog	A listing of all the books, periodicals, and other materials a library owns; organized by author, title, and subject, and stored on cards in a file or on computer
Dictionary	A book of alphabetically listed words with definitions, word histories, pronunciations, and other information
Encyclopedia	A set of books containing articles with information on many subjects; arranged alphabetically
Newspaper	A periodical containing current information about local, national, or international events; published daily or weekly
Readers' Guide to Periodical Literature	An index of articles published in major magazines in the United States; listed by author and subject

UNIT 5

THE COUNTRIES OF ASIA

CONTINENTAL HANDBOOK

TABLE OF COUNTRIES

CONNECTIONS

What are some of the products you use daily that come from Asia?

TERMS

Pacific Rim

FOCUS

What makes Asia a region?

Japan Is Said To Be Richest

TOKYO, Aug. 1, 1987—Japan became the world's richest nation on paper in 1987, surpassing the United States in national assets for the first time with $43.7 trillion worth of land, factories, stock and other wealth, a leading Japanese newspaper said today.

A. Growing Ties Between the United States and Asia

This newspaper article probably startled some Americans who are used to thinking of the United States as the richest country in the world. In recent years, however, the economies of Japan and many other Asian countries have grown dramatically. These countries have become important customers of American-made goods. Asian countries also produce many of the goods we buy in the United States, such as televisions, videocassette recorders, and other electronic goods.

In addition to being important trade partners with the United States, Japan and other Asian countries are taking on new responsibilities. For example, Japan is giving some of its new wealth to poor countries around the world, just as the United States does. In the future, Japan is also expected to help maintain international peace by contributing money and troops to peace-keeping forces. Americans must learn about Asia to cooperate with our economic and diplomatic partners.

B. Large and Small in Asia

No other continent on earth has as many great contrasts between large and small countries, cities, and physical features as Asia does. For example, Asia includes six of the world's ten most populated countries. China has more peo-

Asia is the largest continent on the globe. It includes the deserts of the Middle East and the snow-covered peaks of the world's highest mountains.
▶ What mountain range is Mt. Everest located in?

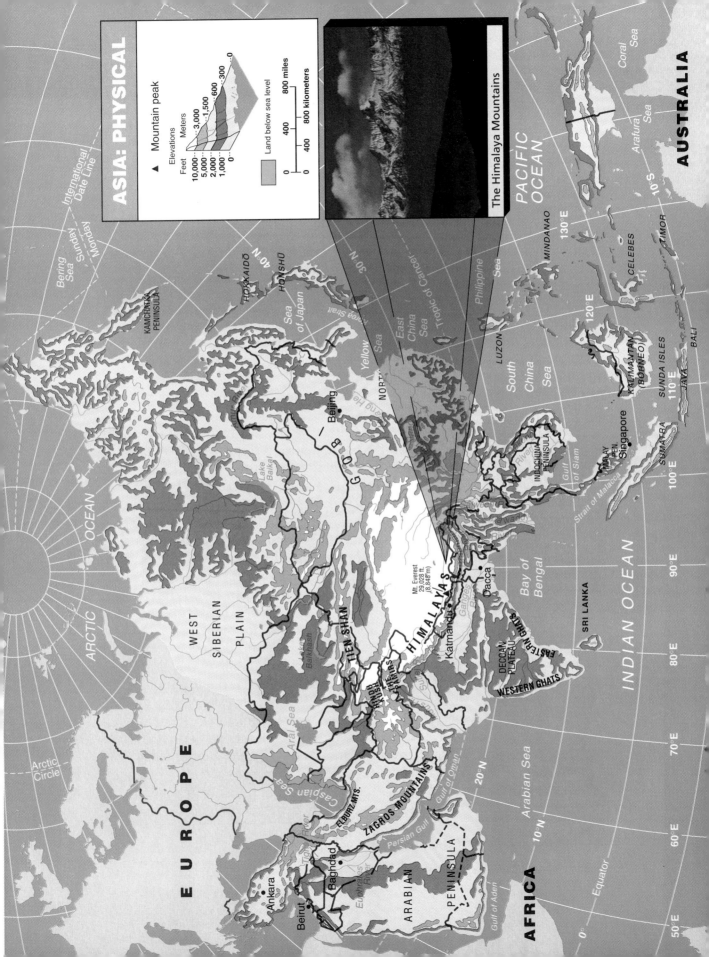

ASIA: PHYSICAL

Elevations

Feet	Meters
10,000	3,000
5,000	1,500
2,000	600
1,000	300
0	0

▲ Mountain peak

Land below sea level

0   400   800 miles

0   400   800 kilometers

The Himalaya Mountains

EUROPE

AFRICA

AUSTRALIA

ARCTIC OCEAN

PACIFIC OCEAN

INDIAN OCEAN

Bering Sea

Sunday
Monday
International Date Line

KAMCHATKA PENINSULA

HOKKAIDŌ

HONSHŪ

Sea of Japan

Korea Strait

Yellow Sea

East China Sea

NORTH

Beijing

Huang He

GOBI

Lake Baikal

Lake Balkhash

WEST SIBERIAN PLAIN

TIEN SHAN

THE PAMIRS

HINDU KUSH

Aral Sea

Caspian Sea

ELBURZ MTS.

ZAGROS MOUNTAINS

Tigris River

Euphrates River

Persian Gulf

Gulf of Oman

Gulf of Aden

ARABIAN PENINSULA

Arabian Sea

Ankara

Beirut

Baghdad

HIMALAYAS

Mt. Everest 29,028 ft. (8,848 m)

Katmandu

Ganges River

Indus River

DECCAN PLATEAU

WESTERN GHATS

EASTERN GHATS

Dacca

Bay of Bengal

SRI LANKA

Tropic of Cancer

Philippine Sea

LUZON

MINDANAO

South China Sea

Gulf of Siam

INDOCHINA PENINSULA

Mekong River

MALAY PEN.

Singapore

Strait of Malacca

SUMATRA

KALIMANTAN (BORNEO)

SUNDA ISLES

JAVA

BALI

TIMOR

CELEBES

Arafura Sea

Coral Sea

Arctic Circle

Equator

40°N

30°N

20°N

10°N

10°S

0°

50°E

60°E

70°E

80°E

90°E

100°E

110°E

120°E

130°E

ple than any other country on earth, over 1.2 billion people. India is the second largest, with nearly 950 million people.

Yet Asia also includes countries with small populations. For example, the nation of Qatar (ke TAHR) has just over half a million people.

In area, too, Asia has both large and small countries. China is one of the largest countries of the world, with 3,691,502 square miles (9,560,990 sq km) of territory. This means that China is slightly larger than the United States. On the other hand, the tiny state of Singapore is really just a large city. Singapore covers an area of 225 square miles (583 sq km). The smallest state of the United States, Rhode Island, is more than five times as large as the nation of Singapore.

C. What Makes Asia a Region?

Why are such different countries called the region of Asia? One reason that they are grouped together is they share the same landmass. Bodies of water meet most of the edges of this landmass. The Pacific Ocean marks the eastern edge of Asia, and the Indian Ocean defines the southern edge. Along the western edge of Asia is the Red Sea, which separates Asia from Africa. The Mediterranean Sea divides Asia from Europe.

The northern border of Asia runs along Russia's northern border. As you read in Chapter 15, most of Russia's territory is in Asia. But it is not considered an Asian country, because its largest cities and most of its people are in the European part of the country.

Within Asia itself there are several regions. These are East Asia, which in-

cludes China and Japan; South Asia, which includes India and its neighbors; the countries of Southeast Asia; and the Middle East, which stretches from Afghanistan to Lebanon.

Within Asia's gigantic landmass are some of the world's most dramatic landscapes. The mighty Himalayas form a huge, rugged knot near the center of this region. These mountains stretch across the border of China into the nations of India and Nepal.

Mount Everest, the world's highest mountain, is located in the Himalayas. Mount Everest is 29,028 feet (8,848 m) high. This means that if you climbed to the peak of Mount Everest, you would be almost 6 miles (9 km) above the earth's surface. Many teams of mountain climbers have tried to do just that, and some of them have actually reached the top.

In addition to having the highest mountain, Asia also has the lowest point on the earth's surface. This is the Dead Sea, 1,302 feet (397 m) below sea level.

Along with high peaks and low lands, the huge landmass of Asia also has great contrasts in climate. One of the driest regions on earth, the Arabian Desert, is found on the Arabian Peninsula. Some areas of the Arabian Peninsula receive almost no rainfall for many years and have almost no vegetation or people.

But not all of Asia is this dry. The islands of Indonesia, the Philippines, and the coasts of countries such as Vietnam, Malaysia, and Thailand are covered with thick, dense rain forests that receive over 80 inches (203 cm) of rainfall each year. People in these regions grow crops such as rice, which requires large amounts of water and a warm climate.

The countries of Asia include some of the richest and poorest nations in the world.
▶ How many nations share the island of Borneo?

ASIA: POLITICAL

⊛ National capitals
• Other cities

| 0 | 400 | 800 miles |
| 0 | 400 | 800 kilometers |

PACIFIC OCEAN

Tropic of Cancer

30°N
40°N
50°N
20°N

ARCTIC OCEAN

AUSTRALIA

PAPUA NEW GUINEA
Port Moresby
Coral Sea
NEW GUINEA
Arafura Sea

TIMOR

INDONESIA
SULAWESI (CELEBES)
BALI
Semarang
Surabaja
JAVA
Bandung
Jakarta
SUMATRA
SINGAPORE
KALIMANTAN (BORNEO)
Singapore
Kuala Lumpur
MALAYSIA
BRUNEI
Bandar Seri Begawan
Medan
Strait of Malacca

PHILIPPINES
Quezon City
Manila
Philippine Sea

Bering Sea
180

KURIL ISLANDS (RUSSIA)

Sapporo
JAPAN
Tokyo
Yokohama
Kawasaki
Nagoya
Kyōto
Ōsaka
Kōbe
Hiroshima
Kitakyūshū
Fukuoka
Sea of Japan

Khabarovsk
Vladivostok

NORTH KOREA
Pyongyang
SOUTH KOREA
Seoul
Inchŏn
Taegu
Pusan

RYUKYU ISLANDS (JAPAN)

East China Sea
TAIWAN
Taipei
Kao-hsiung

Yellow Sea

Harbin
Changchun
Fushun
Shenyang
Anshan
Beijing
Luda
Tianjin
Qingdao
Jinan
Shanghai
Nanjing
Wuhan
Taiyuan
Lanzhou
Xi'an
Chongqing
Chengdu
Huang He

Hong Kong
MACAO (PORTUGAL)
Guangzhou
Xi Jiang

South China Sea

VIETNAM
Hanoi
Ho Chi Minh City
Phnom Penh
CAMBODIA
LAOS
Vientiane
THAILAND
Bangkok
Gulf of Siam

EUROPE

RUSSIA

Yekaterinburg
Chelyabinsk
Omsk
Novosibirsk
Barnaul
Kemerovo
Novokuznetsk
Krasnoyarsk
Irkutsk

URAL MOUNTAINS

Amur River

Ulan-Bator
MONGOLIA

CHINA

Karaganda
KAZAKHSTAN
Aral Sea

UZBEKISTAN
Tashkent
Alma-Ata
Bishkek
KYRGYZSTAN
Dushanbe
TAJIKISTAN
TURKMENISTAN
Ashkhabad
Islamabad

Kabul
AFGHANISTAN
PAKISTAN
Faisalabad
Lahore
New Delhi
Delhi
NEPAL
Katmandu
Thimbu
BHUTAN

BANGLADESH
Dacca
Chittagong
MYANMAR
Rangoon
Mandalay
Brahmaputra River

ANDAMAN ISLANDS (INDIA)

NICOBAR ISLANDS (INDIA)

Bay of Bengal

SRI LANKA
Colombo

INDIAN OCEAN

MALDIVES
Male

LACCADIVE ISLANDS (INDIA)

INDIA
Kanpur
Nagpur
Ahmadabad
Bombay
Pune
Bangalore
Madras
Hyderabad
Karachi
Calcutta

Ganges River
Indus River

Istanbul
Ankara
Izmir
TURKEY
LEBANON
Beirut
SYRIA
Damascus
IRAQ
Baghdad
Jerusalem
ISRAEL
Amman
JORDAN

Tehran
Meshed
Isfahan
IRAN

Al-Kuwait
KUWAIT
Manama
BAHRAIN
QATAR
Doha
Riyadh
SAUDI ARABIA
Jidda
Abu Dhabi
UNITED ARAB EMIRATES
Masqat
OMAN
San'a
YEMEN
Gulf of Aden
Red Sea
Persian Gulf
Gulf of Oman
Arabian Sea
Caspian Sea

Euphrates River
Tigris River

AFRICA

Equator

50°E
60°E
70°E
80°E
90°E
100°E

D. Old and New in Asia

Some of the world's oldest civilizations began in Asia. Three thousand years ago the area along the Huang He, a river of northern China, became the heartland of Chinese civilization. The area between the Tigris and Euphrates rivers in Iraq also held important ancient civilizations.

Asia has a long history, but the region is not trapped in the past. In many ways, Asia is as modern as the countries of Europe and the United States. The people of Japan, South Korea, and Taiwan have earned a reputation as brilliant engineers who have developed new electronic goods, scientific equipment, and automobiles.

Nearly 40 percent of Asia's people live in small villages and on farms. Only Africa has a greater proportion of people who live in rural areas. But Asia also has some of the world's largest cities. Tokyo, the capital city of Japan, has grown so large that it has spilled over into the nearby city of Yokohama. Together these two cities have over 26 million residents and form the world's largest urban center.

The people in Asia's cities communicate with people all over the world through radio, telephone, television, and newspapers. Asia's cities also have many of the same problems that are found in large American and European cities, such as housing shortages, pollution, and traffic jams.

E. The Future of Asia

Asia has valuable resources, although some countries lack certain minerals. Nations in the southwestern part of Asia, such as Saudi Arabia, Kuwait, and Iran, have gigantic reserves of petroleum. Countries all over the world depend on this oil to run factories and vehicles, and to make plastic products.

Some Asian countries, such as Taiwan, South Korea, and Japan, have built industries that produce goods bought by millions of people throughout the world, but especially by those in North America and South America. The Taiwanese, South Koreans, and Japanese also buy many products produced in the United States, Canada, Mexico, and the other countries of Latin America.

For this reason, we say that most of the countries around both sides of the Pacific Ocean belong to the region known as the **Pacific Rim.** Trade, cultural exchange, and diplomatic relations are growing stronger each year among nations of the Pacific Rim. Many people believe that the Pacific Rim countries will become the world's largest and strongest economic area.

Review

REVIEWING MAIN IDEAS
A. In what ways is Japan an important economic partner of the United States?
B. Which Asian country has the largest territory and the largest population?
C. What are the highest and lowest points in Asia?
D. In what ways are Asian cities like cities in the United States or Europe?
E. Why is the Pacific Rim an important region?

SKILLS CHECK
MAP SKILL
Turn to the world map on pages 688–689 of the Atlas. Name the countries that form the Pacific Rim of North and South America.

ASIA

	FLAG AND PRINCIPAL LANGUAGE(S)	POPULATION AND LANDMASS	PRINCIPAL PRODUCTS EXPORT	IMPORT

AFGHANISTAN

Kabul ★

Pashto, Dari

POPULATION
21,252,000
85 per sq mi/33 per sq km

LANDMASS
250,775 sq mi/649,507 sq km

Natural Gas

Vehicles

BAHRAIN

★
Manama

Arabic, English, Persian

POPULATION
576,000
2,259 per sq mi/873 per sq km

LANDMASS
255 sq mi/660 sq km

Crude Oil

Crude Oil

BANGLADESH

★Dacca

Bengali, English

POPULATION
128,095,000
2,324 per sq mi/898 per sq km

LANDMASS
55,126 sq mi/142,776 sq km

Jute Products

Crude Oil

BHUTAN

★Thimbu

Dzongkha, Nepali

POPULATION
1,781,000
98 per sq mi/38 per sq km

LANDMASS
18,150 sq mi/46,990 sq km

Cement

Food

BRUNEI

Bandar Seri
Begawan ★

Malay, English, Chinese

POPULATION
292,000
131 per sq mi/51 per sq km

LANDMASS
2,226 sq mi/5,765 sq km

Crude Oil

Machinery

CAMBODIA

Phnom Penh ★

Khmer

POPULATION
10,561,000
153 per sq mi/59 per sq km

LANDMASS
68,898 sq mi/178,446 sq km

Rubber

Machinery

CHINA

Beijing ★

Chinese

POPULATION
1,203,097,000
326 per sq mi/126 per sq km

LANDMASS
3,691,502 sq mi/9,560,990 sq km

Crude Oil

Machinery

INDIA

★ New Delhi

Hindi, English, Assamese, Bengali

POPULATION
936,546,000
762 per sq mi/294 per sq km

LANDMASS
1,229,424 sq mi/3,184,208 sq km

Tea

Crude Oil

ASIA

	FLAG AND PRINCIPAL LANGUAGE(S)		PRINCIPAL PRODUCTS EXPORT	IMPORT

INDONESIA

★Jakarta

Indonesian, Dutch English

POPULATION
203,584,000
261 per sq mi/101 per sq km

LANDMASS
779,675 sq mi/2,019,358 sq km

Crude Oil

Machinery

IRAN

★Tehran

Farsi, Turkish, Kurdish, Arabic

POPULATION
64,625,000
102 per sq mi/39 per sq km

LANDMASS
635,932 sq mi/1,647,064 sq km

Crude Oil

Machinery

IRAQ

★Baghdad

Arabic, Kurdish, Persian, Turkish

POPULATION
20,644,000
122 per sq mi/47 per sq km

LANDMASS
168,927 sq mi/437,521 sq km

Crude Oil

Machinery

ISRAEL

Jerusalem

Hebrew, Arabic, English

POPULATION
5,143,000
644 per sq mi/249 per sq km

LANDMASS
7,992 sq mi/20,699 sq km

Diamonds

Machinery

JAPAN

Tokyo

Japanese, English

POPULATION
125,506,000
874 per sq mi/338 per sq km

LANDMASS
143,619 sq mi/371,973 sq km

Electrical Machinery

Crude Oil

JORDAN

★Amman

Arabic, English

POPULATION
4,101,000
109 per sq mi/42 per sq km

LANDMASS
37,737 sq mi/97,739 sq km

Phosphates

Crude Oil

KUWAIT

★Kuwait

Arabic, English

POPULATION
1,817,000
264 per sq mi/102 per sq km

LANDMASS
6,880 sq mi/17,812 sq km

Crude Oil

Vehicles

LAOS

★Vientiane

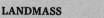
Lao, French, English

POPULATION
4,837,000
53 per sq mi/20 per sq km

LANDMASS
91,428 sq mi/236,799 sq km

Timber

Rice

	FLAG AND PRINCIPAL LANGUAGE(S)	POPULATION AND LANDMASS	PRINCIPAL PRODUCTS EXPORT	IMPORT

LEBANON

Beirut ★

Arabic, French, English

POPULATION
3,696,000
936 per sq mi/362 per sq km

LANDMASS
3,949 sq mi/10,228 sq km

 Services

 Food

MALAYSIA

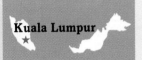

Kuala Lumpur ★

English, Malay, Chinese, Tamil

POPULATION
19,724,000
153 per sq mi/59 per sq km

LANDMASS
128,727 sq mi/333,403 sq km

 Crude Oil

 Machinery

MALDIVES

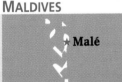

★ Malé

Divehi, English

POPULATION
261,000
2,270 per sq mi/877 per sq km

LANDMASS
115 sq mi/298 sq km

 Fish

 Petroleum

MONGOLIA

Ulan Bator ★

Mongolian

POPULATION
2,494,000
4 per sq mi/2 per sq km

LANDMASS
604,247 sq mi/1,565,395 sq km

 Livestock

 Machinery

MYANMAR

Rangoon ★

Burmese, English

POPULATION
45,104,000
172 per sq mi/66 per sq km

LANDMASS
261,789 sq mi/678,034 sq km

 Teak

 Machinery

NEPAL

Katmandu ★

Nepali

POPULATION
21,561,000
397 per sq mi/153 per sq km

LANDMASS
54,362 sq mi/140,798 sq km

 Textiles

Food

NORTH KOREA

P'yŏngyang ★

Korean

POPULATION
23,487,000
504 per sq mi/195 per sq km

LANDMASS
46,609 sq mi/120,717 sq km

 Metals

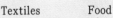 Machinery

OMAN

★ Masqat

Arabic

POPULATION
2,125,000
26 per sq mi/10 per sq km

LANDMASS
82,000 sq mi/212,380 sq km

 Crude Oil

Machinery

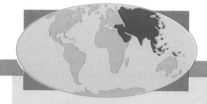

ASIA

	FLAG AND PRINCIPAL LANGUAGE(S)	POPULATION AND LANDMASS	PRINCIPAL PRODUCTS EXPORT	IMPORT

PAKISTAN
Islamabad ★

Urdu, Baluchi, Punjabi, Pushtu

POPULATION
131,542,000
424 per sq mi/164 per sq km

LANDMASS
310,403 sq mi/803,944 sq km

Cotton

Machinery

PHILIPPINES
★Manila

Filipino, English, Spanish

POPULATION
73,266,000
634 per sq mi/245 per sq km

LANDMASS
115,651 sq mi/299,536 sq km

Electronics

Crude Oil

QATAR
★Doha

Arabic, English

POPULATION
534,000
121 per sq mi/47 per sq km

LANDMASS
4,400 sq mi/11,396 sq km

Crude Oil

Machinery

SAUDI ARABIA
★ Riyadh

Arabic

POPULATION
18,730,000
21 per sq mi/8 per sq km

LANDMASS
873,972 sq mi/2,263,587 sq km

Crude Oil

Machinery

SINGAPORE
Singapore ★

Chinese, English, Malay, Tamil

POPULATION
2,890,000
12,844 per sq mi/4,960 per sq km

LANDMASS
225 sq mi/583 sq km

Petroleum

Crude Oil

SOUTH KOREA
★ Seoul

Korean

POPULATION
45,554,000
1,198 per sq mi/463 per sq km

LANDMASS
38,022 sq mi/98,477 sq km

Ships

Crude Oil

SRI LANKA
Colombo ★

Sinhali, Tamil, English

POPULATION
18,343,000
724 per sq mi/289 per sq km

LANDMASS
25,332 sq mi/65,610 sq km

Tea

Crude Oil

SYRIA
Damascus

Arabic, Kurdish, Armenian, Turkish

POPULATION
15,452,000
216 per sq mi/83 per sq km

LANDMASS
71,498 sq mi/185,180 sq km

Crude Oil

Crude Oil

TABLE OF COUNTRIES

	FLAG AND PRINCIPAL LANGUAGE(S)	POPULATION AND LANDMASS	PRINCIPAL PRODUCTS EXPORT	IMPORT

TAIWAN

★Taipei

Chinese

POPULATION
21,501,000
1,548 per sq mi/598 per sq km

LANDMASS
13,887 sq mi/35,967 sq km

Electrical Machinery

Crude Oil

THAILAND

★Bangkok

Thai (Siamese), Chinese, English

POPULATION
60,271,000
304 per sq mi/117 per sq km

LANDMASS
198,445 sq mi/513,998 sq km

Rice

Crude Oil

TURKEY

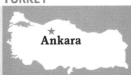
★
Ankara

Turkish

POPULATION
63,406,000
210 per sq mi/81 per sq km

LANDMASS
301,380 sq mi/780,574 sq km

Clothing

Crude Oil

UNITED ARAB EMIRATES

Abu Dhabi★

Arabic

POPULATION
2,925,000
91 per sq mi/35 per sq km

LANDMASS
32,278 sq mi/83,600 sq km

Crude Oil

Machinery

VIETNAM

★Hanoi

Vietnamese, English French, Chinese

POPULATION
74,393,000
570 per sq mi/220 per sq km

LANDMASS
130,486 sq mi/337,912 sq km

Clothing

Crude Oil

YEMEN

★
San'a

Arabic

POPULATION
14,728,000
72 per sq mi/28 per sq km

LANDMASS
205,356 sq mi/531,667 sq km

Petroleum

Crude Oil

JAPAN AND THE KOREAN PENINSULA

Land and Sea in Japan and the Two Koreas

CONNECTIONS
Thinking back on the units you have already studied, name as many island nations and peninsula nations as you can.

TERMS
Ring of Fire

FOCUS
What are the principal landforms of Japan, North Korea, and South Korea?

A. Making a Geographical Comparison

Two Island Nations You might think that the nation of Great Britain could not possibly be similar in any way to the nation of Japan. After all, they are almost on opposite sides of the earth. But surprisingly, these two nations have quite a few things in common.

For example, if you compare the map on page 398 with the map on page 264, you can see that Japan's location off the east coast of Asia is somewhat similar to Great Britain's location off the west coast of Europe. Both Japan and Great Britain are island nations. Japan is separated from the mainland of Asia by the Korea Strait, which is only about 120 miles (193 km) wide, and by the Sea of Japan. The English Channel and the North Sea separate Great Britain from the European continent.

Another feature shared by both nations is their dependence on the seas and channels around them. Like the people of Great Britain, the Japanese use the ocean and the nearby seas as transportation routes. In the 1800s and 1900s, Great Britain established a vast overseas empire. The Japanese also built an empire but it was much smaller than Great Britain's. Like the British, they are trading experts. Today,

Japanese products are famous around the world, and Japanese companies have offices in many countries.

Both Japan and Great Britain have economies that depend on trade and manufacturing. Both countries import food and raw materials for their industries and export manufactured goods to pay for these imports. Foreign trade is the lifeblood of Japan and Great Britain.

B. Japan, a Nation of Islands

Four Islands One of the great gifts of the Japanese people to the world is a style of poetry called *haiku* (HY koo). A haiku is a verse form in which there are only 17 syllables. The syllables are usually divided into three lines, with 5 syllables in the first line, 7 in the second line, and 5 in the third line, as in this example.

Wet snow is sweeping
Over the red-berry bush. . .
Two sparrows chirping.

A haiku often paints for the reader a scene from nature and usually gives an impression of peace and tranquility. Through their haiku, the Japanese describe their land with great affection.

What is their land like? Japanese poets never run out of scenes to describe, because the Japanese landscape is full of fascinating and varied views. Japan is an archipelago, or a group of islands quite close to each other. The Japanese archipelago consists of 4 main islands. The largest island is Honshu (HAHN shoo). To its north is the island of Hokkaido (hah KYD oh). The southernmost of the islands are Shikoku (shi-KOH koo) and Kyushu (kee OO shoo). Nearly 4,000 small islands are found in the ocean that surrounds these 4 large islands.

Ring of Fire Most of Japan's islands are the peaks of a large mountain chain that rises from the floor of the North Pacific Ocean. A number of the mountains are

▶ Hirosaki Castle on the main island of Honshu

397

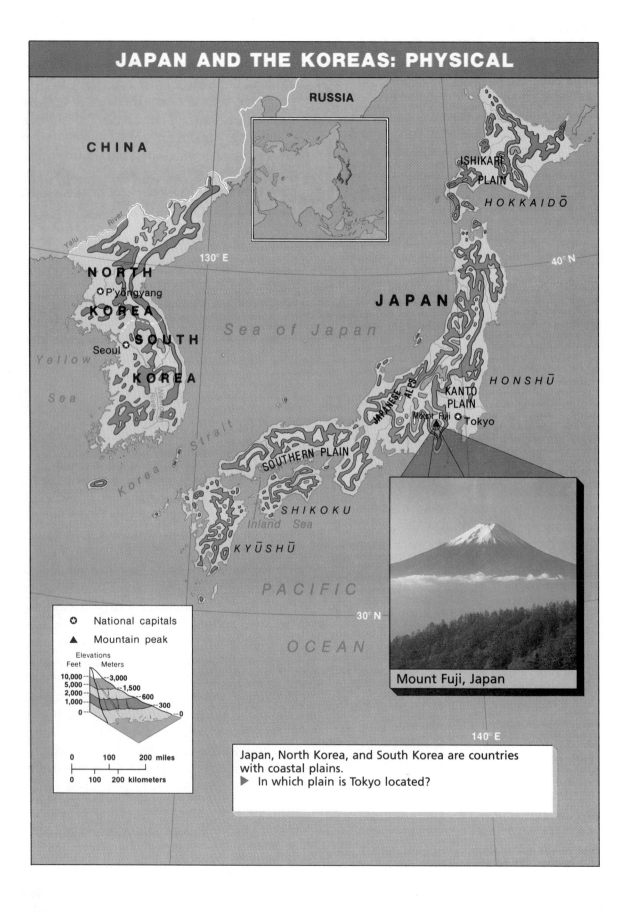

JAPAN AND THE KOREAS: PHYSICAL

RUSSIA

CHINA

ISHIKARI PLAIN

HOKKAIDŌ

Yalu River

NORTH

P'yŏngyang

KOREA

SOUTH

Seoul

KOREA

Han River

Yellow

Sea

Sea of Japan

JAPAN

40° N

130° E

JAPANESE ALPS

KANTO PLAIN

HONSHŪ

Mount Fuji

Tokyo

SOUTHERN PLAIN

Korea Strait

SHIKOKU

Inland Sea

KYŪSHŪ

PACIFIC

30° N

OCEAN

140° E

Mount Fuji, Japan

National capitals

Mountain peak

Elevations
Feet   Meters
10,000 ---- --3,000
5,000 ---- --1,500
2,000 ---- --600
1,000 ---- --300
0 ---- --0

0   100   200 miles
0   100   200 kilometers

Japan, North Korea, and South Korea are countries with coastal plains.
▶ In which plain is Tokyo located?

volcanos, and many are still active. As you read earlier, volcanic eruptions are caused when heat and pressure build up deep inside the earth. This process is similar to the way that bubbles in a pot of soup rise to the surface and burst, releasing heat and steam. When the volcanos erupt, they vent smoke, fumes, and sometimes lava. Because of the many fiery eruptions, the mountain ranges on the coasts around the Pacific Ocean, including that of Japan, make up what is called the **Ring of Fire.**

The earthquakes in Japan that often accompany volcanic activity are usually mild. But an earthquake that struck Japan in 1923 destroyed the entire city of Yokohama and much of the city of Tokyo. Approximately 100,000 people died in that earthquake. Since more than 1,000 earthquakes occur in Japan each year, it is no wonder that the Japanese appreciate the peaceful settings that they describe in their haiku poetry.

The highest, most scenic mountains of Japan are the Japanese Alps, which are located near the center of Honshu. Mount Fuji, the highest peak in the Japanese Alps, rises more than 12,300 feet (3,700 m) above sea level. Of all the mountain peaks in the world, the beautiful snowy peak of Mount Fuji is perhaps the most photographed. The Japanese regard Mount Fuji as a sacred mountain. Many poems have been written about it, including this one.

Struck with awe by high
and sacred Fuji's summit
towering in the sky,
Even the clouds dare not go
over it, but trail below!

C. From Snowy Peaks to Sunny Plains

Climates The islands of Japan stretch out about 1,400 miles (2,253 km) from northeast to southwest. By looking at the map on page 398, you can see that the most northern point of Japan is located at a latitude of about 45°N and that the most southern point is at about 31°N.

Imagine that we could move the islands of Japan into the Atlantic Ocean and spread them along the East Coast of the United States. Japan would reach as far north as the northern borders of Vermont and New Hampshire. It would then stretch south along the coast all the way to the northern edge of Florida.

Japan has a range of climates similar

The cold, snowy winters in northern Japan are perfect for winter sports.
▶ Which East Coast states in our country have similar winter weather?

399

to that of our East Coast. In northern Hokkaido, winters are long and icy, as are winters in northern Vermont and New Hampshire. Winter temperatures rarely go above 32°F (0°C). Heavy blankets of snow cover the ground and fill the roads, blocking the routes of travelers. Winters in Hokkaido are so difficult that people look forward with great joy to the coming of spring.

On Kyushu, the southernmost island of Japan, winters are mild. During the daytime the temperature usually reaches 45°F (7°C). The air is clear and crisp, and little snow falls.

Japan Current Kyushu, Shikoku, and Honshu are warmed by the Japan Current, an ocean current that brings warm water to Japan from the southern part of the Pacific Ocean. The waters of this current warm the air above the water's surface and keep temperatures mild. The Japan Current flows north along Kyushu, Shikoku, and Honshu, but just at the northern tip of Honshu, the Japan Current veers toward the east. Its warmth doesn't reach as far north as Hokkaido. That is why Hokkaido's winters are colder and harsher than winters in other parts of Japan.

On Honshu, Shikoku, and Kyushu, summers are long, hot, and humid. In Tokyo, the temperature often reaches as high as 85°F (29°C) during the day. Farther south on Kyushu, summer temperatures frequently climb to 90°F (32°C). This is a time of the year when vacationers appreciate Hokkaido's cooler temperatures and travel to the northern island for rest and relaxation.

D. The Four Islands of Japan

Japan has a population of over 125 million people, which is about one-half the population of the United States. But Japan's land area is only 143,619 square miles (371,973 sq km), whereas the land area of the United States is 3,615,123 square miles (9,363,169 sq km), which makes the United States approximately 25 times larger than Japan. As a result, Japan has an average of 874 people per square mile (338 people per sq km), compared with 73 people per square mile (28 people per sq km) in the United States.

Japan's population is not evenly spread out over all its islands. Honshu, the largest island, has the largest population, and most people are concentrated in two important

JAPAN: POPULATION DENSITY

National capital
Other cities

Persons per
square mile	square kilometer
0	0
250	100
750	300
1,250	500
2,500	1,000

0   200   400 miles
0   200   400 kilometers

THE 25 LARGEST CITIES OF JAPAN

City	Population	City	Population
...kyo	8,129,000	Sakai	808,000
...kohama	3,299,000	Kumamoto	636,000
...saka	2,604,000	Okayama	601,000
...goya	2,162,000	Hamamatsu	558,000
...pporo	1,717,000	Sagamihara	552,000
...be	1,499,000	Kagoshima	538,000
...oto	1,457,000	Funabashi	538,000
...wasaki	1,195,000	Higashiōsaka	516,000
...kuoka	1,162,000	Amagasaki	497,000
...roshima	1,097,000	Niigata	489,000
...akyūshū	1,021,000	Hachiōji	482,000
...ndai	942,000	Shizuoka	474,000
...iba	842,000		

Almost one half of the 25 largest cities of Japan have a population of more than 1 million.
▶ What is Tokyo's population density?

400

The fine harbor at Yokohama is vital to the city's large shipbuilding industry.
▶ Why is a good harbor important to the success of shipbuilding?

urban areas, Tokyo and Yokohama. Tokyo is the capital city and industrial center of Japan. Nearby is the city of Yokohama. Together their metropolitan area population is 22 million. They have more people, industries, shipyards, and businesses than any other cities of Japan.

The remaining three large islands of Japan are quite different from Honshu and from one another. Forests, farms, and fishing villages are typical of Hokkaido. Shikoku and Kyushu look across the beautiful Inland Sea to the large island of Honshu. Shikoku is the smallest of the four main islands. Mountains cross the island from east to west. Kyushu also has steep mountains, which are covered by forests. But Kyushu does have a small level area in the north, with cities and industries.

E. Comparing North Korea and South Korea

Like Japan, most of the land of North Korea and South Korea is mountainous. A few small valleys and narrow plains provide a limited amount of level land. Until recently this peninsula consisted of one country, Korea. Japan ruled Korea before World War II. When Japan was defeated in 1945, Soviet troops occupied northern Korea, and the United States Army moved into southern Korea to help South Koreans build a new government. In 1945 a border was drawn across the peninsula near the 38th parallel (38°N), separating the two regions.

In 1948 the people north of this line formed their own country, called the Democratic People's Republic of Korea, or North Korea. Their capital city is P'yongyang (pee ONG yahng). North Korea has a Communist form of government and a strong friendship with communist China. The people south of the dividing line formed their own country, called the Republic of Korea, or South Korea. Its capital city is Seoul (sohl). South Korea has a democratic form of government and strong friendships with the United States and Japan.

LESSON 1

Review

REVIEWING MAIN IDEAS

A. What similarities are there between Great Britain and Japan?
B. Why do earthquakes occur in Japan?
C. How is the climate of Japan similar to the climate of the East Coast of the United States?
D. How is Honshu different from the other three regions of Japan?
E. How did Korea become separate nations?

SKILLS CHECK

MAP SKILL

Use the Gazetteer on pages 707–720 to find the latitude and longitude of these cities: Tokyo, Seoul, P'yongyang. Write your answers on a separate sheet of paper.

401

Japan's Economic Miracle

CONNECTIONS

Japan is famous for producing automobiles, cameras, and electronic equipment. Name a Japanese product in each of these categories that is available in the United States.

TERMS

seedbed, paddy, synthetic material

FOCUS

How do the Japanese produce so many goods with so few natural resources?

A. Living on a Farm in Honshu

Raising Rice Most of Japan is made up of hills and mountains. There is little level land for farming. On Honshu, only the Kanto Plain near Tokyo has level land.

Tadashi Matsumoto, a Japanese schoolboy, knows how much effort it takes to farm in Japan. Tadashi lives with his family in a small village near the city of Kobe (KOH bee), in the foothills of the Japanese Alps. Tadashi's family raises rice, tea, bamboo, mushrooms, melons, and onions in its fields. Tadashi attends school, and after school he does homework or plays baseball. Often he must help his family with the farm work.

One such task is the care of rice seedlings, or young rice plants. Rice seeds are planted in a special area called a **seedbed** at the edge of an irrigated rice field, called a **paddy**. The rice seeds are sprouted in the seedbed, and then planted in the paddy.

When the paddy has been prepared and the seedlings shoot up in the seedbed, the family transplants the tender seedlings into the paddy. To make sure that the seedlings thrive, each seedling must be planted at just the right depth and with the right amount of space around it. Although a person working carefully can perform this delicate task much better than a machine, today some people use a motorized planter to set the seedlings in place.

The photograph on the left shows people harvesting a crop of rice.
▶ What stage in rice farming is shown in the photograph on the top right?

Hiroshima was the first city ever to be attacked with an atomic bomb. It was almost completely destroyed. Today the city has been rebuilt.
▶ What do you think is shown in the right photo?

Terrace Farming Tadashi's family also uses hilly areas on its land by making terraces. On the terraces, paddies can be irrigated. If Tadashi's father planted rice on a hillside slope without terraces, the water would just run off the hill and the seedlings would not survive. As in the Andes, terraces turn useless land into productive farmland.

On slopes where terraces are too difficult to construct, Tadashi's family and neighbors raise peach, apple, or mandarin orange trees, or they grow potatoes, vegetables, or tea bushes.

Very little land in Japan is used for grazing cattle or other animals. This is true even on the Kanto Plain and in the lower hills of Honshu. In countries where land is scarce, farmers use their small plots of land for growing food crops rather than for grazing livestock. They can produce more food by cultivating each acre of land than by leaving it as pastureland.

B. Japan's Economic Growth

A New Economy Today, names of Japanese corporations such as Honda, Toyota, Sony, and Mitsubishi are known all over the world. But a few decades ago, it seemed as though Japan's economy was crushed and would never recover. When Japan was defeated in World War II and forced to surrender, its economy was greatly weakened. Many large cities, such as Hiroshima (hihr uh SHEE muh) and Nagasaki (nahg uh SAHK ee) had been destroyed. Many factories throughout Japan had been leveled, and thousands of people had been killed.

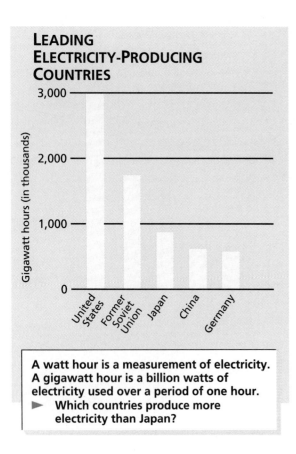

LEADING ELECTRICITY-PRODUCING COUNTRIES

Gigawatt hours (in thousands)

A watt hour is a measurement of electricity. A gigawatt hour is a billion watts of electricity used over a period of one hour.
► Which countries produce more electricity than Japan?

In the years after World War II, Japan received many loans and much aid from the United States and other countries. But money alone could not work the economic recovery that Japan experienced, because Japan lacks almost all the raw materials needed for industry.

Resources A list of Japan's natural resources is short. It includes a small amount of coal on Hokkaido and Kyushu, and mountain forests that produce lumber and wood pulp for making paper. Iron ore and minerals such as silver, lead, and copper are found only in limited amounts. Japan has a severe shortage of petroleum. Almost every drop of oil that Japan uses must be imported. To reduce the expense of im-

porting oil, factories in Japan use electricity as much as possible.

In the Japanese Alps near the industrial zones of Honshu, there are short, swift rivers that have been dammed to generate massive amounts of hydroelectric power. Except for the United States and the former Soviet Union, Japan produces more electricity than any other country. Yet Japan still cannot produce enough power for all its factories and industries. So Japan imports large amounts of oil and natural gas. Indonesia and the Middle East, especially Saudi Arabia, are Japan's main suppliers of oil.

With few raw materials or fuels, how does Japan continue to be an industrial giant? Its secret is to buy raw materials from other countries and import them through excellent harbors at Yokohama, Nagasaki, and Osaka. Factories then use the most modern equipment and techniques to produce goods efficiently. With large amounts of high-quality goods to export, Japanese industries earn a great deal of money. They spend this money on even more efficient machinery, better methods of manufacturing, and high wages for their workers.

Japan began this policy of exporting goods soon after World War II. The country's leaders believed that this would be the best way for Japan to develop its economy. One of the first export industries developed in the country was the textile industry. The profits earned from the export of textiles were then used to build new factories. These factories produced more sophisticated goods, such as cameras and televisions, for export.

C. Honshu's Industrial Zones

Three Industrial Centers Honshu has more than farms like the one belonging to Tadashi's family. It also has most of Japan's industries and large cities. In the industrial city of Tokyo and its neighboring city Yokohama, huge factories produce steel, children's toys, optical equipment, and parts for oceangoing ships. Yokohama has an especially fine harbor and a large shipbuilding industry. Japan is a major world producer of steel, cement, electronic equipment, automobiles, and chemicals. It is also a major world producer of microchips. Microchips are the "brains" of computers.

Most of these industries are located in the Tokyo–Yokohama industrial zone.

Japan's engineers are working hard to make Japan a leader in the production of computer products such as microchips. In fact, the country hopes to be able to build the world's fastest computer soon. It has also invested huge sums of money to create artificial intelligence programs for computers.

MAKING COMPUTER MICROCHIPS

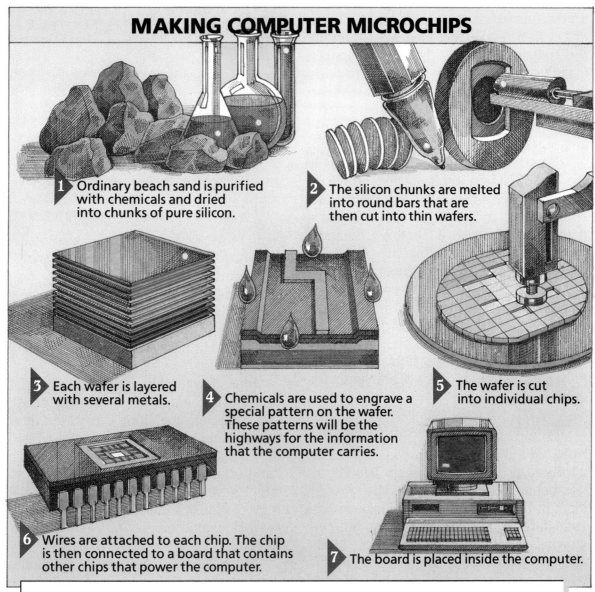

1 Ordinary beach sand is purified with chemicals and dried into chunks of pure silicon.

2 The silicon chunks are melted into round bars that are then cut into thin wafers.

3 Each wafer is layered with several metals.

4 Chemicals are used to engrave a special pattern on the wafer. These patterns will be the highways for the information that the computer carries.

5 The wafer is cut into individual chips.

6 Wires are attached to each chip. The chip is then connected to a board that contains other chips that power the computer.

7 The board is placed inside the computer.

Microchips are the source of the computer's power and speed. The chips must be manufactured in an extremely clean environment.
▶ What skills, do you think, are required to create a microchip?

Honshu's second industrial zone is shared by the cities of Kobe and Osaka. Together, Kobe and Osaka have approximately 4 million people. Until World War II, Osaka was Japan's leading trade and manufacturing city. Osaka's economy was built on trade with China, carried out by ships that crossed the Inland Sea and the Sea of Japan. Find these bodies of water on the map on page 398. Osaka was especially famous for its many textile factories, which used cotton brought in by ship up the Inland Sea to Osaka's harbor. Most of Osaka's textile factories were built in the 1940s and 1950s. They can no longer make textiles as cheaply as newer factories in Taiwan and South Korea. Today, other factories in Osaka and Kobe produce parts for ships, engineering equipment, clothes, and other manufactured goods.

The third industrial zone of Honshu is the city of Nagoya (nuh GOI uh), which is located between the Tokyo-Yokohama and Osaka-Kobe industrial zones. Nagoya's population of nearly 2.5 million is much smaller than that of the other two industrial zones. Yet Nagoya is now the first-ranking Japanese city for producing cotton, wool, and textiles made from **synthetic materials**. A synthetic material is made from materials produced by people, not by nature, and is often made from chemicals. Polyester, nylon, and rayon are synthetic materials.

D. Hokkaido, Shikoku, and Kyushu

Hokkaido Plain Hokkaido, the most northern of Japan's four main islands, is less populated than Honshu. The Ishikari Plain in the southern part of Hokkaido has enough level land for agriculture, but the growing season is short and cool. Many farmers on the Ishikari Plain raise a special type of rice that grows quickly and does not need a warm climate. They also produce crops that are typical of Eastern Europe's

Many of Japan's major products are in turn used in the manufacture of another of its major products, automobiles.
▶ How does this help Japan's economy?

farms, such as oats, hay, and potatoes. Some farmers on Hokkaido also grow pasture grasses and graze dairy cattle and beef cattle. This is a young and growing form of agriculture in Japan. As a result, the Japanese are eating much more meat than ever before.

Hokkaido also has an important tourist industry. The long, snowy winters create ideal conditions for skiing and other winter sports. Tunnels and bridges connect Honshu with Japan's three other main islands. One tunnel allows high-speed trains to travel between Hokkaido and the large cities of Honshu, allowing city people to get to Hokkaido quickly to enjoy a winter weekend.

There are no large plains on Shikoku as there are on Honshu and Hokkaido. Instead, Shikoku has rugged mountains covered by forests, and a narrow strip of coastal land along the Inland Sea, where small cities and rice paddies cover the landscape. Many people live in fishing villages and around the edge of the island.

Commercial Fishing Japan has one of the largest and most productive fishing industries in the world. In contrast to the small-scale fishing of Shikoku, commercial fishing is done by companies that own huge modern ships. These ships travel through the Pacific Ocean and fish off the coasts of Alaska and South America, catching salmon, tuna, and other ocean fish. The ships are large enough to carry the supplies needed for the crew to live at sea for weeks. Often a "factory ship" accompanies the fishing vessel. Workers on the factory ship clean and refrigerate or freeze each day's catch so that the fish do not spoil before the ship anchors in a harbor. Some of the catch is exported to North and South America. The bulk of the fish is used in Japan, because fish is an important part of the Japanese people's diet.

Coal Mining Kyushu, the most southern of Japan's large islands, has Japan's largest coalfield. Coal mines are located along the northern coast of Kyushu. You can see from the map on page 390 that coal can be loaded onto ships in northern Kyushu and sent eastward through the Inland Sea toward the three industrial zones of Honshu. Unfortunately for Japan, most of Kyushu's coal is of a poor quality and unsuitable for industrial use. And Kyushu's coal supplies have decreased, because the mines have been operating for many years. Most of Japan's coal mines will be depleted by the year 2000. Much of the country's coal is now imported from Australia, China, and Canada and the United States.

WORLD FISH CATCH

China 17%
Japan 8%
Other 51%
Peru 8%
Chile 6%
U.S. 6%
Russia 4%

Japan is a world leader in the fishing industry. Most of the fish caught is eaten by the Japanese.
► What percentage of the world total is caught by Japan and China?

LESSON 2

Review

REVIEWING MAIN IDEAS
A. Why is farming so difficult in Japan?
B. Why is it so remarkable that Japan has become an economic giant?
C. Where are the three industrial zones of Honshu located?
D. What are the main economic activities of Hokkaido, Shikoku, and Kyushu?

SKILLS CHECK

THINKING SKILL
Imagine that you are asked to visit a small country that has few mineral resources and only small areas of level land. Make a list of the materials the country might import, and the products that could be manufactured and exported with those materials.

Old and New Lifestyles in Japan

CONNECTIONS

What topics would you consider if you wanted to compare ways people in Japan live with the ways in which people in the United States live?

TERMS

futon, tatami

FOCUS

In what ways, do you think, is Japan's culture a blend of old and new life styles?

A. Japan, a Nation Without Minority Groups

Few Immigrants One of the unique features of Japan's people is that hardly anyone belongs to a minority group. Almost everyone in Japan today is simply Japanese, whereas in the United States there are many minority groups. Ancestors of today's Americans came to the United States from all over the world and blended their cultures to create an American culture. In Japan, almost everyone has kept the same culture for many centuries.

Why does Japan have hardly any minority groups? One reason is that in the sixteenth century, Japan almost completely closed its doors to outsiders, especially Europeans. The Japanese feared that Europeans would take over their land. So they forced foreign missionaries, traders, and visitors to leave Japan.

Allowing Visitors Japan kept its doors closed to foreigners until 1853. In that year, Commodore Matthew Perry arrived at Tokyo Bay with three United States Navy warships. He persuaded Japan's leaders to sign a treaty giving the United States trading

Like haiku, traditional Japanese watercolors usually have nature as their theme.
▶ What is shown in the watercolor?

rights and other privileges. Slowly, Japan began accepting outside people, but only a very few. Even recently, Japan has been reluctant to allow foreigners to immigrate permanently. In the 1970s, when hundreds of thousands of Vietnamese fled from the war in their homeland, many countries around the world allowed the Vietnamese to come to their nations. Altogether, nearly 1 million of these people left Vietnam, but the Japanese allowed fewer than 200 of them to enter Japan.

B. What Is Japan's Culture Like?

Early Settlers Before Japan closed its doors to outsiders in the sixteenth century, its islands were settled by people from all over Asia. Many of the early settlers arrived in Japan by traveling through China and the Korean peninsula and then crossing the Korea Strait.

The early Japanese adopted many ideas and techniques from the Chinese and from the Koreans. In past centuries, Japanese students went to China to study its *philosophy*, or basic ideas about the nature and meaning of life, its laws, and its government. The Japanese used some of China's ideas in organizing their own governments.

The Japanese adopted some Chinese ways and rejected others. For example, the Japanese borrowed and simplified the Chinese form of writing. They then created a new written language, Japanese, which has different characters from Chinese.

Religion Many Japanese believe in Shintoism, a collection of ideas about gods who lived in mountains, in the sea, and everywhere in nature. Some Shinto ceremonies and festivals are designed to ask the gods in nature for help in growing a good crop or in avoiding floods in the rainy season. Other ceremonies thank the gods for a rich harvest or for good weather. Shintoism is not quite the same as other religions, because it does not call people together for

Many Japanese people today believe in two religions, Shintoism and Buddhism.
▶ What do you think this Shinto shrine is used for?

worship. In the beginning there were not even any Shinto priests.

Beginning in the sixth century, many Buddhists began arriving in Japan from China and Korea. Buddhists believe in the teachings of Buddha, the founder of the Buddhist religion. He taught that happiness comes from being kind to others. He also taught that material things are not important for happiness.

The early Japanese added the teachings of Buddhism to their beliefs of Shintoism. Many people in Japan today follow both religions, celebrating some events with a Shinto ceremony and others with a Buddhist ceremony. The combination of Shinto and Buddhist beliefs is unique in Japan and not found extensively in other parts of Asia.

409

This photograph shows the Ginza district, one of the busiest sections of Tokyo. The Ginza is famous for its shops, restaurants, and nightclubs.

▶ What cities in the United States have sections famous for shops, restaurants, or entertainment?

C. Busy Tokyo

Daily Life City life in Japan is much like city life everywhere in the world. For example, the morning rush hour in Tokyo is similar to rush hours in most large cities. As you read the following paragraph, think of other cities that fit the same description.

It is morning in a Tokyo train station, and you are being pushed along by a great crowd of people hurrying toward the train that will take them to work. The crowd is so dense that you could not turn back even if you wanted to. If you dropped a package or a shoe, you would not dare stoop down to pick it up for fear of being trampled. When you reach the train, there are no seats left, so you crowd against

the other people standing in the aisle. On schedule the doors close, and the train begins to move.

Yoshiko Uchimura is a young Japanese girl who lives with her family in Tokyo. Life in Tokyo is busy and hectic for Yoshiko, her family, and her friends. Tokyo is one of the most crowded cities in the world. Yet many Japanese customs make it possible for people to live together in crowded conditions and still maintain peace.

Like most people in Tokyo, the Uchimura family lives in a huge building containing many apartments, each with only one or two rooms. Yoshiko's entire family shares one large room that is used as a bedroom at night, as a dining room for meals, and as a living room for relaxing and studying. Many Japanese homes do not have solid wood walls, but have sliding walls of heavy paper. The walls can be opened or shut to make smaller rooms out of one large room. Heavy padded quilts called **futons** are rolled out at night for sleeping. They are stored away in chests during the day, so they don't take up much valuable space.

When Yoshiko goes out shopping or visiting friends, she usually wears blue jeans and a blouse or sweater. But at home she often wears a comfortable kimono, a soft, warm robe with a large sash around the waist. Like most Japanese, Yoshiko removes her shoes when entering her home. The most common type of floor covering in Japanese homes is the **tatami**, a soft woven floor mat. Wearing street shoes in the home would dirty the tatami, so by custom, people remove their shoes on entering a room and use soft slippers instead.

Japanese Culture Popular western culture and ways are becoming more common every day in Japan. Western culture comes from the United States and Europe, and includes things that are familiar to American teenagers, such as rock music, comic books, and movies. Tokyo even has its own Disneyland, built in 1983 on the edge of the city.

But the Japanese also follow many old traditions. Yoshiko and her family sometimes spend January 1, New Year's Day, visiting the Imperial Palace, near downtown Tokyo. This huge complex of buildings contains the modern palace where the emperor of Japan lives with his family. This section of the Imperial Palace is open to the public only on special holidays. Parts of the old palace where former emperors lived are also located here.

Gardens and nature are important to the Japanese, perhaps because their cities

Several Japanese people enjoy their lunch while sitting in Ueno Park in Tokyo.
▶ What are some of the sights found in Ueno Park?

are so congested. Tokyo's beautiful Ueno (WAY noh) Park has several large museums, an art gallery, and a zoo. It is a favorite place for people to stroll and enjoy nature right in the middle of the city.

LESSON 3

Review

REVIEWING MAIN IDEAS

A. Why does Japan have so few minority groups?
B. How has Japan's culture been influenced by the cultures of China and Korea?
C. In what ways is daily life in Japan different from daily life in the United States?

SKILLS CHECK

WRITING SKILL
Imagine that you are visiting Tokyo. Write a short letter home describing what you have seen on your visit.

North Korea and South Korea

CONNECTIONS

Using what you have already learned about the Korean peninsula, name what you think are important economic activities of North Korea and South Korea.

TERMS

demilitarized zone

FOCUS

How do the economies of North Korea and South Korea differ?

A. Korea as a Colony of Japan

Korea's Modernization Like the Japanese, the Koreans tried to avoid contact with outsiders for several centuries. Their culture, which had adopted many features of Chinese culture, did not change much while Korea's doors were closed to people from other countries.

In 1895, Japan took Korea as a colony and imposed rapid changes on the people of the peninsula. The people of Korea had always farmed, but the Japanese forced them to modernize, or change to meet the needs of the times. The Japanese built more irrigation canals in order to build new rice paddies. They also introduced basic farm machinery to the Koreans and showed them how to grow crops such as tobacco and cotton. The Japanese also modernized Korean fishing boats and taught the Koreans how to fish more efficiently and catch greater numbers of fish. Although the Japanese helped to improve the Korean economy, the Koreans were not happy to be a colony of Japan.

Independence By the time Japan was defeated in World War II and had to give up its colony of Korea, life was quite different for the Koreans. They had begun to cut large amounts of wood from their forests

for fuel. People worked in coal mines and iron ore mines that the Japanese had opened up in the northern part of Korea. The Japanese had built roads and railroads to connect important cities and ports on the peninsula. With good transportation the Japanese could ship coal, iron ore, and other minerals to their own factories in Japan. After Korea became independent, the Korean people built and added on to what the Japanese had introduced to them.

In 1950, Communist North Korea invaded South Korea. This action grew into the Korean War. The United States and some other members of the United Nations fought to protect South Korea. The Chinese Communists fought for North Korea, which also received help from the Soviet Union. North Korea was unable to take over South Korea. In 1953, North Korea and South Korea agreed to a division of the Korean peninsula at the 38th parallel. A narrow strip of land called a **demilitarized zone** lies on either side of the boundary. That zone is an area where there are no troops or weapons. It helps to keep the two countries separate.

South Gate, shown above, is a famous landmark in Seoul, South Korea.
▶ How does South Gate differ from the surrounding buildings?

B. Northern and Southern Agriculture

Rugged North Korea The northern end of the Korean peninsula has rugged mountains along the border between North Korea and China. These mountains are not especially high, and most of the peaks do not even reach 9,000 feet (2,743 m). But between the peaks, rivers have cut through the mountains like knives, leaving deep, narrow gorges that are almost impossible to travel through.

The land of North Korea is difficult for people to live in, and the climate of the northern mountains is hostile. Summers are warm, with temperatures often reaching 85°F (29°C). In contrast, winters are long and bitterly cold. Cold winds from Siberia bring frigid temperatures. Daytime temperatures usually reach only about 27°F (-3°C). Rivers in North Korea are frozen for three or four months every winter. Ice forms along the coasts and blocks the harbors.

Under these conditions, farmers have a difficult time growing crops. Cool-weather crops, such as corn, potatoes, and wheat, are commonly grown in North Korea. Most of North Korea's level land is located around the capital city of P'yŏngyang. In rural areas, there is little land for growing food for North Korea's population of about 22 million people.

South Korea's Agriculture The climate of South Korea is milder than that of North Korea. High temperatures in wintertime often pass 32°F (0°C). With less frigid winters, farmers in South Korea are able to grow vegetables such as cabbage, potatoes, and sweet potatoes in the cooler months. In warmer summer months, farmers grow rice, soybeans, and onions. By planting crops during their longer growing season, South Korean farmers produce more food than North Korean farmers.

South Korea also has another advantage for agriculture. A large, level plain is

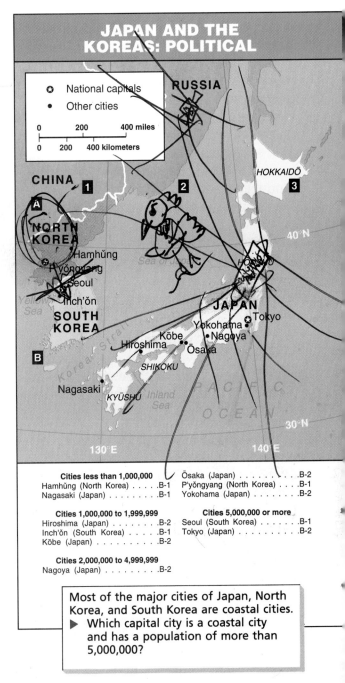

JAPAN AND THE KOREAS: POLITICAL

- ⊛ National capitals
- • Other cities

0   200   400 miles
0   200   400 kilometers

RUSSIA

CHINA **1**

A

NORTH KOREA

Hamhŭng

P'yŏngyang

Seoul

Inch'ŏn

SOUTH KOREA

B

Kōbe

Hiroshima

SHIKOKU

Nagasaki

KYŪSHŪ   Inland Sea

HOKKAIDŌ **3**

2

40°N

Sea of Japan

HONSHU

JAPAN

Yokohama

Nagoya   Tokyo

Ōsaka

PACIFIC OCEAN

30°N

130°E   140°E

Korea Strait

Yellow Sea

Cities less than 1,000,000
Hamhŭng (North Korea) B-1
Nagasaki (Japan) B-1

Ōsaka (Japan) B-2
P'yŏngyang (North Korea) B-1
Yokohama (Japan) B-2

Cities 1,000,000 to 1,999,999
Hiroshima (Japan) B-2
Inch'ŏn (South Korea) B-1
Kōbe (Japan) B-2

Cities 5,000,000 or more
Seoul (South Korea) B-1
Tokyo (Japan) B-2

Cities 2,000,000 to 4,999,999
Nagoya (Japan) B-2

Most of the major cities of Japan, North Korea, and South Korea are coastal cities.
▶ Which capital city is a coastal city and has a population of more than 5,000,000?

located between the Naktong River and the capital city of Seoul. The plain provides farmers with much more level land than the North Korean farmers have.

Before 1945 the lack of agriculture in North Korea was not a serious problem, because North Korea had not yet been separated from South Korea. As part of the nation of Korea before 1945, South Korea supplied food to all the people of Korea.

Today, North Korea is working hard to modernize its farms. The government controls most of the farmland and organizes farm households into collective farms, with about 300 families on each farm. Families are usually paid with part of the crops and some cash, too. North Korea's farmers now produce almost all the food needed to feed their country's population.

C. Two Different Paths of Industrialization

An Industrial Nation North Korea's mountains make farming difficult, but they hold valuable resources, such as coal, iron ore, tungsten, and zinc. Steel and machinery are two of North Korea's main industrial products, but chemicals and fertilizers are valuable products, too. Most of North Korea's industries are located near the capital city of P'yŏngyang.

North Korea has most of the Korean peninsula's important minerals. But the standard of living in North Korea is low. Why? One reason is the Communist economic system. All economic decisions are made by the government. Individual factory owners must follow government plans about what to produce and how much to produce. As you read in Chapter 15, this is how the Soviet Union's economic system used to work. Perhaps North Korea's government will also make changes in its economic system now that communist rule in the Soviet Union has ended.

An Economic Power South Korea's economy offers an interesting contrast to North Korea's. South Korea has few mineral or energy resources. The country used to pay for electricity sent by transmission lines from North Korea. When Korea was divided in 1945, the transmission lines were cut and South Korea was left without a reliable source of cheap power. But South Korea has one of the world's fastest growing

North Koreans stand in front of a monument as they wait to visit a museum in P'yŏngyang.
▶ What, do you think, does the monument intend to show?

South Korea is a leading producer of steel, and in turn, shipbuilding has become a major industry there.
► What part of a ship is shown here?

economies; in fact, South Korea is said to have experienced an economic miracle much like Japan has.

South Korea's economic success is the result of several factors. One is that South Korea's people are better educated than North Korea's. Another reason is that the government borrowed money from other countries to create new industries.

Another factor has been South Korea's development of its few mineral resources. Recently, small deposits of iron ore were found in the southeast, and coalfields were discovered in the east. With these resources and imported petroleum, South Korea is growing as an industrial nation. It is one of the world's leading producers of steel. Shipbuilding, which depends on steel production, is a major industry in South Korea. At the same time, its business leaders have worked hard to build industries that produce clothing, shoes, computer equipment, televisions, and other electronic goods. South Korea's own people and many millions more in other countries purchase these products in great numbers. As a result, South Korea's economy has grown rapidly in the past 20 years.

Unfortunately, not all of South Korea's people have benefited from the economic miracle. People in the cities have a higher standard of living than people who live in rural areas.

LESSON 4

Review

REVIEWING MAIN IDEAS

A. How did Japan influence the economy of the country of Korea before World War II?

B. Why do farmers in North Korea have more difficulty producing food than South Korean farmers do?

C. What kinds of industries are most important in North Korea and South Korea?

SKILLS CHECK

THINKING SKILL

Why do you think South Korea's economy has become more developed than North Korea's economy?

CHAPTER 16 REVIEW

REVIEWING TERMS

On a separate sheet of paper, write the term that best completes each sentence.

paddy
synthetic material
futon
tatami
demilitarized zone

1. Many Japanese homes have a type of floor covering called a _____.
2. A _____ is made from materials produced by people, not by nature.
3. A _____ helps to keep two countries separate and does not allow troops or weapons within its boundaries.
4. Rice seedlings are transplanted into an irrigated rice field, which is called a _____.
5. In Japan, a heavy padded quilt called a _____ is often used for sleeping.

REVIEWING THE FACTS

On a separate sheet of paper, answer the following questions in complete sentences.

1. Why are the mountain ranges on the coasts around the Pacific Ocean called the Ring of Fire?
2. How does the Japan Current affect the climate of Japan?
3. On what island is Tokyo, the capital of Japan, located?
4. How do the governments of North Korea and South Korea differ?
5. What are some of the ways Japanese industries continue to improve their products?

6. What are some goods produced in Honshu's industrial zones?
7. What are the two main religions practiced in Japan?
8. Why did Japan give up its colony of Korea?
9. How does the geography of North Korea differ from the geography that is found in South Korea?
10. Why are the mountains of North Korea important?

WRITING ABOUT CULTURE

In addition to rock music, comic books, and movies, what other parts of western culture, do you think, may eventually become common in Japan? Write a paragraph or two explaining your views.

THINKING CRITICALLY

On a separate sheet of paper, answer the following questions in complete sentences.

1. Why can potatoes and fruit trees, but not rice, be grown on slopes that do not have terraces?
2. Why is the ship that usually accompanies a fishing vessel called a factory ship?
3. What reasons might Japan have for wanting to limit the number of immigrants it allows?
4. What minority groups does the United States have?
5. Why would Japan want to have Korea as a colony?

On a separate sheet of paper, draw a graphic organizer like the one shown here. Copy the information from this graphic organizer on the one you have drawn. Under the main idea of each lesson, write three statements that you think best support that main idea.

CHAPTER THEME

Japan's historical development was mostly separate and isolated. Today, Japan is a modern, industrialized nation. Its neighbors, the Koreas, offer many contrasts.

Lesson 1 Japan, North Korea, and South Korea have a variety of landforms.
1. _____
2. _____
3. _____

Lesson 2 The Japanese produce many goods even though their land has few natural resources.
1. _____
2. _____
3. _____

Lesson 3 Japan's culture is a blend of old and new lifestyles.
1. _____
2. _____
3. _____

Lesson 4 North Korea and South Korea have different economies.
1. _____
2. _____
3. _____

17

CHINA AND ITS NEIGHBORS

China, the Giant of East Asia

CONNECTIONS

Name the ways in which you think China is different from Japan.

TERMS

alpine, tableland

FOCUS

What are the differences between eastern and western China?

A. Planning a Trip to China

Climbing Mount Everest One day in 1984, Peter Jenkins, a writer and mountain climber from Tennessee, received an important telephone call from his friend Skip. After the phone call, Peter was so excited that he was hopping around like a dancing stork. Skip had just invited him to join a mountain-climbing expedition. The team would climb to the top of Mount Everest, the highest mountain in the world. Mount Everest rises to a height of 29,028 feet (8,848 m). This incredibly high mountain belongs to a long mountain range called the Himalayas. The Himalayas stretch across China's southwestern border. The Himalayas cover a part of China that is now called Xizang (SHEE ZANG), but it was once known as Tibet.

Peter and Skip tried to imagine where Tibet and Mount Everest are. In his journal, which was later published in his book, *Across China,* Peter wrote down the following conversation.

> *"Where is Tibet?" I asked. Skip paused, trying to figure it out himself.*
> *I could not picture that part of the world.*
> *"Tibet's in the far southwestern corner of China. . . . I think Tibet borders with India, Nepal, and Bhutan."*
> *Every country he mentioned sounded more intriguing.*

China's Neighbors Skip correctly named India, Nepal, and Bhutan as China's neighbors. China has eleven other neighbors as well. China shares its northern border with Russia and Mongolia. Mongolia is landlocked between Russia and China.

North Korea touches China along China's northeastern border. China shares its southern border with India, Bhutan, Nepal, Vietnam, Laos, and Myanmar, which used to be named Burma. China's western border includes Pakistan, Afghanistan, and three former republics of the Soviet Union that are now independent—Tajikistan, Kyrgyzstan, and Kazakhstan.

B. Crowded East, Empty West

A Vast Country China, which is officially called the People's Republic of China, occupies most of eastern Asia. China's total area of 3,691,502 square miles (9,560,990 sq km) makes China slightly larger than the United States.

When Peter's mountain-climbing team left for China in August 1984, they flew from Seattle, Washington, to Beijing, formerly Peking, the capital city of China. This almost 17-hour trip took them about 5,500 miles (8,850 km) across the Pacific Ocean. Once the team arrived in China, they had to fly another 1,600 miles (2,574 km) to reach the city of Lhasa, which is near Mount Everest. But this was only the beginning of the trip. It would be two more months before they reached the peak of Mount Everest.

The team left Lhasa and traveled in old trucks to the foot of Mount Everest, a distance of about 300 miles (480 km). On a modern highway in the United States, a car could travel that distance in about six hours. For Peter's team, the trip took several days. They had to travel slowly because the **alpine**, or mountainous, roads were narrow, twisted, and dangerous. Getting to the bottom of Mount Everest was almost as difficult as climbing to its peak!

419

▶ One of the six temples in the Forbidden City in Beijing, China

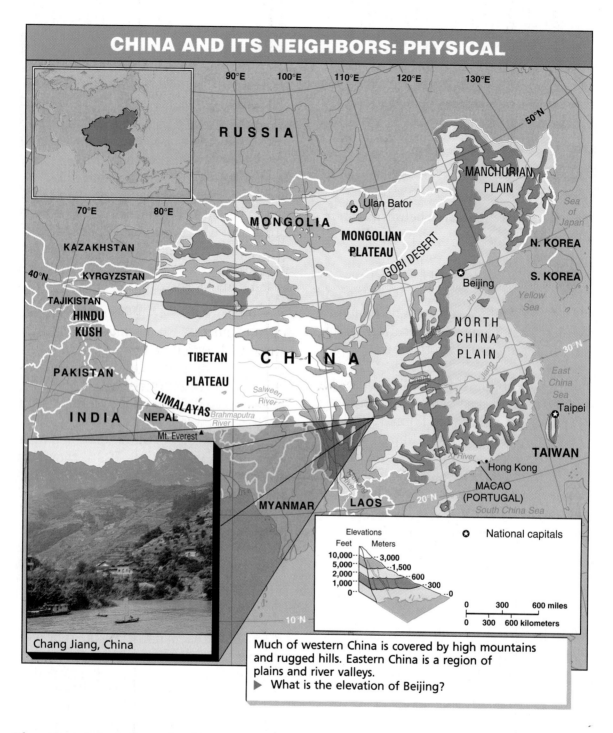

CHINA AND ITS NEIGHBORS: PHYSICAL

90°E 100°E 110°E 120°E 130°E

RUSSIA

50°N

MANCHURIAN PLAIN

Ulan Bator

MONGOLIA

MONGOLIAN PLATEAU

GOBI DESERT

Sea of Japan

N. KOREA

Beijing

S. KOREA

KAZAKHSTAN

40°N KYRGYZSTAN

TAJIKISTAN

HINDU KUSH

PAKISTAN

TIBETAN PLATEAU

C H I N A

NORTH CHINA PLAIN

Yellow Sea

HIMALAYAS

Salween River

Brahmaputra River

INDIA NEPAL

Mt. Everest

East China Sea

Taipei

TAIWAN

Hong Kong

MACAO (PORTUGAL)

MYANMAR LAOS

South China Sea

30°N

20°N

10°N

Chang Jiang, China

Elevations
Feet   Meters
10,000   3,000
5,000   1,500
2,000   600
1,000   300
0   0

National capitals

0   300   600 miles
0   300   600 kilometers

Much of western China is covered by high mountains and rugged hills. Eastern China is a region of plains and river valleys.
► What is the elevation of Beijing?

The Populated East As Peter and his team made their way to Mount Everest, they saw only a few houses, farms, or other travelers. Why was this western part of China so empty when China has the largest population of any country on earth—over 1.2 *billion* people? The answer is that most of China's people live in eastern China. Western China is mainly barren, a land of mountains, plateaus, and deserts.

Much of eastern China is covered by broad river valleys. If you look at the map above, you can see that the northernmost river is the Huang He (hwang hih), or Yellow

The Pinyin System

How would you translate the Chinese characters for the word *Beijing*? Translating Chinese characters into the alphabet used in English and many other languages has always been a difficult task. In the early 1900s, two Englishmen developed the Wade-Giles (jiles) system of translating Chinese. The Wade-Giles system was used for most of this century, and many people still recognize place-names based on that system.

In the 1950s the Chinese govern-ment introduced the Pinyin system for writing Chinese words in the Roman alphabet. The Chinese believe that the Pinyin spelling comes closer to the correct pronunciation of Chinese.

In this book, we are using the Pinyin system. Whenever we have used the Pinyin term, we have also mentioned its older, Wade-Giles spelling. That is why we tell you that Xizang was once called Tibet and that Beijing was once known as Peking.

River. This 2,903-mile-long (4,671-km-long) river begins in central China and makes two large loops as it crosses the country. Before it empties into the Yellow Sea, the Huang He crosses the wide North China Plain, which is China's most important agricultural region.

South of the Huang He is China's longest river, the Chang Jiang (chahng jee-AHNG), or Yangtze River. The Chang Jiang also begins in central China, but it winds eastward for 3,434 miles (5,525 km) before it empties into the East China Sea.

The Western Region Western China, where Peter's group traveled to Mount Everest, is a rugged, sparsely populated region. Only a few towns and villages are found in its narrow valleys. To the north of the Himalayas is a high, dry region called the Tibetan plateau. The plateau is level and flat, so it is called **tableland**, but the cold, dry climate makes farming difficult.

C. The People of China

About 95 percent of China's citizens belong to one ethnic group—the Chinese. Although the Chinese speak the same language, they use many different dialects. Some of the dialects are so different from each other that they sound almost like other languages. More than 50 other ethnic groups with different languages and customs also live in China. The Tibetans are among the most important of these groups. They speak Tibetan and live mainly in southern and western China.

The Mongols are an important ethnic group in northern China. Their language, Mongolian, is completely different from Chinese and is similar to the languages of the Muslim people who live in the Central Asian nations of the former Soviet Union.

LESSON 1

Review

REVIEWING MAIN IDEAS
A. Which countries are neighbors of China?
B. Why is eastern China more densely populated than western China?
C. What are three important ethnic groups in China?

SKILLS CHECK

MAP SKILL
Using the map on page 423, name the river that is nearest to each of these Chinese cities: Guangzhou, Shanghai, Tianjin.

China's Varied Regions

If you were going on a trip to China, what kinds of clothes would you pack for your stay there?

TERMS

triple cropping, loess, alluvial soil

FOCUS

How are China's three regions different from one another?

A. The Three Regions of China

Studying China Peter Jenkins had studied China's geography before he began his trip, so he was not surprised to see large areas of uninhabited land in the west. He had learned that China has three regions—the western interior, northeastern China, and southeastern China. Peter's trip to China took him to all three regions. These regions can be seen on the map on page 420.

Peter began his trip in the western interior. This region includes Mount Everest and the rest of the Himalayas. The second region Peter traveled through is southeastern China, which is located between the Chang Jiang and the southern border of China. Finally he traveled through the third region, northeastern China. The Chang Jiang forms this region's southern border, and the coast of the Yellow Sea makes up its eastern border.

Two Different Climates Before Peter packed his suitcase for his trip, he made two lists of clothing to take. One list included wool socks, wool pants, a wool sweater, gloves, and a heavy parka. These were the clothes he would need while traveling in the western interior.

At the top of the second list, Peter wrote "For travel in China—hot and humid weather." This list was completely different from the first one. It included sandals, cotton socks, a lightweight sweater, jeans,

T-shirts, and sunglasses. These were the clothes Peter needed for traveling in northeastern and southeastern China. Peter knew he would need a variety of clothing because the lands and climates in China's three regions are very different.

B. The Western Interior

I'd never experienced so many mountains. There seemed to be a million of them. . . . Over every pass, around every cliff, and through every narrow valley arose more and more mountains.

This was Peter's journal entry as the mountain-climbing team traveled through the Himalayas toward Mount Everest.

The Himalayas are one of the four major landforms of the western interior. The three other landforms are the Tibetan plateau and two deserts, the Xinjiang and the Gobi.

In the Himalayas, Peter's team took tanks of oxygen to help them breathe at elevations above 20,000 feet (6,096 m). They also had to wear heavy parkas and gloves to keep warm. It was a tough climb to the top. As the leader of Peter's team said later, everyone finally reached the summit of Mount Everest "despite a cracked rib, frozen eyeballs, bad avalanches and winds faster than a race car."

The climate in most areas of the Himalayas is cold. Peter noted that his team

passed several clusters of . . . homes with smoke fluffing out from the tops of their flat roofs. It was the dead of summer [August] and a chilly high forties this morning.

The Rooftop of the World Located north of the Himalayas is the Tibetan plateau. This plateau is often called the "Rooftop of the World," because it is the world's largest high-elevation plateau. The Tibetan plateau is crisscrossed by mountain ranges,

The map

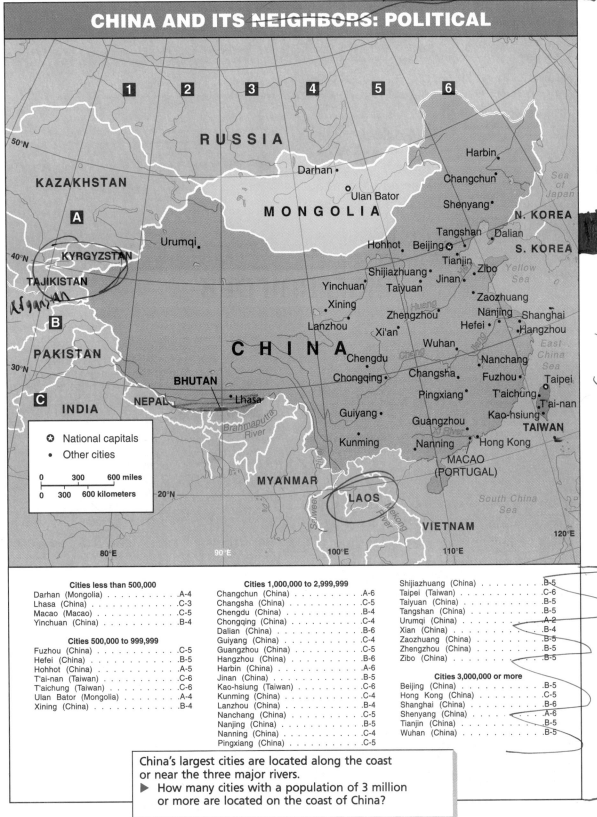

CHINA AND ITS NEIGHBORS: POLITICAL

| 1 | 2 | 3 | 4 | 5 | 6 |

RUSSIA

KAZAKHSTAN

A

KYRGYZSTAN

TAJIKISTAN

Afghanistan

B

PAKISTAN

C

INDIA

NEPAL

BHUTAN

Darhan

Ulan Bator

MONGOLIA

Urumqi

Lhasa

Brahmaputra River

MYANMAR

Harbin

Changchun

Shenyang

N. KOREA

Tangshan   Dalian

Hohhot   Beijing   S. KOREA

Tianjin

Shijiazhuang   Zibo   Yellow Sea

Yinchuan   Jinan

Xining   Taiyuan

Zhengzhou   Nanjing   Shanghai

Lanzhou   Hefei   Hangzhou

Xi'an

Wuhan   East China Sea

Chengdu   Nanchang

Chongqing   Changsha   Fuzhou

Pingxiang   T'aichung   Taipei

Guiyang   Kao-hsiung   T'ai-nan

Guangzhou   TAIWAN

Kunming   Nanning   Hong Kong

MACAO (PORTUGAL)

South China Sea

LAOS

VIETNAM

CHINA

Huang   Chang   Xi River   Salween   Mekong

Sea of Japan

❖ National capitals
• Other cities

0   300   600 miles
0   300   600 kilometers

50°N
40°N
30°N
20°N
80°E   90°E   100°E   110°E   120°E

Cities less than 500,000
Darhan (Mongolia) A-4
Lhasa (China) C-3
Macao (Macao) C-5
Yinchuan (China) B-4

Cities 500,000 to 999,999
Fuzhou (China) C-5
Hefei (China) B-5
Hohhot (China) A-5
T'ai-nan (Taiwan) C-6
T'aichung (Taiwan) C-6
Ulan Bator (Mongolia) A-4
Xining (China) B-4

Cities 1,000,000 to 2,999,999
Changchun (China) A-6
Changsha (China) C-5
Chengdu (China) B-4
Chongqing (China) C-4
Dalian (China) B-6
Guiyang (China) C-4
Guangzhou (China) C-5
Hangzhou (China) B-6
Harbin (China) A-6
Jinan (China) B-5
Kao-hsiung (Taiwan) C-6
Kunming (China) C-4
Lanzhou (China) B-4
Nanchang (China) C-5
Nanjing (China) B-5
Nanning (China) C-4
Pingxiang (China) C-5

Shijiazhuang (China) B-5
Taipei (Taiwan) C-6
Taiyuan (China) B-5
Tangshan (China) B-5
Urumqi (China) A-2
Xian (China) B-4
Zaozhuang (China) B-5
Zhengzhou (China) B-5
Zibo (China) B-5

Cities 3,000,000 or more
Beijing (China) B-5
Hong Kong (China) C-5
Shanghai (China) B-6
Shenyang (China) A-6
Tianjin (China) B-5
Wuhan (China) B-5

China's largest cities are located along the coast
or near the three major rivers.
▶ How many cities with a population of 3 million
   or more are located on the coast of China?

Jaffe
scied

but they are not as high or spectacular as the Himalayas.

In the valleys of these mountains, farmers grow barley, wheat, and vegetables in small plots. Most people on the Tibetan plateau make their living by herding yaks, animals that are similar to oxen.

Peter's group hired yak herders to help carry their climbing gear to their base camp at Mount Everest. There were no roads in that area, but each yak could carry about 100 pounds (45 kg) of food and equipment on the rocky trails.

The yak herders told Peter and his friends that yaks have several uses. The herders use their yaks to carry food and clothing or to pull a plow in a farmer's field. Yak hair is woven into clothing, and yak milk is made into butter. When yaks

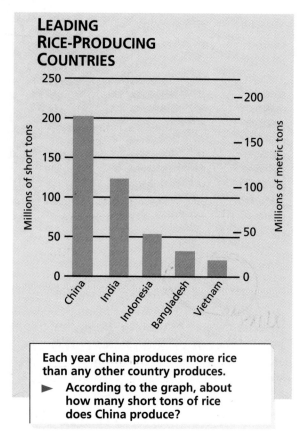

LEADING RICE-PRODUCING COUNTRIES

Each year China produces more rice than any other country produces.

▶ According to the graph, about how many short tons of rice does China produce?

Most people who live on the Tibetan plateau make a living by herding yaks.
▶ What do you think the climate is like on the Tibetan plateau?

become very old or must be killed, their meat is eaten and their hides are used to make sandals and other products that are usually made from leather.

The Xinjiang Desert The Xinjiang Desert is the third major landform of the western interior. It is found north of the Tibetan plateau. This dry region includes several broad basins and a few small rivers. All of the western interior is far from the Pacific and Indian oceans, and it rarely receives any precipitation. Total annual precipitation in the western interior is less than 10 inches (254 mm).

The Gobi Desert The fourth major landform of the western interior is the Gobi Desert. The Gobi, like other parts of the western interior, is sparsely populated. Scorching hot summers and frigid winters make life difficult in both the Gobi Desert and the Xinjiang Desert. Fierce winds there carry blinding dust but little moisture.

C. Southeastern China

A Humid, Rainy Climate After leaving the Himalayas, Peter traveled by plane to Chengdu, a city in southeastern China. As soon as Peter's plane landed in Chengdu, he noticed that the weather there was much warmer and more humid than that of the Himalayas and the Tibetan plateau. In his journal, Peter wrote, "My clothes stuck to my skin and palm trees sagged under the hammer of summer in tropical China. . . . It was about 95° [35°C]."

The Chang Jiang, which runs along the northern edge of southeastern China, is this region's most important river. Many smaller rivers flow out of the western mountains and across southeastern China to the South Sea. Between the rivers are rolling hills and broad, flat valleys.

Triple Cropping Southeastern China's level land and warm, rainy climate provide excellent conditions for agriculture. Most farmers here can plant crops throughout the year. As soon as they harvest one crop, they begin planting another. This is called **triple cropping**. Triple cropping allows farmers to get three times as much food from their land as farmers in cold climates, who plant only one crop a year.

Rice is the main crop grown in southeastern China. The tremendous amount of rice grown here helps to make China the world's largest rice producer.

Peter learned about the other crops grown in southeastern China by studying the menus of Chengdu's restaurants. In the western interior, he had mainly eaten goat meat, butter made from yak's milk, and bread made of uncooked dough. In Chengdu the foods were quite different. Chengdu is located in the province of Sichuan (SEE-chwahn), and Sichuan cooking is famous everywhere, including the United States.

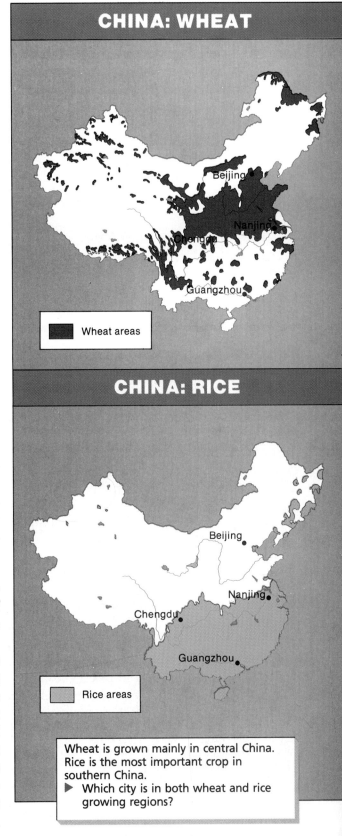

CHINA: WHEAT

Wheat areas

CHINA: RICE

Rice areas

Wheat is grown mainly in central China. Rice is the most important crop in southern China.
▶ Which city is in both wheat and rice growing regions?

Water wheels are used on the Huang He, or Yellow River, to irrigate farmland. ▶ Across what important agricultural region of China does the Huang He flow?

Peter ate many tasty dishes made of pork, chicken, and fish. In a restaurant he watched a chef cook onions, green peppers, garlic, and vegetables with these meats. He also drank a lot of tea, which is another major product of southeastern China, and he ate many bowls of rice and special Sichuan noodles.

Shanghai and Guangzhou Huge cities are found throughout southeastern China. The largest is Shanghai, which is located near the mouth of the Chang Jiang. Shanghai has a population of over 7.5 million people. For centuries, Shanghai has been one of China's most important trade centers. Many of the goods and crops produced in southeastern China are shipped down the Chang Jiang to Shanghai. There they are loaded onto large boats and ships. The products are sold to buyers in other parts of China or are exported.

Shanghai also receives agricultural products and manufactured goods from northern China. Coastal shipping lines carry the products to Shanghai. They are then sent up the Chang Jiang and sold to the millions of people in small towns and villages of southeastern China.

Shanghai is also an important industrial center. Tungsten, which is found in great quantities in southern China, is processed here. Other industries include shipbuilding, rice milling, processing of fruits and vegetables, and new industries that produce metals and chemicals.

Guangzhou (GUAHNG joh), or as it was once called, Canton, is the second largest city in southeastern China. It is much smaller than Shanghai, with 2.9 million people. Guangzhou is located near the mouth of the Xi (shee) Jiang, or West River, making the city a major port. In turn, shipbuilding has become a major industry in Guangzhou.

Farmers from all over southern China send their products to Guangzhou. The raw materials needed for the city's textile industry are among these products. Guangzhou has several cotton mills and silk mills for manufacturing cloth.

Guangzhou's main industry is the processing of tea, sugarcane, and rice. Hydroelectricity generated from the Xi Jiang powers other factories, which produce textiles, fertilizers, and farm machinery.

Guangzhou is a center of international trade. In fact, twice each year the city plays host to China's largest trade fair, the Export Commodities Fair, which attracts thousands of foreign merchants.

D. Northeastern China

China's Heartland Northeastern China is the cultural and industrial heartland of China. It is also the oldest inhabited region in China. Archaeologists have discovered human fossils showing that people lived

CHINA AND ITS NEIGHBORS: POPULATION DENSITY

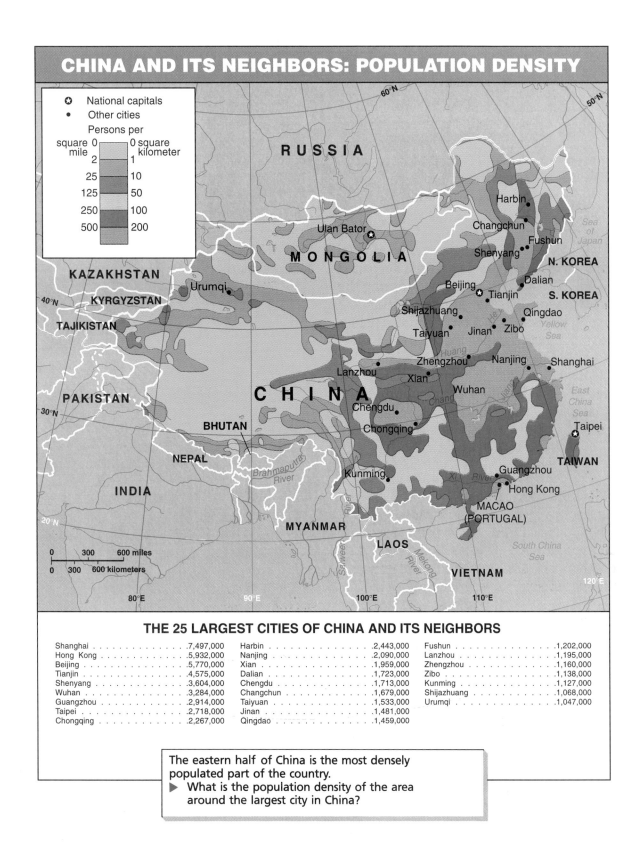

Legend:

- ⊛ National capitals
- • Other cities

Persons per

square mile	square kilometer
0	0
2	1
25	10
125	50
250	100
500	200

Scale: 0 300 600 miles / 0 300 600 kilometers

THE 25 LARGEST CITIES OF CHINA AND ITS NEIGHBORS

City	Population	City	Population	City	Population
Shanghai	7,497,000	Harbin	2,443,000	Fushun	1,202,000
Hong Kong	5,932,000	Nanjing	2,090,000	Lanzhou	1,195,000
Beijing	5,770,000	Xian	1,959,000	Zhengzhou	1,160,000
Tianjin	4,575,000	Dalian	1,723,000	Zibo	1,138,000
Shenyang	3,604,000	Chengdu	1,713,000	Kunming	1,127,000
Wuhan	3,284,000	Changchun	1,679,000	Shijazhuang	1,068,000
Guangzhou	2,914,000	Taiyuan	1,533,000	Urumqi	1,047,000
Taipei	2,718,000	Jinan	1,481,000		
Chongqing	2,267,000	Qingdao	1,459,000		

The eastern half of China is the most densely populated part of the country.

▶ What is the population density of the area around the largest city in China?

near Beijing in 600,000 B.C. Farmers began to practice agriculture along the Huang He about 5000 B.C.

The name *Huang He* means "yellow river" in Chinese. The river's color comes from the yellowish soils that have been washed into the river from the Loess (LOH-es) Plateau. A powdery, fertile soil, **loess** is excellent for agriculture since it holds moisture so well.

Rich **alluvial soils** are found along other stretches of the Huang He. Alluvial soils are rock fragments and silt deposited on the land when a river floods during the rainy season. For thousands of years the Huang He has flooded every spring, spreading a blanket of rich soil across the Huang He valley and the North China Plain.

The North China Plain is a large, flat area of alluvial soils near the mouth of the Huang He. The North China Plain and Huang He valley make up China's most important agricultural region. More than one fourth of all of China's agricultural products comes from this area. It is the country's largest wheat-growing region. In fact, as you can see from the map on page 14, China is one of the world's largest producers of wheat.

This region also produces enormous amounts of corn, tobacco, cotton, and soybeans. Soybeans are used for animal feed, food products, and in industrial products, such as paint.

Climate and Resources The crops grown in northeastern China are different from those grown in southeastern China. Why? Using the climographs on this page, compare the temperatures of Beijing and Shanghai. The area around Beijing has a colder and drier winter than Shanghai does. This makes it impossible to grow in Beijing the

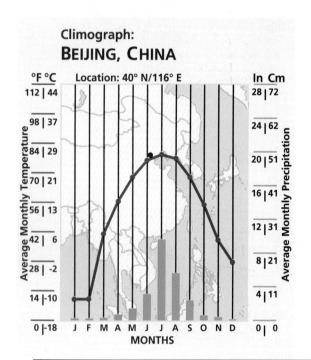

Climograph:
BEIJING, CHINA

Location: 40° N/116° E

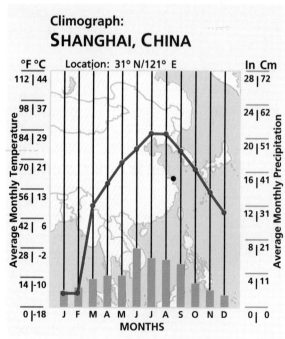

Climograph:
SHANGHAI, CHINA

Location: 31° N/121° E

Winter in the area around Beijing, in northeastern China, is generally colder and drier than winter in the area around Shanghai, in southeastern China.

► During which month is the difference between the temperature in Beijing and the temperature in Shanghai the greatest?

tea, rice, sugarcane, and other crops grown in southeastern China.

Northeastern China has many of China's mineral and fuel resources. Most of China's enormous deposits of coal—which are the largest in the world—are found in the northeast. Important coal and iron ore deposits are found near the city of Shenyang.

Near the border with North Korea, China has large deposits of minerals such as lead, zinc, tin, and copper. Factories and steel mills in Shenyang process these raw materials into heavy machinery, tools, bicycles, and other metal goods.

Beijing and Tianjin are the two largest cities in northeastern China. Since it is China's capital city, Beijing has many important government offices. It also has ancient palaces, shrines, and beautiful gardens. Tianjin, to the east of Beijing, is northeastern China's industrial center. The government has enlarged and modernized Tianjin's port and has encouraged the growth of industries such as chemicals, textiles, and iron and steel mills.

Transportation Northeastern and southeastern China have most of the country's people, farms, and industries. However, it is difficult to transport goods across the enormous distances that separate the cities in each region. Because of the mountains and rivers that cross these regions from east to west, only a few roads, highways, or railroads have been built to connect the cities of northeastern and southeastern China. However, over the centuries the Chinese have built many canals that crisscross the rivers that flow through these two regions. The longest is the Grand Canal, which extends for over 1,000 miles (1,600 km) and connects Beijing and the city of Hangzhou near Shanghai. This and other canals have made it possible to ship foods, minerals, and manufactured goods cheaply from the north to the south.

The Grand Canal is the longest of the canals that connect China's rivers and allow trade between the southeastern and northeastern regions.
▶ How long is the Grand Canal?

LESSON 2

Review

REVIEWING MAIN IDEAS

A. What are China's three regions?

B. What are the four major landforms of the western interior region of China?

C. Why is Shanghai an important trading center for southeastern China?

D. What makes northeastern China a fertile farming region?

SKILLS CHECK

THINKING SKILL

Why is triple cropping practiced only in southeastern China, and not in the western interior or northeastern China?

Ways of Life in China

CONNECTIONS

What are some of the ways in which life in a mountainous region might be different from life on a plain?

TERMS

dynasty, commune

FOCUS

Why do people living in the desert and mountain areas of China have different languages and religions from other Chinese?

A. Beijing, the "Northern Capital"

Beijing One of the first things tourists notice when they visit Beijing is the bicycles. Hundreds of bicycles wheel through the streets, carrying business people, workers, and students to their work or homes. Bicycles are found throughout China's cities, but Beijing has the most—over 3 million, more than any other city in the world. Beijing is special for another reason—it is China's capital city and home to an incredible number of fascinating palaces.

Bicyclists on a street in Beijing.
► What do you think is one of the benefits of using bicycles instead of cars in a city?

Beijing, whose name means "northern capital" in Chinese, has been the capital of China since 1421. For thousands of years before then, it had been only a small town. It became an important political center beginning in the 1200s, when the great Mongol emperor Kubla (KOO bluh) Khan took over China. Kubla Khan decided to rebuild Beijing and create two sections for the city, the Inner City and the Outer City. The Outer City, in southern Beijing, was where ordinary people lived and worked. The Inner City was the section where the rulers lived. This section of Beijing was surrounded by high walls.

Inside the Inner City was another enclosed area, called Imperial City. This zone held the offices of the ruler's closest advisors. The Imperial City enclosed yet another city—the Forbidden City.

The Forbidden City The Forbidden City was a protected area where the emperors of China lived and worked. China's emperors usually belonged to a **dynasty**, or a family that ruled China for many generations. No one was allowed to pass through the gates into the Forbidden City without permission. Most ordinary people never saw the inside of the Forbidden City. When the Communist party took control of China in 1949, the government opened up the Forbidden City as a museum for the public, making it possible for all to marvel at its great treasures and architecture.

The Forbidden City is huge, covering 250 acres (101 ha). Inside are many palaces, temples, bridges, roadways, and courtyards. The most important part is an area of six palaces. Here the emperors of China presided over ceremonies, watched military parades, met with their advisors, and held huge banquets.

These six palaces stretch out along a straight walkway. Like the emperor and his visitors in the past, tourists today can walk down this walkway, passing through many gates and archways with names such as the Gate of Supreme Harmony and the Gate of Heavenly Purity.

Outside the Forbidden City is a huge plaza called Tiananmen (TEE en ahn mun) Square. This has been the traditional meeting place for the Chinese people to voice criticism of the government. It was here in 1989 that thousands of students and workers demonstrated for democracy in China. The Communist government would not accept their demands and decided to end the demonstration by sending in soldiers. Over 1,000 of the demonstrators were killed by the soldiers in the areas around the square.

B. The Mongols and China

The Great Wall In the third century B.C., the Chinese became worried about invaders and built a massive fortified wall to protect themselves from Asians who might attack from the north. This wall, which is called the Great Wall, is about 4,000 miles (6,400 km) long and wide enough to allow five

horses to travel together along the road built on top of it. The Great Wall winds across northern China from its border with North Korea to the edge of the Xinjiang Desert. This remarkable structure is the only object made by humans that is visible from the moon.

The Mongols The Great Wall was not an effective barrier to invaders. In fact, China was invaded many times both before and after the Great Wall was built. One of the most important invaders was Kubla Khan, the emperor who rebuilt Beijing. Kubla Khan was a Mongol from the Gobi Desert of the western interior. Although the Mongols ruled China between the thirteenth and the fourteenth centuries, their culture did not influence Chinese culture. Even today, Mongols are quite different in their culture.

Peter Jenkins desperately wanted to visit a Mongolian village while he was in China. He had read about the ancient Mongolian horsemen and wanted to see

A lone man stopped a convoy of tanks in Beijing only days after soldiers had shot demonstrators.
▶ Why would a person risk his or her life because of what he or she believes in?

how their descendants live today. He received permission from the government to visit a village near the city of Hohhot, on the southern edge of the Gobi Desert.

The Mongol family that Peter visited herded cattle and sheep, and raised horses to help with the livestock. Many Mongol families live in mud-brick houses in small villages that have only a few families. The people and their language, Mongolian, are related to Turkish. Their way of life is similar to that of people in the nearby nation of Mongolia.

The language of the Mongols is completely different from Chinese. As you read earlier, even the Chinese language has many different dialects. Chinese dialects spoken in northern China are distinct from the Chinese spoken in Shanghai, Guangzhou, or other parts of China. Often two people speaking different dialects of Chinese cannot speak each other's language at all.

C. Religions of China

Lamaism in Tibet Religions in China also vary. For example, Tibetans living in the valleys of the Himalayas and in the Tibetan plateau practice Lamaism, which is a form of the religion called Buddhism. For centuries the Tibetan people considered their religious leaders to be their political leaders as well. Many young Tibetan men studied to be *lamas*, or holy men, in Tibet's thousands of monasteries and temples.

Tibet was part of the Chinese empire for centuries. In 1911, China granted Tibet independence. Independence did not last long, however, because China took over Tibet again in 1951. Then Chinese troops destroyed monasteries and shrines through-

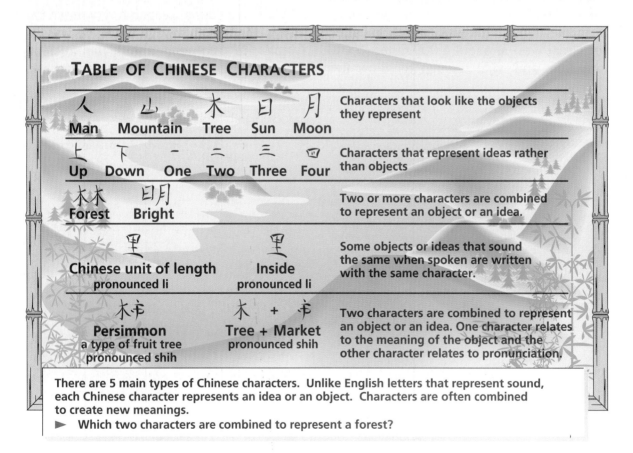

TABLE OF CHINESE CHARACTERS

| 人 | 山 | 木 | 日 | 月 | Characters that look like the objects they represent |
| Man | Mountain | Tree | Sun | Moon | |

| 上 | 下 | 一 | 二 | 三 | 亖 | Characters that represent ideas rather than objects |
| Up | Down | One | Two | Three | Four | |

| 林 | 明 | Two or more characters are combined to represent an object or an idea. |
| Forest | Bright | |

| 里 | 裏 | Some objects or ideas that sound the same when spoken are written with the same character. |
| Chinese unit of length pronounced li | Inside pronounced li | |

| 柿 | 木 + 市 | Two characters are combined to represent an object or an idea. One character relates to the meaning of the object and the other character relates to pronunciation. |
| Persimmon a type of fruit tree pronounced shih | Tree + Market pronounced shih | |

There are 5 main types of Chinese characters. Unlike English letters that represent sound, each Chinese character represents an idea or an object. Characters are often combined to create new meanings.
► Which two characters are combined to represent a forest?

432

out Tibet and the other regions of China. The Chinese believed that to be good Communists, people must not believe in any religions. Many Tibetan monks and religious leaders escaped to the neighboring nations of Nepal and India. Recently the Chinese government has allowed the Tibetans to rebuild some of their shrines and temples.

Buddhism The Chinese government has tried to crush religion, but religious teachings and writings still influence people's everyday behavior. Most Chinese practice Buddhism, a religion that first appeared in northern India in the sixth century B.C. Buddhists learn self-discipline and the correct way to do even small daily tasks. Buddhist *monks* study meditation and learn to ignore hunger and pain. In China, most Buddhists also follow the teachings of Confucius (kun FYOO shus), a Chinese philosopher who lived during the fifth century B.C. Confucius taught people that they should do good deeds and treat others the way they would like to be treated themselves. His teachings are collected in a book called the *Analects*. Here are some of his ideas.

> *The Master said, Even when walking in a party of no more than three, I can always be certain of learning from those I am with. There will be good qualities that I can select for imitation and bad ones that will teach me what requires correction in myself.*
>
> *A follower asked, Is there any single saying that one can act upon all day and everyday? The Master said, Perhaps the saying about consideration: Never do to others what you would not like them to do to you.*

D. Rural Life in China

An Agricultural Nation China is unusual in that over half of its people live in villages and small towns; only about a fourth of the people in the United States live in small

The Chinese philosopher Confucius lived from about 551 B.C. to 479 B.C.
▶ About how old was Confucius when he died?

communities. Most Chinese are farmers, although some may have second jobs in small factories or businesses. Despite this fact, Chinese farmers have difficulty producing enough food to feed a steadily growing population.

Chinese farmers and consumers are careful not to waste farmland or food. Farmers grow grain and vegetables instead of using their scarce land to raise pasture grasses to feed cattle and large animals. For much of China's history, however, Chinese farmers have tried to grow crops without the equipment or technology to fight floods, droughts, and insects. The

FROM: **The Good Earth**

by Pearl S. Buck

Pearl S. Buck, an American who grew up in China where her parents were missionaries, is famous for her books about life and people in China. Her best-known novel, *The Good Earth*, tells about a farmer named Wang Lung who loves the land and struggles for many years to keep his crops growing. Wang Lung endures droughts, floods, and locusts, insects that eat farmers' crops.

. . . **I**n these parts, where Wang Lung had lived all his life and his father and his father's father had lived upon the land, there were famines once in five years or so, or if the gods were lenient, once in seven or eight or even ten years. This was because the heavens rained too much or not at all, or because the river to the north, because of rains and winter snows in distant mountains, came swelling into the fields over the dykes which had been builded by men for centuries to confine it.

Time after time men fled from the land and came back to it, but Wang Lung set himself now to build his fortunes so securely that through the bad years to come he need never leave his land again but live on the fruits of the good years, and so subsist until another year came forth. He set himself and the gods helped him and for seven years there were harvests, and every year Wang Lung and his men threshed far more than could be eaten. He hired more laborers each year for his fields until he had six men and he builded a new house behind his old one, a large room behind a court and two small rooms on each side of the court beside the large room. The house he covered with tiles, but the walls were still made of the hard tamped earth from the fields, only he had them brushed with lime and they were white and clean. Into these rooms he and his family moved, and the laborers, . . . lived in the old house in front.

434

FAMILY PLANNING—A BASIC NATIONAL POLICY OF CHINA

Huge billboards that tie family planning to patriotism are a common sight in China.
▶ What is the English translation of the slogan on this billboard?

government has tried many agricultural experiments to encourage farmers to produce as much food as possible.

Communes In the 1950s, China's Communist government took control of all farmland and divided it into huge state farms called **communes**. About 20,000 people worked on each commune. The government made all the decisions about what the commune should grow and how it should operate.

The communes did not produce much more food than the old system. So gradually the government broke down the huge communes into smaller units called collectives. Many people were allowed to rent small plots of land and keep any profits they could make with their crops.

Family Planning Food production increased, but the population was increasing even more quickly. By the early 1980s, Chinese officials had adopted a plan to encourage *family planning*. Under the plan,

people would be rewarded for having only one child. The government hoped to slow down population growth and avoid huge famines in the future. Their population control plan has had some success. But China's greatest problem for the future is going to be feeding its growing population.

LESSON 3

Review

REVIEWING MAIN IDEAS

A. How did China's emperors close the Forbidden City to outsiders?
B. Why was the Great Wall built?
C. What are two of the religions of China?
D. How has the Chinese government tried to increase food supplies?

SKILLS CHECK

WRITING SKILL

Write an advertisement for tourists, describing the sights of China.

435

China's Neighbors

CONNECTIONS

Taiwan is known for the production of many small products. Can you name any products in your home that were made in Taiwan?

TERMS

arable, buffer state

FOCUS

How are Taiwan, Hong Kong, and Mongolia different from China?

A. Taiwan, "the Other China"

A Nationalist Island Less than 100 miles (160 km) off the southern coast of China is an island nation that is often called "the other China." This is the nation of Taiwan, or as it is formally called, the Republic of China. The language and religion of the Taiwanese are similar to those of the People's Republic of China. Indeed, their island, sometimes called Formosa, was inhabited by the Chinese and belonged to the Chinese empire for hundreds of years.

The governments of Taiwan and China are different. China is controlled by the

Taiwan's capital, Taipei, has modern department stores.
▶ How are such stores a sign of a high standard of living?

Chinese Communist party, which began to form in 1911. At that time, many people who did not agree with the ideas of the Communists formed a different political party, called the Nationalists. The Communists and Nationalists fought for control of China for several decades. Finally, in 1949, the Communists won control of China, and the Nationalists fled to the island of Taiwan, where they formed their own government.

With money and political support from the United States, the Nationalists built a modern country on their island. This was difficult, because Taiwan has few mineral resources or fuels. The eastern half of the island is mountainous and is covered with dense forests. In the west there is a broad coastal plain, a flat area along the coast of the Taiwan Strait. The map on page 420 shows that the Taiwan Strait is a body of water that separates Taiwan and China.

The farms on the coastal plain are small but highly productive. The most common crop is rice, but farmers there also grow wheat, tea, sweet potatoes, sugarcane, and tropical fruits. Irrigation, rice paddy farming, and terracing allow Taiwan's farmers to produce surplus foods to export to other countries.

Most of Taiwan's 21.5 million people live and work on the western coastal plain. Taipei (tye PAY), the capital city of Taiwan, is located at the northern end of the coastal plain. Smaller cities have grown up along the foothills of the mountains. Factories in these cities use hydroelectric power generated from the rivers that tumble out of the mountains and empty into the Taiwan Strait.

An Export Economy Taiwan's industries are similar to Japan's. The Taiwanese import raw materials such as iron ore, petroleum, minerals, and cotton. They manufacture these materials into machinery, clothing, calculators, radios, televisions, and plastic goods such as toys. These products are then exported around the world. As in the country of South Korea, shipbuilding is another important and profitable industry in Taiwan.

Taiwan is much smaller than China, only 13,887 square miles (35,967 sq km) in area, which is somewhat larger than the states of Massachusetts and Connecticut combined. Taiwan, however, has a higher standard of living than China and more goods and food available for its citizens. It has also moved toward having a democratic form of government.

Taiwan's government continues to claim that it is the rightful ruler of mainland China. Most nations of the world—including the United States—recognize China's Communist government as the legitimate government of mainland China.

B. Hong Kong, the Tiny Dynamo

A British Colony At the mouth of China's Xi Jiang is the former British colony of Hong Kong. Most of Hong Kong's population is of Chinese ancestry, and most of the people speak Chinese. Like Taiwan, Hong Kong was part of China for many centuries. But unlike Taiwan, which is controlled by Chinese Nationalists, Hong Kong came under the control of Great Britain in the 1800s. Under British rule, Hong Kong prospered. It became one of Asia's most important trading centers.

Hong Kong has three main areas, altogether covering about 400 square miles (1,036 sq km). As you can see from the map on this page, the colony stretches across the tiny island of Hong Kong, the mainland area called Kowloon Peninsula, and a large coastal zone called the New Territories. People and businesses are spread over this entire area. Huge apartment buildings, office complexes, and factories crowd almost every corner of the tiny island of Hong Kong.

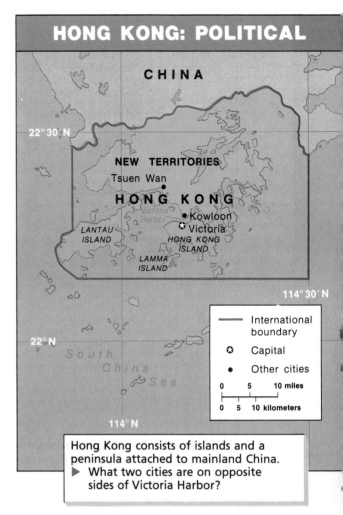

HONG KONG: POLITICAL

Legend:
— International boundary
✪ Capital
• Other cities
0 5 10 miles
0 5 10 kilometers

Hong Kong consists of islands and a peninsula attached to mainland China.
▶ What two cities are on opposite sides of Victoria Harbor?

Hong Kong's population is about 5.5 million. Less than one tenth of the land in Hong Kong is **arable**, or useful for agriculture. This means that most of Hong Kong's food is imported, much of it from China and Japan. However, Hong Kong has one of the strongest export economies in East Asia.

A Busy Economy Hong Kong's busy factories produce textiles, electronics, clocks, toys, and cameras, which are sold around the world. Most of these goods are produced with raw materials that must be imported from other countries. The finished products are sold to industrialized countries, such as the United States, the nations of the United Kingdom, and France.

China and the United Kingdom agreed that Hong Kong would be returned to China in 1997. China promised that it would allow Hong Kong to have special political and economic rights. These would help Hong Kong's economy to continue to prosper.

C. Mongolia, a Buffer State

Between Two Nations Few countries in the world are located between two powerful nations. Mongolia, or the Mongolian People's Republic, has been one such country. In the past, Mongolia was sandwiched between two enemies—China and the Soviet Union.

It might seem that the Mongolian people should have been in constant fear of war between China and the Soviet Union. But Mongolia's location actually helped to keep that from happening. The Soviet Union would never have allowed China to take over Mongolia. And China would never have allowed the Soviet Union to invade Mongolia and approach the Chinese border. So Mongolia is a country that kept these two countries separated. We call such a country a **buffer state**.

Deserts and Grasslands Mongolia is a large country of deserts, grasslands, and forested mountains. The total area of Mongolia is 604,247 square miles (1,564,395 sq km), which makes it about twice the size of Texas. But its population is only 2.5 million, about one-eighth the population of Texas.

The Gobi Desert covers eastern and southern Mongolia. The southern part of the Gobi is covered by grasslands on which herds of cattle, sheep, goats, and horses feed. For centuries, nomadic herders have moved their livestock across the Gobi's grasslands from season to season, searching for grass and water.

The nomads depend on their animals for almost everything. For example, the sheep wool is made into *felt*, a tough woolen fabric used to make clothing and to make the herders' tents, which are called *yurts*.

Even in villages, Mongolians have a

This photograph shows a section of Hong Kong's waterfront.
▶ How can you tell from the photograph that Hong Kong is prosperous?

The southern part of the Gobi Desert is covered by grasslands.
▶ How do Mongolians use the Gobi's grasslands?

difficult life. Dry, cold winds blow constantly, and fresh fruits and vegetables are in short supply. Some people believe that the harsh environment made Mongolians into tough warriors in the past. One of these warriors was Genghis Khan, who ruled an empire that stretched into Russia and Eastern Europe. Genghis, his son, and his grandson, Kubla Khan, conquered much of China and the Middle East.

Today, Mongolia is building modern roads, railways, and industries with the help of other countries. In the capital city of Ulan Bator, factories produce wool products, cement, leather goods, soap, and machinery. Most of Mongolia's exports still come from its livestock and from products made from their milk and hides.

LESSON 4

Review

REVIEWING MAIN IDEAS

A. Why is Taiwan called "the Other China?"

B. What are Hong Kong's main industries?

C. Why is Mongolia called a buffer state?

SKILLS CHECK

MAP SKILL

Use the Gazetteer on pages 707–720 to find the latitude and longitude of each of the following cities. Then determine which city is farthest west:

Ulan Bator   Taipei   Hong Kong

REVIEWING TERMS

On a separate sheet of paper, write the letter of the term that best matches each numbered statement.

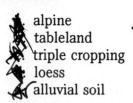
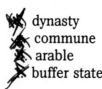

alpine
tableland
triple cropping
loess
alluvial soil

dynasty
commune
arable
buffer state

1. A country that separates two powerful countries
2. A continuous method of planting and harvesting crops that allows farmers to get more food from their land
3. Rock fragments and silt deposited on the land when a river floods during the rainy season
4. A plateau that is level and flat
5. A family that ruled China for many generations
6. A huge farm owned by the state
7. Land that is useful for agriculture
8. Mountainous
9. A powdery, fertile soil

REVIEWING THE FACTS

On a separate sheet of paper, answer the following questions in complete sentences.

1. What is the official name of China?
2. What rivers cross the North China Plain?
3. What mountains are located in the western interior region of China?
4. Why are yaks important to the people of the Tibetan plateau?
5. Why is the Gobi sparsely populated?
6. Why have the Chinese built canals?
7. How is the city of Beijing organized into different sections?

8. What Chinese philosopher taught that people should do good deeds and treat others as they would like to be treated?
9. How is the government of Taiwan different from the government of China?
10. What country controlled Hong Kong until 1997?

WRITING ABOUT CULTURE

Like the yak herders of the Tibetan plateau, other groups of people also depend on animals to help them in many ways. Write several paragraphs describing how people in other parts of the world use animals.

THINKING CRITICALLY

On a separate sheet of paper, answer the following questions in complete sentences.

1. What are some advantages to using bicycles for transportation in the streets of Beijing?
2. Why, do you think, did the Mongol's culture not influence Chinese culture?
3. What reasons might explain why the communes of China did not produce much more food than the old system of agriculture produced?
4. What other countries, like China, face the problem of feeding their growing populations?
5. Why, do you think, was the United States willing to give money and political support to help the Nationalists make Taiwan a strong nation?

On a separate sheet of paper, draw a graphic organizer like the one shown here. Copy the information from this graphic organizer to the one you have drawn. Under the main idea for each lesson, write three statements that you think best support it.

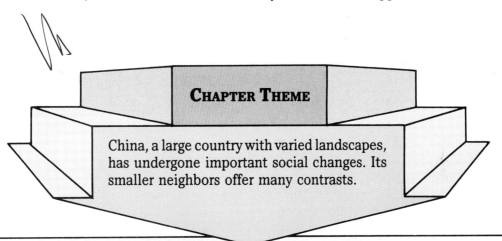

CHAPTER THEME

China, a large country with varied landscapes, has undergone important social changes. Its smaller neighbors offer many contrasts.

Lesson 1 The western part of China is different from the eastern part of China.	**Lesson 2** China has three different regions.
1. _____ 2. _____ 3. _____	1. _____ 2. _____ 3. _____

Lesson 3 The people living in the desert and mountain areas of China have different languages and religions from other Chinese.	**Lesson 4** Taiwan, Hong Kong, and Mongolia are different from China.
1. _____ 2. _____ 3. _____	1. _____ 2. _____ 3. _____

CHAPTER 18

SOUTHEAST ASIA

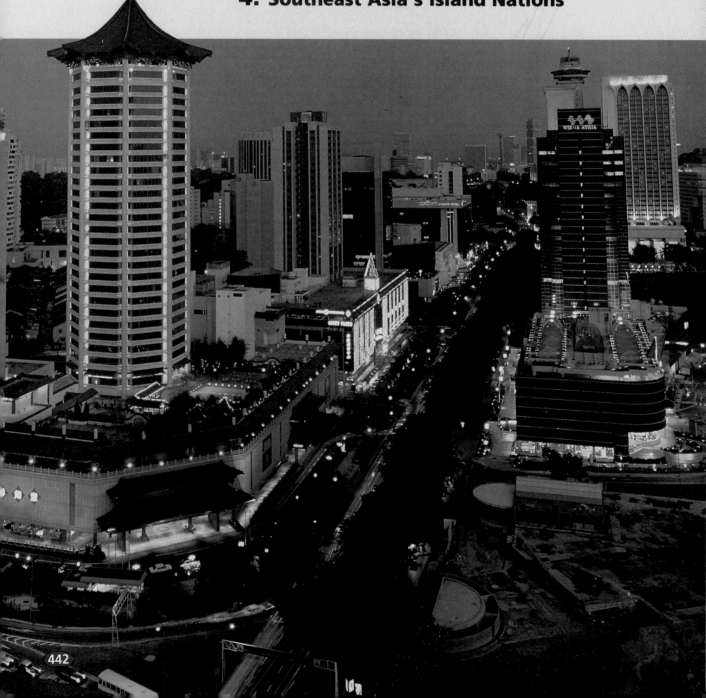

Mainland Nations and Island Nations

CONNECTIONS

Many countries in Southeast Asia have an equatorial climate. List the words you would use to describe such a climate.

TERMS

equatorial climate, ebony

FOCUS

How does Southeast Asia's location affect the region's economy?

A. Mainland Nations and Island Nations

A Green, Lush Land An ancient tale describes how two men from China traveled to Southeast Asia to seek their fortune. If you look at the map on page 444, you can see the route they took. They sailed from China across the South China Sea and the Gulf of Siam toward the city of Bangkok, which is now the capital of Thailand. This is what the men saw during their trip.

> As the [boat] sailed lazily along the coast, they saw in the distance the wealth of bright green rice-fields and all around the spreading trees welcoming them with outstretched arms, and they conjured up in their own minds a vision of abundance and prosperity such as they had never heard or dreamt of before. Never had they seen cultivable land so suited to their nimble minds and hands. . . .

Southeast Asia today is still a land of beauty and of fertile farmland. And like the Chinese travelers, many other Chinese have migrated to Southeast Asia, where they have hoped to live a prosperous life.

Mainland and Islands Using the map on page 444, you can see that seven Southeast Asian countries are located near each other on the mainland of Asia. These are the countries of Myanmar, Malaysia, Singapore,

Terracing is a farming method often used on farmland in Southeast Asia.
▶ How does terracing increase the amount of available farmland?

Thailand, Cambodia, Laos (LAY ahs), and Vietnam. These mainland countries occupy about 46 percent of the area of Southeast Asia. About 44 percent of Southeast Asia's people live in the mainland countries.

The other Southeast Asian countries are located on islands. These are Indonesia, the Philippines, and Brunei (broo NYE). Part of Malaysia is also located on an island. The largest country in Southeast Asia is Indonesia. Indonesia's total area of 779,675 square miles (2,019,358 sq km) makes it about one-fifth the area of the United States. But if you could place the islands on a map of the United States, you would find that they would stretch from the West Coast to the East Coast. Indonesia's population, over 203 million people, is one of the largest in the world, and the largest in Southeast Asia. About 40 percent of all the people of Southeast Asia live on the islands that make up Indonesia. Yet only about 13,700 islands are inhabited.

▶ An evening view of the shopping area along Orchard Road in Singapore.

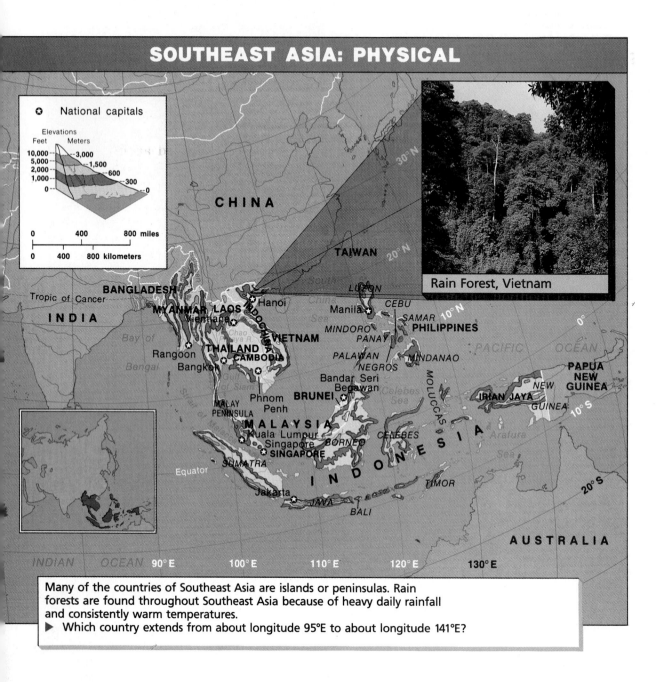

National capitals

Elevations
Feet   Meters
10,000 -- 3,000
5,000 -- 1,500
2,000 -- 600
1,000 -- 300
0 -- 0

0   400   800 miles
0   400   800 kilometers

CHINA

TAIWAN

Rain Forest, Vietnam

BANGLADESH

Tropic of Cancer

INDIA

MYANMAR LAOS

Hanoi

Vientiane

Bay of

LUZON

Manila   CEBU

SAMAR

VIETNAM

MINDORO

PHILIPPINES

PANAY

Rangoon   THAILAND   CAMBODIA

PALAWAN   MINDANAO

Bangkok

NEGROS

Bengal

Bandar Seri
Begawan

PAPUA
NEW
GUINEA

Phnom   BRUNEI

IRIAN JAYA

NEW
GUINEA

Penh

MALAY
PENINSULA

MALAYSIA

Kuala Lumpur

CELEBES

Singapore

BORNEO

SINGAPORE

SUMATRA

INDONESIA

Arafura

Equator

Sea

Jakarta

TIMOR

JAVA

BALI

AUSTRALIA

INDIAN   OCEAN   90°E   100°E   110°E   120°E   130°E

Many of the countries of Southeast Asia are islands or peninsulas. Rain
forests are found throughout Southeast Asia because of heavy daily rainfall
and consistently warm temperatures.
▶ Which country extends from about longitude 95°E to about longitude 141°E?

B. Southeast Asia's Many Cultures

Migrations The Chinese travelers you read about earlier were only two individuals in a steady stream of migrants to Southeast Asia. As you can see from the map above, anyone wishing to travel from the Indian Ocean to the Pacific Ocean along the shortest route would have to pass through the waters of Southeast Asian countries.

Beginning about 2,000 years ago, people from India began moving into Southeast Asia. Many of them introduced their religion, Hinduism, to Southeast Asia, and as a result, today there are many Hindus in this region. India's artistic styles were also adopted by Southeast Asians. Many traditional paintings, drawings, and sculptures in both India and Southeast Asia have a similar style.

In the fifth, sixth, and seventh centuries, Buddhists moved into Southeast Asia and converted many people to Buddhism. This is still the main religion of Thailand, Myanmar, and Cambodia.

As you read earlier, many Chinese migrated to Southeast Asia. Most became traders and merchants, and their descendants quickly grew in number. Today the Chinese are the largest minority group in most Southeast Asian countries.

Arabs and Europeans Arab traders also sailed into Southeast Asia's harbors. Most of the Arab traders were Muslims, and they converted many people in the island nations of Southeast Asia to Islam. Today, Muslims make up a large part of the populations of Indonesia and Malaysia. In fact, the country with the world's largest Muslim population is not in the Middle East—it is Indonesia. More than 175 million Muslims live in Indonesia.

Beginning in the 1550s, Europeans became interested in buying Southeast Asia's silks, spices, jewels, and coffee. The British, French, Dutch, and Spanish established many trading ports and cities, such as Manila and Jakarta (juh KAHR tuh). Only Thailand remained an independent kingdom. After World War II the people of Southeast Asia gradually gained independence from the Europeans. This means that most Southeast Asian countries have been independent less than 55 years.

C. Southeast Asia's Climate

The green rice fields and thick forests described by the Chinese travelers are typical of most of Southeast Asia and other areas of the world located near the Equator. As you can see from the map on page 444, the Equator crosses through Southeast Asia. Because of their location, the nations of Southeast Asia are said to have an **equatorial climate**.

This small village is found in one of the valleys of the rugged, isolated Annamese Mountains.
▶ How do you think the people in this village make a living?

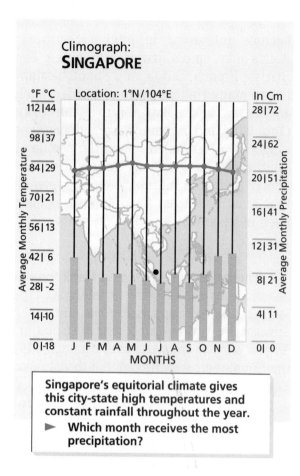

Climograph: SINGAPORE

°F °C Location: 1°N/104°E In Cm

Average Monthly Temperature

Average Monthly Precipitation

112|44
98|37
84|29
70|21
56|13
42| 6
28| -2
14|-10
0|-18

28|72
24|62
20|51
16|41
12|31
8|21
4|11
0| 0

J F M A M J J A S O N D
MONTHS

Singapore's equitorial climate gives this city-state high temperatures and constant rainfall throughout the year.
► Which month receives the most precipitation?

Places with low elevations along the Equator usually have much higher temperatures all year round than do other parts of the world. Most of these warm areas near the Equator also receive heavy rainfall. The air near the earth's surface heats up, and then it rises and cools. Cooler air cannot hold as much moisture as warm air, so warm air that rises and cools usually drops some of its moisture as precipitation. This happens almost all year round in the island nations of Southeast Asia. The weather is both warm and rainy almost every day. In fact, you could say that it is always like summer in an equatorial climate.

The climograph for Singapore on this page shows how little temperature and precipitation vary in an equatorial climate. Temperatures vary by only 2° or 3° at the least, and 7° or 8° at the most. Equatorial climates have the least change in annual temperature range. Rainfall is heavy throughout the year. It is also humid almost every day. Regions that are at a higher elevation, of course, escape some of this heat and humidity.

The abundant rainfall and warm temperatures produce thick vegetation throughout Southeast Asia. Forests provide valuable woods, such as **ebony**. Ebony is a hard, dark, strong wood that comes from various trees found in tropical areas such as Southeast Asia. Ebony wood is used to make the black keys on expensive pianos.

Another plant that grows especially well in an equatorial climate is bamboo. There are more than 700 different kinds of this tall, sturdy plant that is actually a giant form of grass. Bamboo has hundreds of uses and can be used to make items ranging from chairs to food containers.

Farmers' lands produce rich harvests of rice, tea, fruits, vegetables, and sugarcane. No wonder the Chinese travelers felt sure they could make a fortune by moving to Southeast Asia.

LESSON 1

Review

REVIEWING MAIN IDEAS

A. Which countries are located on the mainland of Southeast Asia?
B. What are the three principal religions found in Southeast Asia?
C. How is it always like summer in an equatorial climate?

SKILLS CHECK

MAP SKILL

Use the map on page 444 to name the Southeast Asian countries that have coastlines on these bodies of water:

South China Sea   Pacific Ocean
Gulf of Siam   Strait of Malacca

The Mainland Nations of Vietnam, Laos, and Cambodia

CONNECTIONS

Many people from Vietnam and Cambodia have come to live in the United States because of wars in their countries. How do you think their lives changed when they arrived in the United States?

TERMS

delta, teak, refugee

FOCUS

How have recent wars affected the mainland nations of Southeast Asia?

A. Vietnam, a Land of Mountains and Coasts

Indochina Lisa Bennett, a young American student, excitedly unwrapped a package of photographs from Southeast Asia. Lisa's aunt, a photographer for a newspaper in Vietnam, had sent the photos.

Lisa was curious about these photos because her mother was born and raised in Vietnam. In 1968, Lisa's mother had married Lisa's father, an American soldier who had been sent to Vietnam. Lisa's older brother and sister were born in Vietnam and came to the United States with her parents in 1972. Lisa was born in California, and she had never seen Vietnam or any of the other countries that make up the region called Southeast Asia. So she was fascinated by her aunt's photos.

Lisa separated the photos, making one group for each country. Her mother told her that the mainland countries of Vietnam, Laos, and Cambodia had once been united as a French colony called Indochina. So she decided to put those photos into a single group.

The Annamese Mountains Some of the photos of Vietnam showed rugged mountains. Her aunt had written their name, the Annamese Mountains, on the photos. The Annamese run almost the entire length of western Vietnam along its western border and reach into Laos, Vietnam's western neighbor. These isolated mountains are sparsely populated. Dense forests cover the slopes, and small villages fill the valleys. Most farmers practice subsistence farming.

Like most of Southeast Asia, Malaysia has an equatorial climate, with abundant rainfall and warm temperatures.
▶ How does this climate affect vegetation?

447

Flat-bottomed boats like these are commonly used on the Mekong River.
▶ Into what body of water does the Mekong River flow?

Some of the photos of Vietnam showed farms and cities on level land. They were taken along the Red River, the Mekong River, and the coast of the South China Sea. The Red River begins in China and flows along the northern part of Vietnam to empty into the Gulf of Tonkin.

The Mekong River The Mekong River begins in China and flows 2,600 miles (4,183 km) toward the southeast, where it forms most of the border between Laos and Thailand. The Mekong River then cuts across Cambodia and southern Vietnam to empty into the South China Sea.

Both the Red River and the Mekong River deposit rich alluvial soils along their banks. Villages and rich farmlands prosper along these rivers. But even more valuable are the lands at the mouths of the rivers, where they empty into the sea.

Delta Cities The Red River and the Mekong River both flow more slowly as they enter the sea, just as you slow down when you hit the water after zipping down a slide and splashing into a swimming pool. As the rivers slow, they deposit the heavy loads of sand and soil that they carried down from the Annamese Mountains. This sediment has built up over the centuries and has created a **delta**, which is new land formed at the mouth of a river.

On the delta of the Red River in northern Vietnam is the country's capital city, Hanoi, with over 2 million people. On the delta of the Mekong River in southern Vietnam is Vietnam's largest city, Ho Chi Minh City, with over 4 million people. With a long coastline and rich deltas, Vietnam is not only larger than Laos and Cambodia, but it is also much more densely populated.

B. The Two Vietnams

Two Countries Hanoi and Ho Chi Minh City were the capitals of two different countries at one time. How did this happen? In 1954, an international conference decided that Vietnam should be divided into two countries along the line of latitude at 17°N. This border was needed because two different groups, the Communists in the north of Vietnam and the non-Communists in the south, both claimed to be the leaders of the country. Elections were to be held to decide which group should govern the entire peninsula of Vietnam.

North Vietnam, including Hanoi, was made up of the area to the north of this boundary and was controlled by a Communist government. South Vietnam included the land to the south of the border. Its capital city was in what is now Ho Chi Minh City. At that time, however, it was called Saigon. South Vietnam had a non-Communist government.

The Vietnam War Five years after the border was drawn, guerrillas from North Vietnam began to invade South Vietnam. In 1965 the United States sent troops to help South Vietnam defend itself against the Communist troops from the north. More than 50,000 United States soldiers died in the fighting, which continued until 1973. In that year the United States, North Vietnam, and South Vietnam signed an agreement to end the conflict. United States troops returned home. But the war continued. By 1975, North Vietnam had conquered South Vietnam.

Resources Most of the people who experienced the terror and destruction of the war lived along Vietnam's coast and in its two largest cities. Today these people are rebuilding the irrigation canals and fields that help them produce Vietnam's main food crop, rice.

Northern Vietnam has coal deposits, along with small amounts of iron ore, bauxite, and other minerals. Most of Vietnam's manufacturing centers are in the north, in and around Hanoi. These factories produce textiles, motorcycles, and processed foods.

The Boat People After North Vietnam took control of South Vietnam, many Vietnamese left the country. Lisa's mother told her about many friends and relatives who fled from Vietnam during this time. Perhaps 1 million Vietnamese escaped in small, dangerous boats and crossed the South China Sea to other countries. They were called "Boat People." About one million more crossed the mountains and fled to Thailand and Laos, hoping to someday find a permanent home. Many came to the United States.

C. Laos, a Landlocked Country

Several of Lisa's photos from Laos showed people in traditional dress, with elaborate embroidery and unusual head-pieces. These people lived in the Annamese Mountains, which cover most of the country of Laos. Small tribes of people with different languages and customs lived in villages in the basins and valleys in the mountains. One group, called the Hmong (hmawng), fought with the United States against Communist guerrillas in Laos. When Communists gained control of Laos, many of the Hmong came to the United States.

A large group of South Vietnamese people struggle to board the last American helicopter to leave Saigon.
▶ What is Saigon called today?

449

Thousands of Cambodian refugees have fled to Thailand, bringing with them only the few belongings they can carry.
▶ Why did these people leave Cambodia?

The Mekong River runs along the western border of Laos. Most of the population of Laos lives in the Mekong River valley. The capital city, Vientiane, is located in this valley. The country's only railroad runs from Vientiane across the Mekong River into Thailand.

The farmers in the Mekong River valley grow rice, cotton, and corn. These are Laos's main agricultural products. But its main exports are timber and electricity, both of which come from the mountains. The heavy forests of the mountain slopes contain many **teak** trees. Teak is a hard, yellowish-brown wood that can be used for carving and to make furniture. Teak contains a great deal of oil, which makes it water resistant, so it is also used for shipbuilding.

D. Cambodia, a Nation Torn by War

Cambodia, the third country in the area called Indochina, is different from Vietnam and Laos because it is a mainly flat land with only a few mountains on its southern border.

Lisa's aunt had sent her photographs of people in the capital city of Phnom Penh (puh NAWM pen), located on the Mekong River. Most of the people in these photographs looked quite sad, perhaps because their country has undergone bloody conflicts and invasions for many years. In 1975, Communists called the Khmer Rouge (kuh MER roozh) took over Cambodia and killed hundreds of thousands of Cambodians. Thousands of other Cambodians fled across the western border into Thailand and became **refugees**. A refugee is a person who is forced to leave his or her country. In 1978, Vietnam invaded Cambodia and forced the Khmer Rouge out of power. The Khmer Rouge continued to fight the Vietnamese. In 1989, Vietnamese soldiers left Cambodia. In 1993, elections were held under a new constitution. However, the Khmer Rouge again fought to regain power. Cambodia remained a war-torn country.

Cambodia has fertile soils and large forests. The forests supply firewood and lumber for construction, but roads and railroads are needed to bring these resources out of the forest areas. Farmers grow rice, soybeans, and corn, and raise some cattle. They need fertilizers, modern machinery, roads, and storage facilities in order to produce more food. There is little manufacturing in Cambodia. Some factories produce cement, paper, and textiles.

LESSON 2

Review

REVIEWING MAIN IDEAS

A. How are Vietnam's two most important rivers used?

B. Why was Vietnam once divided into two countries?

C. What are the two most important exports from Laos?

D. How has Cambodia been affected by war?

SKILLS CHECK

THINKING SKILL

Why, do you think, did the United States send soldiers to fight in South Vietnam?

The Countries of the Malay Peninsula

CONNECTIONS

What kinds of economic activities would you expect to find in a country with few natural resources but with a good harbor and port?

TERMS

pagoda, isolationism, latex, city-state

FOCUS

Why are the Malay Peninsula's main cities located on water routes?

A. The Ancient Nation of Thailand

A Growing Country Lisa Bennett, the young American student you read about earlier, watched photos from Thailand tumble through her hands. Scenes of hamburger stands on busy city streets, small fishing boats crowded along rivers, and huge traffic jams caught her eye. Thailand is a country with a long and rich history, but it is growing and modernizing quickly today.

Thailand, along with Myanmar, Malaysia, and Singapore, is part of the long, narrow Malay Peninsula. Most of Thailand is a flat plain crossed by rivers. The Mekong River flows along the edge of this plain, following Thailand's eastern border with Laos. Thailand's most important river is the Chao Phraya (CHOU prah YAH) River. As you can see from the map on page 444, this river flows out of the mountains of Laos and empties into the Gulf of Siam.

Bangkok Thailand's capital city, Bangkok, is located near the mouth of the Chao Phraya River. With about 5.6 million residents, Bangkok is a busy, crowded city. Its population is growing quickly, and could triple in the next twenty years.

What makes Bangkok so special? For one thing, it is a primate city. As you remember, a primate city is the only city in a nation where almost everything im-

portant is found. Almost all of Thailand's businesses, factories, hotels, schools, government offices, and hospitals are located in Bangkok. The concentration of such important services in one place can be a problem for people who live in small towns or in the countryside. They must travel to the primate city for practically everything they need. Living in the primate city itself is much more convenient. So people move into a primate city like Bangkok by the thousands.

Thailand's Products How did Bangkok become so prosperous? Many Bangkok businesses grew wealthy by exporting Thailand's products. For example, Thailand's farmers produce large quantities of food, especially rice. In fact, Thailand is the world's largest exporter of rice. Most of Thailand's rice is grown in paddies similar to the rice paddies of Japan and China.

Thailand's farmers also raise corn, sugarcane, and tobacco. And they grow cassava, a small shrub with roots that can be ground up and eaten or used to make puddings such as tapioca.

This typically busy street in Bangkok is packed with rush-hour traffic.
▶ How does transportation in Bangkok differ from that in American cities?

451

Thailand has deposits of tin, iron ore, lead, bauxite, and tungsten. These are shipped down the Chao Phraya to Bangkok, where they are used to manufacture steel, electronic goods, and automobiles.

B. Myanmar, Land of the Golden Pagodas

The Irrawaddy River Like a horseshoe, mountains ring Myanmar on three sides. Between the mountains, long river valleys reach like fingers toward the south. The Irrawaddy River is the most important of these rivers. It stretches to the south across Myanmar and forms a huge delta before it empties into the sea. The capital city of Myanmar, Rangoon, is located near the mouth of the Irrawaddy River.

Most people of Myanmar live in the Irrawaddy River valley. Mandalay, near the country's center, once was Myanmar's largest and most important city. Today, Mandalay is second to Rangoon in size and importance. When the British began trading in Myanmar in the middle 1800s, they built rice paddies on the delta of the Irrawaddy. They also turned the small settlement near Rangoon into a major trading station and port. Today, Rangoon has over 2.5 million inhabitants and is growing quickly.

Roads, railways, and the Irrawaddy River connect Myanmar's two main cities of Mandalay and Rangoon. Rice, grown in paddies along the river, is sent by boat to Rangoon, where it is milled and then packaged before it is sold.

Elephants are often used in Thailand, Cambodia, and Myanmar to move logs that have been cut from the vast rain forests found in these countries.
▶ How are the elephants carrying the logs?

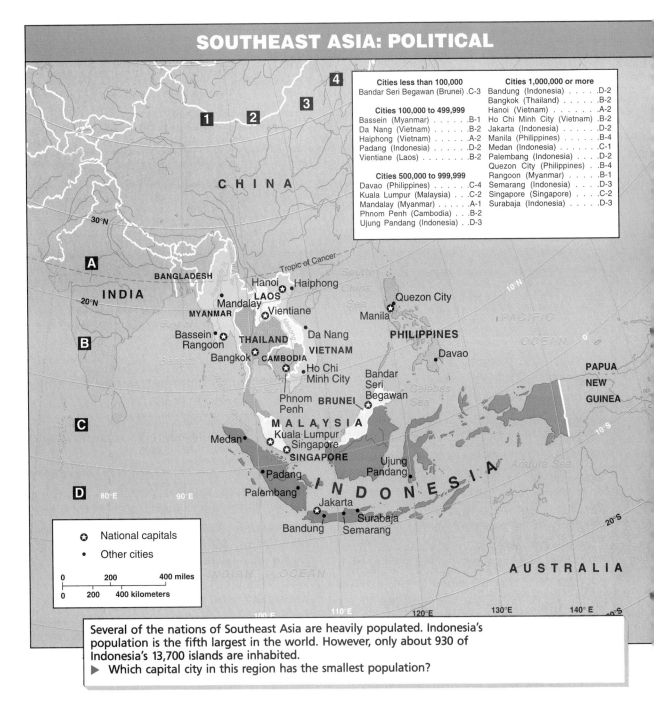

SOUTHEAST ASIA: POLITICAL

Cities less than 100,000
Bandar Seri Begawan (Brunei) .C-3

Cities 100,000 to 499,999
Bassein (Myanmar) B-1
Da Nang (Vietnam) B-2
Haiphong (Vietnam) A-2
Padang (Indonesia) D-2
Vientiane (Laos) B-2

Cities 500,000 to 999,999
Davao (Philippines) C-4
Kuala Lumpur (Malaysia) . . .C-2
Mandalay (Myanmar) A-1
Phnom Penh (Cambodia) . . .B-2
Ujung Pandang (Indonesia) . .D-3

Cities 1,000,000 or more
Bandung (Indonesia) D-2
Bangkok (Thailand) B-2
Hanoi (Vietnam) A-2
Ho Chi Minh City (Vietnam) .B-2
Jakarta (Indonesia) D-2
Manila (Philippines) B-4
Medan (Indonesia) C-1
Palembang (Indonesia) D-2
Quezon City (Philippines) . .B-4
Rangoon (Myanmar) B-1
Semarang (Indonesia) D-3
Singapore (Singapore) C-2
Surabaja (Indonesia) D-3

⚙ National capitals

• Other cities

0   200   400 miles
0   200   400 kilometers

Several of the nations of Southeast Asia are heavily populated. Indonesia's population is the fifth largest in the world. However, only about 930 of Indonesia's 13,700 islands are inhabited.
▶ Which capital city in this region has the smallest population?

Sugarcane, wheat, cotton, and corn are also sent down the Irrawaddy to Rangoon. Huge rafts carry teak logs, which grow in Myanmar's tropical forests, to Rangoon for processing.

A Land of Pagodas Lisa saw several photos of graceful, rounded buildings that reached a point at their tops. Her aunt labeled these **pagodas**, the name for the Buddhist shrines that are found all over Myanmar and the other Buddhist regions of Southeast Asia. Myanmar has so many pagodas, which are decorated with gold, that is is often called "The Land of the Golden Pagodas."

453

This pagoda graces the scenery in Rangoon, capital city of Myanmar— "The Land of the Golden Pagodas."
▶ What is the purpose of a pagoda?

Isolation Myanmar gained its independence from the United Kingdom in 1948. Shortly after, Myanmar's leaders decided to follow a policy of **isolationism**, or cutting off contact with foreign countries. Without information and funds from people in other countries, Myanmar's industries have not grown. Only basic goods such as textiles, soap, cement, glass, and paper are produced in their factories. Since 1988 the army has controlled Myanmar's government. The army has made it difficult for prodemocracy groups to gain power.

C. Malaysia's Many Cultures

A Divided Country From the map on page 444, you can see that Malaysia has a very interesting shape. It includes the southern tip of the Malay Peninsula and part of the island called Borneo. Malaysia shares the island of Borneo with Indonesia and with Brunei.

You might also notice from the map that Malaysia's capital city, Kuala Lumpur, is located along a narrow channel of water called the Strait of Malacca. This strait has been an important passageway for ships traveling between India and China. Kuala Lumpur and other coastal cities became important trading centers because of the strait's location.

Through the centuries, ships brought many different kinds of people to Malaysia. Today, the descendants of the original Malays make up about 59 percent of Malaysia's population. Most Malaysians are Muslim. About 32 percent of Malaysians are of Chinese ancestry, and most of them are Buddhists. And about 9 percent of Malaysia's people are descendants of Indians, who are mostly Hindus. Other religious and ethnic groups are also found in Malaysia.

Rubber Plantations A photo showing dozens of perfectly straight rows of trees puzzled Lisa. Trees don't usually grow in lines! Her aunt's label said this was a picture of a rubber tree plantation in Malaysia. Malaysia, along with Indonesia, Cambodia, and Thailand, is a major world producer and exporter of rubber.

Rubber trees grow naturally in tropical forests, and workers carry buckets from tree to tree to collect a liquid called **latex**. This latex is then boiled and processed and sent to factories to be made into tires and other rubber products. Wild rubber trees are scattered in the forest, so workers waste valuable time searching for them. They work more efficiently when the rubber trees are planted and cared for on a plantation.

Malaysia's economy is strong and growing because of its other products. One of these products, palm oil, is also produced on plantations. A special type of palm tree grown here produces nuts containing oil that is used as a cooking oil. Palm oil is a major export of Malaysia. If you look at the list of ingredients on a box of cookies you might see palm oil on the list.

Malaysia is also fortunate to have huge deposits of tin. Malaysia produces more tin than any other country in the world. Tin can be made into cans, and a layer of tin can prevent steel from rusting.

D. Singapore, a City-State on an Island

The Strait of Malacca between Malaysia and Indonesia is such an important sea route that in 1819 the British decided to build a new port city on this channel, at the tip of Malaysia. They called the new city Singapore.

Today, Singapore is an independent nation and a powerful center of trade and commerce. Singapore is also one of the wealthiest countries in Southeast Asia. This is amazing, because Singapore is small, crowded, and has no natural resources.

Singapore's total area is only 225 square miles (583 sq km), which is a bit smaller than the District of Columbia in the United States. Singapore occupies one large island, which is connected to Malaysia by a causeway. As you have learned, a causeway is a road running along a ridge of land. Other tiny islands surround the main island.

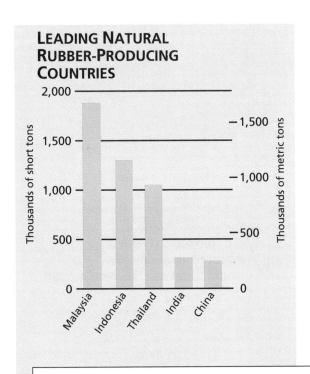

LEADING NATURAL RUBBER-PRODUCING COUNTRIES

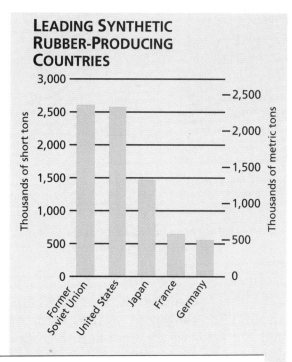

LEADING SYNTHETIC RUBBER-PRODUCING COUNTRIES

Products such as radial tires require natural and synthetic rubber.

▶ Which nations produce more natural rubber than Thailand?

455

The dragon, a symbol of good luck and wealth, is used to celebrate the Chinese New Year in the city-state of Singapore.
▶ Why is Singapore called a city-state?

nearly 3 million people, Singapore has one of the highest population densities in the world, with a density of 12,844 people per square mile (4,960 per sq km).

How did Singapore become so wealthy? Like the Japanese, the people of Singapore learned to import raw materials and manufacture them into goods for export. Singapore's businesses import lumber, food, cotton, petroleum, and rubber. The country's factories then manufacture paper, flour, canned fruits and vegetables, textiles, clothing, plastics, chemicals, and tires for export to other countries.

Singapore's rapid growth into a major economic power in the Pacific Ocean region has attracted the attention of other countries. Many governments in poorer countries would like to follow Singapore's example.

They would also like to follow the economic examples of South Korea, Taiwan, and Hong Kong. These three lands, along with Singapore, have been called the Four Tigers because of their growing economic power.

LESSON 3

Review

REVIEWING MAIN IDEAS

A. Why is Bangkok Thailand's primate city?
B. Why is the Irrawaddy River so important in Myanmar?
C. What products are grown on plantations in Malaysia?
D. How did Singapore become a wealthy country?

SKILLS CHECK

WRITING SKILL

Write a short letter to an imaginary friend in Southeast Asia, asking for photographs of life in that region. Describe what kinds of things you would like to see in the photographs.

Other countries of the world are smaller than Singapore, such as Bermuda and Barbados in the Caribbean Sea. But Singapore is almost entirely a city, which is quite unique. Singapore is called a **city-state** because the whole nation of Singapore is really one huge city. With

456

Southeast Asia's Island Nations

CONNECTIONS

Find the countries of Indonesia and the Philippines on the map on page 453. Make a list of the problems you think a government might have when its territory is made up of thousands of islands.

TERMS

tsunami, green revolution

FOCUS

What are the natural resources of Southeast Asia's island nations?

A. Indonesia, the Giant of Southeast Asia

A Nation of Islands With over 203 million people, Indonesia has nearly three times as many people as the Philippines, the second most populated country of Southeast Asia. Indonesia has over three times as much territory as Myanmar, the second largest country of Southeast Asia.

Indonesia's huge territory is spread across more than 13,000 small islands and two large islands, called Sumatra and Java. Indonesia includes part of the island of Borneo and shares another island, called New Guinea, with the nation of Papua New Guinea.

These islands and many others of Southeast Asia belong to the Ring of Fire that you read about in the chapter on Japan. Many of Indonesia's islands are really the peaks of volcanos that have grown up from the ocean floor. Some of these peaks reach 10,000 feet (3,084 m) in elevation.

Volcanic eruptions and earthquakes are quite common in this part of the world. One of the largest eruptions the world has ever seen occurred on the island of Krakatau (krah kah TOU) in 1883. This island was located between the islands of Java and Sumatra. The volcanic explosion was so powerful that it blew the island to pieces. Thousands of people were killed in **tsunamis** (tsoo NAH meez), or tidal waves, huge walls of water set in motion by an earthquake or a volcano. Tsunamis washed over many coasts of Southeast Asia and wiped out buildings and farms.

A Resourceful Country Volcanos can be destructive, but nature has been kind to Indonesia, too. Nickel, copper, coal, and bauxite are found in Indonesia's mountains. These resources are exported or are used in manufacturing tools, machinery, household appliances, and bicycles.

Most of Indonesia's industry is concentrated in the capital city, Jakarta. Jakarta is quickly becoming one of the largest cities of the world, with about 8.3 million inhabitants. Jakarta, like Bangkok, is also a primate city.

Agriculture and Oil Indonesia is mainly an agricultural country. More than half of its people work in agriculture. Most Indonesians work on or own plantations that produce rice, spices, sugarcane, coffee, and rubber. The Dutch, who colonized Indonesia in the 1600s, traded Indonesia's coffee all over the world. Today, coffee is one

Indonesia's unique culture includes shadow puppets like those shown above.
▶ How are these puppets different from American puppets?

457

of Indonesia's main exports. Because it uses so much land for export crops, Indonesia must import huge amounts of food, including rice.

Indonesia has large petroleum fields and exports oil to many countries. This is perhaps a great source of wealth for the future. But for now, Indonesia is still a poor, overcrowded country without enough education or decent jobs for most of its huge population.

B. Brunei and Papua New Guinea

Brunei As you read earlier, Brunei is the tiny state that shares the island of Borneo with Malaysia and Indonesia. It is surrounded by land belonging to Malaysia.

Brunei has two things in common with Indonesia. First, most of Brunei's people are Muslims, as are most Indonesians. And second, Brunei has petroleum fields, like Indonesia. But Brunei has only 2,226 square miles (5,765 sq km) of area, which makes it a little larger than the state of Delaware. And Brunei has less than half a million people. The earnings they receive from their oil have made many of them quite wealthy. In fact, Brunei has one of the highest per capita incomes in the world: more than $9,000 per person.

Papua New Guinea Another neighbor of Indonesia is Papua New Guinea, which shares the island of New Guinea with Indonesia. Papua New Guinea is a dramatic contrast to Brunei. Over 4.2 million people inhabit its mountains. Over 80 percent of its land is blanketed in dense forests. Most people there live in small villages or rural towns with few schools, hospitals, or industries.

C. The Philippines: A Nation of Scattered Islands

An American Colony The Philippines was a colony of Spain until Spain lost the

Spanish-American War to the United States in 1898. Spain was forced to turn the Philippines over to the United States, which controlled it until independence in 1946. Because of these events, three languages are spoken widely in the Philippines. They are Spanish, English, and Tagalog, a native language.

The Republic of the Philippines is made up of over 7,000 islands in the South China Sea. The two largest islands are Luzon (loo ZAHN) and Mindanao (mihn duh NOU). Luzon has the capital city, Manila. Most of the people in Luzon are Catholic. Mindanao has a smaller population, and most of its people are Muslims. There has been conflict between the Muslims and the Catholics. Some Muslims on Mindanao would like to form their own country, and they have fought a guerrilla war with the government.

The Economy The Philippines has been able to build a strong agricultural economy. Plantations, especially on the flat coastlands, grow sugarcane and coconut palm trees. Coconuts produce an oil used in soap, shampoos, and prepared foods such as breakfast cereal. The fleshy part of the coconut is dried and used in cooking. Coconut products and sugarcane are the Philippines' main agricultural products that are exported.

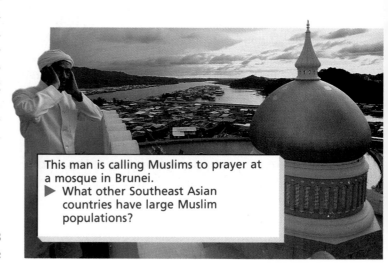

This man is calling Muslims to prayer at a mosque in Brunei.
▶ What other Southeast Asian countries have large Muslim populations?

The Green Revolution Subsistence farmers in valleys and mountainous areas raise rice, corn, tobacco, and fruits. Many of these farmers have very little land and are trying to take advantage of the **green revolution**, which is modern ways of farming rice, wheat, and corn.

The green revolution began in the 1960s when scientists working in the Philippines and in other countries, such as India, invented new kinds of seeds that would produce more food on each acre of land. In addition, experts helped farmers by providing information about fertilizers and new methods of farming. The government helped by giving farmers loans to buy new tools and equipment. Farmers soon were producing twice as much food, and the green revolution spread to many other countries.

The Philippines has become an important manufacturing center in Southeast Asia. Factories produce clothes, shoes, electronic equipment, and chemicals. Some of the Philippines' copper, silver, and nickel deposits are used in manufacturing. The Philippines uses its earnings from exports to import goods such as machinery and petroleum.

A Special Relationship The Philippines has had a special relationship with the United States. For decades, thousands of American soldiers had been stationed at two giant United States military bases in the Philippines. And the United States is the Philippines' largest trading partner.

The United States has also played a role in the Philippines' return to democracy. From 1965 to 1986, the country was ruled by Ferdinand Marcos. Marcos did not allow the Philippine people political freedoms. In 1986, the Philippine people removed Marcos from power. The United States supported the removal of Marcos and gave economic aid to the new president of the country, Corazon Aquino.

Democracy returned to the Philippines under President Corazon Aquino and continued with her successor, Fidel Ramos.
▶ Who did Corazon Aquino replace?

Aquino returned the Philippines to democracy. When her term ended in 1992, Fidel V. Ramos was elected president. He had been one of Aquino's strongest supporters. Under Ramos, the Philippine economy continued to grow. However, poverty and unemployment remained a serious problem.

LESSON 4

Review

REVIEWING MAIN IDEAS

A. Why is Indonesia considered a poor country?
B. How are Brunei and Papua New Guinea different from each other?
C. How did the green revolution help farmers in the Philippines?

SKILLS CHECK

MAP SKILL

Use the map on page 453 and name the countries that occupy the following islands:
Borneo, Java, New Guinea, Sumatra, Luzon, Mindanao

REVIEWING TERMS

On a separate sheet of paper, write the term that best matches each numbered statement.

ebony   isolationism
delta   latex
teak   tsunamis
refugee   city-state
pagodas   green revolution

1. A person who is forced to leave his or her country
2. A country's policy of cutting off contacts with foreign countries
3. New land formed at the mouth of a river
4. Huge walls of water set in motion by an earthquake or a volcano
5. A hard, dark, strong wood found in tropical areas that can be used to build ships
6. Buddhist shrines found in Myanmar
7. Where a whole nation is one city.
8. Modern ways of growing rice, wheat, and corn
9. A hard, yellowish-brown wood used for carving and furniture
10. A liquid from certain trees used to make tires and other rubber products

REVIEWING THE FACTS

On a separate sheet of paper, answer the following questions in complete sentences.

1. How did the people from India who moved into Southeast Asia influence the region?
2. Why did Europeans establish trading ports in Southeast Asia?

3. What two important cities in Vietnam are located on deltas?
4. Why were some Vietnamese people referred to as "boat people?"
5. What are the main exports of Laos?
6. What three countries are in the area that was once called Indochina?
7. What country exports more rice than any other country in the world?
8. What did the British do that helped Rangoon become such a large and important city?
9. Why is Singapore called a city-state?
10. What two things does Brunei have in common with Indonesia?

WRITING ABOUT GEOGRAPHY

If you were a photographer like Lisa's aunt, what pictures would you take of Southeast Asia? Maybe you would choose to photograph people at work, the varied landscapes, or the resources of the region such as rice paddies, or forests. Write several paragraphs describing what you would photograph.

THINKING CRITICALLY

On a separate sheet of paper, answer the following questions in complete sentences.

1. Why, do you think, did the "boat people" want to leave Vietnam?
2. What are some possible reasons to explain why the Cambodian government has not built roads, or supplied its farmers with modern machinery, or developed industries in the country?

3. What other country have you read about that, like Myanmar, had a policy of isolationism at one time in its history?

4. What reasons can you give to support the statement that Thailand has very fertile soil?

5. Why is Indonesia mainly an agricultural country?

SUMMARIZING THE CHAPTER

On a separate sheet of paper, draw a graphic organizer like the one shown here. Copy the information from this graphic organizer on the one you have drawn. Under the main idea of each lesson, write three statements that you think best support that idea.

CHAPTER THEME ➡ Southeast Asia, an area of great ethnic diversity, suffers from political and economic instability.

Lesson 1 The location of Southeast Asia affects the region's economy.

1. _____
2. _____
3. _____

Lesson 2 Recent wars have affected the mainland nations of Southeast Asia.

1. _____
2. _____
3. _____

Lesson 3 The main cities of the Malay Peninsula are located on water routes.

1. _____
2. _____
3. _____

Lesson 4 The island nations of Southeast Asia have many natural resources.

1. _____
2. _____
3. _____

CHAPTER **19**

INDIA AND ITS NEIGHBORS

1. **The Region of South Asia**
2. **India and Its Regions**
3. **Ways of Life in Modern India**
4. **India's Neighbors**

The Region of South Asia

Look at the photograph on the opposite page. What do you think this building was constructed for, and what do you think it is used for today?

TERMS

subcontinent

FOCUS

What are South Asia's principal physical features?

A. The Subcontinent of Asia

The Taj Mahal In a small town in northern India stands one of the world's most beautiful monuments—the Taj Mahal (tahz muh HAHL). This tomb was built in the early 1600s by Shah Jahan, a great emperor of India. Shah Jahan built the Taj Mahal to honor his young wife, who had died shortly after they were married.

Jahan spared no expense in building this magnificent structure. It is built of the world's finest marble and is surrounded by pools and fountains. Marble and ivory archways lead into courtyards lined with balconies of marble that are carved into delicate, lacy patterns.

The Taj Mahal displays two important characteristics of India and the surrounding region. First, the monument serves as evidence that this is a region where great civilizations have thrived for centuries. The people who have lived here have developed advanced techniques of architecture, engineering, and crafts such as weaving and silver working.

Second, the Taj Mahal shows that the people of this region have long conducted trade with other nations. For centuries, traders have brought treasures such as the pearls, ivory, silver, and marble used to decorate the Taj Mahal. Merchants leaving India and neighboring lands have carried cotton, jewels, and precious spices such as pepper to China or Europe. Travelers who have passed through India by land or by sea also have brought philosophies, religions, and languages from other parts of the world.

The Subcontinent India and its neighboring countries form a huge triangle that juts into the Indian Ocean. The Arabian Sea stretches along the western coast of this gigantic triangle. The eastern coast faces the Bay of Bengal. At the southernmost tip of the triangle is the island nation of Sri Lanka (sree LAHNG kuh). Much of the northern edge of the triangle runs through the Himalayas.

This huge triangle of land is cut off from the rest of Asia because it has coasts and high mountains along its borders. Sometimes this triangle of land is called a **subcontinent**. A subcontinent is a landmass that belongs to a larger continent. The term *South Asia* is also used to describe this huge triangle of land. South Asia includes India and most of the countries on its *perimeter*, or edges. These neighboring countries are Pakistan, Nepal (nuh PAWL), Bhutan, Bangladesh, and the island nations of Sri Lanka and the Maldives. India is the largest country on the subcontinent. Its total area is 1,229,424 square miles (3,184,208 sq km). This makes it about one-third the size of the United States.

A Rural Population India's population of 936 million people is one of the largest in the world. Only China has a larger population than India. As in China, most of the people in India and the rest of South Asia live in small villages and rural areas. Less than one fourth of South Asia's population lives in cities.

Nevertheless, India and its neighbors have some of the largest cities of the world, such as Karachi in Pakistan, and Bombay,

▶ The magnificent Taj Mahal, in Agra, is a symbol of India's great civilizations.

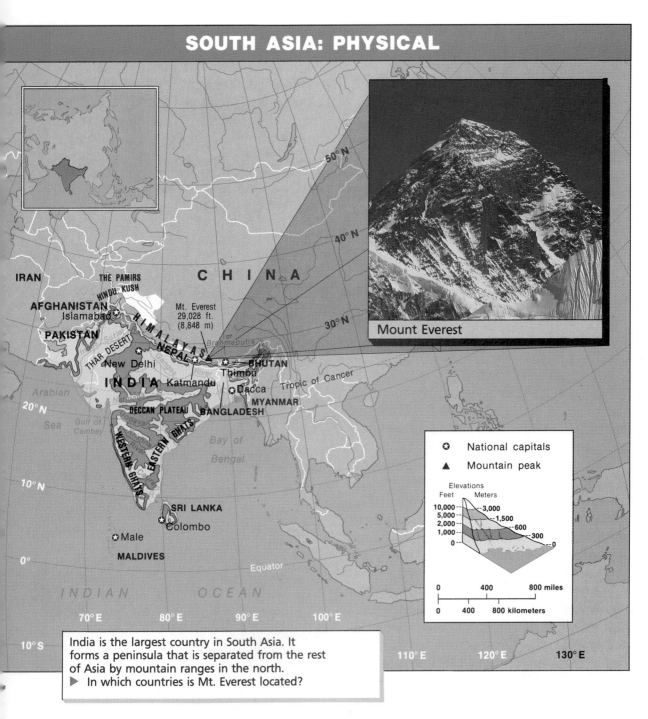

SOUTH ASIA: PHYSICAL

Mount Everest

India is the largest country in South Asia. It forms a peninsula that is separated from the rest of Asia by mountain ranges in the north.
► In which countries is Mt. Everest located?

Madras, and Calcutta in India. Most South Asian cities are crowded and busy. A visitor might see "streetcars. . . bulging with twice as many passengers as they were built to carry—the last few people to have boarded them. . . just dangling from the back platform like a bunch of human bananas."

B. The Mountains and Plains of South Asia

Landforms South Asia has three major landforms. The first of these landforms is the Deccan Plateau. This huge, rugged plateau forms the core of the peninsula of India. On the eastern and western edges of the Deccan Plateau are mountain ranges called the Eastern Ghats and the Western Ghats.

The Ganges (GAN jeez) River and its plain are South Asia's second major landform. The Ganges is a wide river that flows across northern India from west to east for 1,560 miles (2,670 km).

The Himalayas are the third major landform of South Asia. The Himalayas cross through northern Pakistan, northern India, Nepal, and Bhutan. Between the high mountain peaks are valleys and basins where towns, villages, and farms are found.

The Indus River The Indus River and its valley are an important part of the South Asian landscape. The Indus River begins in the Himalayas and flows south across Pakistan. It is 1,976 miles (3,179 km) in length, which makes it longer than the Ganges River. The water of the Indus River is extremely valuable because the area around the river is desert.

South Asia's other important river is the Brahmaputra (brah muh POO truh). This river has both a long name and a long route,

1,802 miles (2,883 km), which is about the same length as the Rio Grande in North America. You can see from the map on page 464 that most of the nation of Bangladesh is located in the broad valley and deltas of the Brahmaputra River.

C. The Importance of Religion

Religion and Politics South Asia has an amazing variety of religions. Hinduism, India's principal religion, has the largest number of followers in South Asia. Islam has the second largest number of followers. There are also many smaller religious groups, such as the Sikhs (seeks) and the Tamils (TAM ulz). Each of these groups has its own beliefs and its own shrines or temples.

Many of South Asia's conflicts and political problems are based on religious differences. For example, some of the borders of South Asia's nations were created because of a past conflict between Muslims and Hindus. In 1947, when the British gave the people of India independence, the Muslims and Hindus faced a difficult problem.

Water buffaloes drag this farmer's wooden plow through a field along the Indus River.
▶ Do you think this work is difficult?

465

When the borders of India and Pakistan were set, millions of Muslims and Hindus had to relocate.
▶ What does this photograph tell you about the people's efforts to relocate?

They did not want to form a single independent nation because their beliefs were so different. So two separate countries were formed, India and Pakistan.

A Violent Beginning The results of this decision were dramatic. If the Hindus and the Muslims had lived in completely separate areas, the boundaries of the new countries could have been drawn between them. This would have been simple and efficient. But the Hindus and Muslims lived in the same villages and towns. When the national borders were established, millions of Muslims living in the new country of India fled across the border into Pakistan, where Muslims were to be the majority of the population. And going in the other direction, millions of Hindus who found themselves living in Pakistan fled to India to live with other Hindus.

There were riots and violence as millions of people tried to move their families and belongings as quickly as possible. Many were farmers who had to leave their land behind. When they arrived in their new country, these farmers had no land and no way to earn a living. This caused terrible hardship and suffering for many people.

LESSON 1

Review

REVIEWING MAIN IDEAS
A. Why are India and its neighbors sometimes considered a separate region?
B. What are the three main rivers of South Asia?
C. Why was India divided into two separate nations?

SKILLS CHECK
MAP SKILL
Use the map on page 464 to name the countries that border the following South Asian nations: Pakistan, Nepal, Bhutan.

India and Its Regions

CONNECTIONS
What are the ways in which we can describe a country's geography?

TERMS
domestic, monsoon, precipice

FOCUS
Which of India's regions produce agricultural products?

A. India's Regions

Geographers have a method for sorting out what they see of the land and people of a country and for learning about the country in an organized way. They study the special features of each region within a country. You have already done this before in studying China's regions, and we can use the same method to study India's vastly different regions.

India's three regions center around the country's major landforms. In the first of these regions, the Ganges River plain, are rolling hills and many shrines and religious sites. Green farmland stretches out alongside rivers and streams, and villages are grouped near clumps of trees. Women walk carefully along narrow paths with big pots or bundles balanced on their heads.

Buses traveling to India's second region, the Deccan Plateau, sputter and groan as they climb up zigzag roads. At the top of the plateau are forests, grasslands, and plantations on which tea and coffee are grown for export.

India's third region is the Himalayas. Dense jungle covers the foothills of the mountains. The jungle has been cut away in many places to allow the building of huge tea plantations and resort towns.

B. The Ganges River and Its Plain

The Sacred Ganges For Indians, the most important river on earth is the Ganges. The Ganges begins high in the Himalayas, where Hindus believe their gods live. Hindus believe the gods send the river through India, so they consider the entire length of the Ganges River holy.

The Ganges provides a valuable re-

To the Hindus of India, the Ganges River is holy. Bathing in it is a religious ritual.
▶ Why else, do you think, is the Ganges River important to India?

source for farmers who live along its banks. Every year this river floods during the rainy season, leaving rich soils on the surrounding farmlands. For thousands of years, farmers have used these rich soils to grow crops, such as wheat, cotton, and rice.

The population of the Ganges River plain has grown considerably over the years, and today this region of India is one of the most densely populated parts of the world. Many areas have more than 1,800 people per square mile. Most of these people live in farm villages and make their living from agriculture.

The Ganges River plain also has large cities. Delhi, which is more than 700 years old, is located on a tributary of the Ganges River in the western part of the plain. Over 8.4 million people live in Delhi, making it the third largest city in India. New Delhi, the capital city of India, is also located on the Ganges River plain.

The Western Plain We usually think of a plain as an area of flat land where there is little variation in climate from place to place. But the Ganges River plain is different from most plains. The climate of the western end of the Ganges Plain is much drier than that at the eastern end. As a result the crops and methods of farming are different in these two areas.

In the western Ganges River plain, farmers grow corn, barley, and wheat, which is the main food crop. India is a major world producer of wheat, growing nearly as much as the United States. Most of the wheat produced in India is for **domestic** use, which means that it is used in India and is not exported to other countries.

Farmers in the western part of the Ganges River plain also grow cotton and sugarcane. India is the world's fourth largest producer of cotton, and the world's second largest producer of sugarcane. The Ganges River and its tributaries provide irrigation water to grow these crops. Hydroelectric power is generated from huge dams built recently along the Ganges River.

The Eastern Plain The eastern part of the Ganges River plain receives far more rainfall than the western area. Rice is the major crop grown here. Only China produces more rice than India, and both countries consume most of the rice they produce. Tropical fruits, such as bananas and oranges, and other crops such as tea and sugarcane are also grown in the eastern plain.

The difference in rainfall in eastern and western India is dramatic. In the western Ganges Plain near Delhi, the total amount of rain that falls during a year is about 25 inches (64 cm). Calcutta, at the eastern end of the Ganges River, receives over 63 inches (160 cm) of rain per year.

C. India's Monsoonal Climate

The Monsoon Why is the eastern part of India so much rainier than the western part? The **monsoon**, a seasonal wind, is responsible for India's climate. From November until March, monsoon winds blow from the northeast and bring dry air from the Himalayas. The winter months are dry throughout most of India. Almost all of

Daily life continues in India during the monsoon rains. The heavy downpour floods the streets of most cities.
▶ What is the monsoon?

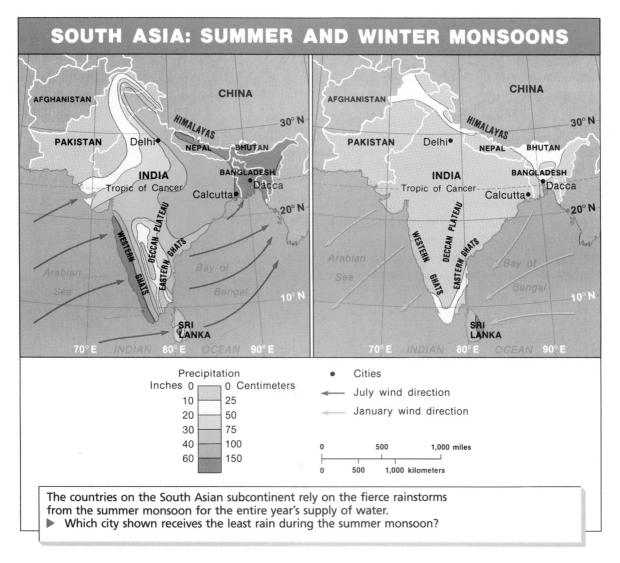

SOUTH ASIA: SUMMER AND WINTER MONSOONS

Precipitation

Inches	0	0	Centimeters
10		25	
20		50	
30		75	
40		100	
60		150	

• Cities

⬅ July wind direction

⬅ January wind direction

0 — 500 — 1,000 miles

0 — 500 — 1,000 kilometers

The countries on the South Asian subcontinent rely on the fierce rainstorms from the summer monsoon for the entire year's supply of water.
▶ Which city shown receives the least rain during the summer monsoon?

India receives less than one inch (2.54 cm) of rainfall per month during the dry season.

In June, July, and August, monsoon winds blow from the southwest to the northeast, carrying moisture from the Indian Ocean and dropping it over the land. Everywhere in India, summer is a rainy season. But some places receive more rain during the summer than others do.

Using the maps of India on this page, you can see that moist air from the Bay of Bengal moving from southwest to northeast must blow along the eastern edge of India. This moist air drops heavy rainfall near the mouth of the Ganges River and in Bangladesh. Calcutta and the eastern part of the Ganges River plain receive a drenching in the summer, with up to 13 inches (33 cm) of rainfall per month.

Moist winds from the Arabian Sea also carry rainfall toward India. But when these winds arrive at India's west coast, they immediately climb up to the Deccan Plateau. These winds leave their rain along the western coast, so they are dry by the time they reach the western part of the Ganges River plain. As a result, Delhi receives only about 7 inches (18 cm) of rain per month in the rainy season.

Calcutta In the early 1700s the British built a port and trading center in Calcutta.

This made the eastern Ganges Plain as important as the western part and Delhi. Today, Calcutta is India's largest city, with over 11 million inhabitants. Calcutta is also the main port for exporting the farm products of the Ganges Plain. Tea, rice, and wheat are processed in Calcutta. Textile mills there turn cotton into clothing and fabrics for export.

India's main coal and iron ore deposits are located to the west of Calcutta. These resources are used to make steel and some of the iron ore is exported. Calcutta is India's main industrial city for producing metals, machinery, tools, and chemicals.

D. The Rugged Deccan Plateau

The Deccan Plateau The Deccan Plateau, India's second region, is a level area cut by **precipices**, or sharp drop-offs. Swirling rivers wind their way between cliffs and steep valleys, and many deep, narrow chasms cut across the plateau.

Most of the Deccan Plateau is at an elevation of 2,000 feet (610 m) or less. Some areas of the plateau are densely forested. Most of it is sparsely populated, with only a few scattered villages. Farmers raise cotton, a few vegetables, and millet. Millet is a wheatlike grain that can be ground up into flour. It is then usually made into bread.

The tableland of the Deccan Plateau drops to sea level along the coasts of the Arabian Sea and the Bay of Bengal. The side of the plateau is steep and nearly vertical along these coasts. The coastal plains at the base of the plateau are narrow and are densely populated.

The coastal plain along the western edge of the Deccan Plateau is called the Malabar Coast. This coastal plain receives heavy rainfall during the rainy season. Farmers along the Malabar Coast produce crops such as rice, rubber, tea, coffee, coconuts, and pepper.

Like most old Indian cities, Bombay has streets crowded with open-air markets.
▶ What kinds of goods do you think are sold in Bombay's open-air markets?

Bombay Bombay is the principal city on the western coast, and it is also India's second largest city. Nearly 10 million people live in Bombay. They work in many different industries, including textiles. Bombay's textile industry uses cotton grown in western and central India.

Other industries in Bombay manufacture leather goods, process foods, and produce chemicals and railway equipment. Many of Bombay's factories use hydroelectric power generated from the rivers that drop off the Deccan Plateau along the western coast. India has some petroleum fields along the coast of Bombay, but there is not enough oil to provide power for all the country's factories.

Madras The eastern coast of the Deccan Plateau is called the Coromandel (kor uh MAN dul) Coast. Here, farmers grow rice, sugarcane, citrus fruits, cashew nuts, and

GROWING UP IN INDIA

Shiv is a young boy who lives in a small village in northern India. Shiv, his brothers, and his younger sister all attend school from 7:00 A.M. until 1:00 P.M. in the summertime. After school they return home and spend about one hour and a half doing homework. They also help out with the housework and farm chores. In the winter-time, they attend school from 9:00 A.M. until 4:00 P.M.

Shiv's family grows most of the food the family eats. Rice is the main dish. It is often flavored with curry, which is a combination of many spices. The family also has vegetables and chapatis (chuh PAHT eez), flat disks of bread that look like pancakes.

In the past, Shiv could look forward to a life of farming. In fact, farming was the occupation of all the males in his family. When Shiv's grandfather grew too old to continue farming, the family followed tradition and divided up the farm among Shiv's father and uncles. But when Shiv's father dies, the land will not be split among Shiv and his brothers. If it was split among the family sons, each would receive only a tiny piece of land. This would not be enough to make a living. Instead, Shiv and his brothers are studying to learn a craft or trade someday. Farming alone will not provide a livelihood for their future families.

Villages everywhere in India are modernizing and changing, but progress is slow. Shiv's village is small, with only 64 houses. It has a population of 500 people. Unlike most villages, Shiv's has a small hospital, electricity, and a school.

Even as the village modernizes, people have kept many customs. For example, Hinduism plays an important role in Shiv's family and village. There are portraits of Hindu gods and goddesses in Shiv's house, and the adults pray every morning.

Shiv's parents hope that a good education will help their children lead healthier, more prosperous lives.

peanuts. These crops grow quickly in the warm, rainy climate. The largest city on the Coromandel Coast is the port city of Madras. Madras is India's fourth largest city, with 5.4 million residents.

Fort St. George is in the oldest part of Madras. This fort was built by the British in 1640, only 20 years after the Pilgrims landed at Plymouth Rock in the American colonies. From Madras the British gained control of trade up and down the coast and later established Calcutta and Bombay.

E. The Himalayan Region

The Northern Border The Himalayas run along the northern border of India. India's territory includes some of the highest peaks of the Himalayas, but lower foothills are also found along India's northern border. These foothills are lower than the Himalayas themselves, but the land is still steep. The city of Darjeeling is built on the steep sides of these foothills. Houses perch on the hillsides or nestle in protected nooks.

In the east the lower foothills have a rainy climate. Here grow thick forests of valuable woods such as teak, which is used for making fine furniture. Large areas of these foothills have been cleared for huge tea plantations. The state of Assam and the city of Darjeeling, both in eastern India, have given their names to teas that are considered to be among the best teas in the world.

Workers on tea plantations must keep an eye on tea plants and cultivate them with care as they grow. The tea plants are trimmed and kept to a height of about 2 or 3 feet (61 or 91 cm). At times they are even cut back down to the ground to begin growing again. This keeps the tea leaves fresh and young, making them the best kind for brewing tea. After the tea leaves are picked, they are weighed, dried, and sifted before being packed.

Kashmir Kashmir is a state in India in the highest and most western reaches of the Himalayas. Although small, it is well

This photo shows workers harvesting tea leaves in the Himalayan foothills.
▶ What happens to the tea leaves after they are picked?

PROCESSING TEA LEAVES

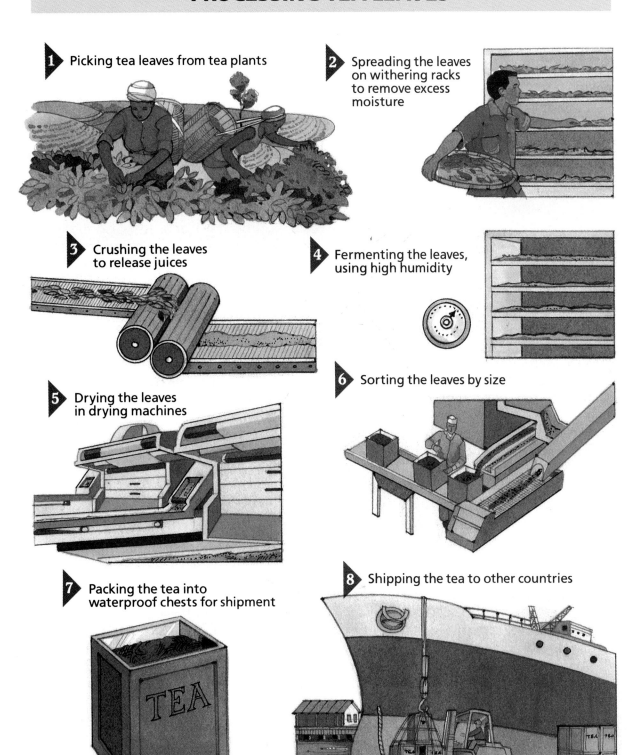

1. Picking tea leaves from tea plants

2. Spreading the leaves on withering racks to remove excess moisture

3. Crushing the leaves to release juices

4. Fermenting the leaves, using high humidity

5. Drying the leaves in drying machines

6. Sorting the leaves by size

7. Packing the tea into waterproof chests for shipment

8. Shipping the tea to other countries

TEA

Cashmere wool comes from goats like
the ones shown here.
▶ In what Indian state are goats like
these found?

known for two reasons. One is that its goats
produce a soft, luxurious wool called *cashmere* in English. A cashmere coat or sweater
is an expensive item in the United States.

The second reason for Kashmir's fame
is that India and Pakistan have fought over
this territory for several decades. Most of
the people in Kashmir are Muslim, but
their rulers throughout history have usually
been Hindu. When the new nations of India
and Pakistan were formed, there was much
disagreement about whether Kashmir should
be part of Pakistan or part of India.

Because the majority of Kashmir's population is Muslim, it seemed reasonable
for this state to join Pakistan. But the
Hindu rulers preferred to join India. This
disagreement erupted into violence until
the United Nations sent troops to Kashmir
to maintain peace.

Even today, Pakistan and India continue to disagree about Kashmir. This region is important to both countries because

many rivers begin here. Control of river
water is important during the dry season.

LESSON 2

Review

REVIEWING MAIN IDEAS
A. What are India's three main regions?
B. Why is the Ganges River plain so
   important to India?
C. How do monsoons affect the climate
   of the Ganges River plain?
D. Describe the land of the Deccan
   Plateau.
E. What valuable products come from the
   foothills of the Himalayas?

SKILLS CHECK
THINKING SKILL
On a separate sheet of paper, list the
three regions of India. Now list, under
each region's name, the products grown
in that region.

474

Ways of Life in Modern India

CONNECTIONS

Name as many different religions of the United States as you can and describe some of the different beliefs or traditions of those religions.

TERMS

caste, Aryans, autonomy

FOCUS

How did past migrations of people help to create the variety of religions in India today?

A. Old and New in India's Cities

Delhi and New Delhi In every Indian city, people practice both ancient ways and modern lifestyles. The differences between Delhi and New Delhi are especially surprising. Delhi is one of the most important cities in India's history. For centuries, Delhi was the capital city of huge empires that stretched across most of South Asia. In 1912, the British established their colonial government just outside of Delhi, in a newly built city named New Delhi.

Although Delhi and New Delhi are near each other, they have different landscapes. New Delhi, with its long, straight concrete roads and vast open lawns, has a neat and efficient appearance. Few people stroll in the streets, and the buildings seem large and cold. New Delhi was built as a showcase for the British, and it was laid out to provide plenty of space and room for growth.

In contrast, Delhi has crooked, narrow streets and is filled to the brim with busy people. The older part of Delhi is similar to the older parts of most Indian cities. Vast mazes of narrow alleyways crisscross through marketplaces. Fruit stands, tailors, watch-repair shops, shoemakers, and bread sellers are almost overrun by bicyclists, running children, beggars, and women carrying bundles of purchases.

Indian Dress Most Indian men wear pants and shirts, or a suit and tie. Many Indian women still wear the traditional *sari*, a dress made by draping graceful lengths of material over the shoulders and around the waist. The beautiful colors of the saris— "mustard-yellow and scarlet and petunia," and many shades of blue and green—swish elegantly as women walk through the streets of India's big cities and tiny villages.

Modern shops and businesses are also found in Delhi. Army officers in crisp uniforms and businessmen in well-pressed suits stroll through the streets. Policemen direct traffic, which often includes both ox-drawn carts and luxury cars. Boutiques, cafes, and movie theaters line the spacious streets of newer neighborhoods. Many of these businesses have English names, because English became a widely used language when India was a British colony.

Today many Indian children learn English in school or while traveling in the United States. Many Indian doctors, engineers, teachers, and scientists study in North America or Europe and then return to India to practice their professions.

B. Hinduism, India's Main Religion

Sacred Animals Another unforgettable sight when first visiting India is the respectful behavior Indians show toward animals. Hindus believe that every living creature has a soul and that killing or injuring an animal is a terrible thing. Cattle are especially sacred to Hindus and Hindus are not allowed to eat beef. In many places, cattle roam freely, and traffic stops to let them pass in the streets.

Hinduism is a religion of many gods. It does not have just one written holy book such as the Bible. Instead, Hindu teachings are recorded in poems and stories written in the ancient language of Sanskrit.

Benares (buh NAH reez), on the Ganges River, is a famous holy city. Hindus journey to Benares to bathe in the Ganges. They believe that this will purify, or make clean, their souls. Lining the river's banks are huge steps that lead down into the water of the Ganges. Elaborate Hindu temples and Hindu people dressed in many colors add excitement to the scenery.

Hindus believe that the soul of each living being returns after death in the body of another animal or person. This process is called *reincarnation*. At the time a person is born, his or her place in society is determined for a lifetime. This is how each person becomes a member of a **caste**, or group of people with a similar standing in society.

The Indian government has banned the use of caste to determine a person's social standing, but it is still widely practiced in India. The highest caste is the Brahmans; the lowest is the Untouchables.

The Aryans How did Hindus come to dominate India, while Muslims and Buddhists are common in other parts of South Asia? The answer is found in India's history. Hinduism was brought to South Asia about 1750 B.C. At that time, farming people living on the Ganges Plain were overrun by invaders called **Aryans**. The Aryans were warriors from the northwest who introduced many gods to India. The Aryans' beliefs gradually formed a new religion, Hinduism. All across northern India, people began to practice Hinduism.

The Aryans also introduced their languages into South Asia. Hindi is the most widespread of these languages, but many other languages are also spoken in India.

The Aryans settled across northern India but found the Deccan Plateau, farther south, rugged and difficult to farm. Because of this, the Aryans had only moderate influence on the people of the Deccan Plateau, whose culture and language are called Dravidian. However, most of the people on the Deccan Plateau added Hindu

beliefs to their own beliefs and are now considered Hindus.

C. Other Religions of India

Buddhism In the sixth century B.C., a prince named Siddhartha Gautama (sihd-DAHR tuh GOUT uh muh), who lived in northern India, left his life of luxury and began to teach a new religion that became known as Buddhism. Over many centuries, people in South Asia, Southeast Asia, China, and Japan adopted Buddhism. But Hinduism was still strong in India, and relatively few people there became Buddhists.

Islam's Influence Arab traders from North Africa and the Middle East began arriving at ports on India's western coast in the

Elaborately carved figures are part of this Hindu temple's exterior.
▶ Which group of people brought Hinduism to India?

FROM: **The Bhagavad Gita**

Translated and Interpreted by Franklin Edgerton

Hinduism teaches that a person's soul is immortal. When a person dies, his or her soul is reincarnated in a new body. Hinduism allows its followers to break free from this cycle of death and reincarnation and attain *nirvana*, or heaven. The way to reach *nirvana* is described in "The Song of the Blessed One", a poem which is part of the *Bhagavad Gita*. The poem is one of the most important religious works of the Hindu religion.

Let the disciplined man ever discipline
Himself, abiding in a secret place,
Solitary, restraining his thoughts and soul,
Free from aspirations and without possessions.

In a clean place establishing
A steady seat for himself.
That is neither too high nor too low,

. . . .

There fixing the [mind] on a single object,
Restraining the activity of his mind and senses,
Sitting on the seat, let him practice
Discipline unto self-purification.
[Straight] body, head, and neck
Holding motionless, steady,
Gazing at the tip of his own nose,
And not looking in any direction,

. . . .

Thus ever disciplining himself,
The man of discipline, with controlled mind,
. . . attains [nirvana].

The Golden Temple of Amritsar is the most holy place in the Sikh religion.
▶ In what Indian state is the city of Amritsar located?

fifth century. In the eleventh century, Arab warriors invaded the Hindu kingdoms of India and took over the land. The Arabs introduced Islam into their new empire. Most people in what are today Pakistan and Bangladesh became Muslims, and a large number of people in India follow this new religion as well.

The empire built in India by the Muslim Arabs was known as the Mogul (MOH-gul) Empire. Mogul emperors ruled a large area of South Asia from the 1500s until the middle 1800s. The Moguls were not successful in converting most Indians to Islam. But in the far north of India, in a state called the Punjab, the Muslims left a legacy that still causes conflict today. This legacy was the Sikh religion, which is based on both Hindu and Muslim beliefs. The Sikhs built their own empire and held fiercely to their customs for centuries.

The most holy place in the Sikh religion is the Golden Temple in the city of Amritsar. This beautiful marble building has a solid gold dome and a copper base.

The Sikhs consider themselves different from the Hindus and Muslims of South Asia. Their religion and culture are unique, and their homeland in the Punjab has a higher standard of living than most areas of South Asia. In recent years they have campaigned for special status and **autonomy**, or self-government, for their state. Their campaign has been bloody because the Sikhs have resorted to using terrorism.

LESSON 3

Review

REVIEWING MAIN IDEAS

A. In what ways are Delhi and New Delhi different?

B. Why is Hinduism the main religion of India?

C. How did Buddhism, Islam, and Sikhism develop in India?

SKILLS CHECK

WRITING SKILL

Imagine that you have been chosen to visit India as an exchange student. Write a short letter to the principal of your new Indian school, explaining whether you would prefer to live in Delhi or New Delhi, and why.

India's Neighbors

A. Pakistan and the Indus River

A Desert Country A huge white concrete dam is supported by 66 arches and stretches for 1 mile (1.6 km) across the Indus River of Pakistan. This huge dam holds back the waters of the Indus. The water is released slowly during the dry winter months. The dam is a reminder that the waters of the Indus River are Pakistan's lifeline.

The rains carried by the summer monsoon to India and Bangladesh almost never reach Pakistan. In fact, they never even reach the westernmost stretch of India along the border of Pakistan. The dry zone along this border is called the Thar Desert. With less than 20 inches (51 cm) of rainfall per year, it is one of the driest places in South Asia.

Pakistan's population of over 131 million people is spread out over 310,403 square miles (803,944 sq km). This is about twice the size of California. Its population density of 424 people per square mile (164 per sq km) is much lower than that of India. Most of Pakistan's people, cities, factories, and farms are located along the banks of the Indus River.

Pakistan's farmers continually face the same problem: getting enough water to grow crops. Pakistan's government has built many canals and dams to carry water for irrigation to farmers' fields.

The government began this program of building dams and canals more than a hundred years ago. It was only in recent years, however, that the construction of dams and canals was accelerated, or sped up, as the government began to modernize Pakistan's agriculture.

Besides building these new water-control systems, the government also began to introduce Pakistani farmers to the benefits of the Green Revolution. The new seeds and the new methods of growing crops have helped Pakistan's farmers rapidly increase the amount of food they produce. In fact, Pakistan has experienced an incredible increase in the output of crops such as wheat.

Sugarcane, wheat, cotton, and corn are

The *minarets*, or towers of Muslim mosques are a common sight in the cities and villages of Pakistan.
▶ Why are mosques a common sight?

also important agricultural products. Where farmers have an adequate supply of water, rice is grown as well. Pakistan is one of the world's leading producers of both cotton and rice.

Karachi Karachi, which is located on the Arabian Sea, is Pakistan's largest city, with over 7 million inhabitants. It is also Pakistan's main industrial city. Steel is produced here, using some of Pakistan's small iron ore deposits, which are located in the central part of the country. A factory that assembles automobiles from imported parts is also located in Karachi. But Pakistan's main industry is manufacturing cotton textiles. Plants that produce cotton cloth, yarn, and clothing are important to Pakistan's economy.

Karachi was once the capital city of Pakistan, but today Islamabad is the capital city. Government leaders felt that Islamabad was closer than Karachi to the heartland of Pakistan's culture in central and northern Pakistan.

B. Bangladesh, a Young Nation

When the Muslim nation of Pakistan was formed in 1947, it was divided into two parts. The area that is today the nation of Pakistan was called West Pakistan. The area that is now the nation of Bangladesh was called East Pakistan. Together the people of West Pakistan and East Pakistan belonged to one country, called Pakistan.

In 1971 the people of East Pakistan decided to separate from West Pakistan and form the country of Bangladesh. Why did this happen? And what results did this division create? To answer these questions, we need to compare Pakistan and Bangladesh.

Pakistan and Bangladesh are very different geographically and economically. You have already read about Pakistan's dry climate. Pakistan receives less than 10 inches (25 cm) of rainfall per year. Bangladesh, in contrast, has a rainy climate, with over 80 inches (203 cm) of rainfall per year. Farmers in Bangladesh usually have a problem with too much water in their fields. Their fields

When the monsoon rains arrive in Bangladesh, the Brahmaputra River floods the nearby fields.
▶ What are the advantages and disadvantages of the floods caused by the monsoon rains?

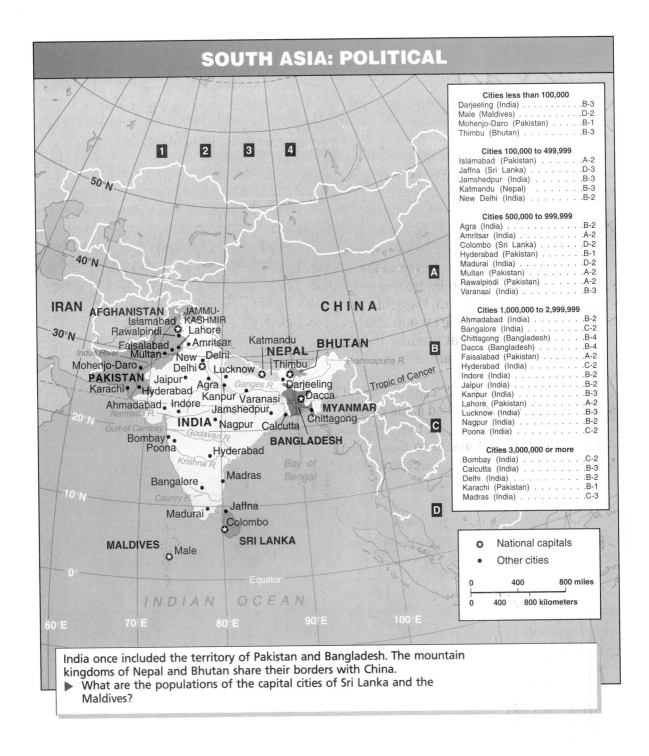

SOUTH ASIA: POLITICAL

Cities less than 100,000
Darjeeling (India) B-3
Male (Maldives) D-2
Mohenjo-Daro (Pakistan) B-1
Thimbu (Bhutan) B-3

Cities 100,000 to 499,999
Islamabad (Pakistan) A-2
Jaffna (Sri Lanka) D-3
Jamshedpur (India) B-3
Katmandu (Nepal) B-3
New Delhi (India) B-2

Cities 500,000 to 999,999
Agra (India) B-2
Amritsar (India) A-2
Colombo (Sri Lanka) D-2
Hyderabad (Pakistan) B-1
Madurai (India) D-2
Multan (Pakistan) A-2
Rawalpindi (Pakistan) A-2
Varanasi (India) B-3

Cities 1,000,000 to 2,999,999
Ahmadabad (India) B-2
Bangalore (India) C-2
Chittagong (Bangladesh) B-4
Dacca (Bangladesh) B-4
Faisalabad (Pakistan) A-2
Hyderabad (India) C-2
Indore (India) B-2
Jaipur (India) B-2
Kanpur (India) B-3
Lahore (Pakistan) A-2
Lucknow (India) B-3
Nagpur (India) B-2
Poona (India) C-2

Cities 3,000,000 or more
Bombay (India) C-2
Calcutta (India) B-3
Delhi (India) B-2
Karachi (Pakistan) B-1
Madras (India) C-3

○ National capitals
• Other cities

0   400   800 miles
0   400   800 kilometers

India once included the territory of Pakistan and Bangladesh. The mountain kingdoms of Nepal and Bhutan share their borders with China.
▶ What are the populations of the capital cities of Sri Lanka and the Maldives?

are only a few feet above sea level when the monsoon rains arrive. With the rains, the Brahmaputra and its tributaries quickly flood and wash over the farmers' fields.

Almost every inch of land in Bangladesh is covered with crops and fields. Bang-

ladesh has an area of 55,126 square miles (142,776 sq km), which means that it is about the same size as the state of Wisconsin. Over 128 million people are crowded onto this land, giving the country a population density of over 2,324 people per square mile (898 per sq km). This is more than six times the population density of Pakistan.

Bangladesh produces many food crops. Rice, tea, sugarcane, and wheat are major farm products. But even more valuable than these products is **jute**, a plant that produces a coarse, tough fiber used in making carpets and rope. Bangladesh is the world's largest producer of jute. Jute exports provide almost three fourths of Bangladesh's export income.

C. Nepal and Bhutan, the Mountain Kingdoms

Nepal High in the Himalayas, the people of the two small nations of Nepal and Bhutan live according to customs and traditions that have barely changed over the centuries. In both countries, almost everyone practices subsistence farming, growing crops such as corn and rice.

Nepal, the larger of these two countries, has about the same total land area as Bangladesh. Nepal's total population is about 21.5 million people.

Nepal has a moderate population density. Yet it has three of the most serious overpopulation problems in the world. First, Nepal's population is growing quickly. Its population size doubles every 28 years. In other words, if Nepal's population was 19 million people in the year 1990, only 28 years later, in 2018, its population would be twice as large, or 38 million people. By comparison, it takes 99 years for the population of the United States to double.

Second, most of Nepal's people are crowded together in the valleys and flat areas, so the population densities of those places are quite high. And third, large areas of Nepal are now deforested. Nepal's people depend on cutting wood for fuel and for timber. People are running out of firewood, and without trees to hold the soil on the hillsides, rocks and soil are running down into the rivers. Further downstream in the Ganges and Brahmaputra rivers, this **sediment**, or soil and other particles, washes into the rivers and clogs irrigation canals as well as the turbines that generate electricity in hydroelectric plants.

Bhutan In mountainous Bhutan, land is terraced, so soil erosion is not as serious a problem as in Nepal. Most of Bhutan's 1.8 million people practice subsistence farming and grow rice, wheat, potatoes, and corn. Many also herd yaks, goats, and sheep. Bhutan is almost self-sufficient in food.

This small country, which is about the size of Vermont and New Hampshire combined, has some coal deposits and minerals such as lead and copper. But it is only just beginning to build modern industries, such as manufacturing of cement, chemicals, and wood products. India has helped Bhutan by building modern transportation and communication facilities.

This hillside in Nepal appears to be terraced, but what you see is actually the results of soil erosion.
▶ What causes soil erosion in Nepal?

D. Sri Lanka and the Maldives

The Island Nations Off the southern coast of India are two island nations. The larger, Sri Lanka, is an island in the southern part of the Bay of Bengal. The Maldives are made up of over 1,000 small islands in the Arabian Sea.

Both island nations have warm, rainy climates, but their economies are different. The economy of the Maldives depends on fishing, coconuts, and tourism. Fresh and dried fish make up about 93 percent of the exports of the Maldives. Food, machinery, and manufactured goods must all be imported.

Unlike the Maldives, Sri Lanka was a British colony. The British built many plantations that produced tea, rubber, coconuts, rice, and spices. When it was a British colony, Sri Lanka was called Ceylon, and it was famous around the world for its excellent teas. Today these products are exported and sold on the world market.

The port city of Colombo became the island's main trading center and capital city. Colombo also has industries that produce jewelry from Sri Lanka's sapphires and rubies, along with cement, textiles, and paper.

Ethnic Conflict Sri Lanka has drawn much of the world's attention lately because of the ethnic conflict that has erupted there. The majority of Sri Lanka's people are Buddhists who speak the Singhalese (sihn huh LEEZ) language. Their ancestors were the Aryans of northern India.

People from southern India also migrated to Sri Lanka in small numbers over the centuries. They were mainly Hindus who spoke Tamil. The Tamils believe that the Singhalese discriminate against them, unfairly preventing them from getting jobs, housing, and schooling. For this reason the Tamils want to form a separate nation in Sri Lanka. To do this, some have begun a guerrilla war against the government.

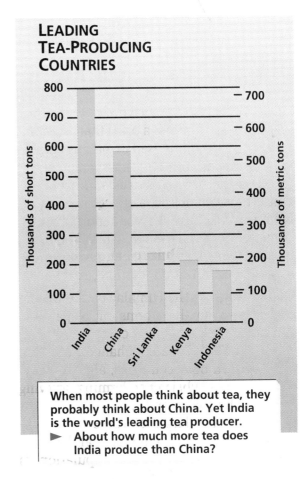

LEADING TEA-PRODUCING COUNTRIES

Thousands of short tons / Thousands of metric tons

India, China, Sri Lanka, Kenya, Indonesia

When most people think about tea, they probably think about China. Yet India is the world's leading tea producer.
► About how much more tea does India produce than China?

LESSON 4

Review

REVIEWING MAIN IDEAS

A. Why is the Indus River so important to Pakistan?

B. Why did Pakistan eventually become two separate nations?

C. How has overpopulation affected the forests of Nepal?

D. What are the main economic activities of the Maldives and Sri Lanka?

SKILLS CHECK

MAP SKILL

Use the scale on the map on page 481 to measure the distance between Karachi, Pakistan, and Dacca, Bangladesh.

THE BALANCE BETWEEN FOOD AND POPULATION

Famine, flood, drought, starvation: Reports of these catastrophes appear often in newspapers and in television news broadcasts. But because of two global changes that have begun to take place, these reports may become more infrequent. These two global changes are the green revolution and the control of population growth.

The Green Revolution

A dramatic revolution in agriculture began in the 1960s. At that time, experts predicted that as a result of increasing populations and decreasing food supplies, the world would run out of food within a few decades. These predictions led scientists working in laboratories in countries such as India, Zimbabwe, the Philippines, and Mexico to step up their efforts to find new ways of producing greater amounts of food.

The scientists developed new varieties of seeds for growing food grains, such as rice and wheat. These new types of seeds were called miracle seeds. Compared with the old varieties of seeds, the new seeds produced much more food on each plant. For example, with the new rice seeds, farmers could grow up to three times as much rice as they could with older types of seeds. Even farmers with small plots of land could grow more food with the miracle seeds.

The scientists' development of miracle seeds was only the first step toward increasing the world's food supply. The second step was to convince farmers in India and other countries to try the new seeds. Many farmers, especially those with small family farms, were reluctant to experiment with new technology. If the new seeds did not work, a farm family could lose its entire harvest and not have enough to eat. In India, for example, few farm families had savings accounts or government welfare, so the families could starve if their farms did not provide most

Scientists in India and other countries developed new types of seeds to produce larger harvests of grains, such as wheat.
▶ What do you think the wheel shown in the right-hand photo is used for?

484

of the household food. For many farmers the risk was too great. They continued to follow the old ways of farming.

For the farmers who were willing to take the risk and try the new seeds, government leaders had to take another step. They had to spend money and effort to help the farmers use the new seeds correctly to get the best results. Miracle seeds require special treatment. They need large quantities of fertilizers and irrigation water. Miracle seeds are also easily ruined by plant diseases and insects, so the farmers had to learn to use chemicals such as pesticides and insecticides.

Government advisors traveled to farms and showed farmers how to get the most out of their miracle seeds. The advisors also helped farmers get loans to buy the seeds, fertilizers, chemicals, and equipment needed to produce good crops. These efforts paid off in India, where many farmers began using the new seeds and new technology. In northern India, for example, farmers who received government help in using the new seeds quickly increased their wheat harvest. Wells were drilled to provide irrigation water for wheat fields, and farmers learned to use fertilizers. In the state called Punjab, over 75 percent of the wheat farms began using miracle seeds.

India is an example of a country that has had success with the *green revolution.* This term refers to the worldwide effort to increase food production through the use of high-yielding seed varieties, pesticides and other chemicals, and improved land management. In India, food production gradually increased, and the world's image of the country began to change. National pride increased, for India evoked images not of starving children but of

Irrigated fields in the Indus River valley produce wheat and other crops.
▶ In what part of India is the Indus River valley located?

local farmers using modern techniques to plant fertile, well-irrigated fields.

Future Food Supplies

By the 1980s, India's farmers were producing twice as much food as they did in the 1950s. In fact, the country was producing more food than it needed and was able to begin exporting grains such as rice and wheat. But in looking toward India's future, experts explain that these food increases are not a permanent solution to India's food shortages. Droughts, floods, or plant diseases could cause a major disaster. If one or two years go by with small harvests, people will have to use their food reserves, or the surplus crops from previous years. Once these reserves are gone, even miracle seeds will not produce enough food quickly enough to feed everyone. India and other countries will then have to turn to the rest of the world for help and food donations.

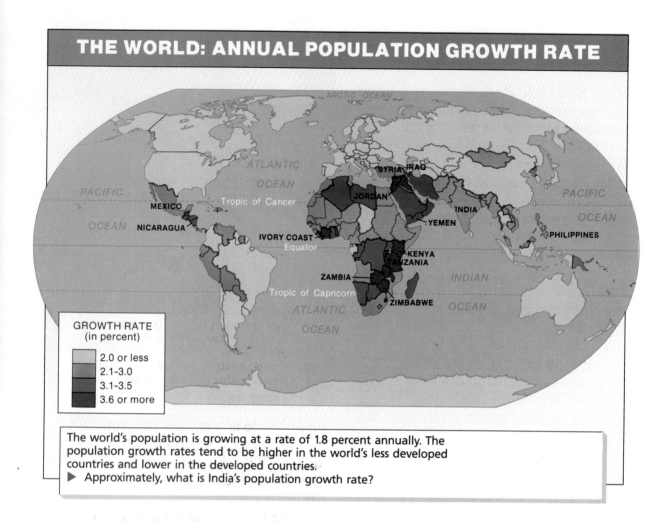

THE WORLD: ANNUAL POPULATION GROWTH RATE

GROWTH RATE
(in percent)

- 2.0 or less
- 2.1–3.0
- 3.1–3.5
- 3.6 or more

The world's population is growing at a rate of 1.8 percent annually. The population growth rates tend to be higher in the world's less developed countries and lower in the developed countries.

▶ Approximately, what is India's population growth rate?

Another factor that threatens the success of the green revolution is the continuing population growth. Although farmers have learned to produce more food, the number of mouths to feed has grown even more quickly. Miracle seeds are barely able to keep up with current population increases. What, then, can India and other countries do to produce enough food to feed their future populations?

A Plan for Producing More Food

The strategy for feeding all the world's people involves two parts: raising even more food and controlling population growth. To raise more food, Indian government leaders plan to continue to take advantage of the research and technology of the green revolution. For example, rice farmers in eastern and southern India have had problems with the miracle seeds. The new rice plants became infected with diseases and insects more often than wheat plants do. More research is needed to help these farmers get good results from miracle seeds and improve their rice harvests.

India's government wants to provide loans and education to farmers who still use the old farming methods and types of seeds. In addition, more food can be produced by encouraging farmers to use land that has never been farmed before. Thus the government wants to build more irrigation canals to allow farming in new areas, and more roads, bridges, and storage facilities for moving and storing farm products.

Another way to increase food production is to reorganize farm boundaries. For example, India's government would like to redraw property boundaries of tiny farms so that each family would own a larger piece of farmland and would produce more crops.

Plans for Limiting Population Growth

The second part of the strategy for feeding all the world's people involves slowing population growth. The populations of countries around the world are growing quickly because modern medicine helps to save lives. Diseases can be prevented or cured more easily than ever before. Also, as a result of the green revolution, people have more food, better nutrition, and healthier lives, so more people live longer and fewer people die. The end result is rapid increases in population.

Many countries, including India, have decided to try to limit population growth by decreasing their birthrates. India's government is encouraging all the country's people to participate in the population control effort. Projects have been organized to convince families that they should have fewer children. For example, thousands of small clinics in the countryside now provide basic medical care for children to ensure that they survive. In this way, healthy children are able to help out on farms and at home, and their families do not need to have as many children as before.

India's leaders have also found that education plays an important role in controlling population. In southern India many more children are being sent to school to learn valuable skills. Then when

India's leaders have found that education plays a role in controlling population.
▶ What subject do you think these schoolchildren are studying?

they become adults, they can work part time or full time to help support their families. With this extra income, the families do not need to have as many children.

The world is watching and waiting to see the results of the green revolution and population control efforts in India. Many countries are only beginning to experiment with these two strategies. India's success could encourage more countries to look ahead and help ensure that our future food supplies will feed all the people of the world.

THINKING CRITICALLY

1. To what countries of the world do you think the green revolution and population control are especially important issues, and why?

2. What problems might some farming techniques of the green revolution present?

3. In what other ways might education be a useful tool in helping to control population growth?

REVIEWING TERMS

From the list below, choose a term that could be used in place of the underlined words in each sentence. Rewrite the sentences on a separate sheet of paper.

subcontinent
monsoon
caste
jute
sediment

1. The people of Bangladesh make carpets and rope from <u>a plant that produces a coarse, tough fiber</u>.
2. <u>The huge triangle</u> formed by India and its neighbors is a <u>landmass that belongs to a larger continent</u>.
3. In the Ganges and Brahmaputra rivers, <u>soil and other particles</u> washes into the rivers and clog irrigation canals.
4. In traditional Indian culture, each person belongs to a particular <u>group of people of similar standing in society</u>.
5. India's climate is affected by the <u>seasonal wind</u> that blows through the country.

REVIEWING THE FACTS

On a separate sheet of paper, answer the following questions in complete sentences.

1. What two important characteristics of India and the surrounding region does the Taj Mahal display?
2. What two geographical features cut the subcontinent of South Asia off from the rest of Asia?
3. In what ways are India and China similar countries?
4. What are the three major landforms of South Asia?

5. How have religious differences caused problems for South Asia?
6. How is the western part of the Ganges River plain different from the eastern part of the Ganges River plain?
7. What are some beliefs of Hinduism, India's main religion?
8. What nations are neighbors of India?
9. How do the climates of Pakistan and Bangladesh differ?
10. What problems in Nepal are caused by deforestation?

WRITING ABOUT GOVERNMENT

If you were a member of the United Nations you might become involved in a debate about whether the state of Kashmir should remain part of India or become part of Pakistan. Write a paragraph that explains why you think Kashmir, which has a largely Muslim population, should be a part of India or Pakistan.

THINKING CRITICALLY

On a separate sheet of paper, answer the following questions in complete sentences.

1. Why is jute a more valuable crop to the economy of Bangladesh than rice, tea, or sugarcane?
2. What problems could be caused by overpopulation?
3. Why do you think the Indian government outlawed the caste system?
4. What steps could Nepal take to decrease its soil erosion?
5. Why do you think the people of Nepal and Bhutan live according to customs and traditions that have changed very little?

SUMMARIZING THE CHAPTER

On a separate sheet of paper, draw a graphic organizer like the one shown here. Copy the information from this graphic organizer to the one you have drawn. Fill in the blanks for each region with important facts about that region. Answers may include the region's landforms, climates, cities, agricultural products, industries, religions, ethnic groups, or other facts that you think are important.

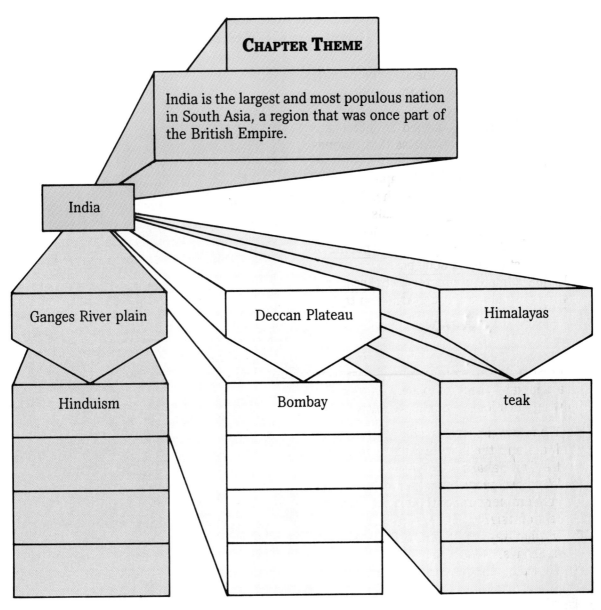

CHAPTER THEME

India is the largest and most populous nation in South Asia, a region that was once part of the British Empire.

India

Ganges River plain

Deccan Plateau

Himalayas

Hinduism

Bombay

teak

20 THE MIDDLE EAST

The Middle East: Crossroads of the World

CONNECTIONS

Look at the photographs in this lesson. What are some of the words that you would use to describe the Middle East?

TERMS

ethnocentrism, oasis, Fertile Crescent

FOCUS

How has the Middle East played an important role in ancient and modern history?

A. The Middle East: A Strategic Region

A Violent Region On the morning of October 24, 1983, Americans woke up to morning newspaper stories similar to this one from the *New York Times.*

> *WASHINGTON, Oct. 23—President Reagan, voicing outrage over the "despicable" destruction of the Marine Corps headquarters in Lebanon, called on the nation today to be more determined than ever to keep a force in that country and resist "the bestial [fierce] nature of those who would assume power."*
>
> *The President, plunging into a day of emergency strategy meetings. . . denounced the unidentified forces behind the attack and said the nation "must be more determined than ever that they [the unidentified forces] cannot take over that vital and strategic area of the earth."*

The terrible act the President was referring to was the bombing of the United States Marine barracks in Beirut, Lebanon. Over 200 Marines were killed in the bombing. President Reagan had sent the Marines to Lebanon to help end the conflict between groups trying to gain control of Lebanon.

Americans and the Middle East Why would the United States be interested in trying to end fighting in Lebanon, one of the smallest countries in the Middle East? Like all important world powers in history, the United States realizes that Lebanon, and all of the Middle East, is in a strategic location. It is here that three of the world's continents—Africa, Asia, and Europe—meet. It is here that by way of the Suez Canal, ships can cross from the Mediterranean Sea to the Red Sea and eastward to India and China. And most important, it is here that more than half of the world's known oil reserves are found.

The United States is also interested in the Middle East for another reason: Israel. This small country on the eastern edge of the Mediterranean Sea is the United States' most important ally, or friend, in the Middle East.

B. The Geography of the Middle East

What is the Middle East? In the previous chapters, we have looked at what was once called the Far East: Japan, China, the countries of Southeast Asia, and India and its neighbors. The countries that stretch from the eastern edge of the Mediterranean Sea down the Arabian Peninsula and all the way west to Afghanistan are called the Middle East. The name Middle East was given to the region by British geographers during the nineteenth century.

The people of the region, however, do not consider themselves to be in the "middle" of the East. Both the terms *Far East* and *Middle East* are examples of **ethnocentrism**. Ethnocentrism is looking at the rest of the world and making judgments about it based only on your own cultural background and experience. Because the British considered themselves to be the center of the world, they thought all other parts of the earth were either east or west of the United Kingdom.

491

▶ Three of the world's major religions consider Jerusalem a holy city.

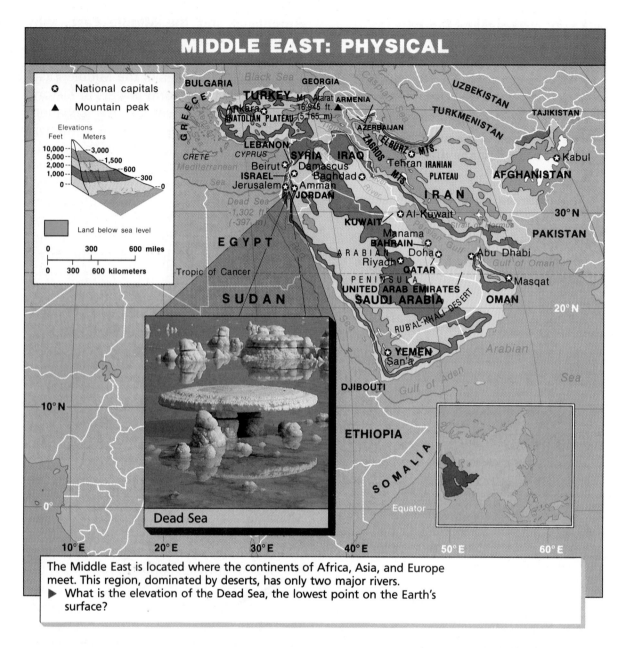

MIDDLE EAST: PHYSICAL

Legend:
- ⊙ National capitals
- ▲ Mountain peak

Elevations
Feet	Meters
10,000	3,000
5,000	1,500
2,000	600
1,000	300
0	0

Land below sea level

0 300 600 miles
0 300 600 kilometers

Dead Sea

The Middle East is located where the continents of Africa, Asia, and Europe meet. This region, dominated by deserts, has only two major rivers.
▶ What is the elevation of the Dead Sea, the lowest point on the Earth's surface?

The Highlands The countries of the Middle East can be divided into three geographic regions: the highlands, the Arabian Peninsula, and the Fertile Crescent. The highland region includes Turkey, Iran, and Afghanistan. As you can see from the map above, a series of mountain ranges stretches across these countries. The rugged Taurus Mountains rise in Turkey, where they are more than 8,000 feet (2,438 m) high. The Zagros Mountains cross the southern reaches of Iran. The Elburz Mountains cross the northern part of Iran and border the Caspian Sea. The mountains of Iran are often the site of devastating earthquakes. The quake that occurred in the northern mountains in June 1990 killed more than 35,000 people, injured more than 100,000, and left more than 500,000 homeless.

Afghanistan is home to the towering peaks of the Hindu Kush, a range of desolate mountains that form the western edge of the Himalayas. The Hindu Kush and the Himalayas come together in a rugged part of Afghanistan known as the Pamir Knot. The Pamir Knot gets its name because it is the meeting point, or knot, that ties together the Himalayas and the Hindu Kush.

The Arabian Peninsula The Arabian Peninsula, the second region of the Middle East, is the easiest to find on a map. Bordered by the Red Sea, the Persian Gulf, and the Arabian Sea, this giant peninsula is about 1 million square miles (3 million sq km) in area. The largest country in the Middle East, Saudi Arabia, occupies most of the peninsula. Much of the Arabian Peninsula is covered by three deserts. One of these, which is called the Empty Quarter, or the Rub 'al-Khali in Arabic, covers 250,000 square miles (648,000 sq km). Here in this desolate, barren region, mountains of sand

reach heights of over 900 feet (300 m). Only a few adventurers have dared to cross this dry, hot desert. Most people live in the cities along the coasts of the Arabian Peninsula or near an **oasis**. An oasis is a place in the desert that has enough water for plants and trees to grow.

The Fertile Crescent The map on page 492 shows an area north of the Persian Gulf that includes the countries of Iraq, Syria, Lebanon, Israel, and Jordan. This is the **Fertile Crescent**. The Fertile Crescent is a 1,000-mile- (1,600-km-) long area of flat, fertile land shaped like a crescent moon and wrapped around the northern end of the deserts of the Arabian Peninsula. Three major rivers flow through the Fertile Crescent: the Tigris, the Euphrates, and the Jordan. With irrigation water from these

Oil production and shipping is vital to the economy of Saudi Arabia.
▶ On what peninsula is Saudi Arabia located?

The Marsh Arabs live at the confluence of the Tigris and Euphrates rivers.
▶ What do you think are the houses shown above made from?

At bedtime you put on *pa-jameh* and sleep on your *matrah*, or mattress.

The people of the Middle East have also made use of many Western ideas and inventions. During the time that Europe was plunged into the Dark Ages, Arab scholars and writers preserved the writings of the ancient Greeks and Romans. They studied the ideas and the practices of these ancient Western civilizations concerning medicine, mathematics, and astronomy, and helped to develop them further.

Three Important Religions The Middle East is known as the birthplace of three of the world's religions: Christianity, Islam, and Judaism. Each religion considers Jerusalem, the capital city of Israel, a holy city. Christians make special pilgrimages to the city to visit the site where Jesus Christ was crucified. Followers of Islam believe that the founder of Islam, Muhammad, ascended to heaven from here. For Jews, Jerusalem is a very special city; it was here that the first temple was built. A visitor to Jerusalem would find churches, mosques, and temples throughout this ancient and historic city.

rivers, farmers grow crops that include wheat, barley, rye, carrots, onions, and garlic.

C. The People of the Middle East

A Mixture of Many Peoples The Middle East is sometimes called the Arab World. Yet while Arabs make up the largest part of the population of the Middle East, they are not the only people who live here. Many other ethnic groups, including Turks, Israelis, Iranians, Armenians, and Kurds, are found throughout the Middle East.

Cultural Influences The people of the Middle East have made many contributions to the world. During the day, you and your family may make use of them. In the morning, your parents may drink *qahwa*, or coffee, which was first roasted by the Arabs. At school, you study *al-jabr*, or algebra. In the evening, you may sit on the *suffa*, or sofa, and read a *makhzan*, or magazine.

LESSON 1

Review

REVIEWING MAIN IDEAS

A. Why is the Middle East important to the United States?
B. What are the major landforms of the three regions that make up the Middle East?
C. How is religion an important part of Middle Eastern culture?

SKILLS CHECK

MAP SKILL

Turn to the map on page 492. List the Middle Eastern countries that touch the borders of the following continents:

Africa   Asia   Europe

The Highlands of the Middle East

CONNECTIONS

What are some of the ways in which religion can influence the way a country is governed?

TERMS

strait, qanat, Shiite, Sunni, theocracy

FOCUS

In what ways is Turkey different from Iran and Afghanistan?

At 16,945 feet (5,165 m), Mount Ararat is the highest peak in Turkey.
▶ How would you describe the land near the base of Mount Ararat?

A. Turkey, Between East and West

The Straits If you look at the map on page 492, you can see that the northern tip of Turkey is split off from the rest of the country by two of the world's most strategic **straits**—the Bosporus and the Dardanelles. A strait is a narrow waterway that connects two larger bodies of water. These two straits connect the Black Sea with the Mediterranean Sea. In the past, these narrow straits provided the main crossing points between Europe and Asia for traders and armies. Today Russia, Ukraine, and many other countries depend on passage through the Bosporus and Dardanelles to transport goods and people.

The tip of Turkey, north of the straits, borders on Bulgaria and Greece. Turkey's southern border faces Iran, Iraq, and Syria. The country's northern boundary is on the Black Sea. Georgia and Armenia, former republics of the Soviet Union, are located to the northeast.

Most of Turkey's territory is south of the straits. This area, which is called the Anatolian Peninsula, is home to the country's major cities and economic regions.

The Taurus Mountains form the northern border of the Anatolian Peninsula. These mountains force the winds to drop their moisture on the peninsula. The rains that fall allow Turkish farmers to grow wheat, cotton, tobacco, and hazelnuts. The Taurus Mountains also hold important deposits of coal, chromium, and other minerals. Turkey has the Middle East's largest nonfuel mineral deposits. The country has worked hard to use these minerals to develop industries.

The Ottomans The modern country of Turkey was once the heart of the Ottoman Empire. This empire stretched from Egypt in North Africa, through the Middle East, and north into Romania and southern Russia. The Ottomans, who were Muslim Turks, ruled their empire for over 600 years. The ancient city of Constantinople, which is now named Istanbul, was the capital of the Ottoman Empire.

The end of the Ottoman Empire came after World War I. During the war the Ottomans fought on the side of Germany. The Ottomans and the Germans were defeated, and in 1918 the winning nations, which included France, Italy, and the United

The ancient city of Constantinople, now called Istanbul, was the capital of the Ottoman Empire in what is now Turkey.
▶ What is the capital of Turkey today?

Kingdom, carved the empire into many smaller countries. The area now known as Turkey is all that is left of the former empire.

Modern Turkey The collapse of the Ottoman Empire brought about enormous changes in Turkey. Most of these changes were the result of one man: Mustafa Kemal. Kemal, who became Turkey's leader, changed the way the Turks were ruled and how they lived. Turkey was proclaimed a republic, with Kemal as its president. The capital was moved to a new city, Ankara, which was in the center of the country's new boundaries.

Kemal was determined to modernize Turkey and to make it more like the countries of Europe. People had to wear European-style clothing, and the Turkish alphabet was changed from Arabic letters to Roman letters. Women were given the right to vote and to receive an education. Because of his enormous influence, Kemal was given the name *Atatürk*, which means "the father of modern Turkey."

Today, Turkey is a member of NATO and considers itself more a part of Europe than a part of the Middle East. The country is poor, however. Millions of Turks in search of jobs have migrated to Western European countries such as Germany. Turkey has also suffered from military dictatorships. But the new democratic government hopes that it can join the European Union and make Turkey into a strong, prosperous nation.

B. Iran: The Land of Ancient Persia

An Arid Land Like Turkey, Iran was once the heart of an empire. This was the Persian Empire, which ruled parts of the Middle East more than 2,000 years ago. The Persian language is still used in Iran, although it is now called Farsi (FAHR see).

The geography of Iran is quite different from that of Turkey. Northern Iran is bounded by the Elburz Mountains. To the east and south are the Zagros Mountains. The center of the country is the Plateau of Iran. The Plateau of Iran consists mainly of flat areas that are actually dried up lake beds. The plateau is an arid region, with few towns and people.

Qanats The ruins of the Persian Empire's magnificent capital city, Persepolis, are found on the dry Plateau of Iran. How did the people of this large city find water in such a dry part of the country? The answer lies in a system of irrigation that has been used throughout the Middle East and North Africa for thousands of years.

Rain and snow that fall on the Zagros Mountains form small streams that run off the mountains and seep, or slowly flow, into the ground to form ground water. Digging wells to pump the ground water into irrigation canals is not useful in the desert; most of the water would evaporate before it flowed to where it was needed. The ancient Persians avoided this problem by developing an ingenious system of un-derground tunnels called **qanats** (kah NATS). The qanats allow the ground water to flow underground until it reaches a flat area with fertile soils.

The qanat system allows farming along the dry edges of the Plateau of Iran. Crops are also grown in the foothills of the Zagros Mountains. There is also farming along the Zayandeh River, which flows out of the Zagros Mountains. This is Iran's largest river, and it is in the most fertile part of the country. Most of Iran's 64.6 million people live in the foothills of the mountain ranges and along the irrigated sections of the plateau.

The Kurds The mountain regions of Iran are home to an ethnic group called the Kurds. There are about 13 million Kurds throughout the Middle East. Large Kurdish populations are found in the mountains of

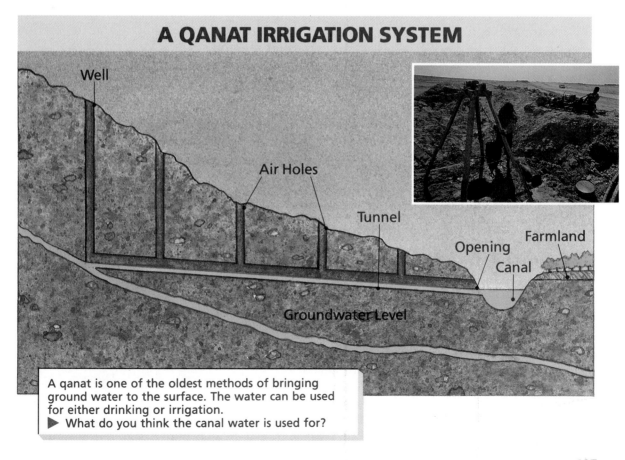

A QANAT IRRIGATION SYSTEM

Well

Air Holes

Tunnel

Opening

Farmland

Canal

Groundwater Level

A qanat is one of the oldest methods of bringing ground water to the surface. The water can be used for either drinking or irrigation.
▶ What do you think the canal water is used for?

During the reign of Ayatollah Khomeini (left), Iranian women were not allowed to wear Western-style clothes (right).
▶ What are these women wearing?

Turkey and Iraq. Most Kurds make a living by herding sheep and goats.

The Kurds have not been treated well by the governments of the countries they live in. For this reason, many Kurds would like to see their traditional homeland, which stretches through the mountains of Turkey and Iraq, become an independent country.

C. Oil, Revolution, and War

Oil and the Shah Iran's economy depends almost entirely on the export of oil. Pipelines carry oil from the huge oilfields near the Zagros Mountains to ports on the Persian Gulf. Supertankers from around the world fill up with the oil.

Iran has used the money from the sale of oil to develop the country's economy. One of the most ambitious efforts to turn Iran into a modern, industrial nation occurred under the shah Mohammed Reza Pahlavi. *Shah* is the Farsi word for "ruler." The shah introduced land reform, giving larger pieces of land to farmers. His government built new factories in the country's cities. Like Turkey's Atatürk, the shah also tried to make Islam less powerful. Women were allowed to vote and to attend school.

Islamic Revolution The shah's reforms were not met with approval, especially by

Iran's **Shiites** (SHEE yts). The Shiites make up one of the two main branches of Islam. The other branch is made up of **Sunnites** (SOON yts). The Shiites and the Sunnites have different beliefs about how to practice their religion.

Over 90 percent of all Iranians are Shiites. A growing number of Iran's Shiites grew dissatisfied with the shah's attempts to make Iran a more secular nation. In 1979 they staged a revolution against the shah. Led by a man called Ayatollah Ruhollah Khomeini (eye yuh TOH luh roo HOH luh koh MAY nee), the Shiite revolutionaries turned Iran into a **theocracy**, a nation ruled according to religious laws instead of laws passed by the people. Strict Islamic laws were to be followed; women were no longer allowed to vote, and Western-style clothes, especially for women, were considered improper.

Attacks on the United States The new revolutionary government also changed Iran's policies toward the United States. Under the shah, Iran and the United States had been good friends. The Ayatollah and his supporters believed that the United

498

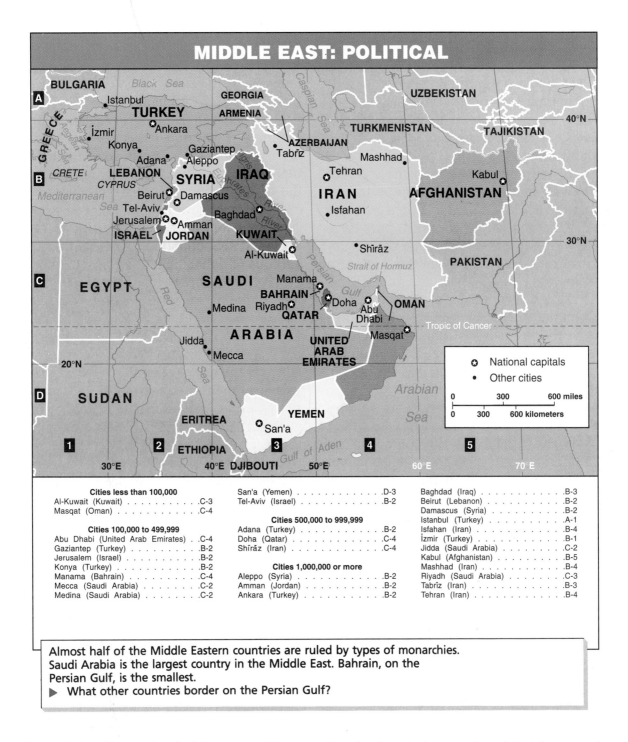

MIDDLE EAST: POLITICAL

Cities less than 100,000
Al-Kuwait (Kuwait) C-3
Masqat (Oman) C-4

Cities 100,000 to 499,999
Abu Dhabi (United Arab Emirates) . .C-4
Gaziantep (Turkey) B-2
Jerusalem (Israel) B-2
Konya (Turkey) B-2
Manama (Bahrain) C-4
Mecca (Saudi Arabia) C-2
Medina (Saudi Arabia) C-2

San'a (Yemen) D-3
Tel-Aviv (Israel) B-2

Cities 500,000 to 999,999
Adana (Turkey) B-2
Doha (Qatar) C-4
Shīrāz (Iran) C-4

Cities 1,000,000 or more
Aleppo (Syria) B-2
Amman (Jordan) B-2
Ankara (Turkey) B-2

Baghdad (Iraq) B-3
Beirut (Lebanon) B-2
Damascus (Syria) B-2
Istanbul (Turkey) A-1
Isfahan (Iran) B-4
İzmir (Turkey) B-1
Jidda (Saudi Arabia) C-2
Kabul (Afghanistan) B-5
Mashhad (Iran) B-4
Riyadh (Saudi Arabia) C-3
Tabrīz (Iran) B-3
Tehran (Iran) B-4

Almost half of the Middle Eastern countries are ruled by types of monarchies.
Saudi Arabia is the largest country in the Middle East. Bahrain, on the
Persian Gulf, is the smallest.
▶ What other countries border on the Persian Gulf?

States helped keep the shah in power. When he was overthrown, the new government showed its hostility toward the United States by taking Americans hostage and engaging in terrorism in the Middle East.

A few years later a war broke out between Iran and its neighbor, Iraq. Hundreds of thousands of Iranians and Iraqis were killed in the fighting, and Iran's economy suffered drastically. The war ended in 1988. A year later the leader of Iran's revolution, Ayatollah Khomeini, died. The new leader of Iran has made some changes in the way the country is governed.

D. Afghanistan: Gateway to the East

A Landlocked Country East of Iran is the nation of Afghanistan. Afghanistan, which is about the size of the state of Texas, is one of the largest landlocked countries in Asia. For more than 20 centuries, invaders and traders have swept through Afghanistan on their way to and from India. They have made their way into India through the Khyber (KYE bur) Pass, which allows passage through the mountains that make up Afghanistan's eastern border.

Almost two thirds of Afghanistan is mountainous. The highest mountain range is the Hindu Kush, which cuts through the middle of the country. The Hindu Kush are rugged, barren, dry mountains. The people who live here are herders.

But Afghanistan is not only a country of dry mountains. Oases on the dry desert plains and rainfall on the valleys of the mountain ranges have made Afghanistan famous for its fruit orchards. Crops grown by Afghan farmers include grapes, apples, cherries, wheat, and cotton.

Invasion and War In 1979 the Soviet Union invaded Afghanistan because of fighting between members of Afghanistan's Communist government. The Soviet Union set up a new Communist government in the capital city of Kabul. Afghans living in the rugged mountain areas refused to accept the new government. Many began a guerrilla war against the Soviet troops. The United States supported the guerrillas with millions of dollars in aid and weapons.

In 1988 the Soviet Union's soldiers left Afghanistan. The Afghan guerrillas continued to fight, hoping to replace the Communist government put in power by the Soviet Union. In 1992 the Communist government resigned as the Afghan guerrillas captured Kabul. However, peace did not return to Afghanistan. Instead, rival guerrilla groups fought for power. The country suffered greatly as fighting continued. By the mid-1990s, 1 million people had died, and 6 million had fled the country.

Many Afghan children attend schools set up by people who fight their government.
▶ How is this school different from the school you attend?

LESSON 2

Review

REVIEWING MAIN IDEAS

A. How did Atatürk modernize Turkey?
B. Why are qanats used in the deserts of Iran?
C. How did Iran's Shiites react to the shah's program to modernize Iran?
D. What effects did the Soviet invasion have on Afghanistan?

SKILLS CHECK

THINKING SKILL

The Constitution of the United States says that there should be a separation between religion and government. Why, do you think, did the Iranian Shiites not want to separate religion from public life?

LESSON 3

The Fertile Crescent

CONNECTIONS
What are some of the ways in which countries can try to solve conflicts that they have with each other?

TERMS
monotheism, Palestinian, Bedouin

FOCUS
Why is there conflict between Israel and the Arab countries of the Middle East?

A. Syria and Lebanon

Two Countries from One The Ottoman Empire included the region that extended along the eastern coast of the Mediterranean Sea. When the European powers divided up the Ottoman Empire, they created several new territories in this region. At first these territories were under the control of the United Kingdom and France. By the 1940s, however, the Europeans had granted them independence. One of these territories under the control of France was divided into the independent countries of Syria and Lebanon.

Syria Unlike most Middle Eastern countries, Syria has few oil deposits. But Syria, which is about the size of North Dakota, is rich in water and agricultural lands. Between 25 and 40 inches (63 and 102 cm) of rain fall along Syria's Mediterranean coast. This is a large amount of rain by Middle Eastern standards, and the farmers along the coast can easily grow wheat, citrus fruits, and olives. Two rivers, the Euphrates in the east and the Orontes in the west, allow irrigated farming in other parts of the country. The abundant crops that grow in the farmland watered by these rivers allow almost 16 million people to live in Syria. Southern Syria is mainly dry, barren desert.

An Ancient City Damascus, the country's largest city, is also the capital. Damascus

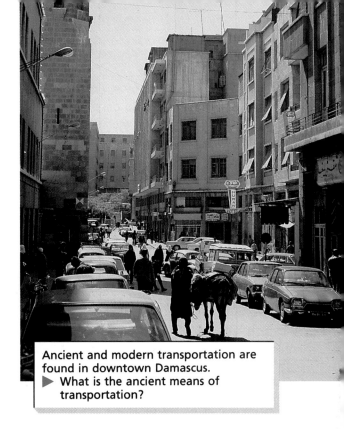

Ancient and modern transportation are found in downtown Damascus.
▶ What is the ancient means of transportation?

is an ancient city; it is considered to be the oldest continuously inhabited city in the entire world. Damascus sits on the site of an ancient oasis that is fed by the Barada River.

City life in Damascus is similar to that found in many other desert cities of the Middle East. Here is how one visitor described a typical day in Damascus.

> *The day begins in the cool dawn, when the streets surrounding the Old City become a vast open-air market, with thousands of carts displaying fresh vegetables and fruit. By ten or so, the shops have opened, both in the darkened souk [bazaar] and narrow streets of the Old City and in the modern downtown. (Even there, the tradition of the small merchant remains the rule; there are no department stores in Damascus.) Until about one o'clock in the afternoon, commerce is intense. . . . As the heat approaches its peak, the shopkeepers lower their shutters. . . . The city naps through the afternoon, waking again as the sun descends and the temperature. . . begins to drop.*

501

At five or so, the shops and most of the business office are open again, but now the city seems less devoted to commerce than to play. Promenading families tour the downtown streets, window-shopping, nibbling pastries from trays in bake shops, sipping coffee in the cafés. . . . At eight, when the offices close, secretaries and clerks pour out onto the streets . . . and by ten, when bright lights are switched off in the store windows, parents have their children in hand and are headed home for bed. . . .

Damascus is located in the southwestern corner of Syria, near a range of mountains. On a clear day a person can stand on these mountains and see into the lands of Syria's neighbor, Lebanon.

Lebanon Compared with Syria, Lebanon is much smaller and has many more problems. Until about 1975, however, Lebanon and its beautiful capital city of Beirut were considered to be "gems" in the Middle East.

Part of Lebanon's appeal comes from its climate and geography. A mild Mediterranean climate makes Beirut somewhat like southern California. In the past, tourists from the surrounding desert countries came to Lebanon's beaches during the hot summers to enjoy the cool sea breezes.

The Lebanon Mountains abruptly rise from the Mediterranean coast. They range upward to 9,000 feet (2,743 m) in height and are snow-covered during the winter. The Lebanon Mountains form the center of Lebanon, and continue almost its entire length. To the east of the Lebanon Mountains is the Bekáa (bih KAH) Valley, where wheat and citrus fruits are raised.

Civil War The Middle East is sometimes called the World of Islam, but that name does not accurately describe all of the Middle East. In Lebanon, for example, over one third of the population is Christian

Large parts of the city of Beirut were destroyed in the civil war between Lebanese Christians and Muslims.
▶ In what year did the civil war begin in Lebanon?

rather than Muslim. For many years after independence, the members of these two religions lived together peacefully. In 1975, however, a civil war erupted between the Christians and the Muslims in Lebanon.

Various Muslim and Christian groups fought for control of the countryside and Beirut, the capital city. The war continued for 16 years. In 1991 the different fighting groups surrendered their weapons to the Lebanese army as a new government was formed. Slowly peace returned to the country as its people rebuilt their beautiful capital city of Beirut. By the mid-1990s, Lebanon seemed to be recovering from war.

B. Israel, the Land of Milk and Honey

The Promised Land Four thousand years ago, a group of nomadic herders traveled from the desert and entered the land they believed their God had promised them. The Hebrews, as these nomads were called, described this new, promised land as "flowing with milk and honey." Part of that land is known today as Israel.

The Hebrews, who were the ancestors of the Jews, practiced **monotheism**. Monotheism is the belief in only one God. The Hebrews were the first people to practice monotheism. Their beliefs were simple, as shown in this passage from the Hebrew Bible.

> *It has been shown to you, O man, what is good*
> > *and what the Lord requires of you;*
> *Only to do justice*
> > *and to love loyally*
> > *and to walk humbly with your God*

Exile and Return By about 900 B.C., the Jewish people had built a great kingdom in their promised land. The capital was Jerusalem, which was the site of a huge temple built of stone and gold. The temple and the kingdom were destroyed when the Romans conquered this region in A.D. 72.

Israeli children celebrate a harvest on a kibbutz, a type of farm-village in which the people who live there share the work, property, and income.
▶ What kind of crop is shown here?

The Romans forced most of the Jews to leave their land, which the Romans called Palestine. Over the next 1,900 years, Palestine was conquered by many peoples. Among the last to occupy Palestine were the Arabs and the Turks. During all this time, there was always a small Jewish population in Palestine.

In the nineteenth century, Jews who were scattered throughout the world began to dream of returning to their ancient homeland. Fleeing persecution, numbers of Jews, especially from Eastern Europe, came to Palestine. They either bought or rented land from the Arabs and Turks and began to try to rebuild the land of milk and honey. The movement for a modern Jewish homeland grew, and finally, in 1948, the independent state of Israel was established.

Transforming the Land In the years since independence, Israel has become one of the Fertile Crescent's most prosperous, modern countries. But this nation, which is only about the size of Massachusetts, has few natural resources, has a small population, and shares borders with hostile neighbors. What, then, accounts for its growth?

One factor has been Israel's climate and land. Israel's main geographic features are a coastal plain, some hills and mountain highlands, and the deep Jordan River valley. Much of the coastal region and the northern hills around Lake Tiberias receive enough rainfall for agriculture. The southern part of the country is a desert known as the Negev. The Israelis have built a pipeline to transport the water from the Jordan River to irrigate farmland in the Negev.

The major reason for Israel's success, however, has been the hard work and energy of the Israeli people. By the early twentieth century, Israel was as one writer said,"a country whose valleys were largely malarial swamps, whose pastures had been grazed down to the ground and turned into dust-bowls, whose hills had been [stripped] of forests.'' By the mid-1960s, the Israeli settlers had changed this landscape to make the desert bloom with fruit orchards and cropland.

Industry Aid from other countries, especially the United States, and funds from Jewish people around the world, have helped Israel develop some thriving industries. These industries produce electronic goods, metal products, and beverages. Israel also has a large armaments industry. The guns, missiles, and planes made in Israel have been used to defend the country against its Arab neighbors.

Another important industry is diamond-cutting, which is centered in the city of Tel Aviv. This city is also home to most of Israel's other industries. Located on the Mediterranean Sea, Tel Aviv is the second-largest city in Israel, with nearly 400,000 people. It is a modern city with skyscrapers, sidewalk cafes, and crowded beaches.

Israel's other main city is the ancient religious center of Jerusalem, with a population of over 550,000. Jerusalem is located in the dry highlands that make up central Israel.

C. The Arab-Israeli Conflict

The Conflict's Beginning Israel has faced intense hostility from the neighboring Arab states from the day it became an independent nation. As the map on page 506 shows, Israel and the Arab states have fought several wars. The wars have occurred because the land of Israel is claimed by two peoples: the Israelis and the Arab **Palestinians**.

The Palestinians lived in most of what now is Israel until 1948. In that year the United Nations decided Palestine should be divided between the Jews who wanted to return to their homeland and the Palestinians. The neighboring Arab countries believed the Jews did not have a right to a homeland in the Middle East and began the first of many wars with Israel.

Israel won the wars fought with the Arab nations. It also won large areas of new territory from the Arab states, especially after the 1967 war. In 1979, one Arab country, Egypt, decided to make peace with Israel.

The West Bank After the 1967 war, Israel gained a large section of land claimed by

In 1993, Prime Minister Yitzhak Rabin of Israel (left) and Yasir Arafat, leader of the Palestinian Liberation Army, (right) met in Washington, D.C.
▶ Why did the two leaders meet?

504

ANWAR SADAT'S SPEECH BEFORE THE ISRAELI PARLIAMENT

On November 20, 1977, an Arab named Anwar Sadat, the President of Egypt, made history. On that day, Sadat stood before the Israeli Parliament and said he wanted to live in peace with Israel.

I come to you on solid ground to shape a new life and to establish peace. . . .

Any life that is lost in war is a human life, be it that of an Arab or an Israeli. A wife who becomes a widow is a human being entitled to a happy life, whether she be an Arab or an Israeli.

Innocent children who are deprived of the care and compassion of their parents are ours. They are ours, be they living on Arab or Israeli land. . . .

You want to live with us, in this part of the world.

In all sincerity I tell you we welcome you among us, with full security and safety. This in itself is a tremendous turning point, one of the landmarks of a decisive historical change. We used to reject you. We had our reasons and our fears, yes. . . .

Yet today I tell you, and I declare it to the whole world, that we accept to live with you in permanent peace based on justice. . . .

What is peace for Israel? It means that Israel lives in the region with her Arab neighbors in security and safety. . . .

Peace is not a mere endorsement of written lines. Rather it is a rewriting of history.

This is Egypt, whose people have entrusted me with their sacred message. A message of security, safety, and peace to every man, woman and child in Israel. I say, encourage your leadership to struggle for peace.

1. What consequences of war are shared by Arabs and Israelis according to Sadat?
2. How does President Sadat define peace?
3. Why, do you think, have some other Arab countries made peace with Israel in recent years?

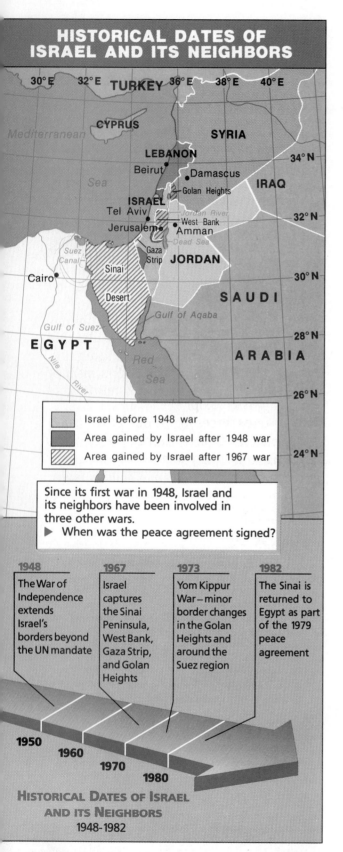

TURKEY

CYPRUS

Mediterranean

SYRIA

LEBANON

Beirut · Damascus

Golan Heights

IRAQ

ISRAEL

Tel Aviv

Jordan River

West Bank

Jerusalem · Amman

Dead Sea

Gaza Strip · JORDAN

Suez Canal

Sinai

Cairo ·

Desert

SAUDI

Gulf of Aqaba

Gulf of Suez

EGYPT

ARABIA

Nile River

Red Sea

	Israel before 1948 war
	Area gained by Israel after 1948 war
	Area gained by Israel after 1967 war

Since its first war in 1948, Israel and its neighbors have been involved in three other wars.

▶ When was the peace agreement signed?

1948 The War of Independence extends Israel's borders beyond the UN mandate

1967 Israel captures the Sinai Peninsula, West Bank, Gaza Strip, and Golan Heights

1973 Yom Kippur War—minor border changes in the Golan Heights and around the Suez region

1982 The Sinai is returned to Egypt as part of the 1979 peace agreement

1950
1960
1970
1980

HISTORICAL DATES OF ISRAEL AND ITS NEIGHBORS
1948-1982

Jordan known as the West Bank. The West Bank is home to the majority of the Palestinians. In 1993, Israel and the Palestinians signed a peace accord, or agreement. They agreed to work together to create an independent country for the Palestinians. In late 1995, Israel began to move its soldiers out of the West Bank. Palestinians elected mayors in some towns there and looked forward to the day they would govern themselves.

D. The Arab Kingdom of Jordan

A Desert Land Jordan is about the size of the state of Indiana, and almost all of the country is desert. Much of Jordan's most productive land is along the east side of the Jordan River valley. This extensively irrigated region makes agriculture the most important part of Jordan's economy.

Jordan also held the land west of the Jordan River until 1967. The West Bank was Jordan's most fertile land.

The Dead Sea The Jordan River flows south along Jordan's border and empties into the Dead Sea. This body of water is called the Dead Sea because there is almost no life in or around it. But the waters of the sea are useful because they contain many minerals, such as phosphates. These phosphates are Jordan's most important mineral export.

The Bedouins Most of Jordan's land east of the Jordan River is sparsely populated. This region of desert and patchy grassland is home to a nomadic people called the **Bedouins** (BED oo ihnz). *Bedouin* is an Arabic word that means "people who live in open country." The Bedouins move with their herds of sheep, camels, and goats among the oases, towns, and villages of the desert. They camp wherever they find pasture for their animals.

The Bedouins have kept alive many of the traditions of the Middle East. They dress in long robes and wear *footas,* or turbans, around their heads. This long, loose clothing protects them from the hot daytime sun, the cool desert nights, and the blowing sand of desert sandstorms.

E. Iraq, a Nation Between Rivers

The Land and Its People Much of the nation of Iraq lies between the Tigris and Euphrates rivers. In ancient times this region was called Mesopotamia, which means "between the rivers." The Tigris and Euphrates begin in the Taurus Mountains of Turkey and flow south toward the Persian Gulf. About 120 miles (193 km) from the gulf, the waters merge into a channel, named the Shatt-al-Arab, and flow southeasterly into the Persian Gulf.

Most of Iraq's 20.6 million people live in the cities and villages built on the lowlands along the Tigris and Euphrates. Iraq's most important cities are here— Baghdad, the capital, which has a population of 3.8 million, and Basra. Basra is Iraq's main port for its largest export: oil. It makes up about 90 percent of Iraq's exports.

War with Kuwait Following the war between Iran and Iraq, (1980–1988), which you read about on page 499, Iraq was heavily in debt. In 1990, Iraq attacked Kuwait, its neighbor to the south, and quickly seized control of that oil-rich country. Iraq's President Saddam Hussein accused Kuwait of plotting with the United States to keep oil prices low. He also insisted that Kuwait settle a long-standing border dispute in Iraq's favor.

The United Nations Security Council and the United States strongly condemned the Iraqi invasion and demanded the immediate withdrawal of Iraqi troops from Kuwait. Saddam Hussein refused to back off. Early in 1991 an international force led by the United States launched air and missile attacks on Iraq and Iraqi-occupied Kuwait. The war against Saddam Hussein was called the Persian Gulf War. General H. Norman Schwarzkopf, Jr., commanded the United States forces in the offensive known as Operation Desert Storm. Within six weeks the Iraqi army was defeated.

The Bedouins move across the desert of Jordan in search of pasture for their herds of sheep, camels, and goats.
▶ What does the word *Bedouin* mean?

LESSON 3

Review

REVIEWING MAIN IDEAS

A. What caused Lebanon's continuing civil war?
B. How have the Israelis changed their land since 1948?
C. Why is there conflict between the Israelis and the Palestinians?
D. What is the source of Jordan's mineral wealth?
E. Why did United States troops participate in a war against Iraq in 1991?

SKILLS CHECK

WRITING SKILL

Write several paragraphs explaining how you think the Israelis and the Palestinians might end their fighting.

The Arabian Peninsula

CONNECTIONS

List some uses of oil. How would daily life and activities be affected if oil were not available?

TERMS

Koran, hajj

FOCUS

How have most of the countries on the Arabian Peninsula benefited from oil?

A. Saudi Arabia: Desert, Sand, and Oil

A Huge Tilted Landform The Arabian Peninsula is like a giant tabletop that tilts downward toward the east and the north. The physical map of the Middle East, which is found on page 492, shows that the peninsula has this tilt because of high elevations in the south. The highest points are along the Hejaz Mountains. The land north of the mountains gradually slopes downward toward the Persian Gulf. Here, at its northern edge, the Arabian Peninsula is flat, dry, and sandy.

The Desert Country Saudi Arabia, the largest country on the Arabian Peninsula, is about the size of Alaska and Texas combined. But Saudi Arabia has a total population of only about 15 million people. Why do so few people live in this large country?

Most of Saudi Arabia is covered by desert. The southern part of the country is mainly the huge desert called the Empty Quarter, which you read about in Lesson 1. No one lives in the Empty Quarter, and few people have ever traveled through this huge "sea" of sand dunes.

Life in the other parts of this desert country is centered around oases. Here are the country's towns and villages. Some oases have grown into large cities. One of these is Riyadh, the capital city of Saudi Arabia. This growing, modern city is in the center of the country.

Along the Persian Gulf are towns and cities that have grown because of the large oil fields located near them. This area is dry and has few sources of water, so the government has built *desalination plants* to produce fresh water from the salt water of the Persian Gulf. Creating fresh water this way is expensive, but it is the only way Saudi Arabia can supply water to the work-

Riyadh, the capital of Saudi Arabia, is one city that grew around an oasis.
▶ What vegetation shown in this photo is typical of an oasis?

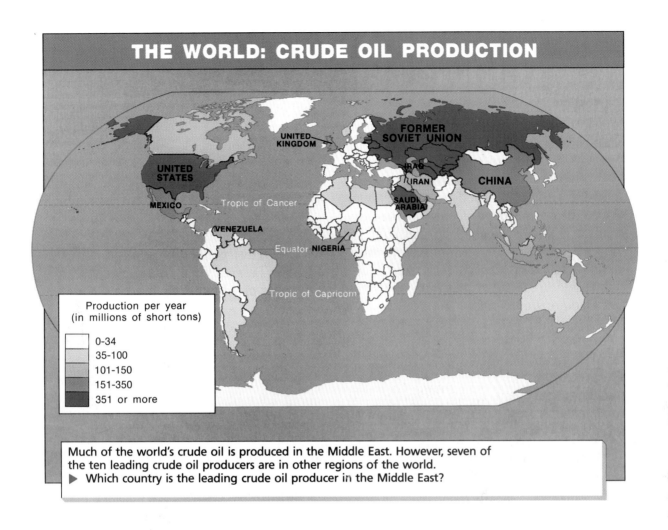

THE WORLD: CRUDE OIL PRODUCTION

UNITED KINGDOM

FORMER SOVIET UNION

UNITED STATES

IRAQ

IRAN

CHINA

MEXICO

Tropic of Cancer

SAUDI ARABIA

VENEZUELA

Equator NIGERIA

Tropic of Capricorn

Production per year
(in millions of short tons)

- 0-34
- 35-100
- 101-150
- 151-350
- 351 or more

Much of the world's crude oil is produced in the Middle East. However, seven of the ten leading crude oil producers are in other regions of the world.
▶ Which country is the leading crude oil producer in the Middle East?

ers and other people who support the country's vital oil industry.

The Region's Oil Leader Saudi Arabia is the world's third largest oil producer and the world's largest oil exporter. The Saudi Arabian government has used the profits from oil sales to build new schools, hospitals, and highways. It has also built two new cities to refine oil, produce chemicals, and make cement and steel. One of these cities, Yenbo, is on the Red Sea coast; the other, Jubail, is on the Persian Gulf. Many people from other countries, such as Pakistan, Egypt, and South Korea, have come to Saudi Arabia to work in the new cities and in the oil fields.

B. The Persian Gulf States

The Benefits of Oil The countries that spread along the Persian Gulf coast of the Arabian Peninsula are small. However, they are among the world's most important countries, since they hold the largest known supplies of oil reserves in the world.

The second largest of these countries is Kuwait, which forms a wedge of land between Iraq and Saudi Arabia. Kuwait is slightly smaller than the state of New Jersey. This flat, sandy desert country has little fresh water and no forests. But Kuwait does have oil—lots of it. In fact, this small country is situated on top of the richest single oil deposit in the world.

On page 507 you read that Kuwait was attacked by Iraq in 1990. Toward the end of the Persian Gulf War, Iraqi troops set afire hundreds of oil wells in Kuwait. The damage to the Kuwaiti oil industry was enormous. Burning oil consumed about 6 million barrels of oil per day. That represented a daily loss of nearly $100 million.

In addition to the damage to the oil industry, the fires caused monstrous damage to the environment. Dense smoke from burning oil wells blocked out sunlight for long periods of time. Oil spurting from wells that were damaged created huge flammable lakes of petroleum. Some wells released poisonous gas.

Shortly after the war had ended, a delegate from the United Nations Environment Program compared the situation to Chernobyl, the 1986 disaster at a Soviet nuclear power plant. It was estimated that the consequences of the damages would be felt for years.

The Other Gulf States Bahrain, Qatar (ke-TAHR), and the United Arab Emirates are also wealthy because of oil. Bahrain consists of one large island and many smaller islands. It has a population of about 576,000. Before it became an oil exporter, Bahrain was an important trading port. It was also well known for its pearls, which come from the surrounding waters of the Persian Gulf.

Qatar, too, was best known for its pearls before oil become an important export. This peninsular nation juts out into the Persian Gulf. About 534,000 people, most of whom are foreign oil workers, live here.

The United Arab Emirates is actually composed of seven small city-states that have formed a political union. The total population of the United Arab Emirates is about 2.9 million. As in Qatar, most of the population is made up of workers from other countries.

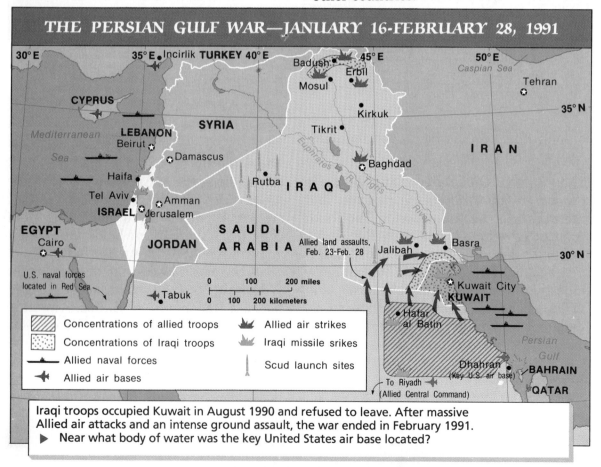

THE PERSIAN GULF WAR—JANUARY 16-FEBRUARY 28, 1991

Concentrations of allied troops
Concentrations of Iraqi troops
Allied naval forces
Allied air bases
Allied air strikes
Iraqi missile srikes
Scud launch sites

Iraqi troops occupied Kuwait in August 1990 and refused to leave. After massive Allied air attacks and an intense ground assault, the war ended in February 1991.
▶ Near what body of water was the key United States air base located?

OPEC The nations of the Persian Gulf and 13 other leading oil-producing nations all belong to the Organization of Petroleum Exporting Countries. This group is often referred to as OPEC. It decides how much oil the members will produce and controls the prices other countries pay for the oil.

C. Oman and Yemen

Oman Along the southern end of the Arabian Peninsula are two countries that do not have as much oil as other countries in the Middle East. One of these countries is Oman. This ancient coastal nation is about the size of our state of Kansas. Unlike most of the other countries on the Arabian Peninsula, farming is possible in some parts of Oman. This is because of the monsoon rains that cross the Indian Ocean each year.

Yemen Along the southern and western coasts of the Arabian Peninsula is Yemen, a country with almost no natural resources. Yemen was formerly two countries—North Yemen and South Yemen. In 1990 the leaders of both countries agreed on unification for economic reasons. San'a (sah NAH), once the capital of North Yemen, was made the new capital.

Yemen has a narrow plain all along its coastline. This gives way to a chain of low-lying mountains. Farther inland, in the north and west, is the high interior section. More than 3 times as many people live in the higher part of the country than in the lower.

Most people in Yemen are farmers or herders of cattle and sheep. Farmers in the north grow wheat, vegetables, grapes, and coffee. Only a few crops grow well in the hot, dry south. Most people in the south live near the port of Aden. Ships moving between the Gulf of Aden and the Red Sea use the port for refueling, transferring cargo, and making repairs.

A unique feature of Yemeni architecture is decorative windows like those above.
▶ What other feature of this building is unique?

D. The Birthplace of Islam

Islam's Holy Land The countries on the Arabian Peninsula are known for their oil, and so they are of interest to many industrial countries. But Saudi Arabia, in particular, has a special interest to Muslims, since it is the location of Mecca and Medina. These two cities make up the holy land of Islam. Mecca and Medina are considered to be holy because they were important in the life of Muhammad, the man who spread the religion of Islam.

Muhammad, an Arab, was born in the oasis town of Mecca in A.D. 570. He taught that people should submit to the will of Allah, or God. On the next page, you can read an example of Muhammad's teachings, which are written in Islam's holy book, called the **Koran**.

When a [courteous] greeting
is offered you, meet it
with a greeting still more
Courteous, [at least]
Of equal courtesy.
Allah takes careful account
Of all things.

Because of his beliefs, Muhammad was forced to move to Medina. From there his followers quickly spread the religion of Islam from Arabia westward across North Africa and into Spain. Islam also spread eastward as far as the Philippines.

The Hajj Muslims are required to visit Mecca once during their lifetime if they can afford it. This trip is called the **hajj** (haj), or pilgrimage. A pilgrimage is a journey made for religious purposes.

Each year during Ramadan, the holiest month of the year in Islam, thousands of Muslims from across the world make the hajj. They travel by train, boat, and plane to the holy city of Mecca. Many first arrive at Jidda, a port city located to the west of Mecca.

Abdul, a teenager who lives in Oman, recently made the hajj with his family. They were not able to afford the plane trip to Mecca, so they made the journey by *dhow* (dou). A dhow is an Arab sailboat that has a distinctive triangular sail.

Abdul and his family left the harbor at Muscat and then followed the coast of the Arabian Peninsula as they sailed southwest toward the Gulf of Aden. Then they sailed northward through the Red Sea until they reached the port of Jidda. There the family joined thousands of other Muslims who were beginning the 46-mile (74-km) walk over the Hejaz Mountains to Mecca.

Finally reaching Mecca, Abdul and his family and the other Muslim pilgrims entered the central mosque in the city. Once inside the mosque, they went to the courtyard. Here they circled seven times

Muslim pilgrims visit the Kaaba, the most sacred shrine of Islam. The Kaaba is in the Great Mosque.
▶ In what city is the Great Mosque?

around the Kaaba (KAH buh), the sacred shrine of Islam.

While in Mecca, Abdul's family stayed at a modern hotel. The hotel and all the other sights and sounds of Mecca were new and exciting to Abdul. It was the first time he had traveled away from Masqat. He told himself that he would always remember the experience.

LESSON 4

Review

REVIEWING MAIN IDEAS

A. How have Saudi Arabia's cities changed because of oil?

B. Why are the small Persian Gulf states important to the world today?

C. How are Oman and Yemen different from the Persian Gulf states?

D. Why is Saudi Arabia considered to be the holy land of Islam?

SKILLS CHECK

THINKING SKILL

Turn to the bar graph of world petroleum producers on page 737. Which leading oil-producing countries are not in the Middle East?

REVIEWING TERMS

On a separate sheet of paper, write the letter of the term that best matches each numbered statement.

a. ethnocentrism
b. oasis
c. Fertile Crescent
d. strait
e. qanat
f. theocracy
g. monotheism
h. Bedouins
i. Koran
j. hajj

1. The belief that there is only one God
2. A place in the desert that has enough water for plants and trees to grow
3. A nation ruled according to religious laws instead of laws that have been passed by the people
4. A system of underground tunnels that is used in the Middle East to supply water to dry areas
5. A nomadic group of people who live on the Arabian Peninsula
6. The pilgrimage to Mecca that every Muslim is required to try to make at least once during his or her lifetime
7. A way of looking at the world and making judgments about it based only on your own cultural background and your own experience
8. Islam's holy book that contains the teachings of Muhammad
9. A long, flat, fertile area north of the Persian Gulf that includes the countries of Iraq, Syria, Lebanon, Israel, and Jordan
10. A narrow waterway that connects two larger bodies of water

REVIEWING THE FACTS

On a separate sheet of paper, answer the following questions in complete sentences.

1. Why is the Suez Canal in a strategic location?
2. Why is it incorrect to refer to the Middle East as the "Arab World"?
3. How did the Ottoman Empire come to an end?
4. What natural resource supports most of Iran's economy?
5. How did the revolutionary government of the Ayatollah Khomeini show its hostility toward the United States?
6. How does Syria differ from most other Middle Eastern countries?
7. Why has Israel fought many wars with the neighboring Arab countries?
8. What Arab country made peace with Israel in 1979?
9. What is OPEC?
10. What impact did the Persian Gulf War have on the environment and economy of the Arabian Peninsula?

WRITING ABOUT ECONOMICS

Imagine that OPEC has decided to cut back the amount of oil produced by its members and wants to substantially raise the selling price of its oil. Write several paragraphs explaining how the economies of many nations around the world might be affected by these decisions.

THINKING CRITICALLY

On a separate sheet of paper, answer the following questions in complete sentences.

1. Where does the water come from that supplies an oasis?
2. Why would a visitor find churches, mosques, and temples in Jerusalem?
3. What reasons can you give to defend the statement that a nation should be ruled by laws passed by the people and not by religious laws?
4. What effect, do you think, did losing the West Bank have on Jordan's economy?
5. Why, do you think, did the nations of the Persian Gulf and other leading oil-producing nations join together to form OPEC?

SUMMARIZING THE CHAPTER

On a separate sheet of paper, draw a graphic organizer like the one shown here. Copy the information from this graphic organizer to the one you have drawn. Under the main idea for each lesson, write three statements that you think support the main idea.

CHAPTER THEME

The Middle East is a region that is experiencing rapid change, mainly because of oil and ethnic or religious conflict.

Lesson 1 The Middle East has played an important role in ancient and modern history.
1. _____
2. _____
3. _____

Lesson 2 Turkey is different from Iran and Afghanistan in several ways.
1. _____
2. _____
3. _____

Lesson 3 There is conflict between Israel and the Arab countries of the Middle East.
1. _____
2. _____
3. _____

Lesson 4 Many of the countries on the Arabian Peninsula have benefited from oil.
1. _____
2. _____
3. _____

COOPERATIVE LEARNING

In this unit you learned about important places in Japan, China, Southeast Asia, India, and the Middle East. Sometimes people and places are the basis for works of literature, such as plays. How could you write a play about a certain event in a country?

PROJECT

Work with a group of classmates to plan, write, and perform a play about a real place from Unit 5. For example, a play could be written about Japan's economic miracle. The setting could be in a corporation. A group of Japanese sales people are talking about a new kind of product they could invent. The plot could tell how their invention made the corporation successful.

Meet as a group and look through the chapters to select a subject for your play. Be sure to discuss each other's ideas politely and try to stay on the job.

Once you have chosen the subject for your play, discuss specific ideas for the characters, setting, and plot. Take notes to record each group member's ideas.

Once you have planned your play, the group is ready to begin writing. Divide the play's characters among the group members. Each group member should suggest what lines his or her assigned character or characters might say. You may want to have a narrator introduce and explain the action of the play. Decide together which group member will play each role.

PRESENTATION AND REVIEW

Rehearse your play. When you are ready, present your play in front of your classmates.

Meet again with your group to evaluate your project. How well did your group members work together? How could your play have been improved?

REMEMBER TO:
- Give your ideas.
- Listen to others' ideas.
- Plan your work with the group.
- Present your project.
- Discuss how your group worked.

SKILLBUILDER

HYPOTHESIZING FROM TABLES AND GRAPHS

WHY DO I NEED THIS SKILL?

Hypothesizing is an intellectual skill used in explaining facts or solving problems. The skill involves forming a *hypothesis*, a possible explanation or solution. A hypothesis is an "educated guess" based on information that is already available. When you form hypotheses, you are interpreting information and proposing conclusions that may be drawn from that information. One way to hypothesize is to use information presented in tables and graphs.

LEARNING THE SKILL

The table and pie graph on these pages present facts about Japan's imports and ex-

ports in one year. The table lists different categories of products and the amount of import and export trade for each category. For example, the table tells you that Japan imported $19,432,000,000 worth of food and food product, and exported $1,567,000,000 worth. The last two columns of the table give percentages of the total import and export dollars for each category. Here you can see that food and food products made up 15 percent of Japan's total import dollars and 1 percent of its total export dollars.

The pie graph on the next page presents the same import percentages presented in the table. But the pie graph is easier to understand at a glance because it gives you proportions in pictures.

The information in the table and graph can be used to make various hypotheses

JAPAN'S IMPORTS AND EXPORTS

Products	Imports (in millions of dollars)	Exports (in millions of dollars)	Percentage of total import dollars	Percentage of total export dollars
Food and food products	19,432	1,567	15	1
Fuels and raw materials	54,196	2,002	43	1
Chemicals	9,733	9,484	8	4
Machinery and transportation equipment	13,283	133,326	10	62
Other manufactured goods	21,023	60,725	17	29
Miscellaneous products	8,742	2,048	7	1
Total	126,409	209,152	100	100

JAPAN'S IMPORTS

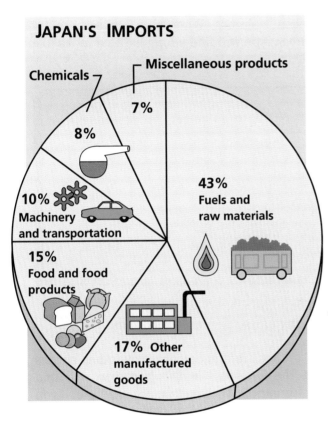

Chemicals ⌐

⌐ Miscellaneous products

7%

8%

10%
Machinery
and transportation

15%
Food and food
products

17% Other
manufactured
goods

43%
Fuels and
raw materials

about Japan's economy. For example, the information provided shows that Japan imported more than $54 billion in fuels and raw materials but exported only about $2 billion. Based on this information, you might hypothesize that Japan has limited amounts of fuels and raw materials and must rely on imported supplies.

How do you think Japan used many of the fuels and raw materials that it imported? You could look at the data for the country's exports to get an idea. You can see that Japan exported almost $200 billion in machinery, transportation equipment, and other manufactured goods. You might hypothesize that

Japan uses imported fuels and raw materials in its manufacturing industries.

PRACTICING THE SKILL

Use the table and graph in this Skillbuilder to answer the following questions.

1. What product category accounts for the greatest percentage of Japanese trade, either import or export?
2. Based on what you already know about Japan, what specific types of products do you think are included in the category called "Machinery and transportation equipment"?
3. What other types of products do you think are included in the category "Other manufactured goods"?
4. For which product category is there the greatest difference between the percentage of total import dollars and the percentage of total export dollars?
5. In what kinds of jobs do you think many people in Japan are employed?

APPLYING THE SKILL

As you continue reading your geography textbook, form hypotheses by using information in tables, graphs, photographs, maps, and other visuals. Use all the related information in the chapters to see if your hypotheses are correct and you have drawn the right conclusions. You can also use the hypothesizing skill in other subject areas—such as in science, in which hypothesizing is an important part of the scientific method.

USING THE *READERS' GUIDE TO PERIODICAL LITERATURE*

WHY DO I NEED THIS SKILL?

It is necessary to learn how to gather information by using many sources. You may have questions that are not answered in your social studies book. If you know how to do additional research, you can find the information you need to answer those questions.

One important source of information is magazines, which are also called *periodicals*. A valuable reference tool to help you find information in magazines is the *Readers' Guide to Periodical Literature*. The *Readers' Guide* is an index that will tell you the names of magazines in which articles on specific topics are located. Knowing how to use the *Readers' Guide* is an important research skill, for it will allow you to use magazines as sources of information for reports and for answering questions.

LEARNING THE SKILL

The *Readers' Guide* lists articles that are found in about 185 popular magazines. It is published each year in a large volume and in smaller supplements for recent months. The *Readers' Guide* lists entries by authors and by subjects. Usually, you will be looking for information on a specific topic, so this Skillbuilder will focus on finding subject entries in the *Readers' Guide*.

Imagine that your teacher has asked everyone in your class to prepare an oral report about current events in an Asian country. You have selected Japan. You have decided to begin your research with the 1995 *Readers' Guide to Periodical Literature*. You can then work forward by looking in more recent volumes. When you locate the entry *Japan*, you will find a long list that looks like this.

> **Japan**
>   *See also*
>   Airports—Japan
>   Architecture—Japan
>   Baseball, Professional—Japan
>   Computers—Japan
>   Opera—Japan
>   Space research—Japan
>   Television broadcasting—Japan
>   Tokyo—Japan
>   Women—Japan

These are just a few of the many cross-references for *Japan*.

Cross-references give you other entries in the *Readers' Guide* where you will find information about Japan. For example, if you wanted to learn about professional baseball in Japan, you would look under *Baseball, Professional—Japan*.

Following the cross-references is a long list of articles on Japan. However, you have now become interested in Japan's largest city, Tokyo. You would use the cross-reference information and find the entry for *Tokyo—Japan*. There you will find entries such as the following.

> Ambassador and Mrs. Walter F. Mondale in Japan [embassy residence in Tokyo]
> C. Lutfy. il pors *Architectural Digest*
> v52 p218-24+ O '95

To conserve space in the *Readers' Guide,* you will notice that the editors use various abbreviations for things such as dates (O '95 = October 1995), and other information (il = illustrated; pors = portraits). Sometimes the title does not explain what an article is about, so the editors add information in brackets. For example, in the entry on page 518 we learn that the article is about the American ambassador's residence in Tokyo.

PRACTICING THE SKILL

On a sheet of paper, answer these questions about the following *Readers' Guide* entries on Japan.

The secret of Japanese education. S. Goya
   il *Phi Delta Kappan* v75 p706–12 O '93
Japan's big environmental challenges. J.
   D. Hair il *International Wildlife* v23
   p26 N/D '93
Nintendo: no more playing around. N.
   Gross il *Business Week* p71 F 21 '94
Japan boosts spending for space by 7.2%.
   E. Sekigawa il *Aviation Weekly and
   Space Technology* v140 p23 Mr 7 '94
Into the trenches: the Japanese search for
   deep-sea earthquake clues. L. Cuyvers il
   Sea Frontiers v40 p42–5 O '94

1. What article would give you information about the Japanese space program?
2. How many pages long is the article by J. D. Hair?

3. Which articles have illustrations?
4. Where could you go to learn something about Japanese video games?
5. In what volume of *Sea Frontiers* will you find the article by L. Cuyvers?
6. Who wrote the article in *Business Week*?
7. When was the *Phi Delta Kappan* article published?

APPLYING THE SKILL

Use the *Readers' Guide* when you need to research any topic. Important information can be found in magazines. By using the articles referenced in the main entries and by looking under cross-references, you should be able to find the information you need.

You can also use the *Readers' Guide* to locate information on events that happened in the distant past. For example, if you want to find out about the 1994 Winter Olympic Games that were held in Lillehammer, Norway, you could look in the 1994 *Readers' Guide* under *Olympic Games* to find where articles on that subject appeared. Your public library keeps back issues of many of the periodicals listed in the *Readers' Guide,* and the librarian will help you locate the articles you need.

UNIT 6

THE COUNTRIES OF AFRICA

CONTINENTAL HANDBOOK

TABLE OF COUNTRIES

CONTINENTAL HANDBOOK
AFRICA

CONNECTIONS

What are some of the ways in which a rich country can help poor countries?

TERMS

savanna

FOCUS

What are Africa's main geographic regions?

Peace Corps is Widening Its Role in Africa
By James Brooke

NDJAMENA, Chad—At 24, Lori Leonard is younger than most of her students at Chad University.

But discipline is rarely a problem. After losing school years to civil war and Libyan invasion, Chadians are serious students. They are also delighted that an American has come all the way from La Crescent, Minn., to teach them English.

Miss Leonard is a volunteer with the Peace Corps, an enduring aid program that . . . is poised for a new spurt of growth.

A. The United States and Africa

The Peace Corps is a United States-sponsored group of volunteers who work in other countries. These volunteers—often young people—teach new skills to people in developing countries. These skills include using new farming methods, building fisheries, using forests wisely, and developing water supplies.

The countries of Africa have the largest number of Peace Corps volunteers. Many African countries are struggling to develop their economies and welcome the help of groups like the Peace Corps.

B. A Huge Continent

Over 50 countries are found in Africa. With about 12 million square miles (31 million sq km) of total area, Africa is the world's second largest continent. It is so big that all the United States except Hawaii and Alaska would fit into Africa nearly four times.

Almost all of this huge continent is a vast plateau, high above sea level. Only a few small areas could be called coastal plains. Near the coastline of the continent, the plateau drops off to the narrow coastal plains. This sharp drop in elevation is marked around the edge of the African continent by a series of mountain ranges and cliffs.

The coastline of Africa is fairly smooth, with few natural indentations that would make good harbors. Just a few

---

Much of Africa is located on a plateau that is 1,000 feet (300 m) above sea level. Deserts stretch across the northern part of the continent. Many large lakes are found in the eastern region.
▶ What is the average elevation along the coasts of Africa?

522

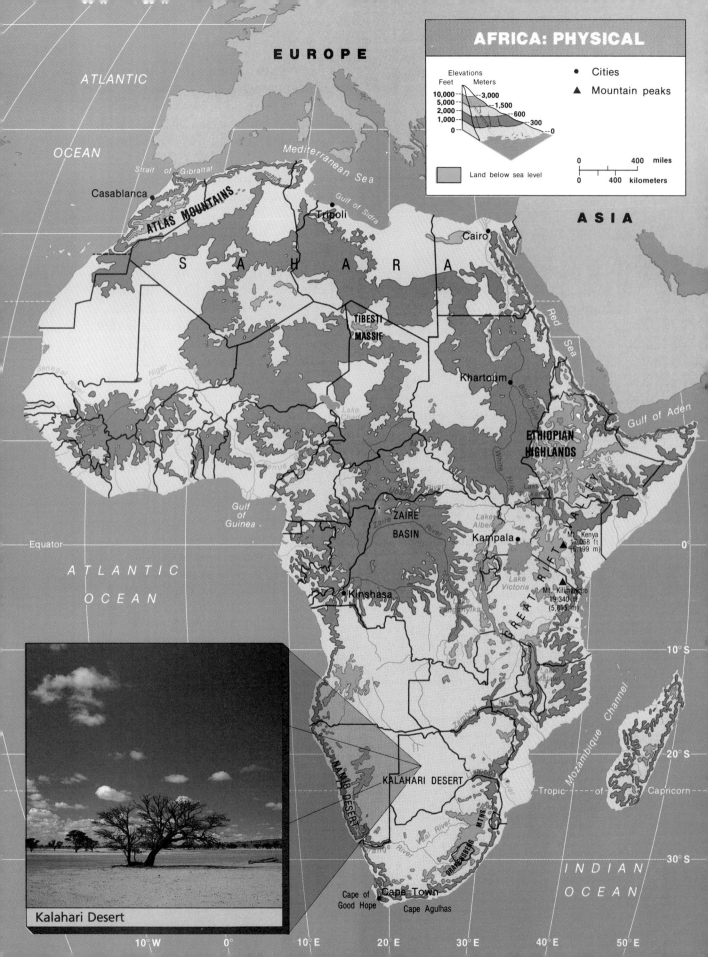

ATLANTIC

OCEAN

EUROPE

ATLANTIC

Strait of Gibraltar

Mediterranean Sea

Gulf of Sidra

ASIA

AFRICA: PHYSICAL

Elevations

Feet	Meters
10,000	3,000
5,000	1,500
2,000	600
1,000	300
0	0

● Cities

▲ Mountain peaks

Land below sea level

| 0 | | 400 | miles |
| 0 | 400 | kilometers |

Casablanca

ATLAS MOUNTAINS

Tripoli

Cairo

S A H A R A

TIBESTI
MASSIF

Red Sea

Khartoum

Blue Nile

Niger

Senegal River

Lake Chad

Benue

ETHIOPIAN
HIGHLANDS

Gulf of Aden

White Nile

Shebelle

Gulf of
Guinea

ZAIRE

BASIN

Zaire River

Ubangi River

Lake Albert

Lake
Turkana

Kampala

Mt. Kenya
17,058 ft
(5,199 m)

Equator

ATLANTIC

OCEAN

Kinshasa

Lake Victoria

Mt. Kilimanjaro
19,340 ft
(5,895 m)

GREAT RIFT VALLEY

Tanganyika

Lake Malawi

10° S

NAMIB DESERT

KALAHARI DESERT

Zambezi

Mozambique Channel

20° S

Tropic of Capricorn

Vaal River

Orange River

DRAKENSBERG MTS.

Cape of
Good Hope

Cape Town

Cape Agulhas

INDIAN

OCEAN

30° S

Kalahari Desert

10° W   0°   10° E   20° E   30° E   40° E   50° E

miles upstream on Africa's major rivers, there are waterfalls and rapids. These natural barriers prevented early explorers and traders from traveling to the continent's interior. Because of this lack of exploration, the interior of Africa remained virtually unknown to outsiders for many years. As recently as the mid-1800s, maps of Africa showed large blank spaces in the interior.

C. Africa's Climates

Most people know that the Equator passes through Africa, and many automatically associate the region with hot, humid conditions and dense jungle vegetation. Yet in some places just a few miles from the Equator, there are mountains that are covered with snow year-round. There are some areas of tropical forests along the Gulf of Guinea.

But most of the continent is covered by extensive grasslands. Scattered around the grassland regions are clumps of trees and bushes. These areas of tall natural grasslands found in tropical regions are called **savannas.** These savanna regions cover about two fifths of Africa.

Much of Africa's population lives in the area north of the Equator, where the savanna is like the steppes of the Soviet Union. In recent years, this region has been hit by many droughts.

Across the northern part of the continent, and extending almost 4,000 miles (6,436 km) from the Atlantic Ocean to the Red Sea, is the world's largest desert—the Sahara. Desert climates extend southward along the Red Sea and down the eastern coast of the continent as far as the country of Kenya.

The highest mountain in Africa is Mount Kilamanjaro. Find its elevation on the map on page 523. Mount Kenya, at more than 17,000 feet (5,182 m), is right on the Equator and is covered with snow year-round. Two huge lakes, Lake Victoria and Lake Tanganyika, are found to the west of these mountains.

D. Africa's Resources

Unlike many mountains in other places, the mountains in Africa do not hold mineral resources. But a huge crescent-shaped region that extends from Central Africa to Southern Africa is rich in mineral resources, such as copper, coal, iron ore, gold, and diamonds.

Africa's other resources include tropical plantation products, such as cacao, palm oil, rubber, coffee, and tea. Most of these come from a region that extends from the rain forests of West Africa across to the highlands of East Africa.

Review

REVIEWING MAIN IDEAS
A. How do Peace Corps volunteers help people in developing countries?
B. What prohibited the exploration of Africa by Europeans?
C. What vegetation zone covers two fifths of Africa?
D. Where are Africa's mineral resources found?

SKILLS CHECK
MAP SKILL
Look at the map of Africa on the next page. Use the scale on the map to determine how wide Africa is from its farthest western and eastern points.

AFRICA: POLITICAL

⊛ National capitals
• Other cities

0   400   800 miles
0   400   800 kilometers

EUROPE

ASIA

30°W   20°W

40°N

30°N

20°N

0°   Equator

10°S

20°S   Tropic of Capricorn

30°S

MADEIRA
ISLANDS
(PORTUGAL)

CANARY
ISLANDS
(SPAIN)

Strait of   Gibraltar

Mediterranean   Sea

Algiers   Tunis
TUNISIA
Tripoli

Rabat
Casablanca
MOROCCO

WESTERN
SAHARA
(MOROCCO)

ALGERIA

LIBYA

Alexandria   Cairo
Giza
EGYPT

Nile   River

Red   Sea

MAURITANIA

MALI

NIGER

CHAD

Khartoum

SUDAN

ERITREA
Asmara

DJIBOUTI
Djibouti

Gulf of Aden

Nouakchott

Dakar
SENEGAL
Banjul
GAMBIA   Bamako
GUINEA-BISSAU
Bissau   GUINEA
Conakry
SIERRA
LEONE
Freetown
Monrovia
LIBERIA

Niamey

BURKINA FASO
Ouagadougou

BENIN
CÔTE   GHANA   TOGO
D'IVOIRE
Yamoussoukro
Abidjan   Accra
Lomé   Porto-
Novo

NIGERIA
Abuja
Ibadan
Lagos

Lake
Chad
N'Djamena

CENTRAL
AFRICAN REPUBLIC
Bangui

CAMEROON
Yaoundé
Malabo

EQUATORIAL GUINEA
SÃO TOMÉ E PRÍNCIPE
São Tomé
Libreville
GABON   CONGO
Brazzaville
Kinshasa
Cabinda
(Angola)

Addis Ababa
ETHIOPIA

SOMALIA

Mogadishu

UGANDA
Kampala
RWANDA
Kigali
BURUNDI
Bujumbura

KENYA
Nairobi

Lake
Victoria

ZAIRE

Zaire   River

TANZANIA
Dodoma   ZANZIBAR
Dar es Salaam

COMOROS
Moroni

MAYOTTE
ISLAND
(FRANCE)

ATLANTIC

OCEAN

Luanda

ANGOLA

ZAMBIA
Lusaka

MALAWI
Lilongwe

NAMIBIA

Windhoek

BOTSWANA
Gaborone

Harare
ZIMBABWE

Zambezi   River

MOZAMBIQUE

Antananarivo

MADAGASCAR

Mozambique   Channel

INDIAN

OCEAN

Pretoria
Maputo
Mbabane   SWAZILAND
Bloemfontein   Maseru
LESOTHO   Durban

SOUTH
AFRICA
Cape Town

There are 53 independent countries on
the continent of Africa.
▶ Name the countries in Africa through
which the Equator passes.

AFRICA

	FLAG AND PRINCIPAL LANGUAGE(S)	POPULATION AND LANDMASS	PRINCIPAL PRODUCTS EXPORT	IMPORT
ALGERIA  Algiers	Arabic, French, Berber	**POPULATION** 28,539,000 31 per sq mi/12 per sq km **LANDMASS** 919,591 sq mi/2,381,741 sq km	Crude Oil	Food
ANGOLA ★Luanda	Portuguese, Bantu	**POPULATION** 10,070,000 21 per sq mi/8 per sq km **LANDMASS** 481,351 sq mi/1,246,669 sq km	Crude Oil	Machinery
BENIN Porto-Novo ★	French	**POPULATION** 5,523,000 127 per sq mi/49 per sq km **LANDMASS** 43,483 sq mi/116,621 sq km	Footwear	Textiles
BOTSWANA Gaborone ★	English, Setswana	**POPULATION** 1,392,000 6 per sq mi/2 per sq km **LANDMASS** 219,916 sq mi/569,582 sq km	Diamonds	Food
BURKINA FASO Ouagadougou ★	French, Sudanic languages	**POPULATION** 10,423,000 98 per sq mi/38 per sq km **LANDMASS** 105,869 sq mi/274,201 sq km	Cotton	Food
BURUNDI Bujumbura ★	French, Kirundi	**POPULATION** 6,262,000 582 per sq mi/225 per sq km **LANDMASS** 10,759 sq mi/27,866 sq km	Coffee	Petroleum
CAMEROON ★Yaoundé	French, Ewondo, English, Donala	**POPULATION** 13,521,000 74 per sq mi/29 per sq km **LANDMASS** 183,591 sq mi/475,501 sq km	Crude Oil	Machinery
CAPE VERDE ISLANDS  ★Praia	Portuguese	**POPULATION** 436,000 280 per sq mi/108 per sq km **LANDMASS** 1,557 sq mi/4,033 sq km	Fish	Food
CENTRAL AFRICAN REPUBLIC  Bangui ★	French, Sango	**POPULATION** 3,210,000 13 per sq mi/5 per sq km **LANDMASS** 240,533 sq mi/622,980 sq km	Diamonds	Vehicles

Country	Capital	Flag and Principal Language(s)	Population	Landmass	Export	Import
CHAD	N'Djamena	French, Massa, Sara, Arabic, Kanembou	5,587,000 / 11 per sq mi/4 per sq km	495,752 sq mi/1,283,998 sq km	Cotton	Machinery
COMOROS	Moroni	French, Arabic, Swahili	549,000 / 804 per sq mi/311 per sq km	863 sq mi/2,235 sq km	Cloves	Rice
CONGO	Brazzaville	French, Lingala, Kokongo	2,505,000 / 19 per sq mi/7 per sq km	132,012 sq mi/342,000 sq km	Crude Oil	Food
CÔTE D'IVOIRE	Yamoussoukro	French	14,791,000 / 119 per sq mi/46 per sq km	124,503 sq mi/322,463 sq km	Coffee	Food
DJIBOUTI	Djibouti	Arabic, French, Afar, Somali	421,000 / 48 per sq mi/19 per sq km	8,800 sq mi/22,999 sq km	Livestock	Food
EGYPT	Cairo	Arabic	62,360,000 / 161 per sq mi/62 per sq km	386,660 sq mi/1,001,449 sq km	Crude Oil	Food
EQUATORIAL GUINEA	Malabo	Spanish, Fang, Bubi	420,300 / 39 per sq mi/15 per sq km	10,825 sq mi/28,037 sq km	Cocoa	Food
ETHIOPIA [1]	Addis Ababa	Amharic, Galligna, Tigrigna	55,979,000 / 119 per sq mi/46 per sq km	471,775 sq mi/1,221,897 sq km	Coffee	Crude Oil
GABON	Libreville	French, Bantu	1,156,000 / 11 per sq mi/4 per sq km	103,347 sq mi/267,667 sq km	Crude Oil	Machinery

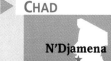

[1] Eritrea declared itself free from Ethiopia and an independent nation in 1993. See political map of Africa on page 698.

AFRICA

	FLAG AND PRINCIPAL LANGUAGE(S)	POPULATION AND LANDMASS	PRINCIPAL PRODUCTS EXPORT	IMPORT

GAMBIA

★Banjul

English, native languages

POPULATION
989,000
247 per sq mi/95 per sq km

LANDMASS
4,003 sq mi/10,368 sq km

Groundnuts

Food

GHANA

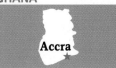

Accra

English, Twi, Fanti, Ga, Ewé, Dagbani

POPULATION
17,763,000
193 per sq mi/75 per sq km

LANDMASS
92,100 sq mi/238,539 sq km

Cocoa

Crude Oil

GUINEA

★Conakry

French, Malinké, Susu, Fulani

POPULATION
6,549,000
68 per sq mi/26 per sq km

LANDMASS
94,925 sq mi/245,856 sq km

Bauxite

Machinery

GUINEA-BISSAU

Bissau
★

Portuguese, Crioulo

POPULATION
1,125,000
81 per sq mi/31 per sq km

LANDMASS
13,948 sq mi/36,125 sq km

Groundnuts

Food

KENYA

★Nairobi

Swahili, English, Kikuyu

POPULATION
28,817,000
128 per sq mi/49 per sq km

LANDMASS
224,960 sq mi/582,646 sq km

Coffee

Crude Oil

LESOTHO

★Maseru

English, Sesotho

POPULATION
1,993,000
170 per sq mi/66 per sq km

LANDMASS
11,716 sq mi/30,344 sq km

Diamonds

Food

LIBERIA

★Monrovia

English, tribal dialects

POPULATION
3,073,000
71 per sq mi/27 per sq km

LANDMASS
43,000 sq mi/111,370 sq km

Iron Ore

Food

LIBYA

Tripoli

Arabic

POPULATION
5,248,000
8 per sq mi/3 per sq km

LANDMASS
679,358 sq mi/1,759,537 sq km

Crude Oil

Machinery

MADAGASCAR

Antananarivo

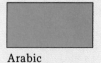 
Malagasy, French

POPULATION
13,862,000
61 per sq mi/24 per sq km

LANDMASS
226,657 sq mi/587,042 sq km

Spices

Crude Oil

	FLAG AND PRINCIPAL LANGUAGE(S)		PRINCIPAL PRODUCTS	
			EXPORT	IMPORT

MALAWI

Lilongwe

Chichewa, English, Nyanja, Yao

POPULATION
9,808,000
217 per sq mi/84 per sq km

LANDMASS
45,193 sq mi/117,050 sq km

 Tobacco

 Chemicals

MALI

★Bamako

French

POPULATION
9,375,000
20 per sq mi/7 per sq km

LANDMASS
478,652 sq mi/1,239,709 sq km

 Cotton

 Machinery

MAURITANIA

Nouakchott
★

French, Arabic, Tucolor

POPULATION
2,263,000
5 per sq mi/2 per sq km

LANDMASS
397,955 sq mi/1,030,703 sq km

 Iron Ore

 Food

MAURITIUS

Port Louis

English

POPULATION
1,127,000
1,565 per sq mi/604 per sq km

LANDMASS
720 sq mi/1,865 sq km

 Sugar

 Food

MOROCCO

★Rabat

Arabic, Berber, French, Spanish

POPULATION
29,169,000
169 per sq mi/65 per sq km

LANDMASS
172,413 sq mi/446,550 sq km

 Phosphates

 Crude Oil

MOZAMBIQUE

Maputo

Portuguese, Bantu, English

POPULATION
18,115,000
61 per sq mi/24 per sq km

LANDMASS
297,846 sq mi/771,421 sq km

 Fish

 Food

NAMIBIA

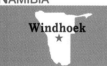
Windhoek
★

Afrikaans, English, German

POPULATION
1,652,000
5 per sq mi/2 per sq km

LANDMASS
317,887 sq mi/823,327 sq km

 Diamonds

N/A

NIGER

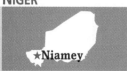
★Niamey

French, Fulani

POPULATION
9,280,000
20 per sq mi/8 per sq km

LANDMASS
459,073 sq mi/1,188,999 sq km

Uranium

 Cereals

NIGERIA

Abuja

English, Hausa, Yoruba, Ibo

POPULATION
101,232,000
284 per sq mi/110 per sq km

LANDMASS
356,669 sq mi/923,773 sq km

 Crude Oil

Machinery

AFRICA

	FLAG AND PRINCIPAL LANGUAGE(S)	POPULATION AND LANDMASS	PRINCIPAL PRODUCTS EXPORT	IMPORT
RWANDA Kigali	French, Kinyarwanda	**POPULATION** 8,605,000 846 per sq mi/327 per sq km **LANDMASS** 10,169 sq mi/26,338 sq km	Coffee	Machinery
SÃO TOMÉ E PRÍNCIPE São Tomé	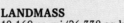 Portuguese	**POPULATION** 140,000 376 per sq mi/145 per sq km **LANDMASS** 372 sq mi/963 sq km	Cocoa	Food
SENEGAL ★Dakar 	French, Wolof, Serer	**POPULATION** 9,007,000 118 per sq mi/46 per sq km **LANDMASS** 76,124 sq mi/197,161 sq km	Petroleum	Food
SEYCHELLES ★Victoria 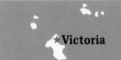	English, French, Creole	**POPULATION** 73,000 417 per sq mi/161 per sq km **LANDMASS** 175 sq mi/453 sq km	Petroleum	Petroleum
SIERRA LEONE ★Freetown 	English, Krio	**POPULATION** 4,753,000 172 per sq mi/46 per sq km **LANDMASS** 27,699 sq mi/71,740 sq km	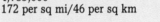 Diamonds	Crude Oil
SOMALIA Mogadishu ★	Somali, Arabic, English	**POPULATION** 7,348,000 30 per sq mi/12 per sq km **LANDMASS** 246,154 sq mi/637,539 sq km	Livestock	Machinery
SOUTH AFRICA Pretoria ★ 	 Afrikaans, English, Bantu	**POPULATION** 45,095,000 96 per sq mi/37 per sq km **LANDMASS** 471,445 sq mi/1,221,043 sq km	Gold	Machinery
SUDAN Khartoum	Arabic, English, tribal dialects	**POPULATION** 31,120,000 32 per sq mi/12 per sq km **LANDMASS** 967,500 sq mi/2,505,825 sq km	Cotton	Food
SWAZILAND Mbabane ★	English, Siswati	**POPULATION** 967,000 144 per sq mi/56 per sq km **LANDMASS** 6,705 sq mi/17,366 sq km	Sugar	Machinery

TANZANIA

Dodoma

English, Swahili,
Bantu, Arabic

POPULATION
28,701,000
79 per sq mi/30 per sq km

LANDMASS
364,943 sq mi/945,202 sq km

Coffee

Crude Oil

TOGO

Lomé

French, Ewé, Mina,
Kabyé, Cotocoli

POPULATION
4,410,000
202 per sq mi/78 per sq km

LANDMASS
21,853 sq mi/56,599 sq km

Phosphates

Food

TUNISIA
Tunis ★

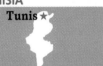

Arabic, French

POPULATION
8,880,000
141 per sq mi/54 per sq km

LANDMASS
63,170 sq mi/163,610 sq km

Crude Oil

Machinery

UGANDA

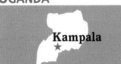
Kampala

English, Swahili,
Luganda, Ateso, Luo

POPULATION
19,573,000
215 per sq mi/83 per sq km

LANDMASS
91,134 sq mi/236,037 sq km

Coffee

Machinery

ZAIRE

★Kinshasa

French, Ishiluba,
Kikongo, Lingala

POPULATION
44,061,000
49 per sq mi/19 per sq km

LANDMASS
905,063 sq mi/2,344,113 sq km

Copper

Machinery

ZAMBIA

Lusaka
★

English, Bantu

POPULATION
9,446,000
33 per sq mi/13 per sq km

LANDMASS
290,585 sq mi/752,615 sq km

Copper

Machinery

ZIMBABWE

Harare ★

English, Chishona,
Sindebele

POPULATION
11,140,000
74 per sq mi/29 per sq km

LANDMASS
150,820 sq mi/390,624 sq km

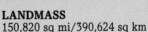
Tobacco

Machinery

531

THE COUNTRIES OF NORTH AFRICA

North Africa: A Desert Region

The Sahara Desert covers much of North Africa. Imagine that you are in the Sahara. What do you see around you? What is it like to be in the desert?

TERMS

erg, desert pavement, hammada, diffusion

FOCUS

What are the differences between the three main physical features of North Africa?

A. North Africa's Physical Features

The Mystery Plane During the Second World War, airplanes called B-24's flew from North Africa to Italy to drop bombs on enemy positions there. In 1943, one of these B-24 bombers, named the *Lady Be Good* by its crew, took off from Benghazi, Libya. After many hours, when all the other airplanes had returned, the *Lady Be Good* was missing. Everyone thought that it had probably crashed in the Mediterranean Sea.

Sixteen years later an exploration team was searching for new oil fields in remote areas of southern Libya. Unexpectedly they came upon the *Lady Be Good*.

The *Lady Be Good* had crash-landed on a giant sea of sand, 450 miles (724 km) south of Benghazi. Canteens of water and some food were found in the plane, and the radio still worked! However, there was no sign of the eight crew members.

About 75 miles (121 km) north of the crash site, the skeletons of five of the crew were found. With the skeletons was a diary that told the crew's story.

The crew had parachuted out of the plane when it ran out of fuel. They started walking north, mistakenly thinking they were close to the Mediterranean Sea. The

men traveled only at night and rested during the 130°F (54°C) days beneath shelters made out of their parachutes. They shouldn't have lasted more than three or four days in the harsh desert. But they rationed their tiny water supply and trekked on for eight days, through the Sahara.

The five men whose bones were found had decided to stop. The three strongest men pushed on northward in search of help. Entries in the diary during the next couple of days ranged from "all want to die" to "have hope for help very soon." The last entry read, "no help yet, very cold nite." The bodies of the three men who went on have never been found.

Three Main Regions As the story of the *Lady Be Good* shows, there are huge empty areas in the Sahara. In the Arabic language the word *Sahara* means "emptiness." It is a vast desert that stretches across the northern end of the continent of Africa. Only the Red Sea separates northeastern Africa from Asia, which begins on the Arabian Peninsula. Together the nations of Egypt, Libya, Tunisia, Algeria, Morocco, and the territory of Western Sahara form the area referred to as North Africa.

There are two other physical regions of North Africa besides the Sahara—the Atlas Mountains and the coastal margin. The Atlas Mountains are found in Morocco, as well as in parts of Algeria, Tunisia, and the Western Sahara. The coastal margin is the land between the Atlas Mountains and the coastline of the Atlantic Ocean and the Mediterranean Sea.

B. The Sahara

Landscape Features It is the Sahara's 3.5 million square mile area (9.1 million sq km) that dominates North Africa. This makes the Sahara about the same size as the United States.

Some parts of the Sahara are giant sand seas like the one in which the *Lady*

▶ The Sphinx and the Pyramids at Giza, near Cairo, Egypt.

Be Good crashed. These large areas called **ergs** are what most people picture when they think of a desert—loose sand blown into tall dunes by the wind. But most of the Sahara is made up of **desert pavement** and **hammadas**. Desert pavements are vast plains of gravel and boulders, and hammadas are rocky plateaus. Both surfaces are the result of the erosion of the soil due to the wind.

Located in the center of the Sahara are huge clusters of mountains. These mountains are actually the high peaks of extinct volcanoes. The highest peak in the Ahaggar Mountains, which are found in southern Algeria, has an elevation of 9,843 feet (3,000 m).

Not all of the Sahara is barren land. Oases are found scattered throughout the desert wherever water is available. Oases are the key to living in the Sahara because the oasis land is arable, or suitable for growing crops. The Nile River valley in Egypt is the largest oasis area found in the region of North Africa.

A Wet Sahara? The Sahara has not always been as dry as it is today. It is believed that 10,000 years ago much of the region was once covered with grass, like the Great Plains of the United States. A huge lake once covered much of the central Sahara, and large animals, such as elephants and hippopotamuses, roamed the grasslands. Ancient carvings of elephants and other types of animal life have been discovered throughout the region of the central Sahara.

About 5,000 years ago the climate of the Sahara started becoming drier, which slowly created the desert. Animals could no longer survive there and either died or moved south. Many scientists believe that this process is still continuing. The Sahara is slowly becoming larger as the grasslands to the south of this desert gradually get drier.

C. The Atlas Mountains and the Coastal Margin

Atlas Mountains The second major geographical feature of North Africa is the Atlas Mountains. The Atlas Mountains stretch 1,500 miles (2,414 km) along the northwest coast of the African continent. The name Atlas comes from the ancient

DESERT LANDSCAPE

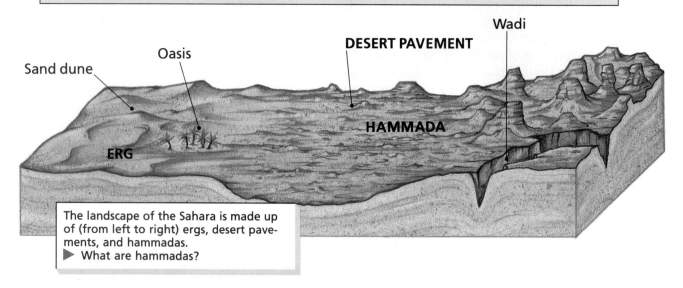

Sand dune

Oasis

DESERT PAVEMENT

Wadi

ERG

HAMMADA

The landscape of the Sahara is made up of (from left to right) ergs, desert pavements, and hammadas.
▶ What are hammadas?

534

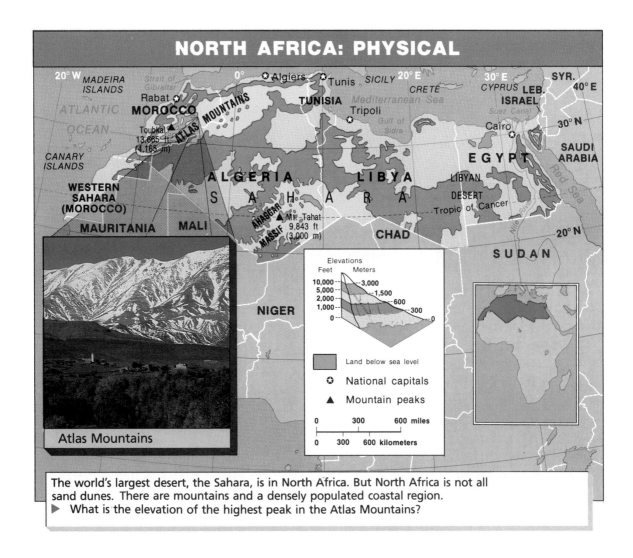

NORTH AFRICA: PHYSICAL

Elevations

Feet	Meters
10,000	3,000
5,000	1,500
2,000	600
1,000	300
0	0

Land below sea level

✪ National capitals

▲ Mountain peaks

0   300   600 miles

0   300   600 kilometers

Atlas Mountains

The world's largest desert, the Sahara, is in North Africa. But North Africa is not all sand dunes. There are mountains and a densely populated coastal region.

▶ What is the elevation of the highest peak in the Atlas Mountains?

Greeks, who told a myth about a giant named Atlas. For his part in a revolt against the gods, Atlas was condemned to hold up the heavens above the earth. To the Greeks, this range of mountains literally rose high enough to support the heavens. Tunisia, Algeria, Morocco, and Western Sahara benefit from the mineral resources of this mountain range.

The Coastal Margin The coastal margin is the region north of the mountains that slopes down to the sea. The height of the Atlas Mountains acts as a barrier to the moist air flowing in off the Atlantic Ocean and Mediterranean Sea. The air flows up the mountain slopes and cools enough so that clouds form and some rain falls. The valleys in the mountains and the foothills north of the range receive about 30 inches (76 cm) of rain per year. With the exception of the Nile River valley, this area is the best watered and the most populated region of North Africa.

D. North Africa and the Middle East

Much in Common Some geography books put the Middle East and North Africa together in the same chapter because they

535

The Al Azhar Mosque and University in Cairo has been a center of learning for over 1,000 years.
▶ What other city in Egypt has been a center of learning?

have much in common. Both the Middle East and North Africa have a desert environment. The people who live in the deserts of both regions depend on oases. The majority of the people of these two regions also have the same religion and culture.

The Berbers, a nomadic people, are the oldest surviving inhabitants of the western part of the Sahara. The biggest change in their way of life came when the Arab people spread into North Africa from the Middle East. The Arabs moved across North Africa early in the eighth century A.D., converting people to Islam. Many of the Berbers were gradually absorbed into the

Arab culture. The mixture of Arabs and Berbers created a new ethnic group—the Moors. Over time the Moors crossed the Strait of Gibraltar into Spain.

Arabs Preserved Knowledge While the Moors made their way across Spain, Europe was in the midst of the Dark Ages. This was a time when the knowledge and learning of the Greek and Roman empires was forgotten in Europe. European civilization collapsed under the weight of barbarian invasions. Greek and Roman discoveries about mathematics, science, geography, and literature were lost to the Europeans.

536

TABLE OF NUMERALS

Hindu	Arabic	Modern
٥	٥	0
١	١	1
٢	٢	2
٣	٣	3
٨	٩	4
٩	ع	5
٢	٧	6
٦	٧	7
٤	٨	8
٤	9	9
١٥	١٥	10

The writing of numbers has changed over time as it has passed from culture to culture.

► How would you write the current year with each type of numeral?

However, the Arab world of North Africa carried on that body of knowledge and merged it with their own. The Arabs had inherited this knowledge from the ancient Greek and Roman education centers, such as Alexandria, in Egypt. The Arabs preserved that tradition of learning and took it with them as they spread their people and culture across North Africa.

Diffusion The Moors carried the knowledge with them on into Spain. It was from there in the fifteenth and sixteenth centuries that the Europeans finally began to rediscover the knowledge of the classical Greek and Roman world. This spread of knowledge from one group of people to another is known as **diffusion**.

Look at the table of numerals on this page. Numerals are the written symbols of mathematical numbers. Notice the similarity between the three types of numerals. Which numbers were written the same way?

Some of them appear the same because they passed by diffusion from Hindu to Arab to European society.

The way we write numbers today can be traced back to Hindu and Arabic origins. Arab merchants and armies reached India and learned the Hindu numeral system. The use of this system spread throughout the Arab world. Contact with Europeans brought the Arabic system into Europe. Arabic numerals, like the ones shown in the table, were first used in a European book in the tenth century A.D. Modern numerals first appeared in a book in the year 1202. This book was a translation of an Arabic book on mathematics written four centuries earlier.

The Berbers, Arabs, and other inhabitants of North Africa have learned how to live in the region's desert environment. Just as the religion and culture of North Africans are like those of people in the Middle East, so too is their way of making a living.

LESSON 1

Review

REVIEWING MAIN IDEAS

A. What are the three main regions of North Africa's physical geography?

B. What are the physical features of the Sahara's surface?

C. How do the Atlas Mountains affect the weather of the western part of North Africa?

D. What do North Africa and the Middle East have in common?

SKILLS CHECK

MAP SKILL

During World War II, American warplanes like the *Lady Be Good* flew from North Africa to Italy. Using the map on page 547, calculate the distance from the southern coast of Italy to the following cities: Benghazi, Tripoli, Cairo, and Tunis.

Living and Working in North Africa

CONNECTIONS

How, do you think, is making a living in North Africa similar to or different from making a living in the Middle East?

TERMS

fellahin, bazaar, caravan

FOCUS

How do people in North Africa make a living from their desert environment?

A. Life in a North African Oasis Village

Oasis Farmers Life in North Africa can be studied by looking at three ways in which people have lived through the centuries—as villagers, as city dwellers, and as nomads. About three fourths of the people in North Africa are farmers. As in the Middle East, these farmers are often called **fellahin** (FEL uh heen), which is an Arabic word that means "peasant." Most fellahin live in small villages. In areas such as the Nile River valley, where there is abundant water available, there are many villages located close together. But across the vast Sahara region, a village is located wherever there happens to be enough water for an oasis.

Oasis Economy Some oases of the Sahara are fed by underground springs that supply enough water to support small towns and villages. The value of each oasis is determined by the number of date palm trees it supports. The number of date palm trees surrounding an oasis can reach as high as 300,000. The date palms are the heart of the desert oasis economy because of the variety of goods that can be made from these trees.

Every part of the date palm tree is useful. The fruit is eaten and also used to make sugar. The leaves are used to make baskets and mats, while other parts of the

Many of the goods sold in the marketplace are made in local workshops.
▶ What is this merchant selling?

tree are used to make rope, sandals, cooking oil, and even medicine.

In addition to raising date palm trees, oasis farmers grow almonds, apricots, oranges, lemons, pomegranates, and some wheat and millet. Millet is a grass similar to hay and is used for its grain. Farmers may also raise a few goats and chickens, and maybe even a water buffalo or two. The chief foods of the villagers are fruits, nuts, bread, and goat cheese.

B. Life in a North African City

The North African City Most North Africans are Arabs who are followers of Islam. Therefore the Islamic mosque is one of the dominant features of any North African city. The mosque is the center of religious life. The people of the city live in housing quarters, or districts, located around the mosque and **bazaar**. The bazaar is the central marketplace.

The bazaar is almost like a huge shopping center where you can buy almost anything you need or want. Many bazaars are a series of small shops or stands lined up along very narrow streets. You can see all kinds of merchandise for sale—from pots and pans to camel saddles; from leather goods and cloth to chickens; from books and religious jewelry to carpets. In the bazaar the nomads and the people from the villages can buy sugar, coffee, tea, glassware, and many other things. The workshops of the craftspeople who make many of the items for sale are often located behind the merchants' stalls.

C. A Nomadic Way of Life

Nomads The nomads lead a third way of life in North Africa. They move from place to place, searching out watering holes and grasses for their herds of goats, sheep, and camels. Nomads sell and trade wool and animal hides to the city dwellers in return for the things the nomads need. Craftspeople and merchants in the city make finished items from the wool and hides. Wool, for example, is made into carpets that are sold in the bazaar.

Caravans For centuries, goods such as ivory, gold, salt, and even slaves were moved overland across the Sahara to the grasslands located south of the desert. The only way to cross the desert safely was to go by camel **caravan**. A caravan is a group of people traveling together, usually on animals or in vehicles.

Caravan trading routes connected the scattered oasis villages in the region. Expert caravan leaders would guide their train of camels by relying on landmarks in the desert. Camels are sometimes called "ships of the desert" because they move cargo across the desert like ships move across the sea. Camels adapt well to the dry environment. A camel's body can store enough water and food to survive for long periods of time in the desert.

One tribe of nomads that has been involved in the caravan trade lives in the western part of the Sahara. These nomads are the Tuaregs (TWAH regz). The Tuaregs

The traditional camel caravan is being replaced by cars and trucks.
▶ Why does the camel driver wear a veil across his face?

539

Because there are few trees to use for wood, homes in this oasis village are made of sun-dried mud bricks.
▶ What kind of trees grow in the oasis?

disappearing in the modern world. To continue trading along the old caravan routes, nomads would have to ignore political boundaries. The governments of modern nations, however, do not like people freely crossing their borders. Today most of the trade is carried on by sea. Also, roads for cars and trucks now cross the desert, replacing the need for caravans. Therefore, many nomads have moved to urban areas to find work.

Three Ways of Life   North Africa's three ways of life are distinctively different, yet they are closely interrelated. Villagers are mostly peasant farmers who raise food crops. Wool and hides are produced by the nomads. For their part, the city dwellers collect and process the crops and other raw materials, and in turn sell certain necessary items to the villagers and the nomads. This three-way interrelationship is found all over North Africa, and it is typical of the way of life in the Middle East. This shows another strong cultural connection between the Middle East and North Africa.

live in tents, often made of leather. In Tuareg societies, all men over the age of 15 or 16 wear a long scarf wrapped around their head as a turban. It also serves as a veil and hides all but their eyes from others. The turban-veil provides cover that keeps the mouth from drying out during hot caravan trips. Also, the dark color of the turbans helps to cut down on the glare of the bright sun. Through the years the turban-veil has become a symbol for the well-dressed Tuareg male.

A Vanishing Way of Life   In the past the Tuaregs and other nomads traveled across the Sahara. But the nomadic way of life is

LESSON 2

Review

REVIEWING MAIN IDEAS
A. How do the fellahin make a living?
B. What would you be likely to see in a North African city?
C. How has the nomadic way of life changed?

SKILLS CHECK

WRITING SKILL
Experienced caravan leaders relied on landmarks in the desert to guide their way. Imagine that you are a caravan leader traveling from the southern tip of Algeria to Cairo, Egypt. Using the map on page 535, describe the route you will take and the landmarks you will use to guide the caravan.

Egypt

What difficulties would a heavily populated country experience if there were very little arable land available for its people to use?

TERMS

distributary, ecology

FOCUS

What influence has the Nile River had on the country of Egypt?

A. The Nile Valley

The Gift of the Nile The ancient Greek historian Herodotus (hih RAHD uh tus) once wrote, "Egypt is an acquired country, the gift of the river." How right Herodotus was! Without the Nile River there would be no Egypt. The 4,187-mile-(6,737-km-) long Nile is the only major river in North Africa. For thousands of years, Egypt has been dependent on the Nile River. The ancient Egyptian civilization emerged and flourished along the narrow gash of green that the Nile cut across the Sahara. In most places the Nile River valley is less than 10 miles (16 km) wide.

Just north of Cairo the river breaks into two main **distributaries**, the Rosetta Mouth and the Damietta Mouth. A distributary is a river branch flowing away from the main stream. It is the opposite of a tributary, which, as you read in Chapter 12, flows into the main stream.

As a major river reaches a flat region, its speed slows, and the silt and sand that it is carrying settles to the bottom of the river. The silt and sand eventually create sandbars and new islands, which cause the river to divide into two or more separate channels of water.

Each of these newly formed channels becomes a distributary. In other words, they distribute the river's flow across the delta and into the sea or ocean. The delta is the land that is formed by the mud and sand deposited at the mouth of the river.

Population Density Almost all of Egypt's 62 million people live in the Nile's narrow river valley and its triangular-shaped delta. Only a few Egyptians live elsewhere, in scattered desert oases. Egypt has about 386,660 square miles (1,001,449 sq km) of territory. That works out to a population

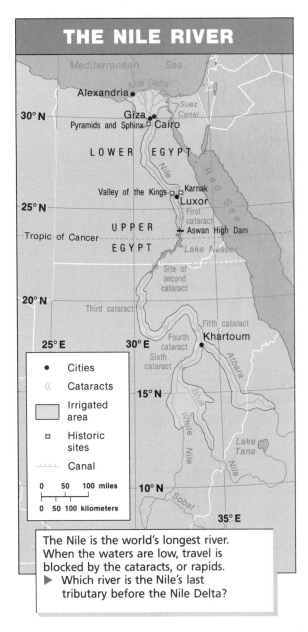

THE NILE RIVER

The Nile is the world's longest river. When the waters are low, travel is blocked by the cataracts, or rapids.
► Which river is the Nile's last tributary before the Nile Delta?

In some places, the desert reaches the Nile's riverbanks. In the past, travel by water was much easier than by land because of the desert.
▶ How is this boat powered?

density of 161 people per square mile (62 people per sq km).

However, about 96 percent of Egypt's land is barren desert and wasteland. Nothing will grow there because there is no water. This leaves only 15,466 square miles (40,057 sq km) of land that is usable for farms, villages, cities, and so on. If we only count the usable land in calculating the population density, then the result is 4,032 people per square mile (1,557 people per sq km). In comparison, the most densely populated state in the United States is New Jersey, with 1,050 people per square mile (406 people per sq km).

A Dry Land Because Egypt is one of the driest countries in the world, it is dependent on the Nile. The most rainfall, about 8 inches (20 cm) per year, occurs along the Mediterranean Sea near the city of Alexandria. The amount of rainfall decreases as you move inland; for example, south of Cairo, less than 2 inches (5 cm) of rain falls each year.

The Nile has the advantage of drawing water from two sources that get rain at two different times. One tributary is the Blue Nile, which flows out of the mountains of Ethiopia. The other tributary is the White Nile, which gathers its waters from the much wetter regions near the rain forests of central Africa.

B. Irrigation from the Nile

The Nile God The ancient Egyptians worshipped more than one god. Among their gods the Nile god was very important because the river was their source of water. Also, every year the Nile would overflow its banks. As the water receded, it deposited new fertile silt onto the farms of the valley. The Egyptians knew the exact day of the year when the Nile would overflow. They also had elaborate systems of gauges and measurements so that they could predict just how high the flood waters would get.

The Aswan High Dam The rulers of Egypt long desired to store the Nile's water and use it to create and irrigate more farmland. In the nineteenth century the first large dams were built along the river. In 1970 the huge Aswan High Dam was completed in the southern part of Egypt. This dam created a huge new reservoir, or artificial lake, called Lake Nasser. The lake is so long that it backs the Nile's waters up into a section of the country of Sudan called Nubia. Many Nubian people and their villages had to be relocated when the dam was built.

The Aswan High Dam provides hydroelectric power, and Lake Nasser gives Egypt an assured year-round water supply for irrigation. Egyptian leaders had hoped that many of their problems would be solved by the Aswan Dam. But that was not to be. Egypt's population continued to increase very rapidly, so that any gains made in new lands for farming were quickly offset by many new mouths to feed.

The Aswan High Dam created a number of disastrous side effects for which no one was prepared. All the rich silt that used to provide natural fertilizer to the farmers' fields was now blocked by the dam and deposited on the bottom of Lake Nasser. Egyptian farmers are now forced to rely on expensive artificial fertilizers that they cannot afford. Also, below the dam the river now flows faster because it is not laden with its load of silt. Many water-lifting devices, like the one shown on this page, have been washed away by the swift current.

The **ecology** of the coastal region has been affected. Ecology refers to the balance between living things and their environment. Silt no longer reaches the coast, and the coastal beaches along the delta are eroding. The sardine industry along the Mediterranean coast has suffered because of the change in the content of the Nile water. Egypt has learned the hard way about how human interference can sometimes cause major changes in the ecological balance of a place.

C. Egypt's Economic Growth

Lower and Upper Egypt As you can see on the map on page 699, the Nile River flows from the mountains in the south and empties through its delta into the Mediterranean Sea in the north. The Nile delta area has traditionally been referred to as Lower Egypt, and farther south on the map is Upper Egypt. These region names might confuse you because often when giving

Devices like this shadoof have been used for centuries to lift water from the Nile to irrigate fields.
▶ How does this device work?

543

directions on a map we wrongly use *up* and *down* instead of *north* and *south*. The terms *upper* and *lower* refer to the flow of a river as it relates to elevation, not placement on the map. All rivers flow downhill, to lower elevations. So the higher elevations of a river are often referred to as its upper end and the delta of a river is often called its lower end.

Rice and wheat are grown in the delta of Lower Egypt. Lower Egypt is also where long-staple cotton is grown. This kind of cotton has long, very fine fibers and is highly prized for making cloth. Sugarcane is grown farther upstream, in the region known as Upper Egypt. Upper Egypt's farmers also harvest fruits, including apricots, nectarines, oranges, lemons, figs, grapes, and olives. For many centuries, agriculture has been Egypt's main source of income.

Suez Canal Another source of income for Egypt is the Suez Canal. Originally built by the French in 1869, the canal was controlled by French and British companies. The Egyptians took control of the canal in 1956. The tolls collected from foreign ships using this 107-mile-long (172-km-long) strategic waterway are an important source of income for Egypt.

Tourism Tourism provides another major source of income for Egypt. Every year thousands of people travel to Egypt to see its historic monuments. The Great Pyramid and the Sphinx at Giza, and the huge temple ruins of Karnak at Luxor are some of the biggest attractions. Also, across the Nile from Luxor is the famous Valley of the Kings, where many of the ancient Egyptian pharaohs, or kings, were buried along with their riches.

COTTON PLANT AND PRODUCTS

FIBERS   LINT   SEEDS

Boll

Flower

Seeds

Lint

Fibers

Stem

Leaves

Different products are made from each part of the cotton plant. Fibers are made into a variety of textile products, from fine fabrics to typewriter ribbons and sailcloth.

▶ What part of the plant would be used to feed livestock?

Cairo, the capital of Egypt, is the largest city in Africa. The Cairo Tower is in the center of the picture.
▶ What river does this bridge cross?

D. Rapid Population Growth

A Giant Metropolis Cairo is a huge, rapidly growing city. The metropolitan area has a population of over 14 million people, making it by far the largest city in Egypt as well as the largest city in Africa. Cairo is an old city, and it has long been one of the leading centers of the Islamic world. The Al Azhar Mosque of Cairo is one of the largest mosques in all of Islam.

Growth Problems Egypt, like other rapidly growing areas of the world, is running into the problem of not having enough space. Thousands of homeless people in Cairo actually live in the large city cemetery because they can find no other space to live in. The population of Egypt continues to increase by about 1 million people per year, or about 2,740 people per day.

All these people have to live somewhere, and cities such as Cairo continue to expand. But Egypt cannot afford the luxury of building more cities on its little, narrow ribbon of irrigated land. Egypt needs this land just as desperately for farming.

This is one of the problems that Egypt will continue to face into the next century.

LESSON 3

Review

REVIEWING MAIN IDEAS

A. What effect does the Nile River have on Egypt's population density?
B. What are some of the benefits and drawbacks of the Aswan High Dam?
C. What are some of the major sources of income for Egypt?
D. What are some of the problems caused by Egypt's rapid population growth?

SKILLS CHECK

MAP SKILL

Locate the Suez Canal on the map on page 547. What two seas does the canal connect? Before the canal was made, what route did ships have to follow to travel between these two seas?

545

Libya and the Maghreb

CONNECTIONS

A part of North Africa has a climate like that in Southern Europe because both border the Mediterranean Sea. What crops would you expect to find in this climate?

TERMS

Maghreb, Tell, phosphate

FOCUS

Where do most of the people of the western part of North Africa live and why do they live there?

A. The Heart of Arid North Africa

Libya Libya is big. With 679,358 square miles (1,759,537 sq km), it is equal to about one fifth of the continental United States. However, it has no major rivers. The only moisture supply other than a few oases is some rainfall along the Mediterranean coast. The rainfall there ranges from 8 inches (20 cm) per year in the east to 24 inches (61 cm) per year in the west.

Libya is so dry that only about 4 million people live there, and almost all of them live within 50 miles (80 km) of the coast. Over half the people of Libya live in two cities—Tripoli, which is the capital, and Benghazi. The population density of Libya is only 8 people per square mile (3 people per sq km), and there are huge areas of empty desert land in Libya's interior where no one can live. No wonder that the *Lady Be Good* was not found for 16 years, and then only by accident!

Libya's Resource Those oil explorers who found the *Lady Be Good* also found the answer to Libya's future. Rich oil fields were discovered in 1959, and the Libyans have used the income from oil production to build up their nation. They have a fairly high per capita income, and they are using oil profits to build irrigation systems to increase farmland. At this time, Libya imports about three fourths of its food, a situation that its leaders would like to change in the future.

Leadership Throughout the 1970s and 1980s, Muammar Al-Qaddafi (MOO uh mahr al kuh DAH fee) tried to make Libya a leader among the Arab nations. He also tried to have a strong influence on other nations. For example, Qaddafi sent troops into Chad, Uganda, and other countries. By doing so, he caused problems with his Arab neighbors, especially Egypt, Tunisia, and Chad. Libya also came into conflict with the United States, which accused Qaddafi of supporting terrorist attacks throughout the world.

Much of Qaddafi's power comes from the money Libya earns from the oil business. Libya's oil industry is owned by the government, which is a dictatorship run by Qaddafi. He has put some of the profit from oil sales into improving farming and into building new schools, houses, and hospitals. His government has also provided free social services to Libya's citizens. Still, many Libyans would like their country to be run democratically.

B. Western North Africa

The Maghreb Tunisia, Algeria, and Morocco form the region of North Africa known as the **Maghreb** (MUH grub). *Maghreb* is an Arabic word meaning "western isle." The

Muammar Al-Qaddafi became the ruler of Libya in 1969.
▶ How has he caused conflict with neighboring countries?

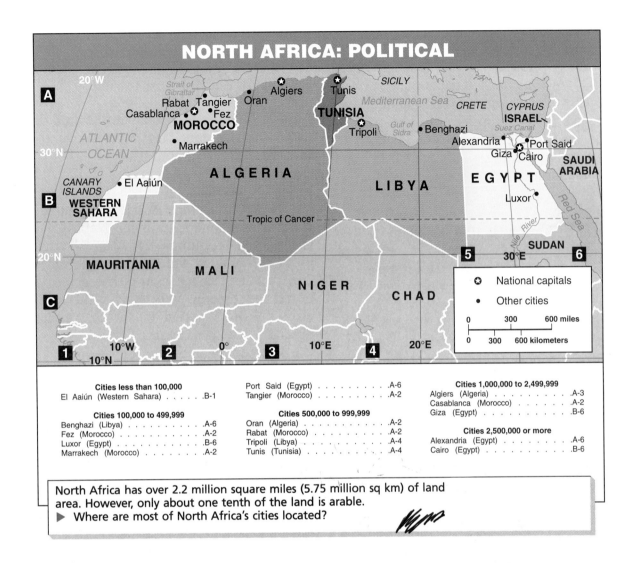

NORTH AFRICA: POLITICAL

○	National capitals	
•	Other cities	

0   300   600 miles
0   300   600 kilometers

Cities less than 100,000
El Aaiún (Western Sahara) B-1

Cities 100,000 to 499,999
Benghazi (Libya) A-6
Fez (Morocco) A-2
Luxor (Egypt) B-6
Marrakech (Morocco) A-2

Port Said (Egypt) A-6
Tangier (Morocco) A-2

Cities 500,000 to 999,999
Oran (Algeria) A-2
Rabat (Morocco) A-2
Tripoli (Libya) A-4
Tunis (Tunisia) A-4

Cities 1,000,000 to 2,499,999
Algiers (Algeria) A-3
Casablanca (Morocco) A-2
Giza (Egypt) B-6

Cities 2,500,000 or more
Alexandria (Egypt) A-6
Cairo (Egypt) B-6

North Africa has over 2.2 million square miles (5.75 million sq km) of land area. However, only about one tenth of the land is arable.
▶ Where are most of North Africa's cities located?

name most likely refers to the fact that here the Atlas Mountains rise like an island out of the western part of the Sahara.

The Atlas mountain range protects the coast along the Atlantic Ocean and Mediterranean Sea from the dry climate of the Sahara. On the coast side of the mountain range there is plentiful rainfall and arable land. On the other side there is useless desert sand.

This land pattern is the same for the entire Maghreb. Along the coast is a hilly region called the **Tell**. *Tell* is an Arabic word meaning "hill." Adjacent to the Tell is a steppe-like plateau, where nomads raise their flocks of sheep. This grassy plateau

region and the coastal Tell are actually parts of the lower elevations of the Maghreb's Atlas Mountains.

Maghreb Economy As with the people of Libya, the people of the Maghreb live on the hills and plains along the coast. These people benefit from the warm, wet winters and hot, dry summers of the Mediterranean climate. Wheat, olives, grapes, and citrus fruits are grown in this climate. Industries that have developed from these crops include wine making, olive oil production, and fruit canning. Fishing and fish canning is another Maghreb industry.

Tourists are also attracted to the sunny North African coast. Algeria receives about

714,000 visitors per year. Tunisia and Morocco each receive more than 2 million tourists a year.

The Atlas Mountains supply Tunisia, Algeria, and Morocco with mineral resources. These countries mine **phosphates**, iron ore, zinc, lead, and copper. Phosphate is a vital mineral used in making fertilizers for the farmers of the world.

C. Tunisia, Algeria, and Morocco

Tunisia Tunisia is the smallest of the countries of North Africa. With an area of 63,170 square miles (163,610 sq km), it is about the size of New England. Tunis, the capital city, has a population of about 1 million, and is the largest city in this nation of 8.9 million people. Tunis is located next to the ruins of the city of Carthage.

In ancient times, Carthage competed with Rome for power. After a series of wars, Carthage was conquered by the Romans and destroyed. Today, along the coast of Tunisia, the ruins of the ancient Roman Empire are visited by tourists.

Algeria Algeria is located in the middle part of the Maghreb. It is the largest country in North Africa. About three fourths of Algeria's 919,591 square miles (2,381,741 sq km) is desert.

Like Libya, Algeria has tremendous reserves of oil and natural gas. Natural gas is exported to Europe from the Algerian port cities of Oran and Algiers in two ways. Some of it is changed from a gas into a liquid and shipped out by tanker. The other way it is transported is through a gas pipeline that goes beneath the waters of the Mediterranean Sea to Italy.

Algeria was a French colony until 1962, when after a bloody revolution that lasted eight years, the Algerians won their independence. Almost 1 million French settlers left Algeria at that time and returned to France. Today Algeria has a population of 24 million, most of whom live in the northern part of the country.

Morocco The High Atlas range slices across the middle of Morocco, the westernmost country of the Maghreb. About the size of the state of California, Morocco has an area of 172,413 square miles (446,550 sq km).

Almost all of Morocco's 29 million people live between the coast and the Atlas Mountains. Marrakech, a city nestled at the base of the Atlas range, is an inland trading center and resort city. It has long been a place that has attracted tourists and other visitors. Here also is Casablanca, the largest city of the Maghreb, with a population of over 2.6 million. The capital city of Rabat is on the Atlantic coast, about 60 miles (97 km) northeast of Casablanca.

Morocco has a fairly large fishing industry, which is based on the abundance of fish found off the Atlantic coast. Tuna

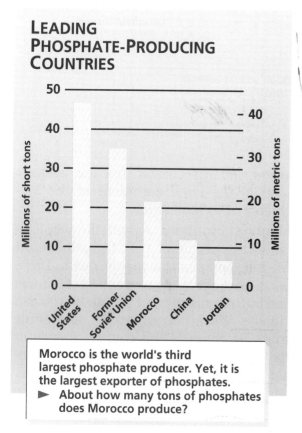

LEADING PHOSPHATE-PRODUCING COUNTRIES

Millions of short tons

Millions of metric tons

United States, Former Soviet Union, Morocco, China, Jordan

Morocco is the world's third largest phosphate producer. Yet, it is the largest exporter of phosphates.
► About how many tons of phosphates does Morocco produce?

These brightly colored spices are for sale in a market in Morocco. The spices are weighed and then packaged in jars and boxes.
▶ How are spices weighed?

and sardines are the most important catches. Much of the catch is processed by Morocco's cannery industry.

Most of Morocco's wealth comes from one mineral resource, phosphates. With over half the world's supply, Morocco has become the world's leading exporter of phosphates.

Western Sahara In 1975, Morocco claimed the region along its southern border. This area, which is called the Western Sahara, was a Spanish colony. In 1975, Spain gave up its claim to the Western Sahara. When Spain pulled out, Morocco's government allowed 350,000 Moroccan people to march into the Western Sahara and claim the land for Morocco. No other nations recognize Morocco's claim to the Western Sahara.

LESSON 4

Review

REVIEWING MAIN IDEAS

A. What is meant when it is said that Libya's economy is heavily dependent on one resource?

B. What do the countries of the Maghreb have in common?

C. What are some sources of income for Tunisia, Algeria, and Morocco?

SKILLS CHECK

THINKING SKILL

Create a bar graph comparing the population density of the countries of North Africa. Population and land area figures to calculate the population density can be found in Lesson 4. Egypt's population density can be found in Lesson 3.

REVIEWING TERMS

Use the following terms to complete the sentences below. Write your answers in sentence form.

erg	caravan
hammada	distributary
diffusion	ecology
fellahin	Maghreb
bazaar	phosphate

1. From the edge of the _____, a vast stretch of desert could be seen below.

2. The Rosetta Mouth is a main _____ that flows away from the Nile River.

3. The _____ of the Hindu numeral system to Europe occurred because of the Arabs.

4. The _____ raise their crops in an oasis.

5. Our tour traveled through the _____ countries of Tunisia, Algeria, and Morocco.

6. I bought a copper bracelet from a vendor in the _____.

7. The *Lady Be Good* crashed in the middle of a giant _____, or sea of sand.

8. The Aswan High Dam has affected the _____ of the Nile River.

9. _____ is a vital mineral that is used in making fertilizers.

10. The _____ of camels could be seen in the distance, moving across the top of a sand dune.

REVIEWING THE FACTS

On a separate sheet of paper, answer the questions in complete sentences.

1. Why are oases the key to living in the desert?

2. What barrier creates abundant rainfall in the coastal margin?

3. What influence did the Moors have on the people of Europe in the fifteenth and sixteenth centuries?

4. Why are date palm trees the heart of the desert oases economy?

5. Why do Tuareg men wear turban-veils?

6. How is a delta formed?

7. What are the two sources of the Nile River?

8. How has Libya spent the profits it has received from the sale of oil?

9. What attracts tourists to the Maghreb region?

10. What are the two ways natural gas is exported from Algeria to Europe?

WRITING ABOUT GEOGRAPHY

Sahara is the Arabic word for "emptiness." In a paragraph, describe how this emptiness is filled with life at an oasis.

THINKING CRITICALLY

On a separate sheet of paper, answer the following in complete sentences.

1. How has water influenced where people live in North Africa?
2. How can the diffusion of knowledge help create a better life for people?
3. In what ways has technology changed the lifestyles of the North Africans?
4. Some people consider the Sahara an empty place. What do you think?
5. Why is it important for North Africans to make good use of their arable lands?

SUMMARIZING THE CHAPTER

On a separate sheet of paper, draw a graphic organizer that is like the one shown here. Copy the information from this graphic organizer to the one you have drawn. For each country, write a plus sign (+) if the country has the characteristic listed. Write a minus sign (−) if the country does not have the characteristic.

CHAPTER THEME

The Sahara Desert has strongly influenced the culture, economy, and lifestyles of the people of North Africa.

CHARACTERISTIC	EGYPT	LIBYA	TUNISIA	ALGERIA	MOROCCO
Atlantic Ocean					
Atlas Mountains					
Coastal margin					
Maghreb					
Mediterranean Sea					
Nile River					
Sahara Desert					

CHAPTER **22** THE COUNTRIES OF WEST AFRICA

1. **West Africa: A Varied Region**

2. **Living and Working in West Africa**

3. **West Africa's Past: From Empires to Independence**

West Africa: A Varied Region

CONNECTIONS
West Africa has four different tropical climates. Describe the climates of tropical areas that you have studied.

TERMS
mangrove, Sahel

FOCUS
In what ways is West Africa a varied region?

A. A Disease Under Control

Looking carefully at the ground, the young boy walks along the pathway, avoiding tree roots or stones. If he were alone, he could easily walk around or jump over any object in his way. But he is not alone. The boy holds on to one end of a stick, leading his father, who holds the other end. On this path the boy must be the eyes for his father. His father is blind.

In West Africa, it is common to see a young person guiding someone who suffers from river blindness. River blindness is a disease given to humans by the bite of a fly called the black fly. The name of the disease comes from the fact that it is commonly found in people who live near rapidly flowing rivers where the flies reproduce in great numbers.

When the black fly bites, it transmits a microscopic-sized worm into the human body. In the body, the worm produces millions of smaller worms. When these smaller worms die, they accumulate under the skin and in the eyes of the victim. Under the skin, they cause itching so severe that some people commit suicide. In the eyes, they block vision to the point of total blindness.

One black fly bite can cause a little itching, but it takes repeated exposure to the flies to create a severe condition. The disease can be controlled by eliminating the flies. It is important to put an end to the disease because people cannot live near rivers where there is fear of the black fly. One result of the fear is that good farmland next to the rivers is not being used.

Since the 1970s, scientists have led the battle against the black fly by spraying pesticides on rivers where the flies breed. The spraying has been a great success. In 90 percent of the area being treated, there have been no new cases of river blindness. Thanks to the efforts against the disease, almost all of the 16 countries of West Africa have opened up new farmland without risk of infection and blindness. Gaining new farmland is important because West Africa is the most populated area on the continent. An estimated 290 million people, or about one third of Africa's total population, live there.

A young boy leads a person from his village who suffers from river blindness.
▶ What causes river blindness?

▶ Thousands of slaves were shipped from Elmina Castle in Ghana.

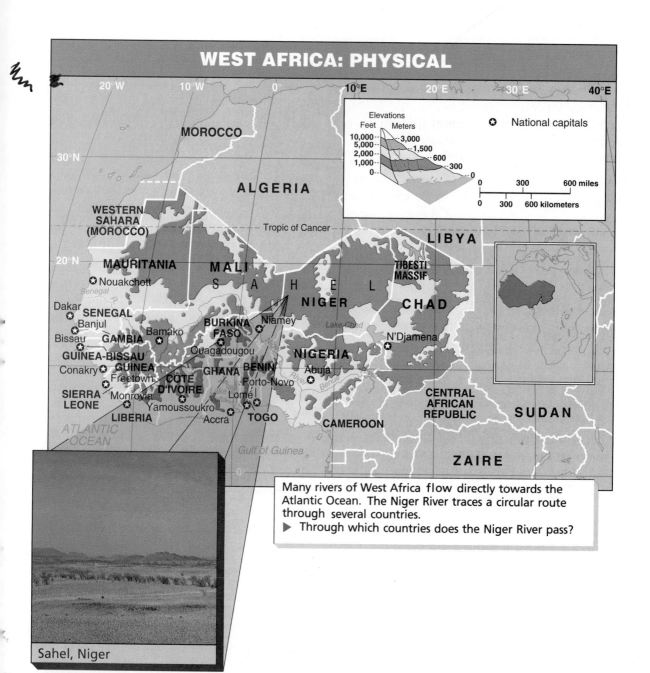

WEST AFRICA: PHYSICAL

Elevations
Feet	Meters
10,000	3,000
5,000	1,500
2,000	600
1,000	300
0	0

⊗ National capitals

0   300   600 miles
0   300   600 kilometers

MOROCCO

WESTERN
SAHARA
(MOROCCO)

ALGERIA

Tropic of Cancer

LIBYA

MAURITANIA   MALI   NIGER   CHAD   TIBESTI
MASSIF
⊗ Nouakchott   S A H E L
Senegal R.
Dakar   Niamey ⊗
⊗ SENEGAL   BURKINA
Banjul   FASO ⊗   N'Djamena ⊗
Bissau ⊗ GAMBIA   Bamako
Ouagadougou   NIGERIA
GUINEA-BISSAU   Abuja ⊗
Conakry ⊗ GUINEA   GHANA BENIN
⊗ Freetown COTE   Porto-Novo
SIERRA   D'IVOIRE Lomé ⊗
LEONE   ⊗ Monrovia ⊗⊗   CENTRAL
        Yamoussoukro ⊗   AFRICAN   SUDAN
LIBERIA   Accra TOGO   REPUBLIC
ATLANTIC   CAMEROON
OCEAN
        Gulf of Guinea   ZAIRE

Many rivers of West Africa flow directly towards the
Atlantic Ocean. The Niger River traces a circular route
through several countries.
▶ Through which countries does the Niger River pass?

Sahel, Niger

As you can see from the map on this page, four of West Africa's 16 countries—Mali, Burkina Faso (bur KEE nuh FAH soh), Niger(NYE jur), and Chad—are landlocked. The remaining 12 countries have coastlines on the Atlantic Ocean. One other country is sometimes included with West Africa. The Republic of Cape Verde is a group of fifteen islands located in the Atlantic Ocean 375 miles (600 km) west of Cape Verde.

Cape Verde is the westernmost point in the continent of Africa.

B. Landforms of West Africa

Coastal Lowland On the map above, you can see that West Africa can be divided into coastal and inland regions. The coastal lowland is one of the largest in Africa. At its western end, in Mauritania (mor uh TAY nee uh), it is part of the Sahara. This is also the coastal lowland's widest point, and it includes nearly all of the country of Senegal.

Mangrove swamps are found along the coast, especially in the delta of the Niger River and other places where rivers reach the sea. The mangrove is a tree that has a very unusual root system. Part of the roots are above the water and look like bare branches. These roots hold the main part of the plant above the water. The rest of the roots go deep into the soil below the water. A mangrove swamp in Nigeria is pictured below.

Inland Plateaus Much of West Africa is made up of plateaus that are between 500 feet (150 m) and 2,000 feet (610 m) in elevation. In the west a highland zone called the Fouta Djallon (FYOOT uh juh LOHN) rises above the plateaus. These highlands are rarely higher than 6,000 feet (1,829 m), but they are where most of the important rivers of West Africa begin. The Senegal, Gambia, and Niger rivers all originate here.

The Niger River is one of Africa's great rivers. From the Fouta Djallon, the Niger River flows north into the country of Mali.

From Mali, the Niger turns southeast to flow for over 1,000 miles (1,600 km) through the countries of Niger and Nigeria (nye JIHR ee uh) before it reaches the sea.

The Tibesti Mountains are located at the eastern end of West Africa in Chad. The elevation of the highest of its five peaks is 11,204 feet (3,415 m). Near the Tibesti Mountains is Lake Chad, West Africa's largest lake. The Chari River feeds into Lake Chad. The lake has no outlet to the sea, so it slowly evaporates in the dry climate. Depending on the season, the size of the lake can vary by as much as 6,000 square miles (15,540 sq km).

C. The Climates of West Africa

From Desert to Rain Forest If you look at the world climate map in the Atlas, you can see that West Africa has four climate zones that stretch from east to west across the region. Most of the territory of Mauritania, Mali, Niger, and Chad extends into the Sahara. These desert lands have little vegetation and are mainly the home of groups of nomadic herders.

The delta of the Niger River has many mangrove swamps that make navigation difficult.
▶ Look at the map on the opposite page. In what country is the Niger delta?

Scattered trees cover this savanna in Burkina Faso. The grasslands of the savanna are used to graze cattle.
► What is the savanna climate like?

Along the coast of the Gulf of Guinea (GIHN ee) is the equatorial climate. As you have learned, the hot, humid, and rainy equatorial climate creates the rain forest environment. Rainfall can exceed 135 inches (343 cm) per year in southern Nigeria, which is in this climate zone.

Transition Zones There are two zones that form a transition between the desert and the rain forest. The first of these two zones has a semidesert climate. This land is known as the **Sahel**, an Arabic word that means "border." The Sahel forms the border between the desert and the more humid lands to the south. In the Sahel, enough rain normally falls to grow the short grasses and scattered trees that support grazing animals. Farming is not usually possible without irrigation.

The second transitional zone has a savanna climate. As you read earlier, the savanna is a grassland that contains scattered trees. The savanna climate has a long rainy season and a long dry season. Farming is possible during the rainy season in the savanna climate. As one moves south through the savanna toward the Equator, the rainfall increases and forest begins to replace the savanna climate grassland.

People who live in each of the four climate zones of West Africa have different ways of life. Since nearly all the countries of West Africa extend across two or more of these climate zones, their people are highly varied in their ways of living.

LESSON 1

Review

REVIEWING MAIN IDEAS

A. How has river blindness affected the countries of West Africa?
B. What are the main landforms of West Africa?
C. In what ways is West Africa a region of contrasts?

SKILLS CHECK

MAP SKILL

Turn to the world climate map in the Atlas. Locate the areas that have the same climates as West Africa. List two countries for each of the four climate types found in West Africa.

Living and Working in West Africa

CONNECTIONS
Think about ways of making a living in your community. What effect do these jobs have on the environment?

TERMS
forage, desertification, drought

FOCUS
How has the environment been affected by the various ways in which people make their living in West Africa?

A. West African Cities

Important Cities West African countries have modern cities with many of the same conveniences found in cities throughout the world. Most West African cities are growing rapidly. The most important cities in West Africa are Lagos and Ibadan in Nigeria, and Dakar, Senegal, and Abidjan, in Côte d'Ivoire (KOT dee vwahr). Lagos, the largest city in West Africa, has over 3 million people. Ibadan has over 1.3 million people. Dakar has more than 1.7 million inhabitants, and Abidjan has over 2.7 million.

If you visited one of these West African cities, you would find it similar to large cities in the United States. You would see large buildings with government and business offices in the downtown areas. You would find wealthy neighborhoods and poor neighborhoods. You would see people dressed in business suits or in traditional African clothing. They would be going to work in offices as well as heading to work in factories. These people might be riding on the many buses going up and down the city streets. You might also notice vendors along the street selling newspapers, candy, and many other items to passersby.

Markets If you explored a bit, you would eventually find a market where people from farming areas bring food to sell. You would find people selling many different kinds of fruit and vegetables. Some of the things you would see would be familiar, like oranges, bananas, pineapples, and corn. But you would surely see many things for sale that you did not recognize. For example, there might be many different kinds of palm fruit and products like palm oil for cooking and palm wine, which is made

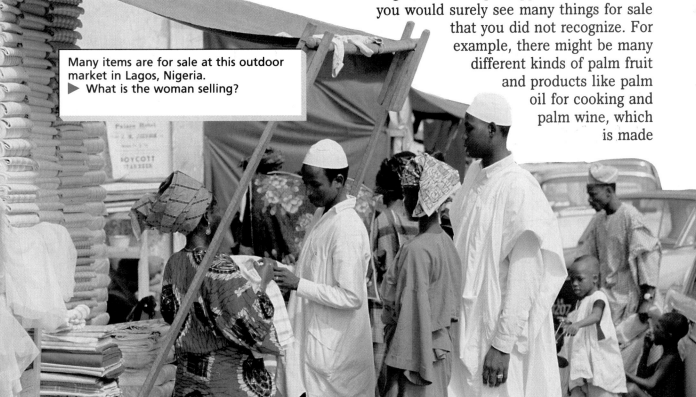

Many items are for sale at this outdoor market in Lagos, Nigeria.
▶ What is the woman selling?

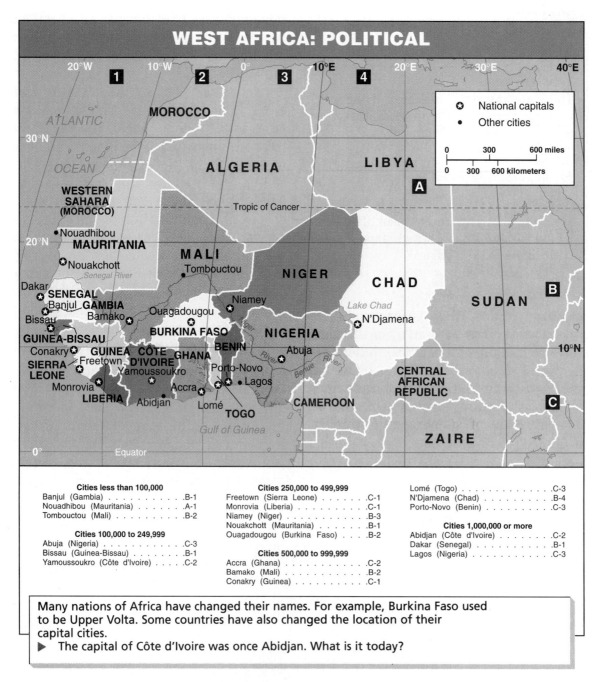

WEST AFRICA: POLITICAL

National capitals
Other cities

0   300   600 miles
0   300   600 kilometers

Cities less than 100,000
Banjul (Gambia) B-1
Nouadhibou (Mauritania) A-1
Tombouctou (Mali) B-2

Cities 100,000 to 249,999
Abuja (Nigeria) C-3
Bissau (Guinea-Bissau) B-1
Yamoussoukro (Côte d'Ivoire) C-2

Cities 250,000 to 499,999
Freetown (Sierra Leone) C-1
Monrovia (Liberia) C-1
Niamey (Niger) B-3
Nouakchott (Mauritania) B-1
Ouagadougou (Burkina Faso) B-2

Cities 500,000 to 999,999
Accra (Ghana) C-2
Bamako (Mali) B-2
Conakry (Guinea) C-1

Lomé (Togo) C-3
N'Djamena (Chad) B-4
Porto-Novo (Benin) C-3

Cities 1,000,000 or more
Abidjan (Côte d'Ivoire) C-2
Dakar (Senegal) B-1
Lagos (Nigeria) C-3

Many nations of Africa have changed their names. For example, Burkina Faso used to be Upper Volta. Some countries have also changed the location of their capital cities.

▶ The capital of Côte d'Ivoire was once Abidjan. What is it today?

---

from the sap of the palm oil tree. Cacao beans, kola nuts, mangoes, and many different kinds of yams and sweet potatoes would also be common. The sweet-flavored kola nuts are used in soft drinks like Coke and Pepsi.

In the coastal cities, you might find a fish market near the water. The fishers often bring their catch to sell as soon as they reach the shore. The fish are usually sold whole. Inland cities might have an animal market where you could see sheep, goats, and camels offered for sale.

B. Farming in West Africa

A Traditional Village Despite the rapid growth of cities, most people in West Africa still live in small villages. In the traditional

African village the houses are round, with cone-shaped straw thatch roofs. The walls of the house are made of mud mixed with dried straw.

The village probably would not have straight streets. Instead, there would be paths that wander between the houses. Aside from the houses, in smaller villages there might be a small health center, a school, and a building for the police and the local government officials.

Houses in most villages do not have electricity, running water, or indoor plumbing. Every day, the women and children go to the nearest well or stream for water. They also have to spend many hours looking for firewood to build cooking fires.

Subsistence Farming Most of the villagers make their living by subsistence farming. As you have learned, subsistence farmers are only able to grow enough food for their family's use. Shifting agriculture is the most common kind of subsistence farming in rain forest areas. Shifting agriculture means that the farmers relocate their fields when the soil is no longer fertile enough to grow crops. Even in the savanna areas, farmers often change fields every few years if they can. If the farmers had fertilizers to use, they could plant the same land year after year. Unfortunately, most poor subsistence farmers have trouble getting enough money to buy chemical fertilizers.

Farmers burn brush and bushes to clear fields for farming. The ashes from the fire act as fertilizer for the crops. Most of the farmwork is done by hand rather than by machine.
▶ What, do you think, is the man doing with the tree branch?

In the rain forest areas, the farmers raise crops that include yams, sweet potatoes, corn, rice, and manioc, which is also called cassava. Cassava is a root crop similar to a potato. It can be made into flour for bread or used in a type of pudding called tapioca. In the savanna areas you would see peanuts, millet, sorghum, and sesame being grown. Millet and sorghum are types of grain that grow well with little rain.

Cash Crops West Africa has become a world leader in the production of coffee, cacao, rubber, and palm oil. These crops are raised on plantations. The plantations are mainly in the rain forest, where the climate is suitable for growing these crops. A plantation is the opposite of a subsistence farm. Instead of raising just for their own use, the plantation farmer raises one or two main crops to be sold. These crops are called cash crops and are usually exported to bring income into the country.

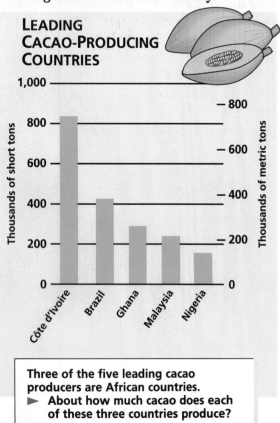

LEADING CACAO-PRODUCING COUNTRIES

Three of the five leading cacao producers are African countries.
► About how much cacao does each of these three countries produce?

In some cases, land that had been used to grow food is now used to grow cash crops. This has led to food shortages that have caused some countries to begin importing food to feed the people in towns and cities. Despite the problems, the income brought into some West African countries by cash crops is greater than the income received from any other products.

C. Herding in West Africa

Herding In the Sahara, the Sahel, and the drier parts of the savanna, livestock herding is the main occupation. Livestock such as sheep, goats, cattle, and camels feed on the **forage** that grows in these areas. Forage is plants such as grass and shrubs that serve as food for livestock.

Once, most of the herders were nomadic, moving their herds in search of green forage. Today nomadic herding is not as common in many parts of West Africa for several reasons.

Governments have built irrigation projects in some of the drier areas so that farmers can use the land. When the land is turned into farms, nomads can no longer use it for their animals. Some governments have dug wells so there is water in one place for animals. This eliminates some of the need for herders to move, but it has caused new problems. When the wells were dug, the herders used the new water to expand their herds. And because the animals stayed close to the wells where there was water, the forage quickly became used up. The area around the wells soon began to look like desert.

Throughout the Sahel, livestock herders have allowed their flocks to overgraze the land. The livestock eat the natural seeds of the grasses and shrubs, so the plant life does not grow back. Without plants, nothing is left to prevent the soil from blowing away. As a result, vegetation disappears completely. The land changes into desert.

People from all over the world have sent help to the famine victims of the Sahel drought. Food and medical care have been supplied to those in need.
▶ What help are these people receiving?

Often, the word **desertification** is used to describe this process.

The Expanding Desert Perhaps you have read in the newspaper or have seen stories on television about **drought** in the Sahel. A drought is an extreme shortage of water. Droughts are common in the Sahel and are part of a natural cycle of wet years followed by dry years. In the 1960s an unusually long period of adequate rainfall allowed more people to move into the Sahel. New farms were started and the number of livestock increased because there was more water and forage.

When the drought came, between 1968 and 1973, disaster occurred. Rivers dried up, crops failed, and millions of cattle died. Over 250,000 people died of starvation. Millions more migrated southward in search of food. A similar drought occurred between 1980 and 1984, driving still more people from the Sahel.

The combination of natural drought and overgrazing has totally destroyed once productive parts of the Sahel. Desertification is an especially important problem along the southern parts of the Sahara. Desertification has quickened the slow natural advance of the Sahara into the Sahel. If farming and grazing continue to expand in the Sahel, the desertification process will make even more land useless.

LESSON 2

Review

REVIEWING MAIN IDEAS

A. In what ways are West African cities different from American cities?

B. How have cash crops affected West African village life?

C. Why are deserts expanding into the Sahel?

SKILLS CHECK

THINKING SKILL

What solutions do you propose to solve the problems discussed in this lesson?

561

West Africa's Past: From Empires to Independence

CONNECTIONS

The European colonies in West Africa were broken into many small countries after independence. In what other areas of the world did this happen?

TERMS

imperialism, enclave

FOCUS

What changes have occurred in the countries of West Africa since independence?

A. Trade Changes West Africa

Trading Empires Today the Sahel suffers from drought and an expanding desert. In the past, however, it was a region of productive farmland. Yet the Sahel's main source of income did not come from farming—it came from trade. The people in the Sahel were located on the trade route between the people in the rain forest and the people in the desert. Market towns emerged in the Sahel and grew into large trading cities.

One of the leading trade cities was Tombouctou (tohn book TOO), or Timbuktu, on the Niger River at the southern edge of the Sahara Desert. Trading cities like Tombouctou became wealthy by placing a tax on camel caravans that passed through the city. They used this tax money to pay for powerful armies. These cities became the centers of a series of trading empires in the savanna region.

The savanna trade empires began around the year 300. The earliest one was Ghana (GAH nuh). Following the decline of Ghana, Mali became the most important trade empire. Two modern African nations are named after these trading empires. After Mali, Songhai became the major trading empire. Songhai declined around 1500, just as the first European trading posts were established in the coastal areas.

Unknown Continent Portuguese sailors had explored the African coast before Columbus made his famous voyage to America in 1492. Still, European knowledge of the

Today Tombouctou is a small city in Mali. Trade still takes place, but it is not the wealthy city it once was.
▶ What protects the merchants from the heat?

interior of Africa was limited up until about 100 years ago. People in Europe knew little about Africa, so they called Africa the "dark continent."

Why were Europeans, who quickly explored and colonized large parts of North and South America, so slow to explore and colonize Africa, which is much closer to Europe than are North and South America?

A Portuguese historian named João de Barros (zhoo OUN day BAHR roosh), writing about 1540, tells one of the reasons why Europeans didn't explore beyond the coast of Africa.

> It seems that for our sins, or for some inscrutable [mysterious] judgement of God, in all the entrances of [the coast of West Africa] that we sail along, He has placed a striking Angel with a flaming sword of deadly fevers, who prevents us from penetrating into the interior. . . .

Africa is the home of some of the most dreaded diseases known to humans. The Europeans who dared to attempt exploration of this continent suffered from many diseases that weakened or killed them. Even their horses and other animals sickened and died. Africa quickly gained a reputation for being the graveyard of Europeans. Many of the young Europeans who were sent to protect or work in the trading posts along the coast never expected to see their relatives or friends again.

Hostile Lands and Independent People
In addition to the diseases that plagued Africa, this large and mysterious continent offered other barriers to European colonization and settlement. The great rivers that flow out of the continent, the Nile, the Niger, the Zaire, the Zambezi, and others, have waterfalls, swampy deltas, or other barriers that make it impossible to sail ships far in from the coast. Another important reason that exploration and colonization were so long delayed was that the

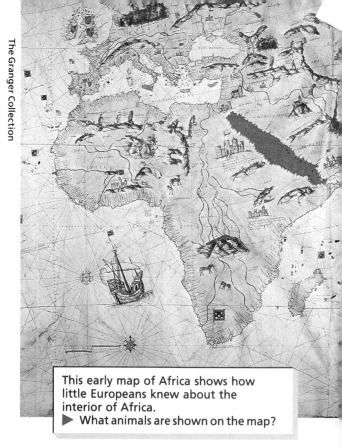

This early map of Africa shows how little Europeans knew about the interior of Africa.
▶ What animals are shown on the map?

native people of Africa were fiercely independent and resisted efforts to bring them under European rule.

The Europeans who wanted to benefit from the many products found in Africa set up trading posts along the coast. From these posts, they traded with the native people for the things they wanted. In this way, they did not have to face the dangers of travelling inland.

The Slave Trade The Europeans named sections of the coast based on each section's main export product. The modern country of Ghana was the British colony called the Gold Coast. The former French colony known as the Ivory Coast still uses the French version of that name (Côte d'Ivoire). It earned this name because of the ivory elephant tusks that were shipped from this coast.

The Atlantic coast of the modern countries of Togo (TOH goh), Benin (be NEEN), and Niger was once called the Slave Coast. Although many slaves were shipped from there, most of the slaves were not native to West Africa. The slave trade had been going on for centuries in Africa before the Europeans became involved. But, once they were involved, the Europeans took millions of slaves from Africa and sent them to the Americas and Europe.

Since the Europeans traded for slaves rather than capturing the slaves, the Europeans cared little where the slaves came from. Many of the slaves were captured far inland and marched to the Atlantic coast by slave traders. Most of the people who became slaves were unlucky people who were caught by the slave traders. Some slaves were criminals or prisoners of war that were sold to the slave traders.

In his book *The Africans*, David Lamb describes Goree Island, located off the coast of Senegal. This island is one of the places where slaves were gathered before being sold and put in ships for the Americas or other destinations.

For millions of West Africans . . . this is where freedom ended and serfdom [slavery] began. It was here, in the dark, dank [damp] slave house, that Arab traders bartered and bickered with European shippers, here that the Africans spent the last weeks in their homeland, chained to a wall in underground cubicles, awaiting a buyer, a boat and, at the end of a long, harrowing voyage, a master.

In the weighing room below the trading office, the men's muscles were examined, . . . the children's teeth checked. Those were the qualities . . . on which human worth was judged. The slaves were fattened like livestock up to what was considered an ideal shipping weight, 140 pounds, and those who remained sickly or fell victim to pneumonia or tuberculosis, were segregated [separated] from the rest . . . , led into a corridor whose open door overlooked the ocean and tossed out for the sharks.

Slaves were held on Goree Island until they were packed onto ships. The journey took several weeks and many slaves died on the way.
▶ What were some of the slaves' destinations?

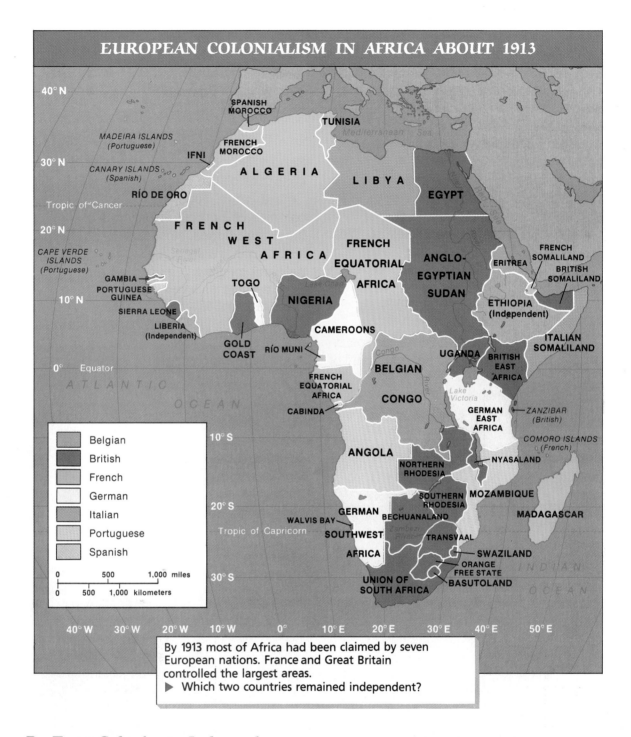

EUROPEAN COLONIALISM IN AFRICA ABOUT 1913

Legend:
- Belgian
- British
- French
- German
- Italian
- Portuguese
- Spanish

0   500   1,000 miles
0   500   1,000 kilometers

By 1913 most of Africa had been claimed by seven European nations. France and Great Britain controlled the largest areas.
▶ Which two countries remained independent?

B. From Colonies to Independence

In the late 1800s, Great Britain, France, Portugal, Spain, Belgium, and Germany extended their control from the coast toward the interior of Africa. These European countries followed a policy of **imperialism**. Imperialism is a policy of conquering new lands to build an empire. Africa was divided into separate European-controlled territories. As you can see from the map above, by 1913 almost the entire continent belonged to the Europeans.

After several decades of European control, the people of West Africa began to demand the right to rule themselves. In 1957, Ghana became the first country in West Africa to gain independence from a colonial power. Independence did not come easily. Kwame Nkrumah (KWAH mee un KROO muh) led the struggle for independence and became Ghana's first president. At the independence celebration, Nkrumah wore the clothing of a prisoner because he had been jailed by the British several years earlier for demanding independence.

By 1965, all the countries of West Africa were independent except for Guinea-Bissau (GIHN ee bih SOU) and the Cape Verde Islands. These two Portuguese colonies gained their independence in the mid-1970s.

Today, there are almost 50 independent countries south of the Sahara. Many of these countries, including those in West Africa, have ties to their former colonial owners. The language and customs of the Europeans are still used, and Europe is a leading trade partner.

C. The French-Speaking Countries

Export Economies All the West African countries of the Sahel as well as Guinea, Côte d'Ivoire, Togo, and Benin were once colonies of France. These former colonies have maintained close ties with France, and they have kept French as the official national language.

In colonial times, the French encouraged farmers to grow cash crops such as cacao, coffee, and bananas for European markets. Today these products are still among the main exports of these countries.

Côte d'Ivoire exports many different products through the port city of Abidjan. Part of the city is located on an island.
▶ How do people get to the island?

PRODUCTS OF PEANUTS

More than 300 uses for the peanut have been found. The fruit is in the form of a pod, or shell, with the seeds, or peanuts, inside. Growing peanuts and making products from them is a major part of the economy of West Africa.
▶ Where does the fruit grow?

The French-speaking countries on the coast are smaller than most of the Sahel countries, but they are more prosperous. The most prosperous of these countries and one of the wealthiest countries in Africa is Côte d'Ivoire. Côte d'Ivoire is a world leader in the production of cacao, leads Africa in the production of coffee, and is Africa's second largest producer of palm oil. The country also produces bananas, coconuts, rubber, cotton, and sugarcane. In the 1980s, oil and natural gas were discovered offshore in the Gulf of Guinea. Crude oil and petroleum products play a part in Côte d'Ivoire's economy.

Isolation In contrast, the countries of the Sahel are among the poorest countries in the world. One cause of their poverty is their isolated location. Of the countries of the Sahel, only Senegal and Mauritania have a seacoast. Mali, Burkina Faso, Niger, and Chad are landlocked. They must bring in food, machinery, and motor vehicles over long routes through neighboring countries. The additional time and distance adds to the cost of the products. Being landlocked also increases the amount of time it takes to export goods to foreign countries.

Transportation Guinea, Côte d'Ivoire, Togo, and Benin all have coastal locations, so they are not isolated in the same sense as the landlocked countries of the Sahel. Still, isolation is a problem.

The French built railroads in Guinea, to bring minerals and agricultural products such as peanuts and cotton from the interior. Similar railroads were built in Côte d'Ivoire, Togo, and Benin. These railroads

567

An elder of the Yoruba ethnic group in Nigeria wears ceremonial clothing for a village council meeting.
▶ Do you think he considers the council meeting to be important?

were intended to bring export goods from the interior of each colony to coastal ports. From these ports, goods could be shipped to France. So, the rail lines extend inland from the coast like delicate threads.

The French were not interested in using the railroads to connect places within each colony, nor did they care about connecting the coastal colonies with each other. Later, roads followed the rail lines into the interior, but none were built along the coast between the newly independent countries. Because of this, the transportation systems do not help to unite these countries which share a common colonial language and colonial heritage.

The isolation of these countries from each other is made even greater by the fact that they have continued to depend on trading one or two goods with the countries

of Europe. If the economies of these countries were better linked, they might be able to develop trade among themselves. In this way, they could reduce their dependence on Europe.

D. The English-Speaking Countries

Isolation Four former British colonies lie scattered along the coast of West Africa. They include Sierra Leone (see ER uh lee OHN), Ghana, Nigeria, and the tiny country of Gambia. A fifth English-speaking country is Liberia. Liberia was settled by American slaves who were freed before and after the American Civil War.

As with the other countries of West Africa, isolation is a problem for the English-speaking countries. They also have transportation systems that were designed to bring goods to the coast for export rather than to *integrate*, or bring together, the different countries. This problem is made greater by the fact that the English-speaking countries are widely separated from each other. This makes it hard for them to take advantage of their common language and colonial heritage.

Diversity Another problem is the great diversity in size and resources of the English-speaking countries. Tiny Gambia, smaller than the state of Connecticut, and with fewer than one million people, is an **enclave**. An enclave is a country that is completely surrounded by another country. Except for its tiny seacoast, Gambia is completely surrounded by the much larger Senegal.

Because of the enclave, Gambia and Senegal have joined in a confederation called Senegambia. The confederation agreement between Gambia and Senegal makes it possible for the governments of the two countries to work together for economic development.

At the other extreme is Nigeria, one of the larger countries in West Africa. Nigeria is also the most populous country in Africa, with about 101 million people. Some experts say that Nigeria's population will more than double by the year 2020 because of that country's high birthrate.

Nigeria is a prosperous country compared with its neighbors. It has some of the best farmland in West Africa. In addition to this, Nigeria has valuable oil reserves and is the largest oil producer in sub-Saharan Africa. The government has used part of the money it has earned from petroleum exports to develop industry. These industries include textile manufacturing, food processing, oil refining, metal processing, and automobile assembly. These industries produce goods mainly for the large population within Nigeria. If the countries of West Africa were less isolated from each other it might be possible for Nigeria to sell manufactured goods to its neighbors and have even more industry.

Setting Boundaries The countries of West Africa did not exist before European colonization. The Europeans extended their control along the coast from the trading posts until they came to the territory of another European power. In this way, the coast was divided up into separate European-controlled territories. Later, as Europeans extended their influence away from the sea, the coastal boundaries were simply pushed inland.

The native people of West Africa belonged to hundreds of different ethnic groups or tribes. Each of these groups had its own language, territory, and way of life. The boundaries drawn by the Europeans paid no attention to the territories of the native people. Later, when the West African colonies became independent, the new countries kept their colonial boundaries. These new countries included many different culture groups, some of which might have been long-time enemies or rivals. This made it very hard to govern the new countries.

A mountain of peanuts is prepared for shipment from a plantation in Senegal.
▶ What are the steps made from?

LESSON 3

Review

REVIEWING MAIN IDEAS
A. In what ways has trade changed in West Africa?
B. How have the European countries affected West African countries?
C. In what ways are the countries of West Africa isolated?
D. What type of economic diversity is found in West Africa?

SKILLS CHECK
WRITING SKILL
Write an article for a newspaper, describing the problems of the modern countries of West Africa.

569

CHAPTER 22 REVIEW

REVIEWING TERMS

mangrove	**imperialism**
forage	**enclave**
drought	

On a separate sheet of paper, match the word with its correct definition. Write your answers in sentence form.

1. Plants such as grasses and shrubs that livestock eat
2. A tree with an unusual root system, usually found in swamps
3. An extreme shortage of water
4. A country enclosed within another country
5. A policy of conquering new lands to build an empire

REVIEWING THE FACTS

On a separate sheet of paper, answer the questions in complete sentences.

1. Why is the Fouta Djallon important?
2. What are the four climate zones of West Africa?
3. In what ways are West African cities similar to cities in the United States?
4. What is the difference between subsistence crops and cash crops?
5. How did Tombouctou become a wealthy city?
6. Why was West Africa difficult to explore and settle?

7. What products are exported by the French-speaking countries?
8. Who settled the country of Liberia?
9. Why did Senegal and Gambia form a confederation?
10. How has Nigeria used the profits from oil exports?

WRITING ABOUT GEOGRAPHY

Independence for most West African countries came about during the 1950s and 1960s. Imagine you are a leader of a West African country at the time of independence. Write a speech outlining the major problems of your country and possible solutions to these problems.

THINKING CRITICALLY

On a separate sheet of paper, answer the following in complete sentences.

1. What are the causes of desertification in West Africa?
2. How has slavery hurt the development of West Africa?
3. Compare the economies of the French-speaking and English-speaking countries. Which countries have experienced the greatest development?
4. What effect has disease had on West Africa?
5. Compare the West African trading empires with European trade in West Africa.

SUMMARIZING THE CHAPTER

Many events discussed in this chapter caused other events to occur. On a separate sheet of paper, draw a graphic organizer that is like the one shown here. Copy the information from this graphic organizer on the one you have drawn. Fill in the missing effects.

CHAPTER THEME

The influence of the Europeans has affected the economic, political, and cultural growth of West Africa.

LESSON 1 The environment affects how people make their living.

Cause	Effect
1. People will not live next to rivers because of the black fly.	1. _____
2. Desert areas in Mauritania, Mali, Niger, and Chad have little vegetation.	2. _____
3. The savanna climate has a long rainy season and a long dry season.	3. _____

LESSON 2 The environment of West Africa has been affected by the way people make a living.

Cause	Effect
1. Governments have built irrigation projects in drier areas.	1. _____
2. Nomads expanded the size of their herds because new wells were built.	2. _____
3. Throughout the Sahel, herders have allowed their livestock to overgraze the land.	3. _____

LESSON 3 Former European control has influenced the development of the modern West African countries.

Cause	Effect
1. Europeans encouraged farmers to grow cash crops.	1. _____
2. Europeans built railroads from coastal ports of each colony to the interior.	2. _____
3. Newly independent African countries have boundaries set by European countries.	3. _____

CHAPTER **23**

THE COUNTRIES OF CENTRAL AFRICA

Central Africa: The Rain Forest

CONNECTIONS

Look at the picture of the rain forest on this page. What, do you think, is it like under that sea of green?

TERMS

canopy, jungle

FOCUS

What are Central Africa's environment and landforms?

A. The Rain Forest

Anyone who has stood in the silent emptiness of a tropical rain forest [feels] overpowered by the heaviness of everything—the damp air, the gigantic water-laden trees that are constantly dripping, never quite drying out between the violent storms that come with monotonous regularity. . . . And, above all, . . . people feel overpowered by the silence . . . and loneliness of it all.

But these are the feelings of outsiders, of those who do not belong to the forest. If you [live in] the forest it is a very different place . . . a cool, restful, shady world with light filtering through the tree tops that meet high overhead and shut out the direct sunlight. . . .

There are a multitude of sounds, but most of them are as joyful as the brightly colored birds that chase one another through the trees, . . . or the chatter of the handsome black-and-white Colobus monkeys as they leap from branch to branch. . . . And the most joyful sound of all . . . is the sound of the voices of the forest people as they sing . . . praise to this wonderful world of theirs.

The author of this description is Colin Turnbull. For several years he lived in the rain forest that is located in the center of Africa. This rain forest region is outlined by the long, curving course of the Zaire (zah IHR) River and its tributaries. The rain forest covers the countries of Gabon, Equatorial Guinea, Congo, and Zaire. It is also found in the southern portions of Cameroon and the Central African Republic. All these countries and the island nation of São Tomé and Príncipe (soun toh ME and PRIHN suh pee) are included in the region that is called Central Africa.

The Canopy From an airplane the rain forest looks like a vast sea of dark green covering the landscape. The surface of this "green sea" is called the **canopy**. The canopy is formed by thousands of leafy, umbrellalike treetops. Some of the trees can reach heights of 200 feet (61 m).

Much of the life of the rain forest is found in the canopy layer. Birds, insects, snakes, small rodents, and monkeys live out most of their lives high above the floor of the forest.

When most people think of a rain forest, they imagine vegetation so thick that you cannot walk through it without cutting a path. But this description of an overgrown, thick tangled mass of tropical

This green landscape is formed by thousands of rain forest treetops.
▶ What shadow appears in the photograph?

▶ A farm village in the Ruwenzori Mountains of Zaire

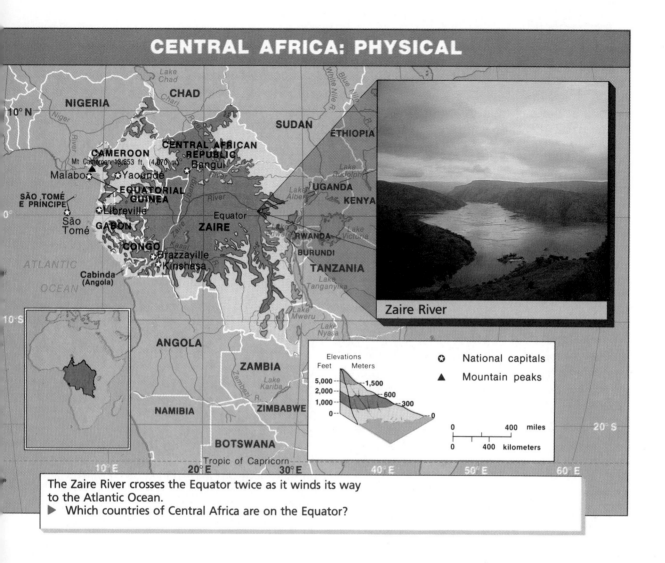

CENTRAL AFRICA: PHYSICAL

Zaire River

Elevations
Feet   Meters

5,000 — 1,500
2,000 — 600
1,000 — 300
0 — 0

⊕ National capitals
▲ Mountain peaks

0   400   miles
0   400   kilometers

The Zaire River crosses the Equator twice as it winds its way
to the Atlantic Ocean.
▶ Which countries of Central Africa are on the Equator?

vegetation characterizes a **jungle**. Wherever sunlight reaches into the rain forest, a jungle is present. For example, jungles appear along river banks or where fields have been cleared and abandoned. A rain forest is different—the canopy is so thick that sunlight cannot easily penetrate. As a result, the ground remains relatively clear of plants.

B. Climate of Central Africa

Central Africa has an equatorial climate. All year long the temperature remains high. The temperature remains around 80°F (27°C) throughout the day and the air does not cool off much when the sun goes down.

Away from the Equator, in Cameroon and the Central African Republic, the rain forest gives way to savanna. Unlike the rain forest, which has a yearlong wet climate, the savanna has alternating wet and dry seasons. The savanna extends along the coast. Because of the cool ocean water, the climate is cooler along the coast than the equatorial climate.

C. Landforms of Central Africa

The Zaire River Basin The landscape of Central Africa is dominated by the Zaire River basin. The Zaire River drains an area covering 1,425,000 square miles (3,690,750 sq km) in five countries. The river's eight

Before the disaster in 1986, the water of Lake Nios was clear.
▶ What caused poisonous gas to be released through the lake?

major tributaries make it second only to the Amazon River in the volume of water that it carries. The Zaire is Africa's second longest river and the world's seventh longest, at 2,716 miles (4,370 km).

Look at the map on page 574. Around the Zaire River basin are highland regions that form its rim. To the east are the Mitumba (mih TOOM buh) and Ruwenzori (roo un ZOR ee) mountains. The peaks of the Ruwenzori Mountains reach heights above 16,750 feet (5,105 m).

Plateaus are located to the north and south of the basin. At the western end of the northern plateau is Mount Cameroon. This mountain is located in Cameroon, near the coast of the Gulf of Guinea.

Volcanic Region Mount Cameroon is a volcano that had its last volcanic eruption in 1959. In 1986 deadly poisonous gases were released from deep underground through the waters of Lake Nios. About 1,700 people who lived on the mountain slopes surrounding the lake were killed.

This lake, near the town of Wum, is located in a dormant volcano crater. Scientists who investigated the disaster believe that the gas was a result of volcanic activity. A similar incident occurred in 1984 when 37 people were killed by gas released from a lake located near Lake Nios.

LESSON 1

Review

REVIEWING MAIN IDEAS

A. What is the difference between a rain forest and a jungle?

B. What different types of climates are found in Central Africa?

C. In what way does the Zaire River basin dominate Central Africa?

SKILLS CHECK

WRITING SKILL

Colin Turnbull described the rain forest environment as he came to see it from living in it. Write a description of the environment where you live.

Living and Working in Central Africa

CONNECTIONS

If you could carry only five items on an expedition into a rain forest, what would you take?

TERMS

Bantu, leaching, humus, tsetse fly

FOCUS

What are the main economic activities in Central Africa?

A. Life in the Rain Forest

Hunters and Gatherers In the rain forest of Central Africa live a group of people known as Pygmies. They are called Pygmies by outsiders because their average height is only 4.5 feet (1.4 m). These people consider the name Pygmy to be offensive and prefer to be called by the name of their ethnic group. One of these ethnic groups is called the Efe (AY fay).

The Efe are nomadic and survive as hunters and gatherers. The men skillfully hunt small animals, using bows and arrows or spears and nets. Efe women search the forest to gather vegetables, roots, berries, fruits, and nuts.

The women also take care of the children and build the small huts in which the families live. These huts are made of bent branches that are tied together and covered with leaves to make them waterproof. The huts are abandoned when the Efe move to a new part of the forest in search of food.

The Efe's way of life seems very primitive compared with the way we live. But the Efe have adapted to their environment. For example, starting a fire in the wet rain forest is difficult. So the Efe keep their fires constantly burning—even when moving to a new location. They carry embers, glowing hot pieces of wood, wrapped in waterproof leaves from one campsite to another. In this way they are able to move their continuously burning campfires with them.

Several Efe prepare arrows to be used in a hunt.
▶ From what are the arrows made?

There are approximately 175,000 people in Central Africa who live as hunters and gatherers. Frequently, hunters and gatherers have close ties to their farming neighbors. The farmers exchange what they grow for the meat that the hunters get in the forest. Honey gathered in the forest is a highly prized item in both groups. Trading is possible between the two groups because they speak the same language and desire each other's products.

The Bantu The majority of the farmers are Bantu-speaking Africans. **Bantu** is a family of African languages. Today there are more than 200 languages and dialects related to Bantu.

The Bantus probably originated in the area of modern Cameroon more than 2,000 years ago. They were farmers who used iron tools. As their population grew, groups of Bantus migrated in search of more farmland. By A.D. 300 the Bantus had spread to eastern and southern Africa.

Many Bantus moved into the rain forest of Central Africa. They cleared the forest for farming and built permanent villages. Today much of the land is farmed the same way it has been farmed for centuries.

B. A Rain Forest Family

Amosa and his family live in the rain forest of Zaire in a small village on the Ikelemba River, a tributary of the Zaire River. The village huts are small, made of sticks and grass, and have cone-shaped roofs. All around Amosa's village are small clearings in the rain forest, where the villagers grow their food crops. Amosa's mother does the farming at the clearing. In Amosa's tribe it is the custom that the women do the farming and the men hunt and fish to provide meat for the village.

Amosa's mother and the other women of the village use simple hoes and pointed digging sticks to prepare the soil for plant-

These boys have been riding their home-made wooden scooters.
► What, do you think, are the scooters made from?

ing and to dig the weeds out of the clearing. The yields from the clearings around Amosa's village are very low because of the poor soil. For this reason, the villagers practice shifting agriculture.

Because of the heat, the people of Amosa's village cannot store food very long before it spoils. There are no refrigerators, freezers, or even electricity in Amosa's village, so gathering food is a daily task. Some of the men, like Amosa's father, leave the village for several weeks or months at a time to work on plantations. In this way, they can earn some money to help buy extra food and other things that the people of the village may need.

C. Farming in Central Africa

Infertile Soil The main difficulty farmers face in Central Africa is infertile soil. Because of almost daily rainfall, **leaching** occurs. Leaching is a process in which nutrients in the top layers of the soil are washed down into the lower soil layers. Farm crops have shallow root systems that cannot reach the nutrients. Trees can survive because their roots reach deep into the soil.

The rain forest also lacks **humus** (HYOO mus). Humus is a very fertile layer of

A swarm of locusts descends on a village in Central Africa.
► What is a locust?

decayed plant material that forms slowly. Leaves that fall off trees, and other vegetation that dies, lie upon the surface of the soil and decay. This decaying process creates a new humus layer. In cooler climate regions, the decay occurs gradually, allowing the humus layer to form. Because of the very hot and humid conditions of the rain forest, the decay occurs very rapidly. As a result, the vegetation does not lie on the surface long enough to form a new layer of humus.

Sleeping Sickness Another major problem facing farmers is disease. One disease found in Central Africa is known as sleeping sickness. Symptoms, or signs of the disease, include fever, weakness, and sleepiness. The result is often a coma followed by death. This dreaded disease is passed by the bite of the **tsetse** (TSET see) **fly.** The tsetse fly also bites livestock, causing cattle to die. The farmer can lose his or her own life as well as cattle and crops.

Locusts The crops are also at risk from swarms of locusts. A locust is a large grasshopper. In Africa giant hordes of millions of locusts swarm every few years. These insects eat almost all the vegetation in their path including farmer's crops. The following is a description of a locust swarm by Nigerian author Chinua Achebe in his book *Things Fall Apart.*

> [Q]uite suddenly a shadow fell on the world, and the sun seemed hidden behind a thick cloud. Okonkwo looked up from his work and wondered if it was going to rain at such an unlikely time of the year. . . .
>
> At first, a fairly small swarm came. They were the harbingers [advance group] sent to survey the land. And then appeared on the horizon a slowly-moving mass like a boundless sheet of black cloud drifting towards [the village]. Soon it covered half the sky, and the solid mass was now broken only by tiny eyes of light like shining star dust. It was a tremendous sight, full of power and beauty. . . .
>
> [A]t last the locusts did descend. They settled on every tree and on every blade of grass; they settled on the roofs and covered the bare ground. Mighty tree branches broke away under them, and the whole country became the brown-earth color of the vast, hungry swarm.

LESSON 2

Review

REVIEWING MAIN IDEAS

A. In what ways have the Efe adapted to life in the rain forest?

B. How does Amosa's family make a living?

C. What difficulties do farmers face in the rain forest?

SKILLS CHECK

THINKING SKILL

Draw a diagram that shows the sequence of events in the leaching process and in the creation of a humus layer.

Zaire and Its Neighbors

CONNECTIONS

Why do we need transportation systems?

TERMS

islet, exploitation

FOCUS

What problems do the countries of Central Africa face?

A. Zaire

Zaire River Basin Zaire is the second largest country south of the Sahara. With an area of 905,063 square miles (2,344,113 sq km), it is slightly larger than Alaska and Texas combined. Zaire's population of 44 million is the fourth largest in Africa. However, because of Zaire's vast size, the population density is only 49 people per square mile (19 per sq km). Most of the land consists of the sparsely populated rain forest of the Zaire River basin.

Before Europeans arrived in Africa, the Africans called the Zaire River the Nzere. *Nzere* means the "river that swallows all rivers." The earliest Europeans to explore the coast called the river the Zaire, after the African word. The Europeans later changed the name to Congo, after the Kongo tribe that lived near the mouth of the river. The region became known as the Belgian Congo because the area was claimed by Belgium. Today the name has come full circle, with Zaire now used for the country and the river for which it was named.

The name change was one of the first acts of Joseph Mobutu (moh boo too), a military officer who took control of the government in 1965. Mobutu changed the name of the capital city from Leopoldville to Kinshasa. He also ordered the people to change their names and style of dress. Even Mobutu changed his first and middle names from Joseph Désiré (day zee ray) to Sese Seko (SES ay SEK oh) to set an example. Business suits and ties were forbidden because they were part of a style of clothing that was not African. By replacing the European colonial names and customs, Mobutu restored his people's pride in their African heritage.

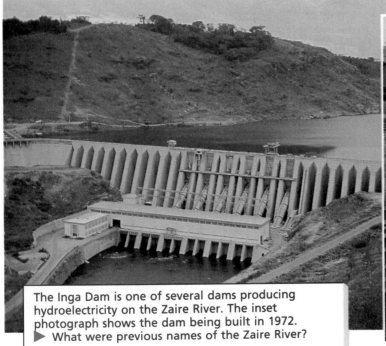

The Inga Dam is one of several dams producing hydroelectricity on the Zaire River. The inset photograph shows the dam being built in 1972.
▶ What were previous names of the Zaire River?

579

Great Potential Zaire is often described as a nation with great potential. With the Zaire River and its many tributaries, Zaire probably has the ability to generate more hydroelectric power than does any other country in the world. It also has tremendous mineral wealth. Zaire is a world leader in the production of copper, cobalt, and industrial diamonds. Southern Zaire has rich deposits of lithium, silver, gold, tin, and manganese, and it has some oil. Lithium is a soft silver-white element that is the lightest metal known. Most of Zaire's mineral wealth has been untapped.

Zaire is unable to exploit some of its vast resources, because it cannot afford to build hydroelectric plants or to mine its minerals. The rain forest makes it difficult to reach these resources. Because of the expense of building roads and railroads, few have been built to tie the different parts of Zaire together.

Railroads and roads have been built to improve transportation on the Zaire River. Entire sections of the river are not navigable; that is, they are not able to be traveled by boat or ship. From Kinshasa to the port city of Matadi, the river drops almost 1,500 feet (457 m) through a series of waterfalls and rapids that river boats cannot pass. A railroad is used to move goods between the two cities. This means that cargo must be transferred between boats and trains at both ends of the rapids. Every time the cargo has to be loaded and unloaded, the cost of transportation increases.

Although some factories have been built near the mines and in the major cities, farming is the main occupation in Zaire. More than 70 percent of the people are farmers. Most of the agricultural production is from plantations. Coffee is a leading export, and cotton is a major product, which has led to a growing textile industry. Food production is limited because much of the farmland is used for cash crops.

Buses pick up passengers on a busy street in Kinshasa, the capital of Zaire.
▶ How does the photograph show that Kinshasa is a modern city?

Kinshasa, Zaire's Capital As you can see on the map on page 582, Kinshasa is located in western Zaire on the southern bank of the Zaire River. Kinshasa is Zaire's largest city and it is the country's national capital. The first settlement that was built on the site of Kinshasa dates back more than 500 years.

Most of the government buildings are in a section of the city located along the river. These are modern high-rise buildings on wide tree-lined streets. Most of Zaire's wealthy citizens live in spacious bungalows. Foreign visitors to Kinshasa stay in modern hotels. But, there are many poor people who work and live in the city. These people live in buildings made from dried mud bricks with thatched roofs.

B. Former French Colonies

Congo Across the Zaire River from Kinshasa is Brazzaville, the capital of the Congo. The Congo is one of four nations, along with Gabon, the Central African Republic, and Cameroon, that were created from the breakup of the former colony called French Equatorial Africa.

With 132,012 square miles (342,000 sq km) of territory, the Congo is about the size of the state of Montana. Nearly 2.5 million people live in the Congo, which serves mainly as a link for its neighboring countries to the outside world. The reason is the rail network that connects the Congo's port of Pointe-Noire (pwant nuh WAHR) with the interior of Central Africa. One rail line goes to the border with Gabon, and the other goes inland to Brazzaville, where it picks up trade coming down the Zaire River. The Congo's main resources are oil and timber.

Gabon Gabon, with an area covering 103,347 square miles (267,667 sq km), is about the size of Colorado and has a population of about 1.2 million. Most of the people live near the capital city of Libreville, located on the Atlantic coast. The Equator passes through Gabon. Most of the country is covered by rain forest. Very little land has been cleared for farming, and the country has to import food. Gabon has some large reserves of oil. Other resources include manganese and iron ore.

Central African Republic Another former French colony in Central Africa is named the Central African Republic. With a total area of 240,533 square miles (622,980 sq km), it is almost as big as the state of Texas. The Central African Republic is landlocked. It is a good example of how a landlocked geographic location causes problems of movement. Its capital, Bangui, is located on the Ubangi River. Goods are shipped down river on the Ubangi to where

LEADING DIAMOND-PRODUCING COUNTRIES

Most of the world's diamonds are used by industry. Zaire is the world's largest producer of these diamonds.
► What other African countries are diamond producers?

it merges with the Zaire River, which borders Zaire and the Congo. Then the goods continue down river to Brazzaville, where they have to be transferred to a railroad to go across the Congo to the port city of Pointe-Noire.

Most of the Central African Republic's about 3.2 million people are subsistence farmers who raise cotton, peanuts, and coffee. The country's major known resource is industrial diamonds, which are found by digging in the gravel of dry stream beds.

There is hope that more resources will be discovered, since the country is located on a highland plateau that is geographically similar to the mineral-rich region of southern Zaire.

Cameroon The northernmost of the Central African countries is Cameroon. Cameroon was originally a German colony that

CENTRAL AFRICA: POLITICAL

1 10°E **2** 20°E **3** 30°E

NIGERIA · CHAD · SUDAN
10°N

CAMEROON · CENTRAL AFRICAN REPUBLIC · **A**
Malabo · Douala · Bangui
São Tomé · Yaoundé
EQUATORIAL GUINEA · Kisangani · UGANDA
Libreville · Equator · 0°
SÃO TOMÉ AND PRÍNCIPE · GABON · ZAIRE · RWANDA
BURUNDI
CONGO · Brazzaville · **B**
Pointe-Noire · Kinshasa · Kananga
Cabinda (Angola) · Matadi · TANZANIA
ATLANTIC OCEAN · ANGOLA
Kolwezi · 10°S
Lubumbashi
ZAMBIA · **C**
BOTSWANA · ZIMBABWE · 20°S

✪ National capitals
• Other cities

0   400 miles
0   400 kilometers

Cities less than 100,000
Malabo (Equatorial Guinea) . . .A-1
São Tomé (São Tomé and Pr.) .A-1

Cities 100,000 to 499,999
Bangui (Central African Rep.) . .A-2
Kananga (Zaire) B-3
Kisangani (Zaire) A-3
Libreville (Gabon) A-1
Matadi (Zaire) B-2

Cities 500,000 to 999,999
Brazzaville (Congo) B-2
Douala (Cameroon) A-1
Kolwezi (Zaire) C-3
Lubumbashi (Zaire) C-3
Pointe Noire (Congo) B-2
Yaoundé (Cameroon) A-2

Cities 1,000,000 or more
Kinshasa (Zaire) B-2

Zaire, the largest country in central Africa, has many natural borders.
▶ What types of natural borders does Zaire have?

extended northward from the Atlantic coast to Lake Chad. After Germany was defeated in World War I, four fifths of the colony was controlled by the French and the remainder was divided into two British sections. In 1960 the French section became independent Cameroon. During 1961, one British section joined independent Cameroon and the other joined Nigeria.

In Cameroon the soils are rich and fertile. As you read earlier, Mount Came-

roon, which is located here, is an active volcano. Soil near a volcano is often very rich and fertile because of the fresh layers of volcanic ash that are periodically deposited. In Cameroon, bananas, coffee, and rubber trees grow on large plantations.

C. Island Countries

Volcanic Islands South of Cameroon, in the Atlantic Ocean, are a series of islands that are a part of the volcanic mountain chain that includes Mount Cameroon. Like Cameroon, these islands have fertile volcanic soil. Coconut, coffee, and cacao are the cash crops that are grown on plantations in these islands.

Two major islands and several **islets** form the nation of São Tomé and Príncipe. An islet is a very small island, usually uninhabited. For four centuries the two islands of São Tomé and Príncipe were owned by the Portuguese. The Portuguese prospered from the slave trade. After the slave trade ended, more prosperity came from cocoa and from coffee plantations.

However, the residents of the islands were victims of **exploitation**. Large profits were taken from the islands, but very little was left for the people who lived there. When independence was granted in 1975, the Europeans departed, leaving nothing behind. Since then, São Tomé and Príncipe has struggled economically.

The island of Bioko is also a part of the volcanic mountain chain mentioned above. Bioko, four islets, and the territory of Río Muni, on the mainland, form Equatorial Guinea. This country of about 420,000 people was a Spanish colony, but it has had ties to other countries, especially France. Since gaining independence in 1968, Equatorial Guinea has experienced political problems and economic failure. By establishing trade with France and former French colonies, Equatorial Guinea hopes to improve its economy.

In 1985, the people of a western province in Cameroon celebrated the fiftieth year of their king's reign. Pictured here are the king's musicians leading the celebration.
▶ What type of instruments are the musicians playing?

Looking at Problems The problems in Equatorial Guinea and in São Tomé and Príncipe are also found in the Congo, the Central African Republic, and other developing nations of Africa. Although there have been nations in Africa for centuries, many of the modern countries of Africa are less than 30 years old. Compared with the ages of other countries throughout the world, these African nations are toddlers. They are only now beginning to stand and walk.

These countries lack political stability, education, and literate populations. They need to develop agriculture and manufacturing. Even the forces of nature are working against development. Disease, locusts, and poor soil fertility in the rain forest contribute to the difficulties.

These nations, especially Zaire, have tremendous potential. Because of the possibility of great hydroelectric power, mineral wealth, and the greatest resource—a growing population—these Central African countries will increase in importance in the future.

LESSON 3

Review

REVIEWING MAIN IDEAS

A. What is Zaire's untapped potential?
B. What are the transportation problems of Central Africa?
C. What problems are the Central African countries working on?

SKILLS CHECK

MAP SKILL

Using the maps on pages 574 and 582, calculate the distance covered by cargo that is moved from Bangui to Pointe-Noire by the route described on Page 581.

REVIEWING TERMS

On a separate sheet of paper, write the term that best completes each sentence.

> leaching
> humus
> tsetse fly
> islet
> exploitation

1. An _____ is a very small island, usually uninhabited.
2. The rain forest of Central Africa lacks _____, a fertile layer of decayed plant material that forms slowly.
3. The process in which nutrients in the top layers of the soil are washed down into the lower soil layers is called _____.
4. The _____ is an insect found in Central Africa that causes the disease known as sleeping sickness.
5. The residents of the island countries of Central Africa were victims of _____ when the Europeans took large profits from the islands but left very little for the people who lived there.

REVIEWING THE FACTS

On a separate sheet of paper, answer the following questions in complete sentences.

1. Why is the climate of the savanna along the coast of Central Africa cooler than the climate of the rain forest?
2. What has been the main economic activity of Bantu-speaking Africans for a long time?

3. Why do trees rather than farmers' crops survive better in the rain forest?
4. What conditions in the rain forest cause vegetation to decay rapidly?
5. What disease in Central Africa can affect both people and cattle?
6. Why do the farmers of Central Africa fear locusts?
7. Why did Joseph Mobutu force many changes upon the people of Zaire?
8. What natural resources are found in Zaire?
9. What makes the soils of Cameroon rich and fertile?
10. What four countries were created from the breakup of the former colony of French Equatorial Africa?

WRITING ABOUT CULTURE

Recall what you have read about other groups of people, beside the Efe, who have successfully adapted to their environment. Describe some of these groups and give examples of how they have adapted to their environment.

THINKING CRITICALLY

On a separate sheet of paper, answer the following questions in complete sentences.

1. Why is much of the life of the rain forest found in the canopy layer and not on the ground of the forest?
2. Why, do you think, did the Africans give the Zaire River a name that means "river that swallows all rivers?"

3. Why does Zaire need to import so much of its food?

4. Why does it seem likely that the Central African Republic may possess the same minerals as those that are found in Zaire?

5. Why might a growing population be considered a valuable resource for a developing country?

SUMMARIZING THE CHAPTER

On a separate sheet of paper, draw a graphic organizer that is like the one shown here. Copy the information from this graphic organizer to the one you have drawn. Complete the chart by writing statements that will support the chapter theme. The first one has been done for you.

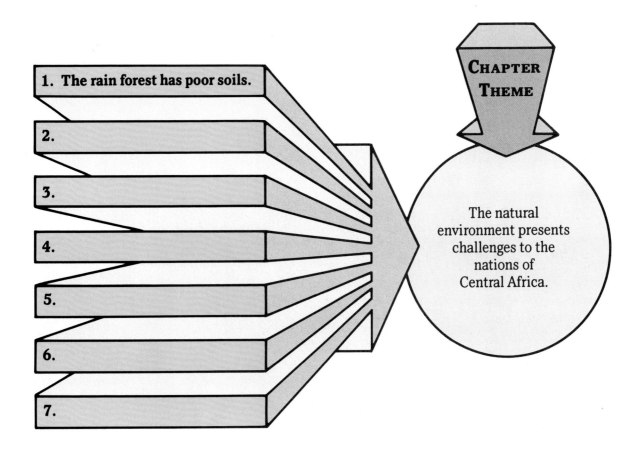

1. The rain forest has poor soils.
2.
3.
4.
5.
6.
7.

CHAPTER THEME

The natural environment presents challenges to the nations of Central Africa.

THE COUNTRIES OF EAST AFRICA

The Lands of East Africa

CONNECTIONS

You have learned that there are hot, humid rain forests in regions near the Equator. How, then, could a person in a region near the Equator get frostbite?

TERMS

Swahili, rift valley, sisal

FOCUS

What are the landforms and climates of East Africa?

A. East African Wildlife

Two black hairy arms circled the tree trunk. A moment later a furry head appeared. Bright eyes peered at me through a lattice [framework] of ferns. . . . The face was familiar, not only by its features but by its impish expression; it belonged to Peanuts.

The person who had this curious encounter was a woman named Dian Fossey. An American zoologist, Fossey spent nearly 18 years living among and studying mountain gorillas in the highlands of Rwanda (roo AHN duh). Peanuts was one of Fossey's favorite gorillas.

Rwanda is home to one of the largest populations of mountain gorillas in Africa. These gorillas are found in forests of the Virunga Mountains, which form the border between Rwanda and Zaire. The Virunga Mountains extend northward into the country of Uganda, and mountain gorillas live there as well. Rwanda, Uganda, and the other nations shown on the map on page 588 make up the region that is known as East Africa.

Dian Fossey set up a research center to study the rare mountain gorillas. She focused her efforts on protecting these animals from *poachers*, or people who hunt illegally, and on preserving the gorillas' mountain habitats. Fossey described her work in the book *Gorillas in the Mist*, which was later made into a movie. Her research helped to make people more aware of the rich wildlife heritage of East Africa.

Endangered Species Mountain gorillas are not the only endangered wildlife species in East Africa. For example, the African elephant—found throughout Kenya, Tanzania, Sudan, Ethiopia, Somalia, and Uganda—faces the danger of extinction. In one week, poachers kill an average of 1,000 elephants for their valuable ivory tusks. The tusks are sold to merchants in Asia, where the ivory is carved into piano keys, jewelry, and decorative figures. A poacher can live for a year on the money from the sale of just one elephant tusk.

Many countries around the world have banned the sale of ivory to try to stop the slaughter of elephants. However, not all countries have agreed to the ban, so the profitable ivory trade has not been eliminated. Many African countries have set aside land as game reserves and national parks in an effort to protect gorillas, elephants, and other important wildlife resources found on this continent.

African Safaris The protection of wildlife is an especially important issue in East Africa. One of the major sources of income in this region, particularly in Kenya, is the safari. *Safari* is the **Swahili** (swah HEE lee) word for "journey." Swahili, a mixture of Arabic and African languages, is spoken throughout much of East Africa.

Since Europeans first came to Africa, people have gone on safaris to hunt the animals of the continent. People have wanted to bring home trophies of the hunt, such as lion heads, zebra hides, and elephant tusks. Today, however, a different kind of safari has become a key part of the East African economy: the photographic safari.

587

▶ Mount Kilimanjaro, the highest peak in Africa

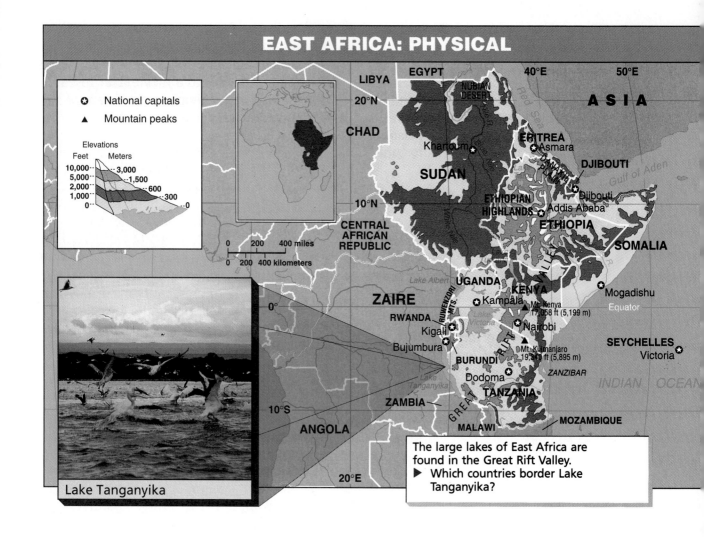

EAST AFRICA: PHYSICAL

Legend:
- ✪ National capitals
- ▲ Mountain peaks

Elevations

Feet	Meters
10,000	3,000
5,000	1,500
2,000	600
1,000	300
0	0

0   200   400 miles
0   200   400 kilometers

LIBYA
EGYPT
40°E
50°E
20°N
ASIA
CHAD
NUBIAN DESERT
ERITREA
Khartoum
Asmara
DJIBOUTI
SUDAN
Djibouti
ETHIOPIAN HIGHLANDS
Addis Ababa
10°N
ETHIOPIA
CENTRAL AFRICAN REPUBLIC
SOMALIA
Lake Albert
UGANDA
KENYA
Mogadishu
ZAIRE
Kampala
Mt. Kenya 17,058 ft (5,199 m)
Equator
RWANDA
Lake Victoria
Nairobi
Kigali
Bujumbura
Mt. Kilimanjaro 19,340 ft (5,895 m)
SEYCHELLES
Victoria
BURUNDI
Dodoma
ZANZIBAR
INDIAN OCEAN
Lake Tanganyika
TANZANIA
ZAMBIA
ANGOLA
MALAWI
MOZAMBIQUE
20°E
10°S
Gulf of Aden
Red Sea
GREAT RIFT VALLEY
RUWENZORI MTS.

Lake Tanganyika

The large lakes of East Africa are found in the Great Rift Valley.
▶ Which countries border Lake Tanganyika?

People from all around the world travel to East Africa to photograph zebras, rhinos, gazelles, giraffes, and the other wildlife found in the region's national parks and game reserves. These safaris are particularly profitable to Kenya and Tanzania.

Although wildlife safaris are an important source of income, not all East Africans favor spending so much effort and large amounts of money to protect wildlife. Some Africans argue that valuable land set aside as game reserves could be put to better use as farmland. This feeling is particularly strong in areas of East Africa that do not have enough land or a climate suitable for farming.

B. The Diverse Climates of East Africa

Desert and Savanna Like most of North Africa, much of northern East Africa has a desert climate. This desert region extends southward along the coast of the Red Sea, the Gulf of Aden, and the Indian Ocean. The area receives less rainfall than might be expected in a coastal region. This is because monsoon winds blow parallel to the coastline and thus do not carry moist air over the land.

South of East Africa's desert region, the landscape changes to savanna, grassy plains with no trees or with some scattered trees and bushes. The savanna region has wet and dry seasons. Rainfall is heavy in winter and very light in summer. The temperatures, however, are high year-round in the savanna region.

Highland Climates Farther south the East African landscape changes abruptly from the savanna plains to the rugged Ethiopian highlands and, still farther south, the highlands of the East African plateau. Scattered around the plateau are mountain ranges with elevations well over 10,000 feet (3,048 m). These high mountains and other landforms of the region contribute to the diversity of East Africa's climates.

Parts of the East African highlands lie along the Equator and receive more rain than other areas. Around Lake Victoria, for example, thunderstorms may occur on 200 or more days a year.

Lower elevations in the East African highlands have enough rainfall to support some forest growth, but much of the region is savanna. At higher elevations, tempera-tures are colder and vegetation is more scarce. Mountain peaks at the highest elevations are snowcapped year-round. Here it is cold enough that mountain climbers trying to reach the summit of one of these peaks could get frostbite.

The cooler climate in the East African highlands makes living conditions there more comfortable than in the savanna or forests found at lower elevations. In addition, the highland savanna of the East African plateau is ideal for the herding of cattle because many disease-carrying insects cannot live at the higher, colder elevations. For example, highland areas above 4,000 feet (1,220 m) are safe from the tsetse fly, which carries the dreaded sleeping sickness.

C. Africa's Great Valley and Highest Peak

Rift Valley Slicing through East Africa from north to south is a gigantic **rift valley**. A rift valley is a deep, trenchlike valley with

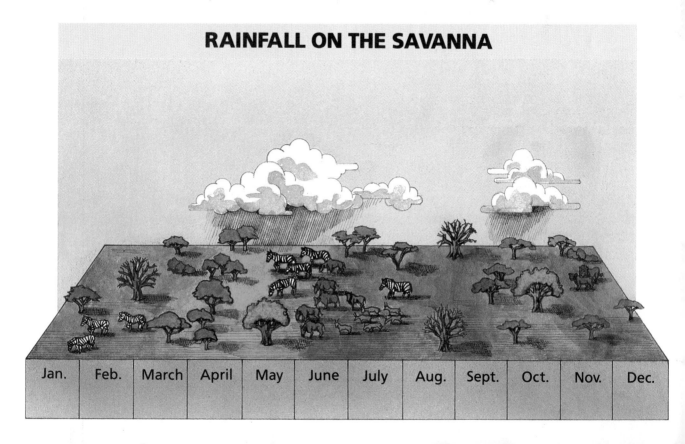

RAINFALL ON THE SAVANNA

| Jan. | Feb. | March | April | May | June | July | Aug. | Sept. | Oct. | Nov. | Dec. |

steep walls. It is caused by the shifting of the earth's crust. The huge East African rift valley, shown on the map on page 523, is called the Great Rift Valley. It begins in the Jordan River valley of the Middle East, extends through the floor of the Red Sea, and then enters the African landmass at Ethiopia. The Great Rift Valley continues south to Lake Victoria. There the valley divides into two sections, one to the east of the lake, the other to the west. South of Lake Victoria the Great Rift Valley continues into Southern Africa.

Many lakes fill parts of the 5,000-mile-long (8,045-km-long) Great Rift Valley. One of these lakes is the Dead Sea, which you learned about in Chapter 20. Other lakes located in the Great Rift Valley include Lake Malawi and Lake Tanganyika. Both of these lakes are found in East Africa. With a depth of 4,710 feet (1,436 m), Lake Tanganyika is the second deepest lake in the world.

In some places, such as at the Dead Sea, the Great Rift Valley is below sea level. In other places, especially in East Africa, the floor of the valley is at an elevation of 6,000 feet (1,829 m). In most places the walls of the Great Rift Valley are cliffs from several hundred to several thousand feet high.

Volcanoes Many volcanoes—some active, some dormant, some extinct—are found along both sides of the Great Rift Valley. The volcanic mountains of the Ethiopian highlands reach elevations of about 13,000 feet (3,962 m). Mount Kilimanjaro is an extinct volcano. Its peak, at 19,340 feet (5,895 m), is the highest point in Africa. Find Kilimanjaro on the physical map on page 588. Another extinct volcano in this region is Mount Kenya, which has an elevation of 17,058 feet (5,199 m). Both Kilimanjaro and Mount Kenya are snowcapped throughout the year.

This photograph, taken in Kenya, shows mountains rising up on both sides of the Great Rift Valley.
▶ Judging from the photograph, how do you think land in this part of the valley is used?

The photograph on the left shows farmland in the East African highlands. The photograph on the right shows workers picking tea leaves in the highlands.
▶ What crops besides tea grow in the highlands?

D. Farming in East Africa

Lowland Crops East Africa's varied climate allows people to raise many different kinds of crops here. In Sudan, for example, over 2 million acres (809,389 ha) of low, flat land between the Blue Nile and the White Nile is irrigated and used to raise cotton and sugarcane. Water is taken from the Blue Nile and channeled across the fields toward the White Nile.

Highland Crops The fertile volcanic soils and cool temperatures in the highlands around Lake Victoria and the Ethiopian highlands make these among the best farming regions of East Africa. One of the main cash crops raised on large farms throughout the highlands is coffee. Tea, tobacco, sugarcane, and rice are other important highland crops.

Coastal Crops The crop **sisal** is one of several crops grown primarily along the East African coast south of the desert region. Sisal is a fibrous plant used to make rope, string, and bags. Cashew nuts and coconuts also come from this East African coastal region. The two islands of Zanzibar and Pemba are world centers for growing cloves, a spice often used in baking. If you have eaten pumpkin pie, you may have tasted cloves from Zanzibar or Pemba.

LESSON 1

Review

REVIEWING MAIN IDEAS

A. Why is the protection of wildlife important to the countries of East Africa?

B. What are the climate regions of East Africa?

C. How do landforms affect the climates of East Africa?

D. What are the major crops grown in East Africa?

SKILLS CHECK

MAP SKILL

Reread Section B, and use the map on page 588 to identify the East African countries that have a desert climate.

Sudan, Ethiopia, and the Horn of Africa

CONNECTIONS

What factors do you think have an effect on how long people live?

TERMS

life expectancy

FOCUS

What are the lands and peoples of Sudan, Ethiopia, and the Horn of Africa like?

A. Sudan—Two Climates, Two Cultures

Northern Sudan Sudan, the largest country in Africa, is a little more than one-fourth the size of the United States. About 31 million people live in Sudan. The northern and southern halves of the country, and the people who live there, are distinctly different from each other.

People in the northern half of the country share the same desert heritage as the people of North Africa. Most people in northern Sudan are Arab Muslims. And as in the desert nations of North Africa, nomadic herding is an important way of life in northern Sudan. Herds of livestock can be found wherever oases or small farming villages are located.

Most people in northern Sudan, however, make their living by farming along the narrow band of fertile land near the Nile River. The population center of the north is found where the Blue Nile and the White Nile meet. Sudan's capital city, Khartoum, and its second largest city, Omdurman, are located in this population center.

Southern Sudan Southern Sudan is very different from northern Sudan. Grassy plains cover much of the southern region, and there is a small area of forest growth along Sudan's border with Uganda.

Sudan's best farmland is in this southern region. The leading crop is cotton. Other agricultural products include sorghum, wheat, groundnuts, and sesame, a plant

Sudan's capital city is located just north of where the White Nile (left) and the Blue Nile (right) meet.
▶ What is the capital of Sudan?

whose seeds are used to flavor breads. Sudan also produces 80 percent of the world's supply of gum arabic, a product that is used in adhesives, candy, medicines, and other products.

The culture of southern Sudan is more closely related to that of Central Africa than to that of northern Sudan and North Africa. For example, most people in southern Sudan follow either the Christian religion or traditional African religions rather than the Islamic religion.

Conflict Sudan was formerly called Anglo-Egyptian Sudan, when it was ruled jointly by Great Britain and Egypt. Since 1956, when Sudan became independent, a series of civil wars has hurt the country. The southerners have tried to break away from the Arabic northerners and start a separate nation. The rulers in the north have kept trying to impose an Islamic government on the whole country.

Rebellion on the part of the southern Sudanese has blocked Sudan's economic development. Petroleum has been discovered in the south, but rebel attacks on oil wells have stopped production. Rebel attacks have also slowed the construction of a canal that Sudan is building with Egypt. When completed, the canal will divert water from the White Nile to irrigate more land for farming.

Sudan has suffered from the same drought and famine that has affected the Sahel of West Africa. Because of the turmoil and poor economic development caused by civil wars, the Sudanese have had to rely on foreign help to deal with the famine.

B. Ethiopia and Eritrea

An Independent Land Ethiopia is a country of about 56 million people. For more than 2,000 years, Ethiopians have prided themselves on their independence. Their country was not claimed by Europeans

Muslims gather outside a mosque in Omdurman, Sudan.
▶ In what part of Sudan is Omdurman located, the north or the south?

during the period of colonialism in Africa. Except for during the period from 1935 to 1941, when Italy invaded and occupied the country, Ethiopia has remained an independent land.

Among the nations of East Africa, Ethiopia has had a unique history. According to Ethiopian tradition, part of the northern region of the country was the rich kingdom known as Sheba. Legend has it that the first emperor of Ethiopia was the son of the Biblical Queen of Sheba and King Solomon of Israel. Many later Ethiopian rulers claimed to be descendants of this king and queen.

Since the fourth century the majority of Ethiopians have been Coptic Christians. They are members of a branch of Christianity that was centered in Alexandria, Egypt. When Muslims conquered lands to the north of Ethiopia in the seventh century, the country's Coptic Christians became isolated. It wasn't until 1490 that ties to other Christians were restored.

The geography of Ethiopia has contributed to its independence and isolation. It is extremely difficult to travel across

EAST AFRICA: POLITICAL

Cities less than 100,000
Dodoma (Tanzania) B-3
Victoria (Seychelles) D-3

Cities 100,000 to 249,999
Bujumbura (Burundi) A-3
Kigali (Rwanda) A-3
Kisumu (Kenya) B-3
Port Sudan (Sudan) B-1

Cities 250,000 to 499,999
Asmara (Eritrea) B-1
Djibouti (Djibouti) C-1
Khartoum (Sudan) B-1
Mombasa (Kenya) B-3

Cities 500,000 to 999,999
Kampala (Uganda) B-2
Mogadishu (Somalia) C-2
Nairobi (Kenya) B-3
Omdurman (Sudan) B-1

Cities 1,000,000 or more
Dar es Salaam (Tanzania) B-3
Addis Ababa (Ethiopia) B-2

✪ National capitals
• Other cities

0   200   400 miles
0 200 400 kilometers

The Nile River and its tributaries begin in East Africa.
▶ Which capital city is located on the banks of three Nile Rivers?

Ethiopia's landscape. The rugged Ethiopian highlands cover most of the country. The highest peak in the highlands is Ras Dashen, at 15,158 feet (4,620 m). The highlands are chopped into sections by the Great Rift Valley. Several rivers, including the Awash and tributaries of the Nile, have cut deep gorges through the region.

Danakil Plain   The Danakil Plain, near the Red Sea, is so hot and dry that any water that flows into the area quickly evaporates. The region is named for the Danakil people who make their home in this desert. For years the Danakil believed that to protect their water supply, they had the right to kill strangers who ventured into this barren land.

Some areas of the Danakil Plain are below sea level. In places, water from the Red Sea slowly seeps up through rock layers below the desert surface. However, the sea water quickly evaporates, leaving behind a layer of salt. The Danakil people cut blocks of this salt from the desert floor. They carry the salt inland by camel or mule caravan to trade for the things they need.

Famine and War   People throughout the world have heard of Ethiopia because of the famine and civil wars that have occurred there. Several years of drought caused a massive famine in Ethiopia in the 1970s and 1980s. The famine killed hundreds of thousands of people.

The people of Ethiopia are very aware of the threat that drought and disease pose to **life expectancy** in their country. Life expectancy is the average number of years a person can expect to live. In Ethiopia, life expectancy is about 40 years; in the United States it is more than 70 years.

For years the people of Eritrea (er uh TREE uh), an Ethiopian province along the Red Sea coast, fought to gain their independence from Ethiopia. In 1991 the Eritreans defeated the Ethiopian forces who controlled

The stone church of St. George, carved into the ground, is one of the Christian churches at Lalibela, Ethiopia.
▶ In what shape has this church been carved?

the area. Two years later, Eritrea declared itself a free and independent nation.

Eritrea is a trumpet-shaped country that is about the size of the state of Indiana. Its most valuable natural resources are gold, iron, and copper. The capital city, Asmara, is located in the country's highlands.

C. Somalia and Djibouti: On the Horn of Africa

Somalia Wrapping around the Horn of Africa is the desert country of Somalia. The name Horn of Africa refers to the easternmost part of Africa, which is shaped like the horn of a rhinoceros. Rainfall in Somalia rarely exceeds 20 inches (50 cm) per year. Only a few inches of rain fall each year along the Indian Ocean coast. Mogadishu, the capital city, is located in Somalia's dry coastal region.

Somalia is a poor country. Because it is so dry, it has little land suitable for agriculture. Most of Somalia's 7.3 million people are Muslims, who have traditionally practiced nomadic herding. For centuries, Somalia's herders have migrated from coastal pastures to inland pastures, according to the season of the year.

Today, herding provides a living to 75 percent of the people in Somalia. Eighty percent of the country's export income comes from livestock. The main exports are skins, canned meat, butter, and live animals. The rest of Somalia's export income is from bananas, sugarcane, and cotton. These crops are grown using irrigation water from the Juba and Shebelle rivers.

Djibouti To the north of the Horn of Africa is the small nation of Djibouti (jih BOOT-ee). With an area of about 8,880 square miles (23,000 sq km), it is slightly larger than the state of Massachusetts. Approximately half of Djibouti's 421,000 people live in the capital city, which is also called Djibouti. A railroad connects this city with Addis Ababa, Ethiopia. Most of Ethiopia's trade goes through the port in the capital city of Djibouti.

Like Somalia, Djibouti is a dry, poor country. The average amount of rainfall is less than 5 inches (13 cm) per year. Farming here is difficult, so livestock herding is the only major agricultural activity.

LESSON 2

Review

REVIEWING MAIN IDEAS

A. In what ways is Sudan a divided country?
B. How has the geography of Ethiopia helped the country maintain its independence?
C. How do the people of Somalia and Djibouti make a living in their dry climates?

SKILLS CHECK

THINKING SKILL
Create a bar graph showing a comparison of the populations of Sudan, Ethiopia, Somalia, and Djibouti.

595

Kenya and Uganda

Jomo Kenyatta became Kenya's prime minister in 1963 and president in 1964.
▶ What was the theme of Kenyatta's presidency?

CONNECTIONS

You have already read about countries that have had political turmoil. How do countries recover from the problems that political turmoil creates?

TERMS

pyrethrum

FOCUS

How do the lands and peoples of Kenya differ from those of Uganda?

A. Kenya

Kenyans Pull Together Kenya was a British colony for many years. In the late 1800s the British built a railroad from the port of Mombasa (mahm BAH suh) inland to Lake Victoria. The British then began to move to the highlands of Kenya's interior to establish coffee and tea plantations.

The largest African ethnic group in the highlands at that time was the Kikuyu people. Many of the Kikuyus resented the British farmers who were now living where the Kikuyus herded cattle. The bad feelings built up over many years and finally grew into a freedom movement.

After several years of turmoil, Kenya gained its independence from Great Britain in 1963. Kenya struggled at first, but it had a strong president named Jomo Kenyatta. Kenyatta had been a leader in the freedom movement. As president he earned respect by working for equal rights for all Kenyans. The theme of his presidency was the call "Harambee!" This is a Swahili word that means "Let us all work together!"

Nairobi, the capital city of Kenya, is located in the country's highland region.
▶ What characteristics of a modern city can you see in this photograph of Nairobi?

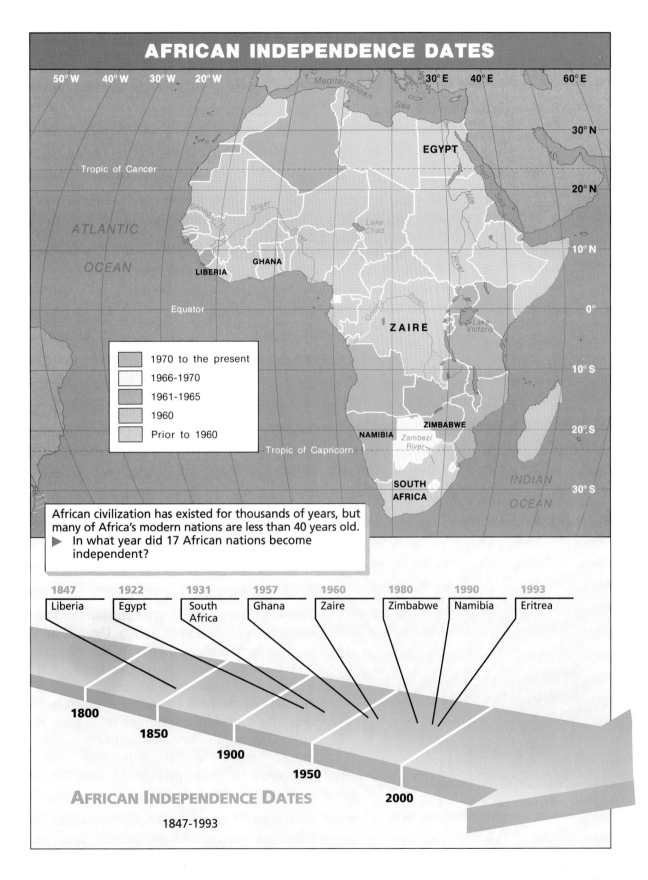

AFRICAN INDEPENDENCE DATES

50° W 40° W 30° W 20° W 30° E 40° E 60° E

30° N

Mediterranean Sea

EGYPT

Tropic of Cancer

20° N

Senegal *Niger River*

ATLANTIC

10° N

Lake Chad

Nile

Red Sea

OCEAN

LIBERIA GHANA

Equator

0°

ZAIRE

Congo River

Lake Victoria

10° S

	1970 to the present
	1966–1970
	1961–1965
	1960
	Prior to 1960

ZIMBABWE

NAMIBIA *Zambezi River*

20° S

Tropic of Capricorn

INDIAN

SOUTH AFRICA

30° S

OCEAN

African civilization has existed for thousands of years, but many of Africa's modern nations are less than 40 years old.
▶ In what year did 17 African nations become independent?

1847	1922	1931	1957	1960	1980	1990	1993
Liberia	Egypt	South Africa	Ghana	Zaire	Zimbabwe	Namibia	Eritrea

1800

1850

1900

1950

2000

AFRICAN INDEPENDENCE DATES

1847–1993

Kenya's Economy Most of the land in northern and eastern Kenya is semiarid steppe and desert. The southwestern part of the country, however, is highland savanna. Most of Kenya's 29 million people live in the highlands. The mile-high capital city of Nairobi is located there.

The highland region and the coastal lands around Mombasa are areas of high economic productivity. Coffee and tea are the main crops raised in the highlands. Highland farms also produce wheat, corn, millet, and dairy cattle. Some farmers in the highlands grow **pyrethrum**, a small flower that is dried and crushed and then used to make a natural insecticide. The fertile coastal land around Mombasa produces coconuts and sisal.

The safari-tourist industry is an important source of income for Kenya.
▶ What kind of safari did these tourists go on?

Kenya's highland region, with its parks and game reserves, is the center of the country's large and highly profitable safari-tourist industry. Kenya also has industries that process the country's agricultural products. These industries include sugar refining, textile production, and coffee bean processing.

Many of these industries are located in Nairobi. This modern capital city is the country's commercial and industrial center. In addition, Nairobi's railway system makes the city the center of Kenya's shipping and transportation industries.

Future Challenges Kenya is one of the most economically developed countries in East Africa. But the country has its problems. For example, Kenya has one of the highest population growth rates in the world—almost 3 percent per year. With this high growth rate, experts predict that by the year 2010, Kenya's population will be about twice what it was in 1990.

Although Kenya has a productive agricultural system, the country today still has to rely on imported food to feed all its people. In the future, Kenya must find better ways to use its land and resources to support its growing population.

B. Uganda, Land of Conflict

The Land Uganda is a small, landlocked country located west of Kenya. Uganda sits on the high plateau between the eastern and western branches of the Great Rift Valley. The Ruwenzori Mountains and a string of lakes mark Uganda's western border. The southeastern border is formed by Lake Victoria, the largest lake in Africa and one of the sources of the Nile River. In the southwest are the Virunga Mountains, home to mountain gorillas.

Years of Turmoil Like Kenya, Uganda was once a British colony. It takes its name from the *Buganda* people who live around

The Ruwenzori Mountains and a string of lakes mark the western border of Uganda.
▶ The Ruwenzori Mountains are part of what major landform of East Africa?

Kampala, the capital city. The British used the Buganda people as administrators in the colony. This caused resentment among some of the other ethnic groups who live in Uganda.

After independence was granted, in 1962, Uganda experienced much turmoil and instability. In a military coup in 1971, a soldier named Idi Amin was made president of Uganda. Amin was a brutal dictator who killed his opponents. Nearly 300,000 people were killed while he was in power. Many others were forced to leave the country or fled to safety in neighboring Sudan and Zaire. Amin was finally removed from power in 1979, but Uganda's government has continued to be unstable.

Uganda's Economy The political turmoil and violence of the 1970s and 1980s has had a lasting effect on Uganda's economy. The country has some minerals, including copper and cobalt, but has not fully developed those resources. Coffee is the leading export crop in Uganda, but most of the country's farmers are subsistence farmers who raise crops such as cassava, beans, and corn. These farmers must use their crops to feed themselves and their families.

Uganda has a great deal of potential. The climate and soils are ideal for agricultural development, and mineral resources are available. Hydroelectricity from the waters of the White Nile River could be used to power industries. Perhaps if the people of Uganda work together, their country could surpass Kenya in successful economic development.

LESSON 3

Review

REVIEWING MAIN IDEAS

A. What threat does a high population growth rate pose to the economy of Kenya?
B. Why has Uganda had difficulty developing its resources?

SKILLS CHECK

MAP SKILL

Using the scale of miles on the map on page 594, find the distance between Nairobi, the capital of Kenya, and Kampala, the capital of Uganda.

599

Tanzania and Its Neighbors

CONNECTIONS

Based on what you have already learned about other East African countries, what problems do you think might affect the countries of Tanzania, Rwanda, and Burundi?

TERMS

kraal

FOCUS

What different ethnic groups influence the cultures of Tanzania, Rwanda, and Burundi?

A. Tanzania

Land and Population Tanzania is a large nation about the size of Texas and Colorado combined. The country stretches westward across the East African plateau from the Indian Ocean to Lake Tanganyika and Lake Victoria. Tanzania also includes the islands of Zanzibar and Pemba. The main port of Tanzania is Dar es Salaam, an Arabic name that means "harbor of peace."

Much of the land in central Tanzania is dry savanna. As a result, most of the population is scattered around the outside edge of the country in a few economically productive areas. This geographic distribution of the population makes it difficult to unite the various regions of Tanzania. This in turn has been a hindrance to the country's economic development.

Tanzania is made up of two former colonies, Tanganyika and the island of Zanzibar. The population of the country is mainly African, but the presence of other ethnic groups reflects the history of the region. Many Arabs still live along the coast and on the islands of Zanzibar and Pemba, where they once practiced the slave trade. There are also Europeans and Indians.

Herders of East Africa On the high plateau of East Africa, many of the people are traditionally cattle herders. In Kenya and northern Tanzania lives one of these groups, called the Masai (mah SYE). The Masai are nomadic people who practice transhumance. They keep their cattle on the plateau grazing lands during the wetter months of the year. During the dry season, the herds are moved to the grassier pastures found in the mountains.

Sometimes a Masai kraal is surrounded by a barrier made of thorny branches.
▶ What purpose do you think the thorny barrier serves?

Some of the Masai live in small, round huts made of thatch. The huts are arranged in a large circle with only one entrance, forming a settlement called a **kraal** (krahl). At night the cattle are kept in pens inside the kraal. During the day the Masai lead the cattle out onto the grazing lands.

A Need for Conservation Mount Kilimanjaro and the Serengeti Plain are located in Tanzania. You have already learned that Kilimanjaro is the highest peak in Africa. The Serengeti Plain is world famous for its wildlife. Many tourists go on photographic safaris in Serengeti National Park.

Tanzania, like the other nations of East Africa, must be cautious in caring for its wildlife resources. If wildlife starts disappearing, then a large, healthy source of income for East Africa will also disappear.

B. The Landlocked Countries of Rwanda and Burundi

Land Use Rwanda and Burundi are two of the smallest countries in Africa. They are also the most crowded nations on the African mainland. Rwanda has a population density of about 846 people per square mile (327 people per sq km). Burundi has a population density of about 582 people per square mile (225 people per sq km).

Almost every piece of available land in Rwanda and Burundi is used for farming. Even so, if drought occurred, these countries would face problems. The potential for famine is high because of the dense populations. Because both countries are landlocked, it would be difficult to get relief supplies to where they are needed.

Ethnic Disputes Like neighboring Uganda, the small countries of Rwanda and Burundi have faced ethnic disputes and rivalries. Over 80 percent of the people of both countries are members of the Hutu ethnic group. The rest of the people belong to the Tutsi ethnic group.

The Masai people live in Kenya as well as in Tanzania. This Masai woman wears traditional face paint and jewelry.
▶ What animals do the Masai herd?

For hundreds of years the Tutsi minority ruled over the Hutu majority. But during the African independence movement of the 1950s and 1960s, the Hutus began to fight to gain control. The resulting conflicts left thousands of people, both Hutus and Tutsis, dead. Another outbreak of fighting in the mid-1990s led to more deaths. Many people fled Rwanda.

LESSON 4

Review

REVIEWING MAIN IDEAS
A. How do the Masai people use their land?
B. Why is the threat of famine so great in Rwanda and Burundi?

SKILLS CHECK

WRITING SKILL
Write a paragraph describing how the countries of East Africa could protect their wildlife resources and still support growing human populations.

PROTECTING THE EARTH'S WILDLIFE

In many semiarid regions of the world, huge seas of grass provide a rich environment for many kinds of human activity. Grasslands cover about one fourth of the earth's land surface. Because grasses die almost every year, new organic material is continually added to the soil. As a result, grasslands are areas of great soil fertility. Some of the world's richest farming regions have developed in grasslands, including the Wheat Belt in the United States, the steppes in Ukraine, and the Pampas in Argentina.

On the African continent the high plateaus are covered with extensive grasslands. The African grasslands provide lush grazing for hundreds of kinds of wildlife. In turn, the grazing animals provide food for the many types of predatory animals that live on the grasslands. But how do human populations affect the grasslands and other environments, and the wildlife these environments support?

East Africa's Wildlife Habitats

The plateau grasslands in the East African nations of Kenya and Tanzania are among the largest natural habitats for wildlife left in the world today. Both countries have established large national parks and game reserves to try to preserve some of the natural grasslands and the wildlife that lives there. The Serengeti Plain of Tanzania is home to one of Africa's largest parks, Serengeti National Park. This magnificent nature reserve covers an area of about 5,600 square miles (14,504 sq km) and continues across Tanzania's border into Kenya, where it is known as the Masai Mara Game Reserve.

This part of Africa inspires a feeling of unlimited open space and awe. Across the gently rolling grasslands of the Serengeti Plain are literally thousands of animals and birds. As far as the eye can see are vast herds of wildebeests, zebras, giraffes, and gazelles and other types of antelopes. The list could go on and on. Scattered here and there are groups of lions and elephants. Together they create an impression of an animal paradise.

This grassland environment of East Africa has existed for thousands of years. The balance of nature has been at work here to ensure the survival of the healthiest, strongest animals. But the balance of nature has been upset by the influence of humans.

Dian Fossey (bottom right) studied mountain gorillas, one of the many rare and beautiful animal species found in Africa.
▶ In what country did Fossey study the gorillas?

Human Interaction with the Environment

In the 1950s and 1960s, anthropologists Louis and Mary Leakey discovered fossils of early humans in this part of East Africa. In Olduvai (AWL doo vye) Gorge, on the eastern edge of the Serengeti Plain, the Leakeys unearthed human bones that were almost 2 million years old. These and other fossils and artifacts found in the region have allowed anthropologists to paint a picture of how humans have changed over the years. For example, scientists have learned that because of the ability to use tools and weapons, humans eventually became hunters and began to dominate this part of Africa.

In the twentieth century, rapid human population growth and the search for new lands to settle have led people to invade land that once belonged only to wildlife. Some of these people are nomadic herders who move around the grasslands in search of water and better pastures for their livestock. Others are farmers who have moved farther into the grasslands in search of new, fertile land.

As little as 30 years ago, there were largely unsettled zones surrounding nature reserves like Serengeti. These zones protected the reserves from the pressures of farming and grazing. But as the need for more food and more grazing land and cropland increased, many people moved closer to the reserves.

The Threat to Wildlife

Hunting is illegal in East Africa's parks and reserves, which have been set up

603

THE WORLD: ENDANGERED SPECIES

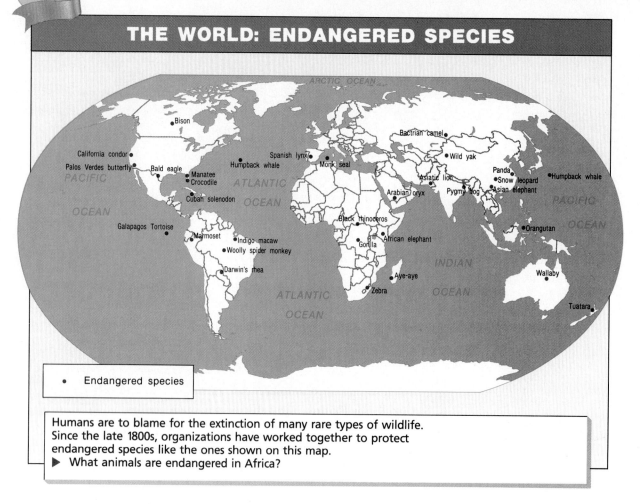

- Endangered species

Humans are to blame for the extinction of many rare types of wildlife. Since the late 1800s, organizations have worked together to protect endangered species like the ones shown on this map.
▶ What animals are endangered in Africa?

largely to protect gorillas, elephants, and other wildlife. But many people in this region of Africa live in poverty, and some turn to poaching as a way to survive. Each year, poachers kill thousands of animals. As you have already learned, elephants are hunted for their ivory tusks. Rhinoceroses are hunted for their horns, which are ground into medicines that are considered valuable in some parts of the world. Some types of animals are caught illegally and sold to zoos, and some are killed for their meat or to be sold as trophies to collectors around the world.

What are some of the results of poaching? In the past 20 years, the number of elephants in Kenya has decreased from over 130,000 to fewer than 20,000. During the same period, the rhinoceros

population has fallen from over 20,000 to fewer than 600. Many African animals are now endangered—that is, their numbers are greatly reduced. Unless strong measures are taken to protect these animals, they will die out.

People are part of nature and part of the grassland environment of East Africa. Like the animals here, the people are trying to survive in this semiarid region. but as you can see from the map showing endangered species, above, people pose a serious threat to the survival of wildlife in Africa and, indeed, around the world.

Solutions in East Africa and Beyond

National parks and game reserves rich in wildlife can be an important source of income for a country, as they are for Kenya and Tanzania. Tourism is worth millions of dollars to these two countries—and the tourists go there primarily to see the African wildlife. If the animals were to die out, the countries would be hurt financially as well as ecologically.

Realizing the importance of wildlife to their national economies, the governments of Kenya and Tanzania have created a strong force of park rangers and game wardens to catch and arrest poachers. Kenya's government is considering building fences around some of the most important wildlife habitats to protect the wildlife by keeping the animals in and the poachers out.

Kenya and Tanzania are actively promoting tours and safaris in their national parks and game reserves. With more money from tourism coming in, more people can be hired to protect wildlife. Also, the tourist dollars help to raise the income levels of the people living in these countries. Perhaps in the future, poverty will decrease to the point where poaching will be eliminated—that is, people will no longer need to illegally hunt animals to survive.

These tourists are on a photographic safari in Kenya's Masai Mara Game Reserve, which extends into Tanzania.
▶ What kind of animals are shown here?

The protection of wildlife is of worldwide concern. People around the world must cooperate with efforts to protect wildlife if these efforts are to be successful. For example, governments must help to enforce the worldwide ban on the sale of ivory. Zoos must purchase animals from sources that follow strict regulations regarding the types and number of animals that can be removed from their natural habitats. Individuals can support international organizations formed for the purpose of raising money to help protect wildlife. Through these and other efforts, we can protect wildlife around the world.

In Zimbabwe and other countries, game wardens use spotter planes to search for poachers in parks and reserves.
▶ How else might poachers be found?

THINKING CRITICALLY

1. Why have humans moved closer to areas where African wildlife lives?
2. What is the connection between poverty and poaching?
3. How could *you* help to protect wildlife in Africa or somewhere else in the world?

605

REVIEWING TERMS

From the list below, choose a term that could be used in place of the underlined words in each sentence. Rewrite the sentences on a separate sheet of paper.

Swahili   **life expectancy**
rift valley   **pyrethrum**
sisal

1. The people of the East African coast make rope, string, and bags from <u>a fibrous plant</u>.
2. <u>A deep, trenchlike valley with steep walls</u> is caused by the shifting of the earth's crust.
3. <u>A mixture of Arabic and African languages</u> is spoken throughout much of East Africa.
4. Some farmers in the highlands of Kenya make a natural pesticide from <u>a small flower that is dried and crushed</u>.
5. In Ethiopia the <u>average number of years a person can expect to live</u> is about 40 years.

REVIEWING THE FACTS

On a separate sheet of paper, answer the following questions in complete sentences.

1. Why is the African elephant in danger of extinction?
2. What geographic region is located south of East Africa's desert region?
3. What is Africa's highest peak?
4. In what ways do the people of northern Sudan make a living?
5. What religions are practiced in Sudan?

6. Where is the Danakil Plain located?
7. What desert country is located on the Horn of Africa?
8. Why is Nairobi Kenya's most important city?
9. What two major problems does Kenya face today?
10. What ethnic groups live in Tanzania?

WRITING ABOUT GEOGRAPHY

Pretend you are the leader of an East African country. Write a speech giving reasons why your country's land should be used for game preserves instead of farming.

THINKING CRITICALLY

On a separate sheet of paper, answer the following questions in complete sentences.

1. How might the civil wars in Sudan be partly responsible for the famine that occurs in that country?
2. In the statement "Ethiopia is an independent land," what does *independent* mean?
3. How might the history of Ethiopia have been different if its geography did not include rugged highlands?
4. Why, in your opinion, is life expectancy so much higher in the United States than it is in Ethiopia?
5. Why does Kenya still rely on imported food to feed its people even though it has a productive agricultural system?

On a separate sheet of paper, draw a graphic organizer like the one shown. Copy the information from this graphic organizer to the one you have drawn. Under the main idea for each lesson, write three statements that support the main idea.

CHAPTER THEME

The countries of East Africa face many obstacles to economic growth and political stability.

Lesson 1 East Africa has varied landforms and climates.

1. _____
2. _____
3. _____

Lesson 2 The lands and peoples of Sudan, Ethiopia, and the Horn of Africa are different from one another.

1. _____
2. _____
3. _____

Lesson 3 The lands and peoples of Kenya differ from those of Uganda.

1. _____
2. _____
3. _____

Lesson 4 Many different ethnic groups influence the cultures of Tanzania, Rwanda, and Burundi.

1. _____
2. _____
3. _____

THE COUNTRIES OF SOUTHERN AFRICA

The Lands of Southern Africa

CONNECTIONS

The plateau that covers much of East Africa also covers much of Southern Africa. Knowing this, what type of climate would you expect to find in the plateau region of Southern Africa?

TERMS

escarpment, High Veld, Afrikaans

FOCUS

What are the landforms and climates of Southern Africa?

A. A Region of Independent Nations

The date was March 21, 1990. The place was a sports stadium in a capital city called Windhoek. The time was just past midnight. As thousands of people looked on, the blue, white, and orange flag of South Africa was taken down and a new blue, red, green, and gold flag was raised. And with that, an independent African nation was officially born: the nation of Namibia (nuh MIHB ee uh).

For more than 70 years, Namibia had been under the control of the country of South Africa, its neighbor to the southeast. Before independence, Namibia was often referred to as South-West Africa, a name that symbolized both the country's location and its political standing in relation to South Africa.

For more than 20 years, a strong nationalist movement had been fighting for Namibia's independence. Now, in the early morning hours of that day in March, the moment had arrived. Sam Nujoma, a major leader of the movement, was sworn in as the country's first president. He proclaimed before the cheering crowd, "In the name of our people, I declare that Namibia is forever free, sovereign, and independent."

Cape Town, South Africa, was built near the edge of the Southern African plateau.
▶ How do you think people might travel to the top of the plateau?

Namibia and South Africa are just two of the independent nations that make up the region known as Southern Africa. The different peoples, landforms, climates, and cultures of these nations, which are shown on the map on page 610, make Southern Africa unique.

B. The Plateau of Southern Africa

The Plateau's Edge In some ways, the southern region of the African continent is similar to the other parts of Africa that you have already read about. The same high

609

▶ The mighty Victoria Falls, a major scenic attraction of Southern Africa plateau that dominates much of East Africa extends into the countries of Southern Africa. The plateau in Southern Africa is surrounded by mountains, hills, and valleys. This rugged landscape forms a barrier between the narrow coastal plain and the gently rolling plain atop the plateau.

In many places there are sudden changes in elevation and you can see the great **escarpments** that form the edge of the plateau. An escarpment is a steep slope or cliff formed by erosion or by movements of the earth's rock layers. Not too far inland from the Atlantic coast of Angola, for example, the land abruptly rises up in a series of giant steps to the top of the Southern African plateau.

Mountain Ranges Along the southern coast of Africa, a region called the Karroo separates the narrow coastal plain from the plateau. In this region, several major mountain ranges run from east to west. Separated by valleys, each of these mountain ranges

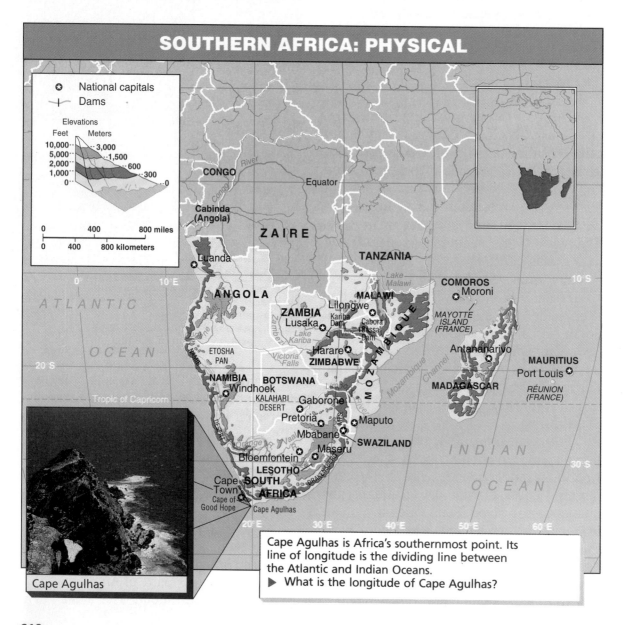

SOUTHERN AFRICA: PHYSICAL

⊙ National capitals
⊢ Dams

Elevations
Feet   Meters
10,000····3,000
5,000····1,500
2,000····600
1,000····300
0·····0

0   400   800 miles
0   400   800 kilometers

CONGO
Equator
Cabinda (Angola)
ZAIRE
Luanda
TANZANIA
ANGOLA
Lake Malawi
COMOROS
Moroni
MALAWI
Lilongwe
ZAMBIA
Lusaka
Kariba Dam
Cabora Bassa Dam
MAYOTTE ISLAND (FRANCE)
Lake Kariba
Victoria Falls
Harare
ZIMBABWE
Antananarivo
MAURITIUS
Port Louis
ETOSHA PAN
MOZAMBIQUE
MADAGASCAR
RÉUNION (FRANCE)
NAMIBIA
BOTSWANA
Windhoek
KALAHARI DESERT
Gaborone
Pretoria
Maputo
Mbabane
SWAZILAND
Bloemfontein
Maseru
LESOTHO
Cape Town
SOUTH AFRICA
Cape of Good Hope
Cape Agulhas
ATLANTIC OCEAN
INDIAN OCEAN
Tropic of Capricorn

Cape Agulhas

Cape Agulhas is Africa's southernmost point. Its line of longitude is the dividing line between the Atlantic and Indian Oceans.
▶ What is the longitude of Cape Agulhas?

People in the region around Cape Town can grow crops typical of other Mediterranean climate regions around the world.
▶ What kind of crops are shown here?

becomes successively higher in steplike fashion as you move northward from the coast to the top of the plateau.

Farther east and extending north along the edge of the continent is the Drakensberg Mountain range. These and the many other mountains in the southern third of Africa make it difficult to travel from the coast to the interior plateau.

C. A Variety of Climates

High Veld Because of its southerly location and high elevations, much of the plateau of Southern Africa is grassland. This is the type of climate and vegetation found in Kansas and other places in the central United States. In Southern Africa this high plateau grassland is called the **High Veld**. The word *veld* means "grassland" in the **Afrikaans** language. Afrikaans, a language that is widely used in South Africa, is a variation of Dutch influenced by various African languages.

Mediterranean There are other types of climates in different parts of Southern Africa. A small coastal region around the city of Cape Town, South Africa, has a Mediterranean climate. This is one of the more comfortable climates in all of Africa. The winter season is rainy but mild, and the summer is sunny and dry. Residents and tourists alike can be almost certain of beautiful weather all summer long. As in other Mediterranean climate regions of the world, such as Greece, Italy, and southern California, people in this region of Southern Africa can grow crops such as wheat, barley, oats, apricots, plums, citrus fruit, and grapes.

Subtropical Another kind of climate is found along the coast of the Indian Ocean in southeastern Africa. A region of humid subtropical climate, it has warm and humid summers, mild winters, and year-round rainfall. People in this region can grow a variety of crops, including pineapples,

611

Workers on a Namibian beach construct barriers to hold back the waves so they can search for diamonds in the sand.
▶ Where do these diamonds come from?

bananas, and citrus fruits. However, the most important cash crop raised in this part of Southern Africa is sugarcane.

D. The Dry Regions of Southern Africa

The Namib Stretching up the coast of southwestern Africa from the mouth of the Orange River into Angola is a dry, barren landscape covered with sand and gravel. This arid part of Africa is the Namib Desert. Like Chile's Atacama Desert, the Namib is a coastal desert. It extends about 60 miles (97 km) inland to the escarpments that mark the edge of the African plateau.

The Namib Desert, however, is not a useless wasteland. It is the site of profitable diamond mines. In addition, millions of dollars worth of diamonds are found in the sand of its beaches. The Orange River erodes mineral-rich areas of South Africa's interior, and the gravel that washes downstream includes millions of tiny diamonds no bigger than large grains of sand. Much of this gravel washes all the way into the Atlantic Ocean.

The Benguela Current, a cool current shown on the map on page 199, sweeps the gravel northward and deposits it and the tiny diamonds on the beaches of the Namib desert region. These beaches are fenced off and patrolled by armed guards. Diamond-mining companies have developed large machines to sort the tiny diamonds from the sand. Larger diamonds are used as gem stones; smaller diamonds are used industrially, for example, to make strong, hard drill bits.

The Kalahari The second major desert region in Southern Africa is the Kalahari, which is located on the interior plateau. The Kalahari is actually a semidesert region. It does receive a little rain, and grass and scrub grow in some areas. The Kalahari is mostly in the country of Botswana and is home to the San people, an ethnic group of Southern Africa.

LESSON 1

Review

REVIEWING MAIN IDEAS
A. When did Namibia become independent?
B. What is the High Veld?
C. What different types of climates are found in Southern Africa's coastal regions?
D. What valuable resource is found in the Namib Desert?

SKILLS CHECK

MAP SKILL
Using the map on page 610, find the lines of latitude between which the countries of Southern Africa are located.

LESSON 2

Zimbabwe and Its Neighbors

CONNECTIONS
You have already read about European colonialism. What European countries had colonies in Africa?

TERMS
Malagasy

FOCUS
What are the lands and peoples of the northern half of Southern Africa like?

Great Zimbabwe, the most famous of the African zimbabwes, was constructed by the Shona people and took about 400 years to build.
▶ What are zimbabwes?

A. Zimbabwe: From Colony to Country

Zimbabwe's History Zimbabwe was once a British colony called Southern Rhodesia (roh DEE zhuh). It and another British colony, Northern Rhodesia, were named for Cecil Rhodes, a British colonizer and businessman. Rhodes acquired land for Britain and played a major role in governing its empire in Southern Africa. Southern Rhodesia was an important part of that empire.

When the first British colonizers moved into Southern Rhodesia in the late 1800s, they found a land inhabited by various African ethnic groups. The country today has a population of more than 11 million people, about 96 percent of whom are black. In the 1960s, Great Britain had said that it would grant independence to Southern Rhodesia only if the black majority there were allowed to rule. However, the white minority in the country refused to agree to the British plan. They declared independence in 1965 and governed the country under their own rules.

After years of turmoil caused by protests from other countries and an all-out civil war, Southern Rhodesia's white minority finally agreed to give control of the nation to the black majority in 1980. The country was renamed after *zimbabwes*, great stone communities built for the kings of an ancient trading kingdom that dominated this part of Africa in the twelfth to fifteenth centuries.

Zimbabwe's Resources Zimbabwe, a landlocked country about the size of Montana, is agriculturally productive. It has a humid subtropical climate that receives enough rainfall for people to be able to raise crops. These include tobacco, corn, cotton, wheat, sugarcane, vegetables, and the country's leading export crop, tobacco.

Zimbabwe is also part of the mineral-rich crescent of Southern Africa. Beginning near the country's capital city, Harare, and running southwest toward the industrial city of Bulawayo is what is called the Great Dyke. This mineral-rich rock formation is from 3 to 6 miles (5 to 10 km) wide and about 320 miles (516 km) long. It is a source of gold, copper, coal, iron ore, and nickel. In addition, about two thirds of the world's supply of chromite, a chromium ore, comes from the Great Dyke.

Another of Zimbabwe's major resources is the mighty Zambezi River, which forms the border between Zimbabwe and Zambia. One of the main scenic attractions in Africa, the impressive Victoria Falls, is located on the Zambezi. Several hundred miles downstream is Kariba Dam, which Zimbabwe and Zambia jointly built and own. The hydroelectric power plant at this dam provides almost all of the electricity used by the two countries.

B. Zambia and Malawi, Former British Colonies

Zambia The country of Zambia, Zimbabwe's neighbor to the north, was once the British colony called Northern Rhodesia. It is a country that is rich in mineral deposits. The Copper Belt, part of Southern Africa's mineral crescent, extends from Zaire into Zambia, and copper is the major mineral resource of Zambia. The country also produces gold, silver, and cobalt.

Zambia is about the size of Texas and West Virginia combined. The country is similar to Zimbabwe in that it is also landlocked and sits on the high African plateau. Over 7 million people live in Zambia, mostly in the capital city, Lusaka, and in mining and manufacturing cities such as Ndola (en DOH luh) and Kitwe, which are located in the Copper Belt.

Malawi The country of Malawi, Zambia's neighbor to the east, used to be a British colony called Nyasaland. It gained independence in 1964.

Malawi is a small country, about the size of Mississippi. Like Zimbabwe and Zambia, Malawi is landlocked. However, it is more mountainous than either Zambia or Zimbabwe because it is located along

Kariba Dam and its hydroelectric plant are located on the Zambezi River, downstream from Victoria Falls.
▶ To what two countries does this plant provide hydroelectricity?

the Great Rift Valley, with its bordering ranges of volcanic peaks. Because of the rich volcanic soils found here, the people of Malawi can grow and export many kinds of crops, including rice, corn, sugarcane, tea, cotton, and tobacco.

C. Madagascar and the Comoro Islands

A Mixed Heritage Just off the Southern African coast is the world's fourth largest island, Madagascar. It is about as big as Colorado and New Mexico combined. Running down the middle of Madagascar is a high plateau where many of the country's 14 million people live. Here in the island's center is the capital city, which is called Antananarivo (an tuh nan uh REE voh).

Madagascar's central plateau divides the island into eastern and western halves, which have different cultural backgrounds. On the western side of the island, across from the African coast, the people are descendants of black Africans who spoke traditional African languages.

In many parts of eastern Madagascar, you can see rice fields up and down terraced hillsides. This part of the island reflects the influence of Southeast Asia. Many of Madagascar's people trace their ancestry back to Malay and Polynesian peoples who sailed here in outrigger canoes about 2,000 years ago.

A third major ethnic influence in Madagascar is French. For many years the island was a French colony. Many of Madagascar's people are Christians as a result of this French-European heritage, and many still speak the French language. However, the island's chief language is **Malagasy** (mal-uh GAS ee), an Asian language.

Agriculture Madagascar's climate is mostly tropical, and a variety of agricultural products grow here. In addition to rice, the island's farmers raise coffee, sugarcane,

Rice fields on the terraced hillsides of eastern Madagascar reflect the influence of Southeast Asia.
▶ What other crops grow in Madagascar?

peppers, and cloves. Two specialty crops also grown here are vanilla beans and ylang-ylangs (EE lahng EE lahngz). Madagascar grows over half of the world's natural vanilla. If you have ever eaten vanilla ice cream with real vanilla beans ground into it, you have probably tasted vanilla from Madagascar. Ylang-ylangs are trees with fragrant flowers. The oil from these greenish-yellow flowers is used to scent perfumes. Madagascar also has some mineral resources, including coal, iron ore, chromite, graphite, and mica.

Comoro Islands The original settlers of the Comoro Islands were Muslims who came from the African mainland and who spoke Swahili. Later the Comoros, like Madagascar, became a French colony. In fact, one of the four main islands in this archipelago still belongs to France. The other islands, however, make up a fully independent nation.

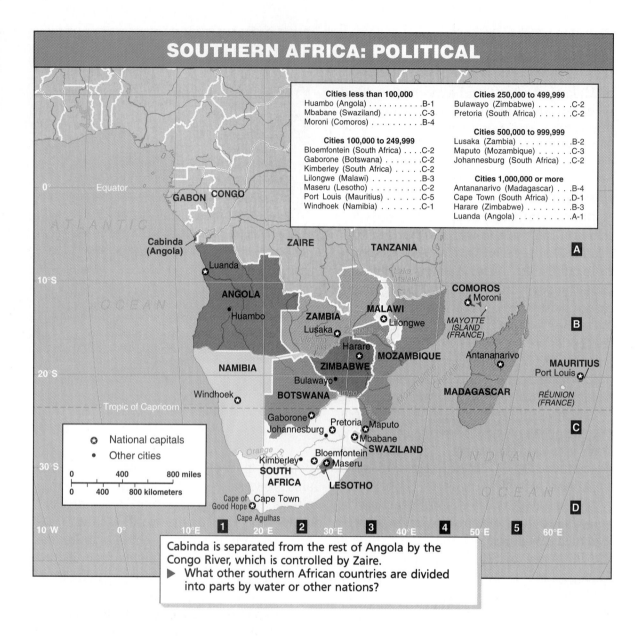

SOUTHERN AFRICA: POLITICAL

Cities less than 100,000
Huambo (Angola) B-1
Mbabane (Swaziland) C-3
Moroni (Comoros) B-4

Cities 100,000 to 249,999
Bloemfontein (South Africa) C-2
Gaborone (Botswana) C-2
Kimberley (South Africa) C-2
Lilongwe (Malawi) B-3
Maseru (Lesotho) C-2
Port Louis (Mauritius) C-5
Windhoek (Namibia) C-1

Cities 250,000 to 499,999
Bulawayo (Zimbabwe) C-2
Pretoria (South Africa) C-2

Cities 500,000 to 999,999
Lusaka (Zambia) B-2
Maputo (Mozambique) C-3
Johannesburg (South Africa) . .C-2

Cities 1,000,000 or more
Antananarivo (Madagascar) . . .B-4
Cape Town (South Africa) D-1
Harare (Zimbabwe) B-3
Luanda (Angola) A-1

☉ National capitals
• Other cities

0   400   800 miles
0   400   800 kilometers

Cabinda is separated from the rest of Angola by the
Congo River, which is controlled by Zaire.
▶ What other southern African countries are divided
into parts by water or other nations?

The Comoro Islands are volcanic in origin and, like Madagascar, have a mostly tropical climate. Much of the land here supports abundant tropical vegetation. The main agricultural products of the islands are rice, maize, and tropical fruits. Fishing is another important industry.

D. Botswana, Land of the San

Land and Resources Botswana, a former British colony, is a country about the size of New Mexico and Nevada combined. The capital city, Gaborone, and most other towns are located near the railroad running along Botswana's eastern border. This railroad connects Zimbabwe to South Africa.

Only about 1 million people live in Botswana. Most live in the eastern part, where the African plateau is higher in elevation and so there is enough rainfall to allow cattle herding. However, most of Botswana's income is from minerals, including copper, diamonds, and nickel.

People of the Desert A large part of Botswana is covered by the Kalahari Desert, which forms the dry interior of Southern Africa. Here live most of the San people of Africa. This ethnic group, formerly called Bushmen, leads a traditional and vanishing way of life on the desert plateau.

Once the San people roamed over much of Southern Africa. But in the 1600s, Europeans began pushing into the region from the south and other African peoples from the north began moving south with their cattle. The San tried to hold their ground, but many were killed and others were eventually forced to move. Finally the San retreated into the Kalahari Desert. Here they found a place that no one else wanted. The heat and scarcity of water offered the San some protection from their enemies.

Today about 5,000 San still lead a traditional life in the desert. They do not practice farming or herding but use hunting and gathering to survive. The San people have learned how to find water underground and to extract moisture and food from the few plants they can gather in the desert, such as roots, berries, and nuts. The San people also hunt game with bows and arrows or spears.

These San live in family groups of anywhere from a dozen people to more than 50. When they use up the resources of a part of the desert, they gather their few belongings and move on. The nomadic San travel light because they move around the desert on foot.

About 55,000 San people still live in the Kalahari region. Most are no longer nomadic hunters and gatherers. Many work as laborers on farms and ranches or in villages. To many people in the modern world, the life of the still-nomadic San people is primitive. But they know the secrets of survival in a harsh desert land that seems as if it could not possibly support human life.

Some of the San people of the Kalahari still lead a traditional nomadic life.
▶ How do the nomadic San people get food to survive in the desert?

LESSON 2

Review

REVIEWING MAIN IDEAS

A. What are some of Zimbabwe's valuable resources?

B. Historically, what do Zambia and Malawi have in common?

C. Which ethnic groups have had an influence on the culture of Madagascar?

D. How do the San people of Botswana survive in the Kalahari Desert?

SKILLS CHECK

THINKING SKILL

Suppose you were going to the Kalahari Desert to spend a month studying the San way of life. Make a list of the things you would want or need to take with you to survive in the desert. Also make a list of the things the San use to survive. Then compare the two lists.

Angola and Mozambique

CONNECTIONS

Why did European countries establish colonies in Africa?

TERMS

exclave

FOCUS

What characteristics do Angola and Mozambique have in common?

A. Angola and Its Resources

Portuguese Colonies The Southern African countries of Angola and Mozambique (moh zum BEEK) were once part of Portugal's colonial empire. Portugal's official policy toward its colonies could best be described as exploitation, the use of something or someone purely for profit. Portugal wanted all the resources and raw materials that it could possibly get from its colonies. The country did almost nothing to develop or improve the colonies but merely took their cash crops, such as sugar and cotton, and used their people as slaves and laborers.

Portugal finally bowed to world pressure and granted independence to Angola and Mozambique in 1975. Since then, both countries have been plagued by civil war, with several different groups of people seeking power.

Angola Today Angola, the largest nation in Southern Africa, is about the size of Arizona, Nevada, New Mexico, and Alabama combined. About 10 million people live in Angola, mostly scattered across the high plateau country, away from the plain along the Atlantic coast.

Angola's narrow coastal plain is the site of the capital city, Luanda. However, the plain is sparsely populated because it is so dry. The cold Benguela Current that

flows offshore has an effect on Angola's coastal region. One benefit is that the cool ocean water is rich in nutrients that fish feed on, so fish are abundant in this region. Therefore, fishing is an important industry along the coast of Angola.

The northern part of Angola receives more rainfall than the rest of the country does and even has a few areas of dense tropical forest. During the colonial period the Portuguese had tried to establish their own agricultural industry in this part of Angola, but those efforts were largely unsuccessful. However, in the mid-twentieth century, the northern coffee plantations began to make a profit. Coffee is now Angola's main export crop.

Oil is Angola's main export. The country's offshore oil fields are vital to its economy.
▶ Where are Angola's oil fields located?

B. Mozambique and Its Resources

On the Indian Ocean coast of Southern Africa is the nation of Mozambique, which is about the size of Texas and South Carolina combined. Like Angola, Mozambique has some mineral resources, including coal, iron ore, bauxite, and tungsten. There is a variety of crops, including cotton, sugarcane, tea, and cashew nuts. This coastal country also has a profitable fishing industry, with catches of tuna, lobster, and shrimp.

Mozambique has been able to develop some of its other resources. An example is the massive Cabora Bassa Dam project on the Zambezi River. This dam produces hydroelectricity for use in Mozambique and also for export to the neighboring country of South Africa.

Another source of income for Mozambique is its ports. This country has a fairly wide coastal plain with some major rivers, including the Zambezi and the Limpopo, emptying across it. The major port cities of Beira and Maputo, serve not only Mozambique but also the landlocked nations of Southern Africa. Railroads connect these port cities to the countries of Malawi, Zimbabwe, Zambia, and Botswana.

The coastal plain of Mozambique has ports that are important to the country's fishing industry.
▶ How else do you think Mozambique's coastal plain might be used?

Mineral Resources One small but very important coastal territory of Angola is separated from the rest of this large country. If you look at the map on page 616, you will see that part of Zaire protrudes, or extends, west to the Atlantic. Above this protrusion is the Angolan **exclave** (EHKS-klayv) of Cabinda. An exclave is a territory surrounded or nearly surrounded by the territory of another country. Cabinda is important to Angola because oil fields are located offshore. Oil is Angola's most important resource and its main export. The other major mineral resources found in Angola include diamonds, iron ore, gold, manganese, and copper.

LESSON 3

Review

REVIEWING MAIN IDEAS

A. What important resources does Angola have?
B. Why are waterways a valuable source of income for Mozambique?

SKILLS CHECK

WRITING SKILL

Write a paragraph or two explaining why you think Portugal would have wanted to establish colonies on opposite coasts of Southern Africa.

South Africa and Its Neighbors

CONNECTIONS

What country gave up control of Namibia in 1990?

TERMS

Boer, Great Trek, apartheid, homeland

FOCUS

What lasting effect has European colonialism had on the southernmost countries of Africa?

A. Europeans in South Africa

At the end of a long peninsula just south of Cape Town is a cape named the Cape of Good Hope. Many people mistakenly believe that the Cape of Good Hope is the southern tip of the African continent. This is probably because people learn in school that the Portuguese explorer Vasco da Gama sailed around this cape in 1498 on his voyage to discover a sea route to India. Actually, the southernmost point in Africa is Cape Agulhas, which lies about 100 miles (161 km) southeast of the Cape of Good Hope.

The Portuguese had been the first Europeans to see the South African coast when they discovered the Cape of Good Hope. But until the first Dutch colonizers arrived in 1652, South Africa was inhabited only by several different African ethnic groups. Among these groups were the Hottentots, San, Zulus, Swazis, and Basutos.

In 1652 the Dutch landed at Table Bay, the inlet that forms the harbor at Cape Town. There the Dutch East India Company established a supply station for their ships that were sailing back and forth between the Netherlands and the East Indies, a source of such valuable spices as pepper, cloves, nutmeg, and ginger. The Dutch who settled at Table Bay began to set up farms

After the British took control of Cape Town and the surrounding area, many of the Dutch settlers began to move to the South African interior.
▶ What were the Dutch settlers called?

and ranches. Soon other Europeans—French, German, and British—also settled at Table Bay. Many Europeans used the African peoples as slaves on their farms and ranches.

B. Growth of Colonies in South Africa

The Great Trek In 1806 the British decided they needed Table Bay as part of their African empire. They took control of the area and established the city of Cape Town as the capital of their new Cape Colony. The British began to force their way of life on the Dutch settlers, who were generally called the **Boers**. Many Boers decided it was time to seek out new lands in the South African interior. And thus

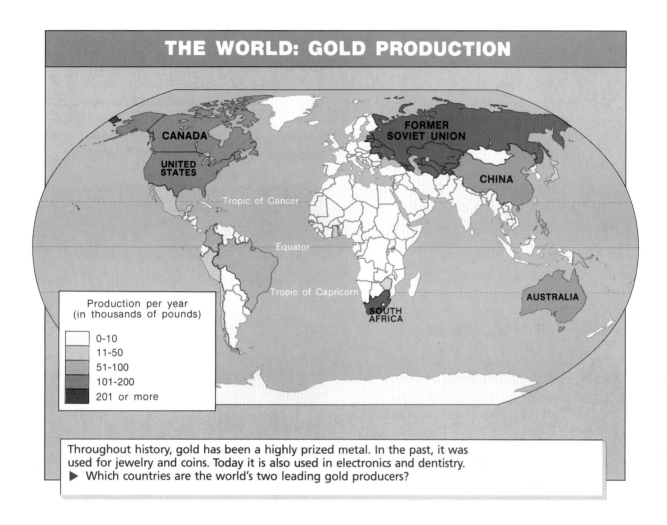

THE WORLD: GOLD PRODUCTION

Production per year (in thousands of pounds)

- 0-10
- 11-50
- 51-100
- 101-200
- 201 or more

Throughout history, gold has been a highly prized metal. In the past, it was used for jewelry and coins. Today it is also used in electronics and dentistry.
▶ Which countries are the world's two leading gold producers?

began the **Great Trek**, the mass migration of thousands of Boers to the High Veld between 1835 and 1838.

Many of the Boers settled between the Orange and Vaal rivers. Find this area on the map on page 610. Here the Boers established an independent republic called the Orange Free State. By the mid-1800s they had established another republic, the Transvaal, farther to the northeast.

Dutch-British Conflict In 1867, diamonds were discovered along the Vaal River near where it joins the Orange River. Within four years the town there, Kimberley, had become the second largest town in South Africa as people rushed to the Orange Free State to search for diamonds.

During this "diamond rush," many British moved to the region around Kimberley. Then the British changed the official boundary of their colony to put Kimberley and its diamond riches within the borders of the Cape Colony, not within the Orange Free State. Many of the Boers, feeling cheated by the British, were outraged.

The tension between the Boers and the British increased with a second valuable mineral discovery. In the 1880s, gold was discovered in the Transvaal, another region that had been settled by the Boers. The gold rush that resulted here created the largest city in South Africa, Johannesburg. It also brought more British and other Europeans to the Transvaal region.

Eventually the tension between the

621

FROM: **Kaffir Boy** by Mark Mathabane

In his autobiography, *Kaffir Boy,* Mark Mathabane describes the story of a black youth's childhood in apartheid South Africa.

Mathabane spent the first eighteen years in Alexandra, a black ghetto of Johannesburg. Mark writes about the feelings of hate, bitterness, hunger, pain, and terror he experienced as he grew up.

... **W**hereas in the past I had been more or less conscious of their [the police's] presence in black life—as they stopped people in the streets and demanded passes, as they chased after *tsotsis* [gangsters] and other hoodlums, as they raided shebeens [places where liquor is sold without a license] in search of illicit liquor, and they launched an occasional pass raid into the neighbourhood—they now moved permanently into my consciousness. Scarcely a week passed without the neighbourhood being invaded by waves of black and white policemen.

They always came unannounced, at any time of day or night, and gradually I came to accept, and to dread, their presence as a way of life. They haunted me in real life and in my dreams, to the extent that I would often wake up screaming in the middle of the night, claiming that the police were after me with dogs or flashlights, trying to shoot me down. Word had it that our neighbourhood, because of the increasing presence of people whose papers were not in order, had been designated a "hot spot," which meant that it had to

be raided constantly. So, barely six years old, I was called upon to deal with constant terror. . . .

Mark was an especially talented tennis player, and it was this ability that allowed him to escape the system of apartheid. In 1978, he received his passport to freedom when he was granted a tennis scholarship to an American college. Because of his experiences in America, Mark came to understand the meaning of human rights and a life without fear.

Boers and the British led to the Anglo-Boer War, which lasted from 1899 to 1902. The British won this war and, in 1910, created the new nation of South Africa, which united the Cape Colony, the Orange Free State, the Transvaal, and the eastern colony of Natal.

C. South Africa Today

A Modern Nation South Africa today has three capital cities, one for each branch of government. The president's office is in Pretoria. Parliament, the legislative branch, meets in Cape Town. The courts, the judicial branch, are in Bloemfontein.

South Africa has developed into the most modern, industrialized nation in Africa because of its tremendous mineral riches. About 65 to 70 percent of all the gold in the world comes from South Africa. A large proportion of the world's gem diamonds also comes from this country, and it also has iron ore, coal, and other valuable minerals. Most of these minerals lie in the Witwatersrand area, near Johannesburg. This region is the southern end of the mineral-rich crescent that extends through much of Southern Africa.

Racial Conflict For many years the government of South Africa was controlled by the country's white minority. The whites enforced **apartheid** (uh PAHR tayt), a policy of social control. *Apartheid* is an Afrikaans word that means "separateness." Apartheid called for the complete separation of South Africa's racial groups.

South Africa has a population of about 45 million. It is divided into four main racial groups. The whites, descendants of the Europeans, only make up about 13 percent of the population. The largest population group is the black African group, who make up about 76 percent. About 3 percent of the population is Asian, mainly people from India. Another 8 percent are people of mixed race. They are called Coloreds.

A large proportion of the world's gem diamonds come from South African mines.
▶ About 65 to 70 percent of what other mineral comes from South Africa?

Apartheid was a government policy of segregation. This policy resulted in separate jobs, schools, communities, transportation, and other facilities for the different ethnic groups. Whites were the privileged group. Nonwhites were denied many basic freedoms. Many South African blacks were forced to move to special reserves called **homelands**.

Opposition Nonwhites in South Africa struggled for years to end apartheid and to gain equal rights. The United Nations asked South Africa to end apartheid. A worldwide movement developed to demand that the policy be ended, since apartheid violated human rights. Many countries would not buy South African goods. Even many white South Africans spoke out against apartheid.

GROWING UP IN SOUTH AFRICA

Stephen Ndotshoni is 15-years-old. He lives with his father, mother, and three little brothers in a one-room shack in South Africa. His father built the shack from old metal roofing panels, old boards, and pieces of cardboard.

The sleeping arrangements are simple. Stephen's mother sleeps on a small cot in the corner of the room. Stephen, his father, and his brothers sleep on mats and bedding on the dirt floor of the hut. During the day, the bedding is folded and stuffed into the corner to make room for other daily activities.

Every day Stephen has to walk a half mile to the nearest water source to fill the family's water containers. Stephen often has to wait in long lines because several thousand families use the same source of water.

Like Stephen's, many black families in South Africa do not have modern luxuries. There are few cars, televisions, phones, or washing machines. Many families do not even have electricity or gas in their homes.

One of the bright spots in Stephen's day is going to school. He is in the seventh grade at school in the township of Leauadi. The school is an old wooden building with four classrooms. There is one teacher for both the sixth and seventh grades. The school does not have enough textbooks for members of the class. It has no computers, no gym, and no cafeteria. Yet Stephen enjoys being with the other students, and he works hard on his lessons.

Since apartheid ended in the mid-1990s, life for black South Africans has begun to improve. Blacks and all ethnic groups now can vote and have equal rights with whites. All restaurants, theaters,

sports arenas, parks, and all public places are now open to all citizens of South Africa.

However, many black families like Stephen's still do not have a high standard of living. Families are now free to move out of Leauadi, the township where Stephen lives, and move to Cape Town and Durban or any city they like. Stephen's parents have talked about moving to Cape Town so that they can get jobs there and move the family into a bigger home. Yet they have heard from friends that many black families have already gone there in search of work. As a result, jobs are often hard to find in Cape Town and other large cities.

Getting a decent place to live in cities is also difficult. Stephen's family realizes that it may take time for President Mandela's government to create new economic opportunities for blacks. But they also know that apartheid has ended and that their future in South Africa is brighter than ever before.

The 1993 Nobel Peace Prize was awarded to South African President Frederik de Klerk (left) and African National Congress President Nelson Mandela (right). They were honored for their efforts to bring peace and democracy to South Africa.
► Why were the efforts of both leaders needed to end apartheid?

In 1990 the white South African government made some changes. It lifted its ban on the African National Congress, a group that had long worked to gain equality for black South Africans. Nelson Mandela, a leader of the African National Congress, was released in 1990, after spending more than 27 years in jail. Then, early in 1991, President de Klerk of South Africa declared that all of the laws enforcing apartheid would soon be ended.

A Change of Power In 1992 South Africa's government began to negotiate with the African National Congress and other antiapartheid groups to end white minority rule. These negotiations led to an agreement to write a new constitution for South Africa and to hold elections. All South Africans were allowed to vote in these elections. In April 1994 the African National Congress received a large majority of the vote, winning a sweeping victory. Nelson Mandela was chosen as the new president of South Africa. Mandela took the oath of office in November 1994. He became the first black in South Africa's history to lead the country's government.

D. South Africa's Neighbors

Namibia The country of Namibia is large, about the size of Texas and North Carolina combined. However, only about 1.5 million people live in Namibia; more than 24 million people live in Texas and North Carolina. Only about 99,000 of Namibia's people are white, and since the country has become independent, many of them who are Afrikaners have moved to South Africa.

You have already read about the Namib Desert. This coastal desert covers most of Namibia. Inland is a high, arid plateau. The country's capital, Windhoek, is located on the plateau. Recall that the sports stadium in Windhoek was the site of Namibia's independence celebration.

Besides having diamonds in mines and along the beaches of the Namib Desert, Namibia has some copper and uranium. And as in the country's neighbor to the north, Angola, fishing is an important industry. Tuna and sardines are harvested from the cool waters of the Atlantic. In addition, some areas of Namibia have enough grazing land to support livestock, and both cattle and sheep are raised.

Swaziland Nestled between South Africa and Mozambique is the tiny country of Swaziland. About the size of Connecticut, Swaziland has a population of about 967,000. Located where the High Veld descends over an escarpment to a low, hilly area, the country has good soils. Many kinds of agricultural products grow here. Forest products, sugarcane, cotton, pineapples, cattle, and dairy products are Swaziland's chief sources of income. In addition, Swaziland and its capital, Mbabane (em bah BAH nay), are important tourist centers. Many South Africans travel to Swaziland to see certain movies and find other types of entertainment banned in their own country.

Lesotho As you can see on the map on page 616, the small nation of Lesotho (le-SUT hoh) is within the country of South Africa. How has this black African country

The people of Swaziland celebrate their independence day, September 6, 1968, at a ceremony in the capital city.
▶ What is the capital of Swaziland?

managed to survive where it is, completely surrounded by the white-controlled country of South Africa?

Many years ago the Basuto ethnic group moved to the Drakensberg Mountains of Southern Africa to escape hostile enemies to the north. Later, when the Boers started moving closer to this area, the Basutos asked the British government in the Cape Colony for protection. The British established a colony called Basutoland.

When the nation of South Africa was formed, Basutoland remained a British colony. Because the land here is so mountainous and the soils are so poor, there was nothing here that South Africa wanted. When Britain granted the colony its independence, it was renamed Lesotho.

Lesotho is only about the size of the state of Maryland, and the country's population is about 2 million. The capital city is Maseru. The country provides many workers for the industries of South Africa. People from Lesotho can commute across the border daily to work in the South African factories. And in this way, Lesotho—like Namibia and Swaziland—is tied to its large neighbor, South Africa.

LESSON 4

Review

REVIEWING MAIN IDEAS

A. Who were the main groups of people living in South Africa when the Europeans first arrived?
B. Why did the Boers move to the South African interior?
C. What was apartheid?
D. What country is found within South Africa?

SKILLS CHECK

WRITING SKILL
Write an editorial describing how you think apartheid hurt both black and white South Africans.

REVIEWING TERMS

On a separate sheet of paper, rewrite the sentences using the term from the list that best completes each sentence.

escarpment
exclave
Great Trek
apartheid
homeland

1. A territory that is surrounded or nearly surrounded by the territory of another country is called an _exclave_.
2. The _Great Trek_ began in South Africa when thousands of Boers migrated to the High Veld between 1835 and 1838.
3. The policy of _apartheid_ called for the complete separation of South Africa's racial groups.
4. In South Africa, each special area reserved for blacks to live in was called a _homeland_.
5. An _escarpment_ is a steep slope or cliff formed by erosion or by movements of the earth's rock layers.

❖❖❖❖

REVIEWING THE FACTS

On a separate sheet of paper, answer the following questions in complete sentences.

1. How is the southern region of Africa similar to the other parts of Africa?
2. What two deserts are found in Southern Africa?
3. Where is Madagascar located?
4. What nation colonized Madagascar and the Comoro Islands?
5. What ethnic group inhabits the Kalahari Desert?

6. Why is Mozambique important to the landlocked nations of South Africa?
7. Why did the Dutch East India Company establish a colony at Table Bay?
8. What conflicts eventually led to the Anglo-Boer War?
9. What natural resource found in South Africa has allowed it to develop into the most modern, industrialized nation in Africa?
10. What is the largest population group in South Africa?

❖❖❖❖

WRITING ABOUT ECONOMICS

Colonialism has a long history, not only in South Africa but in other areas of the world. Write several paragraphs that give examples of colonization in other areas of the world and explain why those areas were valuable.

❖❖❖❖

THINKING CRITICALLY

On a separate sheet of paper, answer the following questions in complete sentences.

1. Why, do you think, would a country be an independent nation rather than a colony?
2. Why don't the San people of the Kalahari Desert practice farming or herding?
3. What actions could a country take to avoid exploitation of its colonies?
4. What mineral "rush" took place in the United States in 1849 that was similar to the "diamond rush" that took place in the Orange Free State?
5. How does the geography of Madagascar help explain why the island has a mixed cultural heritage?

SUMMARIZING THE CHAPTER

On a separate sheet of paper, draw a graphic organizer that is like the one shown here. Copy the information from this graphic organizer to the one you have drawn. Complete the chart by writing in the appropriate item for each box. Some of the boxes have been done for you.

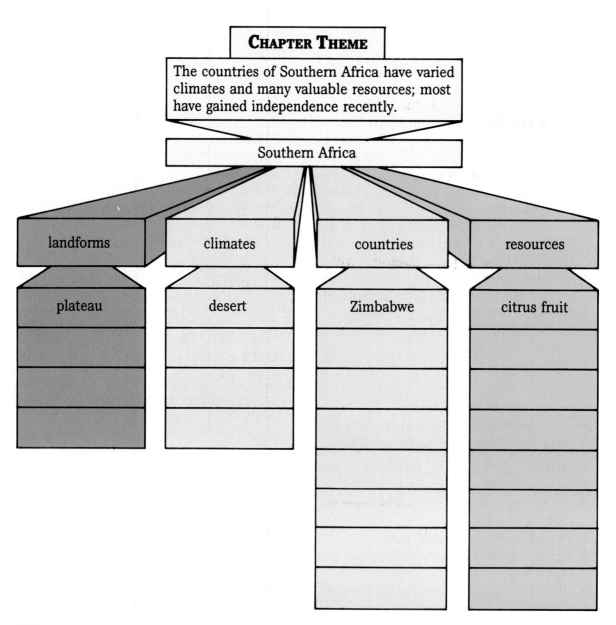

COOPERATIVE LEARNING

In Unit 6 you learned about the continent of Africa. The regions of northern, western, central, eastern, and southern Africa will be the subjects of your class project.

PROJECT

Your teacher will assign one of the regions you studied in Unit 6 to your group. This region will be the name of your group. There must be five groups. Each group will be responsible for a different region of Africa.

Your group's project is to create a television game show similar to the famous game show "Jeopardy." The teacher will be the host of the game show, which will be called "Africa." He or she will choose a scorekeeper.

The game will have a point system of 10, 20, 30, 40 and 50-point questions. Each group must write two questions about their region of Africa for each point category. The 10-point questions will be the easiest to answer, while the 50-point questions will be the most difficult.

Meet with your group to choose a leader. The leader will distribute the type of questions each member will write. Each group will write 10 questions.

Use the information in your chapter to write questions. Questions can be asked about the physical features, farming, economy, ways of life, and living and working conditions in a region of Africa.

The teacher will help you understand how the game is to be organized. He or she will draw the game on the blackboard for you and answer any questions you may have.

PRESENTATION AND REVIEW

Each group will give 10 questions to the teacher. The teacher will distribute the questions in the 10-, 20-, 30-, 40-, or 50-point pile. There will be piles of 10 to 50 point questions for the teacher to ask each group.

Each group will take turns and choose a box on the board. For example, one of the groups may want to try to answer a 30-point question. After the teacher asks the question, the group will try to come up with an answer. If the answer given by the group leader is correct, the group will receive 30 points and an *X* will be placed in the box by the scorekeeper. The points will be added on the scoreboard. At the end of the game, the points will be added up and a winner will be determined.

After the game is over, your group should meet to evaluate your project. How well did your group's members work together? How could your project have been improved?

REMEMBER TO:
- **Give your ideas.**
- **Listen to others' ideas.**
- **Plan your work with the group.**
- **Present your project.**
- **Discuss how your group worked.**

SKILLBUILDER

ANALYZING AND INFERRING FROM A POPULATION DENSITY MAP

WHY DO I NEED THIS SKILL?

Analyzing information and making inferences from it are two important thinking skills. They help you "get more out of" the information. You can develop the skills of analyzing and inferring by using a population density map. Population density maps show how people are distributed throughout an area of the world.

LEARNING THE SKILL

The term *population density* refers to the average number of people per square mile or square kilometer in a particular place, such as a state, country, or region. To find population density, you divide the number of people living in a place by the area—that is, by the size of the place in square miles or square kilometers.

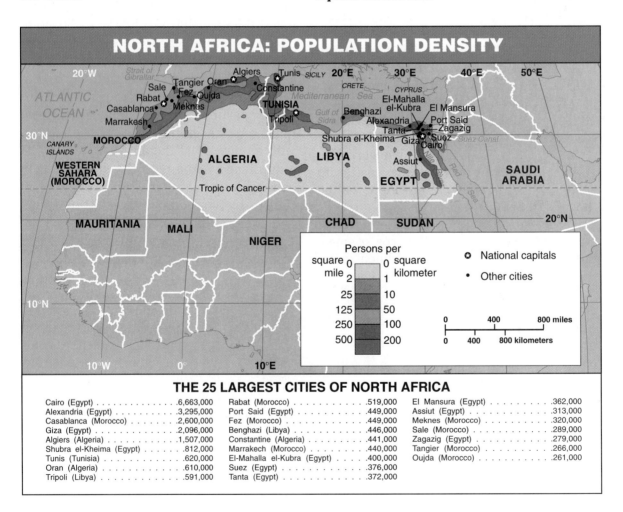

NORTH AFRICA: POPULATION DENSITY

Persons per square mile / square kilometer

square mile	square kilometer
0	0
2	1
25	10
125	50
250	100
500	200

⊕ National capitals

• Other cities

THE 25 LARGEST CITIES OF NORTH AFRICA

Cairo (Egypt) 6,663,000	Rabat (Morocco) 519,000	El Mansura (Egypt) 362,000
Alexandria (Egypt) 3,295,000	Port Said (Egypt) 449,000	Assiut (Egypt) 313,000
Casablanca (Morocco) 2,600,000	Fez (Morocco) 449,000	Meknes (Morocco) 320,000
Giza (Egypt) 2,096,000	Benghazi (Libya) 446,000	Sale (Morocco) 289,000
Algiers (Algeria) 1,507,000	Constantine (Algeria) 441,000	Zagazig (Egypt) 279,000
Shubra el-Kheima (Egypt) 812,000	Marrakech (Morocco) 440,000	Tangier (Morocco) 266,000
Tunis (Tunisia) 620,000	El-Mahalla el-Kubra (Egypt) 400,000	Oujda (Morocco) 261,000
Oran (Algeria) 610,000	Suez (Egypt) 376,000	
Tripoli (Libya) 591,000	Tanta (Egypt) 372,000	

For example, the area of the country of Egypt is 386,660 square miles (1,001,449 sq km). The population of the country is 62,360,000. By dividing the population by the area, you find that the population density of Egypt is about 161 people per square mile (62 people per sq km). This means about 161 people live in each square mile of land.

Of course, each square mile or kilometer does not have exactly the same number of people. Population density refers to the *average* number of people per square mile or square kilometer. The higher the average number of people per square mile or kilometer, the higher the population density.

A population density map shows the variation of population density within an area. For example, the population density map of North Africa shows the variation of population density from place to place within that region. The various colors show the degree of population density in the different parts of the region. As the key indicates, areas shown in beige have between 0 and 2 people per square mile (0 and 1 person per sq km). Areas shown in purple have the highest population densities, 500 people per square mile (200 people per sq km) or more.

This population density map also has a table that lists the 25 largest cities in North Africa. Notice that in Egypt, for example, the largest cities are located where the highest population density is found. On most population density maps, you will find that the largest cities are usually located in the more densely populated areas. Thus, even when a population density map does not list the largest cities in a table, you can usually infer that the largest cities are located in the more densely populated areas.

PRACTICING THE SKILL

Use the population density map of North Africa to answer the following questions.

1. How many different population density areas does the map show?
2. What geographical characteristic do you think the most densely populated areas have in common?
3. What is the population density in the area along the Nile River?
4. What is the population density in the area around the city of Tripoli, Libya?
5. Do any cities in Morocco have a population density greater than 500 people per square mile (200 people per sq km)?
6. What is the population density around the capital city of Algeria?
7. Why, do you think, is the population density in Western Sahara so low?
8. In which country is the fifth largest city in North Africa located?
9. How many of the 25 largest cities are located along the Mediterranean?
10. How many areas shown on the map have population densities between 125 and 250 people per square mile (50 and 100 people per sq km)?

APPLYING THE SKILL

You can analyze and make inferences from the information presented in all the maps in your geography textbook. Use the specific map skills you have just learned when you study the population density map of Australia and New Zealand, which is found on page 651 of Chapter 26.

UNDERSTANDING CAUSE AND EFFECT

WHY DO I NEED THIS SKILL?

The connection between events or actions is called a *cause-and-effect relationship*. It can help to explain why events occur or why people act as they do. The *cause* is an event or action that results in the *effect*, another event or action. Recognizing and understanding cause-and-effect relationships will help you comprehend and learn from your geography book and other textbooks.

LEARNING THE SKILL

Some causes and effects are simple. For example, think about the story you read in Chapter 21 of the World War II bomber *Lady Be Good*.

Cause:
Lady be Good ran out of fuel

Effect:
Crash-landed in the Sahara.

Sometimes there are signal words, such as *because, so, since, therefore, as a result*, to suggest that there might be a cause-and-effect relationship.

Cause:
Because they rationed their water and traveled at night

Effect:
Crew of the *Lady Be Good* lasted eight days

Some cause-and-effect relationships are more complex. For example, one cause could have multiple effects.

C1: Plane ran out of fuel

E1: Fliers parachuted out
E2: Plane crashed
E3: Fliers ultimately died

Sometimes, multiple causes contribute to one effect.

C1: Lack of water
C2: Extreme heat
C3: Exhaustion

E1: Fliers died

Often, causes and effects overlap and result in a cause-and-effect chain:

C1: Crew was lost

E1 (C2): Plane ran out of fuel
E2 (C3): Plane crashed (and so on)

PRACTICING THE SKILL

On pages 542–543 of Chapter 21, you read about the construction of the Aswan High Dam in Egypt. The dam was the cause of many different effects, some of them good and some of them bad.

Copy the partially completed cause-and-effect diagram shown on the next page and fill in the missing causes and effects. Draw additional boxes to represent other causes and effects. Use arrows to show the cause-and-effect relationships.

CAUSE-AND-EFFECT RELATIONSHIPS

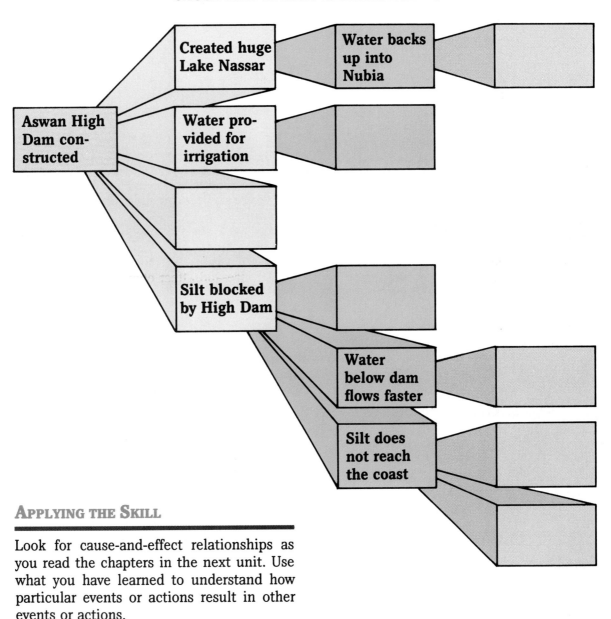

Created huge Lake Nassar

Aswan High Dam constructed

Water backs up into Nubia

Water provided for irrigation

Silt blocked by High Dam

Water below dam flows faster

Silt does not reach the coast

APPLYING THE SKILL

Look for cause-and-effect relationships as you read the chapters in the next unit. Use what you have learned to understand how particular events or actions result in other events or actions.

UNIT 7

AUSTRALIA, NEW ZEALAND, AND THE PACIFIC ISLANDS

CONTINENTAL HANDBOOK

CONNECTIONS

Look at the map on page 637. Why would the United States want to have island territories in the Pacific Ocean?

TERMS

typhoon

FOCUS

How has Oceania changed in recent years?

Australian Reassures Reagan of Commitment to Alliance
By Gerald M. Boyd

WASHINGTON, April 17, 1986— Administration officials said today that Prime Minister Bob Hawke of Australia had assured President Reagan that Australia would continue a security pact with the United States, even if the alliance did not include New Zealand.

A. The United States in the Pacific

In 1986 the United States and New Zealand had a disagreement about the defense treaty the two countries had signed. The treaty, which was also signed by Australia, was designed to protect Australia, New Zealand, and the United States. Problems occurred when New Zealand said it would not allow a ship to dock in New Zealand unless the ship's captain first announced whether the ship held nuclear weapons. The United States said that American ships would not follow New Zealand's request, since the request violated United States military policy. When New Zealand refused to make any exceptions, the United States decided to break its treaty commitments with New Zealand. The United States and New Zealand are still on good terms, however, and both countries continue to trade with each other.

The defense treaty with Australia is only one example of how important the countries and territories of the Pacific Ocean are to the United States. Our fiftieth state—Hawaii—is located in the Pacific Ocean. Two United States territories are also located here. American Samoa lies south of the Equator in the region called Polynesia. Guam, in the region called Micronesia, is west of the International Date Line. When it is Monday afternoon on the American mainland, it is Tuesday morning in Guam.

The people of Guam are American citizens. American Samoans are American nationals but not citizens. Both territories elect their own governors and legislatures. Their voters also send a nonvoting delegate to the United States Congress.

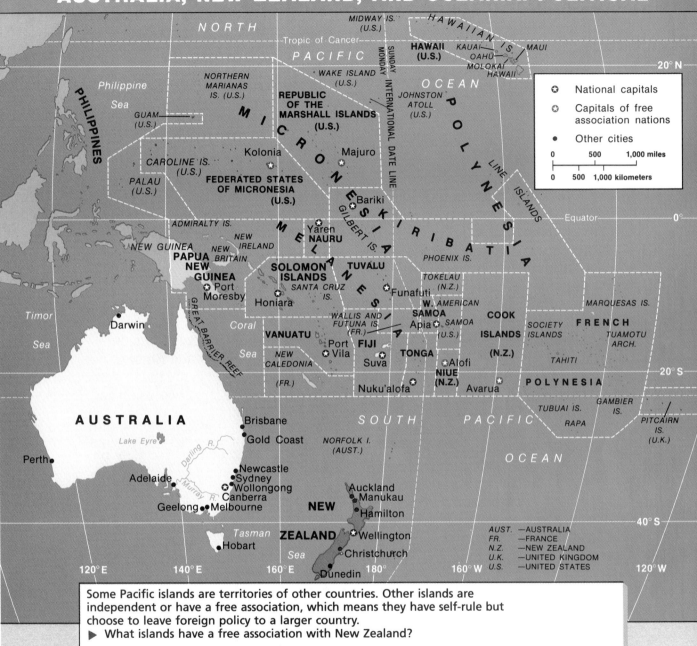

AUSTRALIA, NEW ZEALAND, AND OCEANIA: POLITICAL

Legend:
- ⊛ National capitals
- ⊛ Capitals of free association nations
- • Other cities

0   500   1,000 miles
0   500   1,000 kilometers

AUST.	—AUSTRALIA
FR.	—FRANCE
N.Z.	—NEW ZEALAND
U.K.	—UNITED KINGDOM
U.S.	—UNITED STATES

Some Pacific islands are territories of other countries. Other islands are independent or have a free association, which means they have self-rule but choose to leave foreign policy to a larger country.
▶ What islands have a free association with New Zealand?

The United States possesses several very small islands in the Pacific. Wake and Midway islands are little more than landing fields for airplanes. Johnson Atoll and Howland Island each have an area of only 1 square mile (2.6 sq km). Tiny Baker Island is even smaller.

After World War II the United States took over a number of islands in the region called Micronesia. It was agreed that the peoples of these islands would decide their own future. These islands now have separate governments: the Commonwealth of the Northern Marianas, the

Federated States of Micronesia, the Republic of the Marshall Islands, and the Republic of Palau.

B. The World's Largest Ocean

Oceans and seas cover about 70 percent of the earth's surface. The Pacific Ocean with its marginal, or bordering, seas makes up half of the earth's watery cover. The Pacific is nearly twice as large as the Atlantic Ocean.

The Pacific is the deepest of the world's oceans. A depth of over 36,000 feet (10,973 m) has been measured east of the Mariana Islands. That is almost 7 miles (11 km) deep. If Mount Everest, the world's tallest mountain, rose from the floor of the Pacific, its top would still be more than a mile below the surface.

The name Pacific means "peaceful" or "calm." Ferdinand Magellan, the first European to sail across the great ocean, in 1520, gave the Pacific its name. When he first saw the open sea after a storm-tossed voyage around the tip of South America, the ocean appeared peaceful and calm. But do not let the name mislead you, because the Pacific Ocean is not always peaceful. During certain seasons, tropical storms called **typhoons** sweep over the Pacific and its islands. Typhoons are similar to the Atlantic storms called hurricanes.

C. Oceania: Scattered Islands in the Ocean

Scattered across the Pacific Ocean are thousands of islands. They range in size from Australia, the world's smallest continent and largest island, to tiny islets, islands so small that no one has ever lived on them. Most of the islets are too small to be shown on a map.

Some of the islands in the Pacific, such as Japan, Indonesia, and the Philippines, are so close to Asia that they are usually considered part of that continent. However, Australia and other Pacific Islands differ so greatly from Asia that they are considered a separate region of the world. Years ago a geographer thought that this region of scattered islands should have a name. He decided that since it was located in the greatest of oceans, he would call it Oceania.

D. The Countries of Oceania

The political map of Oceania has changed greatly since 1959. Earlier maps showed only two independent countries: Australia and New Zealand. All other lands were shown as possessions or territories of outside countries.

Since 1959 a number of islands have formed independent countries. These new countries include the ones you read about earlier in this lesson. Others include the former Gilbert and Ellice islands. Once a British colony, these islands divided and became two countries, Kiribati and Tuvalu.

Port Moresby is Papua New Guinea's capital and largest city. This island nation became independent in 1975.
▶ Is Port Moresby a modern city?

Huge stone statues mark the landscape of Easter Island. Scientists think that the statues were carved by early explorers from the Pacific Islands.
► What were these statues carved from?

Fiji and the Solomon Islands have kept the same names, but they are now independent countries rather than parts of the British Empire. So, too, is Tonga, which the British at one time called the Friendly Islands. The New Hebrides, once controlled by both Britain and France, is now the country of Vanuatu.

Papua New Guinea is one of the largest countries of the Pacific Islands. It consists of New Guinea plus New Britain, Bougainville, and other small islands. Australia once controlled this land as well as tiny Nauru, which has an area of only 9 square miles (22 sq km). Western Samoa, now independent, was formerly governed by New Zealand.

French Polynesia and New Caledonia remain French. An independence movement exists in New Caledonia, but 40 percent of the people are of French descent and have opposed separation from France in the past.

Review

REVIEWING MAIN IDEAS

A. What agreement did the United States and Micronesia have?
B. Why is the Pacific Ocean's name misleading?
C. How did Oceania get its name?
D. How has the political map of Oceania changed in recent years?

SKILLS CHECK

MAP SKILL

Turn to the map on page 637. What line of longitude does the International Date Line run parallel to?

Australia, New Zealand & Oceania

FLAG AND PRINCIPAL LANGUAGE(S)		PRINCIPAL PRODUCTS
		EXPORT — IMPORT

TABLE OF COUNTRIES

AUSTRALIA

Canberra

English

POPULATION
18,322,000
6 per sq mi/2 per sq km

LANDMASS
2,967,909 sq mi/7,686,884 sq km

Coal   Machinery

FEDERATED STATES OF MICRONESIA

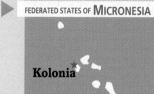
Kolonia

English

POPULATION
123,000
149 per sq mi/58 per sq km

LANDMASS
825 sq mi/2,137 sq km

Food   Coconut Oil

FIJI

★Suva

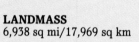
English, Fijian,
Hindustani

POPULATION
773,000
111 per sq mi/43 per sq km

LANDMASS
6,938 sq mi/17,969 sq km

Sugar   Petroleum

KIRIBATI
Bairiki ★

English

POPULATION
79,000
238 per sq mi/92 per sq km

LANDMASS
332 sq mi/860 sq km

Copra   Food

MARSHALL ISLANDS

Majuro

English

POPULATION
56,000
800 per sq mi/309 per sq km

LANDMASS
70 sq mi/181 sq km

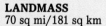
Coconut Oil   Food

NAURU

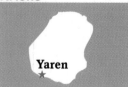
Yaren

Nauruan, English

POPULATION
10,100
1,122 per sq mi/433 per sq km

LANDMASS
9 sq mi/22 sq km

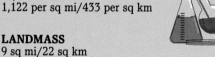 
Phosphates   Food

NEW ZEALAND

Wellington

English, Maori

POPULATION
3,407,000
33 per sq mi/13 per sq km

LANDMASS
103,736 sq mi/268,676 sq km

Meat   Machinery

NORTHERN MARIANAS

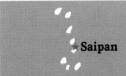

★Saipan

English

POPULATION
43,000
234 per sq mi/90 per sq km

LANDMASS
184 sq mi/477 sq km

Coconut Oil   N/A

PAPUA NEW GUINEA

Port Moresby

Pidgin English,
Chinese

POPULATION
4,295,000
24 per sq mi/9 per sq km

LANDMASS
182,700 sq mi/473,193 sq km

Gold   Machinery

SOLOMON ISLANDS

Honiara ★

English,
Pidgin English

POPULATION
399,000
58 per sq mi/22 per sq km

LANDMASS
6,938 sq mi/17,969 sq km

Copra   Petroleum

TONGA

Nukualofa ★

Tongan, English

POPULATION
105,600
391 per sq mi/151 per sq km

LANDMASS
270 sq mi/699 sq km

Coconut Oil   Food

TUVALU

Funafuti ★

Tuvaluan, English

POPULATION
10,000
1,111 per sq mi/429 per sq km

LANDMASS
9 sq mi/23 sq km

Copra   Food

VANUATU

★Port Vila

English, French

POPULATION
174,000
37 per sq mi/14 per sq km

LANDMASS
4,707 sq mi/12,186 sq km

Copra   Food

WESTERN SAMOA

★Apia

Samoan, English

POPULATION
209,000
191 per sq mi/74 per sq km

LANDMASS
1,097 sq mi/2,841 sq km

Coconut Oil   Food

CHAPTER 26

AUSTRALIA AND NEW ZEALAND

1. Australia: Continent and Country

2. Living and Working in Australia

3. New Zealand: Land of the Kiwi

Australia: Continent and Country

CONNECTIONS

What are the benefits of being located a great distance from other places on the earth?

TERMS

outback, marsupial, coral, reef, Aborigine, anthropologist

FOCUS

What is the landscape of Australia, and how was the continent settled?

A. The Southern Continent

The Mystery In 1768, Captain James Cook and his crew set sail aboard the *Endeavour* in search of the solution to a mystery. From the time of the ancient Romans to the travels of Marco Polo, geographers believed in the existence of a southern continent. Clues to the existence of this southern land were gained by Spanish, Portuguese, Dutch, and English explorers.

The Clues From the beginning of the 1500s, brave ship captains led sailing expeditions throughout the vast unknown waters of the Pacific Ocean. Spanish ships searched in vain for the continent. It is believed that one expedition passed within several miles of the continent, but no crew members sighted it. The Portuguese may have landed on the shore but kept it a secret from their rivals, the Spanish.

In 1605 a Dutch ship exploring New Guinea headed south and discovered the northern tip of Australia, which would later be named Cape York. Within the next forty years, more clues came in from other Dutch ships that found parts of the coastline. One expedition, led by Abel Tasman, missed the mainland but discovered New Zealand and the island that would later be named Tasmania.

The Answer The British sent Captain Cook and the *Endeavour* after several British explorations also failed to find the continent. By March of 1770, Cook and his crew had decided to return home. After sailing for almost two years, they were ready to give up their search. They had explored various islands, including New Zealand, but had not found the missing continent. It was during the voyage home on April 19 that the Australian coast was sighted. Ten days later, they went ashore in a smaller boat called a longboat.

It was time to land. A young midshipman [naval officer] named Isaac Smith was in the bow [front of the boat]. Years later, after many promotions, Admiral Smith . . . would proudly tell how the greatest navigator in history hesitated before quitting the longboat, touched him on the shoulder and said, "Isaac, you shall land first." The lad sprang into the green bottle-glass water . . . and waded ashore. Cook and the others followed, and the seal of distance and space that had protected the east coast of Australia . . . was broken.

A Land Close to Asia Because it takes so long to get to Australia from Europe and North America, most people think of Australia as being a long way from anywhere. But Australia is not far from Asia. It is only about 100 miles (161 km) from the northern tip of Australia to the island of New Guinea. From there, it is relatively easy to travel through the islands of East Asia to mainland Asia. People from Indonesia, Japan, or China don't think of Australia as being far away and isolated.

You might expect that a country that is so close to Asia would have many people from densely populated China or Japan. But there are few Asians in Australia. Today, most Australians are of European origin, especially from Great Britain and Ireland. For many years, Australia had laws that made

▶ One of Sydney, Australia's, most prominent landmarks is the Sydney Opera House.   **643**

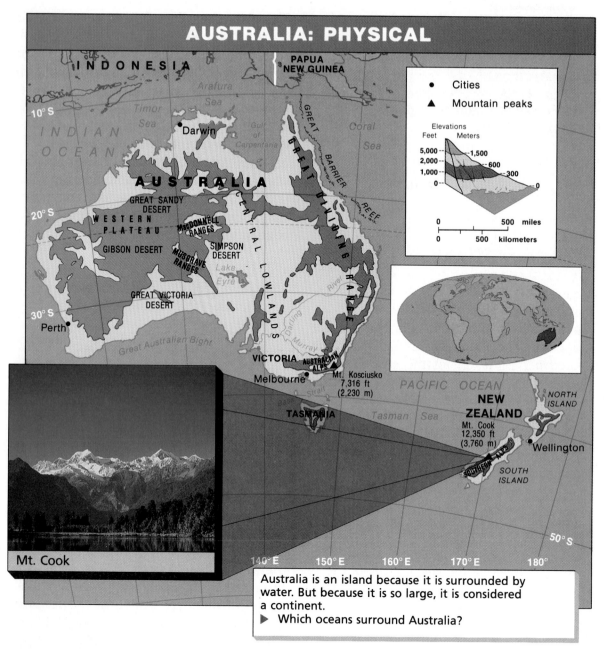

AUSTRALIA: PHYSICAL

INDONESIA

PAPUA NEW GUINEA

10° S

INDIAN OCEAN

Arafura Sea

Timor Sea

Darwin

Gulf of Carpentaria

Coral Sea

AUSTRALIA

GREAT SANDY DESERT

WESTERN PLATEAU

MacDONNELL RANGES

20° S

GIBSON DESERT

SIMPSON DESERT

MUSGRAVE RANGES

CENTRAL LOWLANDS

GREAT DIVIDING RANGE

GREAT BARRIER REEF

Lake Eyre

River

30° S

GREAT VICTORIA DESERT

Perth

Great Australian Bight

Darling

Murray

VICTORIA

AUSTRALIAN ALPS

Mt. Kosciusko
7,316 ft
(2,230 m)

Melbourne

Bass Strait

TASMANIA

PACIFIC OCEAN

Tasman Sea

NEW ZEALAND

NORTH ISLAND

Mt. Cook
12,350 ft
(3,760 m)

Wellington

SOUTHERN ALPS

SOUTH ISLAND

50° S

140° E   150° E   160° E   170° E   180°

- Cities
▲ Mountain peaks

Elevations
Feet   Meters
5,000 -- -- 1,500
2,000 -- -- 600
1,000 -- -- 300
0 -- -- 0

0   500   miles
0   500   kilometers

Mt. Cook

Australia is an island because it is surrounded by water. But because it is so large, it is considered a continent.
▶ Which oceans surround Australia?

it almost impossible for people from Asian countries to move there. Those laws were changed during the 1950s and 1960s to allow small numbers of people from Asia to immigrate to Australia, and the number of Asians is growing.

B. The Island Continent

The Smallest Continent Australia is so small compared to the other continents that you might wonder why it isn't called an island instead of a continent. The answer is that Greenland, the largest island in the world, is just over 839,999 square miles (2,175,597 sq km) in area. By comparison, Australia is 2,967,909 square miles (7,686,884 sq km) or roughly four fifths the size of the United States. Even though Australia is the smallest continent, it is still much closer in size to Europe, the second smallest continent, than it is to the world's largest island.

644

A Land with Few Mountains Australia does not have many tall mountains. The highest point in Australia, Mount Kosciusko (kahs ee US koh) in the Snowy Mountains, reaches an elevation of only 7,316 feet (2,230 m). Even the name *Snowy Mountains* is misleading, since the mountains have snow only in the winter. The Snowy Mountains are part of a highland area called the Great Dividing Range that extends most of the length of Australia's east coast. This highland area is the only part of Australia that has mountains.

The rest of the continent is rather low and flat. The western half of Australia is a large plateau with elevations of 1,000 to 1,600 feet (305 m to 488 m). Between the plateau and the mountains of the east is a low plain. The southern part of this plain near the cities of Adelaide (AD ul ayd) and Melbourne is one of Australia's best farming areas.

Australian Climates Australia's six climate zones can be seen on the world climate map in the Atlas. Most of the continent is dry. The **outback**, as the interior of the continent is known, is desert and semidesert grassland. Only about 10 percent of the country, mostly in the southeast, can be considered well watered. This area is where most of the Australian people live.

The northern section of Australia has a tropical climate. This area has scattered tropical forests and savannas. The southern areas around Perth and Adelaide have a Mediterranean climate that is similar to that of Southern Europe.

Little Land for Farming With a dry climate throughout much of the country, it is not surprising that Australia has little land that is good for farming. Only about one fourth of Australia's land gets enough rain for farming. Most of that land is in the mountains, where it is too rugged for farming. This leaves less than 10 percent of the land of the continent suitable for farming. However, that is more than enough land to

Ranches and mining towns are widely scattered throughout the sparsely populated outback.
▶ What is the climate of the outback?

provide food for Australia's people and for export to other countries.

The Animals of Australia There are many unusual animals that are native only to Australia. You may have seen kangaroos or koala bears, two of Australia's unique animals. The koala and kangaroo are **marsupials**. These are mammals that carry their young in a pouch. There is a greater variety of marsupials in Australia than in any other continent. Europe has none and North America only has the opossum.

Perhaps the most unusual Australian animal is the duck-billed platypus. This little animal looks as if it can't make up its mind what it wants to be. It has a large, flat bill and webbed feet like a duck. But it is a mammal with a furry body like a beaver. And, even stranger, the duck-billed platypus lays eggs like a bird, something that mammals do not normally do.

The Great Barrier Reef The largest structure ever built by living creatures was not made by human hands. It is made of **coral**. Coral is a hard, chalky, rocklike material that is made of the shells of sea animals called coral polyps. Polyps are tiny sea animals that live in warm seawater. They have hard outer skeletons, somewhat like hard cups, into which their bodies fit.

When coral polyps are alive, they fasten to each other. When the polyps die, they leave their connected shells behind as a rocky covering on the sea floor. Then new polyps attach to this covering. When billions of polyps mass together over a long

The koala, kangaroo, and platypus are among Australia's many unusual animals.
▶ Which of these animals are marsupials?

Scuba divers from around the world travel to the Great Barrier Reef to view its beautiful wonders. In some places, the water is shallow enough to see the coral from the water's surface.

▶ What is the length of the Great Barrier Reef?

period of time, they form rocklike ridges or mounds in the water called **reefs**.

The world's largest coral reef stretches 1,250 miles (2,011 km) along the northeast coast of Australia. The Great Barrier Reef, as it is known, is made up of thousands of individual coral reefs and islets. In 1979, Australia set aside part of the Great Barrier Reef as a marine park. In doing this, the government hoped to protect this remarkable coral structure and the different creatures that live there.

C. The People of Australia

The First Australians Australia's first human inhabitants, the **Aborigines** (ab uh RIHJ uh neez), probably migrated from Asia over 30,000 years ago. The Aborigines crossed over a land bridge that connected Asia and Australia. Later, the sea level rose, and the land bridge was flooded, ending the migration.

For thousands of years, the Aborigines lived by nomadic hunting and gathering. They used only simple tools, such as spears and the boomerang. The boomerang is a flat curved stick shaped somewhat like a bent wing. When thrown, the boomerang will sail out toward its target. If it misses, it curves back to land near the feet of the person who threw it.

The British explorers who first met the Aborigines thought the Aborigines were very primitive people. It wasn't until later that **anthropologists** learned about the Aborigines' rich and complex spiritual life and folklore. An anthropologist studies humans and their culture. Anthropologists study both the past and the present cultures of a people.

There may have been over 300,000 Aborigines living in Australia when Cook first landed. Today, there are only about 145,000 Aborigines left, which is less than 1 percent of Australia's 18.3 million people. Just like the Indians of the Amer-

THE JOURNALS OF JAMES COOK

The following excerpt is a passage from the journal of James Cook. In it he gives an account of the Aborigines, whom Cook often referred to as Indians.

. . . *From what I have said of the natives of New Holland they may appear to some to be the most wretched people upon earth; but in reality they are far more happier than we Europeans, being wholly unacquainted not only with the superfluous [unnecessary] but the necessary conveniences so much sought after in Europe; they are happy in not knowing the use of them. They live in a tranquility which is not disturbed by the inequality of their condition. The earth and sea of their own accord furnishes them with all things necessary for life. They covet [desire] not magnificent houses, household stuff, etc.; they live in a warm and fine climate, and enjoy every wholesome air, so that they have very little need of clothing; and this they seem to be fully sensible of, for many to whom we gave cloth, etc., left it carelessly upon the sea beach and in the woods, as a thing they had no manner of use for. In short, they seemed to set no value upon anything we gave them, nor would they ever part with anything of their own for any one article we could offer them. This, in my opinion, argues that they think themselves provided with all the necessaries of life.*

1. Why might the Aborigines have appeared to some people as the "most wretched people upon earth"?
2. According to Captain Cook, in what ways were Aborigines different from Europeans?
3. What were some of the necessities of life that the earth and the sea provided for the Aborigines?

Several Aborigines watch convicts being taken ashore. The first group of convicts, which numbered more than 700, reached Australia in 1788. They were accompanied by about 300 soldiers who guarded the prisoners.
► Why was Australia used as a prison colony?

icas, many were killed or died of diseases brought by European colonists.

Australia Becomes a Colony The British claimed Australia because of James Cook, but they did not have much use for it. Australia was far from England and it did not seem to have many natural resources that the British could use. Still, England wanted to keep its colony. So, the British used Australia as a prison colony. Both prisoners and free settlers were sent to Australia.

From Colonies to Country It was nearly impossible for the convicts to get back to England when they finished their prison sentences. Before long, more people who were not convicts began to move to Australia, looking for land to settle. As the population grew, the continent was divided into seven English colonies. In 1901 the colonies became the six states and one

territory of the independent country of Australia. Today, there is a second territory, the Australian Capital Territory, where Canberra, the capital of Australia, is located.

LESSON 1

Review

REVIEWING MAIN IDEAS

A. What efforts were made to discover the southern continent?
B. How has Australia's climate affected its population?
C. How is Australia's history reflected in its population?

SKILLS CHECK

MAP SKILL

Turn to the map on page 657. Use the scale of the map to calculate the distance from Australia's capital, Canberra, to each of the state capitals.

Living and Working in Australia

CONNECTIONS

At least once during the school day, you may take a drink of water from a water fountain or faucet. What is the source of that water?

TERMS

core, aquifer, station

FOCUS

What are Australia's most important resources?

A. Southeastern Australia

The Heart of a Nation When geographers talk about countries, they often use the word **core**. The word *core* refers to the part of a country that has the largest population, the largest cities, the most productive economy, and the best transportation facilities and other services.

It might help to think of the core area as the heart of the nation. But this does not mean that the core area will be found in the center of the country. In fact, usually, the core of a country is located in or near a coastal area so that goods can be shipped in and out easily.

Australia's Core In the case of Australia, the core is easy to identify. If you look at the population density map on page 651, you can pick out the core very easily. It is the area that lies along the eastern and southern coasts of Australia between the cities of Brisbane and Adelaide. Over 13 million of Australia's 18.3 million people live in this region.

Four of Australia's five largest cities—Sydney, Melbourne, Adelaide, and Brisbane—are in the core area. The city of Perth in southwestern Australia is the only large city in Australia that lies outside of the core. The core has most of the industry, roads, railroads, electrical plants, schools, hospitals, and other services that are demanded by a large urban population. In fact, Australia is a very urban country. About 85 percent of Australians live in cities. Because so many of Australia's people live in cities, the rural population density is low—less than one person per square mile or kilometer.

B. Farming in Australia

Little Land for Farming The best land for farming lies in the east, and nearly all of that land is in or close to the core. In Lesson 1 you read that only about 10 percent of Australia's land is good for farming. Still, farming is one of the most important parts of Australia's economy. The farms are mechanized, and some of the machines that are used have been invented just for use on Australia's large farms.

Sporting events, such as the Australian Open tennis tournament, are popular in the large cities of Australia's core.
▶ Where is Australia's core?

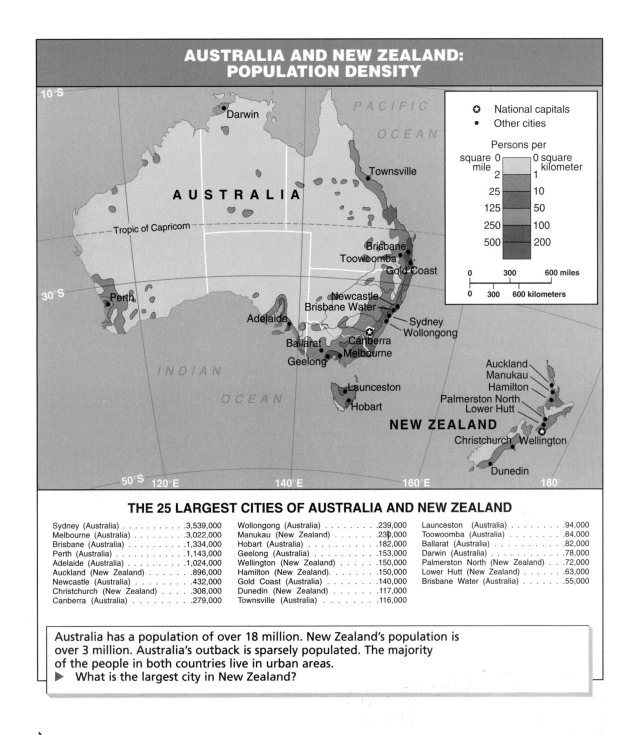

AUSTRALIA AND NEW ZEALAND: POPULATION DENSITY

○ National capitals
• Other cities

Persons per

square mile	0 square kilometer
0	0
2	1
25	10
125	50
250	100
500	200

0   300   600 miles
0   300   600 kilometers

PACIFIC OCEAN

Darwin

Townsville

AUSTRALIA

Tropic of Capricorn

Brisbane
Toowoomba
Gold Coast

Perth

Newcastle
Brisbane Water

Adelaide

Sydney
Wollongong

Ballarat   Canberra
Geelong   Melbourne

INDIAN OCEAN

Launceston

Hobart

Auckland
Manukau
Hamilton
Palmerston North
Lower Hutt

NEW ZEALAND

Christchurch   Wellington

Dunedin

10°S   30°S   50°S   120°E   140°E   160°E   180°

THE 25 LARGEST CITIES OF AUSTRALIA AND NEW ZEALAND

Sydney (Australia) 3,539,000
Melbourne (Australia) 3,022,000
Brisbane (Australia) 1,334,000
Perth (Australia) 1,143,000
Adelaide (Australia) 1,024,000
Auckland (New Zealand) 896,000
Newcastle (Australia) 432,000
Christchurch (New Zealand) 308,000
Canberra (Australia) 279,000

Wollongong (Australia) 239,000
Manukau (New Zealand) 230,000
Hobart (Australia) 182,000
Geelong (Australia) 153,000
Wellington (New Zealand) 150,000
Hamilton (New Zealand). 150,000
Gold Coast (Australia) 140,000
Dunedin (New Zealand) 117,000
Townsville (Australia) 116,000

Launceston (Australia) 94,000
Toowoomba (Australia) 84,000
Ballarat (Australia) 82,000
Darwin (Australia) 78,000
Palmerston North (New Zealand) . . .72,000
Lower Hutt (New Zealand) 63,000
Brisbane Water (Australia) 55,000

Australia has a population of over 18 million. New Zealand's population is over 3 million. Australia's outback is sparsely populated. The majority of the people in both countries live in urban areas.

▶ What is the largest city in New Zealand?

Wheat Farms Australia's most important crop is wheat. The main wheat growing belt extends across the southeastern part of the country in the states of Victoria and South Australia. Australia does not have many rivers, so irrigation is often difficult. The longest and most important rivers of the continent—the Murray and its tributary, the Darling—pass through Australia's wheat belt. The Murray and the Darling are each about 1,650 miles (2,655 km) long. However, the Murray is more important than the Darling because it has more flat land that is good for farming along its banks.

651

GROWING UP IN AUSTRALIA

Imagine what it would be like to have summer in January and winter in July. That is what you could expect if you grew up in Australia. Because Australia lies south of the Equator, its seasons are opposite to those in the United States.

December comes in the middle of the summer, when the temperatures in Sydney and other Australian cities reach as high as 90° F (32°C) or even higher. Yet Christmas decorations still show snowy scenes of Santa Claus.

In July and August, Australians go to ski areas in the Snowy Mountains to enjoy winter sports. This happens while people in the Northern Hemisphere are going to the beach to swim and enjoy the hot summer weather.

There are other differences that you would notice if you grew up in Australia. For example, the school year is very different from that of North America. Summer vacation is only about six weeks, from the week before Christmas to the end of January. Australian students are dismissed from school for two weeks in May and about two weeks in September.

About half the students in Australia attend private schools, most of which are operated by churches. Many students go to schools that are for all girls or all boys. Australians take courses similar to those of North American students, except that everyone is required to take a second language beginning in the sixth grade. Latin and French are the two most popular languages.

All students in Australia wear uniforms to school. In the summer, boys wear a shirt and tie with slacks. The girls wear a blouse, tie, and skirt along with a wide-brimmed hat for shade. In the winter, sweaters and

blazers are added to the uniforms. Each school has its own uniform colors and style.

Food is different in Australia. Australians eat lamb as often as we eat beef. Tropical fruits are enjoyed here. Kiwi fruit, pineapple, or pomegranates are eaten at breakfast. A pomegranate is a fruit that has a hard rind and looks similar to an orange. It has a deep, yellow-red color.

Australia's wildlife is also different. It is not unusual to see "Kangaroo Crossing" signs on the highway. Trucks and buses are equipped with sets of heavy steel bars on the front and back called "kangaroo bars." These bars protect vehicles that run into wild kangaroos. Sometimes panic-stricken kangaroos run into the back of slow moving trucks and buses.

Another important wheat-producing area is located on the west coast around Perth. About 60 percent of Australia's farmland is used to grow wheat. Some of the wheat is used in Australia, but most is exported to other countries. Australia is the world's fourth largest wheat exporter.

Other Crops Wheat is not the only important farm product of Australia. Sugarcane is also grown on farms in Queensland, where the climate is warm all year round. Most of Australia's sugar is exported to its main trade partner, Japan.

Australia's farms also produce barley, rice, oranges, grapes, and a variety of other fruits and vegetables. Much of this produce is sold in the grocery stores and supermarkets of Australia's cities, but some is exported to Europe and Asia. *1*

C. Sheep and Cattle Ranching

The Great Artesian Basin Australia's outback is too dry for farming. There is a lack of both rainwater and surface water, such as lakes and rivers, to irrigate the land. But the scrubby grasses that grow in the outback are good for sheep and cattle ranching. Yet cattle, like plants, need water to survive. The lack of water has been overcome by drilling wells into the Great Artesian Basin, a vast underground water supply.

The Great Artesian Basin is beneath an area covering 670,000 square miles (1,735,300 sq km). The water from rains that fall on the highlands in the eastern part of Australia slowly seeps westward through the ground. The water collects underground in huge **aquifers**, layers of rock, sand, or gravel that can absorb or collect water. The ranchers drill deep holes to tap into the water to supply their cattle. The aquifers are so deep that the water brought out through a bore is very hot. The water has to run through a ditch above ground for at least 1 mile (1.6 km) to cool enough for cattle to drink it.

A helicopter, instead of a cowboy on a horse, does the job of rounding up the cattle on this ranch in Australia.
▶ Why, do you think, would a helicopter be used to round up cattle?

You may be wondering, why isn't the water used for farming? The problem is that the water is generally too salty for farming. Although the salty water does not harm cattle, the salt content of the water would cause problems if used to grow crops. After the water evaporates, the salt would be left, making the land unsuitable for future farming. So, the Great Artesian Basin region is used mostly to raise millions of sheep and cattle.

Sheep for Meat and Wool Sheep are raised mainly for their wool, and as you can see on the graph on page 659, Australia is the world's leading producer of wool. Meat is another product of sheep. The meat of young sheep is called lamb, and the meat of older sheep is called mutton. Mutton is a popular meat in Australia. Australians eat far more mutton than they do beef. Frozen lamb and mutton are also important exports from Australia.

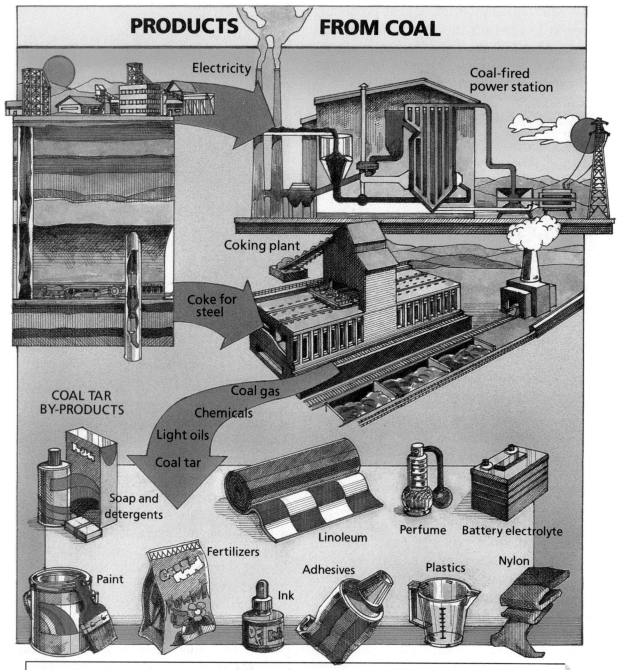

PRODUCTS FROM COAL

Electricity

Coal-fired power station

Coking plant

Coke for steel

Coal gas

COAL TAR BY-PRODUCTS

Chemicals

Light oils

Coal tar

Soap and detergents

Linoleum

Perfume

Battery electrolyte

Fertilizers

Paint

Ink

Adhesives

Plastics

Nylon

Coal products come from different stages of processing coal. The production of electricity and coke are the main uses of coal. By-products of the coking process such as coal tar are used to produce goods like the ones shown.
▶ Which coal products can be used in the home?

Large Ranches Cattle and sheep are raised on large ranches that the Australians call **stations.** Some stations are huge, covering up to 12,000 square miles (31,080 sq km), an area larger than the entire state of Maryland! Large stations use helicopters and planes to track the thousands of sheep and cattle that graze on the ranch.

654

Dairy cattle are raised in southeast Australia and on the island of Tasmania. Those areas have enough rain for good pastures. Dairy cattle are also raised near the large cities where there are good markets for milk and other dairy products, such as cheese and butter.

D. Australia's Mineral Resources

Gold Opens the Way Australia's lack of good land for farming is made up for by the country's vast mineral riches. In 1851, a gold rush similar to the one in California in 1848 and 1849 brought thousands of miners to this continent. Life was hard and few people grew rich. As one miner at the gold diggings wrote in a poem,

> *I've come back all skin and bone*
> *From the diggins-oh.*
> *And I wish I'd never gone*
> *To the diggings-oh.*
> *Believe me, 'tis no fun, . . .*
> *At the diggins-oh!*

The gold rush ended quickly, but many of the migrants who came seeking their fortune stayed to help build a country. Gold mining today is much different than it was in the mid-1800s. Today, large companies own the mines and the mining is done with machines. Also gold is no longer Australia's most important mineral resource.

Other Minerals Australia is the world's leading producer of bauxite and lead. These minerals are among Australia's most valuable resources. Australia is one of the world's top producers of iron ore, manganese, nickel, zinc, tungsten, silver, gold, and coal.

Australia uses some of these minerals in its own manufacturing industry. About 25 percent of Australia's workers have jobs in manufacturing. The main industries include food processing and manufacturing different kinds of machinery.

Steel is made at this plant in New South Wales.
▶ What are Australia's main industries?

LESSON 2

Review

REVIEWING MAIN IDEAS

A. Why is Australia's core important?
B. What are Australia's most important agricultural products?
C. What products does Australia get from sheep?
D. What minerals are mined in Australia?

SKILLS CHECK

WRITING SKILL

A larger population is needed in order to have Australia's industry grow. Write a paragraph explaining the problems that might occur if Australia's government encouraged many people to move to Australia.

New Zealand: Land of the Kiwi

CONNECTIONS

New Zealand is even more isolated than Australia. What, do you think, do these two countries have in common?

TERMS

emblem, Maori

FOCUS

How is New Zealand different from Australia?

A. Getting to Know New Zealand

A Strange Bird New Zealand is a small country in the southern part of the Pacific Ocean. New Zealanders call themselves Kiwis (KEE weez). Why did they choose such an unusual nickname for themselves? The name comes from a strange bird called a kiwi. Kiwis cannot fly and they are nocturnal, meaning they hide during the day and come out to hunt for food at night. Because of this, kiwis are hard to find. This distinctive bird is New Zealand's national **emblem**, or symbol. Its picture is on New Zealand's seal and money and on some of its postage stamps.

Like Australia, New Zealand has many unique animals and plants. In fact, Australia and New Zealand have much in common. However, there are differences between them, beginning with the landscape.

Larger Than It Looks New Zealand is about 1,200 miles (1,935 km) from Australia. Usually, when we look for New Zealand on a map, we look at a world map or a map of the Pacific Ocean. Because the world and the Pacific Ocean are such large areas, they must be greatly reduced to fit on a small map. Islands like New Zealand look very tiny on such maps.

In reality, the two main islands of New Zealand combined—North Island and South Island—are about 10 percent larger than the United Kingdom. They only look small because they have been included on a map of such a large area.

Two Islands The two main islands are both mountainous. South Island, however, has higher and more rugged mountains than North Island. The mountains of South Island are called the Southern Alps. They are snow-capped and have glaciers, much like the western part of Canada and the state of Alaska. North Island has many volcanos, some of which are active. North Island has many geysers and hot springs, like those found in Yellowstone National Park in the United States.

A Temperate Climate New Zealand has a cool, rainy climate, much like the climate of the northwestern part of the United States. Snow is common in the Southern Alps but not elsewhere. The mountain ranges greatly affect rainfall, particularly on South Island. Rainfall on the western side of the range may average from 60 to more than 100 inches (152 to 254 cm) a year. The east side averages less than 30 inches (76

The kiwi uses its long, narrow, curved bill to poke into the ground to find worms to eat.
▶ How is the kiwi used as an emblem?

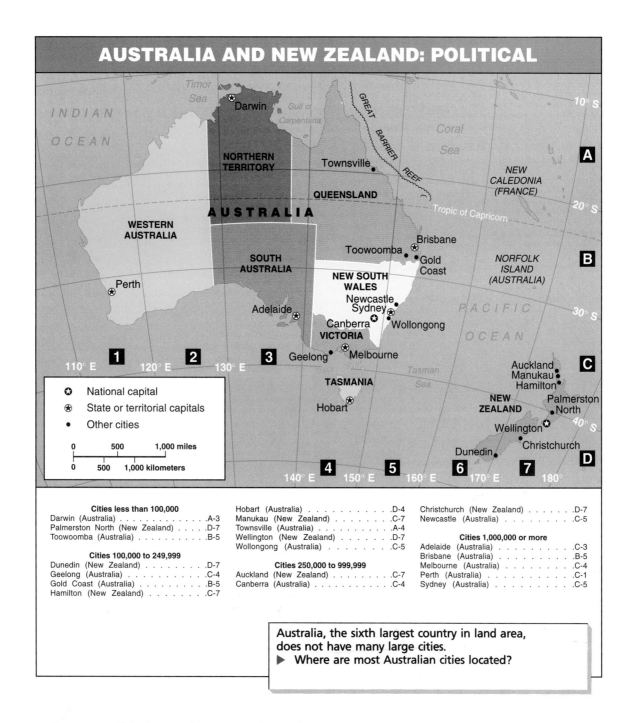

AUSTRALIA AND NEW ZEALAND: POLITICAL

Legend:

- ✪ National capital
- ✪ State or territorial capitals
- • Other cities

0   500   1,000 miles
0   500   1,000 kilometers

Australia, the sixth largest country in land area, does not have many large cities.
► Where are most Australian cities located?

cm) a year. This is another example of the rain shadow effect.

New Zealand's Largest Cities Auckland, on the North Island, is the largest city in the country. It has a population of nearly 900,000 people. Auckland is located on a narrow neck of land at the base of the long northern peninsula. The city covers the whole width of the peninsula between two deep bays, so it is nearly surrounded by water. This peninsula of New Zealand extends over 200 miles (320 km) north from Auckland.

657

Sheep are raised on the hills below Mount Cook.
▶ How many sheep are in New Zealand?

Wellington, New Zealand's capital, is at the southern tip of North Island. Visitors to Wellington enjoy driving to the top of Mount Victoria, a high peak in the city. From there visitors can see the whole city of Wellington spread out below. On a clear day, you can even see the northern tip of the South Island, only 20 miles (32 km) away.

Christchurch, the largest city on South Island, has over 300,000 people. It lies on the eastern side of the island, in the middle of New Zealand's best farming area. Because New Zealand lies close to Antarctica, Christchurch has long been a headquarters for Antarctic explorers.

B. The People of New Zealand

The First New Zealanders The first people to settle in New Zealand were not Europeans. About 600 years ago, sailors from small Pacific islands far to the northeast sailed to New Zealand in giant canoes.

These people are called the **Maoris** (MAH oh reez). No one is sure from what island they sailed for New Zealand, but it may have been one of the islands near Tahiti.

Europeans Find New Zealand European explorers didn't find New Zealand until 1642, when Abel Tasman, the Dutch sea captain, sailed there. The Maoris, who were skilled warriors, were not friendly to Tasman, who sailed away without landing.

It was over 100 years later, in 1769, when Captain Cook's expedition aboard the *Endeavour* claimed the islands for England. For four months he explored the coastline, mapping every detail. But England had little interest in these distant islands, and no effort was made to colonize them for many years.

Over several decades some settlers from Britain did move to New Zealand. The settlers cleared forests to create pastures

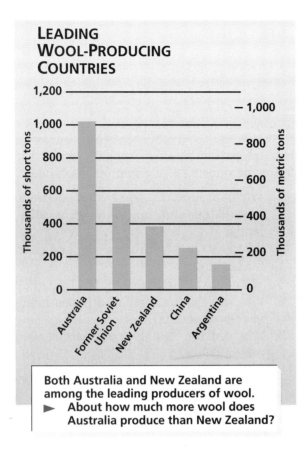

LEADING WOOL-PRODUCING COUNTRIES

Thousands of short tons / Thousands of metric tons

Both Australia and New Zealand are among the leading producers of wool.
▶ About how much more wool does Australia produce than New Zealand?

New Zealand has a pastoral economy and raising sheep and cattle is the most important part of the economy.

New Zealand accounts for over 40 percent of the world's wool exports. It is also a major exporter of lamb, mutton, beef, butter, cheese, and dried milk. You may have seen frozen New Zealand lamb in a grocery store near where you live. But most of New Zealand's meat exports go to the United Kingdom. Wool and meat account for 75 percent of New Zealand's income earned from exports.

Productive Farms   Only 3 percent of New Zealand's land is farmed, but that land produces enough wheat, vegetables, and fruit to feed the country's population. New Zealand's farms also produce hay and grain to feed its many millions of cattle and sheep. The best farmland is located on the Canterbury Plain, a large, flat area near Christchurch.

New Zealand has few mineral resources. There is some coal and iron ore, and a steel mill was opened in the 1980s near Auckland. The most important industries are textiles, wood products, fertilizers, cement, and building materials.

and farmland. Because of the islands' growing population, Britain made New Zealand a colony in 1840. The Maoris didn't like the settlers moving into their land. Fierce battles were fought until 1872, when the Maoris were finally defeated.

A Proud Heritage   Today, about 10 percent of New Zealand's more than 3 million people are Maori. The New Zealanders are proud of their Maori heritage and have built many museums to display crafts such as wood carving, for which the Maori are famous. But the dominant culture of New Zealand is British. New Zealanders speak English, and they have many other customs that have come from England.

C. Earning a Living in New Zealand

Sixty-eight Million Sheep   Only 3.4 million people live in New Zealand, but the islands are home to over 68 million sheep!

LESSON 3

Review

REVIEWING MAIN IDEAS

A. What are the differences in the physical landscapes of New Zealand's two main islands?

B. How have the Maoris and the British influenced life in New Zealand?

C. How do New Zealanders earn a living?

SKILLS CHECK

THINKING SKILL

Look at the world political map on pages 688–689. Why is New Zealand sometimes called "the land where the day begins"?

REVIEWING TERMS

On a separate sheet of paper, write the letter of the term that best matches each numbered statement.

    a. outback
    b. marsupial
    c. coral
    d. reef
    e. Aborigine
    f. anthropologist
    g. aquifer
    h. station
    i. emblem
    j. Maori

1. A symbol
2. A layer of rock, sand, or gravel that can absorb or collect water
3. A mammal that carries its young in a pouch
4. A scientist who studies humans and their past and present cultures
5. The name of the first people to settle in New Zealand
6. The interior of Australia, which is largely desert and semidesert grassland
7. A large ranch in Australia on which sheep and cattle are raised
8. A rocklike ridge or mound in the water made of the connected shells of coral polyps
9. A hard, chalky, rocklike material made of the shells of sea animals
10. The name of Australia's first human inhabitants

REVIEWING THE FACTS

On a separate sheet of paper, answer the following questions in complete sentences.

1. Why is it incorrect to say that Australia is isolated and far away from other lands?
2. Why is so little of Australia's land good for farming?
3. Where is the Great Barrier Reef located?
4. Why are there so few Aborigines living in Australia today?
5. Why did the British use Australia as a prison colony?
6. Why is the core of a country usually located near a coastal area?
7. What animals are raised on the ranches of Australia?
8. What are the two main islands that make up the country of New Zealand?
9. What is the mixed heritage of New Zealand?
10. Why are sheep and cattle so important to the economy of New Zealand?

❖❖❖

WRITING ABOUT GEOGRAPHY

Imagine that you are a member of Captain Cook's crew and that you are going ashore to visit Australia for the first time. Write several paragraphs describing what you see.

THINKING CRITICALLY

On a separate sheet of paper, answer the following questions in complete sentences.

1. What could be some possible reasons to explain why Australia has so many unusual animals?
2. Why, do you think, did the British explorers think that the Aborigines were a very primitive people?
3. What reasons could the European colonists have had for killing Aborigines?
4. Why would many people prefer to live in the core area of a country?
5. How might the history of New Zealand have been different if the Maoris had been friendly to Abel Tasman in 1642?

SUMMARIZING THE CHAPTER

On a separate sheet of paper, draw a graphic organizer like the one shown here. Copy the information from this graphic organizer to the one you have drawn. Next to the main idea for each lesson, write three statements that you think best support the main idea.

CHAPTER THEME Australia and New Zealand each have a unique geography, economy, and history.

Lesson 1	Australia has varied landforms, climates, and wildlife.	1. _____ 2. _____ 3. _____
Lesson 2	Australia has important mineral resources.	1. _____ 2. _____ 3. _____
Lesson 3	There are differences between New Zealand and Australia.	1. _____ 2. _____ 3. _____

CHAPTER 27
PACIFIC ISLAND NATIONS AND ANTARCTICA

1. Locating the Pacific Islands

2. Living and Working in the Pacific Islands

3. A Continent of Ice and Snow

Locating the Pacific Islands

CONNECTIONS

How would you describe the physical landscape of an island in the Pacific?

TERMS

catamaran, continental island, atoll, lagoon

FOCUS

Why are the Pacific Islands considered isolated locations?

A. A Vast Area

A Perilous Voyage There were tearful farewells as the men and women loaded their few belongings into the **catamaran**. This catamaran was made of two large canoes that had been fastened together with wooden boards, making one raftlike boat that would not tip over easily in rough seas. There was enough space on the catamaran for 30 people and for some of the food and water the travelers would need on their long voyage. They carried dried and green bananas, sugarcane, coconuts, and sweet potatoes. The travelers also were taking along some dried fish, but they expected to be able to catch fresh fish along the way.

Soon everything was ready. The men paddled the catamaran from the shore into the open sea. Then they opened the sail to catch the wind and began to travel north. Their destination was about 1,800 miles (2,900 km) away. With good winds and no storms, it would take about two weeks of steady sailing for the group to complete their voyage.

These people were leaving their home in the Marquesas (mahr KAY zuz) Islands to sail to islands that had been discovered far to the north. There they would plant crops from the seeds they also carried with them. What were the islands that these brave voyagers were sailing to more than 1,000 years ago? Today we know them as the Hawaiian Islands.

Many of the thousands of islands that are scattered across the Pacific Ocean were settled by other small groups of people looking for new homes and a new life. The islands of the Pacific were the last places on earth that people discovered and occupied. In order to travel to these islands to settle them, people had to learn to make seagoing canoes. They also had to discover how to navigate over hundreds of miles of open ocean. When the people of the Pacific mastered these skills, they were able to make the long voyages that were necessary to cross the vast Pacific.

The Largest Ocean The Pacific Ocean covers nearly one third of the earth's surface, or an area of about 70 million square miles (181 million sq km). The world map on pages 688–689 seems to show that most of the Pacific Ocean between Australia and the United States is empty. However, there are thousands of islands strewn across the Pacific, many of them separated by hundreds of miles of ocean.

Four Kinds of Islands There are four kinds of islands in the Pacific. The largest islands, such as New Guinea (noo GIHN ee) and the islands of New Zealand, are the kind called **continental islands**. They are connected to a continent by land that has been flooded by the sea. Some continental islands are large enough to have many different landforms and climates, like continents.

Many of the smaller islands are volcanic islands, such as the Caribbean islands you studied in Chapter 6. A volcanic island forms when a volcano extends from the floor of the sea to above the water's surface. The Hawaiian Islands, Tahiti (tuh HEET ee), and Fiji (FEE jee) are examples of volcanic islands in the Pacific Ocean.

Coral islands are the third kind of

▶ A coral reef off a tropical island

THE MAKING OF A CORAL ATOLL

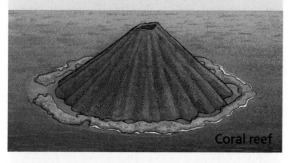

Coral reef

Barrier reef

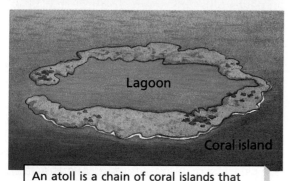

Lagoon

Coral island

An atoll is a chain of coral islands that surrounds a lagoon.
▶ How does a coral reef become a coral island?

reef around a volcanic island. Shifts in the ocean floor may cause the center of the island to sink. As it sinks, a shallow body of water, which is called a **lagoon**, forms inside the reef.

B. Island Groups of the Pacific

Polynesia Look at the map on page 637. The Pacific Islands are divided into three large areas—Polynesia, Micronesia, and Melanesia. Different groups of people live in each of these areas. The inhabitants of the islands in the central part of the Pacific Ocean are Polynesians. The name *Polynesia* means "many islands." A triangle drawn to connect Hawaii in the north with Easter Island in the southeast and New Zealand in the southwest would include most of the thousands of islands of Polynesia. The area encompassed by the Polynesian triangle is over 8 million square miles (21 million sq km), an area nearly as large as North America. But the total land area of Polynesia is only a tiny fraction of the total surface of the Polynesian triangle.

Polynesians speak similar languages. Because of this similarity, anthropologists believe that all Polynesians may have originated from one culture. It is believed that people from this single culture migrated across the Pacific. The story of the catamaran voyage at the beginning of this lesson is an example of such a migration.

Micronesia To the west of Polynesia there are several groups of small islands. Together, these island groups are known as Micronesia. The name *Micronesia* means "small islands." This name relates to the fact that the islands of Micronesia are all very small; some are less than 1 square mile (3 sq km) in area.

Probably the best-known island of Micronesia is Guam, a territory of the United States. Guam is only 210 square miles (544 sq km) in area, but it is the largest island of Micronesia. It is part of a group of islands

island found in the Pacific. Coral islands are actually coral reefs, like the Great Barrier Reef you studied in Chapter 26, that have been pushed above the ocean's surface. Only a few of the Pacific Islands were formed in this way.

Shifts in the ocean floor can also create **atolls**. An atoll is a circular coral island that encloses or partly encloses an area of shallow water. An atoll begins as a coral

MARGARET MEAD IN SAMOA

In 1925, a famous anthropologist named Margaret Mead set sail for the islands of the Pacific. She planned to study the people of Samoa and to describe their culture. She was especially interested in how Samoans raise children and teenagers.

When she first arrived in Samoa, Dr. Mead had to learn the language and many customs of the Samoans. She lived like the Samoans, eating Samoan food and participating in the life of the village. Several years later she described some of her experiences.

The life of the day begins at dawn. . . . Restless little children roll out of their sheets, and wander drowsily down to the beach to freshen their faces in the sea. Boys, bent upon an early fishing, start collecting their tackle. . . . The whole village, sheeted and frowsy, stirs, rubs its eyes, and stumbles toward the beach. . . .

. . . Families who will cook today are hard at work. . . . The children are scuttling back and forth, fetching sea water, or leaves to stuff the pig. . . . Those whose excursions have been short return to the village. . . .

It is high noon. The sand burns the feet of the little children . . . as they creep into the shade of the houses. The women who must go [outdoors] carry great banana leaves as sun-shades or wind wet cloths about their heads. . . . The fishermen beach their canoes, weary and spent from the heat. . . .

Finally the sun sets. . . . Children straggle home, dark little figures etched against the sky; lights shine in the houses, and each household gathers for its evening meal.

. . . Again quiet settles upon the village, as first the head of the household, then the women and children, and last of all the patient boys, eat their supper. After supper the old people and little children are bundled off to bed. . . .

. . . Sometimes sleep will not descend upon the village until long past midnight; then at last there is only the mellow thunder of the reef . . . as the village rests until dawn.

1. Why, do you think, did Dr. Mead try to speak and live as the Samoans did?
2. Why was the sea important to the people of Samoa?
3. What observations made by Dr. Mead about life in Samoa do you find most interesting?

A tropical forest grows in this volcano crater on Krakar Island in Papua New Guinea. The crater is about 7 miles (11 km) wide.
► Of which island group is New Guinea a part?

called the Marianas. The map on page 637 shows that most of the islands in Micronesia form groups of islands. Besides the Marianas, other island groups of Micronesia include the Caroline Islands and the Marshall Islands.

Unlike the Polynesians, Micronesians speak many different languages. Often the people of one island group cannot understand the language of people from another Micronesian island group.

Melanesia South of Micronesia is the large island of New Guinea—the second largest island in the world, after Greenland. Stretching south and east of New Guinea is a string of middle-size and small islands that includes the Solomon Islands, New Caledonia, Vanuatu (vahn wah TOO), and Fiji. These are the main island groups that make up Melanesia, the third group of Pacific Islands. It was named *Melanesia*, which means "islands of black-skinned people," because the first inhabitants of these islands had very dark skin and hair.

The ways people in Melanesia make their living vary from farming in New Guinea to fishing in the small islands of Fiji. As in Micronesia, different languages are spoken in Melanesia. Neighboring ethnic groups on New Guinea may not understand each other's languages.

LESSON 1

Review

REVIEWING MAIN IDEAS

A. Why did it take so long for humans to settle the Pacific Islands?

B. What similarities are there between the three different population groups that live on the Pacific Islands?

SKILLS CHECK

MAP SKILL

Use the map on page 637 to find the distance between the following Pacific Islands.

1. Fiji and New Guinea
2. Tahiti and Fiji
3. Guam and Hawaii
4. Palau and Hawaii

666

Living and Working in the Pacific Islands

CONNECTIONS

How do you think you might earn a living if you lived on one of the Pacific Islands?

TERMS

copra, trust territory, compact

FOCUS

In what ways are the lives of Melanesians, Micronesians, and Polynesians similar?

A. Melanesia

The Countries of Melanesia The islands of Melanesia make up about 70 percent of the total land area of the Pacific Islands. These islands are divided into several countries. The island of New Guinea is split into two nearly equal halves. The western half is called Irian Jaya. It is part of Indonesia. The eastern half of New Guinea is the country of Papua New Guinea. It was once a colony of Australia, but it became independent in 1975. Other independent countries of Melanesia are the Solomon Islands, Vanuatu, and Fiji.

Working in Melanesia The countries of Melanesia do not have much industry. Many people are subsistence farmers who raise pigs and grow crops of yams and plantains, or cooking bananas. Some farmers grow cash crops such as sugarcane, coconuts, cassava, and bananas.

In the coastal areas, Melanesian people catch turtles, fish, shellfish, and other sea animals to eat and to sell. In the past, seashells were made into beads and other ornaments that could be sold. Today, food processing is one of the leading industries in Melanesia.

Fiji If you look at the map on page 637, you can see that Fiji is centrally located in the southwest Pacific. Fiji is a major refueling stop for airplanes traveling between North America and Australia or New Zealand. This has made Fiji an important tourist center and the most prosperous country in Melanesia.

Fiji is the only country in Melanesia in which Melanesians are not a majority of the population. About 46 percent of Fiji's population is of Indian origin. Most of these people were brought from India by the British, Fiji's former colonial rulers, to work on the island's sugar plantations.

Papua New Guinea Papua New Guinea is the largest country in Melanesia. It is about the same size as California. Volcanic mountains that reach elevations of over 16,000 feet (4,879 m) make this a rugged land. Navigable rivers wind their way across the country's swampy coastal lowlands.

Papua New Guinea has mineral resources such as gold, silver, copper, and natural gas. Coffee, coconuts, and cacao are important agricultural products. However, only small amounts of these crops are grown for export.

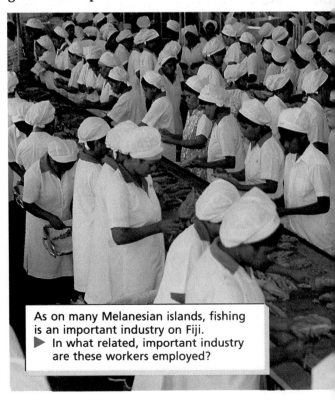

As on many Melanesian islands, fishing is an important industry on Fiji.
▶ In what related, important industry are these workers employed?

The meat of coconuts is dried to produce copra, which is squeezed to produce oil.
▶ How is the fruit of the breadfruit tree (inset) used?

B. Micronesia

Atolls Micronesia provides a striking contrast to Melanesia. Unlike Melanesia, which is made up of large islands with mountains and other landforms, Micronesia is made up of groups of tiny islands. Most of these islands are atolls.

Travel posters that advertise trips to islands in the Pacific often include pictures that make atolls look very attractive. There are white sandy beaches with rows of palm trees and thatched huts. All of these can be found on an atoll. But to the people who live there, an atoll is a hard place to survive on.

Some of the atoll islands barely rise above the waves of the Pacific. Because these islands are low in elevation, there isn't much rain. Think about the way the rain shadow effect relates to mountains. Without higher elevations, there is little rain. On an atoll, water for drinking and for irrigation is often hard to find.

In addition, the atolls' sandy soils are not very fertile, making farming difficult. Because of the lack of water and the difficulty of farming, only a few people live on most atolls. Often the entire population of an atoll may be no more than several hundred people.

Sources of Food Two kinds of trees have adapted to the sandy soils of the atolls—the breadfruit and the coconut palm. In the past, these trees provided much of the food and material that islanders needed. Both trees are still widely used today, but imported foods have been added to the islanders' meals.

Breadfruit can be baked, roasted, or dried into flour. It is called breadfruit because it resembles baked bread. A single full-grown breadfruit tree produces enough fruit to feed a family. These tall trees also provide lumber, and breadfruit juice is made into glue and caulking for canoes.

The coconut tree was and still is another major source of food on the islands. The uses for the coconut palm tree are similar to those of the date palm tree, which you read about in Chapter 21. The inside of a ripe coconut contains a sweet, watery juice that people drink. The coconut provides food in the form of *coconut meat*, which is squeezed to get coconut milk and cream. This milk is used the way we use cow's milk. And oil is squeezed from **copra** (KAH pruh), or dried coconut meat.

Trust Territory Nearly all of the islands of Micronesia were turned over to the United States as a **trust territory** after World War II. A trust territory is a land that is temporarily held by a larger country. The larger country administers the area until the people are ready to rule themselves.

The former member islands of the United States Trust Territory have now reached various levels of independence. The Commonwealth of the Northern Marianas has its own elected government, but its people are citizens of the United States, like the people of Puerto Rico. They have most of the rights of citizens in the 50 states except the right to vote for President.

The Commonwealth of the Northern Marianas does not include Guam, the largest island of the Marianas. Guam is a United States territory that is working toward commonwealth status.

The Republic of the Marshall Islands, the Federated States of Micronesia, and the Republic of Palau are independent. Both the Marshall Islands and the Federated States of Micronesia have chosen to remain associated with the United States by signing **compacts,** or agreements, with the United States. These compacts provide that the United States is responsible for these islands' military defense. The Republic of Palau did not approve a compact but may do so in the future.

The climate and scenery of the Pacific Islands attract thousands of tourists.
▶ What type of island is shown here?

C. Polynesia

Scattered Islands The islands of Polynesia, like those of Micronesia, include atolls as well as volcanic islands. However, there are more volcanic islands in Polynesia. Volcanic islands are good for farming because of the rich volcanic soils. These islands can support many crops. The crops grown in Polynesia are similar to those grown in Micronesia and Melanesia. A popular crop in Polynesia is taro. Taro is a plant with a starchy root that can be cooked whole or ground up into a paste that is used as food. The Hawaiians call it poi. As in other Pacific regions, the economy of the Polynesian islands is based on tourism and farming.

If you look at the map on page 637, you can see that some islands of Polynesia are independent and others belong to different countries. Two island groups, Tonga and Western Samoa, are independent countries. The islands in the center of Polynesia, including Tahiti and the Marquesas Islands, are territories of France. Other islands of

FROM: Tales of the South Pacific

by James A. Michener

The author James Michener describes the unusual features of a cacao tree which is found on the islands of the South Pacific. The cacao is an evergreen tree whose seeds, or beans, are used to make chocolate and cocoa. The beans also supply cocoa butter, which is used in candies and medicines.

. . . The cacao is small, hardly more than a bush, reaching at most twenty feet in height. It has a sturdy trunk, thick branches about five feet from the ground, and grows symmetrically [balanced]. Its leaves are brilliantly glistened like poison ivy, only more shimmering. And they are of myriad [varied] color! Some are pale green, others darkest green, some purple, some almost blue, or gray or bright yellow. And on most trees at least fifty leaves are brilliant vermillion [red pigment], shading off to scarlet and deep red. Each leaf is iridescent [rainbowlike], and dead leaves drop immediately from the tree.

. . . In late January and February the cacao puts out buds that will later grow into pods. They appear without reason at the strangest places! Two inches from the ground on a barren, stiff trunk, a pod will suddenly appear. On one branch there may be a dozen pods. On another, none. In the crevice [crack] formed where a branch leaves the trunk a cluster of pods may appear and the branch itself may be bare. A mature cacao in full season looks as if someone had stood at a distance and flung a huge handful of random pods upon it.

At first the miniature pods are light purple. Then as they grow to full size, they become a weird greenish purple, . . . Next they are all green, and from then on they become the chameleons [lizards] of the jungle. On one tree mature pods, which now look like elongated cantaloupes seven and eight inches long, will be bright green, golden yellow, reddish yellow, red, purple, and greenish purple. And on each tree a few will be dead, charred, black, ugly, with small holes where rats had eaten out the sweet seeds, which, when toasted and ground, become cocoa.

Many people who work at the military base at Pearl Harbor (inset) use sophisticated equipment like that shown here.

▶ What do you think this equipment is used for?

Polynesia belong to Australia, England, New Zealand, Chile, and the United States.

Many of the islands of Polynesia continue to be territories because they are small, scattered far apart, and lightly populated. American Samoa is a United States territory that includes several small volcanic islands. American Samoa's population is only about 55,000 people. The islands' main occupation is canning fish, especially tuna caught by fishing ships from the United States, South Korea, and Taiwan. Tourism is important. The islands are connected by local airlines to Hawaii, New Zealand, and Fiji.

Strategic Locations Why would countries such as the United States and France want to control tiny islands in the middle of the Pacific? One reason is that the Pacific Islands have strategic locations. Airplanes that fly across the Pacific Ocean often stop at Hawaii, Fiji, and Tahiti. These and other islands are also important naval ports and army bases for the countries that control them. So for countries that want to control transportation and trade across the Pacific, these tiny islands can be very important.

Strategic location was one of the main reasons for settlement of the Hawaiian Islands. Russian, British, French, and American merchants, whalers, and missionaries competed during the 1800s for control of the islands. Finally, in 1959, they became the United States' fiftieth state.

Hawaii is still a very strategic location. There are several military bases on the islands, such as Pearl Harbor. Hawaii is the headquarters of the Pacific Command, which is responsible for all United States military in the Pacific and Indian ocean areas.

LESSON 2

Review

REVIEWING MAIN IDEAS

A. How do people make a living in Melanesia?
B. Why is life on an atoll difficult?
C. Why do many of the islands of the Pacific still belong to some large countries?

SKILLS CHECK

WRITING SKILL
The tourist industry in the Pacific Islands has grown in recent years. In a paragraph, explain what might be the advantages or disadvantages of this growth.

A Continent of Ice and Snow

CONNECTIONS
Make a list of things you might need if you went to Antarctica.

TERMS
ice shelf, crevasse, whiteout

FOCUS
Why are so many countries interested in Antarctica?

A. The Race to the South Pole

Exploring Antarctica Early explorers who sailed into the southern waters of the Pacific Ocean looking for land found huge cliffs of ice blocking their way. These cliffs were the edge of giant **ice shelves**. An ice shelf is a mass of ice that floats on the water but is attached to a glacier—that is, the ice on the land. The Ross ice shelf, which can be seen on the map on page 675, covers about 130,000 square miles (336,700 sq km) during the winter. Around the Antarctic coast, large pieces of ice called icebergs continually break off from the ice shelves. These icebergs can be quite large and can drift hundreds of miles or kilometers, making ship travel difficult.

In 1820, explorers discovered the continent that lay beyond the icebergs and ice shelves. As you might guess, exploring this giant, frozen land was not an easy task. But at the beginning of the twentieth century, there was a race to see who would be first to reach the South Pole.

The Amundsen Expedition A Norwegian expedition, led by Roald Amundsen (ROH ahl AH moon sun), reached the South Pole on December 14, 1911. Amundsen's words here describe what it was like to finally arrive at the goal after almost eight weeks of walking across the vast Antarctic ice and snow.

> *We reckoned now that we were at the Pole. Of course, every one of us knew that we were not standing on the absolute spot; it would be an impossibility with the time and the instruments at our disposal to ascertain [locate] that exact spot. But we were so near it that the few miles which possibly separated us from it could not be of the slightest importance. . . .*

Members of the Amundsen expedition prepare for their long trip to the South Pole.
▶ When did Amundsen reach the Pole?

After we had halted we . . . congratulated each other. . . . After this we proceeded to the greatest and most solemn act of the whole journey—the planting of our flag. Pride and affection shone in the five pairs of eyes that gazed upon the [Norwegian] flag, as it unfurled itself with a sharp crack, and waved over the pole. . . . Five weather-beaten, frostbitten fists they were that grasped the pole, raised the waving flag in the air, and planted it as the first at the geographical South Pole.

The Scott Expedition A month later a British expedition, led by Robert Scott, reached the Pole only to find that Amundsen had arrived there first. They were bitterly disappointed and exhausted after nearly ten weeks of struggling over glaciers and snowfields. Scott and his four companions began the long, hard trip back to the coast, where the rest of their expedition waited.

Two months later, they were nearly out of supplies and confronted by constantly worsening weather. One man had died and another was near death, suffering from severely frostbitten feet. Scott wrote the following entry in his journal.

Friday, March 16 or Saturday March 17. Lost track of dates, but think the last correct. Tragedy all along the line. At lunch, the day before yesterday, poor Titus Oates said he couldn't go on; he proposed we should leave him in his sleeping bag. That we could not do, and we induced him to come on, on the afternoon march. In spite of its awful nature for him he struggled on and we made a few miles. At night he was worse and we knew the end had come.

[Oates] slept through the night before last, hoping not to wake; but he woke in the morning—yesterday. It was blowing a blizzard. He said 'I am just going outside and may be some time.' He went out into the blizzard and we have not seen him since.

We knew that poor Oates was walking to his death, but though we tried to dissuade him, we knew it was the act of a brave man and an English gentleman. We all hope to meet the end with a similar spirit, and assuredly the end is not far.

Two days later the three survivors were trapped in their tent by a blizzard. Their bodies were found there in November 1912 by a search party. Scott and his companions died only 11 miles from a store of supplies that might have saved their lives.

B. Antarctica: the Frozen Continent

A Land of Ice and Snow As you can see on the map on page 675, Antarctica faces three oceans—the Indian, Atlantic, and Pacific. Nearly all of Antarctica lies south of the Antarctic Circle. All but a small part of the continent—the northern tip of the Antarctic Peninsula—is covered with ice and snow. The ice that covers the continent reaches a maximum thickness of about 14,000 feet (4,267 m). Antarctica has about 90 percent of all the world's ice. If this ice

A giant ice shelf towers over this visitor to Antarctica.
▶ What is dangerous about the ice shelves?

melted, the resulting water would raise the sea level around the world by about 200 feet (61 m)!

Antarctica has the highest average elevation of any continent, 8,000 feet (2,438 m). The high elevation adds to the polar cold, making Antarctica the coldest place on earth. Temperatures as low as -128.6°F (-89.2°C) have been recorded during the intense polar winter. During the summer the temperature has reached 59°F (15°C) at the northern end of Antarctic Peninsula. But temperatures rarely rise above freezing elsewhere on the continent.

A Desert Although there is a tremendous supply of water in its ice, Antarctica is considered to be a frozen desert. The interior receives only about 2 inches (5 cm) of precipitation per year. Because of the intense cold, there is no liquid water, so people must melt snow for drinking water. Without fuel to melt the ice, explorers could face the ironic situation of dying of thirst while sitting on top of thousands of feet of frozen water. Of course, without fuel, they would most likely freeze to death long before they died of thirst.

C. Modern Polar Exploration

Why Go to Antarctica? Why would anyone want to go to a place like Antarctica? The answer is that scientists want to learn about the world's coldest and most remote landmass. They have learned that Antarctica has an important influence on the weather and climate of the entire world. Scientists have also discovered that Antarctica may possess valuable mineral deposits. Among the minerals that lie under the ice and snow of Antarctica are coal, oil, gold, and iron.

People have also gone to Antarctica to hunt and fish. The interior has no animals or plants except for some mosses and bacteria. But near the coast, one can find seals, whales, penguins, porpoises, dolphins, and about 45 types of birds.

Modern Equipment The story of the race for the Pole tells something of how hard it was to live in Antarctica. Today, life is much different for people who live and work in Antarctica. Expeditions that visit Antarctica are supplied with the most modern equipment. They have airplanes, helicopters, large snow tractors, and the best communications equipment that can be acquired. The scientists live in buildings that are designed for the intense cold.

Still, Antarctica is a dangerous place for humans. Temperatures at the South Pole are so cold that simply touching a metal object with bare hands can instantly freeze a person's fingers to it. People must wear several layers of clothing, including thermal underwear, thickly padded trousers and jackets, and waterproof parkas and pants for the outer layer. Of course, they must also wear several layers of socks under insulated boots and insulated gloves under mittens. However, people rarely stay outdoors for long because it is very easy to

There are about 50 permanent research stations in Antarctica for scientists from all over the world.
▶ What clothing do the scientists wear?

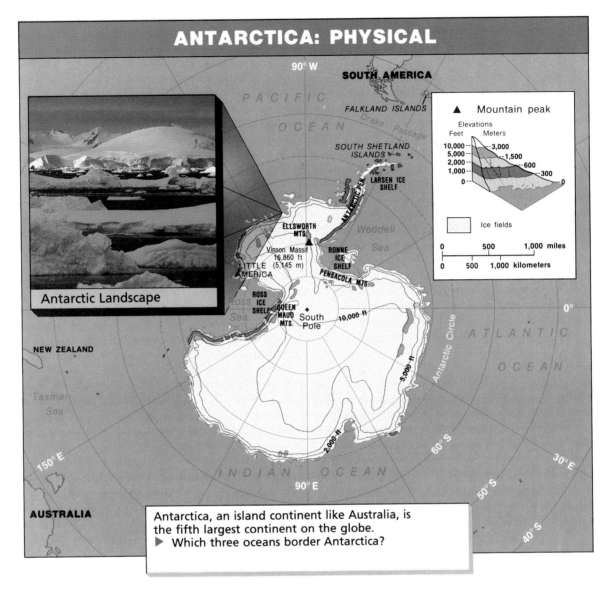

ANTARCTICA: PHYSICAL

Antarctic Landscape

▲ Mountain peak

Elevations
Feet   Meters
10,000 ── ──3,000
5,000 ──
2,000 ── ──1,500
1,000 ── ──600
0 ── ──300
──0

Ice fields

0   500   1,000 miles
0   500   1,000 kilometers

SOUTH AMERICA
FALKLAND ISLANDS
Drake Passage
SOUTH SHETLAND ISLANDS
LARSEN ICE SHELF
Weddell Sea
ELLSWORTH MTS.
Vinson Massif 16,860 ft (5,145 m)
RONNE ICE SHELF
LITTLE AMERICA
PENSACOLA MTS.
ROSS ICE SHELF
Ross Sea
QUEEN MAUD MTS.
South Pole
10,000 ft
Antarctic Circle
ATLANTIC OCEAN
PACIFIC OCEAN
NEW ZEALAND
Tasman Sea
AUSTRALIA
INDIAN OCEAN
5,000 ft
2,000 ft
60°S
50°S
40°S
30°E
0°
90°W
90°E
150°E

Antarctica, an island continent like Australia, is the fifth largest continent on the globe.
▶ Which three oceans border Antarctica?

become frostbitten, even through all the insulated clothing.

Dangers Any outdoor activity in Antarctica requires great care. In many areas, especially on the glaciers that flow from the center of the continent to the coast, there are deep cracks in the ice called **crevasses** (kruh VAS ihz). Many times these deep cracks get covered with snow. A hiker could easily walk across the thin snow and fall through into the crevasse.

Another danger is the **whiteout**. Sometimes the white snow-covered ground blends with the white sky, making it impossible to see shadows or even the horizon. People who are caught in a whiteout are unable to locate directions and can become hopelessly lost in a world without landmarks.

For these reasons, people who live in Antarctica almost always travel in pairs or in larger groups. That way, if one person gets into trouble, someone else will be there to help out.

D. The Continent We All Own

Who Owns Antarctica? Over the years, many nations, including Argentina, Australia, Norway, and the United Kingdom,

These chinstrap penguins are just one type of animal found in Antarctica's coastal areas.

▶ What other animals are found there?

have claimed parts of Antarctica. On the other hand, a large section of the continent called Marie Byrd Land has not been claimed by any country. Some countries, like the United States, have permanent research stations in Antarctica. Yet these countries do not claim any land there.

Many people believe that Antarctica should not belong to any country. They think it should belong to all the world's people and that its resources should not be used for the benefit of any single country.

A Place to Protect Antarctica is a unique place in the world. It was the last continent on earth to be discovered, and it is the only continent that has no land suitable for farming, herding, or any other common way of earning a living. But as people explore Antarctica and use its resources, there is a need to take care of its environment. Governments and private groups are working together to protect the unspoiled beauty of

this remote land. Many people consider this a unique opportunity to study and care for a land that is somewhat untouched by humans.

LESSON 3

Review

REVIEWING MAIN IDEAS

A. What difficulties did Amundsen and Scott face while racing for the Pole?
B. Why are scientists interested in Antarctica?
C. What precautions must people take when living in Antarctica?
D. Why is it important to protect Antarctica?

SKILLS CHECK

THINKING SKILL

Australia, New Zealand, Argentina, and Chile claim land in Antarctica. Look at the map on pages 688–689. What do you think is the explanation for their claims?

676

GLOBAL ISSUES

GLOBAL WARMING AND THE GREENHOUSE EFFECT

In 1958, a young scientist named Charles Keeling was hired by a scientific organization to test how much carbon dioxide was in the atmosphere. Carbon dioxide is the colorless, odorless gas that humans and other animals exhale when they breathe. It is also created by cars and other machines powered by fossil fuels.

Keeling set up special equipment to monitor the atmosphere at the South Pole and on Mount Loa, in Hawaii. He soon was able to confirm what other scientists had thought: the amount of carbon dioxide in the atmosphere was increasing.

Continued monitoring at Mount Loa from 1958 to 1984 showed a continued increase in the amount of carbon dioxide in the atmosphere. Keeling's initial work and the later observations at Mount Loa have helped make the issue of carbon dioxide in the atmosphere a global concern.

Why is the amount of carbon dioxide in the atmosphere a global concern? Because carbon dioxide strongly influences the world's climates. Too little carbon dioxide in the atmosphere leads to cooler temperatures on earth. Too much carbon dioxide in the atmosphere, scientists believe, will lead to warmer temperatures throughout the world. And that could have dramatic consequences. Water shortages, farmland unable to support crops, rising sea levels, and creeping deserts are only a few of the effects that could occur.

What Is the Greenhouse Effect?

The possible consequences of the buildup of carbon dioxide and other gases in the atmosphere are the result of what

Fossil fuels, such as coal and oil, are the main sources of carbon dioxide in the atmosphere.
▶ Why is the increasing amount of carbon dioxide in the atmosphere a problem?

scientists call the greenhouse effect. A greenhouse is a building made of clear plastic or glass that is used to grow plants. The heat from the sun penetrates the glass of the greenhouse, where it is trapped inside.

The earth's atmosphere acts like the glass in a greenhouse. The atmosphere allows heat from the sun to pass through and continue on to the earth. And like the glass in the greenhouse, the atmosphere traps much of the heat that is on the earth.

The greenhouse effect itself is not bad. In fact, without it, life on earth could not occur. The greenhouse gases keep the earth at a livable temperature. The problem scientists now see is that the

THE GREENHOUSE EFFECT

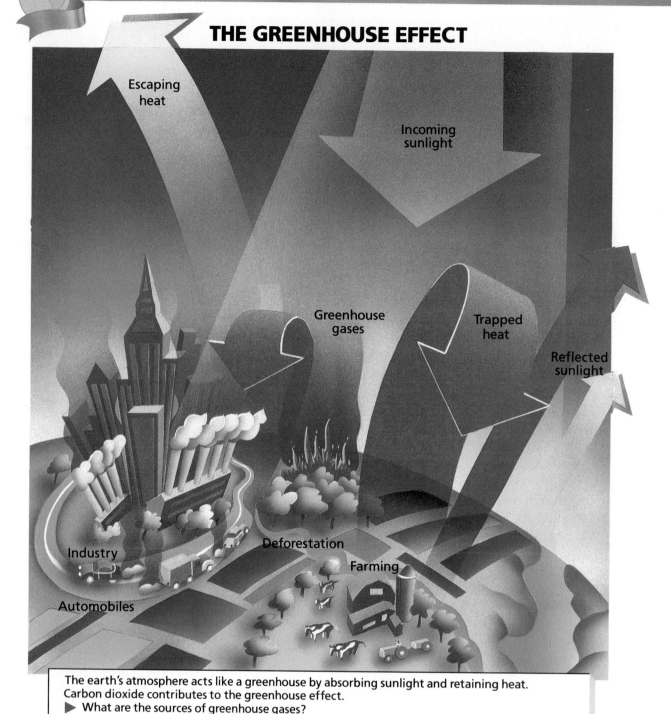

Escaping heat

Incoming sunlight

Greenhouse gases

Trapped heat

Reflected sunlight

Industry

Automobiles

Deforestation

Farming

The earth's atmosphere acts like a greenhouse by absorbing sunlight and retaining heat. Carbon dioxide contributes to the greenhouse effect.
▶ What are the sources of greenhouse gases?

increasing amount of carbon dioxide and other gases may be making the greenhouse effect stronger. Carbon dioxide and other gases in the atmosphere also absorb or trap heat as it tries to escape the earth. More heat trapped in the atmosphere means higher temperatures. And higher temperatures could have a tremendous impact on the world's climates.

You may remember the difference between climate and weather. The weather is the way the atmosphere of a place is on any given day. It may be sunny one day and stormy the next. As a result, the daily weather is hard to predict in advance.

Climate, however, is more predictable. Climate is the pattern of weather over a period of time. We know that a place with an equatorial climate will usually have daily rainfall and consistently high temperatures. An area with a humid continental climate will have cold winters and hot, humid summers.

The climate of a place can change, however. The change, though, is usually slow and gradual. An example of the most recent change in climate is the last Ice Age the earth experienced.

The Consequences

The scientists studying the greenhouse effect are not sure how higher temperatures will affect climate. This is because climate is affected by more than temperature. Ocean currents and clouds are among the factors that also determine climate. Because of this uncertainty, there is disagreement among scientists about the consequences of global warming.

Some scientists believe global warming might cause an increase in the earth's sea level. This could occur for two reasons. One would be the result of ice sheets melting near the North and South poles as temperatures increased. As they melted, the ice sheets would drop into the ocean. This would force the world's sea levels upward.

Many scientists have adopted a second theory to explain why the earth's sea level may rise. As temperatures across the globe rise, the world's oceans could become warmer and expand. This would occur because warm water takes up more room than cold water. If global temperatures increased by the amount predicted, the seas would rise by about 1 foot (31 cm).

One foot does not seem like much of an increase, but it could have immense consequences. The Maldive Islands, for example, are only 2 feet (61 cm) above sea level. An increase of only 1 foot would leave the island at the mercy of storms that would push high tides far inland.

Carbon Emissions from Fossil Fuels, Selected Countries, 1960 and 1987

Country	Carbon			Country	Carbon	
	1960	1987			1960	1987
	(million tons)				(million tons)	
United States	791	1,224		France	75	95
Canada	52	110		South Korea	3	44
Australia	24	65		Mexico	15	80
Former Soviet Union	396	1,035		China	215	594
Saudi Arabia	1	45		Egypt	4	21
Poland	55	128		Brazil	13	53
Germany	149	182		India	33	151
United Kingdom	161	156		Indonesia	6	28
Japan	64	251		Nigeria	1	9
Italy	30	102		Zaire	1	1
				World	2,547	5,599

The table shows the amount of carbon that various countries produced in the years 1960 and 1987.
▶ Which five countries had the largest increases in carbon emissions?

International Solutions to an International Problem

Scientists are unsure about many of the issues concerning the greenhouse effect. They are all united, however, in concluding that carbon dioxide has increased in the atmosphere and could cause global warming. As a result, many countries throughout the world have taken notice of the possible consequences of the greenhouse effect and have pledged to decrease their output of carbon dioxide.

It will be difficult for the industrial countries to cut back on carbon dioxide output. Fossil fuels power the factories that have made these countries industrial powers. There is no easy way to change over to fuels that do not produce carbon dioxide, such as solar power or even nuclear power.

The same problem holds true with cutting back on carbon dioxide emissions from cars. Governments would have to invest heavily in mass transit and other means of allowing people to commute, or travel, to their workplaces.

However, the broad solutions are in place at this time: cut back on carbon dioxide emissions. If the countries of the world continue to cooperate on this issue, global warming may be avoided.

In 1988, President Bush visited farmers after the drought in the Midwest. Many people thought the drought was a sign of the greenhouse effect.
▶ What is a drought?

Scientists continue to debate the extent of other changes that might be caused by global warming. They do agree that temperatures in equatorial climates would increase dramatically. Droughts, such as the one that occurred in the midwestern United States in 1988, might happen more often. This could force farmers in the Great Plains to give up wheat farming because of decreased rainfall.

Not all predictions of global warming see harmful results to the planet. Warmer temperatures would mean that parts of northern Canada and Russia would be warm enough for farming. These countries could then increase their grain output. Other countries might receive more rainfall than they do now, which would cut down on water shortages they now face.

THINKING CRITICALLY

1. How has the creation of a modern, manufacturing economy contributed to the greenhouse effect?

2. How could countries work together to decrease the creation of gases that lead to the greenhouse effect?

3. Some people have argued that nuclear power could be used instead of coal-powered plants to produce electricity. Do you think the risks of nuclear power plants are less than the risks of increasing global warming because of the use of coal-powered plants?

REVIEWING TERMS

On a separate sheet of paper, write the term that best matches each numbered statement.

catamaran
continental island
atoll
lagoon
copra

trust territory
compact
ice shelf
crevasse
whiteout

1. A _____ happens when the white snow-covered ground blends with the white sky, making it impossible to see shadows or even the horizon.
2. A _____ is made of two canoes that have been fastened together to make one boat that will not tip over in rough seas.
3. _____ is dried coconut meat.
4. A circular coral island, called an _____, encloses or partly encloses an area of shallow water.
5. A _____ is connected to a continent by land that has been flooded by the sea.
6. A _____ is a land that is temporarily held by a larger country.
7. The shallow body of water inside a reef is called a _____.
8. The Marshall Islands and the Federated States of Micronesia have each signed a _____, or agreement, with the United States.
9. An _____ is a mass of ice that floats on the water but is attached to a glacier.
10. A deep crack in the ice of a glacier is called a _____.

REVIEWING THE FACTS

On a separate sheet of paper, answer the following questions in complete sentences.

1. What skills did people need to master in order to travel to the islands of the Pacific Ocean?
2. New Guinea and the islands of New Zealand are what kind of island?
3. What islands in the Pacific are volcanic islands?
4. Of what island group is Guam a part?
5. Why is Fiji the most prosperous country in Melanesia?
6. What are two major sources of food for the people of Micronesia?
7. What are the two major activities that support the economy of Polynesia?
8. Why is Hawaii's location important to the United States today?
9. Why is Antarctica considered a frozen desert?
10. What are three minerals that lie under the ice and snow of Antarctica?

WRITING ABOUT GEOGRAPHY

Imagine four travel posters. Each poster shows the climate and scenery of a different island in the Pacific Ocean. Write a caption for each poster that includes the name of the island and tells why tourists should visit the island.

THINKING CRITICALLY

On a separate sheet of paper, answer the following questions in complete sentences.

1. Why would you have wanted to or not wanted to be one of the travelers who sailed a thousand years ago in search of islands on which to make a new home?

2. What evidence might lead you to believe that the people of Micronesia come from many different cultures?
3. How are atoll islands and Antarctica alike?
4. Why, in your opinion, do animals live near the coast of Antarctica and not in the interior of the continent?
5. What do you think should happen to Antarctica in the future?

SUMMARIZING THE CHAPTER

On a separate sheet of paper, draw a graphic organizer like the one shown. Copy the information from this graphic organizer to the one you have drawn. Under the main idea for each lesson, write three statements that you think best support the main idea.

CHAPTER THEME

The Pacific Islands are scattered over a vast area of the Pacific Ocean. Antarctica, with no permanent inhabitants, is a base for scientific study.

Lesson 1 The Pacific Islands are isolated nations.

1. _____
2. _____
3. _____

Lesson 2 The lives of the Melanesians, Micronesians, and Polynesians are similar to one another.

1. _____
2. _____
3. _____

Lesson 3 Many countries are interested in Antarctica.

1. _____
2. _____
3. _____

REVIEW

COOPERATIVE LEARNING

In Unit 7 you learned about Australia, New Zealand, the Pacific Island nations, and Antarctica. Each area has unique characteristics.

A report is a beneficial way for your group to learn more about a country or island.

PROJECT

Work with a group of classmates to write a report about a country or island in Unit 7. The purpose of the report will be to learn more about a certain place and to help your classmates learn about it also.

The first step in the project will be brainstorming. Hold a group meeting to talk about all the interesting material that you would like to focus on in your report. Try to come up with at least ten different ideas. Choose one member to write down all your group's ideas. When you are finished brainstorming, that person should read the list aloud and ask group members to vote on what they think are the five best ideas to research.

After you have decided on the five best ideas, divide the following tasks among group members.

- One group member will be the leader. This leader will gather all the information from the others and present the report to the class. Each member in the group will gather information. Information can be found in your textbook and different encyclopedias.
- One person should draw and label the location studied. This could be the cover for the report.
- One group member will be responsible for writing or typing the report.
- One person should gather interesting photographs for the report.

PRESENTATION AND REVIEW

The group leader will present the report to the class. The students in other groups should ask questions based on the report. The members of the group will answer these questions.

Finally, hold another group meeting to evaluate your project. Did everyone in your group have a job to do? Did the group work well together? Did the class think your report was well organized?

REMEMBER TO:
- Give your ideas.
- Listen to others' ideas.
- Plan your work with the group.
- Present your project.
- Discuss how your group worked.

SKILLBUILDER

UNDERSTANDING A CARTOGRAM

WHY DO I NEED THIS SKILL?

A *cartogram* is one type of special-purpose map. Like all maps, a cartogram is a tool that can help you understand a particular characteristic of a geographic area. Like a graph, a cartogram presents data visually. Most cartograms use different sizes to illustrate data. What do *all* cartograms have in common? They are dramatic, visual tools that can help you understand data quickly and easily.

LEARNING THE SKILL

Suppose you want to find out how the states in the United States rank according to population. The unusual map of the United States on page 685 could help you do that quickly. As you can see, all 50 states are shown in their usual shapes, but their sizes are different. Compare this map with the political map of the United States on page 692. How are the sizes of the states different between the two maps, and what do the differences mean?

The states on the cartogram on page 685 are drawn according to population size, not according to land area. How much larger or smaller a state is drawn depends on the proportion of its population in relation to the population of other states. If each state had the same number of people, all the states would be the same size on the cartogram. A state that has twice the population of another state is twice as large on the cartogram.

A cartogram has a map key to tell you how to interpret the cartogram. The key for the United States cartogram has different size boxes. Each box represents a certain number of people. To estimate the population of California, for example, you would determine about how many times the largest box would fit into the state and multiply that number by the population that the box represents.

PRACTICING THE SKILL

Use the cartogram of the United States and the political map on page 692 to answer the following questions.

1. Which western states have populations of less than 1 million people?
2. What eastern state has a population about the same as Texas?
3. Which state has the largest population?
4. Which half of the United States has the greater population, the eastern half or the western half?
5. Which southern state has about twice as many people as Virginia?

APPLYING THE SKILL

You can make your own cartogram to illustrate data for a geographic area. For example, you can draw a cartogram to show the student population of an area of your school. First, select a section of the school and do a survey to determine how many students there are in each classroom. In the key for your map, draw a small box to represent 2 students. Next, draw a box about five times larger to represent 10 students. Then draw a box twice as large as the 10-student box to represent 20 students.

Now you are ready to make your cartogram. Draw each classroom in the correct location and shape on your map, but use the scale in the key to draw the classroom size according to the number of students. Check the sizes of the classrooms you draw by comparing the populations they represent. For example, a classroom that has 40 students should be drawn twice as large as a classroom that has 20 students. Any classrooms that have the same number of students are drawn the same size.

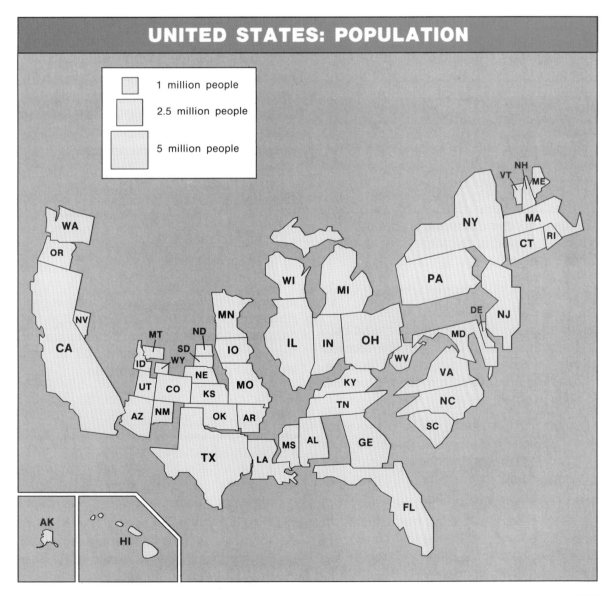

UNITED STATES: POPULATION

1 million people
2.5 million people
5 million people

SKILLBUILDER

EVALUATING FACTS AND OPINIONS

WHY DO I NEED THIS SKILL?

Some things that people write or say are facts. *Facts* are statements that can be proved to be true. People also express *opinions*, which express thoughts or beliefs. Opinions cannot be proved to be true or false. Understanding the difference between facts and opinions will help you to become a more critical listener and reader.

LEARNING THE SKILL

Facts can be evaluated to see if they are true.

- Australia is roughly four-fifths the size of the United States.

You can verify this statement by comparing the areas of Australia and the United States, which are found in the tables on pages 69–71 and 640–641.

Opinions express what someone thinks or believes.

- It was wrong for the English to send their convicts to Australia. When the convicts were released from prison, they were unable to return to England, their homeland.

- It was a good idea for the English to send prisoners to Australia, since the growing population there prevented other countries from challenging England's claim to the Australian land.

These two opinions are different, but they are both based on facts. It was difficult for released prisoners to find ships that would take them on the long journey back to England. And England was able to maintain its claim to the land of Australia. Based on these facts, you can decide if you agree with either one of the opinions.

Sometimes, opinions include false statements or illogical arguments.

- It was all right for the English to use Australia as a prison colony because the only English people who went to Australia were convicts.

This opinion includes the false statement that only convicts went to Australia. You read in Chapter 26 that free settlers also went to Australia. Therefore this statement might be an opinion you would disagree with.

PRACTICING THE SKILL

Use the information in Lesson 3 of Chapter 26 to evaluate each statement in the table on the next page. Copy the table on a separate sheet of paper. Then put a check in the appropriate column to indicate whether each statement is a fact or an opinion. In the last column, write facts or information from the lesson to support your evaluation of each statement as a fact or an opinion.

APPLYING THE SKILL

The ability to distinguish opinions from facts is an important skill that you should use whenever you read. The ability to evaluate opinions—to decide whether they are based on facts or on false statements or faulty arguments—is another important skill. Both skills will help you be an informed and critical reader, listener, and thinker.

686

EVALUATING OPINIONS			
Statement	Fact	Opinion	Why?
1. Kiwi birds are hard to find.			
2. The country of New Zealand is not as small as it seems.			
3. The city of Christchurch is a good jumping-off point for explorations of Antarctica.			
4. It was wrong for Captain Cook to claim New Zealand for England in 1769 because the Maori people were already living there.			
5. It is a good thing that New Zealanders are proud of their Maori heritage, since virtually all inhabitants have some Maori blood.			
6. New Zealand has few minerals, so it is not highly industrialized.			

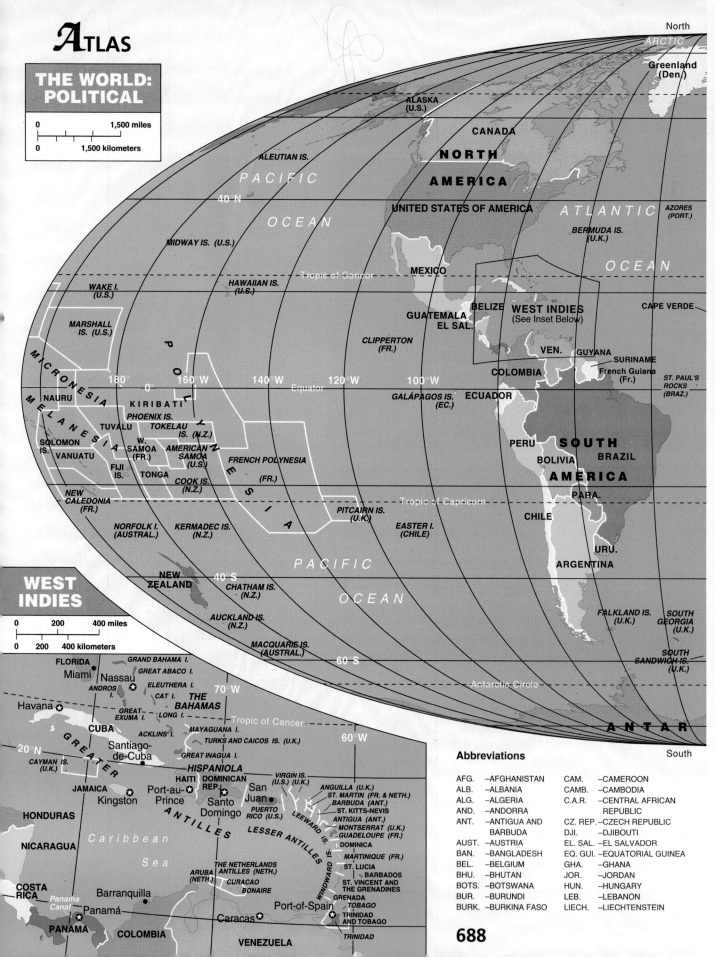

ATLAS

THE WORLD: POLITICAL

0 — 1,500 miles
0 — 1,500 kilometers

North
ARCTIC
Greenland (Den.)

ALASKA (U.S.)

CANADA

NORTH AMERICA

ALEUTIAN IS.

PACIFIC

40°N

OCEAN

UNITED STATES OF AMERICA

ATLANTIC

AZORES (PORT.)

MIDWAY IS. (U.S.)

BERMUDA IS. (U.K.)

OCEAN

Tropic of Cancer

MEXICO

WAKE I. (U.S.)

HAWAIIAN IS. (U.S.)

BELIZE
GUATEMALA
EL SAL.

WEST INDIES
(See Inset Below)

CAPE VERDE

MARSHALL IS. (U.S.)

CLIPPERTON (FR.)

VEN.
GUYANA
SURINAME
French Guiana (Fr.)

MICRONESIA

COLOMBIA

ST. PAUL'S ROCKS (BRAZ.)

MELANESIA

NAURU

180°

0°

160°W

140°W

120°W

100°W

Equator

GALÁPAGOS IS. (EC.)

ECUADOR

POLYNESIA

KIRIBATI

PHOENIX IS.

PERU

SOUTH

BOLIVIA

BRAZIL

TUVALU

TOKELAU IS. (N.Z.)

SOLOMON IS.

W. SAMOA (FR.)

AMERICAN SAMOA (U.S.)

FRENCH POLYNESIA

AMERICA

VANUATU

FIJI IS.

TONGA

(FR.)

PARA.

COOK IS. (N.Z.)

Tropic of Capricorn

NEW CALEDONIA (FR.)

PITCAIRN IS. (U.K.)

CHILE

NORFOLK I. (AUSTRAL.)

KERMADEC IS. (N.Z.)

EASTER I. (CHILE)

URU.

ARGENTINA

PACIFIC

NEW ZEALAND

40°S

CHATHAM IS. (N.Z.)

OCEAN

FALKLAND IS. (U.K.)

SOUTH GEORGIA (U.K.)

AUCKLAND IS. (N.Z.)

MACQUARIE IS. (AUSTRAL.)

60°S

SOUTH SANDWICH IS. (U.K.)

Antarctic Circle

ANTAR

South

WEST INDIES

0 — 200 — 400 miles
0 — 200 — 400 kilometers

FLORIDA
Miami

GRAND BAHAMA I.
GREAT ABACO I.
Nassau
ELEUTHERA I.
CAT I.

THE BAHAMAS

ANDROS I.

Havana

GREAT EXUMA I.
LONG I.

70°W

Tropic of Cancer

CUBA

Santiago-de-Cuba

ACKLINS I.
MAYAGUANA I.
TURKS AND CAICOS IS. (U.K.)
GREAT INAGUA I.

60°W

20°N

CAYMAN IS. (U.K.)

HISPANIOLA

VIRGIN IS. (U.S.) (U.K.)

ANGUILLA (U.K.)
ST. MARTIN (FR. & NETH.)
BARBUDA (ANT.)
ST. KITTS-NEVIS
ANTIGUA (ANT.)

JAMAICA

Kingston

HAITI
Port-au-Prince

DOMINICAN REP.
Santo Domingo

San Juan
PUERTO RICO (U.S.)

LEEWARD IS.

MONTSERRAT (U.K.)
GUADELOUPE (FR.)
DOMINICA

HONDURAS

Caribbean

ANTILLES

LESSER ANTILLES

MARTINIQUE (FR.)
ST. LUCIA
BARBADOS

NICARAGUA

Sea

THE NETHERLANDS ANTILLES (NETH.)

ARUBA (NETH.)
CURACAO
BONAIRE

ST. VINCENT AND THE GRENADINES
GRENADA
TOBAGO

COSTA RICA

Barranquilla

WINDWARD IS.

Port-of-Spain
TRINIDAD AND TOBAGO

Panama Canal
Panamá

Caracas

PANAMA

COLOMBIA

VENEZUELA

TRINIDAD

Abbreviations

AFG.	–AFGHANISTAN	CAM.	–CAMEROON
ALB.	–ALBANIA	CAMB.	–CAMBODIA
ALG.	–ALGERIA	C.A.R.	–CENTRAL AFRICAN REPUBLIC
AND.	–ANDORRA		
ANT.	–ANTIGUA AND BARBUDA	CZ. REP.	–CZECH REPUBLIC
		DJI.	–DJIBOUTI
AUST.	–AUSTRIA	EL. SAL.	–EL SALVADOR
BAN.	–BANGLADESH	EQ. GUI.	–EQUATORIAL GUINEA
BEL.	–BELGIUM	GHA.	–GHANA
BHU.	–BHUTAN	JOR.	–JORDAN
BOTS.	–BOTSWANA	HUN.	–HUNGARY
BUR.	–BURUNDI	LEB.	–LEBANON
BURK.	–BURKINA FASO	LIECH.	–LIECHTENSTEIN

688

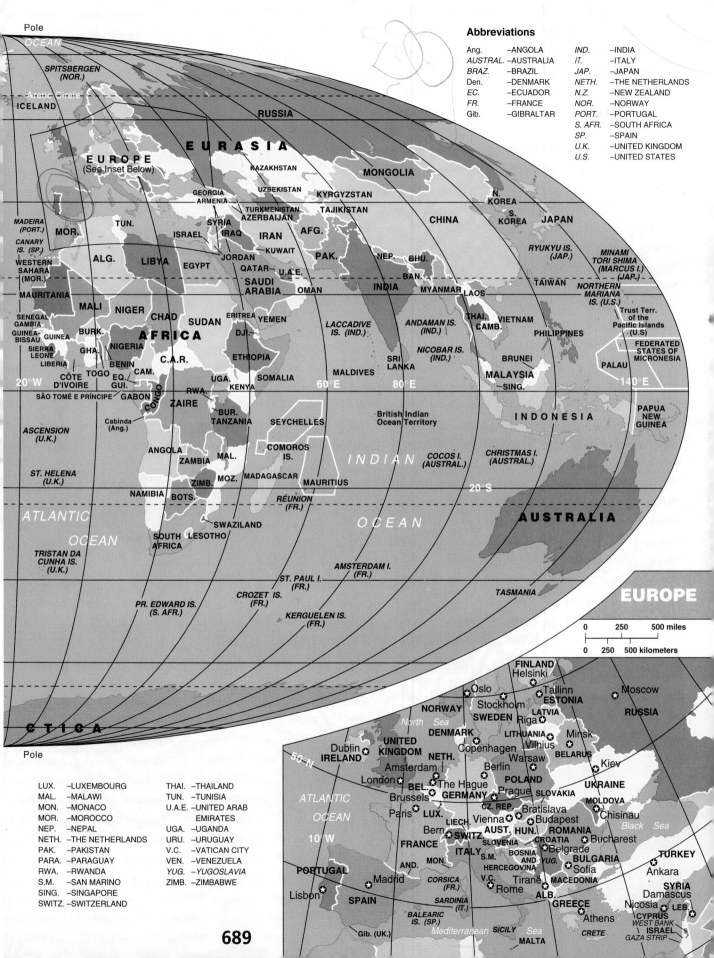

Pole

OCEAN

SPITSBERGEN
(NOR.)

Arctic Circle

ICELAND

RUSSIA

EURASIA

EUROPE
(See Inset Below)

KAZAKHSTAN

MONGOLIA

GEORGIA
ARMENIA

UZBEKISTAN

KYRGYZSTAN

N.
KOREA

MADEIRA
(PORT.)

TUN.

TURKMENISTAN
AZERBAIJAN

SYRIA

TAJIKISTAN

CHINA

S.
KOREA

JAPAN

CANARY
IS. (SP.)

MOR.

ISRAEL

IRAQ

IRAN

AFG.

RYUKYU IS.
(JAP.)

MINAMI
TORI SHIMA
(MARCUS I.)
(JAP.)

WESTERN
SAHARA
(MOR.)

ALG.

LIBYA

EGYPT

JORDAN

KUWAIT

QATAR

U.A.E.

PAK.

NEP.

BHU.

BAN.

TAIWAN

NORTHERN
MARIANA
IS. (U.S.)

MAURITANIA

SAUDI
ARABIA

OMAN

INDIA

MYANMAR

LAOS

MALI

NIGER

CHAD

SUDAN

ERITREA

YEMEN

LACCADIVE
IS. (IND.)

ANDAMAN IS.
(IND.)

THAI.

CAMB.

VIETNAM

Trust Terr.
of the
Pacific Islands
(U.S)

SENEGAL
GAMBIA

BURK.

NIGERIA

AFRICA

DJI.

ETHIOPIA

NICOBAR IS.
(IND.)

PHILIPPINES

FEDERATED
STATES OF
MICRONESIA

GUINEA-
BISSAU

GUINEA

SIERRA
LEONE

GHA.

C.A.R.

SRI
LANKA

BRUNEI

PALAU

LIBERIA

CÔTE
D'IVOIRE

TOGO

BENIN

EQ.
GUI.

CAM.

UGA.

KENYA

SOMALIA

MALDIVES

MALAYSIA

SING.

20°W

60°E

80°E

140°E

SÃO TOMÉ E PRÍNCIPE

GABON

CONGO

ZAIRE

RWA.

BUR.

TANZANIA

SEYCHELLES

British Indian
Ocean Territory

INDONESIA

PAPUA
NEW
GUINEA

Cabinda
(Ang.)

ASCENSION
(U.K.)

ANGOLA

ZAMBIA

MAL.

COMOROS
IS.

INDIAN

COCOS I.
(AUSTRAL.)

CHRISTMAS I.
(AUSTRAL.)

ST. HELENA
(U.K.)

ZIMB.

MOZ.

MADAGASCAR

MAURITIUS

20°S

NAMIBIA

BOTS.

RÉUNION
(FR.)

OCEAN

AUSTRALIA

ATLANTIC

OCEAN

SWAZILAND

SOUTH
AFRICA

LESOTHO

TRISTAN DA
CUNHA IS.
(U.K.)

AMSTERDAM I.
(FR.)

ST. PAUL I.
(FR.)

TASMANIA

PR. EDWARD IS.
(S. AFR.)

CROZET IS.
(FR.)

KERGUELEN IS.
(FR.)

CTICA

Pole

LUX.   —LUXEMBOURG
MAL.   —MALAWI
MON.   —MONACO
MOR.   —MOROCCO
NEP.   —NEPAL
NETH. —THE NETHERLANDS
PAK.   —PAKISTAN
PARA. —PARAGUAY
RWA.   —RWANDA
S.M.   —SAN MARINO
SING. —SINGAPORE
SWITZ. —SWITZERLAND

THAI. —THAILAND
TUN.   —TUNISIA
U.A.E. —UNITED ARAB
        EMIRATES
UGA.   —UGANDA
URU.   —URUGUAY
V.C.   —VATICAN CITY
VEN.   —VENEZUELA
YUG.   —YUGOSLAVIA
ZIMB. —ZIMBABWE

Abbreviations

Ang.   —ANGOLA
AUSTRAL. —AUSTRALIA
BRAZ.   —BRAZIL
Den.   —DENMARK
EC.   —ECUADOR
FR.   —FRANCE
Gib.   —GIBRALTAR

IND.   —INDIA
IT.   —ITALY
JAP.   —JAPAN
NETH.   —THE NETHERLANDS
N.Z.   —NEW ZEALAND
NOR.   —NORWAY
PORT.   —PORTUGAL
S. AFR. —SOUTH AFRICA
SP.   —SPAIN
U.K.   —UNITED KINGDOM
U.S.   —UNITED STATES

EUROPE

0   250   500 miles

0   250   500 kilometers

FINLAND
Helsinki

Oslo

Stockholm

Tallinn
ESTONIA

Moscow

NORWAY

SWEDEN

LATVIA
Riga

RUSSIA

North Sea

DENMARK

LITHUANIA
Vilnius

Minsk

Dublin
IRELAND

UNITED
KINGDOM

NETH.

Copenhagen

Warsaw

BELARUS

Kiev

Amsterdam

Berlin

POLAND

UKRAINE

London

BEL.

The Hague

GERMANY

Prague

SLOVAKIA

MOLDOVA

ATLANTIC

Brussels

Paris

LUX.

CZ. REP.

Bratislava

Chisinau

OCEAN

LIECH.

Vienna

Budapest

Black Sea

10°W

Bern

SWITZ.

AUST.

HUN.

ROMANIA

Bucharest

FRANCE

SLOVENIA

CROATIA

Belgrade

ITALY

S.M.

BOSNIA
AND
HERCEGOVINA

YUG.

BULGARIA

TURKEY

AND.

MON.

V.C.

Sofia

PORTUGAL

Madrid

CORSICA
(FR.)

Tirane

MACEDONIA

Ankara

Rome

ALB.

SYRIA

Lisbon

SPAIN

SARDINIA
(IT.)

GREECE

Nicosia

Damascus

LEB.

BALEARIC
IS. (SP.)

Athens

CYPRUS

ISRAEL

Gib. (UK.)

Mediterranean

SICILY

Sea

CRETE

WEST BANK

GAZA STRIP

MALTA

50°N

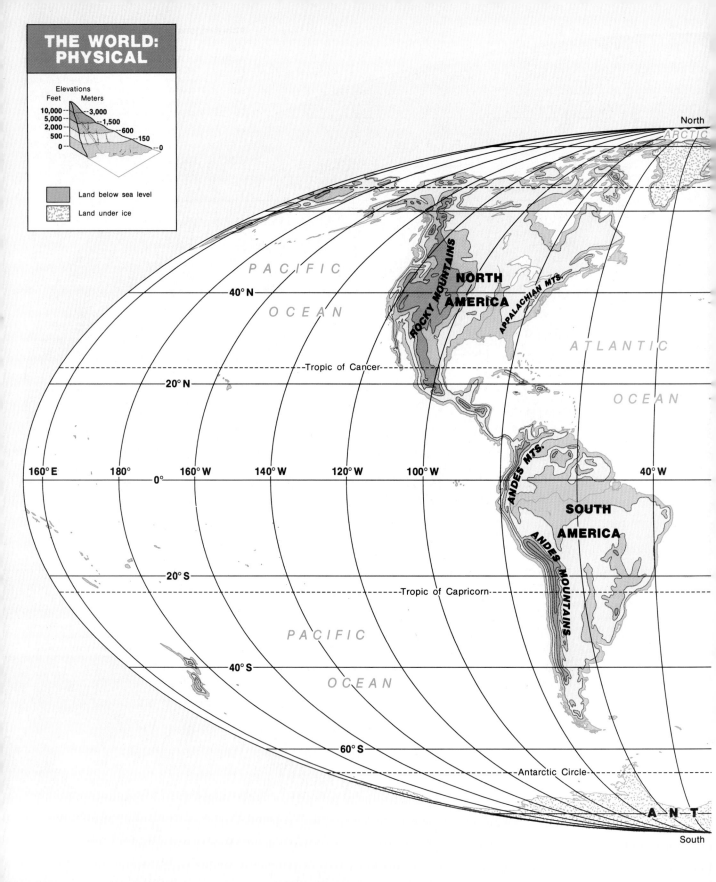

THE WORLD: PHYSICAL

Elevations
Feet   Meters

10,000--- ---3,000
5,000---   ---1,500
2,000---   ---600
500---   ---150
0---   ---0

Land below sea level

Land under ice

PACIFIC

OCEAN

40° N

NORTH
AMERICA

ROCKY MOUNTAINS

APPALACHIAN MTS.

ATLANTIC

Tropic of Cancer

20° N

OCEAN

ARCTIC

North

160° E   180°   160° W   140° W   120° W   100° W   40° W

0°

ANDES MTS.

SOUTH
AMERICA

20° S

Tropic of Capricorn

ANDES MOUNTAINS

PACIFIC

OCEAN

40° S

60° S

Antarctic Circle

A N T

South

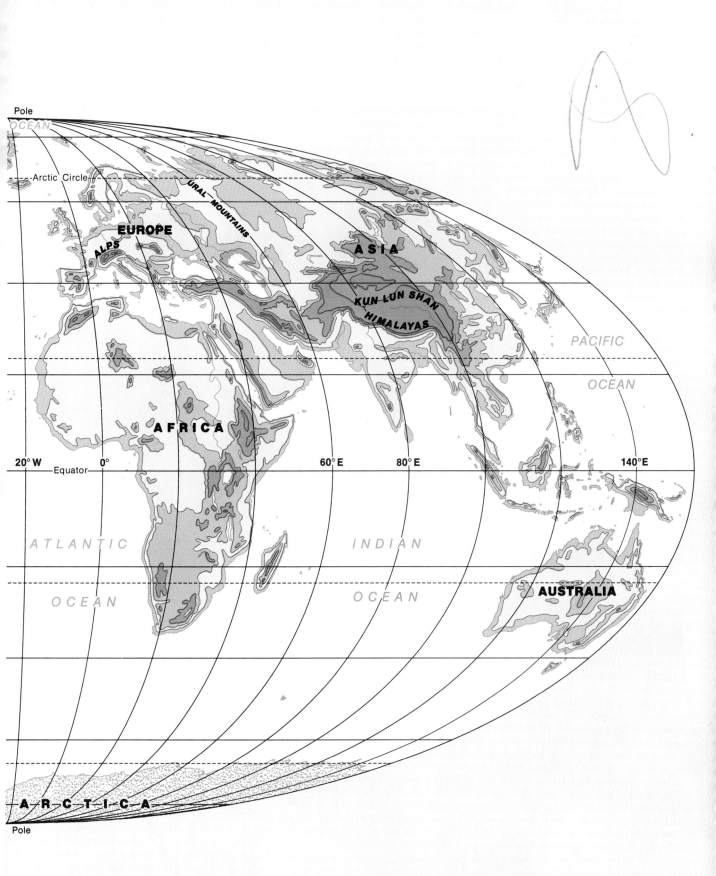

Pole
OCEAN
Arctic Circle
EUROPE
ALPS
URAL MOUNTAINS
ASIA
KUN LUN SHAN
HIMALAYAS
PACIFIC
OCEAN
AFRICA
20° W
Equator
0°
60° E
80° E
140° E
ATLANTIC
INDIAN
OCEAN
OCEAN
AUSTRALIA
A R C T I C A
Pole

THE UNITED STATES: POLITICAL

Legend:
- ✪ National capital
- ✷ State capitals
- • Other cities

0 100 200 miles
0 100 200 kilometers

692

THE UNITED STATES: PHYSICAL

Abbreviations

Mt. —MOUNT
MTS. —MOUNTAINS
I. —ISLAND

Elevations

Feet	Meters
12,000	3,658
9,000	2,743
5,000	1,524
2,000	610
1,000	305
500	152
0	0

CANADA

St. Lawrence River

ADIRONDACK MTS.

Cape Cod
Boston
LONG ISLAND
New York
Hudson R.

L. Ontario
Lake Erie

Philadelphia
Baltimore
Washington, D.C.
Cape May
Cape Charles
Chesapeake Bay
Cape Hatteras

APPALACHIAN MOUNTAINS
BLUE RIDGE
ALLEGHENY MTS.

ATLANTIC COASTAL PLAIN

ATLANTIC OCEAN

Lake Huron
Lake Superior
Lake Michigan

Detroit

Columbus
Ohio River
Indianapolis
Wabash
Cumberland River
Tennessee River

Cape Fear

Atlanta
Mt. Mitchell
6,684 ft.
(2,037 m)

Jacksonville

Milwaukee
Chicago
Illinois R.

Nashville
Memphis

St. Louis
Mississippi R.
Mississippi River

Cape Canaveral

FLORIDA

Cape Sable

Kansas City

Ozark Plateau
Arkansas River
Red River

Oklahoma City

New Orleans
Mississippi Delta

Cape San Blas

Gulf of Mexico

GULF COASTAL PLAIN

Houston

Straits of Florida
FLORIDA KEYS

CUBA

GREAT PLAINS

Missouri River
Platte River
North Platte River
South Platte River

BLACK HILLS
Belle Fourche R.
Cheyenne R.

Longs Peak
14,256 ft.
(4,345 m)
Denver

Pikes Peak
14,110 ft.
(4,301 m)

Mt. Elbert
14,433 ft.
(4,399 m)

Blanca Peak
14,317 ft.
(4,364 m)

LLANO ESTACADO

Canadian River

Pecos R.

Rio Grande

Brazos River

MEXICO

ROCKY MOUNTAINS

Yellowstone River

Green River

Grand Teton
13,766 ft.
(4,196 m)

COLORADO PLATEAU

Colorado River

Albuquerque

CONTINENTAL DIVIDE

Phoenix

COLUMBIA PLATEAU

Snake River

GREAT BASIN

Humboldt River

DEATH VALLEY

MOJAVE DESERT

Los Angeles

SIERRA NEVADA

CENTRAL VALLEY
Sacramento R.
San Joaquin R.

Mt. Whitney
14,495 ft.
(4,418 m)

COAST RANGES

CASCADE RANGE

Mt. Rainier
14,410 ft.
(4,392 m)

Columbia River

Portland
Seattle

Cape Flattery

Cape Blanco

Cape Mendocino

Point Conception

PACIFIC OCEAN

CANADA

BROOKS RANGE
Barrow

ALASKA RANGE
Mt. McKinley
20,320 ft.
(6,194 m)

Yukon River

Anchorage

Gulf of Alaska

KODIAK I.

RUSSIA

ARCTIC OCEAN

Bering Sea

KAUAI
OAHU
Honolulu
MOLOKAI
MAUI
Pearl Harbor
HAWAII

0   100 miles
0   100 kilometers

0   200 miles
0   200 kilometers

200 miles
200 kilometers

45° N
40° N
35° N
30° N
25° N
20° N
50° N

75° W
80° W
20° W
25° W
30° W

120° W
140° W
150° W
160° W
170° W
180°
160° W

693

ASIA

ARCTIC OCEAN

Barrow

Bering Sea

ALASKA
(U.S.)

*Beaufort
Sea*

Thule

**Greenland
(Den.)**

ICELAND

Fairbanks

Anchorage

Dawson

Yukon R.

*Gulf of
Alaska*

Pond Inlet

*Baffin
Bay*

150° W

Juneau

*Great
Bear
Lake*

Godthaab

50° N

Port
Radium — Arctic Circle

*Great
Slave Lake*

Churchill

*Hudson
Bay*

*Labrador
Sea*

PACIFIC

OCEAN

Edmonton
Vancouver
Victoria
Seattle

Calgary

C A N A D A

Goose Bay

40° N

Portland
Spokane

Regina

*Lake
Winnipeg*

Seven Islands

Gander
St. John's

Columbia

Winnipeg

130° W

Missouri R.

San Francisco

*Great
Salt
Lake*

Salt
Lake
City

Minneapolis
St. Paul

Milwaukee

*Great
Lakes*

Quebec
Montreal
Ottawa ⊛

Halifax

Omaha

Toronto
Detroit
Chicago
Cleveland

Buffalo

Boston

Denver

New York

Los Angeles

UNITED STATES OF AMERICA

Pittsburgh

Philadelphia

30° N

San Diego

Kansas City

Cincinnati

Baltimore

Phoenix

St. Louis

Washington ⊛

Ohio R.

Norfolk

GUADALUPE I.
(MEX.)

El Paso

Memphis

Arkansas R.

ATLANTIC

Dallas

Mississippi R.

Atlanta

BERMUDA IS.
(U.K.)

OCEAN

Gulf of California

San Antonio

Houston

New Orleans

Abbreviations

Monterrey

Gulf of Mexico

GRAND
BAHAMA
I.

Den. —DENMARK
FR. —FRANCE
NETH. —THE NETHERLANDS
MEX. —MEXICO
U.K. —UNITED KINGDOM
U.S. —UNITED STATES

M E X I C O

Miami

GREAT ABACO I.

Nassau ⊛

ELEUTHERA I.
CAT I.

**THE
BAHAMAS**

—Tropic of Cancer—

Havana ⊛

ANDROS I.

GREAT
EXUMA I.

LONG I.

MAYAGUANA I.

Guadalajara

CUBA

ACKLINS I.

GREAT INAGUA I.

PUERTO RICO
(U.S.)

VIRGIN IS.
(U.S.&U.K.)

Mexico
City ⊛

Orizaba

Santiago-de-Cuba

DOMINICAN
REPUBLIC

**NORTH AMERICA:
POLITICAL**

CAYMAN
IS. (U.K.)

HAITI

ANTIGUA
& BARBUDA

⊛ National capitals

• Other cities

Belmopan
BELIZE

JAMAICA

Kingston

Port-
au-
Prince

Santo
Domingo

ST. KITTS-NEVIS
GUADELOUPE (FR.)

DOMINICA
MARTINIQUE (FR.)

Caribbean

NETH. ANTILLES
(NETH.)

ST. LUCIA
ST. VINCENT AND
THE GRENADINES
GRENADA

0   250   500 miles

GUATEMALA

Guatemala

San Salvador
EL SALVADOR

HONDURAS

⊛Tegucigalpa

Sea

ARUBA (NETH.)

0   250   500 kilometers

NICARAGUA

Managua

TRINIDAD
AND TOBAGO

694

San José

*Panama
Canal*

Panamá ⊛

COSTA RICA

PANAMA

SOUTH

0°

Equator

100° W

90° W

AMERICA

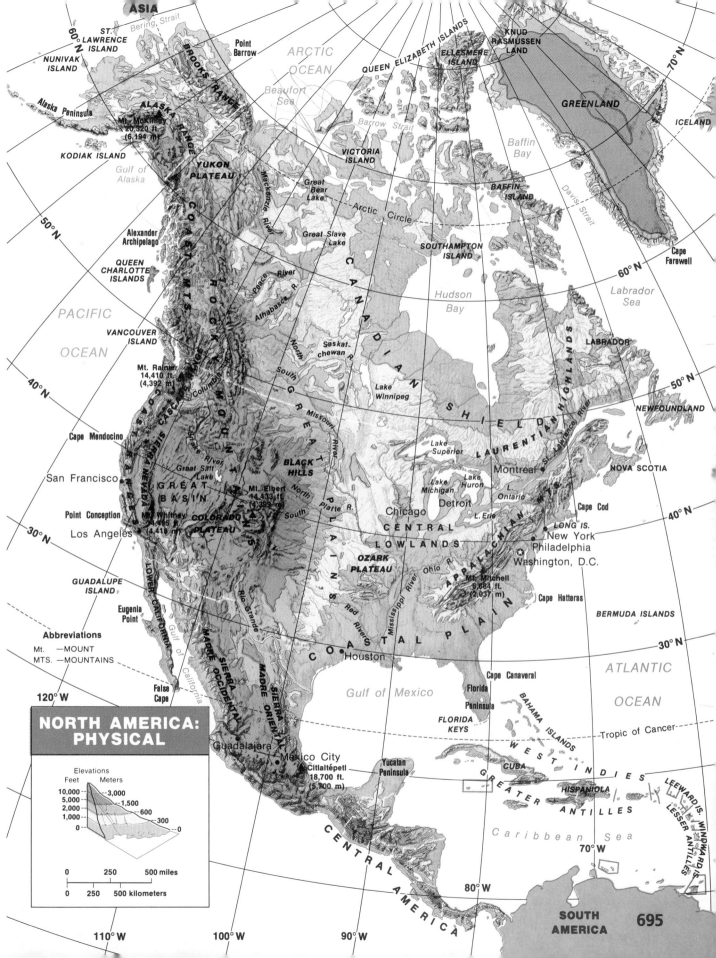

NORTH AMERICA: PHYSICAL

ASIA

ARCTIC OCEAN

ST. LAWRENCE ISLAND

NUNIVAK ISLAND

Point Barrow

Bering Strait

Beaufort Sea

QUEEN ELIZABETH ISLANDS

ELLESMERE ISLAND

KNUD RASMUSSEN LAND

GREENLAND

ICELAND

Alaska Peninsula

KODIAK ISLAND

ALASKA RANGE

Mt. McKinley 20,320 ft. (6,194 m)

Gulf of Alaska

BROOKS RANGE

YUKON PLATEAU

Barrow Strait

VICTORIA ISLAND

Baffin Bay

BAFFIN ISLAND

Davis Strait

Cape Farewell

Great Bear Lake

Arctic Circle

SOUTHAMPTON ISLAND

Alexander Archipelago

QUEEN CHARLOTTE ISLANDS

Mackenzie River

Great Slave Lake

Hudson Bay

Labrador Sea

Peace River

Athabasca R.

CANADIAN SHIELD

LABRADOR

PACIFIC OCEAN

VANCOUVER ISLAND

Saskatchewan R.

North

NEWFOUNDLAND

Mt. Rainier 14,410 ft. (4,392 m)

Columbia R.

South

Lake Winnipeg

LAURENTIAN HIGHLANDS

St. Lawrence River

Cape Mendocino

Snake River

Missouri River

BLACK HILLS

GREAT

Lake Superior

Montreal

NOVA SCOTIA

San Francisco

SIERRA NEVADA

CASCADE RANGE

GREAT BASIN

Great Salt Lake

Mt. Elbert 14,433 ft. (4,399 m)

North Platte R.

PLAINS

Lake Michigan

Lake Huron

Detroit

L. Ontario

L. Erie

Cape Cod

LONG IS.

Point Conception

COAST RANGES

Mt. Whitney 14,495 ft. (4,418 m)

COLORADO PLATEAU

South

Chicago

CENTRAL LOWLANDS

APPALACHIAN MTS.

New York

Philadelphia

Los Angeles

OZARK PLATEAU

Ohio R.

Washington, D.C.

Mt. Mitchell 6,684 ft. (2,037 m)

GUADALUPE ISLAND

LOWER CALIFORNIA

Rio Grande

Red River

Mississippi River

COASTAL PLAIN

Cape Hatteras

BERMUDA ISLANDS

Eugenia Point

Gulf of California

Houston

Cape Canaveral

False Cape

Florida Peninsula

ATLANTIC OCEAN

Abbreviations

Mt. —MOUNT
MTS. —MOUNTAINS

SIERRA MADRE OCCIDENTAL

SIERRA MADRE ORIENTAL

Gulf of Mexico

FLORIDA KEYS

BAHAMA ISLANDS

Tropic of Cancer

WEST INDIES

Guadalajara

Mexico City

Citlaltépetl 18,700 ft. (5,700 m)

Yucatan Peninsula

CUBA

GREATER ANTILLES

HISPANIOLA

LEEWARD IS.

WINDWARD IS.

LESSER ANTILLES

CENTRAL AMERICA

Caribbean Sea

80° W

70° W

SOUTH AMERICA

Elevations

Feet	Meters
10,000	3,000
5,000	1,500
2,000	600
1,000	300
0	0

0   250   500 miles

0   250   500 kilometers

60° N

70° N

50° N

60° N

40° N

50° N

40° N

30° N

30° N

120° W

110° W

100° W

90° W

80° W

Barranquilla
Cartagena
Valencia
Maracaibo
Caracas
Barquisimeto
Cúcuta
San Cristóbal
Georgetown
Paramaribo
Cayenne
Medellín
Bucaramanga
VENEZUELA
GUYANA
SURINAME
French
Guiana
(Fr.)

Bogotá
Cali
COLOMBIA

MALPELO I.
(COL.)

Quito
ECUADOR
Guayaquil
Iquitos

PERU

Trujillo

Callao
Lima
Cuzco

Arequipa

PACIFIC

OCEAN

Chuquicamata
Antofagasta

SAN FELIX I. · SAN AMBROSIO I.
(CHILE)   (CHILE)

Valparaiso
Santiago

JUAN FERNÁNDEZ IS.
(CHILE)
Concepción

Lake Titicaca

BOLIVIA

La Paz

Sucre

PARAGUAY

Asunción

Tucumán

Córdoba
Santa
Fe
Rosario
Paraná
URUGUAY
Montevideo
Buenos Aires
La Plata
ARGENTINA
Bahía Blanca
Mar del Plata

Manaus

Belém
São Luis

Fortaleza

BRAZIL

Recife
Maceió

Salvador

Brasília
(Federal District)

Belo Horizonte

Rio de Janeiro
São Paulo
Niterói
Curitiba
Santos

Pôrto Alegre

ATLANTIC

OCEAN

Tropic of Capricorn

Equator

10° N

0°

10° S

20° S

30° S

40° S

50° S

90° W   80° W   60° W   50° W   40° W   30° W

Amazon

River

River

Paraná

Rio de la Plata

Strait of
Magellan

FALKLAND IS. (U.K.)
(MALVINAS IS.)

696

Punta Arenas

Abbreviations

COL. —COLOMBIA
Fr. —FRANCE
U.K. —UNITED KINGDOM

**SOUTH AMERICA:
POLITICAL**

✪ National capitals
•   Other cities

0   500 miles
0   500 kilometers

Caribbean Sea

Guajira Pen.

MARGARITA I.

Caracas

Orinoco River Delta

G. of Panama

L. Maracaibo

Orinoco R.

LLANOS

Angel Falls

GUIANA HIGHLANDS

DEVILS I.

C. Orange

Abbreviations

ARCH.	—ARCHIPELAGO
C.	—CAPE
G.	—GULF
Mt.	—MOUNT
Pen.	—PENINSULA
Pt.	—POINT
U.K.	—UNITED KINGDOM

MALPELO I.

Mt. Tolima 18,425 ft. (5,616 m)

Bogotá

Meta

Orinoco R.

Rio

Caqueta R.

Negro

Amazon River Delta

MARAJÓ I.

Equator

0°

Mt. Chimborazo 20,561 ft. (6,267 m)

Japura

AMAZON

Amazon R.

C. São Roque

Gulf of Guayaquil

Marañon R.

Juruá

R.

Purus

BASIN

Tapajóz R.

Xingu R.

Tocantins R.

Parnaiba R.

Aguja Pt.

Ucayali R.

Madeira

São Francisco

Mt. Huascarán 22,205 ft. (6,768 m)

10°S

Beni R.

Mamore R.

MATO

Araguaia R.

Tocantins

Lima

Lake Titicaca

GROSSO

PLATEAU

Brasília

BRAZILIAN

Mt. Ancohuma 20,958 ft. (6,388 m)

Potosí

GRAN

HIGHLANDS

20°S

Pilcomayo R.

CHACO

Paraguay R.

Mt. Bandeira 9,495 ft. (2,890 m)

Tropic of Capricorn

ATACAMA DESERT

Parana R.

São Paulo

SAN FELIX I.

SAN AMBROSIO I.

Salado

Parana

C. Frio

Rio de Janeiro

Uruguay R.

ATLANTIC

30°S

Mt. Aconcagua 22,834 ft. (6,960 m)

PACIFIC

ANDES MOUNTAINS

Parana

Santiago

JUAN FERNÁNDEZ IS.

Buenos Aires

Montevideo

OCEAN

Rio de la Plata

PAMPAS

OCEAN

Colorado R.

40°W

30°W

Blanca Bay

SOUTH AMERICA: PHYSICAL

San Matías Gulf

40°S

CHILOÉ I.

Valdés Pen.

Elevations

CHONOS ARCH.

PATAGONIA

Gulf of San Jorge

Feet	Meters
10,000	3,000
5,000	1,500
2,000	600
1,000	300
0	0

Taitao Pen.

C. Tres Puntas

50°S

FALKLAND IS. (U.K.) (MALVINAS IS.)

0   500 miles

Grande Bay

0   500 kilometers

Strait of Magellan

697

90°W   80°W   70°W

TIERRA DEL FUEGO

60°W   50°W

Cape Horn

10°N

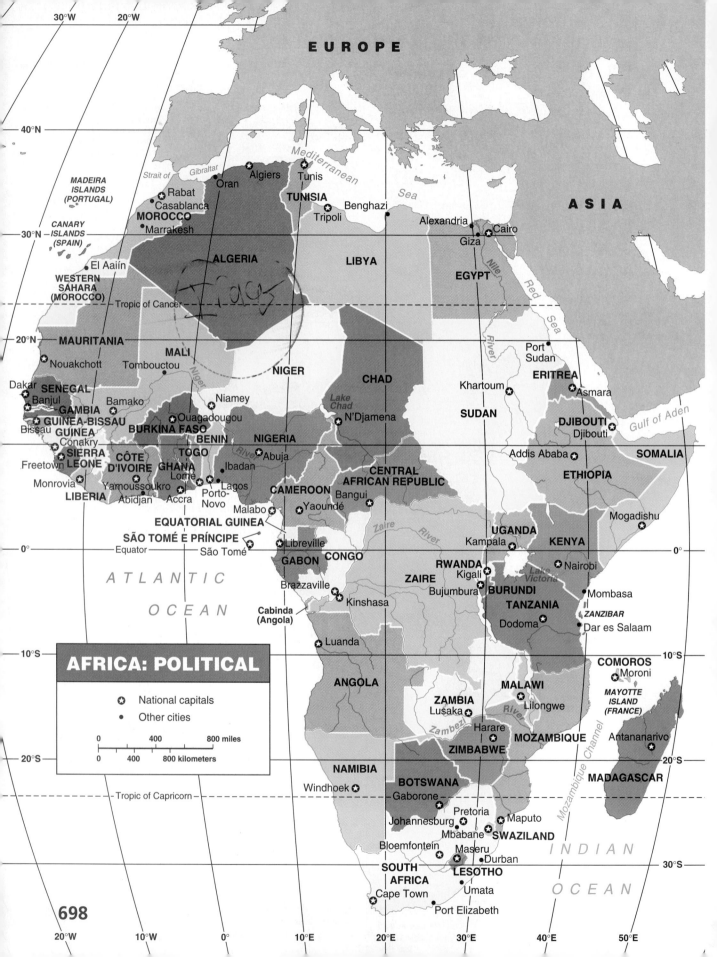

AFRICA: PHYSICAL

EUROPE

ASIA

ATLANTIC OCEAN

AZORES

OCEAN

MADEIRA IS.

CANARY IS.

Casablanca

Strait of Gibraltar

ATLAS MOUNTAINS

Mediterranean Sea

Gulf of Sidra

Alexandria

Suez Canal

Cairo

Sinai

S A H A R A

LIBYAN DESERT

AHAGGAR PLATEAU

TIBESTI MASSIF

NUBIAN DESERT

Red Sea

Tropic of Cancer

Cape Blanco

Senegal River

Cape Verde

Niger River

Lake Chad

Blue Nile

Gulf of Aden

ETHIOPIAN HIGHLANDS

Somali Peninsula

GRAIN COAST

IVORY COAST

GOLD COAST

SLAVE COAST

Cape Palmas

FERNANDO PO

Gulf of Guinea

SÃO TOMÉ

Benue River

Niger River

White Nile

ZAIRE BASIN

Lake Albert

Nile River

Mt. Kenya 17,058 ft. (5,199 m)

Equator

Cape Lopez

Ubangi

Zaire

Zaire River

Lake Victoria

Kilimanjaro 19,340 ft. (5,895 m)

ATLANTIC

OCEAN

Abbreviations

Mt. —MOUNT
Pen. —PENINSULA

Kinshasa

Kasai River

Lake Tanganyika

MASAI STEPPE

ZANZIBAR

Cape Delgado

COMORO IS.

SHABA

BIÉ PLATEAU

Lake Nyasa

Mozambique Channel

NAMIB DESERT

Okavango Swamp

Zambezi

Victoria Falls

Tropic of Capricorn

KALAHARI DESERT

Johannesburg

Limpopo River

INDIAN OCEAN

Orange River

Vaal River

Cape of Good Hope

Cape Agulhas

Elevations

Feet	Meters
10,000	3,000
5,000	1,500
2,000	600
1,000	300
0	0

Land below sea level

0   400 miles
0   400 kilometers

699

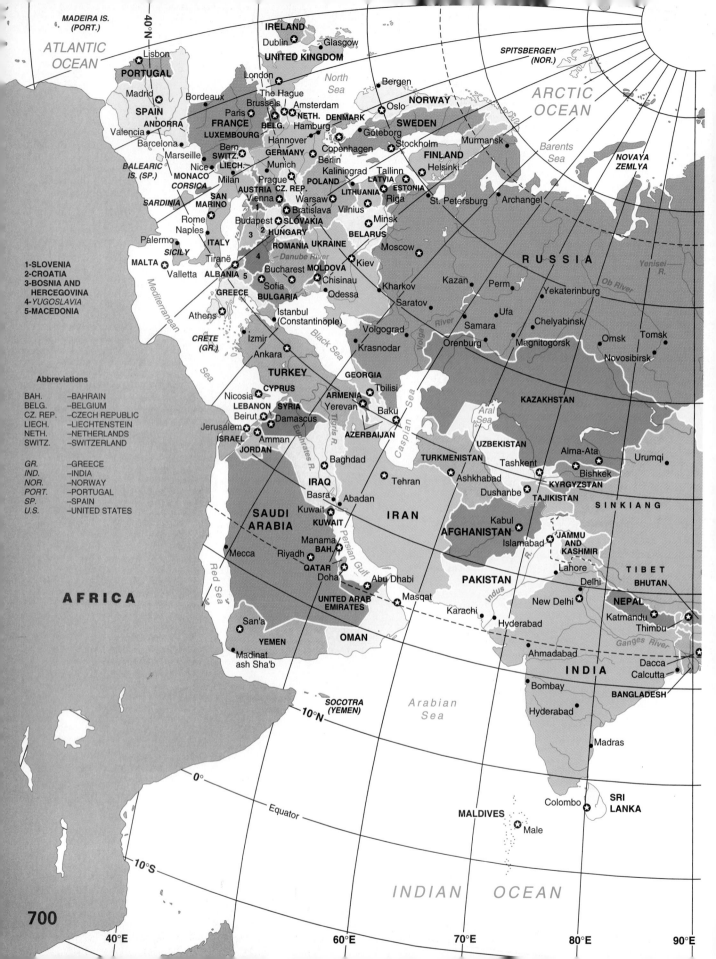

MADEIRA IS.
(PORT.)

ATLANTIC OCEAN

40°N

IRELAND
Dublin ✪   Glasgow ●

SPITSBERGEN
(NOR.)

ARCTIC OCEAN

UNITED KINGDOM
London ●
The Hague ●   Amsterdam
Brussels ✪
BELG.   NETH.   Hamburg
LUXEMBOURG   Hannover
GERMANY   Copenhagen
Bern   Munich   Berlin
SWITZ.   Prague   POLAND
LIECH.   Milan   CZ. REP.   Warsaw
MONACO   AUSTRIA   Bratislava
SAN   Vienna   1   SLOVAKIA
MARINO   2   HUNGARY
Rome   3   Budapest
Naples   ROMANIA   UKRAINE
ITALY   Tiranë   4   Danube River
Palermo   Bucharest   MOLDOVA
SICILY   Valletta   5   Chisinau
MALTA   ALBANIA   Sofia   Odessa
        GREECE   BULGARIA
Athens   Istanbul
        (Constantinople)
CRETE   Izmir
(GR.)   Ankara
        TURKEY
        CYPRUS
Nicosia ✪   SYRIA
LEBANON   Damascus
Beirut ✪
Jerusalem ✪
ISRAEL   Amman
JORDAN

Lisbon ●
PORTUGAL
Madrid ✪   Bordeaux ●
SPAIN
ANDORRA
Valencia ●   Paris ✪   FRANCE
Barcelona ●
Marseille   Nice
BALEARIC
IS. (SP.)
CORSICA
SARDINIA

Bergen ●
NORWAY
Oslo ✪   SWEDEN
Göteborg ●   Stockholm ✪
Murmansk ●
FINLAND
Helsinki ✪
Tallinn
ESTONIA
Kaliningrad   LATVIA
Riga
LITHUANIA   St. Petersburg ●
Vilnius   Archangel ●
Minsk ✪
BELARUS
Moscow ✪
Kiev ✪   RUSSIA
Kharkov ●   Kazan ●   Perm ●   Yekaterinburg ●
Saratov ●   Ufa ●   Chelyabinsk ●
Volgograd ●   Samara ●   Magnitogorsk ●   Omsk ●   Tomsk ●
Krasnodar ●   Orenburg ●   Novosibirsk ●
Black Sea

Barents Sea

NOVAYA ZEMLYA

Yenisei R.
Ob River

Volga River

GEORGIA
Tbilisi ●
ARMENIA
Yerevan ✪   Baku ●
AZERBAIJAN
Caspian Sea
Aral Sea
KAZAKHSTAN
UZBEKISTAN
TURKMENISTAN
Ashkhabad ✪   Tashkent ✪
Dushanbe   Bishkek
Alma-Ata ●   Urumqi ●
KYRGYZSTAN
TAJIKISTAN
SINKIANG

Baghdad ✪
IRAQ
Basra ●
Abadan ●
Tehran ✪
IRAN
Kuwait ✪
KUWAIT
SAUDI ARABIA
Manama
BAH.
Mecca ●   Riyadh ✪
QATAR
Doha ✪
UNITED ARAB
EMIRATES

Kabul ✪
AFGHANISTAN
Islamabad ✪
JAMMU AND
KASHMIR
Lahore ●
Delhi ●
New Delhi ✪
PAKISTAN   TIBET
BHUTAN
Thimbu ●
NEPAL
Katmandu ✪
Ganges River

Abu Dhabi ●
Masqat ●
OMAN
Karachi ●
Hyderabad ●
Ahmadabad ●

INDIA

Persian Gulf
Red Sea

San'a ✪
YEMEN
Madinat
ash Sha'b ●

SOCOTRA
(YEMEN)
10°N

Arabian
Sea

Bombay ●
Hyderabad ●

Dacca ●
Calcutta ●
BANGLADESH

Madras ●

0°

Equator

Colombo ✪
MALDIVES
Male ✪

SRI
LANKA

10°S

INDIAN OCEAN

AFRICA

Mediterranean Sea

Tigris R.
Euphrates R.
Indus R.

1-SLOVENIA
2-CROATIA
3-BOSNIA AND
  HERCEGOVINA
4-YUGOSLAVIA
5-MACEDONIA

Abbreviations

BAH.   —BAHRAIN
BELG.   —BELGIUM
CZ. REP.   —CZECH REPUBLIC
LIECH.   —LIECHTENSTEIN
NETH.   —NETHERLANDS
SWITZ.   —SWITZERLAND

GR.   —GREECE
IND.   —INDIA
NOR.   —NORWAY
PORT.   —PORTUGAL
SP.   —SPAIN
U.S.   —UNITED STATES

40°E   60°E   70°E   80°E   90°E

EURASIA: POETICAL

- ✪ National capitals
- • Other cities

| 0 | 400 | 800 miles |

| 0 | 400 | 800 kilometers |

Bering Sea

NEW SIBERIAN IS.

NORTH LAND

50°N

40°N

30°N

S I B E R I A

Kamchatka Peninsula

• Magadan

Sea of Okhotsk

RUSSIA

Lena R.

SAKHALIN

KURIL ISLANDS

PACIFIC OCEAN

20°N

• Krasnoyarsk

• Irkutsk

• Khabarovsk

Amur River

MANCHURIA

• Harbin

• Vladivostok

• Sapporo

Sea of Japan

• Ulan Bator

MONGOLIA

• Fushun

• Shenyang

N. KOREA

P'yŏngyang ✪

✪ Tokyo

JAPAN

Yokohama

Kyōto • • Nagoya

Kōbe • Osaka

• Seoul

• Pusan

S. KOREA

Great Wall

✪ Beijing • Dalian

• Tianjin

He

Kitakyūshū

• Taiyuan

• Qingdao

• Lanzhou

Huang

• Xi'an

CHINA

• Nanjing

• Shanghai

East China Sea

10°N

• Chengdu

Jiang

• Wuhan

• Chongqing

Chang

• Taipei

TAIWAN

RYUKYU IS. (JAPAN)

Tropic of Cancer

Brahmaputra R.

• Kunming

• Guangzhou

Xi Jiang

Hong Kong

Macao (PORT.)

MYANMAR

• Mandalay

LAOS

• Hanoi

LAOS

South China Sea

• Manila

FEDERATED STATES OF MICRONESIA

0°

✪ Vientiane

Hue •

PHILIPPINES

• Rangoon

THAILAND

• Da Nang

VIETNAM

Mekong

Bangkok ✪

CAMBODIA

Phnom Penh ✪

• Davao

Equator

• Ho Chi Minh City

Bay of Bengal

ANDAMAN IS. (IND.)

Bandar Seri Begawan

NICOBAR IS. (IND.)

BRUNEI ✪

• Manado

Djajapura •

• Lae

IRIAN JAYA

PAPUA NEW GUINEA

M A L A Y S I A

BORNEO

• Medan

Kuala Lumpur ✪

• Samarinda

CELEBES

NEW GUINEA

Port Moresby

• Singapore

Coral Sea

• Pontianak

SUMATRA

• Bandjarmasin

Ujung Pandang

Arafura Sea

• Palembang

I N D O N E S I A

TIMOR

Jakarta ✪

JAVA

BALI

• Bandung

• Surabaja

100°E

AUSTRALIA

701

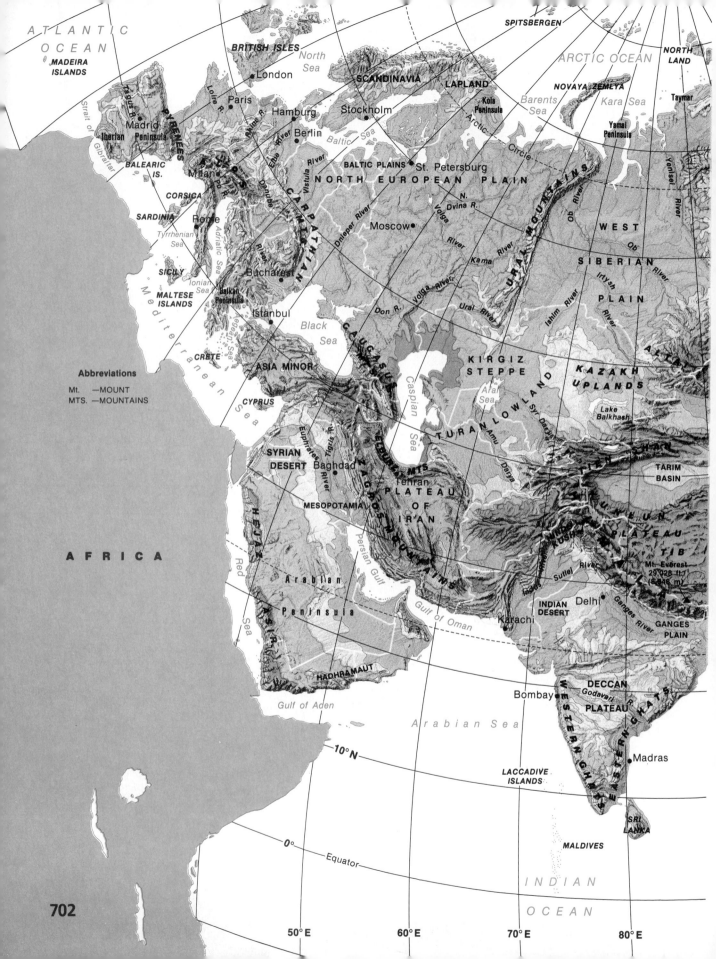

ATLANTIC
OCEAN

MADEIRA
ISLANDS

BRITISH ISLES

SPITSBERGEN

NORTH
LAND

ARCTIC OCEAN

North
Sea

London

SCANDINAVIA

LAPLAND

NOVAYA ZEMLYA

Paris

Loire R.

Kola
Peninsula

Barents
Sea

Kara Sea

Taymar

Hamburg

Stockholm

Madrid

Iberian
Peninsula

PYRENEES

ALPS

Berlin

Rhine R.

Elbe River

Danube River

Vistula River

Baltic Sea

BALTIC PLAINS

St. Petersburg

NORTH EUROPEAN PLAIN

N.
Dvina R.

URAL MOUNTAINS

Yamal
Peninsula

Yenisei
River

Ob River

WEST

BALEARIC
IS.

Milan

Po R.

CORSICA

Adriatic Sea

Rome

SARDINIA

Tyrrhenian
Sea

SICILY

MALTESE
ISLANDS

CARPATHIAN

Danube
River

Bucharest

Balkan
Peninsula

Ionian
Sea

Aegean Sea

Strait of Gibraltar

CRETE

Mediterranean Sea

Istanbul

Black
Sea

Moscow

Dnieper River

Don R.

Volga River

Volga

Kama River

Ural River

SIBERIAN

Ob

PLAIN

KIRGIZ
STEPPE

Irtysh River

Ishim River

Tobol River

KAZAKH

UPLANDS

ALTAI

Caspian
Sea

Aral
Sea

TURAN LOWLAND

Lake
Balkhash

Abbreviations

Mt. —MOUNT
MTS. —MOUNTAINS

ASIA MINOR

CYPRUS

CAUCASUS

Euphrates River

Tigris R.

SYRIAN
DESERT

Baghdad

MESOPOTAMIA

ELBURZ MTS.

ZAGROS MOUNTAINS

PLATEAU
OF
IRAN

Tehran

Syr Darya

Amu Darya

TIEN SHAN

TARIM
BASIN

KUNLUN

PLATEAU

TIB

AFRICA

Red
Sea

HEJAZ

ASIR

Arabian

Peninsula

Persian Gulf

Gulf of Oman

HINDU
KUSH

INDIAN
DESERT

Indus

Sutlej River

Ganges River

Mt. Everest
29,028 ft.)
(8,848 m)

Delhi

Karachi

GANGES
PLAIN

HADHRAMAUT

Gulf of Aden

DECCAN

Bombay

Godavari

PLATEAU

WESTERN GHATS

EASTERN GHATS

Arabian Sea

10°N

LACCADIVE
ISLANDS

Madras

SRI
LANKA

0°

MALDIVES

Equator

INDIAN

OCEAN

702

50°E   60°E   70°E   80°E

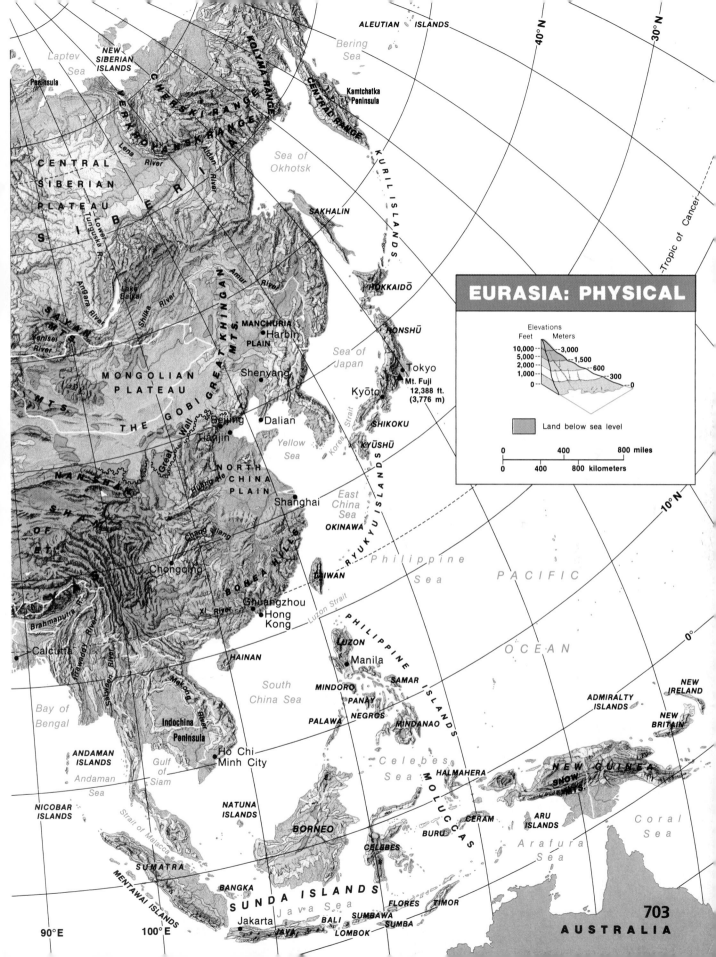

ALEUTIAN ISLANDS

40°N

30°N

Laptev
Sea

NEW
SIBERIAN
ISLANDS

Peninsula

Bering
Sea

Kamtchatka
Peninsula

CHERSKI RANGE

KOLYMA RANGE

CENTRAL RANGE

VERKHOYANSK RANGE

Sea of
Okhotsk

SAKHALIN

KURIL ISLANDS

Tropic of Cancer

C E N T R A L

S I B E R I A N

P L A T E A U

Lena
River

Aldan
River

S I B E R I A

Lower
Tunguska R.

Angara River

Yenisei
River

SAYAN
MTS.

Lake
Baikal

Shilka River

Amur

River

MANCHURIA
PLAIN

Harbin

MONGOLIAN
PLATEAU

GREAT KHINGAN MTS.

Shenyang

HOKKAIDŌ

Sea of
Japan

HONSHŪ

Tokyo
Mt. Fuji
12,388 ft.
(3,776 m)

EURASIA: PHYSICAL

Elevations
Feet   Meters
10,000 ── ─3,000
5,000 ──
2,000 ──   ─1,500
1,000 ──   ─600
0 ──   ─300
           ─0

Land below sea level

0   400   800 miles

0   400   800 kilometers

M T S.

THE GOBI

Great Wall

Beijing

Dalian

Kyōto

Korea Strait

SHIKOKU

Tianjin

KYŪSHŪ

NANSHAN

NORTH
CHINA
PLAIN

Huang He

Shanghai

East
China
Sea

Yellow
Sea

OKINAWA

10°N

OF

TIBET

Chang Jiang

Chongqing

BOHEA HILLS

TAIWAN

RYUKYU ISLANDS

Philippine

Sea

PACIFIC

Brahmaputra R.

Irrawaddy River

Salween River

Mekong River

Calcutta

Guangzhou
Hong
Kong

Xi River

HAINAN

Luzon Strait

PHILIPPINE ISLANDS

LUZON

Manila

OCEAN

0°

Bay of
Bengal

ANDAMAN
ISLANDS

Gulf
of
Siam

Indochina
Peninsula

Ho Chi
Minh City

South
China Sea

MINDORO

PANAY

SAMAR

NEGROS

PALAWAN

MINDANAO

ADMIRALTY
ISLANDS

NEW
IRELAND

NEW
BRITAIN

Andaman
Sea

NICOBAR
ISLANDS

Strait of Malacca

NATUNA
ISLANDS

Celebes
Sea

HALMAHERA

MOLUCCAS

CERAM

BURU

ARU
ISLANDS

NEW GUINEA

SNOW
MTS.

Coral
Sea

SUMATRA

MENTAWAI ISLANDS

BORNEO

CELEBES

Arafura
Sea

BANGKA

SUNDA ISLANDS

FLORES   TIMOR

Java Sea

SUMBAWA

Jakarta

JAVA

BALI

LOMBOK

SUMBA

703

AUSTRALIA

90°E   100°E

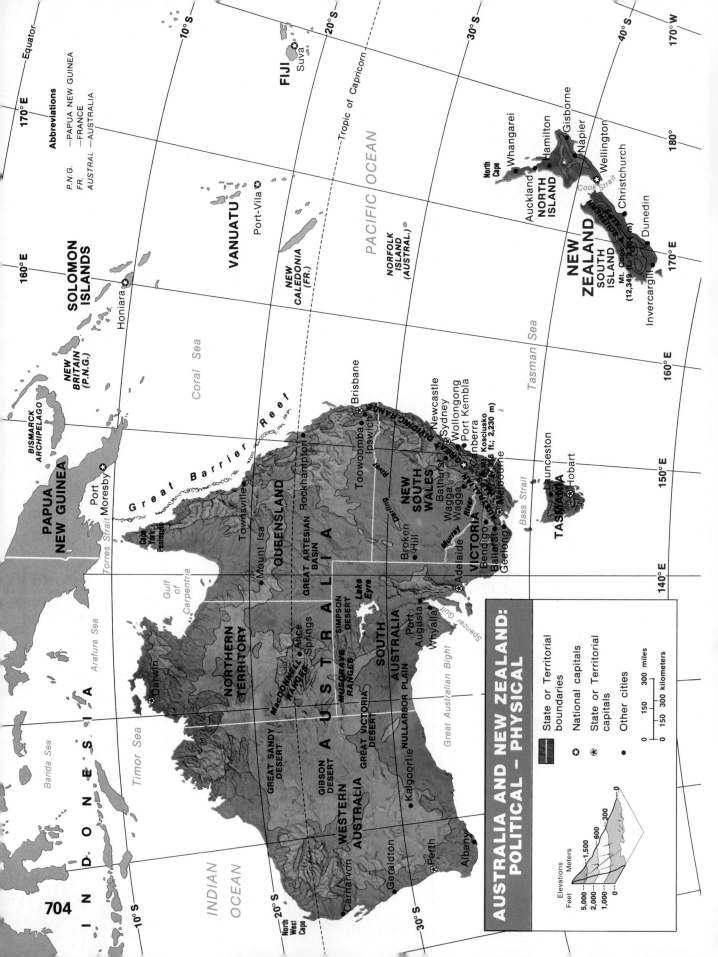

AUSTRALIA AND NEW ZEALAND: POLITICAL – PHYSICAL

704

Elevations
Feet	Meters
5,000	1,500
2,000	600
1,000	300
0	0

State or Territorial boundaries
⊛ National capitals
⊛ State or Territorial capitals
• Other cities

0   150   300 miles
0   150   300 kilometers

Abbreviations
P.N.G. —PAPUA NEW GUINEA
FR. —FRANCE
AUSTRAL.—AUSTRALIA

Equator

10° S

20° S

Tropic of Capricorn

30° S

40° S

170° E
170° E
160° E
160° E
150° E
140° E
180°
170° E
170° W

INDONESIA

PAPUA NEW GUINEA

Port Moresby ⊛

Torres Strait

Banda Sea

Timor Sea

Arafura Sea

Gulf of Carpentaria

BISMARCK ARCHIPELAGO

NEW BRITAIN (P.N.G.)

SOLOMON ISLANDS

Honiara ⊛

Coral Sea

VANUATU

Port-Vila ⊛

NEW CALEDONIA (FR.)

NORFOLK ISLAND (AUSTRAL.)

PACIFIC OCEAN

FIJI

Suva ⊛

INDIAN OCEAN

North West Cape

Carnarvon

Geraldton

Perth ⊛

Albany

Kalgoorlie

WESTERN AUSTRALIA

GREAT SANDY DESERT

GIBSON DESERT

GREAT VICTORIA DESERT

NULLARBOR PLAIN

Great Australian Bight

Darwin ⊛

NORTHERN TERRITORY

MacDONNELL RANGES

Alice Springs

MUSGRAVE RANGES

SIMPSON DESERT

Lake Eyre

SOUTH AUSTRALIA

AUSTRALIA

Port Augusta

Whyalla

Spencer Gulf

Adelaide ⊛

Cape York Peninsula

Great Barrier Reef

QUEENSLAND

Mount Isa

Townsville

Rockhampton

GREAT ARTESIAN BASIN

Toowoomba

Brisbane ⊛

Darling River

Ipswich

Broken Hill

NEW SOUTH WALES

Bathurst

Wagga Wagga

Murray River

Newcastle

Sydney ⊛

Wollongong

Port Kembla

Canberra ⊛

Mt. Kosciusko (7,316 ft.; 2,230 m)

GREAT DIVIDING RANGE

VICTORIA

Bendigo

Ballarat

Geelong

Melbourne ⊛

Bass Strait

TASMANIA

Launceston

Hobart ⊛

Tasman Sea

NEW ZEALAND

North Cape

Whangarei

Auckland

NORTH ISLAND

Hamilton

Gisborne

Napier

Wellington ⊛

Cook Strait

SOUTH ISLAND

Southern Alps

Mt. Cook (12,349 ft.; 3,764 m)

Christchurch

Dunedin

Invercargill

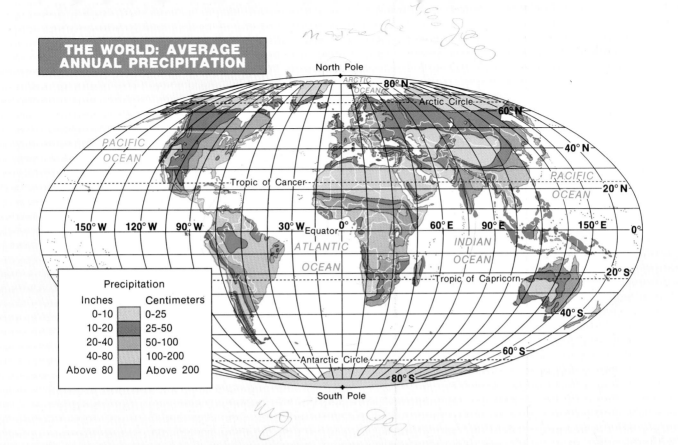

THE WORLD: AVERAGE ANNUAL PRECIPITATION

North Pole

80° N
Arctic Circle
60° N
40° N
PACIFIC OCEAN
Tropic of Cancer
PACIFIC OCEAN
20° N
150° W   120° W   90° W   30° W Equator 0°   60° E   90° E   150° E   0°
ATLANTIC OCEAN
INDIAN OCEAN
Tropic of Capricorn
20° S
40° S
Antarctic Circle
60° S
80° S
South Pole

Precipitation

Inches	Centimeters
0-10	0-25
10-20	25-50
20-40	50-100
40-80	100-200
Above 80	Above 200

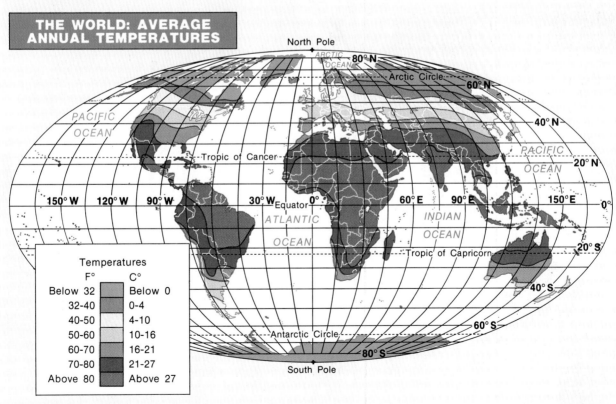

THE WORLD: AVERAGE ANNUAL TEMPERATURES

North Pole

80° N
Arctic Circle
60° N
40° N
PACIFIC OCEAN
Tropic of Cancer
PACIFIC OCEAN
20° N
150° W   120° W   90° W   30° W Equator 0°   60° E   90° E   150° E   0°
ATLANTIC OCEAN
INDIAN OCEAN
Tropic of Capricorn
20° S
40° S
Antarctic Circle
60° S
80° S
South Pole

Temperatures

F°	C°
Below 32	Below 0
32-40	0-4
40-50	4-10
50-60	10-16
60-70	16-21
70-80	21-27
Above 80	Above 27

705

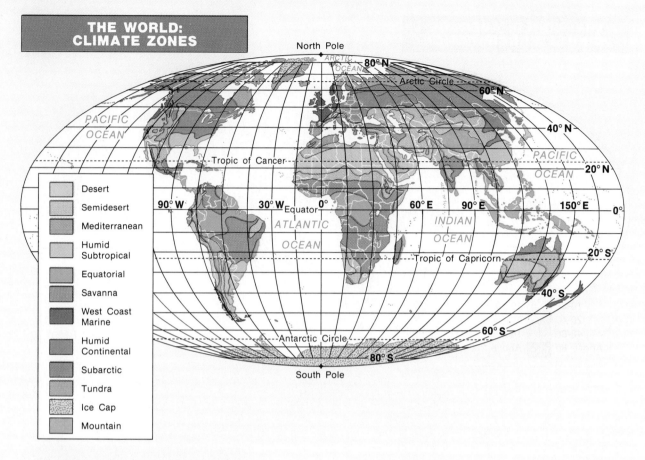

North Pole

ARCTIC
OCEAN

80° N

Arctic Circle

60° N

40° N

PACIFIC
OCEAN

PACIFIC
OCEAN

Tropic of Cancer

20° N

90° W

30° W

Equator

0°

60° E

90° E

150° E

0°

ATLANTIC
OCEAN

INDIAN
OCEAN

Tropic of Capricorn

20° S

40° S

Antarctic Circle

60° S

80° S

South Pole

	Desert
	Semidesert
	Mediterranean
	Humid Subtropical
	Equatorial
	Savanna
	West Coast Marine
	Humid Continental
	Subarctic
	Tundra
	Ice Cap
	Mountain

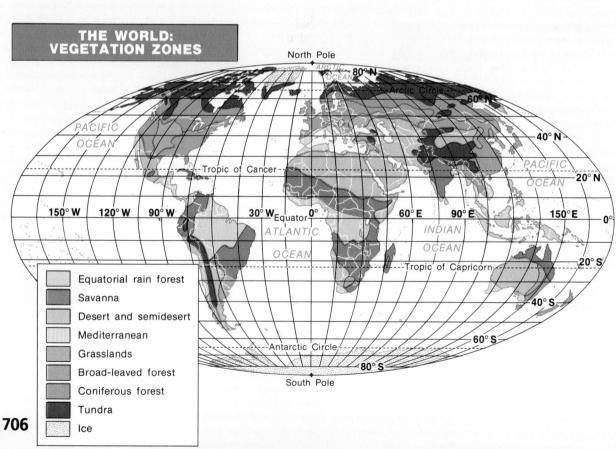

THE WORLD: VEGETATION ZONES

North Pole

ARCTIC
OCEAN

80° N

Arctic Circle

60° N

40° N

PACIFIC
OCEAN

PACIFIC
OCEAN

Tropic of Cancer

20° N

150° W

120° W

90° W

30° W

Equator

0°

60° E

90° E

150° E

0°

ATLANTIC
OCEAN

INDIAN
OCEAN

Tropic of Capricorn

20° S

40° S

Antarctic Circle

60° S

80° S

South Pole

	Equatorial rain forest
	Savanna
	Desert and semidesert
	Mediterranean
	Grasslands
	Broad-leaved forest
	Coniferous forest
	Tundra
	Ice

706

The Gazetteer is a geographical dictionary. It shows latitude and longitude for cities and certain other places. Latitude and longitude are shown in this form: 9°N/39°E. This means "9 degrees north latitude and 39 degrees east longitude." The page reference tells where each entry may be found on a map.

Some words in this book may be new to you or difficult to pronounce. Those words have been spelled phonetically in parentheses. The syllable that receives stress in a word is shown in small capital letters.

For example: **Chicago** (shuh KAH goh)

Most phonetic spellings are easy to read. In the following Pronunciation Key, you can see how letters are used to show different sounds.

PRONUNCIATION KEY

a	after	(AF tur)	oh	flow	(floh)	ch	chicken	(CHIHK un)
ah	father	(FAH thhur)	oi	boy	(boi)	g	game	(gaym)
ai	care	(kair)	oo	rule	(rool)	ing	coming	(KUM ing)
aw	dog	(dawg)	or	horse	(hors)	j	job	(jahb)
ay	paper	(PAY pur)	ou	cow	(kou)	k	came	(kaym)
						ng	long	(lawng)
e	letter	(LET ur)	yoo	few	(fyoo)	s	city	(SIHT ee)
ee	eat	(eet)	u	taken	(TAY kun)	sh	ship	(shihp)
				matter	(MAT ur)	th	thin	(thihn)
ih	trip	(trihp)	uh	ago	(uh GOH)	thh	feather	(FETHH ur)
eye	idea	(eye DEE uh)				y	yard	(yahrd)
y	hide	(hyd)				z	size	(syz)
ye	lie	(lye)				zh	division	(duh VIHZH un)

Abidjan (ab uh JAHN). Former capital of Côte d'Ivoire. Located on the Gulf of Guinea. (5°N/4°W) p. 525.

Abuja (ah BOO juh). Officially replaced Lagos as the capital of Nigeria in 1992. Located in central Nigeria. (9°N/7°E) p. 525.

Acapulco (ah kuh POOL koh). Seaport and international resort located in Mexico, on the Pacific Ocean. (17°N/100°W) p. 132.

Accra (uh KRA). Capital of and most populated city in Ghana. Port city located on the Atlantic Ocean. (6°N/0° long.) p. 525.

Addis Ababa (AD ihs AB uh buh). Capital of and most populated city in Ethiopia. Located at an elevation of 7,900 ft (2,408 m). (9°N/39°E) p. 525.

Adelaide (AD ul ayd). Capital of the Australian state of South Australia. (35°S/139°E) p. 657.

Aden (AHD un). City in Yemen. Located on the Gulf of Aden. (13°N/45°E) p. 389.

Adriatic Sea (ay dree AT ihk see). Arm of the Mediterranean Sea located between Italy and the Balkan Peninsula. p. 257.

Aegean Sea (ee JEE un see). Part of the Mediterranean Sea located between the eastern coast of Greece and the western coast of Turkey. Bounded on the north by the Greek mainland and on the south by Crete. p. 257.

Ahaggar Mountains (uh HAHG ur MOUNT unz). High plateau region in the central Sahara. p. 535.

Alexandria (aligh AZN dree uh). Second most populated city in Egypt. Located in the Nile Delta. (31°N/30°E) p. 547.

Algiers (al GIHRZ). Capital of Algeria. Located on the Mediterranean Sea. (37°N/3°E) p. 525.

Alma-Ata (al muh uh TAH). Capital of Kazakhstan. Located near the borders of Kyrgyzstan and China. (43°N/77°E) p. 372.

Alps (alps). Mountain system extending in an arc from the Mediterranean coast between Italy and France through Switzerland and Austria. p. 255.

Amazon River (AM uh zahn RIHV ur). Second longest river in the world. Tributaries rise in the Andes Mountains and Guiana Highlands. Flows into the Atlantic near Belém, Brazil. p. 171.

American Samoa (uh MER ih kun suh MOH uh). Group of islands of Samoa. Located in the southwestern Pacific Ocean. (14°S/171°W) p. 637.

Amman (AH mahn). Capital of Jordan. (32°N/36°E) p. 389.

Amritsar (ahm RIHT sur). City in northern India. Holy city in the Sikh religion. (31°N/75°E) p. 481.

Amsterdam (AM stur dam). Capital of and most populated city in the Netherlands. Connected to the North Sea by canals. (52°N/5°E) p. 257.

Anatolia (an uh TOH lee uh). Peninsula on which Asian Turkey is located. Lies between the Black and Mediterranean seas. p. 499.

Andes (AN deez). High mountains that stretch north to south along the western part of South America. Highest peak is Mount Aconcagua, with an elevation of 22,834 ft (6,960 m). p. 171.

Angel Falls (AYN jul fawlz). World's highest waterfall, 3,212 ft (979 m) high. Located in southeastern Venezuela. (6°N/63°W) p. 178.

Ankara (ANG kuh ruh). Capital of Turkey. (40°N/33°E) p. 492.

Annamese Mountains (an uh MEEZ MOUNT unz). Range of mountains that runs almost the entire length of western Vietnam and into Laos. p. 444.

Antananarivo (an tuh nan uh REE voh). Capital of Madagascar. (19°S/48°E) p. 525.

Antarctic Peninsula (ant AHRK tihk puh NIHN suh luh). Peninsula in Antarctica that extends toward South America. p. 675.

Antofagasta (ahn taw fuh GAHS tuh). Port city located in northern Chile. (24°S/70°W) p. 219.

Antwerp (ANT wurp). Chief port of Belgium. Located on the Schelde River, about 50 miles (80 km) from the North Sea. (51°N/4°E) p. 296.

Apennines (AP uh nynz). Mountains in Italy. Extend from northwestern Italy to the southern tip of the Italian peninsula. p. 255.

Appalachian Mountains (ap uh LAY chun MOUNT unz). Chain of mountains stretching from Canada to Alabama. p. 65.

Arabian Peninsula (uh RAY bee un puh NIHN suh luh). Large peninsula located east of the Red Sea. p. 387.

Arctic Ocean (AHRK tihk OH shun). Large body of water north of the Arctic Circle. p. 65.

Arequipa (ah ruh KEE puh). Important city in southern Peru. (16°S/72°W) p. 204.

Ashkhabad (ASH kuh bad). Capital of Turkmenistan. Located near the country's southern border with Iran. (38°N/58°E) p. 372.

Asunción (ah soon SYOHN). Capital of Paraguay. Located on the Paraguay River. (25°S/58°W). p. 219.

Aswan (ahs WAHN). Egyptian city known in ancient times as Syene. Located on the Nile River. Site of Aswan High Dam. (24°N/33°E) p. 541.

Atacama Desert (ah tah KAH mah DEZ urt). Very dry area that covers about one third of Chile. Major source of nitrates. p. 212.

Athens (ATH unz). City-state in ancient Greece. Capital of and largest city in modern Greece. (38°N/24°E) p. 257.

Atlantic Ocean (at LAN tihk OH shun). Large body of water separating North America and South America from Europe and Africa. pp. 688-689.

Atlas Mountains (AT lus MOUNT unz). Mountain system located in Morocco, Algeria, and Tunisia, along the northern edge of the Sahara. p. 523.

Auckland (AWK lund). Seaport in northern New Zealand. (37°S/175°E) p. 657.

Baghdad (BAG dad). Capital of and most populated city in Iraq. Located on the Tigris River. (33°N/44°E) p. 389.

Baku (bah KOO). Capital of Azerbaijan. Located on a peninsula in the Caspian Sea. (40°N/50°E) p. 372.

Balkan Peninsula (BAWL kun puh NIHN suh luh). Peninsula in southeastern Europe. Usually thought to consist of Greece, Albania, Bulgaria, Romania, the former Yugoslavia, and European Turkey. p. 255.

Baltic Sea (BAWL tihk see). Part of the Atlantic Ocean, south and southeast of Sweden. p. 257.

Bangkok (BANG kahk). Capital of and most populated city in Thailand. Located on the Chao Phraya River. (14°N/101°E) p. 389.

Bangui (bahng GEE). Capital city of the Central African Republic. Located on the Ubangi River. (4°N/19°E) p. 525.

Barcelona (bahr suh LOH nuh). Important Mediterranean port city in northeastern Spain. (41°N/2°E) p. 325.

Barents Sea (BAR unts see). Part of the Arctic Ocean north of Norway and of the European portion of Russia. p. 257.

Basel (BAH zul). City in Switzerland. Located on both sides of the Rhine River. (48°N/8°E) p. 302.

Basra (BUS ruh). City in Iraq. Country's main port for oil exportation. (31°N/48°E). p. 510.

Bavaria (buh VER ee uh). Region in the foothills of Germany. The capital is Munich. p. 302.

Bay of Bengal (bay uv ben GAWL). Part of the Indian Ocean between the eastern coast of India and the Malay Peninsula. p. 389.

Beijing (BAY jing). Capital of China. Formerly known as Peking. (40°N/116°E) p. 389.

Beira (BAY ruh). Seaport on the southeastern coast of Mozambique. (20°S/35°E) p. 616.

Beirut (bay ROOT). Capital of Lebanon. Located on the eastern shore of the Mediterranean Sea. (34°N/35°E) p. 389.

Belfast (BEL fast). Port city on the eastern coast of Northern Ireland. (55°N/6°W). p. 270.

Belgrade (BEL grayd). Capital of Serbia and the former Yugoslavia. Located where the Sava River joins the Danube River. (45°N/21°E) p. 350.

Belo Horzionte (BAY loh hor uh ZAHN tee). Large industrial city in eastern Brazil. (20°S/44°W) p. 235.

Benares (buh NAH reez). Indian holy city. Located on the Ganges River. Now called Varanasi. (25°N/83°E) p. 481.

Benghazi (ben GAH zee). Port city in Libya. Located on the shore of the Gulf of Sidra. (32°N/20°E) p. 547.

Bering Sea (BER ing see). Part of the North Pacific Ocean bounded on the east by the Alaskan mainland and on the south and southeast by the Aleutian Islands. p. 65.

Bering Strait (BER ing strayt). Narrow body of water connecting the Arctic Ocean and the Bering Sea. Between Russia and Alaska. p. 65.

Berlin (bur LIHN). The capital city of Germany. Berlin is located on the North European Plain. It is the most populated city in Germany. (53°N/13°E) p. 302.

Bern (burn). Capital of Switzerland. (47°N/7°E) p. 257.

Birmingham (BUR ming ham). Second most populated city in the United Kingdom. (53°N/2°W) p. 270.

Bishkek (BISH kek). Capital of Kyrgyzstan. Formerly called Frunze. Located near the border of Kazakhstan. (43°N/75°E) p. 372.

Black Sea (blak see). Large sea bounded by the Ukraine on the north, Russia and Georgia on the east, Turkey on the south, and Bulgaria and Romania on the west. p. 356.

Blue Nile (bloo nyl). River that flows from northern Ethiopia and joins with the White Nile at Khartoum, Sudan. p. 541.

Bogotá (boh guh TAH). Capital of and most populated city in Colombia. Located at 8,563 ft (2,610 m) on a plateau in the Andes Mountains. (5°N/75°W) p. 173.

Bombay (bahm BAY). Indian port city on the Arabian Sea. (19°N/73°E) p. 481.

Bonn (bahn). City in Germany. Located on the Rhine River. (51°N/7°E) p. 257.

Borneo (BOR nee oh). Large island in the East Indies, southwest of the Philippines. p. 389.

Bosporus (BAHS puh rus). Narrow body of water separating European Turkey from Asian Turkey. Connects the Black Sea and the Sea of Marmara. p. 499.

Boston (BAWS tun). Capital of and most populated city in Massachusetts. Important port city. (42°N/71°W) p. 67.

Brahmaputra River (brahm uh POO truh RIHV ur). River that rises in southwestern Tibet and flows south into Bangladesh. Joins the Ganges River near Dacca, India, and flows into the Bay of Bengal. p. 387.

Brasília (bruh ZIHL yuh). Capital of Brazil. Located at the southern edge of the Brazilian Highlands. (16°S/48°W) p. 173.

Brazilian Highlands (bruh ZIHL yun HYE lundz). Highland area located in southeastern Brazil. p. 171.

Brazzaville (BRAH zuh vihl). River port and capital of the Congo. Located on the Zaire River. (4°S/15°E) p. 525.

Brisbane (BRIHZ bayn). Capital of the Australian state of Queensland. Port city located on the eastern coast. (28°S/153°E) p. 657.

Brussels (BRUS ulz). Capital of Belgium. Located on the Senne River. (52°N/4°E) p. 257.

Bucharest (boo kuh REST). Capital of Romania. Located on a tributary of the Danube River. (44°N/26°E) p. 257.

Budapest (BOOD uh pest). Capital of Hungary. Located on both sides of the Danube River. (48°N/19°E) p. 257.

Buenos Aires (BWAY nus ER eez). Capital of and most populated city in Argentina. Located on the estuary of the Río de la Plata. (35°S/58°W) p. 173.

Buffalo (BUF uh loh). City in New York. Located on Lake Erie and the Niagara River. (43°N/79°W) p. 84.

Bulawayo (boo luh WAH yoh). Industrial city in southwestern Zimbabwe. (20°S/29°E) p. 616.

Cabinda (kuh BIHN duh). Territory of Angola, located on the western coast of Africa. Separated from Angola by part of Zaire. p. 525.

Cairo (KYE roh). Capital of Egypt. Most populated city in Africa. Located on the eastern side of the Nile River. (30°N/31°E) p. 525.

Calcutta (kal KUT uh). Port city in northeastern India. (23°N/88°E) p. 481.

Calgary (KAL guh ree). City in the province of Alberta in the prairie region of southwestern Canada. Third largest city in Canada. (51°N/114°W) p. 81.

Callao (kuh YAH oh). Seaport in western Peru. (12°S/77°W) p. 204.

Canadian Shield (kuh NAY dee un sheeld). Upland region of western Canada that extends in a horseshoe shape from the Labrador coast to the Arctic Ocean west of Victoria Island. p. 74.

Canary Islands (kuh NER ee EYE lundz). Islands off the northwest coast of Africa that belong to Spain. p. 525.

Canberra (KAN bur uh). Capital of Australia. Located in the southeast. (35°S/149°E) p. 637.

Cancún (kan KOON). Large tourist resort located at the eastern tip of the Yucatan Peninsula in Mexico. (21°N/87°W) p. 132.

Cape Agulhas (kayp uh GUL us). Southernmost point of Africa. Located at 20°E longitude, which serves as the dividing line between the Indian and Atlantic oceans. (35°S/20°E) p. 523.

Cape of Good Hope (kayp uv good hohp). Cape located on the southwestern coast of South Africa. (34°S/18°E) p. 523.

Cape Town (kayp toun). Port city on the southwestern coast of South Africa. (34°S/18°E) p. 616.

Caracas (kuh RAHK us). Capital of and most populated city in Venezuela. (11°N/67°W) p. 173.

Caribbean Sea (kar uh BEE un see). Part of the Atlantic Ocean that is bounded by South America on the south, Central America on the west, and Cuba, Puerto Rico, and other islands on the north and east. p. 67.

Carpathian Mountains (kahr PAY thee un MOUNT unz). Mountain range that stretches from the Alps in the west to the Balkans in the east. p. 255.

Casablanca (kas uh BLANG kuh). Seaport in northwestern Morocco. Located on the Atlantic Ocean. (34°N/8°W) p. 547.

Caspian Sea (KAS pee un see). Largest inland body of water in the world. Surrounded by Azerbaijan, Russia, Kazakhstan, Turkmenistan, and Iran. p. 356.

Caucasus Mountains (KAW kuh sus MOUNT unz). Mountains located between the Caspian Sea and Black Sea. Highest peak is Mount Elbrus, with an elevation of 18,481 ft (5,633 m). p. 356.

Cayenne (kye EN). Capital of French Guiana. Located on an island in the Cayenne River. (5°N/52°W) p. 173.

Central America (SEN trul uh MER ih kuh). Area that is made up of the countries of Guatemala, El Salvador, Honduras, Nicaragua, Costa Rica, Panama, and Belize. p. 159.

Chaco (CHAH koh). Semiarid plains of the Paraná and Paraguay rivers. p. 171.

Chang Jiang (chahng jee AHNG). Longest river in China. Starts in the central part of the country. Winds eastward before it empties into the East China Sea. p. 420.

Chao Phraya River (CHOU prah YSH RIHV ur). Thailand's most important river. Flows out of the mountains of Laos and empties into the Gulf of Thailand. p. 444.

Chicago (shuh KAH goh). Third most populated city in the United States. Located in Illinois, at the southern tip of Lake Michigan. (42°N/88°W) p. 67.

Chihuahua (chih WAH wah). Capital city of the state of Chihuahua, in northern Mexico. (29°N/106°W) p. 132.

Chisinau (kee shih NOU). Romanian form of name for capital of Moldova. The Russian form is Kishinev. (47°N/29°E) p. 372.

Christchurch (KRYST CHURCH). City in New Zealand. Located on South Island. (44°S/173°E) p. 657.

Ciudad Guayana (syoo DAHD gwuh YAHN uh). City in eastern Venezuela. Located where the Orinoco and Caroní rivers join. (8°N/63°W) p. 188.

Cologne (kuh LOHN). Manufacturing and commercial city in Germany. Located on the western bank of the Rhine River. (51°N/7°E). p. 302.

Colombo (kuh LUM boh). Capital and seaport of Sri Lanka. Located near the mouth of the Kelani River, on the Indian Ocean. (7°N/80°E) p. 389.

Columbia River (kuh LUM bee uh RIHV ur). River that rises in the Rocky Mountains in Canada and flows into the Pacific Ocean along the Washington-Oregon boundary. p. 65.

Comoros (KAHM uh roh). Country of volcanic islands located in the Indian Ocean off the southeastern coast of Africa. p. 525.

Congo River (KAHNg goh RIHV ur). River that rises in southeastern Zaire as the Lualaba River. Flows into the Atlantic Ocean at Matadi, Zaire. Now called the Zaire River. p. 523.

Copenhagen (koh pun HAY gun). Capital of and largest city in Denmark. An important port. (56°N/13°E) p. 257.

Córdoba (KOR doh buh). Second most populated city in Argentina. Located on the western edge of the Pampas. (31°S/164°W) p. 219.

Crete (kreet). Largest island in Greece. Located in the Mediterranean Sea. p. 334.

Cuzco (KOOS koh). City in the Andes of Peru. Was the capital of the Inca Empire. (14°S/72°W) p. 204.

Dacca (DAHK uh). Capital of Bangladesh. Located in west central Bangladesh. (24°N/90°E) p. 389.

Dakar (duh KAHR). Capital and port city of Senegal. Located in western Africa. (15°N/17°W) p. 525.

Damascus (duh MAS kus). Capital of and most populated city in Syria. (33°N/36°E) p. 389.

Danakil Plain (DAN uh kihl playn). Desert region located in East Africa, mostly in the Great Rift Valley. Inhabited by the Danakil people. p. 588.

Danube River (DAN yoob RIHV ur). Second longest river in Europe. Begins in the Alps and flows into the Black Sea in Romania. p. 255.

Dardanelles (dahr duh NELZ). Narrow strait in Turkey, connecting the Sea of Marmara and the Aegean Sea. p. 499.

Dar es Salaam (dahr es suh LAHM). Main port of Tanzania. Located on the Indian Ocean. (7°S/39°E) p. 525.

Darling River (DAHR ling). River in southeastern Australia. Flows southwest into the Murray River. p. 644.

Darwin (DAHR wihn). Capital of Northern Territory, Australia. Port city located on the Timor Sea. (12°S/131°E) p. 657.

Dead Sea (ded see). Salt lake located on the border between Israel and Jordan. (32°N/36°E) p. 492.

Deccan Plateau (DEK un pla TOH). Peninsula of India, between the Eastern Ghats and Western Ghats. p. 464.

Delhi (DEL ee). City in India. Once the capital of Mogul India. (29°N/77°E) p. 481.

Denver (DEN vur). Capital of and most populated city in Colorado. (40°N/105°W) p. 67.

Detroit (dih TROIT). Important industrial city in Michigan. Located on the Detroit River, near Lake Erie. (42°N/83°W) p. 67.

Dinaric Alps (dih NAR ihk alps). Range of the eastern Alps that runs along the Adriatic coast of the former Yugoslavia and northern Albania. p. 340.

Djibouti (jih BOOT ee). Capital of the country of Djibouti. Located on the Gulf of Aden. (12°N/43°E) p. 525.

Dnieper River (NEE pur RIHV ur). River in Europe. Rises in the Valdai Hills of Russia and flows through Belarus and Ukraine and into the Black Sea. p. 356.

Donets Basin (duh NETS BAYS un). Important coal producing and industrial area in the lower valley of the Donets River. The river flows mostly in the Ukraine. p. 373.

Don River (dahn RIHV ur). River in Russia. Connected by canal to the Volga River. p. 356.

Drakensberg Mountains (DRAH kenz burg MOUNT unz). Range of mountains that extends north along the southeastern edge of Africa. Located in the Karroo region. p. 523.

Dresden (DREZ dun). Industrial city in German Located on the Elbe River. (51°N/14°E) p. 302.

Dublin (DUB lun). Capital and port city of Ireland. Located on the Irish Sea. (53°N/6°W) p. 270.

Dushanbe (doo SHAM buh). Capital of Tajikistan. Located near border of Uzbekistan. (39°N/69°E) p. 372.

Eastern Ghats (EES turn gawts). Mountains located along eastern coast of India. p. 464.

Ebro River (AY broh RIHV ur). River in northern Spain. Flows southeast and empties into the Mediterranean. p. 325.

Edinburgh (ED un bur uh). Capital of Scotland. Located in the southeastern part of the country. (56°N/3°W) p. 270.

Edmonton (ED mun tun). Capital of the province of Alberta. (54°N/113°W) p. 81.

Elbe River (el buh RIHV ur). River in Europe rises in the Czech Republic, flows through Germany, and empties into the North Sea. p. 255.

Elburz Mountains (el BOORZ MOUNT unz). Mountains in northern Iran that separate the Iranian Plateau from the Caspian Sea. Highest peak is Mount Damavand, with an elevation of 18,934 ft (5,771 m). p. 492.

English Channel (ING glihsh CHAN ul). Narrow body of water separating the southern edge of the island of Great Britain from France. p. 255.

Equator (ee KWAYT ur). Line drawn on maps at 0° latitude. Circles the earth halfway between the North pole and the South Pole. p. 6.

Euphrates River (yoo FRAYT eez RIHV ur). River that rises in the mountains of eastern Turkey and flows through Syria into Iraq. Joins with the Tigris River to form the Shatt-al-Arab, which flows into the Persian Gulf. p. 492.

Falkland Islands (FAWK lund EYE lundz). Located in the South Atlantic Ocean, east of the southern tip of South America. p. 173.

Fertile Crescent (FURT ul KRES unt). Stretch of land from Jericho to Ebla through Mesopotamia. p. 36.

Fiji (FEE jee). Country formed by a group of islands north of New Zealand, in the southwestern Pacific (between 16° and 19°S and 178°W and 177°E). p. 637.

Florence (FLOR uns). City in Italy. Located on the Arno River at the base of the Apennines. (44°N/11°E). p. 330.

Fraser River (FRAY zur RIHV ur). River that rises in the Canadian Rockies and flows into the Pacific Ocean near Vancouver, British Columbia. p. 74.

Gaborone (gah buh ROH nay). Capital of Botswana. Located in the southeastern part of the country. (25°S/26°E) p. 525.

Ganges River (GAN jeez RIHV ur). Sacred river of India. Rises in the Himalayas. Joined by the Brahmaputra River near Dacca before flowing into the Bay of Bengal. p. 464.

Gdańsk (guh DAHNSK). Important port city in Poland. Located on the Baltic Sea. Formerly called Danzig. (45°N/19°E) p. 350.

Genoa (JEN uh wuh). City in Italy. One of the most important Italian seaports. (44°N/8°E) p. 330.

Georgetown (JORJ toun). Capital and chief port of Guyana. (7°N/58°W) p. 173.

Giza (GEE zuh). City in northern Egypt, near Cairo. Site of the Great Pyramid. (30°N/31°E) p. 547.

Glasgow (GLAS koh). Most populated city in Scotland. Important port located in the west-central part of the country. (56°N/4°W) p. 270.

Gobi Desert (GOH bee DEZ urt). Dry area located in the country of Mongolia and in the Inner Mongolian region of northern China. p. 387.

Gold Coast (gohld kohst). Coast of the Gulf of Guinea between the Ivory Coast and the Slave Coast. Named for large amounts of gold once mined in the area. p. 565.

Grand Canyon (grand KAN yun). Gorge in the Colorado River where the river flows across the northwstern corner of Arizona. More than 1 mi (2 km) deep in places. (36°N/112°W) p. 99.

Great Barrier Reef (grayt BAR ee ur reef). World's largest deposit of coral. Located in the Coral Sea off the northeastern coast of Australia. p. 644.

Great Dividing Range (grayt duh VYD ing raynj). Mountain area of Australia. Extends from north to south along most of the eastern coast. Highest peak is Mount Kosciusko, at 7,316 ft (2,230 m). p. 644.

Greater Antilles (GRAYT ur an TIHL eez). Group of islands in the West Indies. Includes the islands of Cuba, Jamaica, Puerto Rico, and Hispaniola. p. 146.

Great Lakes (grayt layks). Chain of five large lakes—Superior, Michigan, Huron, Erie, and Ontario. Located in central North America, mostly along the border between Canada and the United States. p. 67.

Great Plains (grayt playnz). Elevated plains region east of the Rockies. Extends from northeastern British Columbia and northwestern Alberta in Canada south to western Texas. p. 65.

Greenland (GREEN lund). Large island belonging to Denmark. Located off the northeastern coast of North America. Largest island in the world except for the continent of Australia. p. 67.

Greenwich (GREN ihch). A borough of Greater London in southeastern England. The Prime Meridian, which divides the globe into the Eastern and Western hemispheres, passes through this city. (51°N/0° long.) p. 6.

Guadalajara (gwah duh uh HAHR uh). Second most populated city in Mexico. Located in central Mexico. (21°N/103°W) p. 132.

Guam (gwahm). Largest of the Mariana Islands. Located in the western Pacific Ocean. Territory of the United States. (13°N/145°E) p. 637.

Guanajuato (gwah nah HWAH toh). Rich mining center, especially for silver, in Mexico. (21°N/101°W) p. 132.

Guangzhou (GUAHNG joh). Major port city in southeastern China. Located near the mouth of the Xi Jiang (West River). (23°N/113°E) p. 423.

Guatemala City (gwah tuh MAH luh SIHT ee). Capital city of Guatemala. Largest city in Central Amercia. (15°N/91°W) p. 159.

Guayaquil (gwye ah KEEL). Most populated city and chief port of Ecuador. (2°S/80°W) p. 204.

Guiana Highlands (gee AN uh HYE lundz). Area of low mountains and hills in northern South America. Stretches from eastern Venezuela across northern Brazil, Guyana, Suriname, and French Guiana. p. 171.

Gulf of Aden (gulf uv AHD un). Part of the Arabian Sea located between Africa's Somalia and the Arabian Peninsula. p. 387.

Gulf of Mexico (gulf uv MEKS ih koh). Body of water bordered by the United States, Mexico, and Cuba. p. 67.

Gulf of Thailand (gulf uv TYE land). Inlet of South China Sea. Mostly in Thailand, although its southeastern shore is formed by Cambodia and Vietnam. Often called the Gulf of Siam. p. 444.

Gulf of Tonkin (gulf uv TAHN kihn). Arm of the South China Sea, east of Vietnam. p. 389.

Halifax (HAL uh faks). Capital of Nova Scotia, Canada. Located on the Atlantic Ocean. (45°N/64°W) p. 81.

Hamburg (HAM burg). Port city on the Elbe River in Germany. The country's second largest city. (54°N/10°E) p. 296.

Hanoi (hah NOI). Capital of Vietnam. (21°N/106°E) p. 389.

Harare (hah RAH ree). Capital of Zimbabwe. (18°S/31°E) p. 525.

Havana (huh VAN uh). Capital of Cuba and most populated city in the West Indies. (23°N/82°W) p. 67.

Hawaiian Islands (huh WAH ee un EYE lundz). Group of islands in the North Pacific. State of the United States. Largest island is Hawaii. p. 99.

Helsinki (HEL sing kee). Capital and seaport of Finland. Located on the Gulf of Finland. (60°N/25°E) p. 257.

Hermosillo (er moh SEE yoh). City in northwestern Mexico. (29°N/111°W) p. 132.

Himalayas (hihm uh LAY uz). World's highest mountain system. Located in central Asia. Mount Everest—at 29,028 ft (8,848 m), the highest peak in the world—is located in the Himalayas. p. 387.

Hindu Kush (HIHN doo kush). Mountain range located mostly in Afghanistan. p. 387.

Hiroshima (hihr uh SHEE muh). Industrial city in Japan. City was destroyed by an atomic bomb on August 6, 1945, the first time an atomic bomb was ever used in warfare. (34°N/132°E) p. 413.

Hispaniola (hihs pun YOH luh). Second largest island in the West Indies. p. 695.

Hobart (HOH burt). Capital of the Australian state of Tasmania. (43°S/147°E) p. 657.

Ho Chi Minh City (HOH CHEE MIHN SIHT ee). City formerly called Saigon. Name was changed in 1975 after the Communist takeover of South Vietnam. (11°N/107°E) p. 389.

Hokkaido (hoh KYE doh). Northernmost of the four main islands of Japan. p. 398.

Hong Kong (HAHNG KAHNG). Former British colony in southeastern China. Hong Kong returned to China in 1997. (22°N/114°E) p. 423.

Honshu (HAHN shoo). Largest of Japan's four major islands. Site of many of the country's most populated cities, including Tokyo, Osaka, and Yokohama. p. 398.

Houston (HYOOS tun). Most populated city in Texas and fourth most populated city in the United States. (30°N/95°W) p. 67.

Huancavelica (wahn kuh vuh LEE kuh). Town in Peru, southeast of Lima. (13°S/75°W) p. 204.

Huang He (HWAHNG HIH). Chinese river sometimes called the Yellow River. Rises in the mountains of Xijang and flows into the Yellow Sea. p. 420.

Hudson Bay (HUD sun bay). Large body of water in Canada that is connected with the Atlantic Ocean by the Hudson Strait. p. 67.

Hungarian Plain (hung GER ee un playn). Large plain located mostly in Hungary. The Danube River crosses it. p. 340.

Ibadan (ee BAH dahn). City in southwestern Nigeria. (7°N/4°E) p. 525.

Iberian Peninsula (eye BIHR ee un puh NIHN suh luh). European peninsula southeast of the Pyrenees. Spain and Portugal are on this peninsula. p. 325.

Indian Ocean (IHN dee un OH shun). Large body of water between Africa and Australia. p. 387.

Indus River (IHN dus RIHV ur). River that rises in the Himalayas in Tibet. Flows northwest through the northern tip of India and then southwest through Pakistan to the Arabian Sea. p. 387.

Iquitos (ee KEE tohs). City and port located on the Amazon River, in northeastern Peru. (4°S/73°W) p. 204.

Irian Jaya (ihr ee AHN JAH yuh). Province of Indonesia that covers the western half of New Guinea and some nearby small islands. p. 444.

Irkutsk (ihr KOOTSK). City in Siberia. Located near Lake Baikal and the Lena River. (52°N/104°E) p. 389.

Irrawaddy River (ihr uh WAH dee RIHV ur). River that forms in upper Myanmar. Flows south through Myanmar into Bay of Bengal, near Rangoon. p. 387.

Islamabad (ihs LAHM uh bahd). Capital of Pakistan. Located in the northeastern part of the country. (34°N/73°E) p. 389.

Istanbul (ihs tan BOOL). Most populated city in Turkey. Located on both sides of the Strait of Bosporus. Part of the city is in Europe and part is in Asia. Formerly called Constantinople. (41°N/29°E) p. 499.

Jakarta (juh KAHR tuh). Capital of Indonesia. One of the world's most populated cities. Located on the northwestern coast of Java. (6°S/107°E) p. 453.

Japanese Alps (jap uh NEEZ alps). Highest mountain range in Japan. Located near the center of the island of Honshu. Mount Fuji, the range's highest peak, rises 12,388 ft (3,776 m) above sea level. p. 398.

Java (JAH vuh). Most populated island in Indonesia. Located between the Java Sea and the Indian Ocean. p. 444.

Jerusalem (juh ROOZ uh lum). Capital of Israel. Holy city for Jews, Christians, and Muslims. (32°N/35°E) p. 499.

Jidda (JIHD uh). Port city in Saudi Arabia. Located on the Red Sea. (22°N/39°E) p. 499.

Johannesburg (joh HAN ihs burg). Second most populated city in South Africa. (26°S/28°E) p. 616.

Jordan River (JORD un RIHV ur). River that rises in Syria. Flows south through the Sea of Galilee into the Dead Sea. p. 506.

Juba River (JOO buh RIHV ur). River that rises in the mountains of south-central Ethiopia. Flows south across southwestern Somalia and empties into the Indian Ocean. p. 588.

Jura Mountains (JOOR uh MOUNT unz). Mountains along the border between France and Switzerland. p. 288.

Jutland Peninsula (JUT lund puh NIHN suh luh). Peninsula located between the North and Baltic seas. Denmark and part of Germany are located on the peninsula. p. 264.

Kabul (KAH bool). Capital and most populated city in Afghanistan. (35°N/69°E) p. 389.

Kalahari Desert (kal uh HAHR ee DEZ urt). Dry plateau region located in Botswana, South Africa, and Namibia. p. 523.

Kampala (kahm PAH luh). Capital of Uganda, in East Africa. (0° lat./32°E) p. 525.

Kansas City (KAN zus SIHT ee). Second largest city in Missouri. (39°N/95°W) p. 115.

Karachi (kuh RAH chee). Most populated city in Pakistan. Formerly the capital. Port city located on the Arabian Sea. (25°N/67°E) p. 481.

Katmandu (kaht mahn DOO). Capital of Nepal. Located in the Himalayas. (28°N/85°E) p. 389.

Khartoum (kahr TOOM). Capital of Sudan. Located where the Blue Nile and White Nile join. (15°N/32°E). p. 525.

Kiev (kee EV). Capital of Ukraine. Located on the Dnieper River. (50°N/31°E) p. 372.

Kingston (KINGZ tun). Capital and chief seaport of Jamaica. (18°N/77°W) p. 67.

Kinshasa (keen SHAH sah). Capital city of Zaire. Located on the Zaire River. Formerly known as Leopoldville. (4°S/15°E) p. 582.

Kjølen Mountains (CHUL un MOUNT unz). Mountains that stretch along the border between northeastern Norway and northwestern Sweden. p. 264.

Kobe (KOH bee). City in the foothills of the Japanese Alps. (35°N/135°E) p. 413.

Korea Strait (kuh REE uh strayt). Channel between South Korea and southwestern Japan. Connects the Sea of Japan with the East China Sea. p. 398.

Kourou (koo ROO). Port city in French Guiana. (5°N/53°W) p. 188.

Kraków (KRA kou). Poland's main industrial city. Located in the southern part of the country, on the Vistula River. (50°N/20°E) p. 350.

Kuala Lumpur (KWAH luh loom POOR). Capital of Malaysia. Located along the Strait of Malacca. Important trading center. (3°N/102°E). p. 389.

Kyushu (kee oo shoo). Southernmost of the four islands of Japan. p. 398.

Lagos (LAY gahs). Former capital of and most populated city in Nigeria. Located on the Gulf of Guinea. (6°N/4°E) p. 525.

Lake Baikal (layk bye KAWL). World's deepest lake, 5,715 ft (1,742 m) deep. Located in Russia. p. 356.

Lake Chad (layk chad). Lake located at the borders of Niger, Chad, Nigeria, and Cameroon. p. 523.

Lake Malawai (layk muh LAH wee). Lake located between Malawi, Tanzania, and Mozambique. Formerly known as Lake Nyassa. p. 523.

Lake Tanganyika (layk tan gun YEE kuh). Lake in east central Africa. Four nations—Tanzania, Zaire, Zambia, and Burundi—have coastlines on this lake, which is 4,710 ft (1,436 m) deep. p. 523.

Lake Victoria (layk vihk TOR ee uh). One of the largest bodies of fresh water in the world. Located in East Africa. Kenya, Uganda, and Tanzania all have coastlines on this lake. p. 523.

La Paz (lah pahs). Capital of and most populated city in Bolivia. Third highest city in the world, at 12,001 ft (3,658 m). (17°S/68°W) p. 173.

Larnaca (LAHR nuh kuh). Important port city in Cyprus. (35°N/34°E) p. 320.

Le Havre (luh HAHV ruh). Major port city in France. Located on the English Channel. (50°N/0° long.) p. 294.

Leipzig (LYP sihg). Industrial city in Germany. Country's tenth largest city. (51°N/12°E) p. 302.

Lesser Antilles (LES ur an TIHL eez). Group of islands in the West Indies. Includes the Virgin Islands, the Leeward Islands, and the Windward Islands. p. 146.

Lhasa (LAH suh). Major city in Xizang, at 11,830 ft (3,606 m). (30°N/30°E) p. 257.

Libreville (LEE bruh veel). Capital and seaport of Gabon. Located on the Gulf of Guinea. (0 ° lat./9°E) p. 525.

Lima (LEE muh). Capital of and most populated city in Peru. (12°S/77°W) p. 173.

Limpopo River (lihm POH poh RIHV ur). River that rises near Johannesburg, South Africa. Flows across Mozambique and empties into the Indian Ocean. p. 616.

Lisbon (LIHZ bun). Capital of Portugal. Mainland Europe's westernmost port city. (39°N/9°W) p. 325.

Liverpool (LIHV ur pool). Port city in northwest England. Hometown of the rock group the Beatles. (53°N/3°W) p. 270.

Ljubljana (lee uh blee AHN uh). Capital of Slovenia. Located on Sava River. (46°N/15°E) p. 350.

London (LUN dun). Capital of and most populated city in the United Kingdom. Located along the Thames River. Major industrial and financial center. (52°N/0° long.) p. 270.

Los Angeles (laws AN juh lus). City in southern California. Located on the Pacific Ocean. Second most populated city in the United States; only New York City has more people. (34°N/118°W) p. 67.

Luanda (loo AHN duh). Capital and seaport of Angola on the Atlantic Ocean. (9°S/13°E) p. 525.

Lusaka (loo SAH kah). Capital of Zambia. Located in central Zambia, in the center of a farming region. (15°S/28°E) p. 525.

Luzon (loo ZAHN). Chief island of the Philippines. Manila is located on this island. p. 444.

Macao (muh KOU). Portuguese colony located in southern China, on the South China Sea. Macao will return to China in 1999. (22°N/113°E) p. 423.

Macdonnell Ranges (muk DAHN ul raynj ihs). Mountains in central Australia. p. 644.

Mackenzie River (muh KEN zee RIHV ur). Canadian river. Source in the Northwest Territories. p. 74.

Madagascar (mad uh GAS kur). Island nation located in the Indian Ocean, off the southeastern coast of Africa. World's fourth largest island, excluding Australia. p. 525.

Madras (muh DRAS). City in India. Main port on the country's southeastern coast. (13°N/80°E) p. 481.

Madrid (muh DRIHD). Capital of Spain. Second most populated city in Western Europe. (40°N/4°W) p. 325.

Malay Peninsula (MAY lay puh NIHN suh luh). Peninsula located in Southeast Asia. Parts of Malaysia and Thailand are on this peninsula. p. 444.

Managua (mah NAH gwah). Capital of and most populated city in Nicaragua. (12°N/86°W) p. 159.

Manaus (mah NOUS). City in rain forest of Brazil. Located on the Negro River, a branch of the Amazon River. (3°S/60°W) p. 235.

Manila (muh NIHL uh). Capital of and most populated city in the Philippines. (15°N/121°E) p. 444.

Maracaibo (mar uh KYE boh). Seaport in northwestern Venezuela. Located between Lake Maracaibo and the Gulf of Venezuela. (11°N/72°W) p. 188.

Marianas (mer ee AN uz). Group of islands located in the western Pacific, east of the Philippines. Except Guam, a commonwealth of the United States. p. 637.

Marquesas Islands (mahr KAY zuhz EYE lundz). Group of islands in the eastern South Pacific. p. 637.

Marseille (mahr SAY). Important port city in southern France. Located on the Mediterranean Sea. (43°N/5°E) p. 294.

Marshall Islands (MAHR shul EYE lundz). Group of islands in the western Pacific, east of the Caroline Islands. Since 1947, part of the United States Trust Territory of the Pacific Islands. p. 637.

Maseru (MAZ uh roo). Capital of Lesotho, a country located within South Africa. (29°S/27°E) p. 616.

Masqat (mus KAT). Capital city of Oman. (24°N/59°E) p. 499.

Matadi (mah TAH dee). Zaire's major port city. Located on the Atlantic Ocean. (6°S/13°E) p. 582.

Mbabane (em buh BAHN). Capital of Swaziland. Located in southeastern Africa. (26°S/31°E) p. 616.

Mecca (MEK uh). City in Saudi Arabia. Birthplace of the prophet Muhammad and a holy city for Muslims. (21°N/40°E) p. 499.

Medellín (may day YEEN). Second most populated city in Colombia. Once the heart of a gold-mining region and an important coffee-growing center. (6°N/76°W) p. 188.

Medina (muh DEE nuh). Holy city in Saudi Arabia. (25°N/40°E) p. 499.

Mediterranean Sea (med ih tuh RAY nee un see). Large body of water surrounded by Europe, Africa, and Asia. p. 255.

Mekong River (MAY kahng RIHV ur). River in Southeast Asia. Rises in Tibet and forms most of the boundary between Thailand and Laos. Flows into the South China Sea. p. 44.

Melanesia (mel uh NEE zhuh). Group of islands in the South Pacific, northeast of Australia. Includes New Guinea, the Solomon Islands, New Caledonia, Vanuatu, and Fiji. p. 637.

Melbourne (MEL burn). Capital of the Australian state of Victoria. Located on Port Phillip Bay on the southeastern coast. (38°S/145°E) p. 657.

Mendoza (men DOH zuh). City located in northwestern Argentina. Important wine-producing and industrial center. (33°S/69°W) p. 219.

Mesopotamia (mes uh puh TAY mee uh). One of the earliest centers of civilization. Located between the Tigris and Euphrates rivers. p. 36.

Meuse River (myooz RIHV ur). River that rises in northeast France. Flows north through Belgium and the Netherlands into the North Sea. p. 288.

Mexico City (MEKS ih koh SIHT ee). Capital of Mexico. Most populated city in the Western Hemisphere. (19°N/99°W) p. 67.

Micronesia (mye kruh NEE zhuh). Several groups of small islands located east of the Philippines. Some of the island groups include the Marianas, the Caroline Islands, and the Marshall Islands. p. 637.

Milan (mih LAN). Important industrial city in northern Italy. Country's second most populated city. (45°N/9°E) p. 330.

Mindanao (mihn duh NOU). Largest and second most populated island in the Philippines. p. 444.

Minneapolis (mihn ee AP ul ihs). Most populated city in Minnesota. (45°N/93°W) p. 67.

Minsk (MIHNSK). Capital of Belarus. Official location for the government of the Commonwealth of Independent States. (54°N/28°E) p. 372.

Mississippi River (mihs uh SIHP ee RIHV ur). Second longest river in the United States. Rises in northern Minnesota and flows into the Gulf of Mexico, near New Orleans, Louisiana. p. 65.

Mogadishu (moh gah DEE shoo). Capital and seaport of Somalia. Located on the Indian Ocean. (2°N/45°E) p. 525.

Mombasa (mahm BAH suh). Port city on the eastern coast of Kenya. (40°S/40°E) p. 594.

Monclova (mawng KLOH vuh). Town in northeastern Mexico. Site of copper, silver, and zinc mines. (27°N/101°W) p. 132.

Mont Blanc (mohn BLAHN). Located in the French Alps, near the border with Italy. Highest peak in the Alps, at 15,781 ft (4,810 m). p. 288.

Monterrey (mahn tuh RAY). Industrial city in Mexico (26°N/100°W) p. 132.

Montevideo (mahnt uh vuh DAY oh). Capital of and most populated city in Uruguay. Located on the Río de la Plata. (35°S/56°W) p. 173.

Montreal (mahn tree AWL). Second most populated city in Canada. Located in the province of Quebec, on Montreal Island in the St. Lawrence River. (46°N/74°W) p. 81.

Moscow (MAHS koh). Capital of Russia and former capital of the Soviet Union. Most populated city in Europe. Located on both sides of the Moskva River. (56°N/38°E) p. 257.

Moselle River (moh ZEL RIHV ur). River in northeastern France and western Germany. Flows into the Rhine River. p. 255.

Mount Aconcagua (mount ah kawn KAH gwuh). Highest mountain in the Western Hemisphere, 22,834 ft (6,960 m) high. Located in the Andes Mountains in Chile. (33°S/70°W) p. 212.

Mount Everest (mount EV ur ihst). Highest peak in the world, with an elevation of 29,028 ft (8,848 m). Located in the Himalayas. (28°N/87°E) p. 387.

Mount Fuji (mount FOO jee). Highest peak in the Japanese Alps, rising 12,388 ft (3,776 m) above sea level. (35°N/139°E) p. 398.

Mount Kenya (mount KEN yuh). Located in central Kenya. Second highest point in Africa, with an elevation of 17,058 ft (5,199 m). (0° lat./37°E) p. 588.

Mount Kilimanjaro (mount kihl uh mun JAHR oh). Highest mountain peak in Africa, at 19,340 ft (5,895 m). Located in northeast Tanzania, near the Kenyan border. (3°S/37°E) p. 588.

Mount Kosciusko (mount kahs ee US koh). Highest peak in the Australian Alps, at 7,316 ft (2,230 m). Located in southeastern Australia. (36°S/148°E) p. 644.

Mount McKinley (mount muh KIHN lee). Highest mountain peak in the United States, 20,320 ft (6,194 m) high. Located in Alaska. (63°N/151°W) p. 65.

Mount Vesuvius (mount vuh SOO vee us). Active volcano in southern Italy. About 4,203 ft (1,281 m) high. Erupted and buried the city of Pompeii in A.D. 79. (41°N/14°E) p. 320.

Munich (MYOO nihk). Industrial city in Germany. (48°N/12°E) p. 302.

Murray River (MUR ee RIHV ur). Most important river in Australia. Rises in the Great Dividing Range. Flows into the Indian Ocean near Adelaide. p. 644.

Nagasaki (nah guh SAH kee). Industrial city and seaport in Japan. Located on the island of Kyushu. Destroyed by an atomic bomb near the end of World War II. (33°N/130°E) p. 413.

Nairobi (nye ROH bee). Capital of and most populated city in Kenya. (1°S/37°E) p. 525.

Namib Desert (NAHM ihb DEZ urt). Dry area along coast of Namibia. p. 523.

Naples (NAY pulz). Important port city in Italy. Located on the Mediterranean Sea. (40°N/15°E) p. 330.

New Caledonia (noo kal uh DOHN yuh). French island in the southwestern Pacific, east of Australia. p. 637.

New Delhi (noo DEL ee). Capital of India. (29°N/77°E) p. 389.

New Guinea (noo GIHN ee). Large island located north of Australia. Western half is part of Indonesia; Eastern half is the country of Papua New Guinea. p. 637.

New York City (noo york SIHT ee). Most populated city in the United States. Located at the mouth of the Hudson River, in the southern part of New York State. One of the world's most important ports. (41°N/74°W) p. 67.

Niagara Falls (nye AG uh ruh fawlz). Great falls of the Niagara River, on the United States-Canada border. Divided by Goat Island into Horseshoe (or Canadian) Falls, 158 ft (48 m) high and 2,600 ft (792 m) wide; and American Falls, 167 ft (51 m) high and 1,000 ft (305 m) wide. p. 65.

Nicosia (nihk oh SEE uh). Capital of Cyprus. (35°N/33°E) p. 334.

Niger River (NYE jur RIHV ur). Rises in Guinea, near Sierra Leone border. Flows into Gulf of Guinea in Nigeria. p. 554.

Nile River (nyl RIHV ur). Longest river in the world at 3,473 miles (5,588 km). Flows into the Mediterranean Sea at Alexandria, Egypt. p. 541.

North European Plain (north yoor uh PEE un playn). Large area of flat land curving from southwestern France through Belgium, the Netherlands, Germany, and Poland, then stretching into the former Soviet Union. p. 255.

North Island (north EYE lund). Northernmost of the two major islands of New Zealand. p. 644.

North Pole (north pohl). Most northern place on the earth. Located at 90° north latitude. p. 6.

North Sea (north see). Part of the Atlantic Ocean between Great Britain and the European continent. p. 255.

Ob River (ohb RIHV ur). River in Russia that flows north into the Arctic Ocean. p. 356.

Oder River (OH dur RIHV ur). River that rises in the Czech Republic and flows north through Poland. Flows north to the Baltic Sea, forming the boundary between Poland and Germany. p. 257.

Odessa (oh DES uh). Seaport in Ukraine. Located on the Black Sea. (46°N/31°E) p. 365.

Ohio River (oh HYE oh RIHV ur). River that forms in Pittsburgh, Pennsylvania, by the joining of the Allegheny and Monongahela rivers. Flows into the Mississippi River. p. 99.

Oporto (oh POHR too). Important port city in Portugal. (41°N/9°W) p. 325.

Oran (oh RAN). Seaport in northern Algeria. Located on the Mediterranean Sea. (36°N/1°W) p. 547.

Orange River (OR inj RIHV ur). Longest river in South Africa. Part of it forms the boundary between South Africa and Namibia. Flows into the Atlantic Ocean. p. 610.

Orinoco River (or uh NOH koh RIHV ur). River located in Venezuela. Rises in the Guiana Highlands and flows into the Atlantic Ocean near Trinidad and Tobago. p. 178.

Orlando (or LAN doh). City in east-central Florida. (29°N/81°W) p. 692.

Orontes River (oh RAHN teez RIHV ur). Unnavigable river in western Syria. Flows into the Mediterranean Sea. p. 492.

Osaka (OH sah kah). Third most populated city in Japan. Major seaport, located on Osaka Bay, on Honshu Island. (35°N/136°E) p. 400.

Ottawa (AHT uh wuh). Capital of Canada. Located in southeastern Ontario. (45°N/76°W) p. 67.

Pachuca (pah CHOO kah). City in east-central Mexico. (20°N/99°W) p. 132.

Palau (pah LOU). A group of islands and islets in the western Pacific Ocean. p. 637.

Pampas (PAHM puz). Fertile agricultural plains area in Argentina and Uruguay. p. 171.

Panama Canal (PAN uh mah kuh NAL). Artificial waterway that cuts across the Isthmus of Panama and links the Atlantic and Pacific oceans. p. 159.

Papua New Guinea (PAP yoo uh noo GIHN ee). Country that occupies the eastern half of the island of New Guinea and nearby islands. Capital is Port Moresby. p. 637.

Paraguay River (PAR uh gway RIHV ur). River that flows from southern Brazil through Paraguay. Empties into the Paraná River. p. 171.

Paramaribo (par uh MAR ih boh). Port city and capital of Suriname. (6°N/55°W) p. 173.

Paraná River (pah rah NAH RIHV ur). Forms in Brazil. Flows into the Río de la Plata. p. 212.

Paris (PAR ihs). Capital of and most populated city in France. Located on the Seine River. (49°N/2°E) p. 257.

Patagonia (pat uh GOH nee uh). Barren plains area in southern Argentina. p. 212.

Pearl Harbor (purl HAHR bur). Inlet on the island of Oahu, in Hawaii. Site of the United States naval base attacked by the Japanese on December 7, 1941. (21°N/158°W) p. 693.

Pemba (PEM buh). Island belonging to Tanzania. Located in the Indian Ocean off the coast of East Africa, north of the island of Zanzibar. (13°S/41°E) p. 594.

Pennine Mountains (PE nyn MOUNT unz). Mountain range that runs from north to south through Great Britain. p. 264.

Persian Gulf (PUR zhun gulf). Arm of the Arabian Sea. Separates Iran and Saudi Arabia. Connected with the Gulf of Oman and the Arabian Sea by the Strait of Hormuz. p. 387.

Perth (purth). Capital of the Australian state of Western Australia. Located on the west coast of Australia. (32°S/116°E) p. 657.

Philadelphia (fihl uh DEL fee uh). City at the point where the Delaware and Schuylkill rivers join. The most populated city in Pennsylvania, and the fifth most populated city in the United States. (40°N/75°W) p. 67.

Phnom Penh (puh NAHM PEN). Capital of Cambodia. Located on the Mekong River. (12°N/105°E) p. 444.

Pikes Peak (pyks peek). High mountain located in the Rockies in east-central Colorado. Altitude of 14,110 ft (4,301 m). (39°N/105°W) p. 693.

Pindus Mountains (PIHN dus MOUNT unz). Mountain range in western Greece. p. 320.

Piraeus (pye REE us). Important port city in Greece. (38°N/24°E) p. 320.

Podgorica (PAHD guh reet sah). Capital of Montenegro, a region in the Republic of Yugoslavia. Formerly called Titograd. (42°N/19°E) p. 350.

Pointe-Noire (pwant nuh WAHR). Port city of the Congo. (5°S/12°E) p. 582.

Polynesia (pahl uh NEE zhuh). Groups of scattered islands in the central and south Pacific. It includes Hawaii and Tahiti. p. 637.

Pompeii (pahm PAY ee). Ancient city in southern Italy. It was completely buried under volcanic ash and lava from Mt. Vesuvius. (41°N/14°E) p. 332.

Po River (poh RIHV ur). Longest river in Italy. Starts in the Alps and flows into the Adriatic Sea south of Venice. p. 330.

Prague (prahg). Capital of and most populated city in the Czech Republic. Located on the Vltava River. (50°N/14°E) p. 257.

Pretoria (pree TOR ee uh). One of three capital cities of South Africa. Located on a tributary of Limpopo River. (26°S/28°E) p. 525.

Puerto Rico (PWER tuh REE koh). Self-governing commonwealth in union with the United States. An island of the West Indies. (18°N/65°W) p. 67.

P'yŏngyang (PYUNG yahng). Capital of North Korea. (39°N/126°E) p. 389.

Pyrenees (PIHR uh neez). Mountains along the border between France and Spain. p. 288.

Quebec (kwee BEK). City in Canada, on the north side of the St. Lawrence River. It was founded in 1608 by Samuel de Champlain. Today, it is the capital of the province of Quebec. (47°N/71°W) p. 81.

Queensland (KWEENZ land). State located in northeastern Australia. Its capital city is Brisbane. p. 657.

Quito (KEE toh). Capital city of Ecuador. Lies almost on the Equator, at an altitude of over 9,000 ft (2,743 m). (0° lat./79°W) p. 173.

Rabat (ruh BAHT). Capital city of Morocco. (34°N/7°W) p. 525.

Rangoon (ran GOON). Capital of and most populated city in Myanmar. Located on the Rangoon River. (17°N/96°E) p. 389.

Red Sea (red see). Large inland sea between the Arabian Peninsula and northeast Africa. p. 492.

Rhine River (ryn RIHV ur). Starts in the Alps in Switzerland. Flows north through Germany and then west through the Netherlands, where it empties into the North Sea at Rotterdam. p. 255.

Rhone River (rohn RIHV ur). Starts from a glacier in the Alps in Switzerland and flows south through France, emptying into the Mediterranean Sea at Marseilles. p. 255.

Riga (REE guh). Capital of Latvia and port on the Baltic Sea. Located on the Western Dvina River. (57°N/24°E) p. 372.

Rio de Janeiro (REE oh day zhuh NER oh). The second most populated city in South America. Major port of Brazil. Located on the Atlantic coast. (23°S/43°W) p. 235.

Río de la Plata (REE oh de lah PLAH tah). An estuary of the Paraná and Uruguay rivers. p. 219.

Riyadh (ree YAHD). Capital of Saudi Arabia. (25°N/47°E) p. 499.

Rome (rohm). Capital and most populated city in Italy. Located on the Tiber River. Most important city in the Roman Empire. (42°N/12°E) p. 330.

Rotterdam (RAHT ur dam). City in the Netherlands. Located on the Nieuwe Maas, about 15 mi (24 km) from the North Sea. An important port city. (52°N/4°E) p. 296.

Ruhr River (roor RIHV ur). Small tributary of the Rhine River. p. 255.

Ruwenzori Mountains (roo un ZOR ee MOUNT unz). Mountains located in central Africa, on the boundary between Uganda and Zaire. p. 574.

St. John's (saynt jahnz). Capital of Newfoundland, Canada. Located on the southeast coast of Newfoundland Island, on the Atlantic Ocean. (48°N/53°W) p. 81.

St. Lawrence River (saynt LAHR uns RIHV ur). Flows northeast out of Lake Ontario into the Gulf of St. Lawrence. Forms the boundary between New York State and the Canadian province of Ontario, then passes through southern Quebec province. p. 84.

St. Petersburg (saynt PEET urz burg). Second most populated city in Russia. Located on the Gulf of Finland. Formerly Leningrad and the former capital of Russia. (60°N/30°E) p. 257.

San'a (sah NAH). Capital city of Yemen. (15°N/44°E) p. 389.

San Francisco (san frun SIHS koh). Seaport city situated on the north-central coast of California, between San Francisco Bay and the Pacific Ocean. (38°N/122°W) p. 159.

San José (san hoh ZAY). Capital city of Costa Rica. (10°N/84°W) p. 159.

San Juan (san hwahn). Capital of and largest city in the Commonwealth of Puerto Rico. A major seaport city, located on the north side of the island, on San Juan Bay. (18°N/66°W) p. 151.

San Luis Potosí (san LWEES poh toh SEE). Major industrial city in Mexico. (23°N/101°W) p. 132.

San Salvador (san SAL vuh dor). Capital city of El Salvador. (14°N/89°W) p. 159.

Santiago (sahn tee AH goh). Capital of and most populated city in Chile. (33°S/71°W) p. 173.

Santo Domingo (SAHN toh doh MING goh). Capital city of the Dominican Republic. (18°N/70°W) p. 151.

São Paulo (soun POU loo). The most populated city in South America. Located in southeastern Brazil. (24°S/47°W) p. 235.

Sapporo (SAH poh roh). Industrial city on the island of Hokkaido in Japan. (43°N/141°E) p. 400.

Sarajevo (sar uh YAY voh). Capital of Bosnia and Hercegovina. Located near the Bosna River. (44°N/18°E) p. 350.

Sea of Japan (see uv juh PAN). Body of water that separates the island of Japan from the mainland of Asia. p. 398.

Seine River (sayn RIHV ur). Starts in eastern France, flows westward through Paris, and then empties into the English Channel at Le Havre. p. 288.

Seoul (sohl). Capital of South Korea. Located on the Han River. One of the world's most populated cities. (38°N/127°E) p. 389.

Serengeti Plain (ser un GET ee playn). A region in northern Tanzania noted for its wildlife. The location of the Serengeti National Park. p. 594.

Shanghai (SHANG HYE) China's most populated city. Located on the delta of the Chang Jiang on the East China Sea. (31°N/121°E) p. 427.

Shatt-al-Arab (shat ul AH rahb). Channel in southeastern Iraq formed by the merger of the Tigris and Euphrates rivers. Flows southeasterly into the Persian Gulf. p. 492.

Shikoku (SHEE koh koo). The smallest of Japan's four main islands. p. 398.

Siberia (sye BIHR ee uh). Part of Russia, covering much of the area between the Ural Mountains and the Pacific Ocean. p. 356.

Sierra Nevada (see ER uh nuh VAD uh). High mountain range located mostly in eastern California. Mount Whitney, with an elevation of 14,494 ft (4,418 m), is located in this range. It is the highest peak in the continental United States. p. 65.

Singapore (SING uh por). Capital of the island nation of Singapore. One of the world's busiest ports. Located on Singapore Strait. (1°N/104°E) p. 444.

Skopje (SKAHP yay). Capital of Macedonia. Located on Vardar River. (42°N/21°E) p. 350.

Snowy Mountains (SNOH ee MOUNT unz). Part of the Great Dividing Range, located in eastern Victoria and southeastern New South Wales, in Australia. An important hydroelectric power project is located there. p. 644.

Sofia (SOH fee uh). Capital of Bulgaria. (43°N/23°E) p. 350.

Solomon Islands (SAHL uh mun EYE lundz). Group of islands that includes both the country of Solomon Islands and Bougainville, Buka, and other islands belonging to Papua New Guinea. p. 637.

South Australia (south aw STRAYL yuh). State located in the south-central part of Australia. The capital city is Adelaide. p. 657.

South China Sea (south CHYE nuh see). Part of the Pacific Ocean, enclosed by eastern China, the Indochina and Malay peninsulas, Borneo, the Philippines, and Taiwan. Often called the China Sea. p. 387.

Southern Alps (SUTH urn alps). Range of mountains on South Island, New Zealand. Highest peak is Mount Cook, with an elevation of 12,349 ft (3,764 m). p. 644.

South Island (south EYE lund). Southern island of the two main islands of New Zealand. p. 644.

South Pole (south pohl). The most southern place on the earth. Located at 90° south latitude. p. 6.

Stockholm (STAHK hohm). Capital of and most populated city in Sweden. Located on the country's east coast, on the Baltic Sea. (59°N/18°E). p. 276.

Strait of Gibraltar (strayt uv jih BRAWL tur). Narrow passageway connecting the Atlantic Ocean and the Mediterranean Sea. p. 320.

Strait of Malacca (strayt uv muh LAK uh). A narrow channel of water in Malaysia that is an important passageway for ships traveling between India and China. p. 387.

Sucre (SOO kray). The official capital city of Bolivia. (19°S/65°W) p. 173.

Sumatra (SOO MAH truh). The westernmost of the main islands of Indonesia. Divided into two almost equal parts by the Equator. p. 444.

Sydney (SIHD nee). Capital of the Australian state of New South Wales. Most populated city in Australia. (34°S/151°E). p. 651.

Taipei (tye PAY). Capital of and most populated city in Taiwan. (25°N/122°E) p. 389.

Taiwan Strait (tye WAHN strayt). Body of water that separates Taiwan and China. p. 387.

Tajumulco (tah hoo MOOL koh). Volcano in Guatemala. It is the highest point in Central America, standing 13,845 ft (4,220 m) high. p. 146.

Tallinn (TAL un). Capital of Estonia. Baltic Sea port on the Gulf of Finland. (59°N/25°E). p. 372.

Tampico (tam PEE koh). Port city in Mexico. (22°N/98°W). p. 132.

Tashkent (tash KENT). Capital of Uzbekistan. Located on border with Kazakhstan. (41°N/69°E). p. 372.

Tasmania (taz MAY nee uh). Island off the coast of Australia. Also one of Australia's states. p. 657.

Tbilisi (tuh BIHL uh see). Capital of Georgia. Located on the Kura River. Founded in A.D. 455. For centuries, served as an important trade center between Asia and Europe. (42°N/45°E). p. 372.

Tel Aviv (tel uh VEEV). Most populated city in Israel. Located on the Mediterranean Sea. (32°N/35°E) p. 499.

Thames River (temz RIHV ur). Flows east across south central England. Passes through London before emptying into the North Sea. p. 270.

Thessalonica (thes uh LAHN ih kuh). Busy port city in Greece. Located on the Aegean Sea. Greece's second most populated city. (41°N/23°E) p. 334.

Tianjin (tyen JIHN). Important port city in northeastern China. (39°N/117°E). p. 423.

Tiber River (TYE bur RIHV ur). River in Italy. Rises in the Apennines and flows through Rome to the Mediterranean Sea. p. 330.

Tigris River (TYE grus RIHV ur). Rises in the mountains of southeastern Turkey. Flows through Iraq, where it unites with the Euphrates River to form the Shatt-al-Arab, which flows into the Persian Gulf. p. 492.

Tiranë (tuh RAHN uh). Capital of Albania. (41°N/20°E) p. 350.

Tokyo (TOH kee oh). Capital of Japan. Located on Tokyo Bay, on the island of Honshu. Second most populated city in Asia. (36°N/140°E) p. 389.

Toronto (tuh RAHNT oh). Most populated city in Canada. Capital of the province of Ontario. Located on the northeastern end of Lake Ontario. Is also a port. (44°N/79°W) p. 81.

Tripoli (TRIHP uh lee). Capital of Libya. Port city on the Mediterranean Sea. (33°N/13°E). p. 525.

Tunis (TOO nihs). Capital city of Tunisia. (37°N/10°E) p. 525.

Turin (TOOR ihn). Industrial city located on the Po River, in northwestern Italy. (45°N/8°E) p. 330.

Ulan Bator (oo lahn bah TOR). Capital of Mongolia. (48°N/107°E) p. 389.

Ural Mountains (YOOR ul MOUNT unz). Located in Russia. They form the division between Asia and Europe. p. 356.

Vancouver (van KOO vur). City in British Columbia, Canada. Canada's most important seaport on the Pacific Ocean. (49°N/123°W). p. 81.

Vanuatu (vahn uh WAH too). Island nation in the Pacific Ocean. (16°S/167°W). p. 637.

Victoria (vihk TOR ee uh). State located in the southeastern part of Australia. The capital city is Melbourne. p. 657.

Vienna (vee EN uh). Capital of and largest city in Austria. Located on the Danube River. (48°N/16°E) p. 257.

Vientiane (vyen TYAHN). Capital of Laos. Located in the Mekong River valley. (18°N/103°E) p. 444.

Vilnius (VIHL nee us). Capital of Lithuania. Located near border of Belarus. (55°N/25°E). p. 372.

Vistula River (VIHS choo luh RIHV ur). Poland's most important river. Rises in the Carpathian Mountains, flows north through Warsaw, then empties into the Baltic Sea at Gdańsk. p. 340.

Vladivostok (vlad ih VAHS tahk). City in Russia, at the eastern end of the Trans-Siberian Railway. Located on the Sea of Japan. (43°N/132°E) p. 389.

Volga River (VAHL guh RIHV ur). Most important river in Russia, and the longest river in Europe. Empties into the Caspian Sea. p. 356.

Warsaw (WOR saw). Capital of Poland. Located on the Vistula River. (52°N/21°E). p. 350.

Washington, D.C. (WAWSH ing tun dee see). Capital of the United States. Located between Maryland and Virginia, on the east bank of the Potomac River. (39°N/77°W) p. 65.

Wellington (WEL ing tun). Capital of New Zealand. Located on North Island and Cook Strait. (41°S/175°E) p. 657.

West Indies (west IHN deez). Group of islands stretching about 2,500 mi (4,023) km) from near Florida to near Venezuela. p. 151.

White Nile (hwyt nyl). River rises in Lake Victoria and flows north through Uganda and Sudan, where it joins the Blue Nile. p. 541.

Windhoek (VIHNT hook). Capital of Namibia. (23°S/17°E) p. 525.

Winnipeg (WIHN uh peg). Capital of Manitoba, Canada. Located on the Red River. (50°N/97°W) p. 81.

Xizang (SHEE ZANG). High mountainous area in China, near border with India and Nepal. Formerly called Tibet. p. 423.

Yerevan (yer uh VAHN). Capital of Armenia. Located on Razdan River. (40°N/45°E) p. 372.

Yokohama (yok kuh HAHM uh). Japanese seaport city on the island of Honshu. Located on the western shore of Tokyo Bay. (35°N/140°E) p. 413.

Yucatán Peninsula (yoo kah TAHN puh NIHN suh luh). Located in southeastern Mexico and in Belize and northern Guatemala in Central America. Separates the Gulf of Mexico from the Caribbean Sea. p.126.

Zagreb (ZAH greb). Capital of Croatia. Located on the Sava River. (46°N/16°E) p. 350.

Zambezi River (zam BEE zee RIHV ur). River that rises in Angola. Flows into the Indian Ocean at Mozambique. Forms boundary between Angola and Zimbabwe. p. 610.

Zanzibar (ZAN zuh bahr). Island belonging to Tanzania. Located in the Indian Ocean, off the coast of Tanzania. Also the name of the chief city on the island. (6°S/39°E) p. 594.

Aborigine (ab uh RIHJ uh nee). A member of the earliest group of people known to inhabit Australia. p. 647.

absolute location (AB suh loot loh KAY shun). The latitude and longitude of a place. p. 45.

adobe (uh DOH bee). A building material that is made of sun-dried mud and straw. p. 129.

Afrikaans (af rih KAHNZ). A language that is widely used in South Africa. p. 611.

alloys (AL oiz). Mixtures of metals that are harder or stronger than the individual metals from which they are made. p. 37.

alluvial soil (uh LOO vee ul soil). Rock fragments and silt deposited on the land when a river floods during the rainy season. p. 428.

alpine (AL pyn). Mountain areas above the highest elevation where trees grow. p. 419.

anthropologist (an throh PAHL uh jihst). A person who studies humans and their cultures. p. 647.

antimony (AN tuh moh nee). A mineral used to make a metal harder. p. 207.

apartheid (uh PAHR tayt). The forced separation, by law, of whites and nonwhites in South Africa. p. 623.

aqueduct (AK wuh dukt). An artificial channel for carrying a large quantity of flowing water. p. 108.

aquifer (AK wuh fur). A layer of rock, sand, or gravel that can absorb or collect water. p. 653.

arable (AR uh bul). Suitable for growing crops. p. 437.

archipelago (ahr kuh PEL uh goh). A group or chain of islands. p. 147.

arid (AR ihd). Very dry, usually due to insufficient rainfall, making agriculture difficult. p. 332.

Aryans (ar EE unz). A people who invaded India and introduced their language and their religion. p. 476.

atmosphere (AT mus fihr). The blanket of air that covers the earth. p. 28.

atoll (A tawl). A ring-shaped coral island enclosing or partly enclosing a lagoon. p. 664.

autobahn (AWT oh bahn). West Germany's super-highway system. p. 303.

autonomy (aw TAHN uh mee). Self-government for a state or other political entity. p. 478.

avalanche (AV uh lanch). A giant snowslide that occurs in high mountain areas when too much snow builds up on steep slopes. p. 196.

axis (AK sihs). An imaginary line that goes through the earth from the North Pole to the South Pole. p. 104.

Bantu (BAN too). A family of African languages. p. 577.

basin (BAYS un). A low area almost entirely surrounded by higher land. p. 125.

bazaar (buh ZAHR). The central marketplace in Middle Eastern and North African cities. p. 538.

Bedouins (BED oo ihnz). A nomadic group of people who live in many of the countries of the Arabian peninsula. p. 506.

bilingual (bye LING gwel). Expressed in or using two languages. p. 82.

Boers (boorz). Early Dutch settlers in South Africa; Dutch word for "farmers." p. 620.

bog (bahg). A small marsh or swamp, comprised of wet spongy ground. p. 270.

buffer state (BUF ur stayt). A country that separates two or more countries that are hostile to each other. p. 438.

canopy (KAN uh pee). The interlocking leaves that form the top of a rain forest. p. 573.

canton (KAN tun). A small territorial division of a

country, which functions as a separate political unit. A canton corresponds to a state in the United States. Switzerland is divided into cantons. p. 310.

capital (KAP ut ul). Money used to develop a country's economy. p. 207.

caravan (KAR uh van). A group of people traveling together, usually on animals or in vehicles. p. 539.

cartography (kahr TAHG ruh fee). The making of maps. p. 16.

cash crop (kash krahp). A crop that is sold, usually for export. p. 181.

caste (kast). A system that separates people into groups, or classes, based on birth. p. 476.

catamaran (kat uh muh RAN). Two canoes fastened together to make one boat. Sometimes planks fastened on the framework serve as the deck. p. 663.

causeway (KAWZ way). A raised way or road across wet ground or water. p. 134.

censor (SEN sur). To control the content of publications, radio and television broadcasts, and other forms of free speech. p. 339.

channel (CHAN ul). A strait or a narrow sea between two large areas of land that are close together. p. 265.

chernozem (CHER nuh zem). A rich black soil, which is common in cool or temperate semiarid climates. p. 372.

chromium (KROH mee um). A blue-white mineral that is used to make steel harder. p. 351.

cinder cone (SIHN dur kohn). A small volcano that looks like a cone-shaped hill. p. 130.

city-state (SIHT ee stayt). A self-governing state consisting of a city and its surrounding territory. p. 456.

climate (KLYE mut). The pattern of weather that a place has over a period of time. Temperature and

precipitation are two important parts of climate. p. 28.

coastal plain (KOHS tul playn). An area of flat land that borders a coast. p. 98.

commercial farm (kuh MUR shul fahrm). A farm on which crops are raised for sale rather than for home use. p. 137.

commodity (kuh MAHD uh tee). A product that is bought and sold in commerce. p. 224.

Commonwealth of Nations (KAHM un welth uv NAY shunz). An organization of 48 former British colonies with special defense and economic ties. p. 266.

commune (KAHM yoon). A community, often rural, in which labor, decision making, and profits are shared. p. 435.

communism (KAHM yoo nihz um). A social system in which property and goods are owned in common, or the theory that favors such a system. p. 372.

compact (KAHM pakt). An agreement between nations. p. 669.

compass rose (KUM pus rohz). A small drawing on a map, used to show direction. p. 4.

confederation (kun fed ur AY shun). A union comprised of many different states. p. 310.

confluence (KAHN floo uns). The place where two or more streams or rivers join. p. 212.

conquistador (kahn KWIHS tuh dor). A Spanish soldier of the sixteenth century in the Americas. p. 134.

constitutional monarchy (kahn stuh TOO shuh nul MAHN ur kee). A government in which the monarch, or ruler, serves as head of state and has only those powers given to the ruler by the constitution and laws of the nation. p. 77.

consumer (kun SOOM ur). A person who buys and uses many types of goods. p. 52.

consumer goods (kun SOOM ur goodz). Things

that are grown or made by producers and are used by people. p. 369.

continental island (kahn tuh NENT ul EYE lund). An island that was once part of a continent. It is now separated from the continent by a stretch of water. p. 663.

contour lines (KAHN toor lynz). Lines on a map connecting the points that have the same elevation on a land surface. p. 12.

cooperative (koh AHP ur uh tihv). A cooperative is a plantation or other business that is owned by its workers. p. 137.

copra (KAH pruh). Dried coconut meat from which coconut oil is made. p. 669.

coral (KOR ul). A hard, chalky, rocklike material that is made of the shells of sea animals called coral polyps. p. 646.

core (kor). The part of the country that has the largest population, the largest cities, the most productive economy, and the best transportation facilities and other services. p. 650.

coup d'état (koo day TAH). A sudden overthrowing of a government by a small group. p. 198.

crevasse (kruh VAS). A deep crack in the ice. p. 675.

crop rotation (krahp roh TAY shun). The practice of growing first one crop and then another type of crop on the same land, which preserves the ability of the soil to produce crops. p. 107.

culture (KUL chur). The way of life of a people. p. 31.

czar (zahr). The title given to the rulers of Russia. p. 364.

Czech (chek). A person born or living in the Czech Republic. p. 345.

deforestation (dee for ihst AY shun). The large-scale cutting down of forests. p. 179.

delta (DEL tuh). The land that is formed by mud

and sand deposited at the mouth of the river. p. 448.

demilitarized zone (dee MIHL uh tuh ryzd zohn). An area free of military control, where there are no troops or weapons. p. 412.

desert pavement (DEZ urt PAYV munt). Vast plains of gravel and boulders in the desert. p. 534.

desertification (dih zurt uh fih KAY shun). The process by which livestock eat the seeds of grasses and shrubs, causing vegetation to disappear and the land to change to desert. p. 561.

diffusion (dih FYOO zhun). The spread of knowledge from one group of people to another. p. 537.

dike (dyk). A wall or bank built to control or hold back the water of a river or sea. p. 188.

distortion (dih STOR shun). A twisting or stretching out of shape. p. 16.

distributary (dih STRIHB yoo ter ee). A river branch flowing away from the main stream. p. 541.

distribution map (dihs trih BYOO shun map). A map that shows the range of people, crops, or resources in a country or region. p. 13.

domestic (doh MES tihk). A product that is used in one country and not exported to another. p. 468.

domesticate (doh MES tih kayt). To tame wild animals to live with humans. p. 27.

drought (drout). A long, dry period with no rain. p. 561.

dynasty (DYE nus tee). A family of rulers. p. 430.

ebony (EB uh nee). A hard, dark, strong wood that comes from various trees found in tropical areas. p. 446.

ecology (ee KAHL uh jee). The balance between living things and their environment. p. 543.

ejido (ay HEE doh). Communal farmland in Mexico

that is owned and worked on by several families or by an entire village. p. 129.

emblem (EM blum). A symbol or sign, such as the flag or the seal of a country. p. 656.

emigrate (EM ih grayt). To leave one country or region in order to permanently settle in another. p. 321.

enclave (EN klayv). A country that is completely surrounded by another country. p. 568.

equatorial climate (ee kwuh TOR ee ul KLYE mut). A place with a very warm, humid climate that is near the Equator. p. 445.

equinox (EE kwih nahks). Either of the two times in the year when the sun's direct rays are over the Equator and day and night are of equal length. p. 104.

erg (urg). A large sea of sand in the desert, high-lighted by wind-swept dunes. p. 534.

erosion (ee ROH zhun). The process by which the soil blows away in the wind or washes down the slopes of the hills when it rains. p. 333.

escarpment (e SKAHRP munt). The steep slope, or drop, at the edge of a plateau. p. 610.

estuary (ES tyoo er ee). The mouth of a river into which ocean water flows, mixing fresh water and seawater. p. 211.

ethnocentrism (eth noh SEN trihz um). The process of looking at the rest of the world and making judgments about it based only on your own cultural background and experience. p. 491.

Eurasia (yoo RAY zhuh). The landmass made up of the continents of Europe and Asia. p. 254.

European Union (yoor uh PEE un YOON yen). An organization comprised of 15 Western European countries whose main purpose is to make trade easier among them. p. 300.

exclave (EKS klayv). A territory surrounded or nearly surrounded by the territory of another country. p. 619.

exploitation (eks ploi TAY shun). Taking large profits from a country, leaving very little for the people who live there. p. 582.

expropriate (eks PROH pree ayt). To take over the property of another. p. 150.

fallow (FAL oh). Not cultivated or planted for a season or more. p. 187.

famine (FAM ihn). An extreme shortage of food. p. 274.

federation (fed ur AY shun). A government in which the national government and the governments of the provinces share certain powers. p. 77.

fellahin (FEL uh heen). A group of crop-raising farmers in the Arab countries of North Africa and the Middle East. p. 538.

Fertile Crescent (FURT ul KRES unt). A 1,000-mile-long crescent-shaped region of the Arabian peninsula that is made up of green, flat, fertile land. The Fertile Crescent stretches across Iraq, Syria, Lebanon, Israel, and Jordan. p. 493.

fjord (fyord). A long, narrow, often deep inlet of the sea lying between steep cliffs. p. 79.

flax (flaks). A plant whose fiber can be used to make linen. Oil and livestock feed are obtained from its seed. p. 299.

Fleming (FLEM ing). One of a group of Dutch-speaking people inhabiting Flanders, a region of northern Belgium. p. 299.

forage (FOR ihj). Plants such as grass and shrubs that serve as food for livestock. p. 560.

foreign debt (FOR ihn det). Money a government owes to banks in another country. p. 237.

foreign policy (FOR ihn PAHL uh see). The decisions a country makes about how it will work with other countries. p. 64.

futon (FOO tahn). A heavy padded quilt that is commonly used in Japan. p. 411.

Gaelic (GAYL ihk). Of, relating to, or being the Celtic speech of persons born or living in Ireland, the Isle of Man, and the Scottish Highlands. p. 273.

gasohol (GAS uh hawl). A fuel made by mixing gasoline with alcohol that is made from sugarcane and used to power cars and trucks. p. 234.

geography (jee AHG ruh fee). The study of the earth and how people use the earth. p. 25.

geologic hazard (jee uh LAHJ ihk HAZ urd). A natural event involving the land, such as an earthquake, volcanic eruption, landslide, or flood, that causes problems for people. p. 196.

geyser (GYE zur). A fountain of steam and water that has been heated by hot lava and forced above ground by volcanic gases. p. 279.

glacial till (GLAY shul tihl). The soil and silt deposited by glacial ice sheets as they melted and retreated northward. p. 92.

glacier (GLAY shur). A large mass of ice formed from snow on high ground and moving very slowly down a mountainside or along a valley. p. 44.

great circle (grayt SUR kul). Any circle on the earth's surface that divides the earth into equal parts. The Equator is a great circle. A great circle is the shortest possible distance between any two places on the surface of the earth. p. 18.

Great Trek (grayt trek). The mass migration of thousands of Boers to the High Veld of Southern Africa. The trek began in 1835 and continued into the 1840s. p. 621.

green revolution (green rev uh LOO shun). The growing of more crops on the same amount of land, due to the development of new types of grain by agricultural scientists. p. 459.

grid system (grihd SIHS tum). A network of horizontal lines of latitude and vertical lines of longitude that aids in the location of places on a map. p. 6.

ground water (ground WAWT ur). Rainwater that collects in underground rocks. p. 51.

guerrilla (guh RIHL uh). A person who fights against a government. p. 158.

hacienda (hah see EN duh). A large estate in Spanish-speaking countries. p. 129.

hajj (haj). A pilgrimage that every Muslim must make to Mecca at least once in his or her life if he or she can afford it. p. 512.

hammada (huh MAH duh). A rocky plateau in the desert. p. 534.

harbor (HAHR bur). A protected body of water that is safe for ships. p. 66.

heavy industry (HEV ee IHN dus tree). The production of goods such as tractors, mining equipment, and factory machinery. p. 367.

hemisphere (HEM ih sfihr). Half the earth or the globe. p. 18.

High Veld (hye velt). The upland grassland area of Southern Africa. p. 611.

high-technology industries (hye tek NAHL uhjee IHN dus treez). Industries that produce electronics, computers, and other goods that are extremely complex and specialized. p. 113.

Hispanic (hih SPAN ihk). A Spanish-speaking American. p. 103.

homeland (HOHM land). A special reserve in South Africa where many South African blacks were forced to move. p. 623.

humid continental (HYOO mihd kahn tuh NENT ul). A climate that has a wide range of temperatures, with warm to unpleasantly hot summers and cold to very cold winters. Precipitation also varies considerably in this climate. p. 104.

humid subtropical (HYOO mihd sub TRAHP ih kul). A climate that has very hot temperatures in the summer and mild temperatures in the winter. There is plenty of rain all year but very little snow. p. 105.

humus (HYOO mus). The product of the partial decay of plant or animal matter that forms the organic portion of soil. p. 577.

hydroelectricity (hye droh ih lek TRIHS ih tee). Electricity made from the force of flowing water. p. 87.

ice shelf (eyes shelf). A mass of ice that floats on the water but is attached to a glacier. p. 672.

immigrant (IHM uh grunt). A person who comes into one country from another country to settle permanently. p. 103.

imperialism (ihm PIHR ee ul ihz um). A policy of conquering new lands to build an empire. p. 565.

import (IHM port). A product one country buys from another. p. 52.

industry (IHN dus tree). The manufacturing of goods. p. 109.

inflation (ihn FLAY shun). The decline in the value of money accompanied by an increase in prices. p. 141.

irrigation (ihr uh GAY shun). The watering of crops or other plants by pipes, canals, or ditches. p. 51.

in-migration (IHN mye gray shun). Movement into a region or community. p. 332.

islet (eye liht). A very small island, usually uninhabited. p. 582.

isolationism (eye suh LAY shun ihz um). A national policy of avoiding international political and economic relations. p. 454.

isthmus (IHS mus). A narrow strip of land that connects two larger land areas. p. 148.

jungle (JUNG gul). A thick tangled mass of tropical vegetation. p. 574.

jute (joot). A plant, raised mostly in the Ganges River delta, from which the fiber for burlap and twine is obtained. p. 482.

key (kee). A device on a map that tells what real things and places the symbols cn a map stand for. p. 4.

kilometer (KIL uh meet ur). A measure of distance in the metric system. p. 9.

Koran (kuh RAN). A book of sacred writings accepted by Muslims as revealed to Muhammad by Allah. p. 511.

kraal (krahl). A village commonly found in eastern and southern Africa. p. 600.

lagoon (luh GOON). A shallow channel or pond near or connected with a larger body of water. p. 664.

land bridge (land brihj). A narrow piece of land that connects two larger land masses. p. 76.

landform (LAND form). A feature of the earth's surface, such as a mountain, hill, river, lake, or ocean, that is made by nature. p. 10.

landlocked (LAND lahkt). Not having a seacoast. p. 195.

language family (LANJ gwihj FAM uh lee). A group of languages that all come from one ancestor language. p. 31.

Lapps (laps). A group of people who live in the far north of the Scandinavian Shield, near the Arctic Ocean. p. 278.

latex (LAY teks). A mixture of water and fine particles of rubber or plastic, used especially in paints and adhesives. p. 455.

latitude (LAT uh tood). Distance, measured in degrees, north and south of the Equator. Lines of latitude are used to locate places on a map or globe. p. 5.

lava (LAH vuh). The melted rock forced out of a volcano. p. 66.

leaching (LEECH ing). A process in which nutrients in the top layers of the soil are washed down into the lower layers of soil. p. 577.

life expectancy (lyf ek SPEK tun see). The average number of years a person can expect to live. p. 594.

light industry (lyt IHN dus tree). The production of goods such as textiles, clothing, furniture, and the processing of grains and vegetables. p. 367.

lignite (LIHG nyt). A usually brownish black coal of low quality, sometimes called brown coal. p. 305.

literacy rate (LIHT ur uh see rayt). The percentage of people who know how to read and write. p. 160.

lock (lahk). An enclosed area of a canal, with gates on both sides, used for raising or lowering ships as they go from one water level to another. p. 84.

loess (LOH es). A fine, light silt that is very fertile. p. 428.

longitude (LAHN juh tood). Distance, measured in degrees, east and west of the Prime Meridian. Lines of longitude are imaginary circles that go around the earth and pass through the North Pole and South Pole. p. 6.

Maghreb (MUH grub). The region of Morocco, Tunisia, and Algeria. It receives more rain than any other part of North Africa. p. 546.

magma (MAG muh). Melted rock beneath the earth's surface. p. 66.

Magyars (MAG yahrz). The group of people who settled originally in what is now Hungary. p. 346.

Malagasy (mal uh GAS ee). The language of Madagascar, which is a combination of Malay and Indonesian. p. 615.

mangrove (MANG grohv). A tropical tree whose wood is used for fuel and whose bark is a source of tannin. Mangroves grow in swamps and along riverbanks. p. 555.

Maori (MAH oh ree). A descendant of the first inhabitants of New Zealand. p. 658.

maritime (MAR ih tym). Of, relating to, or bordering on the sea. p. 265.

marsupial (mahr SOO pee ul). An animal, such as a kangaroo, that carries its young in a pouch until the young are fully developed. p. 646.

Mediterranean climate (med ih tuh RAY nee un KLYE mut). A climate that has hot, dry summers and cool, rainy winters. p. 320.

mesa (MAY suh). A large, flat-topped mountain with steep sides. p. 177.

mestizo (mes TEE zoh). A person of Spanish and Native American ancestry. p. 131.

meteorologist (meet ee ur AHL uh jihst). A scientist who studies and forecasts the weather. p. 46.

metropolitan area (me troh PAHL ih tun ER ee uh). An area made up of a large city and the surrounding towns, smaller cities, and other communities. p. 114.

modernize (MAHD ur nyz). To develop the economy of a country. p. 293.

monotheism (MAHN oh thee ihz um). The belief in only one God. p. 503.

monsoon (mahn SOON). A seasonal wind that blows from the land to the water in one season and from the water to the land in the other season. p. 468.

Moors (moorz). A group of people who invaded North Africa and conquered the Iberian Peninsula. p. 327.

mosque (mahsk). An Islamic place of worship. p. 33.

mulatto (muh LAHT oh). A person who is born of one black and one white parent. p. 148.

mural (MYOOR ul). A painting drawn on a wall or ceiling. p. 136.

natural resource (NACH ur ul REE sors). A material made by nature that people can use. p. 28.

navigable (NAV ih guh bul). A lake or river that is deep and wide enough to be traveled by ships and boats. p. 97.

navigator (NAV uh gayt ur). A person who is responsible for directing the course of a ship or airplane. p. 45.

neutral (NOO trul). Not favoring either side in a quarrel, conflict, or war. p. 283.

nitrate (NYE trayt). A mineral that can be used to make fertilizers, explosives, and other products. p. 224.

nomads (NOH madz). People who have no permanent home and who move from place to place p. 35.

nonrenewable resource (nahn rih NOO uh bul REE sors). A resource that, once used, cannot be replaced by nature or people. p. 111.

oasis (oh AY sihs). A place in the desert that has enough water for plants and trees to grow. p. 493.

ore (or). A mineral mined to obtain a substance that it contains. p. 36.

outback (OUT bak). The interior of the continent of Australia. p. 645.

overgrazing (OH vur grayz ing). Allowing livestock to eat too much of the natural vegetation. p. 333.

Pacific Rim (puh SIHF ihk rihm). The nations bordering the Pacific Ocean. p. 390.

paddy (PAD ee). A rice field, particularly a field in which irrigated rice is raised. p. 402.

pagoda (puh GOH duh). A Buddhist shrine that has upward-curving roofs and a pyramidlike shape. p. 453.

Palestinian (pal us TIHN ee un). A person who has a strong commitment to the creation of an independent Palestinian state. p. 504.

Pampas (PAHM puz). The large, fertile grassy plain that covers parts of Argentina, Uruguay, and Paraguay. p. 170.

Parliament (PAHR luh munt). The supreme legislative body of countries that have a parliamentary system of government. p. 273.

pass (pas). A low place in a mountain range. p. 289.

pastoralism (PAS tur ul ihz um). The practice of herding animals for a living. p. 35.

peat (peet). Plant matter used as a fertilizer or fuel. It is made of partially rotted plants and moss. p. 270.

per capita income (per KAP ih tuh IHN kum). The total amount of money that a nation's people earn in a year divided by the total population. p. 152.

permafrost (PUR muh frawst). Permanently frozen ground, sometimes extending to great depths below the earth's surface in very cold regions. p. 75.

petrochemical (pe troh KEM ih kul). A chemical or synthetic material made from petroleum or natural gas. p. 115.

phosphate (FAHS fayt). A vital mineral used in making fertilizers and detergents. p. 548.

physical map (FIHZ ih kul map). A map that shows physical features, such as mountains, plains, and other forms that land and water take. p. 12.

planned city (pland SIHT ee). A city that has been built according to a plan. p. 234.

plantation (plan TAY shun). A large commercial farm that grows only one specific crop. p. 25.

polder (POHL dur). A piece of land reclaimed from the water, usually by building dikes and pumping the water out of the area enclosed by the dikes. p. 297.

population density (pahp yoo LAY shun DEN suh tee). The average number of people who live in a square mile or square kilometer of a state, country, or other area. p. 76.

potash (PAHT ash). A type of mineral salt that is mined from deposits found below the earth's surface. p. 304.

prairie (PRER ee). A large area of level or rolling land that is covered by tall grass and has fertile soil. p. 85.

precipice (PRES ih pihs). A very steep and high face of a rock or mountain. p. 470.

primate city (PRYE mayt SIHT ee). A city that is far more important than any other city in a country. p. 198.

projection (proh JEK shun). The representation on a map of all or part of the earth. p. 16.

pyrethrum (pye RETH rum). A small flower that is dried and crushed and then used to make a natural insecticide. p. 598.

qanat (kah NAT). A tunnel system that allows ground water to flow underground until it reaches a flat area with fertile soils. p. 497.

rain forest (rayn FOR ihst). A large, very thick growth of tall trees that usually have large, broad leaves. Rain forests are found only in areas with an equatorial climate. p. 179.

rain shadow (rayn SHAD oh). An area that does not get much rain, because it is on the protected side of a mountain. p. 217.

reef (reef). A narrow ridge of coral, rocks, or sand at or near the surface of the water. p. 647.

refuge (REF yooj). A safe place that provides shelter or protection from danger. p. 273.

refugee (ref yoo JEE). A person who flees for safety in a time of persecution, war, or disaster. p. 450.

region (REE jun). A part of the earth that has one or more common characteristics. p. 41.

regional specialization (REE jun ul spesh uh lyz AY shun). An economic activity that is the specialty of a particular region. p. 108.

relative location (REL uh tihv loh KAY shun). Gives the location of a place according to some known landmark. p. 46.

relief (rih LEEF). The difference in the elevation or height of the land. p. 43.

renewable resource (rih NOO uh bul REE sors). A resource that once used can be replaced by nature or by people. p. 88.

reserve (rih ZURV). A supply of a resource (such as fuel) that is available or that has been set aside for future use. p. 132.

reservoir (REZ ur vwahr). A place where water is collected and stored for use. p. 51.

rift valley (rihft VAL ee). A canyonlike hollow formed by the sinking of the earth's crust between two parallel faults. p. 589.

Ring of Fire (ring uv fyr). An area of earthquakes and volcanoes in the mountain ranges on the coasts around the Pacific Ocean, including Japan. p. 399.

rural population (ROOR ul pahp yoo LAY shun). People who live outside an urban zone. p. 218.

Sahel (sah HEL). A semidesert area in Africa that lies south of the Sahara. p. 556.

sand dune (sand doon). A mountain of sand that has been formed by the wind. p. 127.

savanna (suh VAN uh). A treeless grassland, or a grassland with scattered trees and bushes, especially in tropical lands that have seasonal rains. p. 524.

scale (skayl). The relationship between distance on a map and distance on the earth. Also, the line drawn on maps that shows this relationship. p. 9.

scrub forest (skrub FOR ihst). A place where trees do not grow very high because of a dry climate. p. 229.

sediment (SED uh munt). The soil, silt, and other material in a river or stream that settles to the bottom. p. 482.

seedbed (SEED bed). The place where seeds are planted. p. 402.

shifting agriculture (SHIHFT ing AG rih kul chur). The process by which subsistence farmers clear plots of forest land to plant crops. p. 187.

Shiites (SHEE yts). Followers of the second largest branch of the Islamic religion. About one fifth of the world's Muslims are Shiite Muslims. Most people in present-day Iran and Iraq are Shiites, followers of the Shi'ah faith. p. 498.

sisal (SYE sul). A fibrous plant used to make rope, string, and bags. p. 591.

Slavs (slahvz). A group of people who were among the first people to live in what is now Eastern Europe. p. 304.

Slovaks (SLOH vahks). A Slavic people who live in Slovakia, which was the eastern region of the former Czecholovakia. p. 345.

smelting (SMELT ing). An extraction process that separates ore from rock. p. 89.

smorgasbord (SMOR gus bord). A self-service luncheon or supper that offers a large variety of foods and dishes. p. 281.

smuggling (SMUG ul ing). The act of exporting or importing goods secretly and unlawfully. p. 182.

Solidarity (sahl uh DAR uh tee). A labor organization that formed Poland's first non-Communist government since World War II. p. 343.

solstice (SAHL stihs). Either of the two times in the year when the sun's most direct rays are as far north or south of the Equator as they will ever be. p. 104.

squatter settlement (SKWAHT ur SET ul munt). A settlement filled with people, known as squatters, who have taken over land they do not own. p. 197.

station (STAY shun). A large ranch in Australia where cattle and sheep are raised. p. 654.

steppe (step). Land in regions of wide temperature range that is dry, usually rather level, and covered with grass. Steppes are found in southeastern Europe, parts of Asia, Africa, and South America. p. 372.

strait (strayt). A narrow waterway that connects two larger bodies of water. p. 495.

strike (stryk). A stopping of work by a group of workers to force an employer to meet demands. p. 343.

subcontinent (SUB kahnt un unt). A landmass of great size but smaller than the continents. p. 463.

subsistence (sub SIHS tuns). An economy in which the people collect only enough food to feed themselves. p. 35.

subsistence agriculture (sub SIHS tuns AG rih kul chur). A family or similar group's practice of growing food chiefly for itself. p. 131.

summit (SUM iht). The highest point of a mountain. p. 289.

Sunnites (SOON yts). The largest branch of the Islamic religion. Most Muslims are Sunnites. p. 498.

superpower (SOO pur pou ur). A large and powerful country that plays a leading role in world affairs. p. 355.

Swahili (swah HEE lee). A language of East and Central Africa. Swahili contains many Arabic, Persian, and Indian words. p. 587.

synthetic material (sihn THET ihk muh TIHR ee ul). A product that is made from materials that are produced by people, not by nature, and is often made from chemicals. p. 406.

tableland (TAY bul land). A level, flat plateau. p. 421.

taiga (TYE guh). The great coniferous forest region of Canada and the southern part of Siberia in Russia. p. 367.

tannin (TAN ihn). A plant extract used to cure leather. p. 217.

tariff (TAR ihf). A tax on imports, or in some countries, on exports. p. 300.

tatami (tuh TAH mee). A soft woven floor mat. p. 411.

teak (teek). A hard yellowish-brown wood that is often used for carving and for furniture. p. 450.

technology (tek NAHL uh jee). The knowledge and skill people use to make things. p. 50.

tell (tel). An Arabic word meaning "hill." p. 547.

terrace (TER us). A flat shelf of land, arranged like wide steps on a mountainside, where crops are grown. p. 200.

theocracy (thee AHK ruh see). A nation that is ruled according to religious laws instead of laws passed by the people. p. 498.

transhumance (trans HYOO muns). The seasonal migration of livestock between lowlands and adjacent mountains. p. 309.

tributary (TRIHB yoo ter ee). A stream or river that flows into a larger body of water. p. 305.

triple cropping (TRIHP ul KRAHP ing). The process of harvesting one crop and then immediately planting another type of crop on the same land. p. 425.

tropics (TRAHP ihks). The zone between the Tropic of Capricorn and the Tropic of Cancer. p. 156.

trust territory (trust TER uh tor ee). A territory, region, or small country administered by another country for the United Nations. p. 669.

tsetse fly (TSET see flye). A kind of fly found mostly in Africa south of the Sahara desert. Some forms of the tsetse fly pass on a one-celled animal that causes a fatal sickness in cattle and sleeping sickness in humans. p. 578.

tsunami (tsoo NAH mee). A great sea wave produced by an earthquake or volcano eruption under the sea. p. 457.

tundra (TUN druh). A rolling plain without trees, found in the Arctic area of the high latitudes. p. 75.

tungsten (TUNJ stun). A mineral that is used to harden steel and to make the filaments in light bulbs. p. 328.

typhoon (TYE foon). A tropical storm accompanied by strong winds and heavy rain. p. 638.

urban population (UR ban pahp YOO LAY shun). People who live in or near cities or towns. p. 218.

vineyard (VIHN yurd). A field of grape vines. p. 293.

volcano (vahl KAY noh). An opening in the earth, usually at the top of a cone-shaped hill or mountain, out of which gases, rock, ashes, and lava may erupt. p. 66.

Walloon (wah LOON). One of a group of French-speaking people inhabiting the southern part of Belgium. p. 299.

weather (WETHH ur). The condition of the air at a certain time, in terms of precipitation, temperature, and other factors. p. 28.

west coast marine (west kohst muh REEN). A climate with temperatures that are warm in the summer and cool in the winter. There is precipitation all year round. p. 105.

whiteout (HWYT out). A condition that occurs when the white snow-covered ground blends with the white sky, making it impossible to see shadows or even the horizon. p. 675.

wood pulp (wood pulp). A wet, soggy mass of ground-up wood chips. p. 89.

GRAPH APPENDIX

THE WORLD: LARGEST COUNTRIES IN AREA

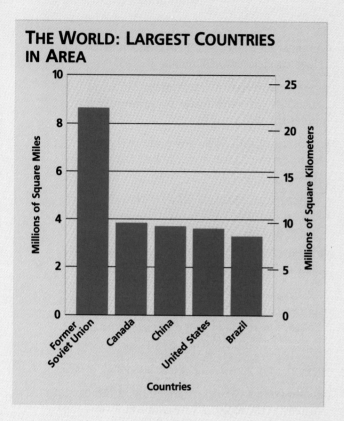

Millions of Square Miles / Millions of Square Kilometers

Countries: Former Soviet Union, Canada, China, United States, Brazil

THE WORLD: LARGEST COUNTRIES BY POPULATION

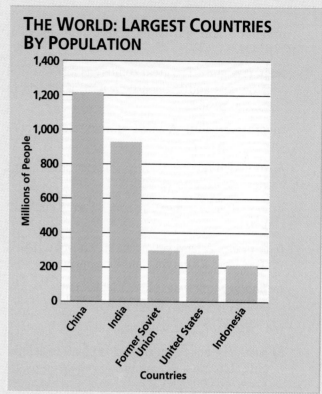

Millions of People

Countries: China, India, Former Soviet Union, United States, Indonesia

THE WORLD: LAND AREA

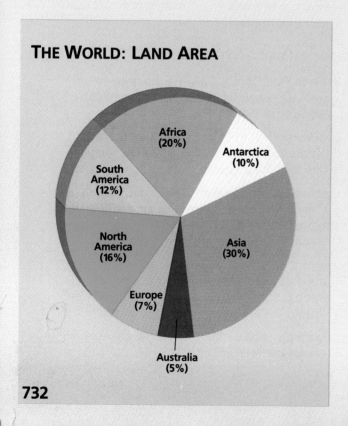

Africa (20%)
Antarctica (10%)
South America (12%)
North America (16%)
Asia (30%)
Europe (7%)
Australia (5%)

THE WORLD: POPULATION

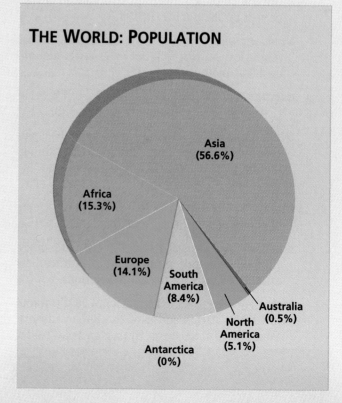

Asia (56.6%)
Africa (15.3%)
Europe (14.1%)
South America (8.4%)
Australia (0.5%)
North America (5.1%)
Antarctica (0%)

THE WORLD: HIGHEST ELEVATIONS BY CONTINENT

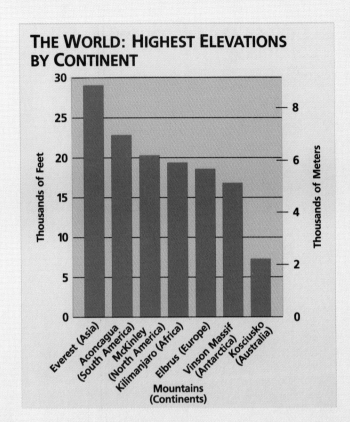

Thousands of Feet

Everest (Asia), Aconcagua (South America), McKinley (North America), Kilimanjaro (Africa), Elbrus (Europe), Vinson Massif (Antarctica), Kosciusko (Australia)

Thousands of Meters

Mountains (Continents)

THE WORLD: LONGEST RIVERS BY CONTINENT

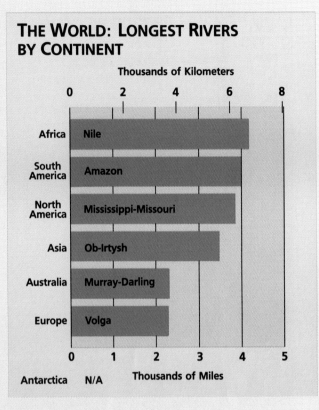

Thousands of Kilometers

Africa — Nile
South America — Amazon
North America — Mississippi-Missouri
Asia — Ob-Irtysh
Australia — Murray-Darling
Europe — Volga
Antarctica — N/A

Thousands of Miles

THE WORLD: FIVE HIGHEST ELEVATIONS

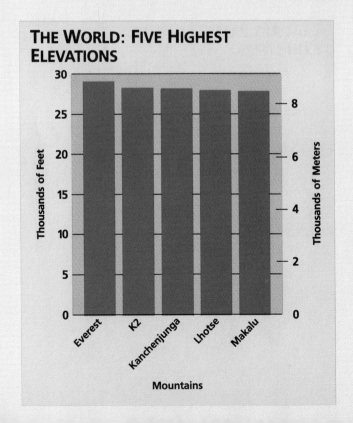

Thousands of Feet

Everest, K2, Kanchenjunga, Lhotse, Makalu

Thousands of Meters

Mountains

THE WORLD: LONGEST RIVERS

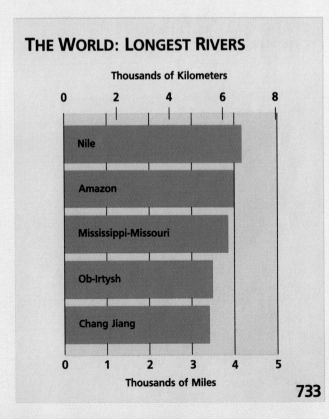

Thousands of Kilometers

Nile
Amazon
Mississippi-Missouri
Ob-Irtysh
Chang Jiang

Thousands of Miles

LEADING BARLEY-PRODUCING COUNTRIES

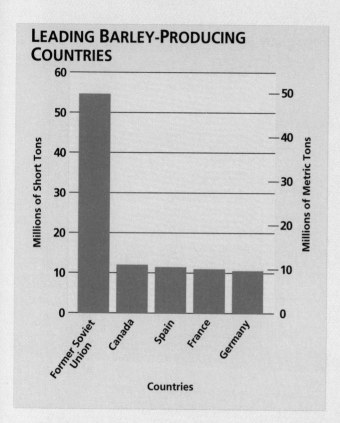

LEADING CATTLE-PRODUCING COUNTRIES

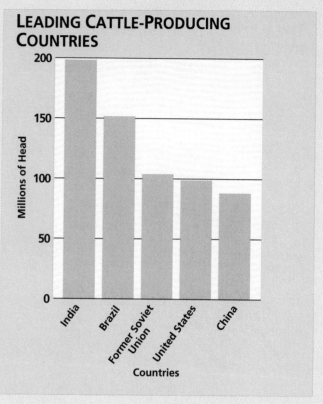

LEADING COTTON-PRODUCING COUNTRIES

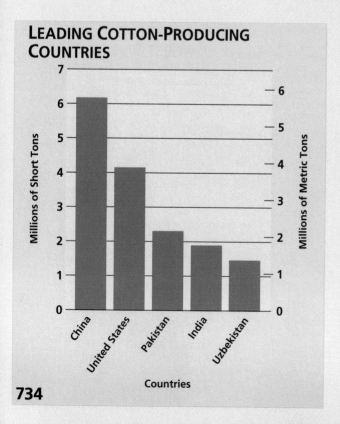

LEADING PALM-OIL-PRODUCING COUNTRIES

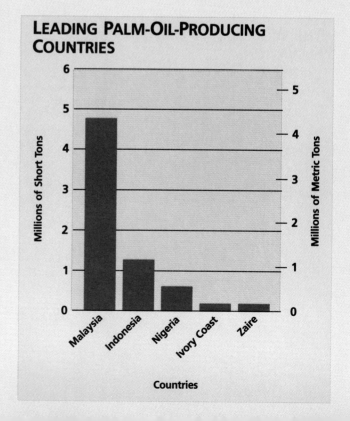

734

LEADING POTATO-PRODUCING COUNTRIES

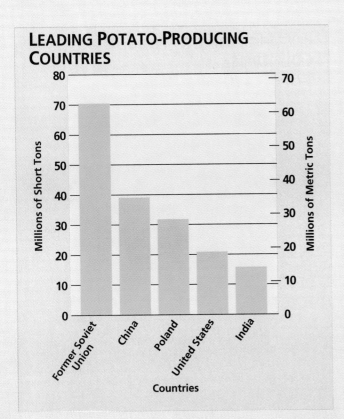

LEADING RYE-PRODUCING COUNTRIES

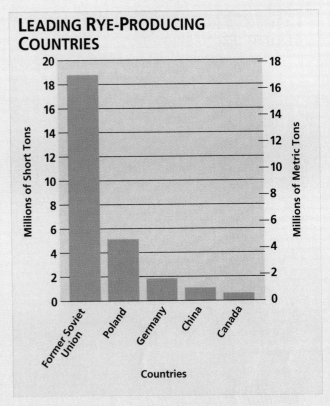

LEADING SOYBEAN-PRODUCING COUNTRIES

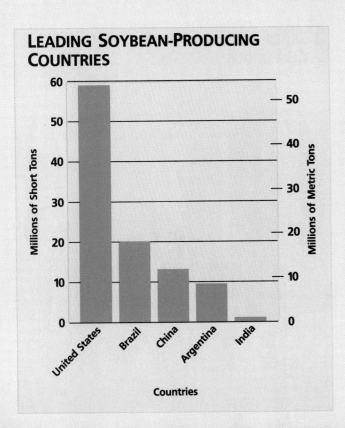

LEADING TOBACCO-PRODUCING COUNTRIES

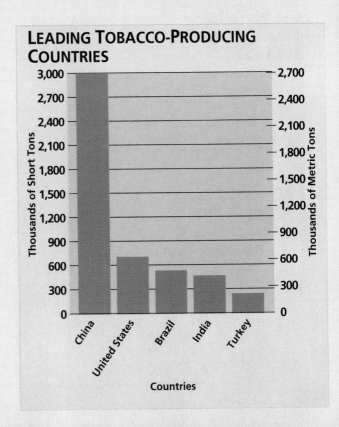

LEADING BAUXITE-PRODUCING COUNTRIES

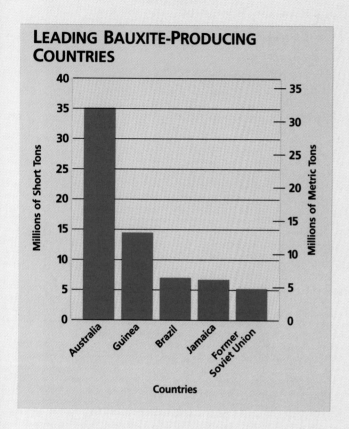

LEADING IRON ORE-PRODUCING COUNTRIES

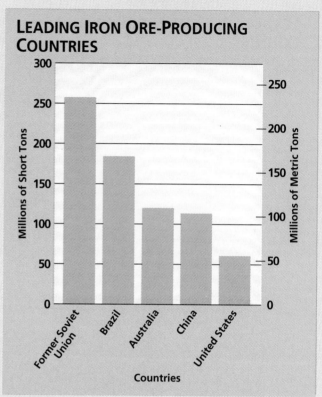

LEADING LEAD-PRODUCING COUNTRIES

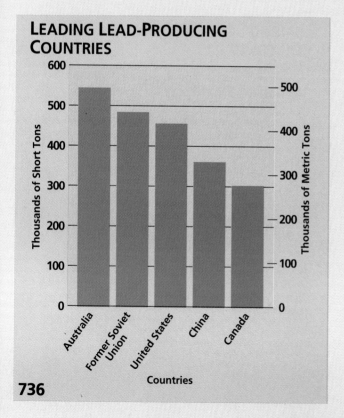

LEADING NICKEL-PRODUCING COUNTRIES

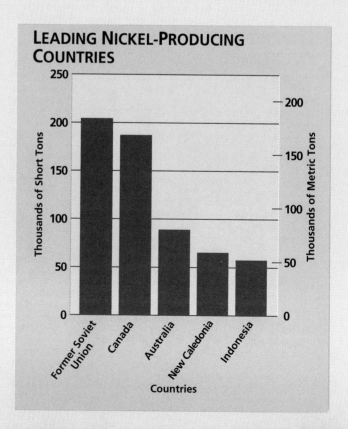

LEADING PETROLEUM-PRODUCING COUNTRIES

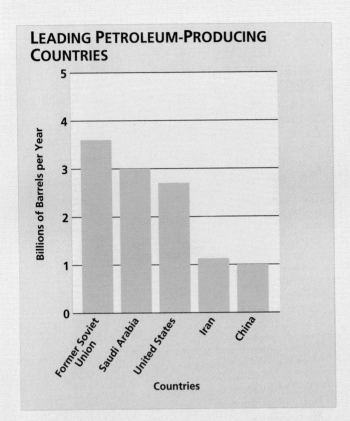

Billions of Barrels per Year

Countries: Former Soviet Union, Saudi Arabia, United States, Iran, China

LEADING SILVER-PRODUCING COUNTRIES

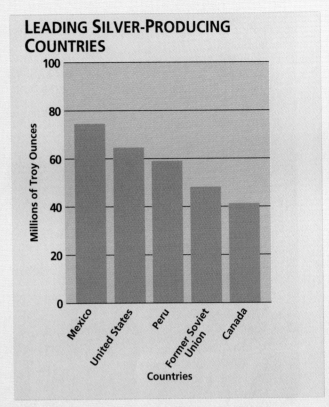

Millions of Troy Ounces

Countries: Mexico, United States, Peru, Former Soviet Union, Canada

LEADING STEEL-PRODUCING COUNTRIES

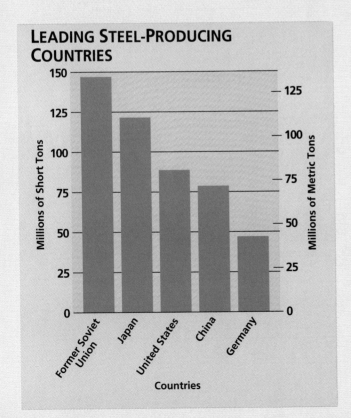

Millions of Short Tons / Millions of Metric Tons

Countries: Former Soviet Union, Japan, United States, China, Germany

LEADING URANIUM-PRODUCING COUNTRIES

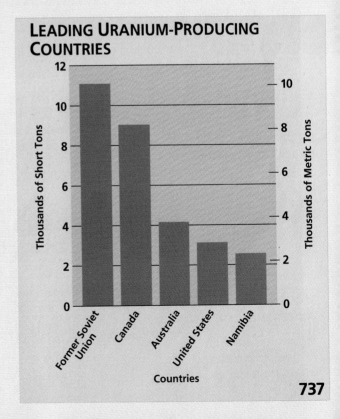

Thousands of Short Tons / Thousands of Metric Tons

Countries: Former Soviet Union, Canada, Australia, United States, Namibia

THE WORLD:
25 LARGEST CITIES BY POPULATION

CITY	POPULATION
1. Seoul, South Korea	10,613,000
2. Mexico City, Mexico	9,816,000
3. Bombay, India	9,910,000
4. Moscow, Russia	8,747,000
5. Jakarta, Indonesia	8,259,000
6. Tokyo, Japan	8,129,000
7. Shanghai, China	7,497,000
8. New York, United States	7,312,000
9. Delhi, India	7,175,000
10. São Paulo, Brazil	7,033,000
11. London, United Kingdom	6,678,000
12. Cairo, Egypt	6,663,000
13. Istanbul, Turkey	6,620,000
14. Tehran, Iran	6,043,000
15. Hong Kong, China	5,932,000
16. Beijing, China	5,770,000
17. Bangkok, Thailand	5,621,000
18. Karachi, Pakistan	5,208,000
19. Rio de Janeiro, Brazil	5,091,000
20. Tianjin, China	4,575,000
21. St. Petersburg, Russia	4,437,000
22. Calcutta, India	4,388,000
23. Baghdad, Iraq	3,841,000
24. Madras, India	3,795,000
25. Los Angeles, United States	3,490,000

UNITED STATES:
25 LARGEST CITIES BY POPULATION

CITY	POPULATION
1. New York, New York	7,312,000
2. Los Angeles, California	3,490,000
3. Chicago, Illinois	2,768,000
4. Houston, Texas	1,690,000
5. Philadelphia, Pennsylvania	1,553,000
6. San Diego, California	1,149,000
7. Dallas, Texas	1,022,000
8. Phoenix, Arizona	1,012,000
9. Detroit, Michigan	1,012,000
10. San Antonio, Texas	966,000
11. San Jose, California	801,000
12. Indianapolis, Indiana	747,000
13. San Francisco, California	729,000
14. Baltimore, Maryland	726,000
15. Jacksonville, Florida	661,000
16. Columbus, Ohio	643,000
17. Milwaukee, Wisconsin	617,000
18. Memphis, Tennessee	610,000
19. Washington, D.C.	585,000
20. Boston, Massachusetts	552,000
21. El Paso, Texas	544,000
22. Seattle, Washington	520,000
23. Cleveland, Ohio	503,000
24. Nashville, Tennessee	495,000
25. Austin, Texas	492,000

CLIMATE TABLES

					MONTHS								
		J	F	M	A	M	J	J	A	S	O	N	D
EQUATORIAL: Rangoon, Myanmar	Temperature °F	77	79	84	87	84	81	80	80	81	82	80	77
	°C	25	26	29	31	29	27	27	27	27	28	27	25
	Precipitation in.	.2	.2	.3	1.4	12.1	18.4	21.5	19.7	15.4	7.3	2.8	.3
	cm	.5	.5	.8	3.6	30.7	46.7	54.6	50.0	39.1	18.5	7.1	.8
SAVANNA: Darwin, Australia	Temperature °F	84	83	84	84	82	79	77	79	83	85	86	85
	°C	29	28	29	29	28	26	25	26	28	30	30	30
	Precipitation in.	15.9	12.9	10.1	4.1	.7	.1	.1	.1	.5	2.2	4.8	10.3
	cm	40.4	32.8	25.7	10.4	1.8	.3	.3	.3	1.3	5.6	12.2	26.2
SEMIDESERT: Tehran, Iran	Temperature °F	34	42	48	61	71	80	85	83	77	66	51	42
	°C	1	6	9	16	22	27	30	28	25	19	11	6
	Precipitation in.	1.6	1.0	1.9	1.4	.5	.1	.2	0	.1	.3	1.0	1.3
	cm	4.1	2.5	4.8	3.6	1.3	.3	.5	0	.3	.8	2.5	3.3

CLIMATE TABLES
Continued

MONTHS

			J	F	M	A	M	J	J	A	S	O	N	D
DESERT: Baghdad, Iraq	Temperature	°F	49	54	61	71	81	90	95	94	88	80	63	53
		°C	10	12	16	22	27	32	35	35	31	27	17	12
	Precipitation	in.	1.2	1.3	1.3	.9	.2	0	0	0	0	.1	.8	1.2
		cm	3.0	3.3	3.3	2.3	.5	0	0	0	0	.3	2.0	3.0
MEDITERRANEAN: Rome, Italy	Temperature	°F	45	47	51	57	64	71	76	76	70	62	53	46
		°C	7	8	11	14	18	22	25	25	21	17	12	8
	Precipitation	in.	3.2	2.7	2.9	2.6	2.2	1.6	.7	1.0	2.5	5.0	4.4	3.9
		cm	8.1	6.9	7.4	6.6	5.6	4.1	1.8	2.5	6.4	12.7	11.2	9.9
HUMID SUBTROPICAL: Montevideo, Uruguay	Temperature	°F	72	72	69	63	57	51	51	51	55	58	65	69
		°C	22	22	21	17	14	11	11	11	13	15	18	21
	Precipitation	in.	2.7	2.8	3.2	4.5	3.5	3.2	2.5	3.6	3.4	2.6	3.2	3.6
		cm	6.9	7.1	8.1	11.4	8.9	8.1	6.4	9.1	8.6	6.6	8.1	9.1
WEST COAST MARINE: Portland, United States	Temperature	°F	39	42	46	51	57	61	67	66	61	54	46	41
		°C	4	7	8	11	14	16	20	19	16	12	8	5
	Precipitation	in.	6.7	5.5	4.8	3.1	2.3	1.6	.6	.6	1.9	3.3	6.5	6.9
		cm	17.0	14.0	12.2	7.9	5.8	4.1	1.5	1.5	4.8	8.4	16.5	17.5
HUMID CONTINENTAL: Vienna, Austria	Temperature	°F	29	33	40	50	59	65	68	67	60	50	39	32
		°C	⁻2	1	4	10	15	18	20	20	16	10	4	0
	Precipitation	in.	1.5	1.3	1.8	2.0	2.8	2.7	3.1	2.7	2.0	1.9	1.8	1.8
		cm	3.8	3.3	4.6	5.1	7.1	6.9	7.9	6.9	5.1	4.8	4.6	4.6
MOUNTAIN: Mexico City, Mexico	Temperature	°F	54	57	61	64	65	64	62	62	61	59	56	54
		°C	12	14	16	18	18	18	17	17	16	15	13	12
	Precipitation	in.	.2	.2	.5	.8	1.9	3.9	4.5	4.6	3.9	1.6	.5	.2
		cm	.5	.5	1.3	2.0	4.8	9.4	11.4	11.7	9.9	4.1	1.3	.5
SUBARCTIC: Okhotsk, Russia	Temperature	°F	⁻11	⁻7	7	21	35	45	55	55	46	27	6	⁻8
		°C	⁻24	⁻22	⁻14	⁻6	2	7	13	13	8	⁻3	⁻15	⁻22
	Precipitation	in.	.1	.1	.1	.2	.5	1.1	.5	1.8	2.1	.7	.2	.2
		cm	.3	.3	.3	.5	1.3	2.8	1.3	4.6	5.3	1.8	.5	.5
TUNDRA: Point Barrow, United States	Temperature	°F	⁻19	⁻13	⁻14	⁻2	21	35	40	39	31	16	0	⁻15
		°C	⁻28	⁻25	⁻26	⁻19	⁻6	2	4	4	⁻1	⁻9	⁻18	⁻26
	Precipitation	in.	.3	.2	.2	.3	.3	.3	1.1	.8	.5	.8	.4	.4
		cm	.8	.5	.5	.8	.8	.8	2.8	2.0	1.3	2.0	1.0	1.0
ICE CAP: Little America, Antarctica	Temperature	°F	22	9	⁻7	⁻24	⁻27	⁻29	⁻34	⁻34	⁻29	⁻14	9	24
		°C	⁻6	⁻13	⁻22	⁻31	⁻33	⁻34	⁻37	⁻37	⁻34	⁻26	⁻13	⁻4
	Precipitation	in.	N/A	N/A	N/A	N/A	N/A	N/A	N/A	N/A	N/A	N/A	N/A	N/A
		cm	N/A	N/A	N/A	N/A	N/A	N/A	N/A	N/A	N/A	N/A	N/A	N/A

Forbidden City, 430-431
Foreign debt, 237
Forest resources. *See also* Rain forests.
  of Africa, 589
  boreal, 75
  of the British Isles, 267
  of Canada, 75, 87, 88
  of East Asia, 404, 412
  of Mexico, 127, 137
  of Russia, 367
  of Scandinavia, 267, 277, 282
  of South America, 196, 204, 229
  of South Asia, 467, 472
  of Southeast Asia, 445, 446, 447, 450, 453
  of the United States, 108
  of Western Europe, 310, 311, 326, 328
Formosa. *See* Taiwan.
Fossey, Dian, 587
Fouta Djallon, 555
France
  African colonies of, 548, 563, 565-568, 581, 582, 615
  and Canada, 73, 77, 80, 82-83, 84
  cities of, 294-295
  colonies of, 153, 447
  economy of, 287, 292, 293
  industrial regions of, 294-295
  land of, 288, 289, 291, 292, 320
  resources of 295
  territories of, 177, 189, 501, 669
Fraser River, 87
French Canadians, 77
French Guiana, 177, 189, 232
French language, 82, 83, 177, 299, 308, 615
Friendship, 7, 41
Fuels. *See* Coal; Natural gas; Oil.
Fuji, Mount, 399
Fundy, Bay of, 82

G
Gabon, 573, 581
Gaelic, 273
Gambia, 568
Gambia River, 555
Game reserves, 588, 598
Ganges River, 465, 467, 469, 475-476, 482
Gasohol, 234
Gathering, 35, 50, 576-577, 617, 647
Gauchos, 213, 218

Gautama, Siddhartha. *See* Buddha.
Gazetteer, 5
Gdańsk, Poland, 342, 343
Genghis Khan, 439
Geography, 25, 45, 309
Geologic hazards, 195-196
Georges Bank, 108
Georgia, 357, 360, 374
German Democratic Republic. *See* Germany.
Germanic languages, 31, 280, 310
Germanic tribes, 303, 308
Germany
  African colonies of, 581-582
  cities of, 301, 303, 305, 306
  culture of, 301, 308, 341
  division of, 301
  economy of, 303-308
  and the environment, 303
  land and climate of 287, 288, 291, 295, 304
  mineral resources of, 299, 304, 305, 306
  reunification of (1990), 301, 303
  and World War I, 495, 582
  and World War II, 301
Germany, Federal Republic of. *See* Germany.
Geysers, 279, 656
Ghana, 562, 563, 566, 568
Gibralter, 319, 536
Ginza district, Tokyo, 410
Glacial till, 92
Glaciers, 44
  in Antarctica, 672
  in Canada, 79, 83, 90-92
  in New Zealand, 676
  in Scandinavia, 276-277, 280
  in South America, 223
Glasgow, Scotland, 273
Glasnost, 359
Gobi Desert, 422, 424-425, 431, 438
Gorillas, 587, 598
Grains, 51, 52, 361, 367. *See also* Rice; Wheat.
Grand Canyon, 101, 102
Grasslands
  of Africa, 556, 611
  of Australia, 645
  of Canada, 85
  of Mongolia, 438-439
  of South America, 215, 229, 232
  of South Asia, 467
  of Ukraine, 372
Grazing lands, 556. *See also* Grasslands.
Great Artesian Basin, 653
Great Barrier Reef, 646-647, 664

Great Britain, 267, 269. *See also* British Isles; United Kingdom.
  African colonies of, 565, 568-569, 596, 598-599, 613, 614, 621-623, 626
  and Australia, 643, 647, 649
  and Canada, 73, 77, 80
  colonies of, 73, 77, 153, 154, 177, 180, 263, 265, 437, 454, 475, 483, 659
  culture of, 31, 32
  empire of, 31, 397, 647
Great circle routes, 18-19
Great Dividing Range, 645
Great Dyke, 613, 614
Greater Antilles, 147, 154
Great Lakes, 84-85, 90, 109
Great Plains
  in Canada, 85
  in the United States, 43, 50, 51, 100, 534
Great Rift Valley, 589-590, 594, 498, 615
Great Slave Lake, 87
Great Wall of China, 431
Greece, 495
  cities of, 321, 334
  climate of, 611
  culture of, 334, 348, 494, 536-537
  farming in 333, 334
  islands of 319, 333
  land of, 322, 333, 334, 348
  language of, 334
Greenland, 17, 265, 644, 666
Green revolution, 459
Grid system, map, 5-7, 45
Ground water, 51
Guam, 664, 669
Guangzhou (Canton), China, 426
Guaraní Indians, 214
Guatemala, 149, 155-159
Guayaquil, Ecuador, 202-203
Guerillas, 158
Guiana Highlands, 178, 179-180, 185, 186
Guianas, 177, 180, 187
Guinea, 566, 567, 575
Guinea-Bissau, 566
Gulf Coastal Plain, 126-127, 128, 131, 132
Gulf Stream, 268
Guyana, 177, 180, 187-189

H
Haciendas, 129, 156, 187
Hadrian's Wall, 273
Haiku, 397
Haiti, 147, 152-153
Hajj (pilgrimage), 510
Halifax, Nova Scotia, 80
Halliburton, Richard, 101, 102

Hamburg, Germany, 303, 347
Hammadas, 534
Hanoi, Vietnam, 448, 449
Harare, Zimbabwe, 613
Hawaii, 104, 671
Hawaiian Islands, 663
Hebrews, 502,503
Hejaz Mountains, 508, 510
Hemispheres, 18
Herding, 35. *See also* Cattle; Sheep.
  in Africa, 560, 592, 595, 600
  in China, 424, 438
  in the Middle East, 498, 500, 507
  in Siberia, Russia, 358
  in South America, 196
  in Switzerland, 309
Hermosillo, Mexico, 128
Highland climate, 156, 589
High Veld, 611, 626
Highways
  in Brazil, 231
  in Germany, 303
  Trans-Canada, 80, 82
  in the United States, 97-98
Himalayas, 44, 493
  in East Asia, 419, 421, 422, 424
  in South Asia, 463, 465, 467, 472
Hindi language, 476
Hindu Kush, 492-493, 500
Hindu numeral system, 537
Hinduism, 32, 33, 465, 467, 475-476
Hindus
  in India, 32, 465-468, 474, 475-478
  in Pakistan, 474
  in Southeast Asia, 444, 454
  in Sri Lanka, 483
Hiroshima, Japan, 403
Hispanic Americans, 103
Hispaniola, 147, 152-153
Ho Chi Minh City, Vietnam, 448, 449
Hokkaido, Japan, 397, 399, 401, 404, 406
Homelands, South African, 623
Home to Poland (Hotchkiss), 344
Honduras, 149, 156, 158, 159
Hong Kong
  colony of Great Britain, 437
  economy of, 437-438
Honshu, Japan, 397, 399, 400, 401, 402-404, 406, 407
Hostages, 499
Hotchkiss, Christine, 344
Houston, Texas, 114
Huang He (Yellow River), 420-421, 428
Huascarán, Mount, 196

Wineries ● Zurich, Switzerland

ACKNOWLEDGMENTS

CREDITS

Country Tables: Scott Wilson **Maps:** Maryland Cartographics, Inc. **Graphs:** Richard Puder Design/JAK Graphics, Ltd. **Contributing artists:** Bryn Barnard: 48-49; Jack Brusca: 678; Susan Johnston Carlson: 44, 435; Rick Cooley: 497, 664; Len Ebert: 233, 242, 298, 473, 544, 567; Dan Fione: 112-113, 405, 589, 654; Polly K. Lewis: 216, 511; Richard Loehle: 281; Tom Powers: 104; Gary Undercuffler: 311, 368-369; Paul Wenzel: 129. **Photographs:** *All photographs by Silver Burdett Ginn (SBG) unless otherwise noted.* **Table of contents:** iii: Larry Lefever/Grant Heilman Photography. iv: Peter Pearson/TSW-Click, Chicago. v: Raphael Koskas/TSW-Click, Chicago. vi: Paul Chesley/Photographers Aspen. viii: Peter Timmermans/Allstock. x: M.P. Kahl/Bruce Coleman. xi: Marc Romanelli/The Image Bank. **Map Skills Handbook:** 2: Joachim Messerschmidt/Bruce Coleman. 3: *t.* Owen Franken/Stock, Boston; *b.* David Lucas for SBG. 5: Joachim Messerschmidt/Bruce Coleman; *inset* ©1993 David Burnett/Contact Press Images/Woodfin Camp & Associates. 11: George Haling/Tony Stone Images. 15: David Lucas for SBG.

Unit 1 opener 22-23: Larry Lefever/Grant Heilman Photography. **Chapter 1** 24: Brian Gill/Globe Photos. 29: Kevin Schafer/TOM STACK & ASSOCIATES. 30: Michal Heron for SBG. 33: Wolinsky/Stock, Boston. **Chapter 2** 40: SuperStock. 41: NASA. 43: Campbell and Boulanger/West Light. 45: SuperStock. 47: Edward Pytlik/West Virginia University. 51: Grant Heilman Photography.

Unit 2 opener 62-63: Peter Pearson/TSW-Click, Chicago. 65: Larry Lee/West Light. 66: Tom Algire/TOM STACK & ASSOCIATES. **Chapter 3** 72: David Barnes/The Stock Market. 74: Harrington Miller/Comstock. 75: *bkgd.* Stephen J. Krasemann/Peter Arnold, Inc.; *t. l.* Wayne Lankinen/Valan Photos; *t. r.* Ester Schmidt/Valan Photos; *b.* Johnny Johnson/Valan Photos. 76: George Hunter/TSW-Click, Chicago. 77: Tim Graham/Sygma. 79: Bruno J. Zehnder/Peter Arnold, Inc. 80: Steve Vidler/After Image, Inc. 82: V. Wilkinson/Valan Photos. 83: Tibor Bognar/The Stock Market. 85: George Hunter/SuperStock. 86: T. Kitchin/TOM STACK & ASSOCIATES. 87: George Hunter/TSW-Click, Chicago. 89: Dan Guravich. 89: T. Kitchin/Valan Photos; *inset* R. Moller/Valan Photos. **Chapter 4** 96: Tony Freeman/Photo Edit. 97: Billy E. Barnes/Stock, Boston. 98: Phylane Norman/Nawrocki Stock Photos. 99: Jean-Paul Nacivet/After Image, Inc. 101: Margaret C. Berg/Berg & Associates. 102: Ronald F. Thomas/Bruce Coleman. 103: Shostal Associates/SuperStock. 108: E. R. Degginger. 109: Cary Wolinsky/Stock, Boston. 113: *l.* Photri; *r.* J. L. Atlan/Sygma. 114: © Allen Green/Photo Researchers, Inc. 117: Steve Vidler/Leo deWys. 118: Martin Rogers/Stock, Boston; *inset* ©1992 R. S. Uzzell III/Woodfin Camp & Associates. 119: D. Dietrich/FPG International. 120-121: *t.* FPG International; *b.* Peter Menzel/Stock, Boston. **Chapter 5** 124: SuperStock. 126: Jack Kerson/DDB Stock Photos. 127: Steven D. Elmore. 128: ©1992 Robert Frerck/Woodfin Camp & Associates. 130: SuperStock. 133: Steven D. Elmore. 134: Robert Frerck/Odyssey Productions. 135: © Wesley Bocxe/Photo Researchers, Inc. 136: ©1992 Alon Reininger/Woodfin Camp & Associates. 137: ©1992 Terrence Morre/Woodfin Camp & Associates. 139: ©1992 Robert Frerck/Woodfin Camp & Associates. 140: Shostal Associates/SuperStock. 141: Bob Thomason/Leo deWys; *inset* George Gerster/Comstock. **Chapter 6** 144: SuperStock. 146: Danny Lehman/After Image, Inc. 147: *l.* SuperStock; *r.* David Muscroft/SuperStock. 148: M. Burgess/H. Armstrong Roberts. 149: © Ed Drews/Photo Researchers, Inc. 152: Donald Dietz/Stock, Boston. 153: *t. l.* Rick Stewart/Allsport; *t. r.* Stephen Green/Sports Illustrated; *b.* Richard Mackson/Sports Illustrated. 154: Joe Viesti/Viesti Associates, Inc. 155: ©1992 Alon Reininger/Woodfin Camp & Associates. 156: © Wesley Bocxe/Photo Researchers, Inc. 157: SuperStock. 158: AP/Wide World Photos, Inc.

Unit 3 opener 168-169: Raphael Koskas/TSW-Click, Chicago. 171: Steve Vidler/Leo deWys. **Chapter 7** 176: SuperStock. 178: Rob Crandall/Picture Group. 179: Collart Odinet/Sygma. 180: Shostal Associates/SuperStock. 181: © 1992 Robert Frerck/Woodfin Camp & Associates. 183: Capa/Magnum. 184: Patrick Rouillard/The Image Bank. 185-187: SuperStock. 189: Sebastiao Salgado/Magnum. **Chapter 8** 192: Manley Photo-Tuscon/Shostal Associates/SuperStock. 193: © Victor Englebert/Photo Researchers, Inc. 194: Don Mason/The Stock Market. 195: *r.* Ernst A. Jahn/The Image Bank; *l.* Robert Frerck/TSW-Click, Chicago. 196: Anna E. Zuckerman/Photo Edit. 197: *l.* © Victor Englebert/Photo Researchers, Inc.; *r.* FPG International. 198: Steele Perkins/Magnum. 200: SuperStock. 201: © H. Silvester/Photo Researchers, Inc. 202: Joe Viesti/Viesti Associates, Inc. 203: Kevin Horan/Picture Group; *inset* D. Donne Bryant. 205: SuperStock. 207: K. Scholz/SuperStock. **Chapter 9** 210: Pedro Luis Raota/Shostal Associates/SuperStock. 211: Claudia Parks/The Stock Market. 212: ©1992 Loren McIntyre/Woodfin Camp & Associates. 213: © Carl Frank/Photo Researchers, Inc. 215: Karl Kummels/SuperStock. 217: Hoa-Qui/Viesti Associates, Inc. 218: © Noel R. Kemp/Photo Researchers, Inc. 220: Ana MacIntyre/Viesti Associates, Inc. 221: Anna Zuckerman/Photo Edit. 222: Bill Parsons/DDB Stock Photo. 223: D. Goldberg/Sygma. 224: © Suen-o Lindbland/Photo Researchers, Inc. **Chapter 10** 228: Ed Rooney/TSW-Click, Chicago. 230: Peter Frey/The Image Bank. 231: Shostal Associates/SuperStock. 232: Claus Meyer/Black Star. 234: S. Jorge/The Image Bank. 236: © Jerry Cooke/Photo Researchers, Inc. 237: J. Messerschmidt/FPG International. 238: Shostal Associates/SuperStock. 240: deWildenberg/Sygma. 241: ©1992 Stephanie Maze/Woodfin Camp & Associates. 244: Martin Rogers/Stock, Boston.

Unit 4 opener 252-253: Paul Chesley/Photographers Aspen. 255: Steve Vidler/Leo deWys. **Chapter 11** 262: Raymond Stott/The Image Works. 263: SuperStock. 264: Shostal Associates/SuperStock. 265: Randy Wells/The Stock Market. 267: Richard Bullard/TSW-Click, Chicago. 268: Masa Uemura/AllStock, Inc. 271: Historical Pictures Service, Chicago. 272-273: James Hargan/Leo deWys. 274: © Porterfield-Chickering/Photo Researchers, Inc. 275: Comstock. 277: Hubertus Kanus/SuperStock. 278: © Farrell Grehan/Photo Researchers, Inc. 279: Shostal Associates/SuperStock. 280: Hubertus Kanus/SuperStock. 282: *l.* Bruce Coleman; *r.* J Messerschmidt/Bruce Coleman. **Chapter 12** 286: J. Messerschmidt/Leo deWys. 288: Floyd Holdman/The Stock Solution. 289: Rick Strange/International Stock Photo. 292: ZEFA, U.K./H. Armstrong Roberts. 295: Kanno Shinichi/FPG International. 297: Globe Photos. 300: Neil Beer/TSW-Click, Chicago. 303: G. and M. Kohler/FPG International. 304: Messerschmidt/FPG International. 306: Terry Qing/FPG International. 307: E. Streichan/Shostal Associates/SuperStock. 308: Tony Craddock/TSW-Click, Chicago. 309: Stockman/International Stock Photo. 310-311: Globe Photos. 312: ©1992 Gernot Huber/Woodfin Camp & Associates. 314-315: Antonin Kratochvil. **Chapter 13** 318: Percy Hennell/TSW-Click, Chicago. 322: Comstock. 323: FPG International. 324, 327: M. Thonig/H. Armstrong Roberts. 328: Robert Frerck/TSW-Click, Chicago. 329: T. Sennett/Magnum. 331: Blaine Harrington/The Stock Market. 332: SuperStock. 333: G. Clyde/FPG International. 335: Erich Lessing/Magnum. **Chapter 14** 338: TSW-Click, Chicago. 339: Chip Hires/Gamma Liaison. 340: DPI. 341: © Photo Researchers, Inc. 342: © 1992 Momatiuk/Eastcott/Woodfin Camp & Associates. 343: Chris Niedenthal/Black Star. 344: Donald Lewis Osborn. 345: Jessie Blackburn/FPG International. 346: Luis Villota/The Stock Market. 347: Eastcott-Momatiuk/The Image Works. 348: Art Zamur/Gamma Liaison. 351: ©1992 Adam Woolfitt/Woodfin Camp & Associates. **Chapter 15** 354: Andy Hernandez/Sipa Press. 355: David Madison/Duomo. 358: © 1993 Howard Sochurek/Woodfin Camp & Associates. 359: Klaus Reisinger/Black Star. 365: Tass/Sovfoto. 366: SuperStock. 368: Focus on Sports. 369: © 1993 Heikki Saukkomaa/Woodfin Camp & Associates. 370: *l.* Tass/Sovfoto; *t. r.* Irv Beckman/FPG International. 371: Arthur Grace/Stock, Boston. 371: Peter Turnley/Black Star. 374: © 1993 Alexander Avakian/Woodfin Camp & Associates. 376: Gilles Saussier/Gamma Liaison.

Unit 5 opener 384-385: Peter Timmermans/AllStock, Inc. 387: Andrea Barrist/The Image Works. **Chapter 16** 396: Steve Vidler/Nawrocki Stock Photos. 398: TSW-Click, Chicago. 399: Joe Viesti/Viesti Associates, Inc. 401: Audrey Gottlier/Monkmeyer Press. 402: SuperStock. 403: FPG International; *inset* Matsumoto/Sygma. 406: Michael Hayman/Stock, Boston. 408: SuperStock. 409: Wolfgang Kaehler. 410: George Hunter/SuperStock. 411: Paul Fusco/Magnum. 412: FPG International. 414: H. Kubota/Magnum. 415: © 1992 Kim Newton/Woodfin Camp & Associates. **Chapter 17** 418: Comstock. 420: Charles Marden Fitch/Shostal Associates/SuperStock. 424: Fred Bavendam/Peter Arnold, Inc. 426: Shostal Associates/SuperStock. 429: Gamma Liaison. 430: © 1992 Alon Reininger/Woodfin Camp & Associates. 431: UPI/Bettmann Newsphotos. 434: Bob Thomason/TSW-Click, Chicago. 435: Michael Springer/Gamma Liaison. 436: Robin Moyer/Gamma Liaison. 438: © Lawrence Migdale/Photo Researchers, Inc. 439: Paul Conklin/Monkmeyer Press; *inset* Elisabeth Weiland. 450: *inset* R. Tsuneo. **Chapter 18** 442: © Alain Evrard/Photo Researchers, Inc. 443: D.J. Forbert/SuperStock. 444, 445: Wolfgang Kaehler. 447: Nik Wheeler/Black Star. 448: © Bruce Gordon/Photo Researchers, Inc. 449: UPI Bettmann Newsphotos. 450: Chauvel/Sygma. 451: Wolfgang Kaehler. 452: Wolfgang Kaehler. 453: J. Wishnetsky/Comstock. 456: Patrick Ward/Stock, Boston. 457: Wolfgang Kaehler. 458: © Paolo Koch/Photo Researchers, Inc. 459: Christopher Morris/Black Star. **Chapter 19** 462: Wolfgang Kaehler. 464: Shostal Associates/SuperStock. 465: Rene Born/Magnum. 467: Lorraine Rorke/The Image Works. 468: Bruno Barbey/Magnum. 470: Mimi Forsyth/Monkmeyer Press. 471: Bruno Barbey/Magnum. 472: © George Holton/Photo Researchers, Inc. 474: Magnum. 476: Mimi Forsyth/Monkmeyer Press. 478: P. Habans/Sygma. 479: Joe Viesti/Viesti Associates, Inc. 480: Sygma. 482: S. Chester/Comstock. 484: *l.* SuperStock; *r.* © 1992 Marc and Evelyne Bernheim/Woodfin Camp & Associates. 485: J. Heil/Leo deWys. 487: Bernhard Pierre Wolff. **Chapter 20** 490: Stockman/International Stock Photos; *l. inset* FPG International; *r. inset* Guy Marche/FPG International. 492: Michaelangelo Durazzo/Ana/Viesti Associates, Inc. 493: © 1992 Robert Azzi/Woodfin Camp & Associates. 494: ©1992 Homer Sykes/Woodfin Camp & Associates. 495: © Fred Maroon/Photo Researchers, Inc. 496: V. Lefteroff/FPG International. 497: Comstock. 498: *l.* Kalari/Sygma; *r.* C. Spengler/Sygma. 500: P. Manoukian/Sygma. 501: The Image Bank. 502: Gamma Liaison. 503: © Nancy Durrell McKenna/Photo Researchers, Inc. 504: Reuters/Bettmann. 505: Gamma Liaison. 507: Bruno Barbey/Magnum. 508: Byron Augustin/TOM STACK & ASSOCIATES. 511: FPG International. 512: Abu Hander/International Stock Photo.

Unit 6 opener 520-521: M.P. Kahl/Bruce Coleman. 523: © Arthur Gloor-Animals Animals/Earth Scenes. **Chapter 21** 532: E. Otto/FPG International. 535: Francois Dardelet/The Image Bank. 536: Robert Frerck/TSW-Click, Chicago. 538: Ted H. Funk/FPG International. 539: *l.* Bob Smith/International Stock Photo; *r.* Ian Steele/International Stock Photo. 540: M. Delledonna/FPG International. 542: Robert Winslow. 543: Erich Lessing/Magnum. 545: Michael Braid/TSW-Click, Chicago. 546: Roule Av/Sygma. 549: Hoa-Qui/Viesti Associates, Inc. **Chapter 22** 552: Dimitri Kessel/The Stock Market. 553: Magnum. 554: © 1992 Wendy V. Watriss/Woodfin Camp & Associates. 555: Dieter Blum/Peter Arnold, Inc. 556: Jacques Jangoux/Peter Arnold, Inc. 557: Shostal Associates/SuperStock. 559: Pedro Coll/The Stock Market; *inset* © 1992 Marc and Evelyne Bernheim/Woodfin Camp & Associates; *r.* © 1992 Wendy Watriss/Woodfin Camp & Associates; *r.* Thierry Rannou/Gamma Liaison. 562: Shostal Associates/SuperStock. 564: © Marc and Evelyne Bernheim/Woodfin Camp & Associates. 566: Shostal Associates/SuperStock. 568: Yoruba/H. Armstrong Roberts. 569: Hoa-Qui/Viesti Associates, Inc. **Chapter 23** 572: James A. Sugar/Black Star. 573: Bruno Barbey/Magnum. 574: Joseph B. Brignolo/The Image Bank. 575: T. Orban/Sygma. 576: FourbyFive, Inc./SuperStock. 577: © 1992 Marc and Evelyne Bernheim/Woodfin Camp & Associates. 578: Tortoli/ZEFA/H. Armstrong Roberts. 579: Abbas/Magnum; *inset* © J.P. Vuillomenet/Photo Researchers, Inc. 580: Millard Thomas/Taurus Photos, Inc. 583: Hoa-Qui/Viesti Associates, Inc. **Chapter 24** 586: C.D. Flannery/Bruce Coleman. 588: Jason Laure. 590: © Dr. Nigel Smith-Animals Animals/Earth Scenes. 591: *l.* © 1992 Kal Muller/Woodfin Camp & Associates. *r.* © Blair Seitz/Photo Researchers, Inc. 592: Robert Caputo/Stock, Boston. 593: © Bruce Brander/Photo Researchers, Inc. 595: Georg Gerster/Comstock. 596: *t.* © 1992 Marc and Evelyne Bernheim/Woodfin Camp & Associates; *b.* TSW-Click, Chicago. 598: E.R. Degginger. 599: Robert Caputo/Stock, Boston. 600: Georg Gerster/Comstock. 601: TSW-Click, Chicago. 602: *t.* Jason Laure; *b.* © 1992 Marc and Evelyne Bernheim/Woodfin Camp & Associates. 603: Wendy Bass/Viesti Associates, Inc. *inset t. r.* S. Franklin/Magnum; *inset b. l.* © 1992 Thomas Nebbia/Woodfin Camp & Associates; *b. r.* Peter Veit. 605: *t.* E.R. Degginger; *b.* © 1992 Stoddart/Katz/Woodfin Camp & Associates. **Chapter 25** 608: © Gregory G. Dimijian/Photo Researchers, Inc. 609: Tom and Michele Grimm/International Stock Photo. 610: Joe Viesti/Viesti Associates, Inc. 611: Joe Viesti/Viesti Associates, Inc.; *inset* Jason Laure. 612: © 1992 Thomas Nebbia/Woodfin Camp & Associates. 613: Photri. 614: Dennis Cox/TSW-Click, Chicago. 615: A. Moldvay/Eriako Associates. 617: © Anthony Bannister-Animals Animals/Earth Scenes. 618: Jason Laure. 619: Shostal Associates/SuperStock. 622: William Campbell/Sygma. 623: Photri. 624: Jason Laure. 625: Reuters/Bettmann. 626: Jason Laure.

Unit 7 opener 634-635: Marc Romanelli/The Image Bank. 638: © 1992 David Austen/Woodfin Camp & Associates. 639: Comstock. **Chapter 26** 642: Paul Steel/The Stock Market. 644: Dallas and John Heaton/TSW-Click, Chicago. 645: Robin Smith/TSW-Click, Chicago. 646: *l.* Dallas and John Heaton/TSW-Click, Chicago; *m.* © Tom McHugh/Photo Researchers, Inc.; *r.* Fritz Prenzel/TSW-Click, Chicago. 647: Peter Hendrie/The Image Bank; *inset* Alvis Upitis/The Image Bank. 648: Historical Pictures Service, Chicago. 650: © World Copyright Pascal Rondeau/AllSport. 652: Ziggy Kalunzy/TSW-Click, Chicago. 653: David Austen/TSW-Click, Chicago. 655: © 1992 Robert Frerck/Woodfin Camp & Associates. 656: © Tom McHugh/Photo Researchers, Inc. 658: Robbi Newman/The Image Bank. **Chapter 27** 662: Pete Seaward/TSW-Click, Chicago. 665: Son Smetzer/TSW-Click, Chicago. 666: FPG International. 667: Wendy Stone/Bruce Coleman. 668: © 1992 Dilip Mehta/Woodfin Camp & Associates; *inset* Comstock. 669: Dallas and John Heaton/TSW-Click, Chicago. 670: Jacques Jangoux/Peter Arnold, Inc. 671: © 1992: Gerd Ludwig/Woodfin Camp & Associates. 672: John Perkins/Globe Photos. 673: © Robert W. Hernandez/Photo Researchers, Inc. 674: TSW-Click, Chicago. 675: Art Wolfe/Allstock, Inc. 676: FourbyFive Inc./SuperStock. 677: © 1992 Chuck O'Rear/Woodfin Camp & Associates. 678: Grant Heilman Photography; *inset* George Mars Cassidy/TSW-Click, Chicago.